EFFECTS OF HABITAT FRAGMENTATION ON BIRDS IN WESTERN LANDSCAPES: CONTRASTS WITH PARADIGMS FROM THE EASTERN UNITED STATES

T. Luke George and David S. Dobkin, editors

Studies in Avian Biology No. 25
A PUBLICATION OF THE COOPER ORNITHOLOGICAL SOCIETY

Cover watercolor painting of a Varied Thrush (*Ixoreus naevius*) in a naturally fragmented western landscape and a Kentucky Warbler (*Oporornis formosus*) in an anthropogenically fragmented eastern landscape, by Wendell Minor

STUDIES IN AVIAN BIOLOGY

Edited by

John T. Rotenberry
Department of Biology
University of California
Riverside, CA 92521

Artwork by
Wendell Minor
Wendell Minor Designs
15 Old North Road
Washington, CT 06793

Studies in Avian Biology is a series of works too long for *The Condor,* published at irregular intervals by the Cooper Ornithological Society. Manuscripts for consideration should be submitted to the editor. Style and format should follow those of previous issues.

Price $22.00 for softcover and $35.00 for hardcover, including postage and handling. All orders cash in advance; make checks payable to Cooper Ornithological Society. Send orders to Cooper Ornithological Society, % Western Foundation of Vertebrate Zoology, 439 Calle San Pablo, Camarillo, CA 93010.

ISBN: 1-891276-34-4

Library of Congress Control Number: 2002114416
Printed at Allen Press, Inc., Lawrence, Kansas 66044
Issued: December 18, 2002

CONTENTS

STUDIES ON FOCAL SPECIES

LIST OF AUTHORS

SARA E. BARKER
Laboratory of Ornithology
Cornell University
Ithaca, NY 14850

JAMES BATTIN
Department of Biological Sciences
Northern Arizona University
Flagstaff, AZ 86011-5694

JAMES C. BEDNARZ
Department of Biological Sciences
Arkansas State University
State University, AR 72467

ANNE E. BLACK
Colorado National Heritage Program
Fort Collins, CO, and
Point Reyes Bird Observatory
4990 Shoreline Highway
Stinson Beach, CA 94970

DOUGLAS T. BOLGER
Environmental Studies Program
HB6182
Dartmouth College
Hanover, NH 03755

L. ARRIANA BRAND
Department of Fishery and Wildlife Biology
Colorado State University
Fort Collins, CO 80523

JOHN F. CAVITT
U.S. Geological Survey
Montana Cooperative Wildlife Research Unit
University of Montana
Missoula, MT 59812
(Present address: Department of Zoology
Weber State University
2505 University Circle
Ogden, UT 84408-2505)

RICHARD M. DEGRAAF
USDA Forest Service
Northeastern Research Station
Holdsworth Hall
University of Massachusetts
Amherst, MA 01003

ANDRÉ A. DHONDT
Laboratory of Ornithology
Cornell University
Ithaca, NY 14850

DAVID S. DOBKIN
High Desert Ecological Research Institute
15 SW Colorado Avenue, Ste. 300
Bend, OR 97702

THERESE M. DONOVAN
SUNY College of Environmental Science and
    Forestry
1 Forestry Drive
Syracuse, NY 13210
(Present address: Vermont Cooperative Fish and
    Wildlife Research Unit
311 Aiken Center
University of Vermont
Burlington, VT 05405)

JOHN FAABORG
Division of Biological Sciences
110 Tucker Hall
University of Missouri
Columbia, MO 65211

ALAN B. FRANKLIN
Colorado Cooperative Fish and Wildlife Research
    Unit
Department of Fishery and Wildlife Biology
Colorado State University
Fort Collins, CO 80523

T. LUKE GEORGE
Department of Wildlife
Humboldt State University
Arcata, CA 95521

R. J. GUTIÉRREZ
Department of Wildlife
Humboldt State University
Arcata, CA 95521
(Present address: Department of Fisheries and
    Wildlife
University of Minnesota
St. Paul, MN 55108)

D. CALDWELL HAHN
U.S. Geological Survey
Patuxent Wildlife Research Center
11410 American Holly Drive
Laurel, MD 20708-4015

RALPH S. HAMES
Laboratory of Ornithology
Cornell University
Ithaca, NY 14850

SALLIE J. HEJL
USDA Forest Service
Rocky Mountain Research Station
P. O. Box 8089
Missoula, MT 59807, and
Sierra Nevada Framework Project
801 I St., Rm. 419
Sacramento, CA 95814
(Present address: Department of Wildlife and
    Fisheries Sciences
2258 TAMU
Texas A&M University
College Station, TX 77843-2258)

RICHARD L. HUTTO
Division of Biological Sciences
University of Montana
Missoula, MT 59812

STEVEN T. KNICK
U.S. Geological Survey
Forest and Rangeland Ecosystem Science Center
Snake River Field Station
970 Lusk Street
Boise, ID 83706

NATASHA B. KOTLIAR
U.S. Geological Survey
Fort Collins Science Center
2150 Centre Avenue, Bldg C
Fort Collins CO 80526-8818

BRIAN D. LOGAN
U.S. Geological Survey
Montana Cooperative Wildlife Research Unit
University of Montana
Missoula, MT 59812

JAMES D. LOWE
Laboratory of Ornithology
Cornell University
Ithaca, NY 14850

JOHN M. LUGINBUHL
College of Forest Resources
University of Washington
Seattle, WA 98195-2100

DIANE EVANS MACK
USDA Forest Service
Pacific Northwest Research Station
3625 93rd Ave SW
Olympia, WA 98512-9193

DAVID A. MANUWAL
College of Forest Resources
Box 352100
University of Washington
Seattle, WA 98195

NAOMI J. MANUWAL
19420 194th Ave NE
Woodinville, WA 98072

THOMAS E. MARTIN
U.S. Geological Survey
Montana Cooperative Wildlife Research Unit
University of Montana
Missoula, MT 59812

JOHN M. MARZLUFF
College of Forest Resources
University of Washington
Seattle, WA 98195-2100

MARY E. MCFADZEN
USDA Forest Service
Rocky Mountain Research Station
P.O. Box 8089
Missoula, MT 59807

CYNTHIA P. MELCHER
U.S. Geological Survey
Fort Collins Science Center
2150 Centre Avenue, Bldg C
Fort Collins CO 80526-8818

MICHAEL L. MORRISON
University of California
White Mountain Research Station
3000 East Line Street
Bishop, CA 93514

BARRY R. NOON
Department of Fishery and Wildlife Biology
Colorado State University
Fort Collins, CO 80523

NADAV NUR
Point Reyes Bird Observatory
4990 Shoreline Highway
Stinson Beach, CA 94970

MARTIN G. RAPHAEL
USDA Forest Service
Pacific Northwest Research Station
Olympia, WA 98512-9193

SCOTT K. ROBINSON
Department of Animal Biology
172 Natural Resource
University of Illinois
Champaign, IL 61820

KENNETH V. ROSENBERG
Laboratory of Ornithology
Cornell University
Ithaca, NY 14850

JOHN T. ROTENBERRY
Center for Conservation Biology and Department of
    Biology
University of California
Riverside, CA 92521

VICTORIA A. SAAB
USDA Forest Service
Rocky Mountain Research Station
316 E. Myrtle St.
Boise, ID 83702

THOMAS D. SISK
Center for Environmental Sciences and Education
Northern Arizona University
Flagstaff, AZ 86011-5694

JOSHUA J. TEWKSBURY
Biological Sciences
University of Montana
Missoula, MT 59812
(Present address: Department of Zoology
Box 118525
University of Florida
Gainesville, FL 32611)

FRANK R. THOMPSON, III
USDA Forest Service
North Central Research Station
202 Natural Resources Bldg.
University of Missouri
Columbia, MO 65211

JOCK S. YOUNG
Division of Biological Sciences
University of Montana
Missoula, MT 59812

Studies in Avian Biology No. 25:3, 2002.

PREFACE

This volume grew from recognition of the need for a forum to address explicitly the contrasts and similarities of fragmentation processes and fragmentation effects in eastern and western landscapes. That recognition arose over the course of several years in informal discussions between the editors, which crystallized at the second North American Ornithological Conference in 1998 in St. Louis, where we conceived of a symposium and outlined the areas that should be covered.

A one-day symposium organized by the editors was held the following year in Portland, Oregon, at the annual meeting of the Cooper Ornithological Society. The central focus of the symposium was to contrast patterns in the western versus eastern United States, and to differentiate and contrast natural versus human-caused fragmentation patterns and associated effects. From the outset, the symposium was intended to serve as the basis for a monograph in the STUDIES IN AVIAN BIOLOGY series. Nearly all of the 16 chapters contained in this volume are based on symposium presentations, although not all topics covered in the symposium are represented here. Each chapter has been peer-reviewed and reviewed by the editors, as well.

We are grateful to the Cooper Ornithological Society for providing logistic support and an excellent venue for the symposium, and to our colleagues who graciously agreed to serve as peer-reviewers for the chapters in this volume. We thank the United States Environmental Protection Agency's Ecosystem Science Branch for generously providing funds to support publication of this volume through Assistance Agreement No. 82772001 to the High Desert Ecological Research Institute. The research contained herein has not been subjected to Agency review, and therefore does not necessarily reflect the views of the Environmental Protection Agency. Additional funds in support of the symposium were provided by the Oregon/Washington office of the United States Bureau of Land Management and the Cooper Ornithological Society. The editors thank Wendell Minor for providing the artwork that graces the cover.

David S. Dobkin
T. Luke George

Studies in Avian Biology No. 25:4–7, 2002.

INTRODUCTION: HABITAT FRAGMENTATION AND WESTERN BIRDS

T. Luke George and David S. Dobkin

Habitat fragmentation and loss due to human activities has been identified as the most important factor contributing to the decline and loss of species worldwide (Noss and Cooperrider 1994). Although the response of species to habitat loss generally is clear, the effects of habitat fragmentation are much more complex (Fahrig 1997, Bunnell 1999). Over the last two decades, our understanding of the effects of habitat fragmentation on bird populations has increased tremendously. Early studies viewed habitat fragments as islands and interpreted patterns of species richness in the context of island biogeography theory (Forman et al. 1976, Galli et al. 1976). It soon became apparent, however, that in contrast to oceanic islands, the habitat or matrix surrounding fragments profoundly influenced the ecological conditions within those fragments. In particular, rates of nest predation and cowbird parasitism of ground-nesting and cup-nesting birds were found to be extremely high close to forest edges (Ambuel and Temple 1983) and in small forest fragments (Wilcove 1985, Robinson 1992). Further study revealed that patterns of nest predation, and especially nest parasitism, were influenced by forest cover in the surrounding landscape (Andrén and Angelstam 1988; Andrén 1992, 1994, 1995; Robinson et al. 1995, Donovan et al. 1997). Taken together, these results suggested that declines and losses of birds from small forest fragments were related to elevated rates of nest predation and parasitism. These observations led to the development of a top-down hierarchical model that included regional, landscape-level, and local effects to explain variation in nesting success across the landscape and subsequent changes in abundance and distribution of the affected species (Thompson et al. *this volume*). Because much of the empirical support for this model derives from studies conducted in the eastern United States (i.e., east of the Rocky Mountains), this model embodies what can be viewed as the "eastern paradigm."

As better understanding of the human-imposed dynamics and the natural ecological processes that govern western landscapes has accrued in recent years, applicability of the eastern paradigm to landscapes of the western United States has become more tenuous. First, the nature of the matrix in most western ecosystems differs dramatically from the East. Habitat fragments studied in the eastern United States frequently are embedded in agricultural or urban landscapes, but most studies of habitat fragmentation in the West have focused on forest fragments created by timber harvest. Logging operations result in fragments of mature or old-growth forest that are embedded in a matrix of young, regenerating forest. Landscapes composed of young forest, in contrast to agricultural and exurban landscapes, may not harbor high densities of predators and brood parasites, and consequently birds inhabiting fragments may not suffer the high rates of nest predation and parasitism observed in the East. While the extent of urban and agricultural development is increasing in the West, it is substantially less than in the East (Fig. 1). As a result, fragments of natural vegetation generally are embedded in a matrix of agricultural and urban land in the East, but urban and agricultural lands generally are isolated in a matrix of unconverted habitat in the West (Fig. 2). Clearly there are some regions in the western United States that exhibit patterns similar to the East. For instance, 71% of California's Central Valley and 63% of Oregon's Willamette Valley have been converted to agricultural or urban uses, which is similar to the high levels of conversion in many eastern and Midwestern regions (T. L. George, unpubl. data).

A second suite of fundamental differences between eastern and western landscapes results in a higher degree of natural heterogeneity in the West. Greater aridity, the greater spatial extent and temporal frequency of fires, and greater topographic diversity made western landscapes inherently more patchy than eastern landscapes long before European settlement (Hejl et al. *this volume*, Kotliar et al. *this volume*). Having contended with the natural heterogeneity of western landscapes for thousands of generations, avian populations inhabiting this region may be less affected by fragmentation processes and consequences than avian populations of the relatively more homogeneous landscapes of the pre-European-settlement eastern United States. If nothing else, these differing selective milieus make it difficult to predict the responses to disturbance (whether natural or anthropogenic) by species inhabiting western landscapes.

The primary objective of this volume was to

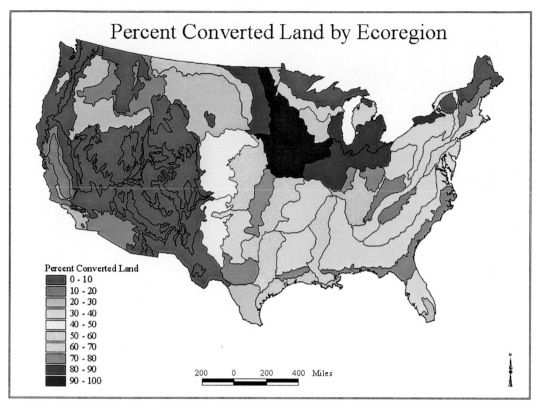

FIGURE 1. Proportion of land converted to agriculture or man-made structures in the conterminous United States in 66 physiographic regions. Proportions were calculated from the U.S. Geological Survey Land Use and Land Cover (LULC) database compiled between 1975–1985 (Mitchell et al. 1977). The LULC database included 45 categories (Anderson et al. 1975); we combined all agricultural and developed land into an "altered" category (see Appendix) and calculated the proportion of altered and unaltered land within each region. The physiographic regions are those used by Robbins et al. (1986) for analyses of the Breeding Bird Survey data.

examine the effects of habitat fragmentation on western bird populations, particularly in the context of predictions derived from eastern paradigms. We defined the western United States as the area from the Rocky Mountains west to the Pacific Coast in the conterminous United States. The following chapters are grouped into three sections covering theory and continental-scale comparisons, effects of fragmentation in specific western ecosystems, and studies of focal species.

Thompson et al. begin by describing and summarizing evidence for the eastern paradigms and provide a multi-scale working hypothesis for the effects of habitat fragmentation on birds. Franklin et al. provide a definition of habitat fragmentation, paying particular attention to the distinction between habitat fragmentation and habitat heterogeneity, and Sisk and Battin review the concept of habitat edge as it applies to western landscapes. The ubiquitous role of fire in shaping western landscapes and their associated avifaunas is addressed by Kotliar et al.

Studies that span the continent offer a unique opportunity to compare the response of birds and their nest predators and parasites to fragmentation in the East and the West. Morrison and Hahn summarize studies of the response of Brown-headed Cowbirds (*Molothrus ater*) to fragmentation in the East and the West. Cavitt and Martin examine differences in rates of nest predation and parasitism between fragmented and unfragmented areas in the East and the West using data on the outcome of tens of thousands of nests in the BBIRD database (Martin et al. 1997). Employing data from the Cornell Laboratory of Ornithology's "Birds in Forested Landscapes" project, Hames et al. compare the responses of tanagers, thrushes, and Brown-headed Cowbirds to forest fragmentation across the United States.

Six chapters focus on individual western ecosystems selected to reflect both the relative importance of specific vegetation communities and the constraint of where fragmentation-related re-

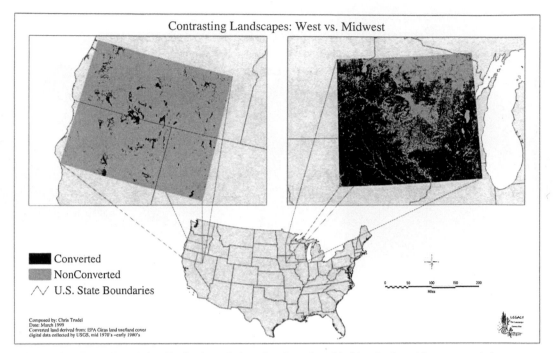

FIGURE 2.   Examples of the distribution of altered and unaltered habitat in the midwestern and the western United States. Land cover data were obtained from U.S. Geological Survey Land Use and Land Cover (LULC) database compiled between 1975–1985 (Mitchell et al. 1977).

search has been conducted in the West. Three chapters focus on coniferous forests. George and Brand summarize studies in redwood (*Sequoia sempervirens*) forests, Manuwal and Manuwal summarize research in the wet coniferous forests of the Pacific Northwest, and Hejl et al. examine forests of the northern Rocky Mountains. Knick and Rotenberry describe avian responses to fragmentation in the Intermountain shrubsteppe, Bolger summarizes a wealth of studies that have been conducted in the highly urbanized coastal sage scrub and chaparral regions of southern California, and Tewksbury et al. analyze riparian bird communities across seven riparian systems in five western states. Notably lacking are summaries of the effects of fragmentation on birds in the southern Rocky Mountains and the desert Southwest. There were too few studies on the effects of habitat fragmentation on birds in these regions to warrant reviews. A recent publication by Knight (2000) provides an overview of the effects of habitat fragmentation in the southern Rocky Mountains.

Finally, as a reflection of the relatively great attention paid to loss and fragmentation of old-growth forests in the western United States, two chapters are devoted to multi-scale assessments of focal species in the context of loss and fragmentation of their old-growth forest habitats. Franklin and Gutiérrez synthesize information across subspecies of Spotted Owls (*Strix occidentalis*), and Raphael et al. examine Marbled Murrelets (*Brachyramphus marmoratus*). Both of these species have had a significant impact on management of western forests.

Although the picture is far from complete, the contents of this monograph illustrate the state of our knowledge regarding fragmentation effects on western bird populations at the beginning of the 21st century. We hope this volume will serve as a landmark contribution to the ecological and conservation literature by presenting a solid synthesis and foundation to buttress future research, and by conveying important policy implications for public land management in the western United States.

APPENDIX. Land Use Categories in USGS Database Designated as Altered (1) or Unaltered (0) for Figures 1 and 2

Anderson[a] land use category	Altered
Urban or built-up land	1
Residential	1
Commercial and services	1
Industrial	1
Transportation, communication, utilities	1
Industrial and commercial complexes	1
Mixed urban or built-up land	1
Other urban or built-up land	1
Agricultural land	1
Cropland and pasture	1
Orchards, groves, vineyards, nurseries, and ornamental horticultural	1
Confined feeding operations	1
Other agricultural land	1
Rangeland	0
Herbaceous rangeland	0
Shrub and brush rangeland	0
Mixed rangeland	0
Forest land	0
Deciduous forest land	0
Evergreen forest land	0
Mixed forest land	0
Water	0
Streams and canals	0
Lakes	0
Reservoirs	0
Bays and estuaries	0
Wetland	0
Forested wetland	0
Nonforested wetland	0
Barren land	0
Dry salt flats	0
Beaches	0
Sandy areas not beaches	0
Bare exposed rock	0
Strip mines, quarries, gravel pits	0
Transitional areas	0
Tundra	0
Shrub and brush tundra	0
Herbaceous tundra	0
Bare ground	0
Wet tundra	0
Mixed tundra	0
Perennial snow or ice	0
Perennial snowfields	0
Glaciers	0

[a] From Anderson et al. (1922).

Studies in Avian Biology No. 25:8–19, 2002.

A MULTI-SCALE PERSPECTIVE OF THE EFFECTS OF FOREST FRAGMENTATION ON BIRDS IN EASTERN FORESTS

Frank R. Thompson, III, Therese M. Donovan, Richard M. DeGraaf, John Faaborg, and Scott K. Robinson

Abstract. We propose a model that considers forest fragmentation within a spatial hierarchy that includes regional or biogeographic effects, landscape-level fragmentation effects, and local habitat effects. We hypothesize that effects operate "top down" in that larger scale effects provide constraints or context for smaller scale effects. Bird species' abundance and productivity vary at a biogeographic scale, as do the abundances of predators, Brown-headed Cowbirds (*Molothrus ater*), and land-use patterns. At the landscape scale the level of forest fragmentation affects avian productivity through its effect on predator and cowbird numbers. At a local scale, patch size, amount of edge, and the effects of forest management on vegetation structure affect the abundance of breeding birds as well as the distribution of predators and Brown-headed Cowbirds in the landscape. These local factors, along with nest-site characteristics, may affect nest success and be important factors when unconstrained by processes at larger spatial scales. Landscape and regional source-sink models offer a way to test various effects at multiple scales on population trends. Our model is largely a hypothesis based on retroduction from existing studies; nevertheless, we believe it has important conservation and research implications.

Key Words: Brown-headed Cowbirds; eastern forests; edge-effects; fragmentation; landscape; *Molothrus ater*; multi-scale; nest predation; predators; songbirds.

Much recent research has focused on the effects of forest fragmentation on breeding neotropical migrant birds and recent reviews have concluded that forest fragmentation generally results in increased nest predation and brood parasitism (Robinson and Wilcove 1994, Faaborg et al. 1995, Walters 1998). For example, numbers of Brown-headed Cowbirds (*Molothrus ater*), brood parasitism, and nest predation are negatively correlated with the amount of forest cover in landscapes in the midwestern U.S. (Donovan et al. 1995b, Robinson et al. 1995a, Thompson et al. 2000). Enough variation or inconsistency exists among studies, however, that it is difficult to develop a general model of the effects of forest fragmentation on songbirds that addresses spatial scale, accounts for local and regional variation in observed effects, and describes mechanisms for observed effects. Most research has been conducted in eastern forests. Differences in ecological patterns and land use between eastern and western North America, however, has led to speculation that the effects of fragmentation on birds may differ among these regions (George and Dobkin *this volume*).

We have been developing a conceptual model that places the effects of landscape-level forest fragmentation within a spatial hierarchy that ranges from biogeographic or regional effects to local effects (Freemark et al. 1995, Donovan et al. 1997, Robinson et al. 1999, Thompson et al. 2000). Our purpose in developing this model is to provide a synthesis of the current understanding of forest fragmentation effects in eastern landscapes, and to stimulate research that will

enhance that understanding in both eastern and western North America. Our model is a simple framework within which factors affecting species viability can be examined. We present the model as a series of hypotheses organized by this framework, and then review key studies that we used to formulate these hypotheses. We present the model as series of hypotheses because it is formed largely by retroduction. Retroduction is the construction of a hypothesis about a process that provides an explanation for observed patterns or facts (Romesburg 1981). Models of this type are often most useful as hypotheses for hypothetico-deductive research (Romesburg 1981), and we review a few studies of this type that test our hypotheses. We do not provide an exhaustive literature review because recent reviews exist (e.g., Robinson and Wilcove 1994, Faaborg et al. 1995, Walters 1998, Heske et al. 2001). We primarily review fragmentation effects at a landscape scale and edge effects at a habitat scale. However, we also discuss effects at larger and smaller scales because of important interactions with edge and landscape effects. For brevity and because of the focus of this volume we focus on biogeographic, landscape, and habitat effects on songbird reproductive success. The context for our review is the eastern deciduous forest, although where possible we make comparisons to western landscapes.

THE MODEL

From a breeding ground perspective, habitat characteristics associated with reproductive success of forest passerines can be evaluated at several spatial scales: (1) *the nest-site scale*—the micro-habitat characteristics directly around the nest or the immediate vicinity of the nest; (2) *the habitat scale*—the features of the habitat patch in which the nest is located; (3) *the landscape scale*—the collection of different habitat patches and the position of a particular habitat within a landscape, the matrix within which the habitat is embedded, and the juxtaposition and proximity of other habitats in the landscape (Freemark et al. 1993); and (4) *biogeographic scales.*

For example, vegetation structure at a habitat scale, or location within a landscape, may be more important than nest site characteristics such as concealment in reducing nest depredation (Bowman and Harris 1980, Leimgruber et al. 1994, Donovan et al. 1997, Burhans and Thompson 1999) or parasitism (Best 1978, Johnson and Temple 1990, Burhans 1997, Morse and Robinson 1999). Furthermore, nest predation or brood parasitism may be related to landscape composition and structure (Robinson et al. 1995a, Donovan et al. 2000, Thompson et al. 2000). Finally, geographic location and abiotic and biotic characteristics at multiple scales can directly impact a population's growth (Hoover and Brittingham 1993, Leimgruber et al. 1994, Thompson 1994, Coker and Capen 1995, Thompson et al. 2000). The essence of our model is that all spatial scales may contribute to the ability of a local subpopulation to replace itself (Sherry and Holmes 1992), but the importance of each may depend on habitat features at other scales or the geographic location within the breeding or non-breeding range. These effects can be arranged in a hierarchy in which larger scale effects provide constraints or context for smaller scale effects (Fig. 1).

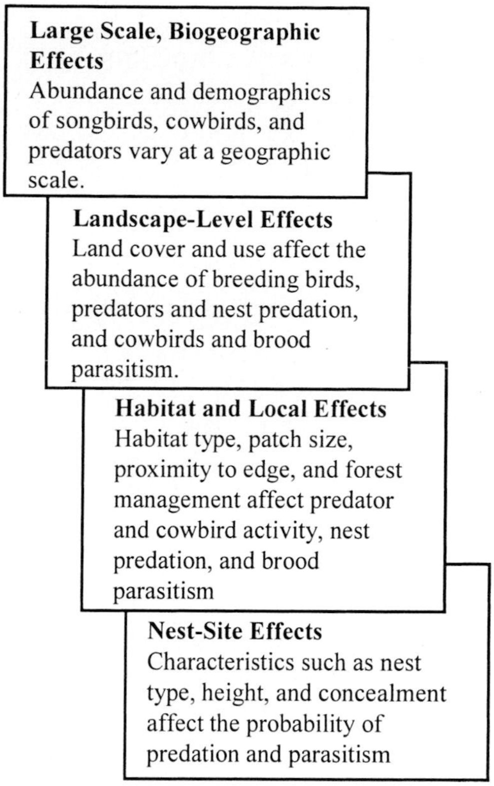

What types of evidence directly support this model? Evidence of top-down constraints comes from observational, experimental, and meta-analysis studies across eastern North America. Although we provide several examples of correlative evidence for such constraints, we emphasize that experimental and meta-analysis approaches that directly test the top-down constraint hypothesis have been very instructive because they attempt to control for factors operating at other spatial scales. For example, we tested the hypothesis that landscape effects are more significant than local edge effects, and that edge effects are dependent on landscape context, in a rigorously-designed, large-scale, randomized field experiment. We found strong evidence that edge effects in nest predation are dependent on landscape context, and that landscape context is a better predictor of cowbird abundance than any other local-scale affect measured (Fig. 2; Donovan et al. 1997). In land-

FIGURE 1. Conceptual model of factors at multiple spatial scales affecting reproductive success of songbirds. Larger scale factors are hypothesized to be more important determinants of species viability because they provide context or constraints for smaller scale effects.

scapes with <15% forest, predation was high in forest edge and interior; at 45–55% forest cover, predation was high in forest edge and low in forest interior; and at >90% forest cover, predation was low in forest edge and interior. Cowbird abundance was much greater in landscapes with high levels of forest fragmentation than those with low levels of fragmentation (Fig. 2). While we could not randomly assign landscape treatments in this study (because the landscape patterns already existed), study sites were randomly selected from a three-state area. As a result, we believe these results allow strong inferences for at least Missouri, Illinois, and Indiana. The results of this research were also confirmed by a meta-analysis of nest depredation studies in which researchers compared the landscape context for studies that documented edge effects on predation patterns with those that failed to find edge effects (Bayne and Hobson 1997, Hartley and Hunter 1998).

We believe that these large-scale analyses are

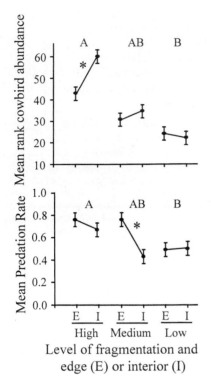

Level of fragmentation and
edge (E) or interior (I)

FIGURE 2. Effects of landscape level of fragmentation and local edge effects on nest predation and cowbird abundance in the midwestern United States. Fragmentation levels were measured as the amount of forest cover and were: high, < 15% forest; medium, 45–55% forest; and low, > 90% forest. Edge (E) and interior (I) treatments were > 50 m and > 250 m from forest edge, respectively. Levels of forest cover with different letters, and edge and interior treatments with an asterisk are significantly different (ANOVA, P < 0.05). Data and figures adapted from Donovan et al. (1997).

critical for understanding how forest fragmentation impacts songbird populations. Although artificial nest experiments at large spatial scales may provide some insights, our hypothesis that larger scale effects provide constraints or context for smaller scale effects depends on observations of nesting success at numerous locations across a species' range. Obviously, collection of these data is not an easy task, and significant advances will likely be made through large-scale collaborations (e.g., Robinson et al. 1995a), large-scale research programs with standardized methodology (e.g., BBIRD; Martin et al. 1997), or through meta-analyses (e.g., Hartley and Hunter 1998, Chalfoun et al. 2002). We have focused on direct measures of nesting success, nest predation, and predator abundance; however, we recognize that indirect measures will be necessary and provide insight at large spatial

scales (e.g., Project Tanager; Rosenberg et al. 1999).

LARGE-SCALE, BIOGEOGRAPHIC EFFECTS

Hypothesis: Breeding birds exhibit geographic patterns in their demographics. These are in part the result of geographic patterns in the distribution of predators and cowbirds, and provide the context for smaller scale effects and can affect local reproductive success.

PREDATOR DISTRIBUTION

Predator abundance and species richness vary across North America. Levels of nest predation could be higher where the total abundance and diversity of predators is higher. For example, Rosenberg et al. (1999) documented biogeographic patterns in predator communities as part of Project Tanager. Tanagers (*Piranga* spp.) were exposed to different combinations of predators across their range, and predators responded differently to forest fragmentation. The highest incidence of the predators they surveyed occurred in the Midwest. General patterns in the distribution of avian predators can be generated from Breeding Bird Survey (BBS) data (Sauer et al. 1997). Detecting biogeographic patterns in nest predation related to predator abundance or diversity will be difficult because of the large number of potential nest predators and variation in their distributions across North America. Further complicating these patterns is the interaction between diversity and abundance; even in areas of low predator diversity a single predator may be very abundant.

BROWN-HEADED COWBIRD DISTRIBUTION

Cowbirds demonstrate strong geographic patterns in abundance; therefore, the potential effects of fragmentation or habitat effects are constrained by this larger-scale effect. More simply put, in regions of the country where cowbirds are rare it is unlikely that fragmentation or local factors will have a strong effect on parasitism levels.

The strongest evidence of this geographic effect comes from BBS data. A distribution map generated from BBS data shows a general pattern of high abundance of cowbirds in the Great Plains and decreasing abundance with distance from the Great Plains (Sauer et al. 1997). Thompson et al. (2000) examined patterns from the BBS data by regressing mean statewide cowbird abundance on distance from the center of their range in the Great Plains and the percent of forest cover in that state. Mean statewide cowbird abundance was negatively related to forest cover in a state and a state's distance from the center of the cowbird's breeding range (R^2 = 0.67). Regression coefficients for distance to center of range and forest cover were both significant. However, the partial correlation of distance to center of range with cowbird abundance was greater than that for forest cover and cowbird abundance. While both partial correlations were significant, the effect of distance to the center of the range was stronger and provides some indication of the importance of biogeographic constraints. Additional evidence of this effect is seen in parasitism levels. Wood Thrush (*Hylocichla mustelina*) parasitism levels decrease from Midwest to Mid-Atlantic to New England (Hoover and Brittingham 1993; see also Smith and Myers-Smith 1998).

LANDSCAPE-LEVEL EFFECTS

Hypothesis: Nest predation and cowbird parasitism increase with forest fragmentation at the landscape scale. Predation and parasitism is greater in fragmented landscapes because of a positive, numerical response by predators and cowbirds that is the result of increase in the availability and interspersion of food, hosts, or other resources.

A landscape is a heterogeneous mosaic of habitat patches in which individuals live and disperse (Dunning et al. 1992), usually ranging in size from a few to hundreds of square kilometers. Most research on landscape-level effects and fragmentation has occurred in the last decade; understanding the logical importance of these factors required a major shift in our concepts of habitat relationships. Biologists, however, have been documenting the distribution of forest passerines in relation to habitat and habitat-patch characteristics for literally decades (e.g., Robbins et al. 1989b; reviewed by Freemark et al. 1995), often using the MacArthur and Wilson (1967) model of island biogeography as a guiding framework (reviewed in Faaborg et al. 1995). Patch size, patch shape, and interpatch distances, as well as forest type, have important effects on bird community composition. However, there is ample evidence to suggest that these local patterns are driven in part by habitat characteristics at the landscape scale, and also vary regionally. Most investigators of fragmentation effects recognized that habitat fragments differed from true islands because the matrix between the fragments was not ocean, but was a different habitat that supported its own set of species. The inclusion of "edge" species in counts on fragments was certainly one form of recognition that effects from the surroundings of the study site could be important. However, to truly understand all the effects of landscape-lev-

el processes upon forest birds we needed to study a variety of landscapes, as opposed to a variety of patches.

PATTERNS OF LAND COVER AND THEIR EFFECTS ON THE ABUNDANCE OF PREDATORS AND NEST PREDATION

Land cover can significantly influence the number and diversity of predators, as well as constrain the importance of more local-scale habitat factors such as patch size, vegetation structure, or distance to edge effects on nest predation. We begin by reviewing the main effects of landscape pattern, and then discuss how landscape factors potentially constrain more local-scale effects on nest predation. Detection of this constraint, however, may be difficult because predators throughout North America vary greatly in habitat use, foraging behavior, and how they collectively contribute to observed nest predation patterns in forest passerines (e.g., Gates and Gysel 1978, Andrén and Angelstam 1988, Yosef 1994, Tewksbury et al. 1998, Marzluff and Restani 1999, Dijak and Thompson 2000).

Robinson et al. (1995a) and Donovan et al. (1995b) were the first to use empirical data from real nests to relate nest predation to forest fragmentation at a landscape scale. They measured many landscape variables but used the percent of forest cover within a 10-km radius as a simple measure of forest fragmentation and examined its correlation with daily nest predation. Correlations for all nine species were in the predicted direction, three correlations were significant ($P < 0.05$), and two additional species had P-values between 0.05 and 0.20. A combined probabilities test on all nine species indicated the overall effect of percent forest cover was significant ($P < 0.02$). Here we present data points and regression lines for two of the species with significant effects, and two with marginally significant effects (Fig. 3). For all these species the highest nest predation rates occurred in landscapes with less than 40% forest cover. Given the high variability in nest predation rates over both time and space, we believe these results are indicative of an important relationship even though some of the correlations were not statistically significant by the conventional criterion.

Two studies have since corroborated the hypothesis that nest predation increases with forest fragmentation in eastern forests. In a rigorously designed observational study, Donovan et al. (1997) tested hypotheses concerning edge and landscape effects on nest predation and parasitism. They randomly selected 18 landscapes from three states with high, moderate, or low levels of fragmentation and determined predation rates of artificial nests in interior and edge habitat.

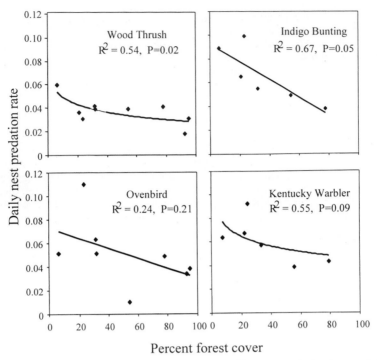

FIGURE 3.   Relationship of daily nest predation to the amount of forest cover in landscapes defined by a 10-km radius in the Midwestern United States. Data are from Robinson et al. (1995a).

Predation rates increased with forest fragmentation, and fragmentation (landscape) effects overwhelmed local edge effects (Fig. 2). Hartley and Hunter (1998) conducted a meta-analysis of a set of artificial nest experiments and showed that predation rates increased as forest cover decreased at 5-, 10-, and 25-km scales of forest cover. Both Donovan et al. (1997) and Hartley and Hunter (1998) addressed factors at multiple scales by investigating the interaction between local edge effects and landscape fragmentation effects, and we discuss this later under edge effects.

Many of the previous studies used percent forest cover in a defined landscape as the independent variable. Most, however, used this measure because it was a convenient index of fragmentation, and hypothesized predation and parasitism were high in fragmented landscapes as a result of increases in the abundance of generalist predators and cowbirds (Donovan et al. 1995b, Robinson et al. 1995a, Thompson et al. 2000).

Tewksbury et al. (1998) reported levels of predation at real nests increased with higher landscape-levels of forest cover. While their results are contrary to our hypothesis and findings for eastern forests, nevertheless they found a landscape effect on nest predation. They believed the primary predator in their landscape

was the red squirrel (*Tamiasciurus hudsonicus*), and red squirrels were more abundant in heavily forested landscapes. We believe this difference can be explained by our overall model as a difference in predator communities resulting from biogeographic and habitat differences in predator communities. Another study (Friesen et al. 1999) found relatively high nesting success in a highly fragmented landscape in Ontario, but it is not possible to conclude if this difference was due to annual variation, biogeographic context, or a lack of generality of the fragmentation effect.

The effects of landscape composition on predator abundance and distribution have received much less attention than patterns in nest success (Chalfoun et al. 2002). Raccoons (*Procyon lotor*) and opossums (*Didelphis virginiana*) reach their highest densities in highly fragmented landscapes (Andrén 1992, Dijak and Thompson 2000), potentially because their distributions are associated with developed and agricultural habitats that are interspersed with forest habitat. In eastern North America Blue Jays (*Cyanocitta cristata*) are significantly more abundant in highly fragmented landscapes with <15% forest cover than in landscapes with moderate or high forest cover (T. M. Donovan, unpubl. data). Rosenberg et al. (1999) surveyed occurrence of some potential nest predators along with tanager species; they generally found positive relationships between predators and fragmentation, but responses were often region or species specific. Abundance of some other predator species, however, may not be affected by forest patterns at a landscape scale, but by more local habitat effects such as edge.

PATTERNS OF LAND COVER AND THEIR EFFECT ON THE ABUNDANCE OF COWBIRDS AND BROOD PARASITISM

Landscape considerations seem logical for cowbirds because cowbirds utilize different habitats for feeding and breeding activities in the midwestern U.S. (Thompson 1994). Cowbirds generally feed in open grassy or agricultural areas, whereas breeding resources (hosts) are often distributed in forested areas (Rothstein et al. 1984, Thompson 1994, Thompson and Dijak 2000). Telemetry studies in Missouri and New York show that although feeding and breeding resources can overlap spatially, cowbirds move between them to optimize the use of each resource (Thompson 1994, Hahn and Hatfield 1995). In Missouri, female cowbirds tend to parasitize nests in host-rich forests in the early morning and move to open grassy or agricultural areas to feed as the day progresses (Thompson 1994, Morris and Thompson 1998, Thompson and Dijak 2000). Also, cowbirds are common in hayfields and mowed roadsides in the White Mountains of New Hampshire, but do not occur in adjacent forest even though permanent openings and clearcuts exist in the forest (Yamasaki et al. 2000). Cowbirds are also more abundant along corridors such as roads that include mowed grass, than in forest interior in New Jersey (Rich et al. 1994). While the specific habitats used differ, the same landscape relationships between feeding and breeding habitat exist in western landscapes (Rothstein et al. 1984). The probability that a cowbird occurs in a forest, therefore, depends at least partly upon the probability that a feeding area is nearby. As areas become more forested, cowbird breeding opportunities may increase but feeding opportunities may decline. Hence, in heavily forested environments such as the Missouri Ozarks, cowbird densities are low and parasitism rates of forest birds have been recorded in the 2–4% range (Clawson et al. 1997). In contrast, fragmented agricultural regions can support massive cowbird populations that attack the limited number of forest breeding birds, resulting in parasitism rates approaching 100%, with high rates of multiple-parasitism in a single nest (Robinson 1992). In this case, cowbirds are probably not

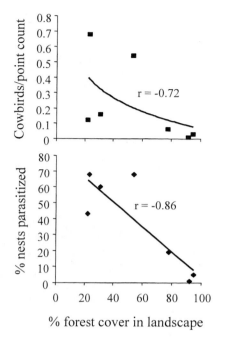

FIGURE 4. Correlation of the amount of forest cover in a 10-km radius with cowbird relative abundance and level of brood parasitism in the Midwestern United States. Data and figures are adapted from Thompson et al. 2000.

food limited but may be constrained by the number of available host nests.

Cowbird abundance and levels of parasitism are closely correlated with landscape statistics reflecting the amount of forest fragmentation, the percent of forest cover, and the amount of potential feeding habitat (agricultural land uses) in the landscape. For example the number of cowbirds and level of brood parasitism are both highly negatively correlated with the amount of forest cover in a 10-km radius (Fig. 4). Landscapes have been defined by 5- to 10-km radii in these studies (Robinson et al. 1995a, Donovan et al. 2000, Thompson et al. 2000), which relates well to the distances most cowbirds commute between breeding and feeding areas (<5 km; Thompson 1994, Thompson and Dijak 2000).

Hochachka et al. (1999) combined numerous data sets from across the United States to test the generality of the midwestern pattern at two different spatial scales. They found that increasing amounts of forest cover within 10 km of study sites was correlated with reduced parasitism rates across the continent. In contrast, when they analyzed the data using forest cover within 50 km of the study site, they found that increasing forest cover resulted in slightly increased parasitism rates in sites west of the Great Plains.

Although there are still details that we do not understand, it appears quite clear that there are landscape-level effects on cowbird densities that affect parasitism rates throughout the range of the Brown-headed Cowbird.

We have suggested that the importance of landscape composition in limiting cowbird numbers is constrained by biogeographic location. Is there evidence that landscape composition constrains the importance of local-scale effects such as host density, nest concealment, or other factors? Several studies suggest that cowbirds select habitats with high host densities (Verner and Ritter 1983, Rothstein et al. 1986, Thompson et al. 2000). However, this relationship may depend upon whether landscapes offer both breeding and feeding opportunities for cowbirds. In Missouri, cowbirds are more abundant in fragments than in contiguous forest with a comparatively greater abundance of hosts (Donovan et al. 2000). We found evidence that cowbird and host abundances were correlated in fragmented landscapes, but not in contiguous forest landscapes, suggesting that landscape composition may constrain the influence of local host abundance on local cowbird abundance. If food or host resources are scarce at the landscape scale, local habitat characteristics may not explain either cowbird abundance or parasitism levels.

Landscape composition may also constrain the importance of local-scale habitat features such as edge or patch size in determining cowbird numbers and parasitism levels. For example, in a heavily forested landscape in Vermont (94% forest cover), cowbird distribution at the patch level was best explained by examining one local-scale habitat characteristic (patch area) and two landscape-scale habitat characteristics (distance to the closest opening and the number of livestock areas [known feeding areas] within 7 km of the patch; Coker and Capen 1995). Similarly, in Missouri the distribution of cowbirds is not as well correlated with patch level statistics such as area or the ratio of perimeter to area, but by landscape-level measures that encompass the known daily movements of cowbirds (Donovan et al. 2000).

HABITAT-SCALE EFFECTS

Hypothesis: Habitat-scale factors affect the probability a nest is depredated or parasitized because of effects on predator and cowbird abundance and activity patterns or nest detectability. The strength of these effects depends on the biogeographic and landscape context.

Within a given biogeographic and landscape context, nest predation and brood parasitism should be related to habitat effects. Species demographics vary among habitats as a reflection of habitat quality. The question of interest here is whether there are consistent features or processes at the habitat scale, or interactions with landscape and biogeographic processes that elevate predation and parasitism. Several possibilities of habitat effects are patch size, proximity to edge, forest management, and nest concealment. These effects have been widely studied, yet there are substantial gaps in our knowledge and inability to explain known effects within a conceptual model. Recent reviews (Martin 1993, Paton 1994, Robinson and Wilcove 1994, Faaborg et al. 1995, Heske et al. 2001) have addressed these topics to various degrees. Here we address edge and forest management effects and how they fit within our general model.

EDGE EFFECTS

Edge effects are not uniform within or among regions (cf. Bolger *this volume*). Many studies show no edge effects or only such effects very close (<50 m) to edges (Paton 1994, Hartley and Hunter 1998). Parasitism levels remain high in forest far from edge in some landscapes (Marini et al. 1995, Thompson et al. 2000), and in at least one landscape parasitism in forest declined gradually from 70% to 5% over a gradient of 1500 m from an agricultural edge (Morse and Robinson 1999).

At least four hypotheses have been suggested for higher predation rates near edges: (1) predators may be attracted to edges because of abundant prey (a functional response; e.g., Gates and Gysel 1978, Ratti and Reese 1988); (2) predator density may be greater near edges than in forest interiors (a numerical response; e.g., Bider 1968, Angelstam 1986, Pedlar et al. 1997); (3) the predator community may be richer near edges (Bider 1968, Temple and Cary 1988, Marini et al. 1995); and (4) predators may forage along travel lanes such as edges (Gates and Gysel 1978, Yahner and Wright 1985, Small and Hunter 1988, Marini et al. 1995).

Results of edge-effects studies have been inconsistent and comparisons among studies have been confounded by lack of experimental control of landscape or habitat context, differences in predator communities, and methodological biases. Problems associated with artificial nests exist (e.g., nest appearance, lack of parental and nestling activity), but even the types of eggs used in artificial nests may bias results. Large eggs (i.e., quail or chicken) exclude predation by some small predators and predation rates are greater when small eggs are used (Haskell 1995a, DeGraaf and Maier 1996). Lack of a mechanistic approach that addresses hypotheses for why predation should be higher near edges has also hampered research. A more mechanistic approach requires studies of predator activities or abundances, not just nest predation patterns.

Equally variable are the results of nest placement studies (i.e., ground vs. shrub/elevated nests). Major and Kendal (1996) reported higher predation at elevated nests in six studies, higher predation at ground nests in four studies, and equal predation rates in three studies. Ground nests containing Japanese Quail (*Coturnix* spp.) and plasticine eggs exhibited increased predation along farm edge and interior in Saskatchewan, but there were no detectable differences in predation rate between ground and shrub nests in logged edge, in logged interior, or in contiguous forest (Bayne and Hobson 1997). Although two studies in the northeastern U.S. did not detect any difference in predation rates between ground and shrub nests (Vander Haegan and DeGraaf 1996, Danielson et al. 1997), DeGraaf et al. (1999) found a strong placement effect (high predation on ground nests) using small eggs, as did Marini et al. (1995).

Our perspective on edge effects is from studies in eastern forests that largely investigated predation of forest bird nests by medium sized mammals such as raccoons and opossums, and corvids such as Blue Jays and American Crows (*Corvus brachyrhynchos*). Based on our studies and others, we offer two predictions that may help account for the variability among previous studies.

Edge effects are dependent on landscape and habitat context

The importance of landscape context is emerging as perhaps one of the few generalities that can be made concerning edge effects. Our hypothesis is that the occurrence of local edge effects is dependent on landscape composition and pattern because of dependence of predators and cowbirds on landscape-level factors. Some evidence exits to support this hypothesis. Edge effects tend not to exist in mostly forested landscapes (Heske 1995, Marini et al. 1995, Bayne and Hobson 1997, Hartley and Hunter 1998, DeGraaf et al. 1999, Chalfoun et al. 2002). Some level of forest fragmentation is necessary to support high numbers of generalist predators in eastern forests. At moderate levels of fragmentation elevated predation rates will be limited to edges because predators depend on agricultural habitats or human settlements. At extreme levels of fragmentation all forest habitat is within close proximity to these habitats and predation is high throughout the forest. We believe edge effects are a result of increases in abundance of predators due to landscape effects (fragmentation) and activity patterns of preda-

tors in fragmented landscapes (Andrén 1995, Chalfoun et al. 2002).

As previously discussed, Donovan et al. (1997) directly tested this hypothesis with a rigorous field experiment using artificial nests, and found strong support for it. Hartley and Hunter (1998) detected the same effects in a meta-analysis of artificial nest studies. In a different meta-analysis Chalfoun et al. (2002) determined that predator responses to edges, patch size, or fragmentation were not independent of landscape context. Predator abundance or activity was related to edge, patch area, or fragmentation in 66.7% of tests when adjacent land use was agricultural, 5.6% when forest, 16.7% when grassland, 5.6% when clearcut forest.

In addition to the effect of landscape context on predator abundance, landscape and habitat contexts also affect the species of predators present. The variability in results among studies of egg predation may reflect differences in nest predator communities or the abundance of particular species in study areas (e.g., Picman 1988). For example, in New England Blue Jays and raccoons were predominant predators of artificial nests in suburban forests, whereas fishers (*Martes pennanti*) and black bears (*Ursus americanus*) were important in extensive forest (DeGraaf 1995, Danielson et al. 1997), and no avian nest predators were detected in the interiors of extensive forest (DeGraaf 1995).

Attempts to identify egg predators include characterizations of predation remains of real eggs (Gottfried and Thompson 1978; but see Marini and Melo 1998), impressions in plasticine (Bayne et al. 1997) and clay eggs (Donovan et al. 1997), hair catchers (Baker 1980), and remotely triggered cameras (DeGraaf 1995). The most promising technique, however, may be the use of subminiature video cameras with infrared illumination at real nests (Thompson et al. 1999, Bolger *this volume*). For example, F. Thompson and D. Burhans (pers. comm.) used this technique and determined 85% of nest predation events in old fields were by snakes, whereas 60% of predation events in forests were by raccoons.

Not all edges are the same

We suggest that negative edge effects are most likely to occur where land-use patterns or topography concentrate activities of predators, and are therefore a functional response by predators. Edge effects are most likely to occur where forest abuts habitats that provide key resources for predators. Agricultural edges generally have stronger edge effects than other types of edge (e.g., regenerating forest, grassland) on nesting success (Hanski et al. 1996, Hawrot and

Neimi 1996, Darveau et al. 1997, Hartley and Hunter 1998, Marzluff and Restani 1999, Morse and Robinson 1999; but see King et al. 1996, Suarez et al. 1996) and on predators (Chalfoun et al. 2002). Differences in results among studies likely are due at least partly to differences in habitat use among predators.

In one of the few studies of predator distributions relative to edges, Dijak and Thompson (2000) showed that raccoons respond differently to different edge types. Raccoon activity was significantly greater in forest adjacent to agricultural fields and riparian areas than in forest adjacent to roads, clearcuts, or forest interior. Studies of raccoon foraging behavior show that the degree of nest cover is much less important than local habitat heterogeneity in preventing depredation (Bowman and Harris 1980). In Illinois Blue Jays used edges differently and preferred gradual shrubby edges (J. Brawn, unpubl. data). Avian predators were more abundant in forest-dividing corridors composed of shrub-sapling vegetation than grass in New Jersey (Rich et al. 1994). Heske (1995), however, found no significant difference in predator activity adjacent to and >500m from edges. Recent work in New England oak forests showed that six species of small mammals represented 99% of captures at both forest edge and interior and their abundance and nest predation rates did not differ between edge and interior (DeGraaf et al. 1999). We believe these differences in edge effects are a result of differences in predator species, type of edge, and landscape context.

SILVICULTURAL PRACTICES

Silvicultural practices such as tree harvest and regeneration of stands (habitat patches) dramatically affect habitat scale characteristics. Bird communities can change greatly in response to these practices, and balancing the needs of species with diverse habitat needs in managed forests is a challenge for land managers and planners (see review by Thompson et al. 1995). Here we focus on two aspects of silvicultural practices that are related to concerns for forest fragmentation: fragmentation of old forests by young forests, and creation of edges between old and young forests.

Fragmentation of mature forest by young forest

Fragmentation of mature forest by young forest created by timber harvest has raised conservation concerns because of the loss of mature forest habitat and potential fragmentation effects. Both even-aged forest management and uneven-aged forest management result in changes in the bird community (Thompson et al. 1992,

Annand and Thompson 1997, Robinson and Robinson 1999). These changes in the bird community can be interpreted as good or bad depending on management objectives. Habitat needs of forest breeding birds need to be addressed by identifying conservation objectives and then evaluating the effects of land management practices on these. Young forests in the East provide habitat for at least some species acknowledged as management priorities (e.g., Kirtland's Warbler [*Dendroica kirtlandii*], Prairie Warbler [*Dendroica discolor*], Golden-winged Warbler [*Vermivora chrysoptera*]); therefore the needs of early and late successional species need to be addressed in forest management plans.

We are aware of no evidence in eastern forests that fragmentation of mature forest by young forest creates the type of negative fragmentation effects that fragmentation by agricultural or developed land uses do. We have suggested that cowbirds and generalist predators benefit from interspersion of agricultural and developed land use in forests because they provide rich food sources, but this would not seem to apply to young forests. For example, in extensively forested northern New England, predation rates on artificial ground and shrub nests were not different among timber size-classes (DeGraaf and Angelstam 1993). Likewise, predation rates on artificial ground and shrub nests were similar in managed and reserved large forest blocks (DeGraaf 1995).

Edge effects between mature and young forest

Not many studies have directly addressed edge effects in managed eastern forests. The evidence for edge effects between mature forest and recently harvested stands is highly variable and suggests results vary locally. In a study of Ovenbird (*Seiurus aurocapillus*) reproductive success in northern New Hampshire in relation to clearcutting (King et al. 1996), nests, territories, and territorial males obtaining mates were equally distributed in edge (0–200 m) and interior (201–400 m) mature forest. Nest survival was higher in forest interior in year 1, but not in year 2. The proportion of pairs fledging at least one young, fledgling weight, and fledgling wing-chord did not differ between edge and interior in either year, nor did the number of young fledged per pair. In another study artificial nests were placed in edge areas (0–5 m from edges) and interior areas (45–50 m from edges) adjacent to clearcuts and groupcuts. The probability of a nest being depredated was higher in edge than interior, and was independent of nest concealment, nest height, or whether adjacent to clearcuts or group-selection cuts (King et al.

1998). In Illinois forest predation of Kentucky Warbler (*Oporornis formosa*) nests was not related to clearcut edges (Morse and Robinson 1999). Nest predation, however, was significantly higher in clearcuts than adjacent older forests, suggesting differences in vegetation structure were important while edge was not. Edge effects can differ among species nesting in the same habitat patch as well. Woodward et al. (2001) determined that nest success of songbirds nesting in regenerating forests and cedar glades varied with distance to mature forest edge, but that patterns were different among species and did not generally increase monotonically with distance from edge.

Given that edge effects seem to vary locally it is important to remember the top down nature of our model. Landscape level fragmentation of forests by habitats that elevate predator and cowbird numbers is likely a more important determinant of nest success at a population level than are local edge effects. While some studies have demonstrated edge effects, no studies have shown a population-level effect on viability.

POPULATIONS ARE STRUCTURED AS SOURCES AND SINKS

Hypothesis: Top-down spatial constraints limit reproductive success in some fragmented landscapes in the Midwest to the point where populations in such landscapes will either decline to extinction or will persist as part of a larger, source-sink system The presence of sink populations may or may not be a detriment to the larger population, depending on the amount of sink habitat in the landscape and to what degree individuals select sink habitat for breeding.

AT A POPULATION SCALE, SINKS EXIST IN HIGHLY FRAGMENTED HABITATS

Source-sink theory (Pulliam 1988) has become a popular framework for describing the population dynamics of organisms that are affected by habitat fragmentation. Pulliam (1988) used models based on births, immigration, deaths, and emigration (BIDE models; Cohen 1969, 1971) to describe geographic subpopulations that are connected by dispersal. All subpopulations contribute individuals that make up the greater population, or the entire source-sink system. At equilibrium, a subpopulation is a source when $B > D$ and $E > I$; and is a sink when $B < D$ but $E < I$. The greater population is at dynamic equilibrium (not changing) when B (all the births) + I (all the immigrants from outside the greater population) − D (all the deaths) − E (all the emigrants that leave the greater population) = 0. If habitat fragmentation subdivides populations into more or less independent breeding subpopulations, then source-sink structure may be an appropriate demographic model.

Is there any evidence that forest passerines exhibit source-sink population structure that is linked to the degree of habitat fragmentation? Several field studies document that reproductive success of neotropical migrant birds varies across a species' range (Probst and Hayes 1987, Robinson et al. 1995a), but few studies examine the interaction of subpopulations from a source-sink viewpoint. One must know the BIDE parameters of each subpopulation to evaluate source-sink dynamics. Measurement of these parameters is extremely field intensive and potentially unachievable with current techniques because of the dispersal capabilities of birds. Surveys of bird abundance may not be capable of establishing source-sink status (Brawn and Robinson 1996).

Most empirical studies documenting sink populations use nesting data and mortality data from the subpopulation, and model population persistence over time in the absence of immigration or emigration (Ricklefs 1973, King and Mewaldt 1987, Stacey and Taper 1992, Pulliam and Danielson 1991, Donovan et al. 1995b). Without immigration, sink populations decline over time and go extinct. With immigration, however, sinks can persist with no detectable declines in numbers over time (Pulliam 1988).

What evidence is there, then, that birds are structured as sources and sinks, and that source-sink status is related to level of landscape-scale fragmentation? The evidence is very weak at this time, in part because we do not yet know the geographic scale that encompasses dispersal movements among sources and sinks. However, there is evidence that reproductive success in fragmented landscapes is too low to compensate for adult mortality (e.g., Donovan et al. 1995b, Trine 1998), and that dispersal occurs among habitat patches. For example, Trelease Woods is an isolated woodlot in central Illinois where bird populations have been censused since 1927 (Kendeigh 1982). In most years, several breeding pairs of Wood Thrush occurred in the woodlot, but three extinction events were recorded that were followed by three colonization events, suggesting that the colonists of unknown origin were not produced locally (Brawn and Robinson 1996).

Although direct evidence to support source-sink structure is weak, predictions generated from population modeling may offer some supporting evidence. Source-sink models suggest that sinks should show relatively higher year to year variation in abundance than source populations (Davis and Howe 1992). As predicted, recent empirical studies demonstrate that populations in fragmented landscapes have greater annual variation than populations in continuous landscapes, which may also affect turnover rates and local extinction (Boulinier et al. 1998). However, it is still unclear whether such variability is due to local processes (such as variability in source-sink status over time), to source-sink dispersal dynamics, or other causes.

THERE IS NO EVIDENCE THAT SINKS OR EDGES FUNCTION AS ECOLOGICAL TRAPS AT A LOCAL SCALE

Although reproductive and survival rates are too low to maintain numbers in sinks, these habitats may benefit the greater source-sink system by "housing" a large number of individuals at any given time. Additionally, a significant number of young may be produced in low-quality habitats, depending on the number of individuals breeding there (Pulliam 1988, Howe et al. 1991).

Is there evidence, however, that maintenance of sink habitat is a detriment to population persistence? Animals often have the opportunity to select among a variety of habitats that vary in quality; preferred habitats are those that are selected disproportionately to other available habitats (Johnson 1980). If individuals avoid low-quality areas, the presence of low-quality habitats may not negatively influence population persistence. However, if individuals select low-quality habitats over available, high-quality habitats for reproduction and survival, then low-quality habitats may function as ecological traps, and their presence may lead to population extirpation (Gates and Gysel 1978, Ratti and Reese 1988, Pulliam and Danielson 1991).

Edges have been suggested to be an ecological trap because they are potentially food rich and have high abundances and diversity of birds, which in turn potentially attract predators searching for food-rich areas (Gates and Gysel 1978, Ratti and Reese 1988). Woodward et al. (2001) examined the ecological trap hypotheses for several species of shrubland-nesting songbirds, and while nesting success varied with distance to edge, they found no evidence that edges acted as ecological traps. Observations of high densities of Wood Thrushes in fragmented Midwest landscapes (Donovan et al. 1995b) have led us to speculate that fragments are similarly acting as traps. High densities of birds in poor-quality fragmented landscapes and low densities in high-quality contiguous landscapes may be the result of: (1) absence of suitable habitat features such as nest sites in contiguous landscapes; (2) displacement of individuals from high quality contiguous landscapes through interspecific competition; or (3) innate preference for habitat

characteristics that more commonly occur in fragmented landscapes, such as edge.

Population models suggest that when individuals in the population selected high- and low-quality habitats in proportion to habitat availability in the landscape, landscapes could contain up to 40% low-quality habitat and still promote population persistence. However, when individuals preferred low-quality habitats over high-quality habitats, populations on landscapes containing > 30% low-quality habitat were extirpated, and the low-quality habitat functioned as an ecological trap (Donovan and Thompson 2001). Clearly, much more work is needed to determine the effect of sink habitats on population persistence.

POPULATIONS STRUCTURED AS SOURCES AND SINKS CAN GROW OR DECLINE

Populations structured as sources and sinks can grow or decline depending on the amount of sink habitat, the selection and use of sinks for breeding, and the magnitude of spatial and temporal variation in demographic parameters. It is critical that we examine how our observations of reduced fecundity or density in fragmented landscapes may impact population trends of a source-sink system. We believe our observations of correlations between nesting success and forest cover at the landscape level in the Midwest (e.g., Robinson et al. 1995a) have been uncritically cited as strong evidence that habitat fragmentation causes bird populations to decline. The negative correlation between fragmentation and nesting success offers support for the hypothesis that fragmentation of breeding habitat is causing declines in some songbird population. No one, however, has attempted to evaluate the number of source and sink populations and their effect on a regional population.

For example, Ovenbirds in the Midwest U.S. are thought to be impacted by habitat fragmentation in several ways: they are area-sensitive (Hayden et al. 1985, Burke and Nol 1998), their pairing success on fragments is often significantly lower compared with larger, contiguous patches (Gibbs and Faaborg 1990, Villard et al. 1993), and they have higher daily nest-mortality and parasitism levels in fragments compared with larger patches (Donovan et al. 1995b, Robinson et al. 1995a). Yet, Breeding Bird Survey data suggest that Ovenbirds are maintaining numbers and even increasing in many areas in the Midwest (Sauer et al. 1997). Overall population growth (the growth rate of the entire source-sink system on the landscape) may not be impacted by the poor reproductive success of birds in fragments if breeding individuals generally avoid small patches or if the landscape is dominated by larger patches that are used for breeding.

We have used modeling approaches to test how landscape composition, habitat selection, and nesting success interact to produce population increases or declines at a regional scale (Donovan and Lamberson 2001). The model combined (1) the frequency distribution of patch sizes in the landscape (e.g., highly fragmented landscapes vs. continuously forested landscapes), (2) the distribution of individuals across the range of patches in the landscape (e.g., area sensitive vs. area insensitive vs. edge distribution patterns), and (3) the fecundity of individuals as a function of patch size in the landscape (e.g., fragmentation effects on fecundity vs. no fragmentation effects on fecundity). We used this model to examine population growth under various landscape, distribution, fecundity, and survival scenarios.

Results from the model indicate that the highly cited observation that fecundity decreases as patch size decreases does not necessarily cause landscape level population declines in songbirds. When total habitat in the landscape is held constant, reduced fecundity associated with patch size could lead to population declines when landscapes are highly fragmented, or when landscapes are more continuous, but individuals occur in high densities in small patches and low densities in large patches. Thus, when landscapes offer both large and small patches for breeding (a more contiguous landscape), area-sensitive species can maintain population sizes in spite of decreased fecundity in small patches because birds achieve their highest densities in patches where fecundity is greatest, and high reproduction in such source habitats can maintain sinks within the landscape (Donovan and Lamberson 2001). Two recent large scale analyses of Breeding Bird Survey data have linked population change to fragmentation. Donovan and Flather (2002) found a significant negative correlation between the proportion of a population occupying fragmented habitat and population trend. Boulinier et al. (2001) found that richness of forest area-sensitive species was lower, and year-to-year rates of local extinction higher, on Breeding Bird Survey routes surrounded by landscapes with lower mean forest-patch size.

RESEARCH AND CONSERVATION IMPLICATIONS

We believe there is adequate corroborative evidence for this multi-scale approach to fragmentation to use this as a working model for research and conservation. We believe one of the most important conclusions from our work in eastern forests is that landscape composition is an important determinant of reproductive success, even at a local scale. In eastern forests where concerns are focused on the effects of cowbird parasitism and on generalist predators associated with agricultural and other human-dominated land uses, fragmentation of forests and a reduction in the amount of forest in the landscape results in increased levels of predation and parasitism. Future research should directly test our hypotheses of top-down constraints on reproductive success as well as hypothesized mechanisms for effects at each scale. Research should address the larger scale context of studies and potential differences among predators. There is already evidence that landscape level effects of fragmentation differ between the western and eastern United States (Tewksbury et al. 1998), which is further indication of the importance of top-down constraints and a multi-scale approach.

This model has important conservation implications as well. The importance of large-scale effects suggests that at high levels of fragmentation, conservation efforts should be focused on restoration of the landscape matrix and a reduction in fragmentation. At some level, where the landscape-level effects of fragmentation are no longer critical, local habitat management practices become important. Local management considerations could include management practices to provide appropriate habitat types, minimize edge, or manage habitat structure. Finally, while we believe fragmentation is a major conservation issue in eastern forests, we caution that not all fragmentation needs to be mitigated. Fragmentation of one habitat provides other habitats, and source-sink dynamics suggest that some proportion of a population can reside in sink habitat. A challenge for researchers, land managers, and policy-makers is to determine when fragmentation at a regional or population level is severe enough to drive population declines, and to balance competing species conservation objectives and land use.

ACKNOWLEDGMENTS

We thank the numerous graduate students, technicians, colleagues, and supporting agencies who have assisted or supported the work that led to the ideas presented in this paper.

Studies in Avian Biology No. 25:20–29, 2002.

WHAT IS HABITAT FRAGMENTATION?

ALAN B. FRANKLIN, BARRY R. NOON, AND T. LUKE GEORGE

Abstract. Habitat fragmentation is an issue of primary concern in conservation biology. However, both the concepts of habitat and fragmentation are ill-defined and often misused. We review the habitat concept and examine differences between habitat fragmentation and habitat heterogeneity, and we suggest that habitat fragmentation is both a state (or outcome) and a process. In addition, we attempt to distinguish between and provide guidelines for situations where habitat loss occurs without fragmentation, habitat loss occurs with fragmentation, and fragmentation occurs with no habitat loss. We use two definitions for describing habitat fragmentation, a general definition and a situational definition (definitions related to specific studies or situations). Conceptually, we define the state of habitat fragmentation as the discontinuity, resulting from a given set of mechanisms, in the spatial distribution of resources and conditions present in an area at a given scale that affects occupancy, reproduction, or survival in a particular species. We define the process of habitat fragmentation as the set of mechanisms leading to that state of discontinuity. We identify four requisites that we believe should be described in situational definitions: what is being fragmented, what is the scale of fragmentation, what is the extent and pattern of fragmentation, and what is the mechanism causing fragmentation.

Key Words: forest fragmentation; habitat; habitat fragmentation; habitat heterogeneity.

Habitat fragmentation is considered a primary issue of concern in conservation biology (Meffe and Carroll 1997). This concern centers around the disruption of once large continuous blocks of habitat into less continuous habitat, primarily by human disturbances such as land clearing and conversion of vegetation from one type to another. The classic view of habitat fragmentation is the breaking up of a large intact area of a single vegetation type into smaller intact units (Lord and Norton 1990). Usually, the ecological effects are considered negative (Wiens 1994). In this paper, we propose that this classic view presents an incomplete view of habitat fragmentation and that fragmentation has been used as such a generic concept that its utility in ecology has become questionable (Bunnell 1999a).

In attempting to quantify the effects of habitat fragmentation on avian species, there is considerable confusion as to what habitat fragmentation is, how it relates to natural and anthropogenic disturbances, and how it is distinguished from terms such as habitat heterogeneity. Here, we attempt to provide sufficient background to define habitat fragmentation adequately and, as a byproduct, habitat heterogeneity. This paper was not intended as a complete review of the existing literature on habitat fragmentation but merely as a brief overview of concepts that allowed us to arrive at working definitions.

There are two ways to define habitat fragmentation. First, there is a conceptual definition that is sufficiently general to include all situations. We feel a conceptual definition is needed for theoretical discussions of habitat fragmentation. Second, there is a situational definition that relates to specific studies or situations. In this paper, we review current definitions and offer a revised conceptual definition of habitat fragmentation. In addition, we propose four requisites for building situational definitions of habitat fragmentation: (1) what is being fragmented, (2) what is the scale(s) of fragmentation, (3) what is the extent and pattern of fragmentation, and (4) what is the mechanism(s) causing fragmentation. To define habitat fragmentation, it is first necessary to review current understanding of how habitat is defined, and to contrast fragmentation and heterogeneity.

FRAGMENTATION—THE HABITAT CONCEPT

Prior to understanding fragmentation of habitat, the term *habitat* must be properly defined and understood. Habitat has been defined by many authors (Table 1) but has often been confused with the term *vegetation type* (Hall et al. 1997; see Table 1). As Hall et al. (1997) point out, habitat is a term that is widely misused in the published literature. The key features of the definitions of habitat in Table 1 are that habitat is specific to a particular species, can be more than a single vegetation type or vegetation structure, and is the sum of specific resources needed by a species. Habitat for some species can be a single vegetation type, such as a specific seral stage of forest in a region (e.g., old forest in Fig. 1a). This might be the case for an interior forest species where old forest interiors provide all the specific resources needed by this species. However, habitat can often be a combination and configuration of different vegetation types (e.g., meadow and old forest in Fig. 1b). In the example shown in Figure 1b, a combination of old forest and meadow are needed to provide the specific resources for a species. Old forest may

TABLE 1. TERMS AND DEFINITIONS FOR HABITAT FRAGMENTATION

Term	Definition	Source
Fragment	—noun: a part broken off or detached; an isolated, unfinished or incomplete part —verb: to collapse or break into fragments; to divide into fragments; disunify	Flexner and Hauck (1987)
Fragmentation	—the act or process of fragmenting; the state of being fragmented —the disruption of continuity —the breaking up of a habitat, ecosystem, or land-use type into smaller parcels	Flexner and Hauck (1987) Lord and Norton (1990) Forman (1997:39)
Heterogenity	—the quality or state of being heterogeneous (composed of parts of different kinds; having dissimilar elements or constituents); composition from dissimilar parts; disparateness —uneven, non-random distribution of objects	Flexner and Hauck (1987) Forman (1997:39)
Habitat	—the resources and conditions present in an area that produce occupancy—including survival and reproduction—by a given organism —the subset of physical environmental factors that a species requires for its survival and reproduction —an area with the combination of resources (like food, cover, water) and environmental conditions (temperature, precipitation, presence or absence of predators and competitors) that promotes occupancy by individuals of a given species (or population) and allows those individuals to survive and reproduce	Hall et al. (1997) Block and Brennan (1993) Morrison et al. (1992:11)
Vegetation type	—vegetation that an animal uses	Hall et al. (1997)
Habitat fragmentation	—the reduction and isolation of patches of natural environment —an alteration of the spatial configuration of habitats that involves external disturbance that alters the large patch so as to create isolated or tenuously connected patches of the original habitat that are not interspersed with an extensive mosaic of other habitat types —landscape transformation that includes the breaking of large habitat into smaller pieces —when a large, fairly continuous tract of a vegetation type is converted to other vegetation types such that only scattered fragments of the original type remain	Morrison et al. (1992:12) Wiens (1989:201) Forman (1997) Faaborg et al. (1993)

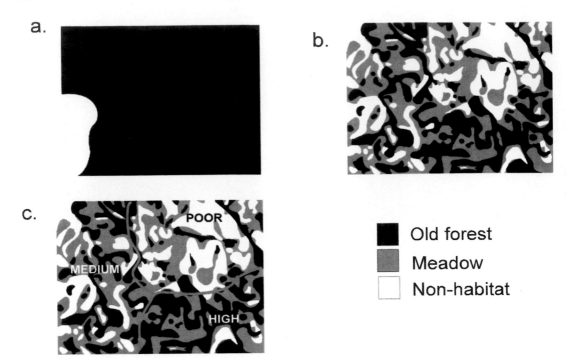

FIGURE 1.   Example of habitat represented as (a) a single vegetation type, (b) a mosaic of different vegetation types, and (c) different mosaics of vegetation types representing different degrees of habitat quality.

provide some resources necessary for survival, whereas meadow might provide resources necessary for reproduction.

In addition to considering habitat versus non-habitat (the intervening matrix), habitat can have a gradient of differing qualities (Van Horne 1983) where *habitat quality* is defined as the ability of the environment to provide conditions appropriate for individual and population persistence (Hall et al. 1997). The idea that habitat can be a specific combination and configuration of vegetation types can be extended further to different combinations and configurations representing different levels of habitat quality (Fig. 1c). Poor habitat quality may result from too much of one vegetation type relative to another. Returning to the example from Figure 1b, too much meadow may provide sufficient resources for reproduction, but not enough for survival (Fig. 1c). Habitat quality is influenced by the mix and configuration of the two vegetation types (Fig. 1c).

An important consideration in both defining and understanding habitat fragmentation is that it ultimately applies only to the species level because habitat is defined with reference to a particular species. Habitat is proximately linked to communities and ecosystems only because these levels are composed of species. There is no con-cept of community or ecosystem habitat. For example, one cannot take a vegetation map and assess habitat fragmentation without reference to a particular species. Therefore, habitat fragmentation must be defined at the species level and those levels below (e.g., populations and individuals within species).

FRAGMENTATION VERSUS HETEROGENEITY

Based on existing definitions (Table 1), *fragmentation* can be viewed as both a process (that which causes fragmentation) and an outcome (the state of being fragmented; Wiens 1994). The definitions in Table 1 suggest that fragmentation represents a transition from being whole to being broken into two or more distinct pieces. The outcome of fragmentation is binary in the sense that the resulting landscape is assumed to be composed of fragments (e.g., forest) with something else (the non-forest matrix) between the fragments. In contrast, *heterogeneity* implies a multi-state outcome from some disturbance process. For example, contiguous old-growth forest can be transformed into a mosaic of different seral stages by some disturbance such as fire (e.g., Fig. 1b). If each seral stage, as viewed by a species, is a distinct habitat, then the result of the disturbance is an increase in habitat heterogeneity. In addition, if habitat is a combination of different vegetation types, then heterogeneity in vegetation types may influence habitat quality (e.g., Fig. 1c), but does not represent fragmentation.

Habitat fragmentation is heterogeneity in its simplest form: the mixture of habitat and non-habitat. However, the effects of habitat fragmentation is also dependent on the composition of non-habitat. The matrix of non-habitat may have a positive, negative, or neutral effect on adjacent habitat. For example, non-habitat consisting of agricultural fields may have a very different effect than non-habitat consisting of younger forest. The key point is whether intervening non-habitat affects the continuity of habitat with respect to the species. We argue that habitat fragmentation has not occurred when habitat has been separated by non-habitat but occupancy, reproduction or survival of the species has not been affected. Under this argument, key components in defining habitat fragmentation are scale, the mechanism causing separation of habitat from non-habitat (i.e., the degree to which connectivity is affected), and the spatial arrangement of habitat and non-habitat. For example, a narrow road dividing a large block of habitat may not affect occupancy, reproduction or survival for a wide-ranging species, such as a raptor. However, the road may affect a species with a narrower range, such as a salamander. Thus, fragmentation is from the species' viewpoint and not ours. We discuss these points in more detail further on.

The analogy of habitat fragmentation as equivalent to the breaking of a plate into many pieces (Forman 1997:408) is of limited utility. First, habitat fragmentation generally occurs through habitat loss; unlike the broken plate, the sum of the fragments is less than the whole. For example, in a uniform landscape composed entirely of a single habitat, fragmentation is only possible if accompanied by habitat loss. Thus, fragmentation usually involves both a *reduction* in area and a *breaking* into pieces (Bunnell 1999b). Second, the transition from being whole to being in pieces may lead to a change in quality of one or more of the fragments if habitat quality is a function of fragment size. For example, fragmentation of continuous forest (accompanied by an inescapable reduction in forest area) may change the quality of the fragments; habitat quality may increase for edge species and decrease for forest interior species (Bender et al. 1998).

When the effects of habitat loss and fragmentation are addressed independently, habitat loss has been suggested as having the greatest consequences to species viability (e.g., McGarigal and McComb 1995, Fahrig 1997). This observation led Fahrig (1999) to suggest the need to distinguish three cases: (1) habitat loss with no fragmentation; (2) fragmentation arising from the combined effects of habitat loss and breaking into pieces; and (3) fragmentation arising from the breaking apart but with no loss in habitat area. These three cases are illustrated in Figure 2. It is possible to illustrate these cases with reference to a common landscape only if the reference landscape is composed of at least one habitat and a surrounding matrix within the bounded landscape (Fig. 2). This occurs because case (3) requires the ability to shift the location of the focal habitat within the landscape boundaries. If there was no matrix within the landscape boundaries (e.g., the landscape was composed entirely of the single habitat), then only cases (1) and (2) in Fig. 2 would apply.

The possibilities illustrated in Fig. 2 are not artificial constructs. Conservation planning usually occurs in a context of habitat mosaics with a diversity of land uses and land ownerships. As such, case 3 is a common result of conservation tradeoffs. For example, wetland mitigation in the U.S. often requires no net loss in wetland area but allows a change in the spatial pattern and location of wetlands. Thus, it is possible to break one large wetland into two or more pieces, mitigate this loss somewhere else on the landscape by creating additional wetlands, and claim no net loss in area.

Fragmentation arising from habitat loss unavoidably leads to an increase in heterogeneity in habitat quality because the fragments may undergo a change in state either directly (through conversion) or indirectly through edge effects (see Bolger *this volume*, Sisk and Batten *this volume*). In light of the previous discussion, this possibility suggests that we need another case in addition to those discussed by Fahrig (1999). This case (case 4 in Fig. 2) includes changes in the spatial pattern of a habitat that are, or are not, accompanied by a change in the quality of the habitat. Case (4) would occur as a byproduct of case (2) depending on the habitat requirements of the species in question.

We attempt to capture these differences in outcome in a dichotomous flow diagram (Fig. 3). Following the diagram from top to bottom requires the investigator to answer a series of questions: "Has there been a reduction in area of the focal habitat?" "Has there been a change in spatial continuity of the habitat?" "Has there been a change in quality of the focal habitat?" Answering this progression of questions allows one to discriminate habitat loss from fragmentation, and to recognize cases where habitat quality has changed.

A final point is that fragmentation of vegeta-

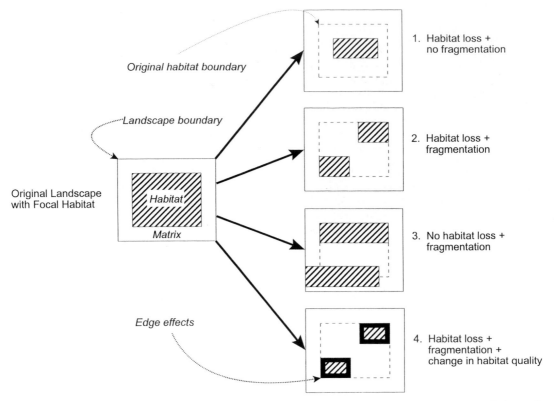

FIGURE 2.   Four cases illustrating the relationship between habitat loss, habitat fragmentation, and change in habitat quality in a bounded landscape.

tion type and habitat fragmentation are often considered synonymous (e.g., the definition by Faaborg et al. (1993) in Table 1). However, the extent and effects of fragmentation can be very different when habitat is considered a single vegetation type or a combination of vegetation types (Fig. 4). Starting with the landscape in Figure 4, forest fragmentation would only be

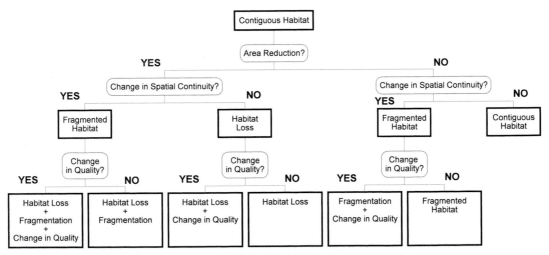

FIGURE 3.   Flow diagram to differentiate between landscapes experiencing habitat loss, habitat fragmentation, and changes in habitat quality.

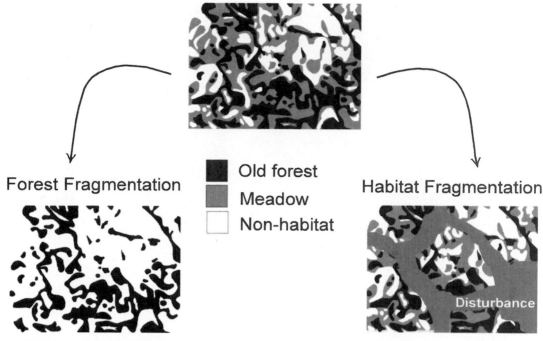

Old forest
Meadow
Non-habitat

Forest Fragmentation

Habitat Fragmentation

Disturbance

FIGURE 4. Schematic differences in forest fragmentation and habitat fragmentation in a landscape composed of a habitat consisting of two vegetation types (old forest and meadow).

considered as habitat fragmentation for a species whose habitat was solely defined as interior old forest (a single vegetation type). However, for the hypothetical example used previously where a species' habitat is composed of two vegetation types (meadow and old forest), habitat fragmentation would occur when some disturbance (such as a flood) disrupted the continuity in the configuration of these two vegetation types (Fig. 4). Thus, to define habitat fragmentation adequately, habitat must first be defined at a scale relevant to the species being examined.

WHAT IS THE SCALE OF FRAGMENTATION?

The second requisite for defining habitat fragmentation is determining the scale at which fragmentation is occurring. Wiens (1973) and Johnson (1980) recognized different scales in understanding distributional patterns and habitat selection, respectively. For example, Johnson (1980) proposed first-order selection at the geographical range of a species, second-order at the home range of individuals or social groups, and third-order at specific sites within individual home ranges. A similar hierarchical scaling can be used in defining and understanding habitat fragmentation. For example, habitat fragmentation could be considered at a *range-wide scale* for fragmentation that occurs throughout a spe-

cies geographic distribution, a *population scale* where fragmentation occurs within populations connected by varying degrees by animal movement, and a *home-range scale* for fragmentation that occurs within home ranges of individuals (Fig. 5). While this scaling can be subdivided into finer intermediate levels, the idea remains the same; habitat fragmentation is scale-dependent with different processes predominating at the different scales for a given species. For example, fragmentation at the range-wide scale can affect dispersal between populations, fragmentation at the population scale can alter local population dynamics, and fragmentation at the home range scale can affect individual performance measures, such as survival and reproduction. Clearly, the different scales are not mutually exclusive, but provide a unifying nested relationship that allows for understanding mechanisms and processes at different levels (Johnson 1980).

Rather than a hierarchical scale, Lord and Norton (1990) proposed a continuous gradient of scale. At one end of the gradient, they defined *geographical fragmentation* where fragments are large relative to the scale of the physiognomically dominant plants (Fig. 6a) and, at the opposite end, they defined *structural fragmentation* where fragments are individual plants or small

Range-wide Scale   # Population Scale

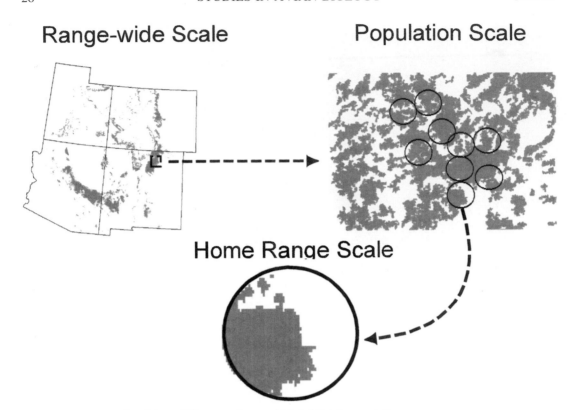

Home Range Scale

FIGURE 5.   Example of three different scales at which habitat fragmentation can occur.

groups of plants (Fig. 6b). While this gradient puts fragmentation on a continuous scale, it lacks the biological connection of the species-centered, hierarchical approach advocated by Johnson (1980). The ideal would be a gradient that is continuous and that has a biological context. Regardless of how scale is measured, a situational definition should include scale because inferences to population and distributional processes for a given species are limited to whatever scale is being examined. Fragmentation that affects processes at the home range scale (i.e., individual survival and reproduction) do not necessarily affect processes at a population or range-wide scale (i.e., dispersal between populations of home ranges). For example, fragmentation that affects foraging sites within the home range of an individual may not impede the ability of the offspring of that individual to disperse across a wider area.

WHAT IS THE EXTENT AND PATTERN OF FRAGMENTATION?

Here, we refer to the *extent* of habitat fragmentation as the degree to which fragmentation has taken place within a specified spatial scale,

whereas the *pattern* of fragmentation describes patch geometry, e.g., size, shape, distribution, and configuration. Extent describes how much fragmentation has taken place (Fig. 7) whereas geometry describes the pattern of habitat fragmentation. For example, the patterns of fragmentation in Figure 8 appear very different even though the total amounts of remaining habitat are the same. Various spatial parameters and statistics (e.g., Turner and Gardner 1991, McGarigal and Marks 1995) can be used to describe the different patterns in Figure 8. A considerable literature exists on how to describe the extent and pattern of habitat fragmentation and we will not review these quantitative methods here. However, a situational definition should include some measure of extent and pattern of fragmentation to place it in context.

WHAT IS THE MECHANISM CAUSING FRAGMENTATION?

Habitat fragmentation often occurs because of some disturbance mechanism. However, habitat fragmentation can be *static,* such as resulting from topographic differences (Forman 1997: 412). For example, habitat used by Mexican

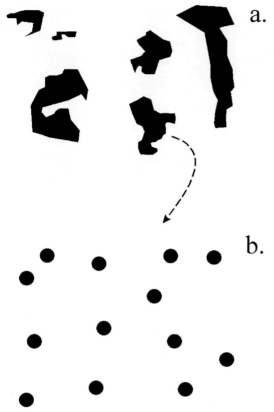

FIGURE 6. Example of (a) geographical fragmentation as illustrated by patches of sagebrush and (b) structural fragmentation as illustrated by the distribution of individual sagebrush plants on a plot within one of the patches (after Lord and Norton 1990).

Spotted Owls (*Strix occidentalis lucida*) is distributed on a range-wide scale in a highly fragmented manner across four states in the U.S. (Keitt et al. 1997; see Fig. 5). This distribution is essentially fixed over an ecological time frame.

Dynamic mechanisms occur with some frequency within a time frame that is applicable to the ecology of the species and the habitat they use. These mechanisms can be "natural" (fire, wind, etc.) or anthropogenic (logging, agriculture, urbanization, etc.; Forman 1997:413). In a given area at a given scale, these mechanisms can simultaneously fragment habitat for some species while creating habitat for others. In conservation issues, the mechanisms causing habitat fragmentation are often of primary concern, especially when these mechanisms are human-induced.

A complete description of fragmentation must include an understanding of how the matrix in-

fluences the ability of the habitat to support a species. If the matrix differs substantially from the original habitat, the impacts on the species may be more severe than if the matrix differs little. That is, fragmentation is also a function of the degree of contrast in quality between the focal habitat and its neighborhood. For example, both selective logging and building homes may cause fragmentation of unharvested forest but the consequences may be very different for the species that inhabit the landscape. Most measures of habitat fragmentation do not consider the effects of the matrix on the survival and reproduction of individuals or populations within the remaining patches.

Understanding what mechanisms are contributing to habitat fragmentation is important for placing habitat fragmentation into the context of either an acceptable ecological process (i.e., resulting from natural mechanisms) or a required conservation action (i.e., fragmentation resulting from anthropogenic mechanisms). Current dogma on habitat fragmentation is value-biased toward a negative connotation (Wiens 1994, Meffe and Carroll 1997); use of the term currently implies that the biological effects are negative. However, habitat fragmentation can be value-neutral or positive, depending on the species.

FRAGMENTATION—A CONCEPTUAL DEFINITION

We propose that the state (or outcome) of habitat fragmentation can be defined conceptually as *the discontinuity, resulting from a given set of mechanisms, in the spatial distribution of resources and conditions present in an area at a given scale that affects occupancy, reproduction, or survival in a particular species.* From this, the process of habitat fragmentation can be defined as *the set of mechanisms leading to the discontinuity in the spatial distribution of resources and conditions present in an area at a given scale that affects occupancy, reproduction, and survival in a particular species.* In developing these definitions, we incorporated definitions proposed by Lord and Norton (1990) and Hall et al. (1997; Table 1) and included three of the four requisites that we previously outlined. The fourth requisite, the extent and pattern of fragmentation, was not included because it hampers the ability of the definition to be general. However, scale and mechanism are included in the definition to avoid, even in general terms, misleading statements. The term habitat fragmentation has acquired a negative connotation over the years (Wiens 1994). Habitat fragmentation can occur naturally and the term should not be interpreted solely in terms of its potential negative impacts. Our definition re-

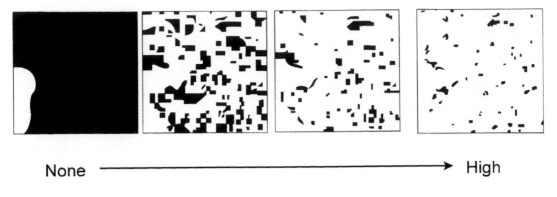

None ⟶ High

Extent of Fragmentation

FIGURE 7.   Schematic representation of changes in the extent of fragmentation (after Curtis 1956).

moves the value-bias that currently is attached to the phrase "habitat fragmentation."

How does our definition differ from previous definitions? We believe our definition is more specific than the definition proposed by Morrison et al. (1992) and explicitly incorporates the concept of continuity (Lord and Norton 1990) that is lacking in the definitions of Wiens (1989) and Forman (1997) (Table1). The definition by Faaborg et al. (1993) does not fit the definitions of habitat by Block and Brennan (1993) and Hall et al. (1997), and is more applicable to vegetation type fragmentation than to habitat fragmentation.

SITUATIONAL DEFINITIONS

To state that "the habitat is fragmented" is insufficient for understanding the scope of a particular conservation problem or the potential effects on the status of a given species in a given area. When defining fragmentation for a given situation (say, within a particular study, conservation plan, or for a given species), statements

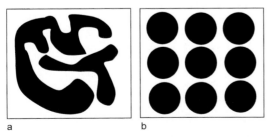

a   b

FIGURE 8.   Examples of different patterns of habitat fragmentation for an area having equal habitat amounts but (a) fewer large patches with higher edge to interior ratio versus (b) greater number of small patches with lower edge to interior ratio.

about habitat fragmentation should include the four requisites discussed earlier. The first requisite, what is being fragmented, requires an understanding of a species' habitat. The second requisite, scale, is essentially a statement as to where inferences are being made and the level of habitat description being considered (e.g., stands of vegetation versus structure of vegetation within stands). The third requisite, extent and pattern of fragmentation, provides a description of the magnitude and type of habitat fragmentation. The fourth requisite, mechanisms, puts habitat fragmentation into a temporal scale (how rapidly changes occur over time) and also into an ecological and conservation context ("natural" versus anthropogenic, or situations in between).

A situational definition for habitat fragmentation will not necessarily be limited to a compact statement as is the conceptual definition. Rather, it should be considered as a series of paragraphs, or even an entire manuscript that includes the four requisites. However, the four requisites should be identified and stated clearly to put habitat fragmentation for a particular situation into its appropriate context.

CONCLUSIONS

By defining habitat fragmentation as we have proposed here, people will have to think more clearly about the characteristic attributes of fragmentation. While some may consider our attempts at defining habitat fragmentation as an over-emphasis on semantics, we agree with Peters (1991) and Hall et al. (1997) that vague and inconsistent terminology in the ecological sciences leads to ineffective and misleading communication, poor understanding of concepts, and generally sloppy science. Habitat is a unifying concept in ecology (Block and Brennan 1993) and central to many of the conservation problems that ecologists face. We believe that developing precise definitions for key concepts at the interface between ecology and conservation is paramount before these concepts become so muddled that ecologists become ineffective in their ability to deal with problems and to communicate those problems to others.

ACKNOWLEDGMENTS

We thank R. A. Askins and J. A. Wiens for their thoughtful reviews of this manuscript. We also thank D. Dobkin and J. Rotenberry for their useful comments and for editing this volume.

Studies in Avian Biology No. 25:30–48, 2002.

HABITAT EDGES AND AVIAN ECOLOGY: GEOGRAPHIC PATTERNS AND INSIGHTS FOR WESTERN LANDSCAPES

THOMAS D. SISK AND JAMES BATTIN

Abstract. Habitat edges are an important feature in most terrestrial landscapes, due to increasing rates of habitat loss and fragmentation. A host of hypothesized influences of habitat edges on the distribution, abundance, and productivity of landbirds has been suggested over the past 60 years. Nevertheless, "edge effects" remains an ill-defined concept that encompasses a plethora of factors thought to influence avian ecology in heterogeneous landscapes. The vast majority of research on edge effects has been conducted in the broad-leafed forests of northeastern and midwestern North America. In general, many western habitats are more heterogeneous and naturally fragmented than their eastern counterparts, and habitat edges are a ubiquitous component of most western landscapes. These differences in landscape structure suggest that edge effects, and the mechanisms underlying them, may differ markedly in the West. We examined over 200 papers from the peer-reviewed literature on edge effects, focusing our efforts on empirical results and trends in research approaches. The relative dearth of western studies makes geographic comparisons difficult, but it is clear that mechanistic understanding of edge effects has lagged behind pattern identification. Bird responses to edge effects tend to vary markedly among species and among different edge types, while no clear pattern emerges regarding species diversity. In the context of the review, we discuss research and modeling approaches that could move our understanding of edge effects toward a more mechanistic and predictive framework.

Key Words: core area model; density; edge effects; effective area model; habitat edge; habitat fragmentation; heterogeneity; species diversity.

Habitat fragmentation increases landscape heterogeneity as continuous patches of native habitats are broken into numerous smaller, isolated patches surrounded by a matrix of different, often heavily disturbed or anthropogenic habitats (Wilcox 1980, Wilcove et al. 1986, Wiens 1994, Franklin et al. *this volume*). The loss of native habitat cover and the increasing isolation of the resulting patches from one another have been the subject of numerous empirical and theoretical studies and several reviews (e.g., Saunders et al. 1991, Faaborg et al. 1995). Since the early 1970s these two factors have dominated debates about conservation planning in increasingly fragmented landscapes (e.g., Diamond 1976; Simberloff and Abele 1976, 1982; Terborgh 1976).

Another result of habitat fragmentation is an increase in the amount of edge habitat, as well as the proliferation of new types of edges, as anthropogenic habitats (e.g., agriculture, logged forest, and urbanized areas) replace native habitats and abut the remaining fragments. The increasing number of smaller patches, and the linear or irregularly shaped patches that often result from fragmentation (Feinsinger 1997), contribute to the rapid, often exponential increase in the amount of edge habitat in the landscape (Fig. 1).

Implications of the proliferation of edge habitat for bird populations are numerous, ranging from the alteration of microclimatic conditions to changes in interspecific interactions, such as competition, predation, and nest parasitism.

These and other edge effects are often distinct from the effects associated strictly with the loss of habitat and the increasing isolation of the remaining patches. By influencing the quality of nearby habitat in the remaining fragments, edges may also directly affect the amount of available suitable habitat (Temple 1986, Sisk et al. 1997). Thus, edge effects constitute a class of impacts that are of increasing importance as fragmentation advances and the heterogeneity and structural complexity of the landscape increases.

Despite over 60 years of active research, our understanding of edge effects remains diffuse and largely site-specific. Interestingly, the literature on "edge effects" predates research on habitat fragmentation by some 45 years, and because of this long history, a summary of the literature on edge effects parallels the development of avian ecology in general. In fact, edge effects can be viewed as the earliest attempt to study avian ecology at the landscape scale, a perspective that received less attention as the focus of field ecology shifted to population dynamics and community ecology in the 1950s through the 1970s. The conservation imperative that emerged in the seventies, driven by the recognition of rapid habitat loss and fragmentation, returned consideration of edge effects to the forefront of avian research, but in a very different context.

Our overview of edge effects traces the development of conceptual approaches through field studies, experiments, and modeling ap-

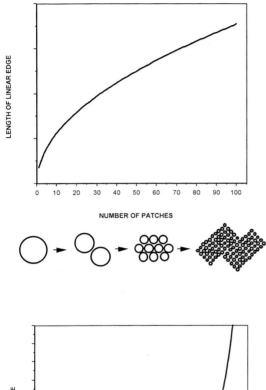

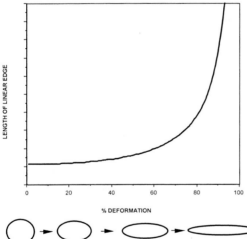

FIGURE 1. Edge habitat proliferates with increasing fragmentation, due both to the increased edge per unit area as the number of patches increases (top), and as individual patches become, on average, more linear or irregularly shaped, as represented here as an increasingly flattened patch (bottom). From Sisk and Margules (1993).

proaches. The paper focuses on patterns in the literature, particularly the disparity in the level of research in the eastern and western United States and the emphasis upon certain habitat types. We list working hypotheses derived from the literature, and we provide brief summaries of supporting and refuting evidence. Finally, we examine more predictive approaches to the study

of edge effects so that the accumulated knowledge might be put to work in efforts to predict the impacts of ongoing fragmentation. Our ultimate goal is to incorporate a consideration of edge effects into efforts to reverse the negative impacts of fragmentation and improve reserve designs, restoration efforts, and management plans for the conservation of avian biodiversity.

EDGE EFFECTS—AN ILL-DEFINED "LAW" OF ECOLOGY

"Edge effect" is among the oldest surviving concepts (some would say "buzz-words") in avian ecology. In 1933, Leopold referred to "the edge effect" to explain why quail, grouse, and other game species were more abundant in patchy agricultural landscapes than in larger fields and forested areas (Fig. 2). He hypothesized that the "desirability of simultaneous access to more than one (habitat)" and "the greater richness of (edge) vegetation" supported higher abundances of many species and higher species richness in general (Leopold 1933). This common-sense definition drew on years of experience as a forester and game manager, and reflects the focus of early wildlife managers on game species, many of which utilize early successional and/or edge habitats preferentially. Lay (1938) provided some of the earliest empirical evidence supporting both increased abundance and greater species richness at woodland edges. His interpretation of these patterns also began a long tradition of deriving management guidelines from studies of bird abundances and species diversity at edges. His claim that the "maximum development of an area for wildlife requires . . . small but numerous clearings" was accepted by many wildlife managers and found its way into many textbooks over a period of several decades, culminating in what has been called the "law of edge effect" (Odum 1958, Harris 1988). General acceptance of the hypothesis that diversity and abundance are higher near edges led wildlife biologists to advocate the creation of edge under the assumption that it would benefit biodiversity (e.g., Giles 1978, Yoakum 1980, Dasmann 1981). This understanding of the beneficial nature of edge effects influenced land management practices for decades and served as a *de facto* prescription for habitat fragmentation in the name of wildlife management. Even today, land managers frequently advocate the creation of edges via (for example) forest clearing and prescribed fire, with the intention of increasing avian abundance and diversity.

More recently, the relationship between forest fragmentation and both nest predation and parasitism has spawned a different view of edge effects. Edges have been shown to support high-

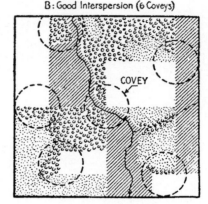

FIGURE 2.   Leopold (1933) coined the term "edge effect" to explain increased abundance of game birds in heterogeneous landscapes with many edges. In this figure, 160 ac (64.7 ha) blocks of 4 habitat types, each 40 ac (16.2 ha), are displayed in the two panels. Panel (a) has 2 mi (3.2 km) of edge, while panel (b) has 10 mi (16 km). Leopold argued that greater bird abundances are associated with the heterogeneous landscapes, such as (b).

er rates of nest predation and parasitism (Wilcove 1985, Paton 1994, Andrén 1995). Current texts are likely to present evidence that edge effects are "bad" and that the creation of edge habitat by fragmentation leads to the decline of "interior species" that are particularly susceptible to nest parasites and predators (e.g., Meffe and Carroll 1997). Again, the focus on certain aspects of edge effects (in this case nest predation and parasitism rates) has led to a widely accepted, general rule of edge effects. However, in this case, the supposedly beneficial effects are often ignored, while the adverse effects, demonstrated for a subset of species in particular habitats and in certain geographic areas, are highlighted.

Thus, perceptions of the relationship between edge effects and habitat fragmentation are often contradictory, and the reality is almost always more complex than perceptions. In some cases, edges are thought to benefit birds; in others they are seen as the primary threat to bird diversity. And in cases where edges support high bird density but low nest productivity, edge effects on population persistence may be particularly negative (Ratti and Reese 1988). Nevertheless, the term continues to be applied with little discrimination, and the assumption that all influences of habitat edges can and should be grouped into a uniform class of ecological impacts persists in the literature. The complexity and diversity of the responses of different species to differing edge types, combined with the lack of an inclusive theoretical framework for organizing the plethora of field observations reported in the literature, has turned "edge effects" into a grab-

bag term, one that too often is used casually to explain anomalous or inconclusive results. Indeed, the term edge effect has become so widely accepted in the management literature that it is commonly used to explain diametrically opposed observations.

Part of the confusion may result from changes in the scale at which species diversity is assessed. Historically, biologists and planners have focused on alpha (local) diversity, which is often high near habitat edges. As conservation planning has shifted to larger areas, and scientists have assessed regional and global patterns in biodiversity, the focus on species diversity has shifted to the gamma (regional) level, which may be lower in fragmented landscapes due to the loss of edge-avoiding species. Until scientists and managers are able to adopt a multi-scaled approach to assessing biodiversity (see Noss 1990), confusion over edge effects is likely to persist.

HISTORICAL PERSPECTIVES: RESPONSE VARIABLES, FOCAL SPECIES, AND GEOGRAPHIC PATTERNS

METHODS

We reviewed the literature on edge effects dating back to the mid-1930s in an attempt to synthesize the large and diverse body of published work in avian ecology and wildlife management. Drawing from on-line searches, published abstracts, examination of literature cited in all papers reviewed, and inquiries with colleagues, we created an annotated bibliography to facilitate analysis of patterns from published studies of edge effects. We limited our review to the peer-reviewed literature after initial attempts to include unpublished reports and other "gray literature" demon-

TABLE 1. ANALYSIS OF THE EDGE EFFECTS LITERA-
TURE BASED ON PARAMETERS LISTED BELOW, RECORDED
FOLLOWING REVIEW OF 215 PAPERS PUBLISHED OVER A
66-YR PERIOD

Study Type—observational, experimental, theoretical,
   or modeling
  Location–country, state/province
  Focal habitat type
  Adjacent habitat
  Edge definition (e.g., is the edge treated as a gradient
     or separate habitat type)
  Focal species
Study design
  Replication
  Response variable(s)
  Explanatory variable(s) measured
Results and Conclusions

strated a tremendous volume of work of highly variable quality. Inclusion of gray literature would have
substantially increased our sample size, particularly in
the West, but that literature could not be accessed in
any consistent manner, and a haphazard sampling of
material would have compromised our analyses. In this
article we attempt to present an unbiased review of the
peer-reviewed literature, and we invite the reader to
critically explore the voluminous gray literature for additional site- and species-specific information on edge
effects.

A total of 215 publications were examined for this
chapter. Of these, we eliminated from further consideration any field studies that did not explicitly address
avian response to edges (for example, studies that employ edge as one of many possible explanatory variables in multivariate analyses of fragmentation effects;

see citations in other chapters in this volume). This left
us with 125 studies, providing a comprehensive perspective on the development of the edge effects concept in the primary literature, current understanding of
edge effects in the context of habitat fragmentation,
and the application of this knowledge in the management of avian populations. Of the 125 publications reviewed, 90 presented original research results involving avian subjects (Appendix), and these are included
in the analyses presented below. For this subset of the
edge literature, we quantified aspects of each study
pertaining to the location, focal habitats, species studied, key results, and several related parameters (Table
1). Conceptual and theoretical treatments of edge effects are discussed in subsequent sections of this chapter.

Unlike the nest predation literature (see recent reviews by Paton 1994, Andrén 1995, Hartley and Hunter 1998), the literature on patterns of bird density and
diversity with respect to habitat edges has not undergone a recent review. For this reason, we analyze this
body of literature in detail. We report the density and
species richness response(s) for every treatment considered in each study (Appendix). For multi-year studies, we consider a treatment to show a response if a
statistically significant response (increased or decreased density or species richness at edges) was observed in at least one year, and a non-significant trend
in the same direction was observed in other years.

GEOGRAPHIC PATTERNS AND RESPONSE
VARIABLES

The majority of published studies of edge effects in avian ecology (88%, N = 60) are from
the eastern half of North America (Figs. 3, 4a).
Furthermore, the West has produced less than
half as much research on this topic than has

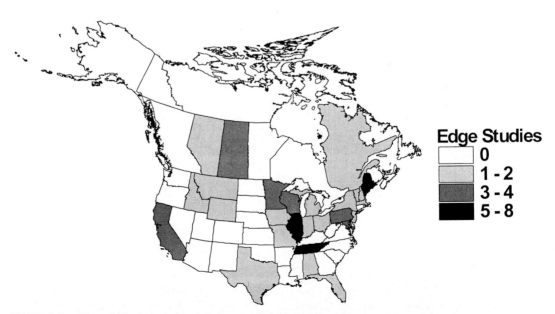

FIGURE 3. Map of North America showing number of studies addressing edge effects in landbirds.

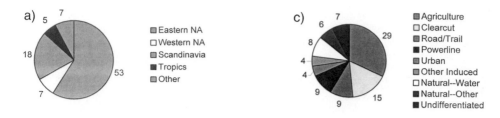

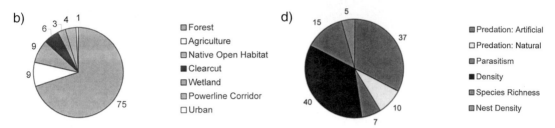

FIGURE 4.   The number of edge studies (a) by region, N = 90; (b) by habitat type, N = 90; (c) by adjacent (matrix) habitat, forest edges only, N = 75; (d) by response variable, N = 112 (some studies involved more than one edge type).

Scandinavia, where conditions are, arguably, more similar to eastern North America (Fig. 4a). Clearly, as measured by the number of peer-reviewed publications, studies in Europe and eastern North America have had a tremendous influence on our understanding of edge effects.

Not surprisingly, since forests are the dominant natural habitats in these regions, 73% of all empirical studies focused on forest edges (Fig. 4b), and 33% of these were edges with agricultural habitats (Fig. 4c). Again, there is a geographic bias, as conversion of forested habitats to agriculture (and the reverse) has been a predominant land-use trend in the East and Midwest, whereas edges in western habitats are most often due to timber harvest and a range of factors that degrade, but less often radically transform, native habitats. When this distribution of research effort is viewed in the context of the overall habitat diversity of North America, and when the range of natural and anthropogenic factors that modify habitats and create edges is considered, it is apparent that our understanding of edge effects is largely the product of research focused on a small subset of edge types in eastern, midwestern, and northern European forest edges.

Examination of the response variables measured in empirical edge studies reveals a strong tendency to focus on patterns in species abundance (44% of all studies) and species richness (17%; Fig. 4d). This work highlights patterns in avian distribution near edges but typically does not examine the factors creating the patterns. Fifty-two per cent of all studies quantified rates of nest predation, but of these only 21% looked at natural nests. The remainder manipulated the placement of artificial nests to estimate relative rates in the wild. Nest parasitism, a topic mentioned at least parenthetically in most recent publications on edge effects, was quantified in only 7 of the papers that we reviewed (8%; Fig. 4d). Many other potentially important variables, including competitive interactions, pairing success, movement and dispersal rates, and edge permeability have received scant attention in empirical studies of avian edge effects.

EDGES AND NEST PREDATION

Three recent reviews that have examined the relationship between forest edges and predation have found that, while evidence exists for higher predation rates at edges, this pattern is far from universal (Paton 1994, Andrén 1995, Hartley and Hunter 1998). These reviews addressed not only the question of how frequently predation edge effects occur, but also looked for explanations regarding why some studies found edge effects and others did not. Landscape context was the primary explanatory variable used by all authors, but they drew markedly different conclusions about its importance.

Paton (1994) examined edge effects in nest predation on artificial nests and in both predation and parasitism on natural nests. He found that 10 of 14 studies using artificial nests showed evidence of differential nest predation at edges, compared with 4 of 7 studies of natural nests. Of the 14 studies showing differences, most showed higher predation at edges. Just under half of the 32 studies examined by Andrén (1995) showed higher predation rates near edges, while only 5 of the 13 North American studies examined by Hartley and Hunter (1988) found a difference in predation rates between habitat edges and interiors. These reviews indicate that high nest predation rates occur near edges, but not consistently. Some studies reviewed by Andrén (1995) and Paton (1994) even found lower predation near edges.

In seeking to explain this variable pattern of edge effects, the three reviews draw strikingly different conclusions, though they consider many of the same papers. Paton (1994) concluded that "significant edge effects were as likely to occur in forested as in unforested habitats." Andrén (1995) concluded that predation near edges was more likely in agricultural than in forested landscapes. Hartley and Hunter (1998), who conducted a substantially more rigorous meta-analysis of the association between forest cover and edge effects, found a marginally significant (P = 0.095) pattern of higher predation in unforested than in forested landscapes. Unfortunately, the power of their analysis was limited, as they considered only two studies from unforested landscapes.

One possible explanation for the inconsistencies in the findings of these different studies is that Andrén (1995) considered both edge effects and patch size effects in a single analysis, while Paton (1994) and Hartley and Hunter (1998) analyzed edge effects and patch size effects separately. In contrast to their equivocal findings on the relationship between landscape context and the presence of edge effects, both Paton (1994) and Hartley and Hunter (1998) found a very strong relationship between nest predation rate and patch size. This result suggests that Andrén (1995) may have confounded effects by lumping patch size and edge effects in his analysis, and that the strong pattern that he detected could be due to patch size rather than edge effects *per se*.

Another difficulty in interpreting these results is that most of the studies of edge effects on nest predation have been conducted using artificial nests. Hartley and Hunter (1998) used only artificial nest studies in their analysis, while Andrén combined artificial and natural nests. Paton considered artificial and natural nest studies separately, but he found only 7 natural nest studies. The use of artificial nests has been questioned repeatedly in recent years (see Willebrand and Marcstrom 1988; Haskell 1995a,b; Major and Kendal 1996, Yahner 1996), and Haskell (1995a,b) suggested that there is a systematic bias toward increased predation on artificial nests in smaller fragments, a finding that could be especially misleading in studies of predation near edges.

While evidence of increased predation rates near edges does exist, it is not clear that this is a widespread phenomenon, or that it is pronounced in the West. We found only two studies of nest predation in the West, one that used artificial nests (Ratti and Reese 1988) and one that used natural nests (Tewksbury et al. 1998). Neither study found a significant edge effect in nest predation.

PATTERNS IN COMMUNITY ORGANIZATION

For several decades, "edge effects" referred almost exclusively to the increase in species diversity and/or density commonly observed near the edge (Johnston 1947, MacArthur et al. 1962, Giles 1978). A total of 21 studies, with 34 separate treatments, examined density or species richness of the entire bird community (Appendix). Of these, 21 treatments reported higher bird densities near edges, while 10 reported no edge response and 3 showed a decrease. The vast majority of these studies (19 studies, addressing 27 treatments) were conducted in forested habitats, so we restrict our more detailed analyses to these results.

Overall, forest studies showed a strong pattern of higher density at edges but a weaker pattern with regard to species richness. Sixteen treatments recorded higher bird abundance near edges, with 8 showing no significant response and 3 a negative response. Nine treatments found higher species richness at edges, while 10 found no difference, and 2 found a decrease. While an unequivocal pattern of higher bird density and species richness at edges does not emerge from this analysis, it seems clear that, in the recent literature, negative responses to edges are relatively rare and positive responses are common. This could be a manifestation of a general ecological principle (i.e., density and species richness increase at most edges) or the result of a bias in the literature (edge responses in areas where studies have been done are different from those in unstudied areas). Because, as we have shown, there is a strong geographical bias in the literature, this second explanation cannot be ruled out.

All studies (9 studies, 9 treatments) conducted

in temperate zone forests that examined total bird abundance at edges between native forests and large anthropogenic openings (matrix = agriculture, clearcut, clearing, anthropogenic grassland; see Appendix) found higher bird densities near the edge. Of the 7 studies that also looked at species richness, 3 found an increase while 4 found no significant pattern. On the other hand, the only study that looked at the difference in overall bird density and species richness along an anthropogenic edge gradient in the tropics found that both decreased near the edge (Lovejoy et al. 1986). Another tropical study, which analyzed edge response by foraging guild, found that two guilds did not differ in abundance and one (insectivores) decreased at the edge (Canaday 1997). These results suggest that even the strongest patterns detected in temperate forests may not generalize well to other habitats and geographic regions.

The effects of linear drivers of habitat fragmentation (roads and powerlines) and natural edges appear to be less consistent. While no studies of road or powerline edges found community-level decreases in avian density, 4 of 7 treatments showed increases and 3 of 7 showed increased species richness. Of the studies that examined natural edges (6 studies, 8 treatments), 3 treatments showed increased density, 4 showed no change, and 1 showed a decrease. Four treatments showed increased species richness at natural edges, with 2 showing no change, and one showing a decrease.

Aside from the suggestion that edge responses may differ between the tropics and the temperate zone, no clear geographical patterns of edge response were evident. No studies from eastern North America recorded decreases in total bird abundance (Fig. 5a) or species richness (Fig. 5b) at edges, but almost as many treatments showed no response in overall bird density (6) as showed an increase (9). As many treatments showed no response in species richness (7) as showed a positive response near edges (7). The only study from western North America had one treatment that showed increased density and species richness at the forest edge and one that showed no change in either variable (Sisk 1992). Two Scandinavian studies showed decreases in density at edges, while 1 reported no change and 2 found increases. We were surprised at the small number of studies that reported on the entire avian community, especially considering the widely held "rule of thumb" associating edges with higher densities and/or species richness. Many of the studies most commonly cited to support this idea examine only part of the bird community present at the study site.

Many explanations for the reported trends in

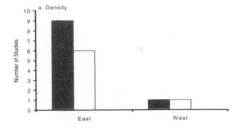

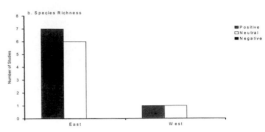

FIGURE 5. Numbers of treatments from studies conducted in eastern and western North America finding positive, negative, or neutral edge responses in total bird density (a) and species richness (b).

avian abundance and diversity near edges have been proposed, and few are mutually exclusive. Few studies have attempted to distinguish among them, and many authors have invoked "edge effects" when discussing any of the myriad influences of habitat fragmentation on disturbance-sensitive species. From this broad range of uses, four general categories of edge effects can be identified:

- *Habitat interspersion.* Species diversity may increase at habitat edges due solely to the proximity of different habitats (Leopold 1933, Giles 1978). At the habitat edge, each community contributes, on average, more than half of its fauna, resulting in higher species diversity at the edge where the two communities mix (MacArthur and MacArthur 1961, Wiens 1989).
- *Resource availability.* Many authors have suggested that birds may utilize more than one habitat type during different activities (e.g., nesting and foraging) or during different life stages. Allocating different activities to the most appropriate habitat may allow some species to maintain higher population densities near edges. It also may provide suitable habitat for species that require more than one habitat type (Kendeigh 1944, MacArthur et al. 1962, Yoakum 1980, Dasmann 1981).
- *Edge as a unique habitat.* Edges may support higher densities of species characteristic of both the adjoining communities, due to in-

creased diversity of the vegetation that typically occurs where two habitats intergrade. Many workers have shown correlations between foliage height diversity and bird species diversity (e.g., MacArthur 1958, Cody 1968, Karr and Roth 1971; but see also Willson 1974). Other studies have shown that floristic composition and the presence or absence of particular plant species are good predictors of both diversity and density of birds (Wiens 1989). Vegetation structure and floristic composition are generally more diverse at edges, so increases in both species diversity and avian density might be expected, even without the addition of edge-dependent species.

- *Interspecific interactions and cascading biotic effects.* Edges, especially those associated with habitat conversion and fragmentation, may permit edge-dependent or habitat-specific species to penetrate some distance into adjacent habitats where they normally do not occur. Their presence can influence the abundance of species in the adjacent habitat, generating cascading effects that penetrate further than the direct environmental changes associated with the edge (Diamond 1978, 1979; Pulliam and Danielson 1991, Fagan et al. 1999). Such secondary effects, including competition, predation, and nest parasitism, are thought to result in the exclusion of forest species from otherwise suitable habitat near habitat edges (Ambuel and Temple 1983, Wilcove et al. 1986, Harris 1988).

SPECIES-LEVEL RESPONSES UNDERLYING COMMUNITY PATTERNS

Each of the definitions of edge effects presented above implies that population densities of some species will change as a function of the distance from the habitat edge. However, few authors have stated explicitly which species they expect to be influenced by habitat edges or how they will respond. In fact, many early studies that support the hypothesis of elevated diversity at edges do not report *which* species contribute to the diverse assemblages found there. Those that do often show that the increase in species richness is due to the addition of common, cosmopolitan, or disturbance-tolerant species, which may mask the loss or decline of sensitive species.

A better understanding of the dynamics in community organization near edges emerges from studies of the responses of individual species near habitat edges (Giles 1978, Dasmann 1981, Harris 1988, Reese and Ratti 1988, Noss 1991, Bolger *this volume*). Many studies have shown that certain species reach their highest or lowest abundance at particular habitat edges

(e.g., Kendeigh 1944, Johnston 1947, Hansson 1983, Kroodsma 1984b, Noss 1991, Bolger et al. 1997, Germaine et al. 1997, King et al. 1997). Species that are encountered more commonly near the edge are often termed "edge species" (e.g., Johnson 1975, Giles 1978, Reese and Ratti 1988), and those whose densities are low near the edge are considered to be habitat-interior species (e.g., Brittingham and Temple 1983, Wilcove et al. 1986, Thompson 1993, Bolger et al. 1997). A more quantitative approach to understanding how species respond to habitat edges involves measurement of a species-specific edge response, defined as the pattern of change in population density at incremental distances from the habitat edge (Noss 1991, Sisk and Margules 1993).

Sisk and Margules (1993) proposed a classification scheme for population-level edge responses based on changes in density along a transect from one interior habitat, across the edge, and into the adjacent habitat (hereafter the edge gradient). For some species, the edge itself has no effect on population density (null responses), and changes in density are attributable to differences between the two adjoining habitats. Other species reach their highest density ("edge exploiters") or lowest density ("edge avoiders") near edges (see also Bolger *this volume*). While classification schemes differ among the published studies reviewed here, it is clear that a diversity of responses is manifest in any particular avian community. Four studies from eastern North America show that edge-exploiting responses are generally more common than edge-avoiding responses, with neutral responses (i.e., no edge effect) more common than either in 3 out of 4 studies (Fig. 6a). The small number of Western studies showed similar patterns, except that edge-exploiting responses outnumbered edge-neutral responses (Fig. 6b).

Villard (1998) compared the edge responses of forest-interior neotropical migrants reported in 4 studies from the eastern seaboard stretching from Florida to New Hampshire. He found that there was little consistency in the way that the authors classified responses for the same species. We extended this analysis to all species that occurred in two or more of the studies (Table 2). While there is considerable variability in the responses reported for these species, some patterns do emerge. Most neotropical migrants are edge avoiders, and all disagreements among authors have to do with whether a species shows a neutral response or a positive or negative response; no species is considered an edge-exploiter by one author and an edge-avoider by another. Conversely, species that are not latitudinal migrants showed neutral or edge-exploiting responses.

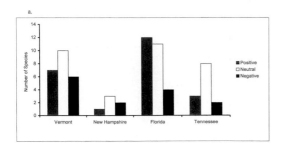

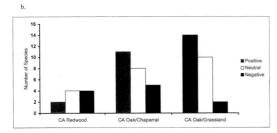

FIGURE 6. Numbers of bird species in four studies showing positive, negative, or neutral responses to habitat edges. Eastern studies (a) were conducted in Vermont (Germaine et al. 1997), New Hampshire (King et al., 1997), Florida (Noss, 1991), and Tennessee (Kroodsma, 1982). Western studies (b) are from California redwood stands (Brand and George *this volume*) and California oak woodlands (Sisk 1992, Sisk et al. 1997).

Again, no species was assigned a positive response by one author and a negative response by another (Table 2). Unfortunately, there are not enough studies of western birds to make similar comparisons, and there is little overlap in species among the few published studies. Three studies from California do, however, seem to show greater variation in the responses of both neotropical migrants and resident species (Sisk et al. 1997, Brand and George *this volume*, Bolger *this volume*).

Ecologists and wildlife managers have often assumed that birds will show consistent, characteristic patterns of habitat selection at edges, even when the adjoining habitats differ in vegetation structure and/or species composition. Implicit in this assumption is the idea that edges of all types share some intrinsic qualities, and that their influence on the distribution of organisms and the composition of assemblages is similar. There is little evidence to support these views. Few studies have measured edge responses at more than one type of edge in a given region, and those that have report differences in the consistency of avian responses at different edge

types. Noss (1991) found considerable variation among species and among sites in longleaf pine (*Pinus palustris*) bird communities. Sisk et al. (1997) showed that over half of the breeding birds in oak woodland showed different responses at edges with grassland versus edges with chaparral, and Kristan et al. (in press) found significant site-to-site variation in edge response in several southern California coastal sage scrub bird species. Brand and George (*this volume*) found general consistency at redwood forest edges adjoining habitats as different as logged forest and grassland.

In summary, our examination of empirical studies of edge effects did not identify a simple pattern in avian responses, but it did uncover several important points regarding patterns in community organization and population responses to habitat edges:

- "Edge effects" is an ambiguous term in avian ecology and conservation. Its usefulness is limited by widely varying assumptions that permeate its history.
- Edge effects do not contribute to species diversity in a consistent manner that is easily generalized among sites.
- The abundances of many species change dramatically near habitat edges.
- Edge responses vary markedly among species.
- A given species often responds very differently at different types of edges (but a few studies show consistency).

MECHANISMS UNDERLYING SPECIES-LEVEL RESPONSES

Mechanisms underlying edge effects are many, but few have been adequately investigated (Bolger *this volume*). Sisk and Haddad (2002) hypothesize that several basic driving factors may underlie the broad range of responses typically grouped together under the term "edge effects". These include:

- *Edges influence movement.* Edges may influence behavior, creating barriers to movement even when animals are clearly capable of crossing them (Ries 1998, Haddad 1999). The influence of edges may prevent dispersal through complex landscapes and isolate animals. Sisk and Zook (1996) have shown that "passive accumulation" of migrating birds may generate widely reported increases in density observed near forest edges.
- *Edges influence mortality.* Particularly for habitat interior species, edges may lead to higher mortality in plants and animals. Higher mortality may occur in three different ways. First, edges create greater opportunity for loss

TABLE 2. VARIATION IN SPECIES-SPECIFIC EDGE RESPONSES REPORTED IN DIFFERENT EMPIRICAL STUDIES FROM THE EASTERN USA

Common name	Scientific name	Tennessee (Kroodsma 1984)	Florida (Noss 1991)	New Hampshire (King et al. 1997)	Vermont (Germaine et al. 1997)
Neotropical Migrants					
Yellow-billed Cuckoo	*Coccyzus americanus*	0	+		
Acadian Flycatcher	*Empidonax virescens*	−	−		
Wood Thrush	*Hylocichla mustelina*	0	−		
Hermit Thrush	*Catharus guttatus*		0	−	−
Red-eyed Vireo	*Vireo olivaceus*	0	−	−	−
Black-and-white Warbler	*Mniotilta varia*	+	0		0
Black-throated Blue Warbler	*Dendroica caerulescens*			0	+
Black-throated Green Warbler	*Dendroica virens*			0	+
Hooded Warbler	*Wilsonia citrina*	0	−		
Ovenbird	*Seiurus aurocapillus*	−	0	0	−
American Redstart	*Setophaga ruticilla*			0	0
Summer Tanager	*Piranga rubra*	+	+		
Scarlet Tanager	*Piranga olivacea*	0		0	0
Temperate Migrants					
American Robin	*Turdus migratorius*		0	0	+
Residents					
Red-bellied Woodpecker	*Melanerpes carolinus*	+	0		
Downy Woodpecker	*Picoides pubescens*	0	0		
Carolina Chickadee	*Parus carolinensis*	0	+		
Northern Cardinal	*Cardinalis cardinalis*	+	+		

Note: Results from four studies allowed the classification of 12 species according to their density responses near edges: '+' for edge-exploiting response; '0' for no edge response; '−' for edge-avoiding response; ' ' if not reported (after Villard 1998).

of dispersers into unsuitable habitat. For example, plants with wind-dispersed seeds that are near the edge will lose more of their propagules into unsuitable habitat. Second, edges alter microclimate, including temperature, light, and moisture (Sisk 1992, Chen et al. 1993, Young and Mitchell 1994, Camargo and Kapos 1995). In doing so, edges impact competitive interactions between species. Third, edges provide points of entry for predators and parasites, such as the Brown-headed Cowbird (*Molothrus ater*; Wilcove et al. 1986, Murcia 1995).

- *Edges provide feeding or reproductive subsidies.* From the edge, species may be able to obtain a greater quantity and quality of food resources from each of the habitats that create the edge, leading to positive effects on population sizes (MacArthur et al. 1962, Fagan et al. 1999).

- *Edges define the boundary between two separate habitats,* creating new opportunities for species to mix and interact. By their very nature, edges influence species interactions because they bring into close proximity species that would not normally be present in the same habitat. Species that are brought together at the edge, including predators and prey, new competitors, and mutualists, generate novel interactions and create new communities of species.

Despite the diversity of hypothesized and documented mechanisms underlying edge effects, surprisingly few studies have attempted to identify the mechanistic basis for edge response and patterns in community organization reported in the literature. Of the 90 field studies considered in this review, most were observational, typically involving some count of individuals or nests in unmanipulated landscapes. The vast majority of experimental studies involved manipulation of artificial nests for the purposes of examining nest predation and parasitism rates; few involved the experimental manipulation of bird habitats (but see Lovejoy et al. 1986).

Forty studies focused on estimates of abundance or species richness, but few examined the mechanisms driving the observed patterns. Donovan et al. (1997) noted that little work has been devoted to exploring the mechanisms underlying observed patterns of edge effects in nest predation and parasitism. This is even more pronounced for studies examining patterns in bird density and species richness. Clearly, the elucidation of mechanisms driving edge effects has lagged far behind pattern identification. Increased attention to the mechanistic drivers underlying edge effects and their relative contribution to observed patterns of distribution and abundance is a fruitful area for future research.

PREDICTIVE APPROACHES TO MODELING EDGE EFFECTS

Despite recent advances in understanding the general consequences of fragmentation, the development of tools for predicting specific impacts has progressed slowly. A growing body of research is demonstrating that edges are often highly influential in determining habitat suitability and population persistence in fragmented landscapes (Robinson et al. 1995a, Donovan et al. 1997, Howell et al. 2000). Like the work focusing explicitly on edges, this landscape-scale research is showing that the importance of habitat edges varies from species to species and from landscape to landscape. Thus, it is increasingly clear that informed habitat management will necessitate the incorporation of our increasing understanding of the role of habitat edges in fragmented landscapes into predictive models that will allow assessment of alternative management options in novel landscapes. Most modeling efforts addressing birds in fragmented habitats have focused on the loss of habitat area and the isolation of remnant patches, typically focusing on a single species (e.g., Thomas 1990, Noon and Sauer 1992, Pulliam et al. 1992). However, models that focus on habitat patches in isolation from matrix and edge effects often prove to be disappointing in management situations (see Saunders et al. 1991). An integrated approach for assessing edge responses and predicting the impacts of increasing edge habitat is needed before the influence of habitat edges can be incorporated into assessments of the effects of habitat fragmentation.

Effective management of habitat edges requires knowledge of population-level responses and a conceptual framework for linking this understanding to spatially explicit information about the landscape. Area-based approaches that treat the edge as an area influenced by adjacent habitats, rather than as a separate habitat type, show some promise for guiding management decisions. In addition, predictive models offer a powerful means for advancing our understanding of the mechanisms that drive observed patterns. The generation of explicit predictions based on empirical measures of species-specific edge responses, followed by field tests and model revision, offer the possibility of more rapid progress in understanding edge effects.

Temple (1986) presented a simple, straightforward approach for including edge effects into a patch-based model of avian abundance. He assumed that the effects of nest predators and par-

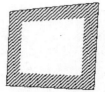

a. Total area 47 ha, core area 20 ha

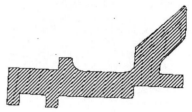

b. Total area 39 ha, core area 0 ha

FIGURE 7. Temple's (1986) original core area model of edge effects used sensitivity to edge as a predictor of habitat use by forest-interior birds. The model assumed that edge effects, in general, penetrate 100 m into a forested patch, dramatically infuencing the "core area" of suitable habitat within a forest patch (contrast panels a, b). The approach motivated a series of efforts that placed edge effects in landscape context and considered edge effects in predictions of the impacts of habitat fragmentation.

asites penetrate about 100 m into remnants of midwestern forest and woodland patches, and that the abundances of species that are "sensitive to fragmentation" would be low or zero within 100 m of the edge patch. He found that linear regressions of species' abundances against the "core area" of the patch—the area greater than 100 m from the edge—were significantly stronger than regressions against total patch area. This idea provided a conceptual foundation for incorporating the effects of edges and patch shape into patch-based approaches to estimating habitat suitability (Fig. 7). Subsequent work relaxed some of the assumptions of the core area model, allowing the distance of edge penetration to vary among species (Temple and Cary 1988) and to vary monotonically with distance from the edge (Laurance and Yensen 1991), adding realism to the approach.

Extension of the core area approach to address all species—those with edge-exploiting as well as edge-avoiding responses—and multiple habitat and edge types, led to the effective area model (EAM; Sisk and Margules 1993, Sisk et al. 1997, Sisk and Haddad 2002). EAM approaches predict species abundances (or other variable of interest) in any number, size, or

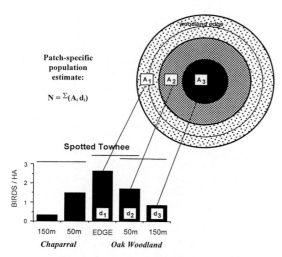

Patch-specific
population
estimate:

$N = \Sigma(A_i\,d_i)$

Spotted Towhee

BIRDS / HA

150m 50m EDGE 50m 150m
Chaparral   *Oak Woodland*

FIGURE 8. Schematic of the effective area model (EAM). Sisk et al. (1997) extended the core area approach to multiple habitat and edge types, using digital habitat maps to describe landscape pattern. The EAM incorporates variation in edge responses among species and at different edge types to estimate the abundances of the breeding bird community in any number of patches of any shape.

shape of habitat patches by projecting density estimates from species-specific edge response curves onto digitized maps of all the habitat patches within the focal landscape. The predicted density of each species within each patch varies with distance from the edge. In the discrete approach illustrated in Figure 8, the patch is divided into sub-regions. These sub-regions correspond to the distance intervals used for field surveys of species abundances, which are used to define species-specific edge responses, illustrated here by the bar graph for Spotted Towhee (*Pipilo maculatus*). Multiplying the area of each sub-region by the corresponding estimate of population density, and then summing the products for all sub-regions, gives a predicted population size for the species in a particular patch (Fig. 8). The degree to which the predicted density differs from predictions that assume equal abundance throughout the patch reflect the importance of "edge effects." Sisk et al. (1997) reported that the EAM performed significantly better than a null model that ignored edge effects and estimated bird abundances based on patch area alone. Other applications of the EAM are presented in Sisk and Haddad 2002.

Several practical considerations influence how the core area and effective area models are applied. First, the spatial resolution of the edge response measured (i.e., the magnitude of the response at various distances from the edge) determines the spatial resolution of the edge ef-

fects modeled. Therefore, the sampling design and survey techniques for measuring the edge response should be scaled to the life history characteristics (e.g., territory size, vagility) of the animals being studied. Logistic and methodological limitations often constrain sampling designs somewhat, but the variety of proven methods for sampling avian populations provides flexibility in quantifying edge responses and facilitates the application of these patch-based models to birds operating at different spatial scales. In complex, heterogeneous landscapes, detailed habitat maps reflecting species-specific requirements are needed. Advances in mapping technologies and the application of remotely sensed data to habitat mapping (e.g., Scott et al. 1993, Imhoff et al. 1997), offer promise for rapid and cost-efficient methods for mapping habitats across large regions.

EDGE EFFECTS IN THE WEST: IMPLICATIONS FOR STUDIES OF HABITAT FRAGMENTATION

After 60 years of attention and relatively little progress toward articulating general principles pertaining to edge effects, it might be tempting to conclude that the topic is intractable. Indeed, the early adoption of simplistic rules of thumb regarding habitat edges—for example, that more edge leads to higher diversity—may have led to poor habitat management and stalled progress in identifying the mechanisms underlying edge effects. However, slow progress in the past is not a reason to ignore the compelling reasons for expanding mechanistic and management-relevant research in the future.

Why study edge effects? First, anthropogenic disturbances are rapidly increasing the prevalence of edges in most terrestrial landscapes. This process is sure to continue, and ignoring edge effects will become increasingly debilitating to conservation efforts. Edge effects may compound the effects of habitat loss and the isolation of fragments on the distribution, abundance, and persistence of many sensitive bird species. Second, edges are amenable to management. The area of habitat protected and its location are often the result of societal decisions based on many factors that often lie outside the purview of conservation biologists. However, management of boundaries often is left to the discretion of the manager. Better understanding of the influences of edges on bird populations will lead to more effective strategies for managing habitat fragments. Third, edges are inherently dynamic environments and, therefore, they offer opportunities for studying avian responses to changing landscape pattern.

What do we know? Not nearly enough, but

the numerous studies from eastern North America offer some important lessons for those pursuing studies in western landscapes undergoing fragmentation.

- Our understanding of the many biological phenomena associated with habitat edges is dominated by the description of patterns from eastern forests.
- Western landscapes are, in general, more naturally heterogeneous than their eastern counterparts, and edges are common components in many landscapes (e.g., riparian corridors).
- The relationship between natural heterogeneity and avian sensitivity to the increased prevalence of edge due to habitat fragmentation is not well understood.
- Mechanistic explanations for avian responses near habitat edges are, in general, poorly developed and inadequately tested. Work in the West should pursue mechanistic understanding and predictive capabilities of use to habitat managers.

These lessons, derived from our review of an extensive literature on edge effects and augmented by landscape-scale studies of avian responses to habitat fragmentation, argue that edge effects occur commonly in many habitats, that they are of increasing importance as habitats become more fragmented, and that we currently know too little about what causes them to predict accurately where and to what degree they will influence bird populations. This knowledge should be sufficient to inspire a more focused, and hopefully more fruitful, effort to understand the many driving factors underlying edge effects and to incorporate this knowledge into strategies for avian conservation.

ACKNOWLEDGMENTS

We are indebted to L. Ries whose role in designing the edge review was fundamental to our efforts. We also thank P. Paton and J. Faaborg for insightful comments on an earlier version of this manuscript. Our work was supported by the Strategic Environmental Research and Development Program (project CS-1100).

APPENDIX. SUMMARY OF STUDIES EXAMINING EDGE EFFECTS IN BREEDING BIRDS

Authors	Focal habitat[a]	Matrix[b]	Avian groupings analyzed[c]	Response[d] Density	Response[d] Species richness	Other variables[e] Predation	Other variables[e] Parasites	Other variables[e] Other
Eastern North America								
		Studies of Density and Species Richness						
Anderson et al. 1977	Forest	Powerline	Individual species	+				
Brittingham and Temple 1983	Forest	Clearing (any opening >0.02 ha.)	Cowbirds				√	
Donovan et al. 1997	Forest	Agriculture, old field, wildlife openings				√		
		1. High fragmentation	Cowbirds	−				
		2. Medium fragmentation	Cowbirds	0				
		3. Low fragmentation	Cowbirds	0				
Evans and Gates 1997	Forest	1. Clearcut	Cowbirds	+				
			All other birds	+	0			
		2. Stream	Cowbirds	+				
			All other birds	+	0			
		3. Powerline	Cowbirds	0				
			All other birds	+	0			
		4. Open-canopy road	Cowbirds	+				
			All other birds	+	0			
		5. Closed-canopy road	Cowbirds	0				
			All other birds	0	0			
Ferris 1979	Forest	Highway	All birds	0	0			
Gates and Giffen 1991	Forest	Stream	All birds	+	+			
			Cowbirds	+	+			
Germaine et al. 1997	Forest	Patch cut	Neotropical edge-open migrants	+				
			Neotropical interior-edge migrants	?				
			Neotropical forest-interior migrants	−				
			Nearctic migrants	0				
			Nonmigrants	0				
			Individual species	0				
Hawrot and Niemi 1996	Forest	Clearcut, natural openings	All birds	0				
Hickman 1990	Forest	Nature trail	Individual species					
King et al. 1997	Forest	Clearcut	Individual species					
Lay 1938	Forest	Clearings	All birds	+	+			

APPENDIX. CONTINUED.

Authors	Focal habitat[a]	Matrix[b]	Avian groupings analyzed[c]	Response[d] Density	Response[d] Species richness	Other variables[e] Predation	Other variables[e] Parasites	Other variables[e] Other
Marini et al. 1995	Forest	Agriculture	Ground nesters	−	−	✓		
			Understory nesters	0	0			
			Canopy nesters	0	0			
Noss 1991	Forest	Old field, open pine, pine/oak, powerline, marsh	All birds	+				
			Individual species					
Rich et al. 1994	Forest	1. Unpaved road	Forest interior neo-tropical migrants	0				
			Other forest nesters	0				
			Avian nest predators	0				
			Cowbirds	0				
		2. Paved road	Forest interior neo-tropical migrants	−				
			Other forest nesters	0				
			Avian nest predators	0				
			Cowbirds	+				
		3. Powerline	Forest interior neo-tropical migrants	−				
			Other forest nesters	0				
			Avian nest predators	+				
			Cowbirds	0				
Small and Hunter 1989	Forest	1. Powerline	All passerines—Site 1	+	+			
			All passerines—Site 2	0	0			
			All passerines—Site 3	+	+			
		2. River	All passerines—Site 4	0	+			
Yahner 1995	Forest	Anthropogenic openings	Ground-shrub foragers	+				
			Trunk-bark foragers	0				
			Sallier-canopy foragers	−				
Kroodsma 1982[f]	Forest	Powerline	All birds	+				
Kroodsma 1984b[f]	Forest	Powerline	Individual species					
Kroodsma 1987[f]	1. Forest	Powerline	All birds	+	0			
			Powerline birds	+	+			
			Forest birds	0	−			
	2. Powerline	Forest	All birds	0	+			
			Powerline birds	−	−			
			Forest birds	+	+			

APPENDIX. CONTINUED.

Authors	Focal habitat[a]	Matrix[b]	Avian groupings analyzed[c]	Response[d] Density	Response[d] Species richness	Other variables[e] Predation	Other variables[e] Parasites	Other variables[e] Other
Strelke and Dickson 1980	1. Forest	Clearcut	All birds	+	+			
	2. Clearcut	Forest	All birds	0	0			
Kroodsma 1984a	Powerline	Forest	All birds	+				
Best et al. 1990	Agriculture	1. Forest	All birds	+	+			
		2. Herbaceous field	All birds	+	+			
Niemuth and Boyce 1997	Savanna	Fuel breaks (<200 ha.)	Cowbirds	+		✓		
			Nest predators	+				
		Wildlife clearings (>1000 ha.)	Cowbirds	+				
			Nest predators	+				
Western North America								
Brand and George 2001	Forest	Natural succession allowed, artificial	Individual species					
Keller and Anderson 1992	Forest	Clearcut	Individual species	0	0			
Sisk 1992	1. Forest	1. Chapparal	All birds	+	+			
		2. Grassland	All birds	+	+			
	2. Chapparal	Forest	All birds	+	+			
	3. Grassland	Forest	Individual species					
Bolger et al. 1997	Shrub, urban	Urban, shrub	Edge/fragment reduced species	−				
			Edge/fragment enhanced species	+				
Scandinavia								
Edenius and Sjöberg 1997	Forest	Mire	All birds	0				
Hansson 1983	Forest	Clearcut	All birds	+				
Hansson 1994	Forest	Clearcut	Individual species	+				
Helle and Helle 1982	Forest	Shoreline	Individual species	−				
Thingstad 1995	Forest	Dam development	All birds	−	−			
Møller 1989	1. Forest	Agriculture	Open-cup ground nesters	−				
			Covered ground nesters	0		✓		
			Open-cup tree nesters	−				
			Hole tree nesters	−				

APPENDIX. CONTINUED.

Authors	Focal habitat[a]	Matrix[b]	Avian groupings analyzed[c]	Response[d] Density	Response[d] Species richness	Other variables[e] Predation	Other variables[e] Parasites	Other variables[e] Other
2. Agriculture								
		Forest	Open-cup ground nesters	−				
			Covered ground nesters	0				
			Open-cup tree nesters					
			Hole tree nesters					
			Individual species					
Berg and Pärt 1994	Agriculture	Forest						
Tropics								
Canaday 1997	Forest	Agriculture, petroleum development	Insectivores	−				
			Frugivores	0				
			Omnivores	0				
Lovejoy et al. 1986	Forest	Clearcut	All birds	−	−			
Other								
Báldi and Kisbenedek 1994	Forest	Agriculture	All birds	+	0			
Cieslak 1992	Forest	Agriculture	All birds	+	+			
Krüger and Lawes 1997	Forest	Anthropogenic grassland	All birds	+	0			
Stroud et al. 1990	Moorland	Conifer plantations	All waders	−				
Other Studies Reviewed								
Eastern North America								
Bayne and Hobson 1997	Forest	Mixed				✓		
Bielefeldt and Rosenfield 1997	Forest	Mixed				✓	✓	
Bollinger and Peak 1995	Forest	Mixed				✓		Nest density
Burke and Nol 1998	Forest	Agriculture				✓		
Danielson et al. 1997	Forest	Mixed				✓		
Fenske-Crawford and Nieme 1997	Forest	Clearcut				✓		
Hahn and Hatfield 1995	Forest	Old field				✓	✓	Predator type
Hannon and Cotterill 1998	Forest	Agriculture				✓		
Hanski et al. 1996	Forest	Clearcut				✓		
Keyser et al. 1998.	Forest	Mixed				✓		
King et al. 1998	Forest	Clearcut				✓		
Linder and Bollinger 1995	Forest	Field				✓		
Small and Hunter 1988	Forest	Mixed				✓		Clutch size
Suarez et al. 1997	Forest	Mixed				✓	✓	Pairing success
Van Horn et al. 1995	Forest	Agriculture						
Vander Haegen and DeGraaf 1996a	Forest	Stream				✓		

APPENDIX. CONTINUED.

Authors	Focal habitat[a]	Matrix[b]	Avian groupings analyzed[c]	Response[d] Den-sity	Response[d] Spe-cies rich-ness	Other variables[e] Pre-dation	Other variables[e] Para-sites	Other variables[e] Other
Yahner et al. 1989	Forest	Mixed				✓		
Rudnicky and Hunter 1993	Forest, clearcut	Clearcut, forest				✓		
Vander Haegen and DeGraaf 1996b	Forest, clearcut	Clearcut, forest				✓		
Yahner and Wright 1985	Forest, clearcut	Clearcut, forest				✓		
Gates and Gysel 1978	Forest, agriculture	Agriculture, forest				✓	✓	Nest density
Strausberger and V. 1997	Forest, grassland	Mixed					✓	
Chasko and Gates 1982	Forest, powerline	Powerline, forest				✓		Nest density
Özesmi and Mitsch 1997	Marsh	Open water						Nest density
Picman et al. 1993	Marsh	Upland				✓		
Fleming and Giuliano 1998	Mixed	Mixed				✓		
Pasitschniak-Arts and Messier 1995	Mixed	Mixed				✓		
Pasitschniak-Arts and Messier 1996	Mixed	Mixed				✓		
Burger et al. 1994	Prairie	Forest					✓	
Johnson and Temple 1990	Prairie	Forest				✓		
Western North America								
Brand and George 2002	Forest	Mixed				✓		
Tewksbury et al. 1998	Forest	Mixed				✓		
Ratti and Reese 1988	Forest, clearcut	Mixed				✓		
Scandinavia								
Berg 1996	Agriculture	Forest				✓		
Berg et al. 1992	Bog	Forest				✓		
Angelstam 1986	Forest	Open				✓		
Huhta 1995	Forest	Road				✓		
Huhta et al. 1996	Forest	Mixed				✓		
Huhta et al. 1998	Forest	Clearcut				✓		
Johnsson et al. 1993	Forest	Agriculture				✓		Cavity use
Kuitunen and Helle 1988	Forest	Mixed				✓		Clutch size, lay date
Pösyä et al. 1997	Forest	Lake				✓		
Sandström 1991	Forest	Agriculture				✓		
Andrén and Angelstam 1988	Forest, agriculture	Agriculture, forest				✓		
Tropics								
Arango-Vélez and Kattan 1997	Forest	Agriculture				✓		
Burkey 1993	Forest	Road				✓		
Latta et al. 1995	Forest	Highway				✓		

APPENDIX. CONTINUED.

			Response[d]			Other variables[e]		
Authors	Focal habitat[a]	Matrix[b]	Avian groupings analyzed[c]	Den-sity	Spe-cies rich-ness	Pre-dation	Para-sites	Other
Other								
Nour et al. 1993	Forest	Agriculture				√		
Santos and Telleria 1992	Forest	Agriculture				√		
Storch 1991	Forest	Agriculture				√		Nest density

[a] Habitats in which edge response was measured.
[b] Habitats bordering focal habitat at which edge response was measured. For studies that combined edges with different matrix habitats together, matrix habitats types are separated by a comma. For studies considering edge types separately, matrix habitats are listed singly with a separate density response for each.
[c] Breakdowns used by authors in analyzing edge effects.
[d] Edge response in bird density and species richness. '+' = density or species richness higher at edge than in interior of focal habitat, '−' = lower at edge, '0' = no significant difference between edge and interior.
[e] Other variables measured by each study; pred = nest predation rate including general nest success calculations, para = nest parasitism rate, other = any other variables measured. √ = variable measured in study.
[f] These three papers are all derived from the same data set. We therefore use only the 1987 results in our analysis, as these represent the most sophisticated analysis.

Studies in Avian Biology No. 25:49–64, 2002.

EFFECTS OF FIRE AND POST-FIRE SALVAGE LOGGING ON AVIAN COMMUNITIES IN CONIFER-DOMINATED FORESTS OF THE WESTERN UNITED STATES

Natasha B. Kotliar, Sallie J. Hejl, Richard L. Hutto, Victoria A. Saab, Cynthia P. Melcher, and Mary E. McFadzen

Abstract.   Historically, fire was one of the most widespread natural disturbances in the western United States. More recently, however, significant anthropogenic activities, especially fire suppression and silvicultural practices, have altered fire regimes; as a result, landscapes and associated communities have changed as well. Herein, we review current knowledge of how fire and post-fire salvaging practices affect avian communities in conifer-dominated forests of the western United States. Specifically, we contrast avian communities in (1) burned vs. unburned forest, and (2) unsalvaged vs. salvage-logged burns. We also examine how variation in burn characteristics (e.g., severity, age, size) and salvage logging can alter avian communities in burns.

Of the 41 avian species observed in three or more studies comparing early post-fire and adjacent unburned forests, 22% are consistently more abundant in burned forests, 34% are usually more abundant in unburned forests, and 44% are equally abundant in burned and unburned forests or have varied responses. In general, woodpeckers and aerial foragers are more abundant in burned forest, whereas most foliage-gleaning species are more abundant in unburned forests. Bird species that are frequently observed in stand-replacement burns are less common in understory burns; similarly, species commonly observed in unburned forests often decrease in abundance with increasing burn severity. Granivores and species common in open-canopy forests exhibit less consistency among studies. For all species, responses to fire may be influenced by a number of factors including burn severity, fire size and shape, proximity to unburned forests, pre- and post-fire cover types, and time since fire. In addition, post-fire management can alter species' responses to burns. Most cavity-nesting species do not use severely salvaged burns, whereas some cavity-nesters persist in partially salvaged burns. Early post-fire specialists, in particular, appear to prefer unsalvaged burns. We discuss several alternatives to severe salvage-logging that will help provide habitat for cavity nesters.

We provide an overview of critical research questions and design considerations crucial for evaluating the effects of prescribed fire and other anthropogenic disturbances, such as forest fragmentation. Management of native avifaunas may be most successful if natural disturbance regimes, including fire, are permitted to occur when possible. Natural fires could be augmented with practices, such as prescribed fire (including high-severity fire), that mimic inherent disturbance regimes.

Key Words: burn severity; cavity-nesters; fire effects; fire suppression; passerine birds; prescribed fire; salvage logging; silviculture; snags; wildland fire; woodpeckers.

Understanding the consequences of anthropogenic activities that alter natural systems requires a thorough knowledge of the natural disturbance regimes that shape communities and landscapes. Often, the ecological consequences of anthropogenic activities have been evaluated in the context of relatively undisturbed, mature forest (e.g., Whitcomb et al. 1977, Mladenoff et al. 1993, King et al. 1997, Morse and Robinson 1999). However, this approach may be inadequate for systems that evolved with major and persistent disturbances, such as fire. In the West, fire has played a dominant role in shaping communities and landscapes. Thus, one of the greatest threats to the ecological integrity of western forest systems may be alteration of natural disturbance regimes and landscape structure through livestock grazing, fire suppression, logging in burned forests (hereafter "salvaging" or "salvage logging"), and other silvicultural activities.

Concern that decades of fire suppression may lead to more frequent, larger wildfires has prompted government agencies to expand prescribed-burning programs and fire-management policies to diminish the chances of large, severe wildfires (U.S. Dept. of Interior and U.S. Dept. of Agriculture 1998). Unfortunately, our understanding of historical fire regimes remains rudimentary and may be inadequate for setting such goals (Tiedemann et al. 2000). Furthermore, the new government-sanctioned program of prescription burning focuses on reducing fuel loads, with relatively little consideration given to the effects on wildlife (Tiedemann et al. 2000). In part, this problem stems from a paucity of rigorous field studies that have evaluated the effects of fire on wildlife communities. Without a better understanding of how historical fire regimes influenced communities (Bunnell 1995) and landscapes, as well as how anthropogenic activities have altered fire regimes, programs of prescription burning and other mitigation measures could be as misguided as widespread fire suppression.

In the review and discussion that follow, we

examine avian communities in post-fire forests in conifer-dominated systems of the West, and compare them to those in unburned forests. We focus in particular on the responses of wood-peckers and passerine birds. Because avian responses to fire may vary with burn severity and size, time since fire, ecological contexts of burns, and post-fire salvage logging, these issues are also discussed. We preface our review by providing an overview of historical fire regimes of western forests and how human activities, particularly fire suppression, may have altered those regimes. This background is essential for understanding the patterns observed among avian communities using unburned and burned forests. We conclude with a discussion of compelling management implications that arise from this review, and we identify essential research questions for improving and enlarging our understanding of how fire shapes and perpetuates avian communities in western forests.

FIRE REGIMES IN CONIFEROUS FORESTS OF THE WESTERN UNITED STATES

Although current knowledge of historical fire regimes in western forests remains somewhat rudimentary, it is possible to place those systems into broad fire-regime categories. The regime that characterizes any one system is an interplay between gradients in burn severity and fire frequency (i.e., fire-return interval). Generally, burn-severity gradients are divided into three levels, based on vegetation responses to fire: (1) low-severity fires kill or temporarily remove above-ground portions of herbaceous and understory layers and sometimes scorch the lower portions of mature trees, typically without killing them; (2) moderate-severity fires may kill but usually do not consume leaves of canopy trees, although some tree mortality may result; and (3) high-severity fires usually burn the canopy, killing the majority of trees (Agee 1993). One level of burn-severity may dominate a given burn, but most burns are mosaics of various fire severities (Agee 1993, Turner et al. 1994). Furthermore, there is variation among tree species' responses to fire intensity (e.g., heat). For example, the thick, fire-retardant bark of mature ponderosa pines (*Pinus ponderosa*) generally provides them protection from understory fires, whereas subalpine firs (*Abies lasiocarpa*) are often killed by understory fires (Agee 1993). Understory fires also typically kill the above-ground biomass of quaking aspen (*Populus tremuloides*) stands, although lateral roots readily respond to fire by resprouting vigorously (Agee 1993). Thus, variations in burn severity can have profound effects on the composition and structure of plant communities.

For simplicity, most forest systems of the West can be characterized by one of three fire-regimes based on the effects of fire intensity on the dominant tree species: high frequency/low severity, moderate frequency and moderate to high severity, or low frequency/high severity (Agee 1993, 1998). High frequency/low severity fires (i.e., 1- to 40-yr fire-return intervals) are characteristic of many dry, warm forests. The combination of dry conditions and pervasive surface fuels (grasses and duff) allows fire to recur frequently. Many tree species in these systems are adapted to fire (e.g., fire-retardant bark, seedling germination requires bare substrates). Generally, fires in these systems are restricted to herbaceous and understory layers, thereby eliminating the majority of saplings and perpetuating a discontinuous forest canopy. Examples of such systems include ponderosa pine forests of foothills along the Rocky Mountains and Sierra Nevada (Arno 1980, Verner and Boss 1980, McKelvey et al. 1996).

In forests characterized by intermediate moisture and temperatures, fire regimes are generally moderate in severity and frequency, although in many cases severity can be high (Agee 1993, 1998). The mix of burn severities often results in heterogeneous burns and multiple-age structures of dominant trees (Agee 1993, 1998). Fire-return intervals tend to be longer (40–150+ yr) than those in drier sites, but can be quite variable (Agee 1993). Examples of this type of system include red fir (*Abies magnifica*) and coastal redwood (*Sequoia sempervirens*) in California (Agee 1993, 1998).

Low frequency/high severity fire regimes typically result in stand-replacement events. Because of the long fire intervals, trees in these systems often lack the ability to withstand fire (Agee 1993), although some species have reproductive adaptations to fire (e.g., serotinous cones of lodgepole pine, *Pinus contorta*; Agee 1993). Typically, climatic conditions (e.g., severe drought and strong winds) necessary for these systems to burn occur only several times per century, and fires spread only if sufficient fuels have accumulated (Romme 1982). Once started, fires in these systems often burn vast areas and may last for months (Agee 1993). Regeneration in larger burns can take decades if viable seed sources are distant (Agee 1993). Fire return intervals range from 200–300 years in lodgepole pine forests (Romme 1982, Veblen 2000) to more than 1000 years for some cedar/spruce/hemlock forests of the Pacific Northwest (Agee 1993).

Local factors, such as elevation, topography, and climate, can modify the general fire regimes described above. For example, surface fires may occur less frequently in naturally dense systems of ponderosa pine with limited herbaceous cover; in turn, canopy fuels may become sufficiently dense to support crown fires (Shinneman and Baker 1997, Brown et al. 1999, Veblen 2000). Especially high probabilities of lighting strikes in mountainous terrain may result in small, frequent surface fires that often perpetuate open meadows in moist forests (Agee 1993, Veblen 2000). Overall, the complex mosaic of western forest systems has been shaped by an equally complex mosaic of fire regimes.

CHANGES IN FIRE REGIMES

Attempts to understand how contemporary human activities have altered natural fire regimes are fraught with difficulties. Fire regimes are inherently dynamic, largely due to variations in climate, both long-term (Clark 1988, Romme and Despain 1989, Johnson et al. 1990) and short-term (e.g., El Niño-driven events; Swetnam and Betancourt 1990, Veblen et al. 2000). In ponderosa pine systems, the degree to which severe fires result from the long-term accumulation of fuels due to fire suppression or the short-term accumulation and desiccation of fine fuels following El Niño/Southern Oscillations is poorly understood and can vary among sites (Veblen et al. 2000). Likewise, decades of fire suppression at Yellowstone National Park, which may have delayed the onset of extensive fires, were apparently overshadowed by severe drought and high winds in August 1988 (Romme and Despain 1989). Thus, the relative contributions of fire suppression and climate on extreme fire behavior remains unclear.

The relatively ephemeral nature of fire records (e.g., fire scars, stand cohorts) limits our reconstruction of fire histories for most locations (but see Agee 1998). Charcoal deposits in lake-bed sediments have revealed longer histories (Millspaugh and Whitlock 1995), but they are influenced strongly by prevailing winds and watershed dynamics so that the overall area they represent may be quite limited. Historic accounts of fire behavior and forest conditions during Euro-American settlement can also be biased (Wagner et al. 2000). Furthermore, humans have influenced fire regimes in North America for at least 6,000–10,000 years. Native Americans used fire in warfare and for driving game (Stewart 1956), and Euro-American settlers used fire to clear land for mining, logging, and even in land disputes (Veblen and Lorenz 1991); settlers also caused many accidental fires (Johnson et al. 1990). Extensive livestock grazing after the mid-1800s coupled with effective fire suppression (particularly after World War II) led to structural changes in forest stands (Saab et al. 1995), which altered fire regimes further (Madany and

West 1983, Covington and Moore 1994; but see Swetnam et al. 1999). Thus, it is difficult to determine what constitutes "natural" or "anthropogenic" changes to fire regimes. For the purposes of this review, we focus on anthropogenic changes that began in the mid 1800s, including grazing, unprecedented fire suppression, and large-scale silvicultural activities (e.g., widespread clearcutting, salvage logging).

Effects of fire suppression

Given the complexity and limited understanding of historical fire regimes, the full ramifications of fire suppression remain unknown. Certainly, the long-term, global-scale effects of fire suppression and their potential interactions with climate changes caused by anthropogenic activities are cause for concern (Leenhouts 1998). On a continental scale, however, it is clear that fire suppression over the last six or seven decades has reduced the number of fires and the total area burned across the U.S. (Ferry et al. 1995). Using satellite imagery, maps of potential natural vegetation, and estimated fire regimes, Leenhouts (1998) concluded that only 8–14% of the area that burned annually in the conterminous United States 200–500 yr ago still burns today.

In western forest systems, effects of fire suppression vary with forest type and inherent fire regime, as well as accessibility (Romme 1982). In many systems adapted to high-frequency/low-severity fire regimes (e.g., ponderosa pine), changes in forest structure since Euro-American settlement have included increased stem densities resulting from decreased mortality of saplings and increased recruitment, and changes in species composition (Gruell 1983, Veblen and Lorenz 1991, Covington and Moore 1994, Swetnam and Baisan 1996, Belsky and Blumenthal 1997, Allen 1998). Accumulation of fuels may promote more extensive, severe fires than those that occurred prior to Euro-American settlement (Barrett 1988, Covington and Moore 1994, Lissoway 1996, Covington et al. 1997, Fule et al. 1997, Veblen et al. 2000). However, wetter climates post-settlement may also contribute to a decrease in fire frequency (Veblen et al. 2000, Wagner et al. 2000).

The consequences of fire suppression in forests characterized by infrequent fires of high severity (e.g., high-elevation spruce-fir forests of the central Rockies) are less apparent, in part because the longer fire-return intervals may delay, or reduce, the effects of fire suppression (Romme 1982, Romme and Despain 1989, Veblen 2000). Even in regions where the frequency of fires has declined, burn severity may not have changed (Romme and Despain 1989). Although the relative contribution of climate and fire suppression is debatable, clearly the effects of both have influenced fire regimes across western landscapes.

Other human activities may amplify or confound the effects of fire suppression. Overgrazing by livestock or elevated populations of native ungulates protected from wolf predation may diminish fire frequency (Hess 1993, Belsky and Blumenthal 1997). For example, during the late 1800s to early 1900s, livestock grazing in many ponderosa pine systems led to decreased surface fuels and increased areas of exposed soil; the result was diminished fire frequencies and increased germination and survival of tree seedlings (Swetnam and Baisan 1996, Veblen 2000). In addition, the combined effects of fire suppression, grazing, and contemporary silvicultural practices in many western forests has promoted the growth of dense, monospecific, even-aged stands (Swetnam et al. 1995, Fule et al. 1997). In turn, this stand structure is believed to present opportunities for more extensive outbreaks of tree-damaging insects than would have occurred prior to the mid-1800s when stands were often more open and complex in structure (Swetnam et al. 1995, Veblen 2000, Veblen et al. 2000). Widespread tree mortality resulting from insect outbreaks can increase a given stand's susceptibility to fire. Although our current knowledge of the interactive effects of fire suppression and other factors is limited, it has become clear that these factors can alter fire regimes significantly.

EFFECTS OF FIRE AND SALVAGE LOGGING ON AVIAN COMMUNITIES

Understanding fire regimes in western forests is essential to understanding forest structure, overall landscape patterns, and the responses of bird communities to fire. Fire affects avian nesting and foraging activities by generating snags, altering insect communities, eliminating foliage, and altering the size, abundance, and distribution of tree species across the landscape (Finch et al. 1997, Huff and Smith 2000). The degree to which fire affects any of these factors depends, in part, on the severity and ecological context of a particular burn. A thorough understanding of the influence of fire and fire-management activities, such as prescribed burning and post-fire salvage logging, on avian communities is essential to both conservation biology and sound management.

Here, we summarize the best current knowledge about the influence of fire and salvage logging on avian communities in conifer-dominated forests (which often include quaking aspen) of the West. Most of the relatively few published studies were conducted in the northern Rocky Mountains. Because these studies encompassed many cover types and were usually poorly replicated, many of our conclusions are preliminary. However, some general patterns, as well as a number of questions, have emerged from four comparisons: (1) avian abundance in burned and unburned forests, (2) avian abundance among different fire severities, (3) changes in avian-community structures associated with post-fire forest succession, and (4) nesting patterns of cavity-nesting birds in salvaged and unsalvaged, burned forests.

AVIAN ABUNDANCE IN RECENTLY BURNED AND UNBURNED FORESTS

We summarized the results of 11 studies that compared the abundance of breeding bird species in early post-fire burns and adjacent mature, unburned forests (Tables 1a–1c; Fig. 1). Although "unburned" forests may have burned previously, these forests were largely mature (i.e., late-successional). All 23 burns surveyed were severe (predominantly stand-replacement) and less than 10 yr old (most were <4 yr old). All but a few burns were greater than 400 ha, and four burns were greater than 1400 ha. Conifers, including ponderosa pine/Douglas-fir (*Pseudotsuga menziesii*), Jeffrey pine (*Pinus jeffryi*)/white fir (*Abies concolor*), lodgepole pine, spruce/fir, and mixed conifers, were the dominant cover types. The studies covered seven western states; seven studies were conducted in the northern Rocky Mountains, one was in the southern Rocky Mountains, two were in the Pacific Northwest, and one was in the Pacific Southwest (Fig. 1). Studies of post-fire bird communities that were older than 10 yr, were predominantly aspen or riparian, or sampled only burn edges were excluded from analysis.

For each species present in ≥3 of the 11 studies, we classified abundance patterns into three response classes by study: (1) occurred only in burns or abundance was ≥50% higher in burns than in unburned forest; (2) occurred only in unburned forest or abundance was ≥50% higher in unburned than in burned forest; and (3) results varied among samples or there were similar abundances in burned and unburned forest (Tables 1a–1c). Because only one study (Johnson and Wauer 1996) included both pre- and post-fire surveys, we used this comparison of abundance patterns to infer response to fire.

Many species showed remarkably consistent patterns, despite the wide geographic area and variety of cover types surveyed. Species that commonly occurred in burns, but were uncommon or absent in unburned forests (Table 1a), included Black-backed Woodpecker, Three-toed Woodpecker, Olive-sided Flycatcher, and Mountain Bluebird (see Appendix for species' scientific names). Species that used unburned forests, but rarely occurred in early post-fire forests (Table

TABLE 1. SUMMARY OF AVIAN ABUNDANCES IN BURNED AND UNBURNED FORESTS

Species	Response categories (number of studies)		
	More abundant in burns	Similar abundance or response mixed	More abundant in unburned
(A) Typically more abundant in burns			
Three-toed Woodpecker	8[a, b, d, e, g, h, i, j]		
Black-backed Woodpecker	6[b, d, e, i, j, k]		1[c]
Olive-sided Flycatcher	8[a, c, d, f, g, h, i, k]		
Mountain Bluebird	9[a, b, c, d, g, h, i, j, k]		
Western Wood-Pewee	7[a, c, d, g, h, i, j]		
Hairy Woodpecker	8[a, b, c, e, f, g, h, j]	2[d, i]	
House Wren	5[a, b, d, g, j]	1[h]	
Tree Swallow	4[b, h, i, j]		1[c]
Northern Flicker	5[a, c, f, i, j]	3[b, g, h]	
(B) Typically exhibited mixed or neutral response to burns			
Mourning Dove	2[d, h]	1[g]	
Common Nighthawk	2[c, h]	1[g]	
Cassin's Finch	4[c, h, i, j]	3[a, d, g]	
Pine Siskin	3[c, f, i]	3[d, g, h]	
Chipping Sparrow	2[a, c]	4[g, h, i, j]	1[d]
Dark-eyed Junco	3[c, f, i]	5[a, d, g, h, j]	
American Robin	4[a, f, j, k]	5[c, d, g, h, i]	
Townsend's Solitaire	1[f]	5[a, c, d, g, h]	
Hammond's Flycatcher	1[f]	3[d, g, h]	
Clark's Nutcracker	2[j, h]	2[d, g]	1[i]
Red-naped Sapsucker	1[h]	1[g]	2[a, b]
Western Tanager	1[c]	4[d, g, h, i]	2[a, j]
White-breasted Nuthatch	1[a]	1[g]	1[d]
Evening Grosbeak	1[g]	1[h]	1[d]
Pygmy Nuthatch	1[a]		2[g, h]
Yellow-rumped Warbler		5[a, c, g, i, k]	3[d, h, j]
Williamson's Sapsucker	1[a]	1[g]	2[h, i]
Red Crossbill		2[g, h]	1[d]
(C) Typically more abundant in unburned forests			
Steller's Jay		1[g]	3[a, f, h]
Plumbeous/Cassin's Vireo		1[g]	2[a, h]
Warbling Vireo		1[g]	2[d, h]
Gray Jay		2[c, h]	3[f, i, j]
Ruby-crowned Kinglet		2[g, h]	3[d, i, j]
Brown Creeper		2[f, g]	5[a, d, h, i, j]
Red-breasted Nuthatch	1[g]	2[h, i]	6[a, b, d, f, j, k]
Hermit Thrush		1[c]	5[a, g, h, i, j]
Mountain Chickadee			6[a, g, h, i, j, k]
Golden-crowned Kinglet			6[a, d, f, h, j, k]
Townsend's Warbler			3[d, f, k]
Swainson's Thrush			3[d, j, k]
Varied Thrush			3[d, f, k]

Notes: Only species observed in three or more studies were included. More abundant in burns = only occurred in burns or abundance was $\geq$50% higher in early post-fire forests than unburned forest; similar or mixed = abundance was similar in burned and unburned forest or results varied among samples; more abundant in unburned = occurred only in unburned forest or abundance was $\geq$50% higher in unburned than early post-fire forests.
[a] Bock and Lynch 1970.
[b] Caton 1996.
[c] Davis 1976.
[d] Harris 1982.
[e] Hoffman 1997.
[f] Huff 1984, Huff et al. 1985.
[g] Johnson and Wauer 1996.
[h] N. Kotliar and C. Melcher, unpubl. data.
[i] Pfister 1980.
[j] Taylor and Barmore 1980.
[k] R. Sallabanks and J. McIver, unpubl. data.

FIGURE 1. Approximate location of study sites referred to in Table 1. Center location of study area is indicated in cases where multiple burns were surveyed. References (dominant cover type; number of burns; survey years post-fire): A—Bock and Lynch 1970 (Jeffrey pine/white fir; 1 burn; 6–8 yrs); B—Caton 1996 (lodgepole pine; 1 burn; 2–4 yrs); C—Davis 1976 (lodgepole pine; 2 burns; 6 yrs, 9 yrs); D—Harris 1982 (ponderosa pine/Douglas fir; 2 burns; 2–4 yrs, 2 yrs); E—Hoffman 1997 (lodgepole pine; 2 burns; 1–2 yrs); F—Huff 1984, Huff et al. 1985 (w. hemlock/Douglas fir; 1 burn; 1–3 yrs); G—Johnson and Wauer 1996 (ponderosa pine; 1 burn; 1 yr pre-fire; 3 yrs); H—N. Kotliar and C. Melcher, unpubl. data (ponderosa pine; lodgepole; spruce/fir; mixed conifer; 8 burns; varied from 0–8 yrs); I—Pfister 1980 (lodgepole pine; 2 burns; 2 yrs, 4 yrs); J—Taylor and Barmore 1980 (lodgepole pine; spruce/fir; 2 burns; 1–3 yrs, 5/7 yrs); K—R. Sallabanks and J. McIver, unpubl. data (mixed conifers; 1 burn; 1–3 yrs).

1c), included Mountain Chickadee, Golden-crowned Kinglet, Hermit Thrush, Varied Thrush, and Townsend's Warbler. Generally, wood drillers and aerial insectivores were more abundant in early post-fire forests, whereas foliage and bark gleaners were usually more abundant in unburned forests. However, there were several exceptions to this generalization. Overall, these results suggest that species with either the strongest affinity for, or aversion to, young burns are responding primarily to the dramatic changes in structural characteristics (e.g., increased availability of snags, decrease in canopy coverage) and/or densities of insect prey brought about by burning.

Numerous species showed more varied, or apparently neutral, responses to burns (Table 1b). For example, Townsend's Solitaire, American Robin, Dark-eyed Junco, Chipping Sparrow, and Cassin's Finch were common in both burned and unburned forests, indicating that both types of forests often may provide suitable habitat for these species. Many species, including Red-breasted Nuthatch, Brown Creeper, Yellow-rumped Warbler, and Western Tanager, were frequently observed in burns, but typically reached their highest abundance levels in unburned forests. Many granivores, bark gleaners, and species that prefer a mixed, open canopy had a varied responses. The mixed results may be due, in part, to the influence of site-specific characteristics (see FACTORS THAT AFFECT SPECIES' RESPONSES TO BURNS).

Several species observed in fewer than three studies exhibited higher abundances in burned compared to unburned forests, including Lewis's Woodpecker (V. Saab, unpubl. data), Rock Wren, Western Bluebird (N. Kotliar and C. Melcher, unpubl. data), Lazuli Bunting (Bock and Lynch 1970), and White-crowned Sparrow (Pfister 1980; N. Kotliar and C. Melcher, unpubl. data). Our personal observations of these species suggest that they readily use burns in certain contexts. Although the generality of these observations is unknown, the apparent suitability of burned forests for these species warrants further study.

A comparison of bird abundances in more than 30 fires that burned in the northern Rockies in 1988, with bird abundances derived from the literature for nine other major Rocky Mountain forest cover types (Table 3 in Hutto 1995), generally corresponds to the results of our review. Most of the species that exhibited higher abundances in burned forests (Table 1a) were more commonly observed in recently burned forests than in all other mature forest types (Hutto 1995). Likewise, species that exhibited higher abundances in unburned forests (Table 1c) commonly occurred in one or more mature forest types but were infrequently observed in recently burned forests (Hutto 1995); however, Mountain Chickadee and Red-breasted Nuthatch occurred in a relatively high percentage (52–74%) of the 1988 burns surveyed by Hutto (1995). Many of the species that showed a mixed or neutral response to burns (Table 1a) also had a higher frequency of occurrence in early post-fire forests compared to mature forest types (Table 3 in Hutto 1995).

Some of the species that showed mixed patterns across studies may use forest edges as well as forest interiors (e.g., Mountain Chickadee, Hermit Thrush; N. Kotliar and C. Melcher, unpubl. data), and because some are rather nomadic (e.g., Red Crossbill), the degree to which burns represent suitable habitat cannot be inferred easily from surveys that abut the edges of burns. Further research is needed to determine how various factors can alter the relative suitability of burned and unburned forests for such species (see next section).

FACTORS THAT AFFECT SPECIES' RESPONSES TO BURNS

The suitability of burns for birds often will depend on burn characteristics (e.g., severity, time since fire, burn geometry) and landscape context (e.g., forest cover types), as well as regional variation (Finch et al. 1997, Huff and Smith 2000). To begin to address these issues, we summarized the results of several studies that evaluated how burn severity and time since fire influenced bird communities. To provide impetus for future studies, we also speculate (based on personal observations and a few limited studies) about the ways in which burn characteristics and context may contribute to variation in results among studies.

Burn severity

Three studies compared avian abundances across various burn severities in reference to unburned forests. Taylor and Barmore (1980) examined two burn severities (moderate, severe) for the first three yr post-fire in a 1414-ha burn in lodgepole pine and spruce/fir forests in Grand Teton and Yellowstone National Parks. Preliminary results (first three yr post-fire) are available from a study of a 9283-ha burn in Oregon in which three burn severities (low, moderate, severe) were examined in mixed coniferous forests (R. Sallabanks, unpubl. data; R. Sallabanks and J. McIver, unpubl. data). In addition, preliminary results are available for a comparison of two understory-prescribed (1 yr post-fire, 200 ha, and 1–3 yr post fire, 1200 ha) and two stand-replacement burns (1 yr post fire, 200 ha, and 3 yr post-fire, 4450 ha) in ponderosa pine/Douglas-fir forests in Colorado (N. Kotliar and C. Melcher, unpubl. data). The trends observed in the burn-severity studies generally are consistent with the patterns we found in our review of severely burned versus unburned forest, which represented the extremes of the burn-severity gradient (Tables 1a–c). The general patterns presented here should be viewed as preliminary and in need of further testing, given that two of the studies are unpublished and only six burns were studied.

Many bird species whose abundances were consistently higher in burned compared to unburned forests (Table 1a) also appeared to use stand-replacement burns more readily than low- and moderate-severity burns. These species included Black-backed Woodpecker (R. Sallabanks, unpubl. data), Three-toed Woodpecker and Cassin's Finch (Taylor and Barmore 1980; N. Kotliar and C. Melcher, unpubl. data), Olive-sided Flycatcher (R. Sallabanks and J. McIver, unpubl. data; N. Kotliar and C. Melcher, unpubl. data), Mountain Bluebird (Taylor and Barmore 1980; R. Sallabanks, unpubl. data; N. Kotliar and C. Melcher, unpubl. data), and Western Bluebird (N. Kotliar and C. Melcher, unpubl. data). Dark-eyed Juncos occurred at similar abundances across all

burn severities (Taylor and Barmore 1980; N. Kotliar and C. Melcher, unpubl. data).

Several species reached their highest abundances in moderate-severity burns. Brown Creeper and Chipping Sparrow exhibited highest abundances in moderate-severity and severe burns (Taylor and Barmore 1980). Townsend's Solitaire was fairly abundant across all severities, but was most abundant in moderately severe burns (N. Kotliar and C. Melcher, unpubl. data). Western Tanager occurred at similar abundances in moderately burned and unburned forests, but was less abundant in severely burned forests (Taylor and Barmore 1980). Cavity nesting species that usually glean the bark of live trees (e.g., nuthatches, Brown Creeper) may respond positively to moderate-severity burns that increase availability of snags for nesting, but retain live trees for foraging. Species common in open canopy forests (e.g., Townsend's Solitaire, Western Tanager, Chipping Sparrow) may use the mixed open canopy of moderate-severity burns, whereas they may avoid large areas of stand-replacement burns. Thus, the varied results observed for these species in our review of severely burned and unburned forests (Table 1b) may reflect, in part, the heterogeneity of burn severities within and across studies.

Species that were consistently more abundant in unburned than in burned forests (Table 1c) also decreased in abundance with increasing burn severity. These species include Plumbeous Vireo, Steller's Jay, and Hammond's Flycatcher (N. Kotliar and C. Melcher, unpubl. data), Gray Jay (Taylor and Barmore 1980); Mountain Chickadee (Taylor and Barmore 1980; R. Sallabanks, unpubl. data; N. Kotliar and C. Melcher, unpubl. data); Ruby-crowned and Golden-crowned kinglets (Taylor and Barmore 1980; R. Sallabanks, unpubl. data); Townsend's Warbler and Varied Thrush (R. Sallabanks, unpubl. data). Many of these species are foliage gleaners; thus their abundance patterns probably reflect the incremental loss of foliage area with increasing burn severity.

Several species showed slightly different patterns across the three studies. Red-breasted Nuthatch and Yellow-rumped Warbler were least abundant in severe burns across all three studies, but their abundances varied across other severities (Taylor and Barmore 1980; R. Sallabanks, unpubl. data; N. Kotliar and C. Melcher, unpubl. data). Western Wood-pewee increased in abundance with burn severity in a lodgepole pine burn (Taylor and Barmore 1980), but was most abundant in low-severity ponderosa pine burns (N. Kotliar and C. Melcher, unpubl. data). Again, variation in results among studies may be due to the heterogeneity of burn severities both within and among studies. Furthermore, if patches of low-

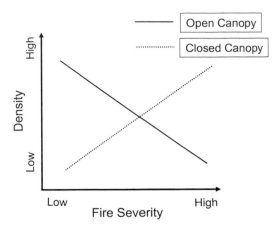

FIGURE 2. Conceptual model of the interactive effects of burn severity and forest structure on the density of avian species preferring open forest structure. In open-canopy forests (e.g., ponderosa pine) avian densities are high in unburned forests but may be low in severely burned forests. In closed-canopy forests (e.g., lodgepole pine), avian densities are low, but may increase as fire opens up the forest canopy. Thresholds responses to degree of burn severity may result in departure from linear relationships depicted here.

and moderate-severity burns occur along the burn periphery, as is often the case, it may be difficult to differentiate between the influence of burn severity and edge effects (i.e., the juxtaposition of burned and unburned forest).

Interactions between burn severity and pre-fire forest structure also may lead to mixed responses to burn severity, particularly for bird species that are sensitive to differences in canopy coverage (Fig. 2). Some species that occur in open-canopy forests (e.g., Western Wood-pewee, Western Tanager) are common in unburned ponderosa pine forests but uncommon in stand-replacement burns in this cover type (N. Kotliar and C. Melcher, unpubl. data). In contrast, these species may be uncommon in dense lodgepole pine (*Pinus contorta*) forests, but common immediately following stand-replacement fires in lodgepole pine forests (N. Kotliar, unpubl. data). Such interactions makes it difficult to predict how a species will respond to burns without a better understanding of how context (e.g., cover type, canopy closure, regional differences, previous silvicultural treatments) can alter suitability of burned forests for a particular species.

Post-fire succession and associated changes in forest structure and avian communities

No studies have followed bird communities from early through late successional stages after fire (but see Bock and Lynch 1970, Bock et al. 1978, Raphael et al. 1987, Johnson and Wauer

1996); therefore, to examine changes in bird communities from early successional to mature forests we also rely on comparisons of stands that vary in time since fire (e.g., Peterson 1982, Huff et al. 1985). In general, forest structure and avian communities change fairly rapidly after fire, although the rates of change depend, in part, on burn severity as well as pre- and post-fire cover type. Because tree mortality is low, and ground cover often rapidly resprouts, evidence of fire in understory burns may be minimal within a few years after fire. In contrast, stand-replacement burns may persist as a forest of snags for decades. The structure of burned snags typically changes within the first few years. First, needles (if remaining) and smaller branches are shed, then bark and larger branches slough away. Smaller snags typically decay faster than larger snags (Morrison and Raphael 1993, Bull et al. 1997). Factors such as topography, root depth, moisture regime, wind, and tree species can all influence how long snags remain standing, which may exceed a century.

Early post-fire forests and associated insect outbreaks attracts cavity-nesting birds due to increases in nest sites and food supplies (e.g., Blackford 1955, Koplin 1969, Lowe et al. 1978, Raphael and White 1984, Bock et al. 1978, Saab and Dudley 1998). Duration of occupancy, however, varies among bird species, presumably due to differences in preferred prey availability, as well as the size, distribution, and age of snags. Black-backed and Three-toed woodpeckers rapidly colonize stand-replacement burns within one to two years of a fire; within five years, however, they become rare, presumably due to declines in bark and wood-boring beetles (Koplin 1969, Bock and Lynch 1970, Bock et al. 1978, Bull 1980, Taylor and Barmore 1980, Apfelbaum and Haney 1985, Dixon and Saab 2000). In contrast, Lewis's Woodpecker is reported to be abundant both in recent burns (2–4 yr; Saab and Dudley 1998) and older burns (10–25 yr; Bock 1970, Linder and Anderson 1998). Hairy Woodpecker and Northern Flicker exhibit more mixed responses, but usually decline within the first 25 yr post-fire (Bock and Lynch 1970, Bock et al. 1978, Taylor and Barmore 1980, Huff et al. 1985, Raphael et al. 1987). Mountain and Western bluebirds are secondary-cavity nesters that commonly nest in recently burned forests (e.g., Hutto 1995, Saab and Dudley 1998; Table 1a), but they typically decline in mid-successional stages (Bock and Lynch 1970, Bock et al. 1978, Pfister 1980, Peterson 1982, Raphael et al. 1987).

Vegetation regrowth after fire also can lead to increases in flower, seed, and insect abundance, which attracts nectarivores, granivores, and aerial and ground insectivores (Lowe et al. 1978, Apfelbaum and Haney 1981, Huff et al. 1985). Olive-sided Flycatcher may appear immediately after fires (Table 1a; Hutto 1995; N. Kotliar and C. Melcher, unpubl. data) and can persist as long as snags are available and canopy cover remains low (Huff et al. 1985; N. Kotliar and C. Melcher, pers. obs.). Seed-eating birds exhibit a mixed response to burns, but there is some evidence that several species readily use burns, Clark's Nutcracker, Pine Siskin, Cassin's Finch, and Red Crossbill in particular (Table 1b; Hutto 1995). Whether theses species are responding to increased seed availability (e.g., serotinous cones), minerals in the ashes (C. W. Benkman, pers. comm.), or other factors remains unclear. Furthermore, these species are rather nomadic, or have large home ranges, and may use burned forests opportunistically.

Many species absent or uncommon immediately post-fire begin to increase in mid-successional stages as snags decay or fall, shrubs and saplings become well-developed, and canopy cover increases. Although Cordilleran and Dusky flycatchers may appear at the edges of early postfire forests (N. Kotliar and C. Melcher, unpubl. data), they sometimes reach peak abundances at mid-successional stages (Peterson 1982, Raphael et al. 1987; N. Kotliar and C. Melcher, unpubl. data). Resprouting aspen stands can attract species commonly associated with deciduous systems (e.g., Warbling Vireo, Dusky Flycatcher; N. Kotliar and C. Melcher, pers. obs.). Red-naped Sapsucker also has been observed drilling holes in lodgepole pine and aspen saplings within 5–10 years following disturbances (N. Kotliar and C. Melcher, pers. obs.). Lewis's Woodpecker may use burned forests 10–20 yr after fires, presumably in response to improved conditions for aerial foraging following a decrease in snag density and an increase in flying arthropods associated with shrub regrowth (c.f., Bock 1970, Linder and Anderson 1998). Species such as Mountain Chickadee, Ruby-crowned Kinglet, and Swainson's and Varied thrushes reach peak abundance in late-successional forests (Bock and Lynch 1970, Bock et al. 1978, Peterson 1982, Huff et al. 1985, Raphael et al. 1987). In contrast, species that favor open canopies (e.g., American Robins) begin to decline in mid- to late-successional stages (Peterson 1982, Huff et al. 1985, Raphael et al. 1987).

Several species that occur in early post-fire forests also may occur in later successional stages. Hammond's Flycatcher occasionally has been detected in young post-fire forests (Harris 1982, Huff et al. 1985, Hutto 1995, Johnson and Wauer 1996; N. Kotliar and C. Melcher, unpubl. data), but they typically reach peak abundance in mature forests (Peterson 1982, Sedgwick

1994; N. Kotliar and C. Melcher, unpubl. data). However, its occasional occurrence immediately after fire suggests that Hammond's Flycatcher may temporarily exhibit site-fidelity. Several species, such as Olive-sided Flycatcher, Brown Creeper, and Dark-eyed Junco, initially may decline in mid-successional stages, but may increase as canopy gaps and snags are created (Huff et al. 1985, Carey et al. 1991).

Fire geometry

Although no studies have explicitly examined how birds respond to burn size or shape, one study examined whether bird abundance was affected by differing patch sizes created by the extensive fires of 1988. Of the 87 species present, only Plumbeous Vireo and Townsend's Solitaire decreased with increasing patch size (Hutto 1995). However, the relatively large minimum patch size surveyed (40 ha) may have masked important area effects at lower size ranges. Thus, the response of birds to total burn area needs additional study.

Given that area effects have been found to be important in other ecosystems, we should consider these effects as they relate to fires as well. For example, post-fire specialists may require a minimum burn size. In contrast, some species may select openings created by small burns and avoid larger burns. Increase in burn size may also lead to increased heterogeneity of burns (e.g., variation in burn severity).

The proportion of burn to edge area is also affected by burn size and shape. Thus, species that show positive responses to burns may be attracted to the juxtaposition of burned and unburned forest. For example, Olive-sided Flycatcher and Townsend's Solitaire (Table 1a) reached their highest abundances at burn edges (N. Kotliar and C. Melcher, unpubl. data). In addition, fire damaged trees (not killed outright by fire), which often occur along the periphery of crown fires, are used by several post-fire woodpecker species (Murphy and Lehnhausen 1998). Many of the species showing mixed response to burns (e.g., American Robin, Townsend's Solitaire, Western Tanager, Dark-eyed Junco, Chipping Sparrow, Pine Siskin, and Cassin's Finch; Table 1b) reached their highest abundances within 50 m of the edges of burns (N. Kotliar and C. Melcher, unpubl. data).

Many crown fires also contain "peninsulas" and "islands" of unburned forest remnants, which can increase edge habitats or retain unburned forest well inside of large burns. For example, the moist microclimate of riparian areas, which may inhibit fire or limit burn severity, can result in riparian remnants. Thus, species not typically associated with early post-fire forests

TABLE 2. NUMBER OF CAVITY-NESTING SPECIES IN UNLOGGED AND SALVAGE-LOGGED POST-FIRE FORESTS DURING THE BREEDING SEASON IN THE NORTHERN ROCKY MOUNTAINS

| Forest type | Number of nesting species | | | | Study |
	Unsalvaged	Partially salvaged	Severely salvaged	Totals	
Mixed conifer/deciduous	16	12	4	17	Caton 1996[a]
Mixed conifer/deciduous	18	—	8	18	Hitchcox 1996[b]
Ponderosa pine/douglas-fir	9	9	—	10	Saab and Dudley 1998[c]
Mixed conifer	8	9	—	9	S. Hejl and M. McFadzen, unpubl. data[d]

[a] Salvage logging of entire 4000-ha burn included clearcuts (all trees were removed except for a few snags) and partial cuts (individual trees or small groups of trees were logged).
[b] Salvage logging of entire 500-ha burn created an interspersion of harvest treatments with unlogged control plots. In severely salvaged areas, all merchantable (>15 cm dbh, >4.5 m tall) fire-killed trees were harvested.
[c] In salvage-logged units, about 50% of all trees >23 cm dbh, and 70% of trees >53 cm, were harvested.
[d] Salvage logging varied among three burns (burns ranged from 494–3,321 ha). The salvaged portions of burns were partially logged with several areas of severe salvage logging. A portion of each burn was left unharvested.

(e.g., Wilson's Warbler, Lincoln's Sparrow; N. Kotliar and C. Melcher, pers. obs.) may be observed in remnant patches immediately post-fire.

In burns, detections of birds more typically associated with unburned forest may be artifacts of study design. Few studies explicitly control for distance from survey points in burned habitats to unburned edges and remnant patches. Yet, some species characteristic of unburned forests (e.g., Mountain Chickadee, Ruby-crowned Kinglet, Hermit Thrush) may use live trees along burn edges (N. Kotliar and C. Melcher, unpubl. data). Thus, these species, which also have highly detectable songs, may appear to use recently burned forests if survey points are too close to edges.

Conclusions: effects of fire on avian communities

Although there are relatively few studies that address the effects of fire on avian communities, the consistent presence of many woodpeckers and aerial insectivores in early post-fire forests, and the near absence of many foliage-gleaning species associated with closed-canopy forests, appear to be robust patterns. Many additional species appear to use post-fire forests in certain contexts. For most species, however, we still have a poor understanding of how fire alters habitat suitability. We clearly need more information about how species' responses to fire can be altered by burn severity (including within-burn heterogeneity), fire geometry, proximity to unburned edges and remnants, pre- and post-fire cover types (e.g., tree species, forest structure, previous silvicultural treatments), and time since fire. Finally, because most burns outside national parks are salvaged, information about the effects of post-fire salvage logging is also critical.

EFFECTS OF POST-FIRE SALVAGE LOGGING ON AVIAN COMMUNITIES

Salvage logging following stand-replacement fires has occurred since the early 1900s (D. At-

kins, pers. comm.). Initially, salvage logging was uncommon due to limited access to burned forests (K. McKelvey, pers. comm.). In the 1950s, however, the demand for lumber increased greatly, and subsequent road-building in national forests provided opportunities to harvest more burns (D. Atkins, pers. comm.). Typically, salvage logging was implemented immediately post-fire, leaving few, if any, standing snags. Only within the past two decades have forest managers begun to retain snags within salvaged areas to benefit wildlife.

The effects of salvaging on avian communities remain poorly understood. Only four studies, all of which were restricted to coniferous and mixed coniferous/deciduous (hereafter "mixed") forests of the northern Rocky Mountains (Montana and Idaho), specifically examined the effects of salvage logging on cavity-nesting bird communities (Caton 1996, Hitchcox 1996, Saab and Dudley 1998; S. Hejl and M. McFadzen, unpubl. data; Table 2). Two other studies evaluated salvaged burns (Blake 1982, Raphael and White 1984) but did not replicate treatments, thus they were not emphasized in this review. As a result, we focus our discussion on cavity-nesting species in the northern Rocky Mountains.

Effects of salvage logging on birds

Severely salvaged burns (Table 2) may decrease the suitability of post-fire forests for most cavity-nesting species. However, the effects of partial salvaging are more equivocal (Table 2). In general, species richness declined only in the most severely salvaged burns, although even partial salvaging altered species composition (Table 2; Raphael and White 1984).

Several cavity nesters showed consistent patterns of abundance in logged or unlogged conditions across studies. Black-backed and Three-toed woodpeckers were most abundant in unsalvaged burns and rarely nested in salvaged areas of burns (Hitchcox 1996, Saab and Dudley 1998; S. Hejl and M. McFadzen, unpubl. data). In contrast, nesting Lewis's Woodpeckers were most abundant in partially salvaged burns (Saab and Dudley 1998; S. Hejl and M. McFadzen, unpubl. data). Mountain Bluebird and Hairy Woodpecker nested in both unsalvaged and salvaged portions of burns, but tended to nest more often in unsalvaged portions (Hitchcox 1996, Saab and Dudley 1998; S. Hejl and M. McFadzen, unpubl. data).

The responses of several species to salvage logging varied among studies. Red-breasted Nuthatch and Williamson's Sapsucker nested primarily in partially salvaged burns in coniferous forest (S. Hejl and M. McFadzen, unpubl. data), whereas in mixed forest they nested only in the unsalvaged portions of severely salvaged burns (Hitchcox 1996). These mixed responses to salvage logging may be due to differences in salvage severity or cover type. In general, it appears that species most closely tied to early successional post-fire forests (Table 1a) may be the most sensitive to salvage logging.

The effects of salvage logging on nesting success also varied among species and studies. In the three studies that examined nesting success (>20 nests per treatment per species), Hairy Woodpecker (Saab and Dudley 1998), Northern Flicker (Hitchcox 1996), and Mountain Bluebird (S. Hejl and M. McFadzen, unpubl. data) experienced significantly higher nesting success in unsalvaged treatments. Three-toed Woodpeckers, House Wrens, and Western Bluebirds had similar nesting success among treatments.

Variation in characteristics of snags used for nests sites and foraging

Salvage-logging practices often call for the harvest of larger, more economically valuable tree species. By altering species composition, sizes, and densities of snags, salvaging may alter resource availability for birds. Therefore, we describe characteristics of post-fire forests required for foraging and nesting cavity-nesting birds and relate those needs to management practices.

Although tree species selected for nest sites varied among bird species and studies, some general patterns were evident. In three studies of mixed forests (both salvaged and unsalvaged) dominated by conifers (95% conifers, 5% *Populus* spp.), a disproportionate percentage of nests (35–80%) were located in deciduous trees (Hutto 1995, Caton 1996, Hitchcox 1996). Most nests were located in snags. In two other studies of coniferous and mixed conifer forests, birds nested in snags of western larch (Hitchcox 1996; S. Hejl and M. McFadzen, unpubl. data) and ponderosa pine (S. Hejl and M. McFadzen, unpubl. data)

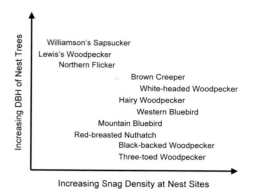

FIGURE 3. General distribution of cavity-nesting birds in burned forests (unsalvaged and salvage logged) as a function of nest-tree diameter (DBH) and snag density at nest sites (Saab and Dudley 1998; S. Hejl and M. McFadzen, unpubl. data).

more often than expected. In one study in Idaho and Montana, 45% of all nests were in Douglas-fir (S. Hejl and M. McFadzen, unpubl. data). Such variation in nest-tree selection among studies may result from variation in species composition and the relative availability of preferred trees (S. Hejl and M. McFadzen, unpubl. data).

The extent of snag decay influences which snags woodpeckers select for nesting. For example, strong excavators such as Black-backed, Three-toed, Hairy, and Downy woodpeckers, nested in snags with intact tops (Caton 1996, Hitchcox 1996, Saab and Dudley 1998; S. Hejl and M. McFadzen, unpubl. data). Weak excavators such as Lewis's Woodpecker, White-headed Woodpecker, and Northern Flicker, nested more frequently in broken-topped snags (many broken pre-fire) that were presumably more decayed than intact snags (Hitchcox 1996, Saab and Dudley 1998; S. Hejl and M. McFadzen, unpubl. data). Because the extent of decay influences nest-tree selection, selective salvaging of less decayed snags likely affects bird species differentially.

Cavity nesters also respond to differences in the sizes and spatial distribution of snags (Fig. 3), which, in turn, could be affected by different salvage prescriptions (Saab et al. 2002). In both coniferous and mixed burns, most cavity nesters selected large-diameter trees more often than expected (Caton 1996, Hitchcox 1996, Saab and Dudley 1998; S. Hejl and M. McFadzen, unpubl. data). Black-backed and Three-toed woodpeckers nested in medium-sized snags (Hitchcox 1996, Saab and Dudley 1998; S. Hejl and M. McFadzen, unpubl. data). This size class was among the smallest used by any woodpecker species, but is within the size-range targeted for salvaging. In general, cavity nesters selected dense patches of snags more often than dispersed or isolated snags (Raphael and White 1984, Saab and Dudley 1998, Saab et al. 2002).

Despite the paucity of foraging studies in post-fire forests, some general patterns regarding preferences of woodpeckers for certain tree species and sizes emerged from our review. Woodpeckers selectively foraged on large snags in both winter (Kreisel and Stein 1999) and summer (Hutto 1995, Powell 2000; S. Hejl and M. McFadzen, unpubl. data). However, use of tree species in summer varied among studies (Hutto 1995, Caton 1996, Powell 2000; S. Hejl and M. McFadzen, unpubl. data), among habitats within one study (Caton 1996, Powell 2000), and among *Picoides* woodpeckers within a study (S. Hejl and M. McFadzen, unpubl. data). In northeastern Washington during winter, Downy, Hairy, Three-toed, and Black-backed woodpeckers selectively foraged on western larch and ponderosa pine, which are also preferentially salvage logged. Thus, by altering the size, distribution, and species composition of post-fire snags, salvage logging differentially affects cavity-nesting species.

Co-occurring species of woodpeckers sometimes select different prey, which could influence avian diversity in post-fire habitats. For example, in a recent study of an unsalvaged burn in Alaska, Murphy and Lehnhausen (1998) analyzed the contents of 33 woodpecker stomachs and found that Three-toed Woodpeckers consumed bark beetle larvae (Scolytidae) almost exclusively, whereas Black-backed and Hairy woodpeckers primarily consumed wood-boring beetles (Buprestidae and Cerambycidae). In an unsalvaged burn in east-central Idaho, Black-backed Woodpeckers were observed feeding their nestlings the larvae and pupae of wood-boring beetles approximately 65% of the time (Powell 2000). Beal (1911), however, reported that 65–75% of the prey consumed by Three-toed and Black-backed woodpeckers were wood-boring beetles. Differences among studies could be due to prey availability (Powell 2000), which in turn is affected by tree species composition, burn severity, and salvage severity.

Conclusions: effects of post-fire salvage logging on cavity-nesting birds

Overall, salvage logging in burned forests can have pronounced effects on cavity-nesting species that use post-fire habitats. In conjunction with a substantial reduction in fire-killed trees due to fire suppression, salvage logging has resulted in dramatic reductions in the availability of snags in these ephemeral habitats. The effects of such reductions have serious implications for the viability of Black-backed and Three-toed woodpeckers, which rarely use even partially- logged post-fire forests. Although forest managers have begun to

retain some snags (including large snags) in salvaged areas, this is not sufficient for species that prefer high densities of snags that characterize unsalvaged burns. Some types of partial salvaging may actually benefit a few species, but historically such species may have been more closely associated with later successional stages of burns after snag densities had decreased naturally, with forests kept open by frequent, low-severity fires, or open post-fire forests. Retention of a diversity of snag species, sizes, and spatial distributions, as well as snags in various stages of decay, in burned forests is essential to the conservation of avian diversity in northern Rocky Mountain forests. The applicability of these conclusion across western forests or other avian communities (e.g., open-cup nesting species) requires further research.

MANAGEMENT IMPLICATIONS

FIRE MANAGEMENT

Given the importance of fire to many bird species, restoration of natural fire regimes may be critical to the ecological integrity of western forests. However, the problems associated with reproducing the complexity and diversity of fire processes at multiple scales pose great challenges (Baker 1993). The recent emphasis on prescribing frequent, low-intensity fires in low-elevation forests of the Rocky Mountains is a good start toward reintroducing fire in systems where frequent understory burns maintained open, old-growth stands (but see Covington and Moore 1994, Tiedemann et al. 2000), but this treatment will not be adequate for bird species that associate with stand-replacement burns. For example, prescribed fire may alter the availability of large snags, depending on fire severity (Horton and Mannan 1988, Tiedemann et al. 2000). In general, the effects of prescribed fire on avian communities are poorly understood (Finch et al. 1997, Tiedemann et al. 2000); the few studies of prescribed fire have been plagued by methodological problems, and thus the conclusions of these studies are suspect (Finch et al. 1997). Furthermore, incorrectly applied prescribed fire can alter landscape structure (Baker 1993). Fire-management practices that include allowing wildland fires of all severities to burn, when and where they are appropriate, may help re-create natural conditions (Hejl et al. 1995). Given the uncertainty about specific, local fire regimes (Baker 1994, Tiedemann et al. 2000, Veblen et al. 2000) and the variation among bird species in response to fire characteristics (Hutto 1995), managers may wish to mimic natural variation in fire regimes (e.g., size, severity, frequency, timing) that may have occurred within a given cover type and geographic area (Baker

1992, Hejl et al. 1995, Veblen et al. 2000). This approach will help to avoid overemphasis on any particular prescription.

Post-fire forests can be altered significantly by salvage logging. Although bird species will vary in their responses to different management options, few cavity-nesting species, if any, will benefit from severe salvaging (i.e., clearcut, or removal of most medium and large snags). Here, we evaluate several alternatives to severe salvage logging based on our knowledge of nesting requirements for six cavity-nesting birds in the northern Rocky Mountains: (1) leave the burn unsalvaged; (2) lightly salvage throughout the burn (e.g., leave many of the biggest snags); (3) salvage the burn (e.g., light or partial) after a delay of several years (Murphy and Lehnhausen 1998, Kreisel and Stein 1999); (4) salvage part of the burn severely and leave the remainder unsalvaged (Hutto 1995); and (5) apply different salvage treatments across the burn (including variation in tree distributions, sizes, and species left uncut).

The species most likely to benefit from unsalvaged burns, or unsalvaged portions of burns, are those most-closely tied to early post-fire conditions. Because Black-backed and Three-toed woodpeckers appear to depend on the short-lived availability of prey resources that quickly invade post-fire habitats, a delay in salvaging may be warranted (Murphy and Lehnhausen 1998). Some species (e.g., American Kestrel, Lewis's Woodpecker) may tolerate or benefit from partial or light salvage logging provided the large snags and tree species (e.g., deciduous trees, Douglas-fir, ponderosa pine, western larch) they tend to select are left uncut (Saab and Dudley 1998; S. Hejl and M. McFadzen, unpubl. data).

Species may inhabit partially salvaged burns (Saab and Dudley 1998; S. Hejl and M. McFadzen, unpubl. data) because they resemble the later successional stages of burns (when snags begin to thin out naturally) or open forests. Given our limited understanding of the cumulative effects of fire suppression and post-fire salvage logging, and their effects on post-fire habitat availability across western landscapes, allowing succession to proceed naturally in unsalvaged burns may benefit the most species.

MIMIC NATURAL DISTURBANCE REGIME

Many bird species are adapted to, and may depend upon, natural disturbance such as fire. Over the last century, however, logging has supplanted fire as the dominant process shaping coniferous forests in many regions of the West. Yet, the consequences of this shift for avian communities is poorly understood (Hansen et al. 1991). It has been suggested that the disturbance created by logging may create adequate habitats for some fire-dependent species in areas where severe fires are impractical (Hutto 1995). Indeed, fire and logging could have similar effects on western landscapes if logging were modified to mimic natural fires more closely (Hunter 1993, Hejl 1994). However, there are profoundly different ways in which past fire and silvicultural activities have affected western forest systems. First, they often operate on vastly different spatial and temporal scales (e.g., disturbance size and frequency), which, in turn, will lead to different landscape structure (Hansen et al. 1991, Gluck and Rempel 1996). Second, there are many unique features produced by fire (e.g., a high density of snags and consequent increases in wood-boring beetles) that may not be replicated readily by current logging practices (Hansen et al. 1991, Hutto 1995). Finally, selective logging often removes larger trees whereas low-severity fires typically kill smaller trees (Finch et al. 1997). Thus, natural disturbances may provide useful models for developing logging and salvaging techniques that would diminish the negative impacts on birds (Hunter 1993, Hejl et al. 1995).

Our understanding of how birds respond to silvicultural activities is based primarily on comparisons of logged versus relatively undisturbed, mature forests (Hejl et al. 1995). However, assessments that include comparisons of logged and naturally disturbed forests with similar disturbance severities (e.g., thinned forests might be compared to moderate or understory burns) would be valuable. For example, a recent study of 16 burned and 16 logged conifer forests in Colorado found that severely logged forests (i.e., logged areas contained few, if any, live or dead trees) were generally unused by most species associated with stand-replacement burns (N. Kotliar and C. Melcher, unpubl. data). Overall, avian species richness was much higher in burns than in logged forests. The pattern was especially salient when comparing clearcuts (i.e., no retention trees) to unsalvaged burns. Of the species that did occur in clearcuts, most also occurred in burns, whereas the reverse was not observed. Hansen et al. (1995b) also found that retaining canopy trees benefits many bird species in the west Cascades of Oregon. In general, clearcut conifer forests do not function as substitutes for burned forests. In many respects, the effects of logging on avian communities in unburned forests may be similar to those of salvage logging in stand-replacement burns.

The high density of snags in burns is the most obvious distinction between burned and clearcut forests. However, the edges of these disturbances can also differ dramatically. For example, clearcut forests often have well-defined edges with few, if any standing snags. In contrast, burn edges are often a heterogeneous mix of burned and unburned trees, except along fire breaks where burn edges are usually more abrupt. The juxtaposition of live and dead forests may be important to many species, such as Olive-sided Flycatcher, which generally sings and conducts foraging sallies from dead trees in open areas but nest in nearby live, mature trees (Altman and Sallabanks 2000). In Colorado, Olive-sided Flycatcher only occurred in cuts that contained both snags and live trees (i.e., not clearcuts; N. Kotliar and C. Melcher, unpubl. data). The complexity of burn edges may also help to diminish deleterious edge effects (e.g., increased nest predation and parasitism) in adjacent undisturbed forests that could result from high-contrast edges of clearcuts. Thus, silvicultural practices that incorporate structural elements of burns (e.g., retaining or creating high densities of snags and patches of live trees, and increasing the complexity of edges) may improve the suitability of logged forests for many post-fire bird species.

There are also important differences between natural and anthropogenic disturbances at larger spatial and temporal scales. For example, in both conifer- and aspen-dominated forests, differences in bird communities among burned and cut forests were most evident in early successional stands, but were still apparent in mid-successional forests (Hutto 1995, Hobson and Schiek 1999). We explore this idea further by comparing the fragmenting effects of severe disturbances: stand-replacement fire, silvicultural activities (e.g., post-fire salvage, clearcuts), and forest conversion. Here, we restrict the meaning of forest fragmentation to the fragmenting effects of anthropogenic disturbance relative to the natural heterogeneity of the landscape. Fragmentation can alter several landscape-scale parameters, including the number, size, and spatial distribution of forest patches, the degree of contrast between disturbed and adjacent undisturbed forests, and the persistence of the disturbed patches. By definition, natural disturbance regimes, such as stand-replacement fires, create and reinforce natural heterogeneity (e.g., spatial configuration of forest patches, variation in successional stages among patches). Because most post-fire forests eventually resemble pre-fire forests (e.g., cover type), persistence and contrast are relatively low compared to the highly persistent patches that result from forest conversion in agricultural or suburban landscapes. The fragmenting effects of silvicultural practices will generally fall somewhere between these two extremes, depending on logging severity (e.g., thinning vs. clearcutting) and frequency (e.g., cut rotation). For some species, however, the negative effects resulting from alteration of landscape structure and dynamics through fire suppression may rival the

negative consequences of forest fragmentation in some western forests. However, few studies have evaluated the consequences of fire suppression or other alterations of fire regimes on avian communities (Lyon et al. 2000).

The degree to which anthropogenic disturbance results in forest fragmentation depends on differences between the scale, intensity, and frequency of natural and anthropogenic disturbance, as well as the natural heterogeneity of the landscape. Species adapted to frequent natural disturbance may tolerate or even prefer the conditions created by disturbance over undisturbed forests. The Pygmy Nuthatch, for example, which is endemic to ponderosa pine forests (relatively short fire return intervals), had higher abundance in prescribed understory burns than in adjacent unburned forests, and was absent in stand-replacement burns (N. Kotliar, unpubl. data). In contrast, species such as the Golden-crowned Kinglet, Varied Thrush, and Townsend's Warbler, which are most often found in association with spruce-fir and cedar-hemlock cover types (relatively long fire return intervals; Hutto 1995), consistently occurred at lower abundances in burned forests (Table 1c). Although many species may tolerate, or be adapted to, natural disturbance, we expect that most bird species (except for some generalists and introduced species) will be extremely sensitive to the high degree of persistence and contrast of forest conversion, regardless of inherent disturbance regimes. Superimposed on these factors are other landscape-scale issues such as local cowbird abundance or the composition of predator communities. Thus, local, landscape, and regional differences need to be addressed when basing silvicultural practices on natural disturbance regimes.

RESEARCH RECOMMENDATIONS

SPECIFIC RESEARCH QUESTIONS

Based on our review of past research, we have identified some general patterns regarding the responses of avian communities to fire. However, the studies have raised more questions than they have answered. Thus, applications of management prescriptions involving fire and fire-related silvicultural practices should be considered experimental and be designed to increase our knowledge about fire effects. For example, we need more information about the basic ecology of post-fire forests, including:

• how various fire characteristics (e.g., severity, size, successional stage, and season of burning), landscape contexts, and cover types (both pre- and post-fire types) affect avian communities;

• the extent to which avian use of burns is pred-

icated on the juxtaposition of burned and unburned forest;

- the effects of fire on life histories (foraging
behavior, nest site selection) and demographics, particularly reproductive success, survivorship, and recruitment for both breeding
and wintering populations (Finch et al. 1997,
Lyon et al. 2000);
- variation in avian use of fire-generated snags
for nest, foraging, or perch sites compared to
use of snags generated by other process (e.g.,
lightning, disease, insects);
- how avian communities differ in naturally disturbed forests compared to managed forests
across successional stages;
- the effects of seed-eaters, flycatchers, and other specialists on seed dispersal, forest regeneration, and overall forest health;
- the manner in which snag characteristics and
distributions affect insect prey and, in turn,
foraging birds; and
- whether or not there is geographic variation
in avian responses to disturbances such as fire.

We also need to understand the ways in which
fires differ from other natural disturbances (e.g.,
blowdowns, insect kills) that can be extensive and
severe. In Colorado, for example, a recent wind-
storm uprooted or damaged trees across 10,000
ha (Flaherty 2000) and, in 1939, an outbreak of
spruce beetles (*Dendrocotonus rufipennis*) killed
nearly 290,000 ha of trees (Veblen et al. 1991).
Information required for sound management includes:

- improved information on the range of natural
variation both within, and among, historic
fires;
- the effects of fire suppression on forest and
landscape structure and wildlife communities;
- the ecological tradeoffs between wildland,
prescribed fire, and mechanical treatments (including thinning and burning; Tiedemann et
al. 2000, Wagner et al. 2000);
- appropriate management of post-fire forests,
including how salvage treatments affect species that require post-fire habitats;
- how wildlife species respond to different stages of succession and whether or not those
stages are similar across disturbance types;
- the responses of forests and wildlife to repeated management treatments in the same location (Andersen et al. 1998);
- the effects of severity in natural compared to
anthropogenic disturbances;
- differences and similarities among fire and
forest harvesting practices and how these disturbances affect avian communities; and
- which management treatments are most likely

to conserve the biological integrity of forest
systems.

RESEARCH DESIGN

The inherent nature of fire limits the opportunities to conduct well-replicated, controlled experiments that evaluate the full spectrum of fire
characteristics across all western forest types.
Rather, we must rely on several complementary
approaches, including: (1) unplanned comparisons of wildfires (e.g., Finch et al. 1997); (2)
meta-analyses that combine data from numerous
studies to generate larger datasets and greater statistical power (e.g., Hutto 1995); and (3) controlled experiments using prescribed (planned)
burns, logged, logged and burned, and unburned
controls. The collective results of all approaches
should help us develop a greater overall understanding of how fire affects wildlife.

Most studies of fire effects on avian communities have been unplanned comparisons of wildfires
(Finch et al. 1997). Although variation among
wildfires (e.g., forest type, burn characteristics) and
post-fire management strategies, plus the lack of
pre- and post-fire treatments, has limited the scope
of inference provided by unplanned comparisons,
they nonetheless provide unique opportunities to
study extensive, severe wildfires. This approach is
most useful immediately after years with extensive
fire, when researchers can establish numerous,
similar-age replicates across regions and in many
forest types. Intensive studies of single sites can
provide useful information as well, especially in
large burns. For example, the effects of burn severity could be studied in one large burn by strat-
ifying survey points across severities (e.g., R. Sallabanks and J. McIver, unpubl. data). In addition,
single-site studies can generate data for use in
meta-analyses.

Meta-analyses provide excellent opportunities
for improving the results of multiple studies that
have little or no replication (Brett 1997). Even
non-statistical compilations of unplanned comparisons can reveal biologically meaningful
trends, as we found in our review that Three-
toed and Black-backed woodpeckers were either
restricted to, or more abundant in, burned forests
(Table 1a). In order for meta-analyses to be possible, however, researchers must publish detailed
study protocols, and they must cooperate with
one another to the extent possible to standardize
protocols and share data.

To complement and expand the existing knowledge gained from unplanned comparisons and
meta-analyses, we need more experiments that
control for and test variations among fire characteristics, forest type, and landscape context (e.g.,
Breininger and Schmalzer 1990). Because annual
variation in bird populations can be considerable,

several years of pre- and post-treatment data ideally should be collected. Whenever possible, researchers should incorporate the full range of fire characteristics provided by natural fire regimes in the systems of interest (Andersen et al. 1998). It will be difficult to find sites for conducting severe burns, but there is increasing support for conducting such studies in national parks (J. Connor, pers. comm.) and wilderness areas. In general, it will be more feasible to conduct experiments of low- to moderate-severity burns in systems that typically experience lower-severity fires.

Research programs must also take into account some important design and interpretation problems that are often ignored in fire studies. Because burn edges and burn severity may have pronounced effects on avian use of burns, survey points must be stratified across burn edges, adjacent unburned forest, and distant unburned forest, and over a range of burn severities to control for these sources of variation. In addition, to determine whether avian species use of post-fire habitats immediately after fire represents a preference for burns, or site-tenacity for breeding territories, studies need pre- and post-fire measures of abundance, as well as measures of reproductive success and recruitment over several years.

Finally, researchers need to implement long-term studies to develop a full picture of post-fire successional changes and how they affect avian communities. Although habitat loss may be the immediate effect of severe fire on species that typically inhabit mature forests (e.g., Golden-crowned Kinglet, Spotted Owl), the long-term effects (e.g., decades or centuries later) may be habitat improvement. Thus, clearing forests of fuels to prevent severe fires that could decrease Spotted Owl habitat in the short term could preclude more significant habitat improvements that would benefit Spotted Owls in the future. Overall, researchers will need to consider a wide variety of research approaches, as well as the full spectrum of fire characteristics and forest types, both unmanaged and managed, to understand how proposed management strategies may affect the future health and integrity of western-forest systems.

ACKNOWLEDGMENTS

We thank W. L. Baker, W. H. Romme, and T. T. Veblen for their gracious assistance in helping us understand the finer points of fire terminology and ecology. H. D. Powell's expertise on insects and woodpecker foraging were instrumental in drafting related sections of the manuscript. W. L. Baker, D. S. Dobkin, T. L. George, and J. E. Roelle all provided valuable suggestions and improvements to earlier drafts of the manuscript. J. Connor contributed to numerous discussions regarding the effects of fire management on bird communities in national parks.

APPENDIX. SCIENTIFIC NAMES OF BIRD SPECIES

Species
American Kestrel (*Falco sparverius*)
Spotted Owl (*Strix occidentalis*)
Mourning Dove (*Zenaida macroura*)
Common Nighthawk (*Chordeiles minor*)
Northern Flicker (*Colaptes auratus*)
Lewis's Woodpecker (*Melanerpes lewis*)
White-headed Woodpecker (*Picoides albolarvatus*)
Black-backed Woodpecker (*Picoides arcticus*)
Downy Woodpecker (*Picoides pubescens*)
Three-toed Woodpecker (*Picoides tridactylus*)
Hairy Woodpecker (*Picoides villosus*)
Red-naped Sapsucker (*Sphyrapicus nuchalis*)
Williamson's Sapsucker (*Sphyrapicus thyroideus*)
Olive-sided Flycatcher (*Contopus cooperi*)
Western Wood-Pewee (*Contopus sordidulus*)
Hammond's Flycatcher (*Empidonax hammondii*)
Dusky Flycatcher (*Empidonax oberholseri*)
Plumbeous Vireo (*Vireo plumbeus*)
Cassin's Vireo (*Vireo cassinii*)
Warbling Vireo (*Vireo gilvus*)
Tree Swallow (*Tachycineta bicolor*)
Steller's Jay (*Cyanocitta stelleri*)
Clark's Nutcracker (*Nucifraga columbiana*)
Mountain Chickadee (*Poecile gambeli*)
Red-breasted Nuthatch (*Sitta canadensis*)
White-breasted Nuthatch (*Sitta carolinensis*)
Pygmy Nuthatch (*Sitta pygmaea*)
Brown Creeper (*Certhia americana*)
Rock Wren (*Salpinctes obsoletus*)
House Wren (*Troglodytes aedon*)
Ruby-crowned Kinglet (*Regulus calendula*)
Golden-crowned Kinglet (*Regulus satrapa*)
Hermit Thrush (*Catharus guttatus*)
Swainson's Thrush (*Catharus ustulatus*)
Varied Thrush (*Ixoreus naevius*)
Townsend's Solitaire (*Myadestes townsendi*)
Mountain Bluebird (*Sialia currucoides*)
Western Bluebird (*Sialia mexicana*)
American Robin (*Turdus migratorius*)
Yellow-rumped Warbler (*Dendroica coronata*)
Townsend's Warbler (*Dendroica townsendi*)
Wilson's Warbler (*Wilsonia pusilla*)
Western Tanager (*Piranga ludoviciana*)
Lazuli Bunting (*Passerina amoena*)
Dark-eyed Junco (*Junco hyemalis*)
Lincoln's Sparrow (*Melospiza lincolnii*)
Chipping Sparrow (*Spizella passerina*)
White-crowned Sparrow (*Zonotrichia leucophrys*)
Pine Siskin (*Carduelis pinus*)
Cassin's Finch (*Carpodacus cassinii*)
Red Crossbill (*Loxia curvirostra*)
Pine Grosbeak (*Pinicola enucleator*)
Evening Grosbeak (*Coccothraustes vespertinus*)

Studies in Avian Biology No. 25:65–72, 2002.

GEOGRAPHIC VARIATION IN COWBIRD DISTRIBUTION, ABUNDANCE, AND PARASITISM

MICHAEL L. MORRISON AND D. CALDWELL HAHN

Abstract. We evaluated geographical patterns in the abundance and distribution of Brown-headed Cowbirds (*Molothrus ater*), and in the frequency of cowbird parasitism, across North America in relation to habitat fragmentation. We found no distinctive parasitism patterns at the national or even regional scales, but the species is most abundant in the Great Plains, the heart of their original range, and least common in the southeastern U.S. This situation is dynamic, because both the Brown-headed and two other cowbird species are actively expanding their ranges in the southern U.S. We focused almost entirely in this paper on the Brown-headed Cowbird, because it is the only endemic North American cowbird, its distribution is much wider, and it has been much more intensively studied. We determined that landscape is the most meaningful unit of scale for comparing cowbird parasitism patterns as, for example, in comparisons of northeastern and central hardwood forests within agricultural matrices, and suburbanized areas versus western coniferous forests. We concluded that cowbird parasitism patterns were broadly similar within all landscapes. Even comparisons between prominently dissimilar landscapes, such as hardwoods in agriculture and suburbia versus coniferous forest, display a striking similarity in the responses of cowbirds. Our review clearly indicated that proximity of feeding areas is the key factor influencing presence and parasitism patterns within the landscape. We considered intensity of landscape fragmentation from forest-dominated landscapes altered in a forest management context to fragmentation characterized by mixed suburbanization or agricultural development. Our review consistently identified an inverse relationship between extent of forest cover across the landscape and cowbird presence. Invariably, the variation seen in parasitism frequencies *within* a region was at least partially explained as a response to changes in forest cover. The most salient geographic aspect of cowbirds' response to landscape fragmentation is the time since fragmentation occurred. Eastern landscapes generally experienced 200 years ago the development and fragmentation that western landscapes experienced less than 75 years ago. Consequently, there is a broad east-west contrast in which more numerous human settlements and smaller unbroken forest stands are found in the East, a difference that permits cowbirds to be more pervasive and ubiquitous. The locality of suitable feeding areas is a hallmark trait of the cowbirds' strategy in exploiting specific forest fragments. Host abundance influences parasitism patterns only secondarily at the landscape scale. These two limiting factors come into play differently in different landscapes. For example, cowbird abundance in unbroken forested landscapes are limited primarily by the availability of foraging areas rather than by host density, whereas cowbirds are limited primarily by host availability in landscapes that are extensively fragmented with feeding areas.

Key Words: Brown-headed Cowbird; cowbird parasitism; fragmentation; geographic variation; host defense; *Molothrus ater*.

The laying of eggs by one species in the nests of another species, allowing the host species to raise their young, is a fascinating evolutionary story (e.g., Rothstein and Robinson 1988, Ortega 1998:37–63). In North America, the Brown-headed Cowbird (*Molothrus ater*) is the primary nest parasite, although two other species are expanding their ranges in the southern U.S. (Cruz et al. 1998, Ortega 1998). The trait of parasitizing nests apparently developed in the Brown-headed Cowbird in the Great Plains. As reviewed below, this cowbird species expanded its range eastward in the 1800s and westward in the 1900s, and now occupies most states and provinces in North America (Rothstein 1994, Peterjohn et al. 2000). Parasitism, along with the cowbird's range expansion, has caused scientists to consider the role that cowbirds might be having in population declines of certain of their host species. Thus, the goal of our paper is to review cowbird abundance, distribution, and parasitism

frequencies across North America so a better understanding of cowbird ecology and its impact on host species can be gained.

In this paper we assumed *no difference* in cowbird parasitism behavior by geographic location. We reviewed the literature (including unpublished manuscripts and reports) in order to characterize the relationship between host and parasite. Given the striking differences in environmental conditions across North America—including the distribution of bird species—we can presuppose that one can easily find some amount of difference in the frequencies of cowbird parasitism just by looking for it. And, in fact, we know this to be the case (see reviews by Ortega 1998, Trine et al. 1998). We were primarily interested in examining the *process* of parasitism. That is, are there fundamental differences in cowbird behavior in different regions that have ecological implications and evolutionary explanations? In our review we considered both feeding behavior and host selection behavior.

VALIDITY OF AN EAST-WEST COMPARISON OF BROOD PARASITISM

Our perception of geographic location is based in part on historic context and tradition. It is also difficult to lump large geographic areas under a common descriptor. Where does the East begin and the West end; where does the East becomes the Southeast? These geographical terms are frequently used subjectively and anthropocentrically in ways that are not supported by ecological characteristics that affect birds. Thus, dividing North America into "East" and "West" is an inappropriate means of examining an ecological relationship such as parasitism and fragmentation. This does not mean, however, that geographic differences do not occur in land-use practices and ecological processes and in the response of animals to these practices and processes. But establishing *a priori* boundaries constrains the analysis to preconceived categories and notions.

THE RESPONSE OF COWBIRD HOSTS TO FOREST FRAGMENTATION

In this section we set the stage for evaluating regional differences in cowbird parasitism by defining fragmentation and placing this concept into an ecological framework. The emphasis of this volume is on fragmentation, and from the perspective of cowbirds, the most important aspects of fragmentation are, first, that it affects the abundance and distribution of host species by altering their habitat and, second, that it alters the abundance and distribution of feeding areas associated with developments. These twin themes about the influence of fragmentation on hosts' breeding habitat and on feeding areas of cowbirds associated with human development recur throughout our review.

The classic description of fragmentation implies extensive landscapes of homogeneous vegetation, but this conception is an artifact of graphic art framed at a large spatial scale. Examined at finer resolutions, most ecological systems are actually a mosaic of different plant associations. Even changes of a few meters can change soils, slope, and aspect, and thus the associated plants. Further, these mosaics are dynamic and change, often rapidly, through succession, catastrophic events (e.g., fire, flood, wind), or development activities such as crop plantings or settlements (Meffe and Carroll 1997:274–275; Franklin et al. *this volume*).

The definition of "fragmented" habitat depends upon the spatial scale of observation. Our analyses use fragmentation at a scale relevant to

selection of habitat by birds, particularly songbirds. Briefly, habitat selection is often viewed as a hierarchical process where individuals first select a broad geographic range, a decision that is largely innate. Within the geographic range the individual then makes a series of decisions based on increasingly refined combinations of vegetation structure, floristics, food resources, and nest sites (Johnson 1980, Hutto 1985).

Thus, in an analysis of brood parasitism, fragmentation is an ambiguous concept unless it is defined in spatial terms relevant to the series of responses a host makes. There are changes that take place in the environment at several scales of resolution (see also Angelstam 1996). Such descriptions of the environment and habitat selection are not restricted geographically, but should apply across eastern and western environs. Consequently, we would not expect different behavioral processes in either host species or cowbirds to be operating geographically. The proportion of birds that show a particular response to fragmentation (e.g., area sensitive, enhanced by edge) may differ geographically depending on the historic factors that formed the initial bird assemblage (e.g., Morrison et al. 1998:16–26). For example, fewer *Dendroica* warblers occur in the West than in central and eastern locations. This is apparently the result of Pleistocene and post-Pleistocene events (Mengel 1964, Morrison et al. 1998:18–21). Thus, there is simply a greater opportunity for fragmentation to cause negative impacts on these warblers in more eastern locations, and perhaps a proportionally more apparent impact to the bird assemblage due to fragmentation.

Fragmentation in managed forests can be considered dynamic in that stands are cut and reforested; stands are not retained in early successional conditions. This means the songbird communities that cowbirds parasitize continue to have extensive natural breeding habitat although the vegetation communities are less stable than they would be in unmanaged forest. In contrast, disturbances due to human development activities result in permanent or static fragmentation (McGarigal and McComb 1995). This eradicates some host-breeding habitat, leaving disjunct fragments separated by patches that have food for cowbirds. They concluded that it is unlikely that the empirical findings on forest fragmentation from urban and agricultural landscapes extend to the dynamic forest landscapes of the Pacific Northwest and elsewhere. Likewise, Keller and Anderson (1992) concluded that fragmentation in Wyoming could not be directly compared with fragmentation occurring in the Pacific Northwest. Freemark et al. (1995) also noted that most studies in the West have been con-

TABLE 1.   COMPARISON OF THE EFFECTS OF LANDSCAPE STRUCTURE ON NEOTROPICAL MIGRATORY SPECIES BREEDING IN NORTHEASTERN AND CENTRAL HARDWOOD FORESTS WITHIN AGRICULTURE AND SUBURBANIZED LANDSCAPES VERSUS WESTERN FORESTS

Landscape structure	Northeastern and central vs. western comparison
Landscape composition	
Forest type	Same
Forest cover	Same; less severe in west
Habitat proportion	Same
Landscape configuration	
Patch size	Same; perhaps less severe in west
Patch shape	N/A[a]
Interpatch distance	Same
Nonforest edge	N/A
Habitat juxtaposition	Same

Note: Information summarized from Freemark et al. (1995).
[a] N/A = comparison not made or comparable.

ducted in forested landscapes fragmented by silvicultural activities—which usually do not have rich food sources for cowbirds—rather than in agricultural and urban landscapes as in the East, which do include sources of food (see also Hejl et al. *this volume*).

Yet, Freemark et al's. (1995) extensive literature review of the response of breeding communities of neotropical migrants to landscape structure across much of North America does show similarities in songbird responses. A subjective comparison of communities nesting in northeastern and central hardwood forests within agricultural and suburbanized areas with communities nesting in western coniferous forests revealed similar responses of birds to broad measures of landscape structure (Table 1). Particularly because this is a comparison among very dissimilar landscape settings (i.e., hardwoods within agriculture and suburbia versus managed coniferous forest), the similarity in response by breeding birds is striking.

Although there are similarities in the responses of host communities in different regions to fragmentation, Freemark et al. (1995) concluded that birds in western (coniferous) forests have not shown as strong a negative response to fragmentation as have birds in northeastern and central hardwood forests. They attributed this several factors: fragmentation is a more recent occurrence in the West; fragmentation has rarely resulted in habitat isolation; and western forests are naturally fragmented and human-induced fragmentation has not had time to negatively impact birds. The key insight here is that there are not inherent differences in the response of bird communities to forest fragmentation. The earlier stage of fragmentation typical of western forest means that many western coniferous forests are actually "perforated" rather than fragmented (Forman and Collinge 1996), or, as Freeman et

al. (1995) described them, "punctuated" by clearcuts. Of course there are also numerous examples of both extensively forested areas and forests perforated by logging and agriculture outside of western environs (e.g., Robinson et al. 1995a, Robinson and Robinson 1999).

McGarigal and McComb (1995), working in the Oregon Coast Range, found that landscape structure (composition and configuration) explained <50% of the variation in each species' abundance among the landscapes. Species' abundances were generally greater in areas with a relatively fragmented distribution of habitat. Note that from the cowbird's perspective this means host abundance increases as fragmentation progresses. They cautioned, however, that species sensitive to fragmentation at the scale of their study may have been rare already and therefore not subject to the approach they used. Again from the cowbird's perspective the species that drop out do not reduce the number of host individuals available to cowbirds. They concluded, however, that their results were generally similar to studies conducted in forest-dominated landscapes in New Hampshire, Missouri, Maine, and Wyoming. Thus, when comparisons are made between similar vegetation types, birds respond in a similar manner across broad geographic regions. They noted that effects of fragmentation in forest-dominated landscapes altered in a forest management context is not comparable with fragmentation caused by urbanization or agricultural development, which is typically how eastern and western regions have been compared in the literature.

In conclusion, the same ecological processes associated with fragmentation seem to operate regardless of geographic region. It is the longevity of those land-use changes that precipitated fragmentation that causes any geographic differences in current responses by birds. Verner

(1986) concluded that in western forests fragmentation was in the early stage and tended to produce two-dimensional islands (clearcuts) in three-dimensional seas (forests), while in eastern forests (as in European forests) the later stages of fragmentation have resulted in three-dimensional islands (forest fragments) in two-dimensional seas (e.g., agricultural lands). Askins et al. (1990) likewise concluded that the longer history of fragmentation in Europe has resulted in the extirpation of most area-sensitive species, a situation now in progress in North America. The localized abundance, breeding success, and survival of birds is related primarily to factors of habitat quality such as resource availability and predator-competitor activity, but these factors can be overridden when patches becomes very small (<10–20 ha) and isolated.

In summary, landscape fragmentation affects the songbird communities that cowbirds parasitize. At one level of intensity, fragmentation refers to the transformation of extensive forests into smaller stands, with the consequence for cowbird hosts of smaller, often shifting, breeding areas, and habitats with a greater edge to interior ratio. As fragmentation progresses, it evolves to a heterogeneous landscape composed of a mix of patches of breeding habitat with patches of development activities such as agriculture and settlements. With these twin aspects of fragmentation—smaller forest stands and increasing food sources associated with development—an increase in cowbird abundance and parasitism is likely.

HISTORIC DISTRIBUTION OF BROWN-HEADED COWBIRD AND POPULATION TRENDS

Peterjohn et al. (2000) described the continental decline in cowbird numbers in North America since the mid-1960s. Maximum cowbird abundance occurs in the northern Great Plains. Regionally, numbers are declining in the southern plains and throughout most of the East. The decline in the East is attributed to substantial increases in forest cover. There appears to be an overall steady abundance of cowbirds in the West. Within the region there is perhaps a slight decrease in the Pacific Northwest, while the Central Valley of California showed perhaps the greatest proportional increase in cowbird numbers in North America.

While there is consensus that the ancestral range of cowbirds in the Great Plains is still the area of their greatest abundance, other aspects of the extent and timing of their range expansions both eastward and westward are less certain. Rothstein (1994) suggested that cowbirds have been in the East in small numbers since at least the 1700s, the earliest era of European colonization. In the West, cowbirds may not be recent additions to the avifauna. While their colonization up the Pacific Coast from southern California to Oregon and Washington has been well documented over the course of the 20th century, there is also evidence of earlier populations in the northwest (Rothstein 1994). They apparently occurred historically, however, across the Great Basin to the eastern edge of the Sierra Nevada (Rothstein 1994). Thus, contrary to popular belief, the cowbird did occur historically in western North America. The Sierra Nevada-Cascade mountain ranges may have served as a barrier to widespread expansion onto the Pacific slope. There is also fossil evidence that cowbirds (of unknown breeding behavior) occurred along the edges of the species' current range in California, Oregon, and Florida in the late Pleistocene (Lowther 1993). Chace and Cruz (1999) suggested that cowbirds formerly ranged to near timberline in the Rocky Mountains because of the historic presence of bison (*Bison bison*). Cowbirds retreated from these elevations with the extirpation of bison from these mountains. The addition of cattle to former bison range is now allowing cowbirds to return to the mountains. If this is the case, we would expect that birds in at least some regions of the Rocky Mountains have had a longer exposure to cowbirds than our recent data indicate, and they may still express behavioral traits that evolved during the bison-cowbird period.

SUBSPECIES DIFFERENCES

Differences among the three subspecies of the Brown-headed Cowbird have been little studied. Rothstein (1994) speculated that the smaller southwestern subspecies, the "dwarf" cowbird, *M. a. obscurus,* might be more vagile or more competitive than *M. a. artemisia,* found to the north, east of the Rockies, because the westward range expansion of the species to the Pacific and up the west coast seems to have been driven by *obscurus.* At some point later *artemisia* appears also to have crossed the Rockies into northern California such that the two have subsequently intermixed as cowbirds moved north into Oregon and Washington.

Recent evidence of the range expansion of the eastern subspecies *M. a. ater* into the Florida peninsula makes it feasible that *ater* may be as successful as *obscurus* was in colonizing the Pacific west coast. Cruz et al. (1998) noted that *ater* has spread rapidly since the 1950s and now has breeding records confirmed halfway down the peninsula, with non-breeding sightings reported throughout the state. The expansion of the Brown-headed Cowbird into Florida is expected to have significant negative consequences for the indigenous breeding passerines, many of which are patchily distributed and breeding in small populations. The character of natural habitats and human settlements in Florida consists of mangrove on the west coast and dunes and beach on the east coast, with relentless human settlement along both coasts. The central section of the peninsula is higher and drier and agricultural and livestock developments are pervasive. Two mangrove-obligate species, the Black-whiskered Vireo (*Vireo altiloquus*) and the Florida subspecies of Prairie Warbler (*Dendroica discolor*), are already reflecting local population extirpation due to parasitism (W. Pranty, pers. comm.).

OTHER COWBIRD SPECIES: RECENT NORTH AMERICAN INVADERS

While it is only speculative to compare the invasive character of Shiny (*Molothrus bonariensis*) and Bronzed (*M. aeneus*) cowbirds to Brown-headed Cowbirds at this stage, recent developments in their respective range expansions suggest that both may be successful and increasingly widespread in the United States. Both are also host generalists, although perhaps not as extreme as the Brown-headed Cowbird (Rothstein et al. 2002). The rapid and impressive northward range expansion of the Shiny Cowbird across the Caribbean and into North America makes it a likely candidate to become established in the southeastern U.S. in the next few decades. While no breeding records have yet been recorded in Florida, the Shiny Cowbird is expected to become established there with little difficulty (Stevenson and Anderson 1994; W. Pranty, pers. comm.). Nothing is known about the extent of habitat specialization for either Brown-headed or Shiny cowbird within Florida.

The Bronzed Cowbird has only recently shown marked range expansion, apparently in association with loss of songbird breeding habitat in lower Rio Grande Valley in Texas. However, it has expanded both eastward and westward and could thus become a factor in regions of the U.S. (Cruz et al. 1998). In Texas, the Bronzed Cowbird parasitizes over 23 species, and at this stage it appears to prefer larger host species than does *M. ater*. The bronzed is thought to have contributed to the extirpation of Audubon's Oriole (*Icterus graduacuada*) in portions of lower Rio Grande Valley. Together with the brown-headed, the bronzed may also have contributed to declines of the Orchard (*I. spurius*), Hooded (*I. cucullatus*), and Northern (*I. galbula*) orioles in south Texas (Cruz et al. 1998).

HOST BEHAVIOR AND GEOGRAPHY

Much interest has focused on the question why most host species of the Brown-headed Cowbird do not show effective anti-parasite behavior. Rothstein's (1975) early experimental study of twelve eastern species used artificial eggs colored to resemble cowbird eggs and showed that only a few species regularly ejected the parasite eggs. Since then a large number of studies have been conducted in a variety of sites both east and west, showing that parasitism defenses (i.e., egg ejection, egg burial, or nest desertion) occur occasionally and unpredictably among species.

Some western-residing species and subspecies show effective anti-parasite behaviors that prevent or minimize deleterious effects of parasitism, which may have developed after contact with cowbirds, or which may have been present as pre-adaptation. For example, the Black-throated Gray Warbler (*Dendroica nigrescens*) regularly buried cowbird eggs in its nests in the Inyo-White mountains of eastern-central California (J. Keane and M. Morrison, unpubl. data), and Rich and Rothstein (1985) showed that Sage Thrashers regularly rejected cowbird eggs throughout their western range.

Egg-ejection behavior is one of the best-studied anti-parasite behaviors, yet a thorough summary of the proportion of acceptor and rejecter species by geographic region is still lacking because that would require systematic comparative studies of different populations of a large number of host species. Although evidence for egg rejection exists for many species, the quantitative estimates of frequency of this behavior can usually only be confirmed through experimentation, usually with artificial eggs (Ortega 1998: 19). Of the >225 species known to be parasitized by Brown-headed Cowbirds, fewer than 20 are known to regularly eject parasitic eggs (Ortega 1998:19–20). Despite the obvious advantages to hosts of removing cowbird eggs, there are also many reasons why birds accept them (Ortega 1998:23–27). The most prominent reason is that parents risk breaking their own eggs when they try to move the cowbird egg.

Little is known about the degree to which egg-ejection behavior is genetically based or learned. Briskie et al. (1992) concluded that some anti brood-parasitic defenses are probably genetically determined. Robertson and Norman (1977) thought that the presence and intensity of aggression should vary widely geographically depending on the length of exposure to brood parasitism. For example, they compared aggression in an area of long-term host-cowbird sympatry (Manitoba) with an area (Ontario) of more recent sympatry. They found that the Manitoba host populations showed more aggression towards a model cowbird, and concluded that this was because of the longer history of sympatry. Hobson and Villard (1998) studied the response of American Redstarts to model cowbirds in western Canada and found that they exhibited more vigorous nest defense in fragmented forests where cowbirds are more common than in extensively forested landscapes.

There is a widespread assumption that all hosts would evolve measurable anti-parasite behaviors given long enough sympatry with cowbirds. According to this hypothesis, some species along the Pacific slope may not have had adequate exposure to parasitism to evolve regular ejection behavior (Rothstein 1975). As discussed above, however, additional evidence must be gathered before any analysis of geographic trends in egg-rejection behavior. We suggest that the variability and relative rarity of anti-cowbird defenses reflects the inconsistent selection pressure exerted by cowbird parasitism in those landscapes where parasitism is relatively low and where the level of parasitism on individual species and communities varies from year to year. In several areas where long-term studies of cowbird parasitism have been conducted and where parasitism pressure is both high and consistent on particular species in the community (such as central Illinois, the Edwards Plateau in Texas and Oklahoma, and southern California), the study populations should be tracked for the emergence of anti-parasite behaviors. Similarly, the evolution of defenses by forest interior birds should be watched in the context of fragmentation in both east and west.

COWBIRD PARASITISM AND GEOGRAPHY

We present a summary of patterns of cowbird parasitism in relation to vegetation structure, host community, and degree of landscape development based on studies conducted across North American a variety of vegetation types in different geographic regions (Table 2).

Our review indicates that proximity of feedings areas is the key factor influencing which host community a local cowbird population will parasitize. Although Payne (1973, 1977) discussed the importance of temporal mismatch of breeding seasons (i.e., differing lengths of exposure, *sensu* Mayfield 1965) and documented the phenomenon for the birds of northern California, temporal mismatch is often overlooked. It is a notable phenomenon in eastern and western locations. The local abundance of cowbirds resulting from fragmentation and feeding opportunities further correlated with parasitization (Payne 1973, 1977).

It is commonly stated that the heavily parasitized riparian communities in the western and southwestern United States are physiographically unique because of the often abrupt change from the relatively mesic riparian vegetation and the xeric surrounding landscape (Ortega 1998: 267, Farmer 1999). However, cowbirds frequently use riparian areas in eastern and central, as well as western regions for passage, nesting, and foraging. Riparian corridors allow passage by cowbirds into an otherwise less suitable landscape matrix, including both eastern and western forests. The primary development impact to western riparian areas is loss of area and fragmentation (isolation), which is the same pattern seen in eastern deciduous forests (i.e., isolated patches of forest in a matrix of different vegetation). Several riparian obligate species in the West and Southwest have been nearly extirpated because of habitat loss. The isolation of these species into small patches exacerbated the effect of cowbird parasitism on their host populations. This situation, however, is not restricted to riparian vegetation of the West and Southwest. In three eastern regions where small and restricted species or subspecies occur in conjunction with a unique and limited habitat, development has created the classic situation in which cowbird parasitism (and nest predation) accelerate the decline of the resident species. In northern Michigan, in jack pine (*Pinus banksiana*) habitat, the species at risk is the Kirtland's Warbler (*Dendroica kirtlandii*). In the coastal mangrove forests of Florida, the species at risk are Black-whiskered Vireo and Prairie Warbler (Cruz et al. 1998, Stevenson and Anderson 1994). In Central Texas and Oklahoma, on the Edwards Plateau, the species at risk are the Golden-cheek Warbler (*Dendroica chrysoparia*) and Black-capped Vireo (*Vireo atricapillus*).

VALIDITY OF GEOGRAPHICAL COMPARISONS OF COWBIRD PARASITISM

One of the most important aspects of geography in analyzing the impact of cowbirds is the use of different spatial scales. Robinson (1999) noted that cowbird ecology can be analyzed at continental, regional, and landscape scales as much as at a local scale in relation to factors such as distances from edges. In this section, we discuss the findings of investigators who analyzed patterns at different scales. Hochachka et al. (1999) emphasized that investigators must define the scale they are using when predicting cowbird abundance and parasitism level.

Several investigators have considered whether aspects of cowbird parasitism vary on a conti-

TABLE 2.   FACTORS CORRELATED WITH INCREASED COWBIRD PRESENCE, ABUNDANCE, OR PARASITISM

Factor	Location	Source
Temporal mismatch	E. Washington	1
	Arizona/California	11
Proximity of feeding	E. Washington	1
	N. Rockies	2, 3, 5
	Sierra Nevada	6, 10
	N. Michigan	7
	Midwest	8, 13, 14, 15
	Vermont	9
	Florida	16, 17
	New Mexico	18
	Texas	19
	Pennsylvania	20
	Virginia	21
Local stand factors[a]	N. Michigan	7
	New York	22
Presence of riparian corridor	N. Rockies	2, 3, 5
	Coastal California	4
	Southern California	23
	Sierra Nevada	10
	Missouri	12
Host density	N. Rockies	2, 5
	Midwest	13
	Nationally	24
Species richness	Sierra Nevada	6
Fragmentation	Illinois	8
	Arizona/California	11a
	Florida	17
	Tennessee	25
Original range	Nationally	26
	Northeast	27

Sources: 1: Vander Haegen and Walker (1999); 2: Young and Hutto (1999); 3: Hejl and Young (1999); 4: Farmer (1999); 5: Tewksbury et al. (1999); 6: Purcell and Verner (1999); 7: Stribley and Hauffler (1999); 8: Robinson et al. (1995a); 9: Coker and Capen (1995, 1999); 10: Lynn et al. (1998); 11: Rosenberg et al. (1991:265, 335); 11a: Rosenberg et al. (1991:282–283); 12: Thompson et al. (1992); 13: Donovan et al. (1997); 14: Thompson (1994); 15: Trine et al. (1998); 16: Cruz et al. (1998); 17: W. Pranty, pers. comm.; 18: Goguen and Mathews (1999); 19: Eckrich et al. (1999); 20: E. Morton, pers. comm.; 21: J. Karr, pers. comm.; 22: Hahn and Hatfield (1995); 23: Kus (1999); 24: Hahn and O'Connor (2002); 25: Miles and Buehler (1999); 26: Smith and Myers-Smith (1998); 27: Hoover and Brittingham (1993).
[a] When in close proximity to feeding areas.

nental scale (Smith and Myers-Smith 1998, Robinson 1999). At a national scale, Hahn and O'Connor (2002) found that the most important factor predicting cowbird abundance is the presence of their preferred mix of host species (i.e., the seventeen most common hosts identified by Friedmann [1963]; Table 2). Landscapes in which host communities are found in close proximity to feeding areas typically occur where considerable habitat fragmentation occurs, that is, intrusion of agricultural activities, including concentrated livestock grazing, into a formerly undisturbed area. When they examined ancestral versus invaded ranges separately, they found that the predictive value of these host species actually operated only in the invaded ranges. Robinson et al. (1995b) suggested that because some western coniferous forests are more open than eastern forests, it was unclear whether or not western and eastern cowbirds differed in their preferences for forests, or if host distribu-

tion or some other factors influenced habitat occupancy by cowbirds. Our review indicates that the relationship between the openness of forests and cowbird abundance holds regardless of region. In fact, the variation seen in parasitism rates *within* a region was at least partially explained as a response to changes in forest cover. Further, many western forests have interlocking canopies with dense understories (e.g., Pacific Northwest, many western riparian forests). Again, sweeping generalizations regarding East and West seem unwarranted.

Hochachka et al. (1999) evaluated the relationship between forest coverage and parasitism among eastern, central, and western regions of the United States to provide a biological explanation for differences in the relationship between forest coverage and rates of cowbird parasitization across the continent. They also examined if variation in forest coverage was associated with the presence or absence of cowbird parasitization in a study area, and, where cowbirds were present, if the frequency at which nests were parasitized was associated with forest coverage. They obtained data on parasitization rates of forest birds from the Breeding Biology Research and Monitoring Database (BBIRD), with data from 23,448 individual nests being analyzed. There were 26 study sites on which the nesting success of forest-nesting birds was monitored.

Hochachka et al. (1999) reported that the conclusions of previous research suggested that larger proportions of forest cover will result in a lower impact of Brown-headed Cowbirds on their hosts. They further suggested that the relationship between forest coverage and parasitization might differ away from the Midwest for a number of reasons. They offered that variation in cowbird abundance may not only affect absolute rates of parasitization, but also the pattern of variation in parasitization rate with varying forest coverage. Cowbirds in different parts of the continent encounter communities of hosts with different lengths of exposure (e.g., Mayfield 1965) and responses (e.g., Briskie et al. 1992) to parasitization, and host species with longer exposure to cowbirds may be resistant to parasitization regardless of the proportion of forest in a landscape. This appears true, but we do not see any evidence of this varying predictably by region in our review—all host responses are seen across the country, and all responses were seen within different localities within a region.

Hochachka et al. (1999) continued that the relationship between cowbird parasitization and forest coverage may also vary as a function of the local area over which forests were measured. Within local areas, forest coverage varied in its power to predict parasitization, depending on the size of the area over which forest coverage was measured (Tewksbury et al. 1998, Donovan et al. 2000). It is clear that vegetated patches surrounded by agriculture are different than those surrounded by more forest; this holds regardless of region.

Hochachka et al. (1999) failed to find any substantial differences in the behavior and habitat requirements among the races of Brown-headed Cowbirds (Lowther 1993). They concluded that although cowbird abundance declined westward—away from the center of the cowbird's range—the lower abundance of cowbirds in the West should result in a lower rate of parasitization, but not in a complete reversal of the relationship between parasitization rate and forest coverage. In the analyses by Hochachka et al. (1999), we see the importance of examining parasitization in a spatially explicit

manner. Local factors, such as presence of agriculture and patch size, will usually override relatively region-wide factors, such as absolute forest coverage and host density, in determining parasitization rates. Our review shows that the major factors determining the impacts of cowbirds on hosts operate continent-wide (Table 2). Fragmentation increases the degree of local sympatry between cowbird and host. Peterjohn et al. (2000) found no evidence to suggest that changes in cowbird populations differentially influenced population changes in cowbird hosts and rejecter species. Trends from BBS data showed that both cowbird host species and species rarely parasitized showed the same pattern of direct association with trends in cowbird abundance, and all of the correlations were low. The general direct relationship between cowbird trends and trends of neotropical migrants reflected the broad regional patterns of increasing bird populations in western North America and declines in the southern United States. They concluded that large-scale changes in weather patterns, land use practices, and habitat availability were primarily responsible for the direct associations they found between population trends in cowbirds and their host species. The strong influence of weather was also used by Johnson (1994) to explain the numerous range expansions of western birds.

Lowther (1993) concluded that fragmentation of eastern deciduous forest leads to increased parasitism by cowbirds. Further, he summarized that similar patterns were becoming evident in western montane areas as human settlement expand. We agree, and conclude that geographic differences in the response of birds to fragmentation—and thus our characterizations of the assemblage of birds in different locations (e.g., species richness)—are largely determined by the time since fragmentation occurred, rather than any inherent differences in the response. Cowbirds respond in distribution to fragmentation first by the location of suitable feeding areas, and secondarily to host abundance. As aptly summarized by Robinson et al. (1995a), cowbirds in heavily forested landscapes appear limited primarily by the availability of foraging areas rather than by host density. In fragmented landscapes, however, cowbirds appear limited primarily by host availability because feeding areas are readily available as a result of the fragmentation.

ACKNOWLEDGMENTS

We thank the editors of this volume for inviting our presentation and for critical reviews of several drafts. We also thank additional comments provided by several anonymous referees.

Studies in Avian Biology No. 25:73–80, 2002.

EFFECTS OF FOREST FRAGMENTATION ON BROOD PARASITISM AND NEST PREDATION IN EASTERN AND WESTERN LANDSCAPES

JOHN F. CAVITT AND THOMAS E. MARTIN

Abstract. The fragmentation of North American forests by agriculture and other human activities may negatively impact the demographic processes of birds through increases in nest predation and brood parasitism. In fact, the effects of fragmentation on demographic processes are thought to be a major underlying cause of long-term population declines of many bird species. However, much of our understanding of the demographic consequences of fragmentation has come from research conducted in North America east of the Rocky Mountains. Thus, results obtained from these studies may not be applicable to western landscapes, where habitats are often naturally heterogeneous due to topographic variation and periodic fire. We utilized data from a large database of nest records (>10,000) collected at sites both east and west of the Rocky Mountains to determine if the effects of fragmentation are consistent across broad geographic regions. We found that forest fragmentation tended to increase the frequency of brood parasitism by Brown-headed Cowbirds (*Molothrus ater*) east of the Rockies but we were unable to detect a significant difference in the West. Within the eastern United States, nest predation rates were consistently higher within fragmented sites relative to unfragmented sites. Yet, in the West, fragmentation resulted in a decrease in nest predation relative to unfragmented sites. This is perhaps accounted for by differential responses of the local predator community to fragmentation. Our results suggest that the effects of fragmentation may not be consistent across broad geographic regions and that the effects of fragmentation may depend on dynamics within local landscapes.

Key Words: brood parasitism; forest fragmentation; nest predation; Western North America.

Forest fragmentation occurs when large, continuous, forested tracts are converted to other vegetation types or land uses so that only a few scattered fragments remain (Faaborg et al. 1995). Fragmentation is a characteristic feature of most human dominated landscapes (Burgess and Sharpe 1981) and is particularly evident in portions of northern Europe and eastern North America (east of the Rocky Mountains) where agricultural production and urban development have reduced once contiguous forests into small, and often isolated patches (Andrén 1992, Donovan et al. 1995b, Robinson et al. 1995a).

For the past several decades considerable attention has been given to the effects of forest fragmentation on avian populations within North America because of widespread population declines (Gates and Gysel 1978, Ambuel and Temple 1983, Wilcove 1985, Askins et al. 1990, Robinson et al. 1995a). The fragmentation of once continuous forests may result in both a quantitative and qualitative loss of habitat for species (Faaborg et al. 1995). Fragmentation can negatively influence avian populations by reducing the total area of native vegetation resulting in the extinction of some species. In addition, as an area is fragmented into increasingly smaller patches, the amount of edge relative to interior area increases. This exposes populations to the conditions of a different surrounding ecosystem and consequently to what are known as "edge effects" (Murcia 1995). Research conducted to date suggests several characteristics of forest

fragments that may negatively affect avian populations. Small forest patches with a high edge to interior ratio have: (1) High rates of nest predation. The abundance of avian and mammalian nest predators (avian and mammalian) often are higher along forest edges than within the forest interior (e.g., Gates and Gysel 1978, Chasko and Gates 1982, Hanski et al. 1996). (2) High rates and intensities of brood parasitism. The Brown-headed Cowbird (*Molothrus ater*) is often more abundant along forest edges, and nests adjacent to edges typically have higher rates of parasitism (Donovan et al. 1995b, Robinson et al. 1995a, Young and Hutto 1999). (3) Reductions in pairing success. Several species within forest fragments and near forest edges have a reduced chance of attracting mates than when in large continuous forests and within the forest interior (Wander 1985, Gibbs and Faaborg 1990, Villard et al. 1993, Burke and Nol 1998). (4) Lower food availability for breeding birds. Burke and Nol (1998) demonstrated that invertebrate biomass was lower within forest fragments than large continuous forests.

These fragmentation effects are thought to be a major underlying influence of long term population declines of many birds, particularly forest-interior species within eastern North America (Whitcomb et al. 1981, Robbins et al. 1989b, Sauer and Droege 1992, Ball et al. 1994). Consequently, many small forest fragments in eastern North America support few if any forest-interior species (Robbins et al. 1989b, Freemark and Collins 1992).

Concern over avian population declines and the potential demographic consequences to fragmentation have led to numerous studies designed to examine the potential effects of forest fragmentation on avian productivity. Previous studies have suffered from two major problems. First, studies of fragmentation effects have often depended on data from artificial nests, which often do not reflect rates or patterns of predation on real nests (e.g., Major and Kendal 1996). Studies using artificial nests also cannot provide information on the rates and patterns of cowbird parasitism. Second, much of our current understanding of the demographic consequences of fragmentation has come from research conducted east of the Rocky Mountains (George and Dobkin *this volume*). Because most fragmentation studies are conducted over a relatively small geographical area (but see Donovan et al. 1995b, Robinson et al. 1995a), often with no replication, the results cannot be generalized to other locations or regions. The effects of forest fragmentation within eastern North America may not automatically be applied to the West for several reasons. Unlike once contiguous eastern forests, forests west of the Rocky Mountains have a naturally heterogeneous pattern due to topographic variation, periodic fire, flooding and other climatic events (Franklin et al. *this volume*, Hejl et al. *this volume*). Thus, human induced fragmentation in the West (e.g., logging) may not have yet created sufficiently different landscape patterns to affect avian populations (Hejl 1992, Freemark et al. 1995, Hejl et al. *this volume*). Unlike fragmentation in eastern North America, fragmentation in the West is a relatively recent phenomenon and thus there may not have been sufficient time for birds to respond (Rosenberg and Raphael 1986). Additionally, the pattern of nest predation may not be comparable between regions because local predator communities likely differ. Large predators found in western North America, but largely absent in the East, may keep mesopredator populations in check (Soulé 1988, Rogers and Caro 1998). Thus, the effects of fragmentation on avian demographic processes in the East may not apply to western North America.

In this paper, we utilized data from 20 replicated study sites to examine the effects of forest fragmentation on the reproductive success and nest predation rates of a suite of forest nesting species breeding at sites east and west of the Rocky Mountains. We also examined if forest fragmentation affects the frequency (number of nests parasitized) and intensity (number of parasite eggs laid per nest) of brood parasitism differently in eastern versus western sites. Finally, we review the available literature on the effects of fragmentation on nest predation by geographic region (east vs. west).

METHODS

We used nesting data from 10,446 nests (103,855 days of exposure) of 23 species of open nesting passerines (Table 1). The data used in these analyses come from the Breeding Biology Research and Monitoring Database, a collaborative effort in which researchers monitor avian breeding productivity and habitat conditions using standardized sampling protocols (Martin et al. 1997) at sites located throughout the continental U.S. Data were utilized from 20 study sites located east and west of the Rocky Mountains (Fig. 1). Examination of Figure 1 illustrates that sites were not evenly distributed across North America and include a grouping centered along the Mississippi River and a grouping along the western side of the Rocky Mountains. For simplicity we refer to sites east of the Rocky Mountains as eastern sites and those along the western side of the Rockies as western sites. Each site utilized was replicated and composed of 4 to 30 separate study plots. Sites were chosen from the database for this analysis if the principal investigator designated them as either largely fragmented by human activities (agriculture or logging), or unfragmented. Because our classification of sites is subjective, we also calculated the proportion of forest within a 10-km radius of each study plot from a GIS layer produced by the USDA Forest Service covering the entire United States. A 10-km radius was chosen because this area relates well to distances most cowbirds commute between breeding and feeding areas (Thompson 1994, Thompson and Dijak 2000), and previous studies have used this area as a simple measure of forest fragmentation (Robinson et al. 1995a, Donovan et al. 1995b, Hochachka et al. 1999, Thompson et al. *this volume*). Forest coverage was calculated using FRAGSTATS (McGarigal and Marks 1995).

Three unfragmented sites in the east and three in the west were paired with a nearby fragmented site to examine local landscape-level effects of fragmentation on daily mortality rates (Table 2). Species were chosen for the analysis if they satisfied all three of the following criteria: (1) they are open nesting passerines that primarily nest in forest habitats, (2) the total number of nests available for each species was greater than 50, and (3) the species were recorded breeding at more than one site. All statistical analyses were conducted using PC-SAS (SAS Institute 1998). Tests were parametric unless transformations of the data could not meet assumptions of normality and homogeneous variances. Results from statistical tests are referred to as significant when $P \leq 0.05$. Values reported in the RESULTS section are means $\pm$ SE.

REPRODUCTIVE SUCCESS

We examined the effects of fragmentation on components of reproductive success by performing paired t-tests on mean clutch size and mean number of offspring fledged per nest, blocking by species and testing for habitat differences. Because cowbirds often remove host eggs before parasitizing nests (Nolan 1978), we

TABLE 1. FOCAL SPECIES USED IN ANALYSES

Common name	Scientific name	Nest placement	Number of nests
Eastern Wood-pewee	*Contopus virens*	Tree	169
Western Wood-pewee	*Contopus sordidulus*	Tree	264
Acadian Flycatcher	*Empidonax virescens*	Tree	1624
Blue-gray Gnatcatcher	*Polioptila caerulea*	Shrub	210
Wood Thrush	*Hylocichla mustelina*	Shrub	814
Swainson's Thrush	*Catharus ustulatus*	Shrub	162
Veery	*Catharus fuscescens*	Shrub	100
American Robin	*Turdus migratorius*	Shrub	1461
Cedar Waxwing	*Bombycilla cedrorum*	Tree	163
Warbling Vireo	*Vireo gilvus*	Tree	468
Red-eyed Vireo	*Vireo olivaceus*	Shrub	673
Yellow Warbler	*Dendroica petechia*	Tree	1276
Kentucky Warbler	*Oporornis formosus*	Ground	115
Hooded Warbler	*Wilsonia citrina*	Shrub	363
Worm-eating Warbler	*Helmitheros vermivorus*	Ground	286
Ovenbird	*Seiurus aurocapillus*	Ground	411
American Redstart	*Setophaga ruticilla*	Tree	335
Northern Cardinal	*Cardinalis cardinalis*	Shrub	307
Indigo Bunting	*Passerina cyanea*	Shrub	492
Black-headed Grosbeak	*Pheucticus melanocephalus*	Tree	180
Song Sparrow	*Melospiza melodia*	Shrub	218
Northern Oriole	*Icterus galbula*	Tree	65
Western Tanager	*Piranga ludoviciana*	Tree	291

included only unparasitized nests in the analysis of clutch size.

BROOD PARASITISM

The frequency of brood parasitism was calculated by determining the number of nests containing cowbird eggs or young for a species within each study site. We calculated parasitism frequency for a species only when evidence of cowbird parasitism could be found within the database. The intensity of cowbird parasitism was calculated by determining the mean number of cowbird eggs laid within each species' nest, within each study site. Each species was classified according to nest placement as either a ground, shrub, or tree nester (Table 1) to determine if nest placement affected a species' response to forest fragmentation. The classification of nest placement was based on Ehrlich et al. (1988) and Baicich and Harrison (1997). Differences in the frequency of cowbird parasitism between fragmented and unfragmented sites were examined using Friedman's nonparametric analysis of variance (ANOVA) for randomized blocks (Sokal and Rohlf 1981) and differences in intensity of cowbird parasitism were examined by using parametric ANOVAs. For each analysis we blocked by species and tested for habitat affects. Nonparametric Wilcoxon 2-sample tests (Sokal and Rohlf 1981) were performed on the arcsine transformed proportion of nests parasitized for each nesting classification to determine if nest placement affected a species' response to fragmentation.

NEST PREDATION

The daily mortality rate of nests and their associated standard errors were estimated using the Mayfield (1961, 1975) method as modified by Johnson (1979) and Hensler and Nichols (1981). We calculated the dai-

ly mortality rate for nests of each species as the total number of failures divided by the total number of days nests were observed, pooled across all nests within each study site. Differences in daily mortality rates between fragmented and unfragmented sites were examined using analysis of variance blocking by species and testing for habitat affects. We also partitioned daily mortality rates into cause-specific components (predation and parasitism) to determine the mechanisms that may influence reproductive success in fragmented versus contiguous sites. As in the parasitism analyses, we classified each species according to its nest placement. Differences in predation rates between paired fragmented and unfragmented sites were examined using the program CONTRAST (Hines and Sauer 1989). This program uses chi-square statistics to test for homogeneity of mortality rates by creating a linear contrast of the rate estimate (Sauer and Williams 1989).

LITERATURE REVIEW

We also reviewed the available literature to summarize the effects of forest fragmentation and edge effects on nest predation rates between sites east and west of the Rocky Mountains. We limited our review to studies conducted in forested systems and to those that examined the effects of anthropogenic fragmentation (e.g., agriculture and forestry practices). Because most nest predation studies have used artificial nests, we have included them in our review, but recognize that there are inherent weaknesses in their use (Haskell 1995a, Ortega et al. 1998).

RESULTS

Sites classified by investigators as fragmented had significantly lower proportion of forest cov-

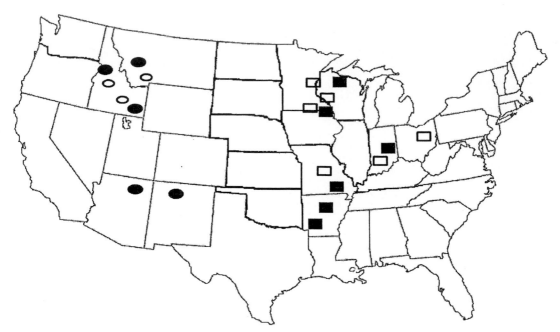

FIGURE 1.   Locations of study sites used in analyses. Squares indicate sites designated as "eastern" and circles as "western." Open symbols indicate fragmented sites and closed unfragmented. Each site plotted on the map is composed of several independent study plots.

er within a 10 km radius (0.45 ± 0.10) relative to unfragmented sites (0.90 ± 0.04, t = −4.199, df = 6.2, P = 0.005).

REPRODUCTIVE SUCCESS

We found no difference in clutch size of un-parasitized nests between fragmented and un-fragmented sites (East −0.01 ± 0.10, t = −0.091, df = 1, P = 0.930; West 0.10 ± 0.07, t = 1.46, df = 1, P = 0.194). Yet, the mean number of offspring fledged per nest attempted was significantly greater in unfragmented rela-tive to fragmented sites in the east (−0.23 ± 0.08, t = −2.72, df = 1, P = 0.02), but we found

no difference between fragmented and unfrag-mented sites west of the Rocky Mountains (0.09 ± 0.08, t = 1.06, df = 1, P = 0.314).

BROOD PARASITISM

The frequency of parasitism by Brown-head-ed Cowbirds was significantly higher in eastern fragmented sites relative to unfragmented sites (χ^2 = 317.34, df = 1, P < 0.001) but there were no significant differences among western sites (χ^2 = 2.29, df = 1, P > 0.1; Fig. 2). In addition, fragmentation resulted in a significantly higher frequency of brood parasitism for all eastern

TABLE 2.   LOCATIONS OF PAIRED FRAGMENTED AND UNFRAGMENTED SITES

Site	Landscape	Latitude–longitude	Location
Columbia	Frag	38.95–92.11	Columbia, MO
Mofep	Unfrag	37.04–91.12	Ozarks, MO
SE Forest 1	Frag	43.61–91.25	Southeastern MN
SE Forest 2	Unfrag	43.61–91.25	Southeastern MN
St. Croix	Frag	45.36–82.72	Eastern MN, Western WI
Cheque. NF	Unfrag	46.06–91.11	Chequemegon NF, WI
Bitterroot 1	Frag	46.10–114.23	Bitterroot Valley, MT
Bitterroot 2	Unfrag	46.10–114.23	Bitterroot Valley, MT
South Fork 1	Frag	43.62–111.63	South Fork of Snake River, ID
South Fork 2	Unfrag	43.62–111.63	South Fork of Snake River, ID
PNFF	Frag	44.67–116.20	Payette National Forest, ID
PNFU	Unfrag	44.67–116.20	Payette National Forest, ID

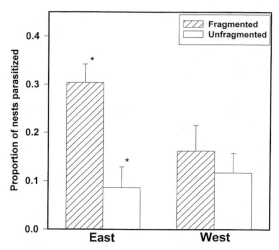

FIGURE 2. Mean frequency of brood parasitism (± SE) by Brown-headed Cowbirds in fragmented and unfragmented eastern and western sites. A * indicates P < 0.05.

nest placement classifications, but no differences were found among western sites (Table 3).

The intensity of brood parasitism was not affected by forest fragmentation east (F = 0.07, df = 1, 10, P = 0.80) or west (F = 0.14, df = 1, 2, P = 0.75) of the Rockies. Within nest place-

ment classifications, shrub nesters at fragmented western sites had a significantly higher intensity of cowbird parasitism relative to unfragmented sites (Table 3). There were no other differences in parasitism intensity by nest placement classification (Table 3).

DAILY MORTALITY

Eastern fragmented sites tended to have higher daily mortality rates than unfragmented sites (F = 3.03, df = 1, 47, P = 0.08) but the difference was not significant (Fig. 3). However, western unfragmented sites had significantly higher daily mortality rates relative to fragmented sites (F = 3.87, df = 1, 30, P = 0.05; Fig. 3). Eastern shrub nesting birds suffered significantly higher daily mortality rates on fragmented than on unfragmented sites, but no other differences by nest placement classification were observed (Table 3).

The daily mortality rate due to nest predation was not significantly different between eastern fragmented (0.031 ± 0.002) and unfragmented sites (0.030 ± 0.003; F = 0.10, df = 1, 31, P = 0.76), but was significantly higher in western unfragmented sites (0.038 ± 0.003; F = 4.04, df = 1, 30, P = 0.05) relative to fragmented locations (0.029 ± 0.003). The daily mortality rate due to parasitism was significantly greater in

TABLE 3. EFFECTS OF HABITAT FRAGMENTATION ON THE FREQUENCY (PERCENTAGE OF NESTS) AND INTENSITY (NUMBER OF EGGS) OF BROWN-HEADED COWBIRD PARASITISM AND DAILY MORTALITY RATES WITHIN NEST PLACEMENT CLASSIFICATIONS FOR SITES EAST AND WEST OF THE ROCKY MOUNTAINS

	Region	Nest placement	Statistics	Fragmented	Unfragmented
Frequency of Cowbird Parasitism			Z, df, P	Median, Upper–Lower Quartiles	Median, Upper–Lower Quartiles
	East	Ground	2.33, 1, 0.02	28.5, 50.0–20.2	2.0, 13.3–0.9
		Shrub	2.01, 1, 0.05	30.1, 62.7–26.5	6.4, 34.8–0.0
		Tree	1.94, 1, 0.05	9.6, 17.0–8.0	1.6, 5.6–0.07
	West	Shrub	0.44, 1, 0.66	35.3, 52.6–0.0	3.1, 19.0–1.4
		Tree	0.0, 1, 1.00	8.6, 21.1–0.0	1.8, 32.0–0.0
Intensity of Cowbird Parasitism			F, df$_{model\ error}$, P	Mean ± SE	Mean ± SE
	East	Ground	1.16, 1, 1, 0.48	1.7 ± 0.4	1.0 ± 0.5
		Shrub	1.25, 1, 6, 0.31	1.7 ± 0.2	1.4 ± 0.3
		Tree	1.07, 1, 2, 0.41	1.1 ± 0.05	1.0 ± 0.1
	West	Shrub	21.36, 1, 2, 0.04	1.6 ± 0.06	1.2 ± 0.06
		Tree	2.2, 1, 2, 0.27	1.2 ± 0.08	1.4 ± 0.08
Daily Mortality Rate			Z, df, P	Median, Upper–Lower Quartiles	Median, Upper–Lower Quartiles
	East	Ground	1.3, 1, 0.20	0.4, 0.06–0.04	0.03, 0.05–0.03
		Shrub	−2.1, 1, 0.04	0.043, 0.05–0.04	0.037, 0.04–0.03
		Tree	0.14, 1, 0.89	0.039, 0.04–0.03	0.034, 0.04–0.03
	West	Shrub	0, 1, 1.0	0.041, 0.04–0.03	0.04, 0.06–0.03
		Tree	−0.3, 1, 0.77	0.031, 0.04–0.03	0.037, 0.06–0.03

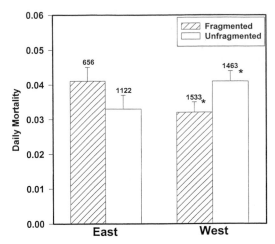

FIGURE 3. Mean daily mortality rate (± SE) of nests in fragmented and unfragmented eastern and western sites. The total number of nests used in analyses are given above each bar. A * indicates P < 0.05.

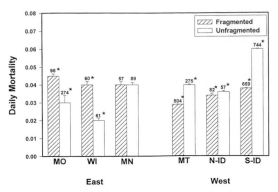

FIGURE 4. Comparison of fragmentation effects on the daily mortality rates (± SE) of paired local sites east and west of the Rocky Mountains. The number of nest records utilized in each comparison is indicated above each bar. A * indicates P < 0.001; other comparison P > 0.05.

eastern fragmented sites (χ^2 = 29.04, df = 1, P < 0.001; median, upper–lower quartiles of fragmented sites 0.005, 0.01–0; unfragmented sites 0, 0.003–0) but not among western sites (χ^2 = 0.278, df = 1, P > 0.5).

In two of the three paired eastern sites, daily mortality rates were significantly higher on fragmented relative to unfragmented plots (Fig. 4). This pattern was reversed in the west where two of the three paired sites had significantly higher daily mortality rates on unfragmented plots relative to fragmented ones.

LITERATURE REVIEW

Our review consisted of 39 studies; the vast majority (33) were located east of the Rockies, with only six studies in the West (Table 4). The results of eastern studies were based on 53 field seasons with a mean duration of 1.6 field seasons per study. Western studies were based on only 11 field seasons with a mean of 1.8 field seasons per study. Of the studies that have tested for edge effects, 56% of 16 studies detected an effect in the East, whereas only one of four studies observed an edge effect in the West. Eastern studies that examined the effect of fragmentation on nest predation rates typically found negative relationships. A negative relationship between fragmentation and nest predation was found in 68% of 19 studies, no relationship in 21%, and two studies (~10%) reported a positive relationship. Only three western studies reviewed tested for fragmentation effects; two of three studies found a positive relationship between nest predation rates and fragment size with the third demonstrating no relationship.

It has been suggested that forest fragments embedded in different matrices may differentially affect patterns of nest predation (Andrén 1995, Bayne and Hobson 1997). According to the "Eastern Paradigm," birds nesting in forest patches imbedded in an agriculture or urban/suburban matrix are expected to have lower reproductive success relative to those nesting in more natural settings (Thompson et al. *this volume*). Thus, we classified studies according to the matrix of the surrounding landscape (e.g., agriculture and forest dominated). Six studies in the East tested for edge effects within an agriculturally dominated matrix and nine within a forested matrix. Five of the six forest-agricultural edge studies demonstrated an increase in nest predation, whereas only four of eight found edge effects within a forested matrix. We were unable to review any western studies that tested for edge effects within an agricultural matrix. Brand and George (2000), however, compared predation rates on artificial nests between sites with different types of adjoining habitat. In contrast to predictions of the "Eastern Paradigm," Brand and George (2000) found predation rates were lower in patches adjacent to urban/suburban areas than those adjacent to natural grasslands. Three of four western studies within forest-dominated landscapes failed to demonstrate an edge effect.

Ten of the eastern studies reviewed tested for fragmentation effects within an agricultural matrix. Two of ten found no relationship between forest area and nest predation rates but the remaining eight reported significant and negative relationships. The results of eastern studies conducted within a logging matrix are not as apparent; of the nine studies reviewed, five report-

TABLE 4. SUMMARY OF STUDIES EXAMINING THE EFFECTS OF EDGE AND FOREST FRAGMENTATION ON NEST PREDATION RATES EAST AND WEST OF THE ROCKY MOUNTAINS

Reference	Location	Nest type[a]	Matrix	Duration of study[b]	Edge effect	Fragmentation effect[c]
Eastern Studies						
Bayne and Hobson 1997	SK	A	Agriculture	2	no	
Burger 1988	MO	A	Agriculture	1	yes	
Donovan et al. 1995	Midwest	R	Agriculture	3		−
Donovan et al. 1997	Midwest	A	Agriculture	1		−
Fauth 2000	IN	R	Agriculture	3	no	0
Gates and Gysel 1978	MI	R	Agriculture	2	yes	
Haskell 1995	NY	A	Agriculture	1		0
Hobson and Baynes 2000	SK	R	Agriculture	4		−
Hoover et al. 1995	PA	R	Agriculture	2		−
Linder and Bollinger 1995	IL	A	Agriculture	1	yes	
Marini et al. 1995	IL	A	Agriculture	1	yes	
Robinson et al. 1995	Midwest	R	Agriculture	5		−
Saracco and Callazo 1999	NC	A	Agriculture	1	yes	
Sargent et al. 1998	SC	A	Agriculture	1		−
Seitz and Zegers 1993	PA	A	Agriculture	1		
Weinberg and Roth 1998	DE	R	Agriculture	2		−
Wilcove 1985	MD, TN	A	Agriculture	1		−
Bayne and Hobson 1997	SK	A	Forested	2	no	
DeGraaf and Angelstam 1993	NH	A	Forested	1		0
Fenske-Crawford and Niemi 1999	MN	A	Forested	1	no	
Gale et al. 1997	CT	R	Forested	2		0
Hanski et al. 1996	MN	R	Forested	1	no	
King et al. 1996	NH	R	Forested	2	yes	
King et al. 1998	NH	A	Forested	1	yes	
Niemuth and Boyce 1997	WI	A	Forested	2	yes	
Rudnicky and Hunter 1993	ME	A	Forested	2	no	0, +
Small and Hunter 1988	ME	A	Forested	1	no	−
Vander Haegen and DeGraaf 1996	ME	A	Forested	1	yes	−
Vander Haegen and DeGraaf 1996	ME	A	Forested	1		+
Yahner and Mahan 1996	PA	A	Forested	1		−
Yahner and Scott 1988	PA	A	Forested	1		−
Yahner and Wright 1985	PA	A	Forested	1	no	
Keyser et al. 1998	AL	A	Residential	1		−
Western Studies						
Hannon and Cotterill 1998	AB	A	Agriculture	2		0, +
Tewksbury et al. 1998	MT	R	Agriculture	2		+
Brand and George 2000	CA	A	Forested	1	yes	
Cotterill and Hannon 1999	AB	A	Forested	3	no	0
Ratti and Reese 1988	ID	A	Forested	1	no	
Song and Hannon 1999	AB	A	Forested	2	no	

[a] R = study monitoring the effect on real nests, A = study monitoring effect on artificial nests.

[b] Number of field seasons on which results are based.

[c] This column indicates the direction of the relationship between forest area and nest predation rates. A "0" indicates no relationship, a "−" indicates a negative relationship and a "+" indicates a positive relationship. Studies with more than one symbol represent annual variation in response.

ed negative relationships between forest area and nest predation rate, two reported a positive relationship, and two reported no relationship. Only two western studies reviewed tested for fragmentation effects within an agricultural matrix, and both of these studies found a positive relationship between nest predation rates and fragment size.

DISCUSSION

We found that the patterns of brood parasitism were not consistent between sites east and west of the Rocky Mountains. The frequency of brood parasitism was significantly higher in eastern fragmented sites relative to unfragmented sites, but not in the West. In addition, all nest placement classifications within fragmented eastern sites had a higher frequency of parasitism relative to unfragmented sites, but we were unable to detect a difference in the West. It appears this differential response may, in part, be due to greater variation in the frequency of parasitism among western sites. For example, some fragmented western sites reported no cowbird parasitism for shrub and tree nesting species and others reported rates as high as 52%, a rate comparable to the most severely affected eastern fragmented sites. This higher variability among western sites in their response to brood parasitism may be attributed to lower cowbird abundance in the West as compared to the East (Sauer et al. 2000). Morrison and Hahn (*this volume*), in an extensive review of the literature, did not find evidence to suggest that cowbird parasitism varied by region. Rather, they suggest that the major factors determining the impacts of cowbirds on their hosts operate continent-wide. The frequency and intensity of cowbird parasitism may be difficult to predict across large geographic regions and may depend primarily on local factors such as the presence of agriculture and patch size (Hahn and Hatfield 1995, Hochachka et al. 1999, Morrison and Hahn *this volume*).

It is clear from this study that the effects of forest fragmentation on nest predation rates are not necessarily consistent across the continent. We found that eastern fragmented sites had fewer offspring fledged per nest attempted, and tended to have higher daily mortality rates relative to unfragmented sites. These results are in agreement with the "Eastern Paradigm" (e.g., Thompson et al. *this volume*). In contrast, western unfragmented sites had significantly higher daily mortality rates due to nest predation relative to fragmented ones. Paired sites east and west of the Rockies also tended to follow this same general pattern, higher daily mortality rates in fragmented eastern sites and unfragmented western sites (see Fig. 4).

Studies reviewed for this paper also suggest that forest fragmentation may not be generalized between sites east and west of the Rockies. Eastern studies typically reported a negative relationship between forest area and nest predation rates (68%). This generality is improved when only studies conducted within an agricultural matrix are examined (80%). Unfortunately, only two western studies could be located, and thus any conclusions regarding the effects of fragmentation on nest predation in the West are speculative. However, both of these studies reported a positive relationship between forest area and nest predation rates and both studies explained their results on the basis of a differential response of nest predators. Tewksbury et al. (1998) demonstrated that nest predation was higher on unfragmented sites relative to sites fragmented by agriculture and human development within the Bitterroot Valley of Montana. They suggested this pattern was due to the re-

sponse of nest predators to fragmentation. Red squirrels (*Tamiasciurus hudsonicus*), important nest predators in their system, were more abundant in forested landscapes and declined with increasing forest cover (but see Bayne and Hobson 2000). Similarly, an artificial nest study conducted in woodlots surrounding agricultural land in Alberta, Canada, found higher rates of nest predation within larger woodlots during one breeding season and no difference during another (Hannon and Cotterill 1998). They suggested that forest interior predators, such as small mammals, were important in driving this response.

Any attempt to uncover patterns associated with nest predation is difficult because predation is an inherently complex phenomenon. Each study site will have a particular suite of reptilian, mammalian, and avian predators (e.g., Miller and Knight 1993, Fenske-Crawford and Niemi 1997, Thompson et al. 1999; Cavitt 1999, 2000) and these predators will either take nests incidentally (Vickery et al. 1992) or deliberately forage for nests (Sonerud and Fjeld 1987). Furthermore, this suite of nest predators will vary from site to site across North America and will likely respond to fragmentation differently (Bayne and Hobson 1998, 2000).

Unfortunately, few studies have been conducted within the western U.S. that examine the effects of forest fragmentation on nest predation rates. Our analyses and literature review are based on only a handful of western sites in comparison to the numerous studies conducted in the East. Consequently, we are not certain of the generality of our results throughout the West. However, these results do suggest that (1) sufficient evidence exists to question the application of patterns observed in the eastern U.S. across broad geographic regions, (2) more studies on the effects of fragmentation are needed throughout the western U.S., particularly studies that simultaneously monitor both the fates of real nests and the response of the predator communities, and (3) long-term studies are needed to separate real effects from stochastic processes.

ACKNOWLEDGMENTS

The results presented here are the products of an extensive list of investigators and their field assistants. Without their collective efforts and generous contributions of data to the BBIRD (Breeding Biology Research and Monitoring Database) project this research would not have been possible. We also wish to thank T. L. George, D. Dobkin, and an anonymous reviewer for comments and suggestions on drafts of this manuscript, and N. Summers for editorial assistance. This research was supported by the BBIRD program under the Global Change Research Program of the USGS Biological Resources Division.

Studies in Avian Biology No. 25:81–91, 2002.

EFFECTS OF FOREST FRAGMENTATION ON TANAGER AND THRUSH SPECIES IN EASTERN AND WESTERN NORTH AMERICA

RALPH S. HAMES, KENNETH V. ROSENBERG, JAMES D. LOWE, SARA E. BARKER, AND ANDRÉ A. DHONDT

Abstract. It is likely that selective forces on forest-specialist birds differ by region across the North American continent, and closely related species that evolved under presumably differing selective regimes may show markedly different responses to human-caused habitat fragmentation. We report the results of research by the Cornell Laboratory of Ornithology that used volunteers to gather data on the effects of habitat fragmentation on forest tanager and thrush species across their ranges and the continent. This large-scale approach permits the comparison of effects between regions within species as well as between species. Although forested landscapes in western North America are often naturally fragmented compared to historically contiguous forests in eastern North America, an identical set of principal components described forest fragmentation in both regions. Response by the Western Tanager (*Piranga ludoviciana*) to overall fragmentation was very similar to that of the Scarlet Tanager (*P. olivacea*) in eastern regions; probability of breeding dropped significantly for both species in highly fragmented landscapes. The Hermit Thrush (*Catharus guttatus*), with both eastern and western populations, is highly affected by fragmentation, with no geographic variation. Additionally, both the Swainson's Thrush (*C. ustulatus*) in the West and the Veery (*C. fuscescens*) in the East showed similar strong effects of fragmentation. Predation and parasitism pressures as estimated by detections of mammalian and avian predators or of Brown-headed Cowbirds (*Molothrus ater*) differed between eastern and western study sites, as did the response by cowbirds to fragmentation gradients in different regions. Overall, however, we found that closely related species and populations showed similar responses to habitat fragmentation, regardless of the historic configuration of the forests in which they occurred.

Key Words: *Catharus fuscescens*; *Catharus guttatus*; *Catharus ustulatus*; geographic variation; *Hylocichla mustelina*; *Molothrus ater*; *Piranga ludoviciana; Piranga olivacea;* predators; principal components analysis.

Selective forces on forest-specialist birds differ by region across the North American continent, with differing levels of disturbance, nest parasitism, and of predation by a variable suite of predators. Further, closely related species, or populations within widely distributed species, that have evolved under differing selective regimes may show markedly different responses to human-caused habitat fragmentation. However, testing whether presumably different selective regimes have indeed led to different responses to fragmentation in western and eastern North America is not a trivial matter. It requires several things that, heretofore, have not been combined in one research project (or even in a series of research projects); these include a large geographic extent, a large sample size, standardized data collection, and a widely applicable measure of fragmentation. Further, the species to be studied must have continent-wide distributions, or comparisons must be made between closely related species with primarily eastern or western geographic ranges. We report the results to date from the Cornell Lab of Ornithology's Birds in Forested Landscapes (BFL) project, which used volunteers to gather data on the effects of habitat fragmentation on forest tanager and thrush species across their ranges and across North America.

Several authors have pointed out the differences between western, often coniferous, forest and eastern deciduous forest landscapes as selective environments for obligate forest-nesting birds (Hejl 1992, Freemark et al. 1995, Tewksbury et al. 1998). For example, western and eastern forests differ both in their original configuration and in their subsequent use by humans (Hejl 1992). Western forests are naturally patchy, and in many areas are confined by moisture regimes to riparian zones or to topographic "islands" (Tewksbury et al. 1998). Further, human-caused fragmentation in western North America has often been due to logging (Hejl 1992), and is of fairly recent origin. In contrast, the formerly contiguous eastern hardwood forests have been cleared for agriculture as long as 200 years before present (Smith et al. 1993, Yahner 1997), and are now increasing from historical lows as abandoned farms revert to forest.

In addition to disturbances caused by humans, naturally occurring disturbances also play a large role in shaping the selective environment in which forest bird species evolve, and it is clear that the type, scale, and frequency of disturbance are different in the two regions. In western North America, the rainiest months occur in winter and spring, with relatively little rain occurring during the summer and fall (Perry 1994). There are also extensive stands of early-successional, serotinous tree species (lodgepole pine, *Pinus contorta*; jack pine, *P. banksiana*; and black spruce, *Picea mariana*) in boreal and temperate montane forest (Perry 1994). Further, dryer forests throughout the West are dominated by the equally fire-adapted ponderosa pine (*Pinus ponderosa*; Perry 1994). This combination of seasonal droughts and fire-adapted vegetation is reflected in frequent disturbance by fire (Freemark et al. 1995). In contrast, eastern deciduous forests are relatively free of fire because of frequent rains during the summer and fall, and because the combination of warmth and high moisture levels leads to rapid decomposition of fallen trees and other potential fuels (Perry 1994).

Other selective forces such as predation and rates of nest parasitism also appear to differ between western and eastern North America. Both the suites of predator species present, nest parasites, and their abundance (Donovan et al. 1995a), appear to combine to alter the selection regimes in the two regions (Tewksbury et al. 1998, Rosenberg et al. 1999). For example, red squirrels (*Tamiasciurus hudsonicus*), which are the most common nest predator in some western landscapes (Bayne and Hobson 1997, Darveau et al. 1997, Tewksbury et al. 1998), are relatively rare in the East where avian predators such as corvid species are much more common (Hogrefe et al. 1998). Moreover, rates of nest parasitism by the Brown-headed Cowbird (*Molothrus ater*) also vary with region, with highest rates in the Midwest region (42.1% of Wood Thrush, *Hylocichla mustelina,* nests) and lower rates in the Mid-Atlantic (26.5%) and Northeast (14.7%) (Hoover and Brittingham 1993). Finally, the responses of both nest predators and parasites to fragmentation has also been shown to vary across physiographic regions (Robinson et al. 1995b, Trine 1998, Rosenberg et al. 1999).

These large differences between eastern and western forest vegetation, historical land uses, disturbance, and between parasitism and predation regimes provide ample grounds to suspect differences in responses to fragmentation between eastern and western landscapes (Freemark et al. 1995). The question becomes how to test for these hypothesized differences. The first requirement is for a measure of fragmentation that is applicable across the continent, and in landscapes with differing conformations of habitat.

Habitat fragmentation implies loss of habitat, a reduction in mean habitat patch size, increases in the mean isolation of patches, and increases in the mean amount of forest/non-forest edge

(Andrén 1994). Most workers agree that loss of habitat is one of the primary mechanisms by which human-caused habitat fragmentation affects populations of birds; some even suggest that habitat loss is the primary (Trzcinski et al. 1999) or only (Fahrig 1997, 1998) mechanism. Others have cited the effects of increased edge (Paton 1994, Hoover et al. 1995, Donovan et al. 1997) and isolation (Robbins et al. 1989a, Villard and Taylor 1994, Villard et al. 1995, Desrochers and Hannon 1997), or of decreased patch size (Schieck et al. 1995, Bellamy et al. 1996a, Keyser et al. 1998, Trine 1998) as also playing an important role. However, it seems most likely that both habitat abundance and configuration (McGarigal and McComb 1995, Villard et al. 1999) play important roles, with the effect of configuration increasing in importance below a critical threshold in abundance (Turner 1989, Andrén 1994, Andrén et al. 1997, With et al. 1997, Andrén 1999). What is needed is a composite measure of habitat fragmentation that captures a large proportion of the information contained within these variables. Such a composite measure should include information captured at the level of the surrounding landscape, as well as at the patch (Freemark et al. 1995), to afford a more complete understanding of the factors affecting the distribution of sensitive species (Hinsley et al. 1995). The Cornell Laboratory of Ornithology's BFL project provides both the fragmentation data needed to calculate such a composite measure, as well as data on species occurrence from across the continent that are necessary to test the hypothesis of different responses to fragmentation in eastern and western landscapes.

BFL is a natural continuation of the Cornell Lab of Ornithology's Project Tanager, which began as a National Science Foundation (NSF) National Science Experiment. Project Tanager used volunteers across North America (north of Mexico) to study the effects of forest fragmentation on four species of tanagers (Rosenberg et al. 1999). BFL uses the same methodology to study the effects of fragmentation on seven species of forest thrushes and two species of *Accipiter* hawks. BFL was undertaken during the 1997 and 1998 breeding season in cooperation with Partners in Flight, an umbrella organization of government agencies, conservation organizations, and industry working together to promote the conservation of birds in the Americas. Birds in Forested Landscapes was continued during the 1999 and 2000 field seasons in cooperation with the United States Department of Agriculture (USDA) Forest Service. For simplicity's sake, we will refer to both Project Tanager and

Birds in Forested Landscapes as BFL hereinafter.

METHODS

DATA COLLECTION

The data-collection protocol for both Project Tanager (Rosenberg et al. 1999) and BFL were essentially identical. Each protocol consisted of four stages: the unbiased selection of one or more study sites; repeated visits to the study sites with the playback of conspecific vocalizations to elicit responses from territorial birds so that they could be counted; the estimation of a number of patch- and landscape-scale measures of fragmentation; and the coding of data onto computer-readable bubble-forms, which were returned to the Lab of Ornithology for collation and analysis.

In both studies, the volunteer participants selected study sites in suitable wooded habitat (e.g., trees >6 m tall, canopy coverage >30%). The instructions stressed that almost any patch of relatively mature forest or woodland was acceptable, and participants were urged to find a range of patch sizes in similar habitat. To avoid bias, participants were cautioned to select their study sites based only on apparent habitat suitability and to not select sites where the species of interest was known to nest (Rosenberg et al. 1999). Each study site was defined as a circle of 150-m radius; point-counts and playbacks were conducted at the center of each study site. Participants made two visits to each site to census for territorial males of the focal species. During a ten-minute point count on each visit, participants looked and listened for territorial individuals of the species of interest within the study site. Participants also recorded the presence of avian and mammalian predators, as well as any detections of Brown-headed Cowbirds during the two point-counts. The two required visits were timed to coincide with pair bonding or nest building, and with the nestling/fledgling stages of the breeding cycle. If no individuals of the species of interest were detected within the point count period, participants used playback of conspecific territorial vocalizations to elicit a response from any previously silent birds in order to verify that no territorial males were present (Villard et al. 1995, Rosenberg et al. 1999). Based on the behavior of birds that were detected, each site was scored as missing, present, possible, probable, or confirmed breeding using breeding atlas codes (Anonymous 1986, Butcher and Smith 1986, Rosenberg et al. 1999). To avoid counting birds passing through on migration, we scored study sites as "possible" breeding sites only if a singing male of the focal species was detected on both visits.

While in the field, participants also used simple techniques to estimate canopy height and amount of canopy closure and noted other site characteristics such as the forest type (coniferous, deciduous or mixed), three most common tree species, and presence or absence of surface water (streams or ponds) at each site. After completion of the fieldwork, participants used USGS topographic maps in conjunction with a clear acetate grid overlay to estimate a number of measures of fragmentation for each site. (The grid was intended for use with 1:24000 maps or aerial photos, and was divided into 1 ha squares at that scale.) Estimated fragmentation measures included the size of the forest patch surrounding the study site, the isolation of that patch from other patches, and the proportion of forest and edge density (amount of forest/non-forest edge corrected for the amount of forest) in the surrounding 1000 ha block. The site's elevation above mean sea level (MSL) was also recorded, as was an estimate of the canopy height. A number of other data were also collected at each site, but were not used in this analysis. For further details on the development of this protocol see Rosenberg et al. (1999). Participants then coded these data onto computer-readable forms and returned the forms to the Lab of Ornithology. At the Lab, we edited each form by hand to ensure it had been correctly completed; simple checks were also performed when the SAS (SAS Institute 1989) dataset was constructed to ensure that each datum was within possible ranges. We excluded all sites with missing data from subsequent analyses.

ANALYSES

At each site participants collected a number of data, including measures of forest fragmentation. We checked the distributions of all fragmentation variables on normal probability plots and transformed variables as needed before analysis began. Many of the measures of fragmentation are highly significantly intercorrelated (Hames et al. 2001). To avoid multicollinearity and the fitting of complicated models with difficult-to-interpret interaction terms, we used principal component analysis (PCA) on the transformed data to simplify the dataset by yielding fewer uncorrelated factors (principal components), which explained a high proportion of the variance in the original dataset (Johnson and Wichern 1982, Villard et al. 1995, Rosenberg et al. 1999). We then used multiple logistic regression to model the probability that territorial birds would be found, based on the principal component values at each site. We also used logistic regression to model the probability of occurrence of the Brown-headed Cowbird. To test the hypothesis that the effects of fragmentation varied between eastern and western landscapes, we compared the magnitude of the fragmentation coefficients derived from logistic regression for each region.

Principal components analysis

To conduct the PCA we combined all unique study points from the 1995, 1996, 1997, and 1998 field seasons of BFL into one dataset. We then used PROC FACTOR (SAS Institute 1989) with the orthogonal varimax rotation option to ensure that there was maximal separation (Johnson and Wichern 1982) and no intercorrelation between the resulting principal components. These rotated factors were then standardized to a mean of zero and a standard deviation of one (SAS Institute 1989) to facilitate comparison of estimated coefficients, before they were used as predictor variables in the logistic regression.

We included a number of transformed variables from each study site in the PCA. These variables were the natural log of the forest patch size (Ln Size), edge density (Ln Edge Density), elevation above msl (Ln Elevation) and canopy height (Ln Canopy Height), as well as the arcsine square-root transformed proportion of forest (Asqrt %Forest; Table 1). The natural log of

TABLE 1.   CORRELATION MATRIX FOR VARIABLES INCLUDED IN PRINCIPAL COMPONENTS ANALYSIS

	Ln(size)	Asqrt(%forest)	Ln(edge density)	Ln(elevation)	Ln(canopy height)
Ln(Size)	1.000	0.556**	−0.386**	0.114**	0.064**
Asqrt(%Forest)		1.000	−0.740**	0.151**	0.029
Ln(Edge Density)			1.000	−0.156**	−0.033
Ln(Elevation)				1.000	−0.031
Ln(Canopy Height)					1.000

Notes: Ln(Size) is the natural log of the patch size; Asqrt(% Forest) is the arcsine square-root transformed % forest in the surrounding 1000 ha; Ln(Edge Density) is the linear measure of forest/non-forest in m/ha; Ln(Elevation) is the natural log of distance above Mean Sea Level, in m; Ln(Canopy Height) is the natural log of canopy height, in m. * $P \le 0.01$, ** $P \le 0.001$.

isolation, measured as distance to the nearest forest patch of 40 or 200 ha, was not included in the PCA because these data were missing from a substantial number of records. As this variable was highly significantly correlated with Ln Size ($r = -0.228$, $P \le 0.001$), Ln Edge Density ($r = 0.413$, $P \le 0.001$), and Asqrt %Forest ($r = -0.567$, $P \le 0.001$), we felt that the increase in sample size gained by omitting this variable more than compensated for any loss of explanatory power caused by its omission.

Logistic regression analysis

We used PROC LOGISTIC (SAS Institute 1996) to model the probability that a singing male of the species of interest would be detected on the two required visits, either vocalizing spontaneously or in response to playback of conspecific territorial calls, based on the level of fragmentation at each site. We fit multiple logistic regressions using all of the calculated predictor variables (Principal Components), and used manual backward elimination of non-significant (Wald chi-square $P > 0.1$) variables to fit the best model. Models were compared using the G^2 statistic (difference in -2 log-likelihood between two nested models; Agresti 1996) and Akaike Information Criterion (AIC; Agresti 1996). The model chosen in each case was the most parsimonious one that minimized the AIC and had a G^2 that was not significant at the $P \le 0.05$ level.

Comparison of fragmentation effects

To compare the effects of fragmentation in eastern and western landscapes, we first subset our data into two parts at the 98th meridian, a natural break in the dataset that coincides roughly with the Great Plains. We focused our analyses on widespread species that had both eastern and western populations (e.g., Hermit and Swainson's, *Catharus ustulatus,* thrushes and Veery, *C. fuscescens*) or congeneric species pairs (e.g., Western, *Piranga ludoviciana,* and Scarlet, *P. olivacea,* tanagers) with one eastern and one western member. In addition to these focal species, we compared the effects of fragmentation on the presence of Brown-headed Cowbird across North America. Additionally, we used contingency table analysis to test for differences in the frequency of occurrence of several species of predators in eastern and western landscapes.

We fit separate regression models for each member of species pairs, and tested for differences in the strength of regression coefficients between the pair using a large sample t-test. We rejected the null hypothesis of no differences if $P \le 0.05$. However, because we had very large sample sizes for several species, we

also compared 95% confidence intervals for the fragmentation coefficient in each model, to avoid rejecting the null hypothesis based on differences that were statistically, but not biologically, significant. We accepted the null hypothesis of no difference in the effects of fragmentation between species pairs if the 95% confidence intervals for the mean estimated effect of fragmentation overlapped substantially. For single species, we fit regression models that included an east/west dummy or indicator variable, and region by factor interaction terms. We rejected the null hypothesis of no difference in effects of fragmentation for widespread species if $P \le 0.05$ (Wald chi-square) for the region by fragmentation interaction term.

Comparison of predator and nest parasite pressure

To characterize differences in predation and nest parasitism pressures between eastern and western landscapes, we used contingency table analysis to test for differences in frequency of occurrence for the Brown-headed Cowbird and for several species of predator. Predator species included nest predators such as squirrels, chipmunks, and corvid species, as well as predators of fledglings and adult birds such as *Accipiter* hawks.

RESULTS

DATA COLLECTION

Volunteers collected data at a total of 1840 sites during the 1995 and 1996 field seasons (tanager species) and at an additional 1298 sites during the 1997 and 1998 field seasons (thrush species), for a total of 3138 sites (Fig. 1). These sites spanned North America, covering 50 states and provinces, and 55 physiographic regions (Robbins et al. 1986). However, many sites were missing required data, and we based subsequent analyses only on sites for which complete data were available. The proportion of sites which contained a territorial male of the focal species on both visits varied from 0.15 for the Swainson's Thrush to 0.325 for the Scarlet Tanager.

ANALYSES

Principal component analysis

Our principal component analysis was based on 2515 unique study sites. These sites included 1933 sites with complete data east of the 98th meridian (East), and 582 west of the 98th me-

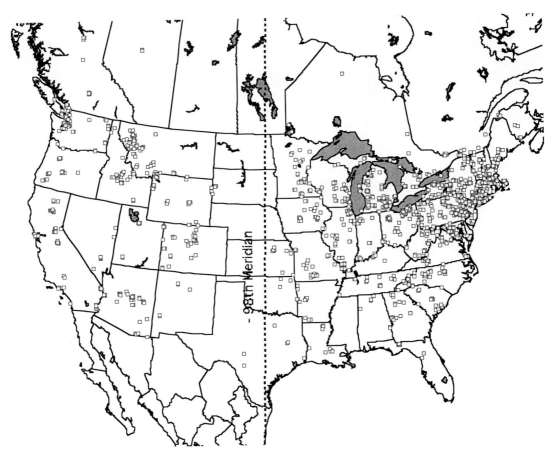

FIGURE 1. Locations of the approximately 2500 study sites on which this analysis is based. Because of the large size of the symbols representing study sites relative to distances on the map, one study site may cover several others.

ridian (West). The correlation matrix for the included variables showed highly significant correlations between patch size, proportion of forest, and edge density (Table 1), which was removed by the orthogonal varimax rotation, thus yielding uncorrelated and easily interpretable principal components (Table 2).

The first three principal components explained 83% of the variance in the data set (Table 2). The first principal component (PC1) had high positive loadings (coefficients >0.5) for patch size and proportion of forest, and high negative loading for edge density in the surrounding landscape; we interpreted this principal component as an overall measure of fragmentation. PC1 varies from negative values for small patches in a landscape with little forest and a large amount of forest/non-forest edge, to posi-

TABLE 2. FACTOR LOADINGS DERIVED FROM PRINCIPAL COMPONENTS ANALYSIS OF 2515 FORESTED SITES

Variable	PC1	PC2	PC3
Ln(Size)	0.742	0.029	0.082
Asqrt(%Forest)	0.921	0.067	−0.041
Ln(Edge Density)	−0.850	−0.090	0.178
Ln(Elevation)	0.093	0.995	−0.016
Ln(Canopy Height)	0.032	−0.016	0.997
Eigenvalue	2.187	1.027	0.923
Cumulative variance explained	0.437	0.643	0.827

TABLE 3. COMPARISONS OF FRAGMENTATION VALUES (PC1) AT SITES SAMPLED IN EASTERN AND WESTERN NORTH AMERICA FOR BIRDS IN FORESTED LANDSCAPES PROJECT

Geographic region	N	Mean	SD	Minimum	Maximum	Range
East	1933	0.036	1.0069	−2.440	2.819	5.259
West	582	−0.127	0.9820	−2.591	2.393	4.984

Notes: Data were included from both the 1997 and 1998 field season of BFL. The mean fragmentation values from eastern and western landscapes were not significantly different (pooled test of H_0: $\mu_1 - \mu_2 = 0$, z = 0.366, df = 2513, P = 0.373).

tive values for large patches in a landscape with high proportions of forest and little edge. Interpretations of the second and third principal components were straightforward: PC2 had a high loading only for elevation and PC3 had a high loading only for canopy height. PC3 was retained in the PCA despite an eigenvalue (0.92), which was less than the commonly accepted cutoff of 1.0, because other studies have suggested that the height of the canopy plays an important role in habitat selection by forest-obligate birds (Cody 1985, Hames 2001). Hereinafter PC1, PC2, and PC3 will be referred to by their interpretations as overall fragmentation, elevation, and canopy height, respectively.

Overall, there was little difference between western and eastern sites in the PCA-derived overall fragmentation values (PC1). The mean overall fragmentation values were not significantly different for western and eastern sites (z = −0.158, df = 2347, P = 0.874) and the minima, maxima, and ranges were very similar (Table 3).

Logistic regression analysis

The effect of fragmentation was a very similar decrease in the probability of detection with increasing habitat fragmentation for both tanager species. Both the Scarlet Tanager in the East,

and the Western Tanager in the West, showed a strong, highly significant increase in probability of "possible" breeding as the fragmentation measure PC1 increased (Table 4). This resulted in an approximately five-fold decrease in the estimated probability of occurrence from the least to the most fragmented site. The probability of detection also increased with increasing elevation in the Scarlet (Fig. 2), but not the Western, tanager (Fig. 3).

Sample sizes for the eastern populations of the Swainson's Thrush, and for western populations of the Veery, were insufficient to make within-species comparisons for these species. We therefore treated these as a species pair and restricted the regression analyses to eastern sites for the Veery and to western sites for the Swainson's Thrush. Both of these thrushes displayed similar highly significant increases in the probability of "possible" breeding as PC1 increased, and fragmentation decreased (Table 4). As in the tanager species, this resulted in an approximately five-fold decrease in probability from the least to most fragmented sites. In both species the probability of detection also decreased with increasing elevation (Figs. 4, 5). The Hermit Thrush (Table 5) also showed a highly significant negative response to fragmentation of approximately the same magnitude as that dis-

TABLE 4. STRENGTH OF THE EFFECTS OF FRAGMENTATION (PC1), ELEVATION (PC2), AND CANOPY HEIGHT (PC3) ON THE PROBABILITY OF DETECTING TERRITORIAL BIRDS, SHOWN AS ESTIMATED COEFFICIENTS DERIVED FROM MULTIPLE LOGISTIC REGRESSION

	Scarlet Tanager	Western Tanager	Veery	Swainson's Thrush	Wood Thrush
Intercept	−0.6174***	−1.4866***	−1.5899***	−0.8660***	−0.7545***
PC1/east	0.3648[a]***	—	0.5755[b]**	—	−0.1668**
PC1/west	—	0.5954[a]***	—	0.7315[b]**	—
95% CI low	0.2304	0.2765	0.3747	0.3054	−0.3089
95% CI high	0.5016	0.9299	0.7835	1.1902	−0.0453
PC2/east	0.3148**	—	−0.2061*	—	ns
PC2/west	—	ns	—	−0.3184*	—
PC3/east	ns	—	ns	—	0.3245***
PC3/west	—	ns	—	ns	—

Notes: The PCA was calculated using all data from across North America; the notations "east" and "west" refer to the region in which each species was studied; — denotes that the corresponding coefficient was not calculated; ns indicates that the coefficient was not significant at the P ≤ 0.05 level.
[a] Test of H_0: no difference between coefficients, z = −1.2812, P = 0.176, ns.
[b] Test of H_0: no difference between coefficients, z = 0.5968, P = 0.334, ns.
* P ≤ 0.10, ** P ≤ 0.01, *** P ≤ 0.001.

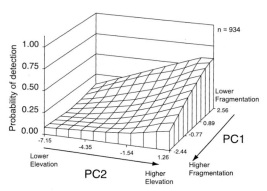

FIGURE 2. The effects of fragmentation (PC1) and elevation (PC2) on the probability of detecting a singing or calling male Scarlet Tanager on both required visits. Probability of occurrence increases as fragmentation decreases and elevation increases. Model is highly significant (−2 log-likelihood = 39.876, df = 2, P < 0.001).

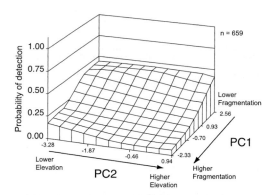

FIGURE 4. The effects of fragmentation (PC1) and elevation (PC2) on the probability of detecting a singing or calling male Veery on both required visits. Probability of occurrence increases as fragmentation and elevation decrease. Model is highly significant (−2 log-likelihood = 35.932, df = 2, P < 0.001).

played by the other thrushes. In addition, the Hermit Thrush showed a highly significant increase in the probability of "possible" breeding with increases in elevation. The best model also contained a significant region by canopy height interaction term, so that we can conclude that the effect of canopy height differed between eastern and western populations. The uniform response to fragmentation across species and also across genera was striking, and somewhat troubling. To test if this trend was universal and potentially an artifact of our analytic design, we also fit a logistic regression model to data for the Wood Thrush, a purely eastern species. The

Wood Thrush showed the opposite trend (Table 4), a somewhat weaker but still significant increase in probability of "possible" breeding with increases in fragmentation. The Wood Thrush was also more likely to be detected in forests with higher canopies (Fig. 6).

In both the East and the West, the Brown-headed Cowbird likewise showed an increase in the probability of occurrence with increases in fragmentation (Table 6). The best model for the cowbird also contained a significant effect of year, an indicator variable used to partition variance due to slight differences in the Project Tanager and BFL protocols as to when cowbirds could be counted. In addition, there was a highly significant year by region interaction term,

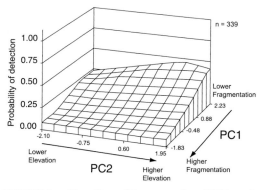

FIGURE 3. The effect of fragmentation (PC1) on the probability of detecting a singing or calling male Western Tanager on both required visits. Probability of occurrence increases as fragmentation decreases. Model is highly significant (−2 log-likelihood = 13.757, df = 1, P < 0.001). Note there is no significant effect of elevation; elevation is only included for comparison between graphs.

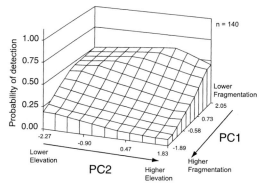

FIGURE 5. The effects of fragmentation (PC1) and elevation (PC2) on the probability of detecting a singing or calling male Swainson's Thrush on both required visits. Probability of occurrence increases as fragmentation and elevation decrease. Model is highly significant (−2 log-likelihood = 12.588, df = 2, P = 0.002).

TABLE 5. RESULTS OF LOGISTIC REGRESSION OF GEOGRAPHIC REGION, FRAGMENTATION, ELEVATION, VEGETATION STRUCTURE, AND THEIR INTERACTIONS, ON THE PRESENCE OF THE HERMIT THRUSH

Variable	Parameter estimate	df	SE	Wald χ^2	P
Intercept	−1.7284	1	0.1724	100.5300	<0.001
West	−0.5680	1	0.3253	3.0498	0.081
PC1	0.6793	1	0.1270	28.6187	<0.001
PC2	0.4099	1	0.1517	7.3037	0.007
PC3	−0.3452	1	0.1432	5.8130	0.016
West*PC3	0.3968	1	0.2245	3.1245	0.077

Notes: Regression based on data from 617 study sites censused for BFL from 1997 to 1998. "West" is an indicator variable: West = 0 east of the Great Plains and West = 1 west of the Great Plains. Overall model χ^2 = 57.879, df = 5, P < 0.001. Concordant pairs = 71.8%.

which showed that fewer cowbirds were detected in the West during the 1997 and 1998 BFL field seasons. Further, there were other highly significant region by fragmentation, and region by elevation interactions, as well as a region by elevation by year three-way interaction.

East/West comparisons

Because we used a standardized measure of fragmentation that included both patch size and the landscape measures proportion of forest and of edge, and because this variable had similar distributions in the East and West, we were able to directly compare fragmentation coefficients from logistic regressions. We tested for differences in the strength of fragmentation between species using a large sample, two-tailed t-test, or between populations within species by using the Wald chi-square for the region by fragmentation interaction term from the logistic regression. We also directly compared the relative strengths of the effects of fragmentation across species by comparing 95% confidence intervals for the es-

timated fragmentation coefficients. We found that the strength of the negative effects was not significantly different (z = −1.281, P = 0.176) in the Scarlet and the Western tanagers (Table 4) and that their 95% confidence intervals showed considerable overlap. Likewise, there was no significant difference in the strength of fragmentation effects (z = 0.597, P = 0.334) between the Veery in the East and the Swainson's Thrush in the West (Table 4), and the 95% confidence interval for the Veery was completely contained within that of the Swainson's Thrush. Logistic regression for the Hermit Thrush (Table 5) did not yield a significant region by fragmentation interaction term (Wald χ^2 = 0.099, P = 0.753), indicating that there was no significant difference in the strength of fragmentation effects between eastern and western populations. Thus, neither objective hypothesis testing, nor a more subjective examination of the degree of overlap in confidence intervals, provided strong evidence to reject the null hypothesis of no difference in eastern and western responses to fragmentation, at least in these tanager and thrush species.

Conversely, although the Brown-headed Cowbird, like the Wood Thrush, showed an overall increase in probability of detection with increases in fragmentation, a significant region by fragmentation interaction term showed that the response to fragmentation was stronger in the West than in the East (Table 6). Additionally, contingency table analysis of the number of sites at which the Brown-headed Cowbird was detected (Table 7) showed a somewhat higher frequency of occurrence in the East than the West, although this difference was not significant (P ≤ 0.058). For predators, however, the picture is more straightforward. Overall the East had a significantly higher proportion of sites with at least one mammalian (49.3%) or at least one avian (64.4%) predator, than did the West (39.3% and 25.4%, respectively.) In fact, the West significantly surpassed the East only in the frequency of occurrence for the red or Douglas (*Tamias-*

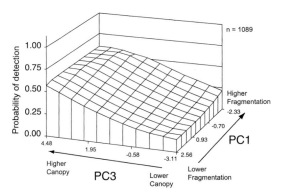

FIGURE 6. The effects of fragmentation (PC1) and canopy height (PC3) on the probability of detecting a singing or calling male Wood Thrush on both required visits. (Note that fragmentation axis is reversed from other graphs.) Probability of occurrence increases as fragmentation increases and canopy height increases. Model is highly significant (−2 log-likelihood = 26.381, df = 2, P < 0.001).

TABLE 6. RESULTS OF LOGISTIC REGRESSION OF PROTOCOL, GEOGRAPHIC REGION, FRAGMENTATION, ELEVATION AND THEIR INTERACTIONS, ON THE PRESENCE OF BROWN-HEADED COWBIRDS

Variable	Parameter estimate	df	SE	Wald χ^2	P
Intercept	−0.8756	1	0.0747	137.37	<0.001
Year	−0.2883	1	0.1259	5.24	0.022
West	−0.3474	1	0.2210	2.47	0.116
PC1	−0.1998	1	0.0571	12.22	<0.001
PC2	0.1398	1	0.0999	1.96	0.162
Year*West	−0.7813	1	0.3562	4.81	0.028
Year*PC2	−0.2965	1	0.1516	3.83	0.050
West*PC1	−0.5577	1	0.1604	12.09	<0.001
West*PC2	−0.7654	1	0.1798	18.12	<0.001
West*PC2*Year	0.8415	1	0.2944	7.65	0.006

Notes: Regression based on data from 2068 study sites censused for Project Tanager and BFL from 1995 to 1998. "Year" is an indicator variable that partitions variation due to differences in the protocols of the two projects. "West" is an indicator variable: West = 0 east of the Great Plains and West = 1 west of the Great Plains. Overall model χ^2 = 101.25, df = 9, P < 0.001. Concordant pairs = 63.0%.

ciurus douglasii) squirrels and for *Accipiter* species. For all other predators the proportion of sites with detections was significantly higher in the East than in the West (Table 7).

DISCUSSION

Despite regional differences in topology, vegetation structure, suites of predators, and land uses past and present, compounded by differences in phylogeny, there is a surprising uniformity in the strength and direction of the responses to fragmentation across the regions and the species studied. This is particularly surprising because Rosenberg, et al. (1999) showed clear regional differences in the strength of responses to fragmentation in the Scarlet Tanager. This lack of regional effects in the present study may be due to the "lumping" of variation occurring at smaller scales, due to the extremely large regions defined for the current study. However, as measured by presence/absence of singing males, for at least the tanager and thrush species we studied, increasing fragmentation is strongly correlated with decreasing probability of detection. What is perhaps not intuitively clear is the correct interpretation of our results.

Our study measured the distribution (presence or absence) of the focal species in relation to fragmentation, not the demographic consequences of that fragmentation. However, demonstrated sensitivity to fragmentation alone (shown as changes in distribution of sensitive species) is sufficient to infer that the tanager and thrush species studied are adversely affected by fragmentation (Winter and Faaborg 1999). For example, in a recent study of fragmentation effects on grassland birds, Winter and Faaborg (1999) make a clear distinction between the distributional consequences (lower densities, lower probability of occurrence) and the demographic consequences (lower nesting success) of fragmentation. Further, their results demonstrate that some area-sensitive species may show distributional effects such as absence from small patches (Robbins et al. 1989a), while other species may show demographic effects such as lower nesting success in fragments (Donovan et al. 1995a, Winter and Faaborg 1999). This useful partitioning of the adverse effects of fragmentation can equally well be applied to forest-dwelling species. This is important because directly determining the demographic consequences of fragmentation requires a skilled field crew and is extremely labor-intensive, making it im-

TABLE 7. PERCENTAGES OF SITES, BY REGION, AT WHICH NEST PREDATORS OR BROWN-HEADED COWBIRDS WERE DETECTED DURING THE 1995, 1996, 1997 OR 1998 FIELD SEASON

	Brown-headed Cowbird	Chipmunk (any species)	Red or Douglas squirrel	Gray or fox squirrel	Crow (any species)	Jay (any species)	*Accipiter* (any species)	Mammalian predator	Avian predator
N	644	783	388	685	1148	1222	161	1429	1838
East %	21.88	29.94	9.86	26.83	44.54	45.59	4.38	49.28	64.40
West %	18.66	12.87	20.98	9.40	16.99	23.42	6.82	39.25	25.41
Δ	3.22	17.07	−11.12	17.43	27.55	22.17	−2.44	10.03	38.99
χ^2	3.603	88.687	64.622	101.356	187.665	118.740	5.058	23.390	69.124
P ≤	0.058	0.001	0.001	0.001	0.001	0.001	0.001	0.001	0.001

Notes: N = Total number of sites at which predators or Brown-headed Cowbird detected; Δ = difference in percentage detected (East − West).

practical for an extensive, volunteer-based study such as this one.

In the future, repeated sampling over several breeding seasons will allow us to use rates of site occupation or turnover (Villard et al. 1992, Winker et al. 1995, Bellamy et al. 1996b), rather than simple presence/absence in one season, as a measure of the effects of fragmentation. For example, Hames et al. (2001) have demonstrated that the proportion of breeding seasons a site is occupied by a territorial male Scarlet Tanager over several years is inversely proportional to the degree of fragmentation. Thus, we eagerly await analyses of multiple-year BFL data, which will allow us to make stronger inferences by using rates of territory occupancy as a currency for the effects of fragmentation on habitat quality and reproductive success. However, although direct demographic data are necessary for a complete understanding of these effects, already documented changes in distribution due to fragmentation are sufficient to demonstrate adverse effects on sensitive species.

Our requirement that singing males be detected on both visits to the study sites reduces the probability that migrant males would be counted as "possible" breeders; that is, as resident males displaying territoriality. However, although the participants were charged to find as many nests of focal species as possible, and to monitor any nests found to determine reproductive success, very few nests were in fact found (Rosenberg et al. 1999). This lack of direct measures of reproductive success, per se, limits our ability to determine the processes that lead to the observed patterns, and hence our ability to make inferences about population effects of fragmentation. In particular, Van Horne (1983) pointed out that the use of density alone as a measure of habitat quality could give rise to misleading results, especially where territorial behavior limits access to high quality habitat. Others (Maurer 1986, Hobbs and Hanley 1990, Winker et al. 1995) have supported her conclusion, and still others (Vickery et al. 1992, Donovan et al. 1995b, Winter and Faaborg 1999) have also pointed out that density does not necessarily track reproductive success. However, although density (measured as number of birds per area) is mathematically equivalent to probability of occurrence (with the same units), probability of occurrence based on presence/absence data is a special case of density measures with density bounded by zero and one. In fact, the only reliable evidence of the effects of fragmentation available from census data is arguably based on the presence or absence of a species (Freemark et al. 1995, Winter and Faaborg 1999). Further, Boyce and McDonald (1999) point out that habitat usage involves both active habitat selection and passive persistence in a habitat. The fitness consequences of utilizing that habitat, expressed as selection on survival or reproduction (Southwood 1977), is what gives rise to the perceived patterns of distribution (Boyce and McDonald 1999). Thus, in most cases, extent of habitat use (or presence/absence) reflects fitness in those habitats (Fretwell and Lucas 1970). The patterns described above (Van Horne 1983, and others) may be exceptions to this generalization (Boyce and McDonald 1999).

Thus, at first glance, it is somewhat surprising that the high sensitivity to fragmentation shown in most of the species studied was not correlated with population trends as measured by the Breeding Bird Survey. For example, while the Veery showed a significant decline survey-wide between 1966 and 1996 (trend = -1.4%, P < 0.01; Sauer et al. 1997), the Hermit Thrush, which displayed approximately the same level of fragmentation sensitivity as the Veery, showed a survey-wide significant increase over the same period (trend = $+1.4\%$, P = 0.01; Sauer et al. 1997). The equally sensitive Swainson's Thrush displayed no significant trend at all survey-wide. Finally, the Wood Thrush, whose probability of occurrence increased with increasing fragmentation, has shown a strong and highly significant negative trend (trend = -1.8%, P < 0.01) over the same 30 years (Sauer et al. 1997). However, this is perhaps not a total surprise.

As migrant species, the thrushes' and tanagers' population trends reflect influences on the birds on their breeding grounds, during migration, and on their wintering grounds. In the case of the Wood Thrush, population decreases coincide with deforestation in their tropical wintering grounds (Morton 1989) and a decrease in the survival of non-territorial "floaters" while over-wintering (Rappole et al. 1989). In contrast, the Hermit Thrush, which is the only thrush exhibiting an increasing population trend, is also the only species we studied that does not winter in the tropics. Thus, demonstrated sensitivity to fragmentation on the breeding grounds alone may not be sufficient for prediction of population trends of these neotropical migrant species. Data from all portions of the annual cycle are important to understand changes in migratory bird demography (Danielson et al. 1997). However, at least in the case of the Wood Thrush, the preponderance of recent evidence suggests that declining trends are due, in large part, to poor reproductive success in fragmented landscapes on the breeding grounds (Robinson and Wilcove 1994, Hoover et al. 1995, Trine 1998).

Another surprising result of our analysis was the uniformly negative correlation between the degree of fragmentation and presence of our focal species (with the exception of the Wood Thrush), which held across western and eastern regions. As recently as five years ago, Freemark et al. (1995) pointed to differences between the landscape contexts of studies of fragmentation in the East and the West as a means to explain the clear differences in levels of response between the regions. They pointed to the fact that most western studies had taken place in forested regions fragmented by silviculture, as opposed to most eastern studies that took place in landscapes where forests were fragmented by agriculture and urbanization (Freemark et al. 1995). Our current analysis did not take the nature and extent of adjacent habitat into account because these data were not always available, but instead made comparison based on patch and landscape configuration alone. Further, Freemark et al. (1995) cited an earlier study by Rosenberg and Raphael (1986), which suggested that the lack of strong reaction by western species may also be due to relatively recent fragmentation combined with a time-lag in response by sensitive birds, as well as a lack of truly isolated forest patches. It is possible that the intervening 16 years was a sufficient time for a time-lagged response to become apparent, or for levels of parasitism by Brown-headed Cowbirds to increase with increasing human populations throughout the West (Tewksbury et al. 1998). It seems just as likely, however, that our study was simply the first that undertook a large scale comparison of fragmentation effects in the East and West using the same methodology and measures of fragmentation in both regions, and that the nature of

adjacent habitat has a far from negligible effect on sensitive species' response to fragmentation.

In summary, it is clear that the trends in probability of detecting tanager or thrush species in landscapes with varying proportions of fragmentation are the same, in both direction and strength, in both western and eastern landscapes. Further, this similarity in response to fragmentation occurs despite differences in both the suites and abundances of predators and of nest parasites, and despite significant regional differences shown in other analyses (Rosenberg et al. 1999). The Brown-headed Cowbird increased in all landscapes with increases in the level of fragmentation, and this effect was stronger in the West. However, all the focal species except the Wood Thrush showed strong negative effects of fragmentation on possible breeding, whatever their distribution and whatever the history of landuse in their ranges. Finally, this study demonstrates that the use of volunteer citizen scientists in conjunction with explicit, rigorous protocols using playback to verify the absence of the species of interest, can be effective at addressing a large-scale question such as this by gathering detailed distributional data about species of interest across North America.

ACKNOWLEDGMENTS

This research was conducted with funding from the National Science Foundation, the National Fish and Wildlife Foundation, the USDA Forest Service, Archie and Grace Berry Charitable Foundation, Florence and John Schumann Foundation, and the Packard Foundation. We also gratefully acknowledge helpful statistical advice from C. E. McCullough, W. M. Hochachka, and fieldwork by hundreds of dedicated volunteers. We also thank the editors, S. T. Knick, and an anonymous reviewer for comments that improved the paper.

Studies in Avian Biology No. 25:92–102, 2002.

THE EFFECTS OF HABITAT FRAGMENTATION ON BIRDS IN COAST REDWOOD FORESTS

T. LUKE GEORGE AND L. ARRIANA BRAND

Abstract. Human activities in the redwood (*Sequoia sempervirens*) region over the last 150 years have changed what was once a relatively continuous old-growth forest ecosystem into a highly fragmented mosaic of young, mature, and old-growth forest patches, agricultural land, and human settlements. We summarize recent studies on the effects of forest fragmentation on diurnal landbirds in redwood forests and present new analyses of the effects of forest patch size on the distribution and abundance of breeding birds. Analyses of the relative abundance of 31 bird species in 38 patches of mature and old-growth redwood forest indicate that six species were positively correlated with forest patch area and may be sensitive to fragmentation: Pileated Woodpecker (*Dryocopus pileatus*), Pacific-slope Flycatcher (*Empidonax difficilis*), Steller's Jay (*Cyanocitta stelleri*), Brown Creeper (*Certhis americana*), Winter Wren (*Troglodytes troglodytes*), and Varied Thrush (*Ixoreus naevius*). These species (except the Steller's Jay) have been identified as sensitive to forest fragmentation in other studies of wet coniferous forests in the western U.S. The American Robin (*Turdus migratorius*), Orange-crowned Warbler (*Vermivora celata*), Dark-eyed Junco (*Junco hyemalis*), and Song Sparrow (*Melospiza melodia*) were negatively correlated with patch area. Song Sparrows and Orange-crowned Warblers are more abundant in young second-growth than mature redwood forests, and American Robins and Dark-eyed Juncos are generally associated with forest openings. Thus, these four species are associated with and likely responding to habitats surrounding forest patches. Previous analyses have shown that four of the species that were positively associated with patch area, Pacific-slope Flycatchers, Brown Creepers, Winter Wrens, and Varied Thrushes, were less abundant at forest edges than the forest interior, suggesting that edge avoidance may be responsible for their sensitivity to fragmentation. Two species, Steller's Jay and Swainson's Thrush (*Catharus ustulatus*), were more abundant along forest edges. In a previous study, we found that predation on artificial nests increased with proximity to forest edge and that Steller's Jays were observed preying on some of the nests. These and other studies suggest that several bird species are sensitive to fragmentation of old-growth and mature second-growth coast redwoods possibly due to changes in microclimate along forest edges or to increased nest predation and subsequent avoidance of forest edges. Implementation of forest practices that reduce the amount of forest edge on the landscape may reduce the potential impacts of fragmentation on bird species in redwood forests.

Key Words: area effects; artificial nests; diurnal landbirds; edge effects; forest fragmentation; nesting success; redwoods; *Sequoia sempervirens*.

Numerous studies have documented the negative effects of forest loss and fragmentation on birds breeding in forests of the midwestern and eastern United States (Ambuel and Temple 1982, Askins et al. 1990, Robinson and Wilcove 1994, Walters 1998, Thompson et al. *this volume*) and Europe (Andrén 1992, 1994). Furthermore, a consensus is emerging among scientists working in these regions that habitat fragmentation results in increased nest predation and parasitism, thereby reducing breeding productivity and possibly leading to population declines. Thompson et al. (*this volume*) have proposed a "top-down" hierarchical model that includes regional, landscape-level, and local effects to explain variation in nesting success across the landscape. However, there is substantial variation among studies and some results in western forests seem to contradict the general pattern (e.g., Tewksbury et al. 1998). This has led to suggestions that the "Eastern Paradigm" may not be applicable to western forests.

Over the last 150 years, Westside forests (for-

ests west of the Sierra Nevada/Cascade crest) have been extensively logged, resulting in a fragmented pattern of late-seral stage forest in a sea of younger forest (Garmen et al. 1999). Because forest fragmentation has had such a dramatic impact on birds in other regions, it has been suggested that similar effects may be occurring in Westside forests. However, while some species such as the Northern Spotted Owl (*Strix occidentalis caurina*) and Marbled Murrelet (*Brachyramphus marmoratus*) show strong negative responses to forest fragmentation, studies of passerines and other small bird species in Westside forests have documented few effects of forest fragmentation (Rosenberg and Raphael 1986, Lehmkuhl et al. 1991, McGarigal and McComb 1995).

A number of hypotheses have been suggested to explain the lack of response of birds to forest fragmentation in Westside forests, including: (1) insufficient time for species to respond (Rosenberg and Raphael 1986, Lehmkuhl et al. 1991), (2) limited extent of forest loss (Rosenberg and

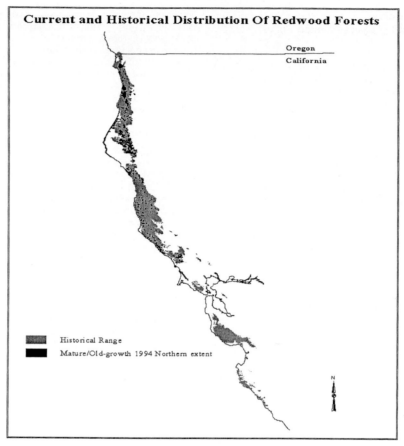

Current and Historical Distribution Of Redwood Forests

Oregon

California

Historical Range

Mature/Old-growth 1994 Northern extent

N

FIGURE 1.   Original distribution of coast redwood (*Sequoia sempervirens*) forests and current distribution of old-growth and mature second-growth coast redwood forest north of Point Reyes National Seashore. Current distributions are based on Landsat satellite imagery (Fox 1997).

Raphael 1986, Lehmkuhl et al. 1991), (3) the matrix (generally young forest) is less detrimental to nesting birds (McGarigal and McComb 1995), and (4) the species are adapted to heterogeneous landscapes and thus to the kinds of changes that logging has produced on the landscape (McGarigal and McComb 1995, Hejl et al. *this volume*). The first two hypotheses do not rule out fragmentation effects but suggest that effects may only be evident in forests that have been logged extensively in the past. The latter two hypotheses imply that forest fragmentation due to logging will have little effect even in heavily logged regions of the western United States.

Coast redwood (*Sequoia sempervirens*) forests have been heavily logged since the mid 1800s. Only about 3.5% of the pre-settlement distribution remains as original growth, and the current distribution of mature and old-growth redwood forest habitat is highly fragmented

(Fig. 1; Larsen 1991). Logging began earlier and has occurred more extensively in redwood than in other Westside forests (Sawyer et al. 2000). Thus, the effects of fragmentation may be more evident in redwood than in other Westside forests.

The birds of the redwood forest have not been extensively studied. However, over the past several years there have been a number of studies that have examined the effects of forest fragmentation on the birds of the region. Our objectives in this paper are to: (1) present new analyses of bird response to patch size and nesting success of Winter Wrens and Swainson's Thrushes (see Table 1 for scientific names of bird species studied) with respect to distance from forest edge, (2) summarize published and unpublished studies on the effects of forest fragmentation on birds in redwood forests, and (3) compare the effects of forest fragmentation on birds in redwood forests to those found in the Midwest and the eastern United States.

METHODS

We describe the methods for the analysis of bird response to patch size and nesting success of Winter Wrens and Swainson's Thrushes in detail, as these analyses have not been published. Methods for estimates of relative bird abundance with respect to distance from forest edge and the artificial nest experiments have been published elsewhere (Brand 1998; Brand and George 2000, 2001).

STUDY AREA

We conducted our studies in redwood forest patches in Humboldt County, California. Point counts that we used for analysis of bird response to patch size were conducted from 1 May to 15 July, 1994. Monitoring of Winter Wren and Swainson's Thrush nests took place during May–August 1998–1999. Study sites consisted of old-growth as well as mature second-growth (>80 years) coast redwood forests. The overstory of all stands was dominated by redwoods (>50%), but other tree species found in these stands included Douglas-fir (*Pseudotsuga menziesii*), Sitka spruce (*Picea sitchensis*), western hemlock (*Tsuga heterophylla*), grand fir (*Abies grandis*), red alder (*Alnus rubra*), California bay (*Umbellularia californica*), big-leaf maple (*Acer macrophyllum*), and tan-oak (*Lithocarpus densiflorus*). The understory was dominated by rhododendron (*Rhododendron macrophyllum*), sword fern (*Polystichum munitum*), salal (*Gaultheria shallon*), California huckleberry (*Vaccinium ovatum*), red huckleberry (*Vaccinium parviflorum*), cascara (*Rhamnus purshiana*), salmonberry (*Rubus spectabilis*), California blackberry (*Rubus ursinus*), Himalayan blackberry (*Rubus discolor*), and red elderberry (*Sambucus racemosa*). The edge of each patch was defined by gaps ≥100 m in the forest canopy occurring adjacent to several features such as rivers, grasslands, young forest (<30 years), residential development, and roads.

Study sites were located on public lands managed by Humboldt Redwoods State Park, Redwood National Park, Prairie Creek Redwoods State Park, the City of Arcata (Arcata Community Forest), Humboldt State University Wildlife Department (Wright Wildlife Refuge), the City of Eureka (Sequoia Park), and Grizzly Creek State Park. Study sites were also located on Simpson Timber Company property and other private lands. Stands on privately owned land have been intensively managed in the past 100 years. Most of the sites on public lands have never been logged; some were logged once and are now mature stands (>100 years).

For the patch size study, we used orthophotographic quadrangles of the region to identify potential forest patches characterized by >50% redwood canopy and a stand age of >80 years. From approximately 90 eligible patches, we randomly chose 38 forest patches to survey. The size of patches ranged from 0.89 ha to 4252 ha. However, 35 of the 38 patches were <160 ha. The study sites were distributed over approximately 700 km², all within 50 km of the Pacific Ocean.

The fate of Winter Wren and Swainson's Thrush nests was studied at the Wright Wildlife Refuge, the Arcata Community Forest, and Redwood National Park. Plots were established along forest edge (edge plots) and in forest interior (interior plots, >400 m from forest edge). One edge plot was established at the Wright Wildlife Refuge, two interior and one edge plot were established in the Arcata Community Forest, and two interior plots were established in Redwood National Park. Both the Wright Wildlife Refuge and the Arcata Community forest bordered on suburban areas.

BIRD RESPONSE TO PATCH SIZE

To examine which passerine bird species are sensitive to forest patch size and shape during the avian breeding season, we investigated the distribution and relative abundance of birds in redwood forest patches using point counts (Verner 1985). The location of the first point in a patch was randomly selected. From that point, a direction was randomly chosen to establish the succeeding points placed 200 m apart, until no further points could be placed within the patch or we had established 4 points. Most points were >100 m from the edge of the patch. In some cases the size and shape of the patch made this impossible, but in all cases points were placed no closer than 50 m from the edge of the patch.

Each patch was surveyed four times (twice by each of two observers), approximately once every two weeks. Point counts lasted 8 min, and were conducted at least 5 min apart. Some patches were too small to contain four points. In these patches, we established fewer points but maintained equal sampling effort by conducting additional counts at the points. If one point was established in a patch, then four, 8-min point counts spaced 5 min apart were conducted at one point. If a patch contained two points, two point counts were conducted 5 min apart at each point. If a patch contained 3 points, two point counts were done at a randomly chosen point, then one point count was conducted at the two remaining points. If four points were established in a patch, one point count was conducted at each point. All point-counts were conducted within four hours after sunrise.

Data were recorded separately for each 8-min point count even if occurring 5 min apart in the same location. During an 8-min point count, birds were not counted twice unless there was a high certainty that it was a different individual of the same species. The number of birds counted at each point in each patch across all visits to each patch was summed to get an index of relative abundance for that patch.

To quantify the landscape variables of habitat patch size and patch shape, we used a planimeter and orthophotoquads to measure the area (ha) of each forest patch and a map wheel to measure the total perimeter (m) of each patch. Because perimeter length is correlated with area, we computed an index of patch shape using the ratio of the perimeter (m) of a given forest patch to the perimeter (m) of a circular forest patch of equal area. Both patch area and patch shape were log transformed for analysis.

Because the bird data are counts, we used Poisson regression (McCullagh and Nelder 1989) to examine the effect of patch area and shape on bird abundance. Only species that were observed in at least 20% of the patches were included in the analysis. We used the natural log of patch area to deal with wide disparity in patch areas. The natural log of patch area and patch shape were correlated ($r^2 = 0.34$, df = 36, $P = 0.037$) and therefore we used only log patch area in the analyses because it explained a higher proportion of the variation in bird abundances than log patch shape, and patch area is generally a better predictor of bird abundance than patch shape (Galli et al. 1976, Blake and Karr 1987, Askins et al. 1990). A scale parameter was included in the model, which allows the variance to be greater than the mean to allow for over-dispersion of bird detections within patches compared to a standard Poisson distribution (McCullagh and Nelder 1989). Species that were positively associated with area were considered sensitive to fragmentation. All analyses were conducted using SAS statistical software (SAS Institute 1999).

NATURAL NESTS

In 1998 and 1999 nests of Swainson's Thrushes and Winter Wrens were monitored in plots established along forest/suburban edges and at locations distant (>400 m) from suburban edges (J. Kranz and T. L. George, unpubl. data). Nests were monitored at 3–4 day intervals until the nest failed or the young fledged. Daily Survival Rate (DSR) was computed for edge (<100 m from suburban edge) and interior (>100 m from suburban edge) nests using the Mayfield method (Hensler and Nichols 1981) and comparisons were performed using program CONTRAST (Hines and Sauer 1989, Sauer and Williams 1989). Because of small sample sizes of nests, we used $\alpha = 0.10$ to reduce the chance of a Type II error.

LITERATURE SURVEY

We surveyed the literature for studies of the response of diurnal landbirds to forest fragmentation in wet coniferous forests of the Pacific Northwest. We classified a species as area sensitive if its abundance increased with patch size (Schieck et al. 1995; this study) or with the amount of mature or old-growth forest within a surrounding buffer. Buffers differed in extent from 100 ha (Manuwal and Manuwal *this volume*) to 250–300 ha (McGarigal and McComb 1995). Rosenberg and Raphael (1986) examined both patch size and the amount of mature or old-growth in a 1,000-ha buffer surrounding the stand. Lehmkuhl et al. (1991) examined three scales: patch size, the area adjacent to the patch (within 400 m of the boundary), and the landscape (circular 2,025 ha area centered on the patch). Hejl and Paige (1994) compared bird relative abundance between a continuous stand of old-growth forest, an old-growth forest with 1–8 year-old clearcuts, and a selectively logged forest. A species was classified as edge sensitive if its abundance declined with proximity to edge (Brand and George 2001) or declined in abundance as the amount of edge increased in a surrounding buffer area. Buffer areas varied from 10 ha (Rosenberg and Raphael 1986), to 100 ha around each patch (Manuwal and Manuwal *this volume*), to 400 m surrounding the patch (Lehmkuhl et al. 1991). Thus there were seven studies that examined area effects and four that examined edge effects. We included fewer studies in our analysis than Manuwal and Manuwal (*this volume*, Table 1) because

we only included studies that specifically addressed area or edge sensitivity. Life history characteristics (nest type, migratory status, and foraging mode) of each species were obtained from the studies included in the summary and from the literature (Ehrlich et al. 1988). Species that showed evidence of area effects in two or more studies are included in Table 3.

RESULTS

Thirty-one species were included in the analysis of bird abundance and patch size (Table 1). Three species, the Golden-crowned Kinglet, Pacific-slope Flycatcher, and Wilson's Warbler, were detected in all of the patches. The abundances of six species, the Pileated Woodpecker, Pacific-slope Flycatcher, Brown Creeper, Steller's Jay, Winter Wren, and Varied Thrush, were positively correlated with log forest patch size (Table 2, Fig. 2). These species spanned the whole range of frequency values, from species that were detected in all of the patches (Pacific-slope Flycatcher) to those that were detected in a small proportion of the patches (Pileated Woodpecker). American Robins, Orange-crowned Warblers, Dark-eyed Juncos, and Song Sparrows were negatively correlated with patch size (Table 2, Fig. 2).

Varied Thrushes and Pileated Woodpeckers showed a threshold response to patch area. Varied Thrushes were detected in only 1 out of 17 patches below and 20 out of 21 patches above 16 ha. Pileated Woodpeckers were detected in 2 of 29 patches below and 6 of 9 patches above 48 ha. None of the other species showed evidence of a threshold response (Fig. 2).

Twenty-three Swainson's Thrush and 48 Winter Wren nests were monitored in the two years. Nest success for both years combined was low for Swainson's Thrushes (25%; DSR $\pm$ SE = 0.940 ± 0.016), whereas Winter Wrens had high nest success (65%; 0.986 ± 0.016). Daily survival rate of Swainson's Thrush nests close (<100m) to forest edges was lower than interior nests (0.92 ± 0.023 vs. 0.974 ± 0.018, respectively; $P = 0.065$) but nest success of Winter Wrens did not differ between edge and interior locations (0.991 ± 0.0053 vs. 0.977 ± 0.009, respectively; $P = 0.17$). None of the nests were parasitized by Brown-headed Cowbirds (*Molothrus ater*).

LITERATURE SURVEY

We found eight studies that had examined the effects of forest fragmentation on diurnal landbirds in Westside forests (Table 3). Because each study used different methods to examine these relationships and species composition varied among sites, the results must be interpreted cautiously. However, we felt this comparison was

TABLE 1. BIRD SPECIES INCLUDED IN ANALYSES OF PATCH CHARACTERISTICS AND BIRD ABUNDANCE IN COASTAL REDWOOD FORESTS

Species	Proportion of patches occupied (N = 38)
Golden-crowned Kinglet (*Regulus satrapa*)	1.00
Pacific-slope Flycatcher (*Empidonax difficilis*)	1.00
Wilson's Warbler (*Wilsonia pusilla*)	1.00
Chestnut-backed Chickadee (*Poecile rufescens*)	0.97
Winter Wren (*Troglodytes troglodytes*)	0.95
Swainson's Thrush (*Catharus ustulatus*)	0.92
Brown Creeper (*Certhia americana*)	0.89
Steller's Jay (*Cyanocitta stelleri*)	0.89
American Robin (*Turdus migratorius*)	0.84
Hermit Warbler (*Dendroica occidentalis*)	0.82
Dark-eyed Junco (*Junco hyemalis*)	0.74
Song Sparrow (*Melospiza melodia*)	0.68
Orange-crowned Warbler (*Vermivora celata*)	0.66
Common Raven (*Corvus corax*)	0.63
Purple Finch (*Carpodacus purpureus*)	0.63
Pine Siskin (*Carduelis pinus*)	0.58
Vaux's Swift (*Chaetura vauxi*)	0.53
Varied Thrush (*Ixoreus naevius*)	0.47
Hutton's Vireo (*Vireo huttoni*)	0.42
Band-tailed Pigeon (*Columba fasciata*)	0.37
Northern Flicker (*Colaptes auratus*)	0.32
Red-breasted Nuthatch (*Sitta canadensis*)	0.32
Western Tanager (*Piranga ludoviciana*)	0.32
Cassin's Vireo (*Vireo cassinii*)	0.29
Hermit Thrush (*Catharus guttatus*)	0.26
Pileated Woodpecker (*Dryocopus pileatus*)	0.24

an important first step in identifying species that consistently show evidence of sensitivity to fragmentation.

Out of seven studies that examined area sensitivity, ten species were identified as being sensitive to fragmentation in two or more and seven in three or more studies (Table 3). There was no tendency for species with particular nest types or foraging modes to predominate, but the majority of the species were residents.

Eight of the ten species that were identified as area sensitive also showed evidence of edge sensitivity in one or more studies (Table 3). Thus, there is high concordance between area sensitive and edge sensitive species in these studies. The association between edge sensitivity and area sensitivity that we found, however, must be viewed with caution. Only one of the studies (Brand and George 2001) was specifically designed to examine response to forest edge; the others were based on point counts, which may be a poor indicator of edge effects (Villard 1998).

DISCUSSION

Six of the 31 bird species we examined in the forest patch size analysis showed a positive association with forest patch area, suggesting that

a substantial portion of the avifauna is sensitive to the effects of forest fragmentation in this region. Four species, American Robins, Orange-crowned Warblers, Dark-eyed Juncos, and Song Sparrows, were more abundant in small than in large forest patches. This is consistent with the habitat associations of these species. Song Sparrows and Orange-crowned Warblers are more abundant in young second-growth than mature redwood forests (Hazard and George 1999) and therefore are likely to be associated with the edges of mature stands. American Robins and Dark-eyed Juncos are generally associated with forest openings (Ehrlich et al. 1988) and therefore it is not surprising that they are more abundant in smaller patches. Because of the extensive loss and fragmentation of mature and old-growth forest in this region, we will focus our discussion on those species that may be negatively affected by loss and fragmentation of mature and old-growth forests.

Other studies in Westside forests have failed to detect strong evidence for edge or area sensitivity among diurnal landbirds (Rosenberg and Raphael 1986, Lehmkuhl et al. 1991, McGarigal and McComb 1995, Schieck et al. 1995). The lack of evidence in other studies may have been due to the landscapes studied and the approaches

TABLE 2. POISSON REGRESSION RELATIONSHIPS BETWEEN BIRD RELATIVE ABUNDANCE AND PATCH AREA IN 38 REDWOOD FOREST PATCHES SURVEYED IN NORTHERN CALIFORNIA IN 1994

Species response to fragmentation	Slope ± SE	P
Negative		
Pileated Woodpecker	0.62 ± 0.25	0.015
Pacific-slope Flycatcher	0.08 ± 0.04	0.037
Steller's Jay	0.17 ± 0.07	0.029
Winter Wren	0.30 ± 0.05	<0.001
Brown Creeper	1.67 ± 0.09	0.055
Varied Thrush	0.71 ± 0.06	<0.001
Positive		
American Robin	−0.44 ± 0.11	<0.001
Orange-crowned Warbler	−0.76 ± 0.26	0.004
Dark-eyed Junco	−0.52 ± 0.24	0.029
Song Sparrow	−0.55 ± 0.27	0.043

Notes: Species that were positively related to area were classified as showing a negative response to fragmentation. Those showing the opposite trend were classified as being positively associated with fragmentation. Only those species that occurred in at least 20% of the patches were included in the analysis.

that were used. Lehmkuhl et al. (1991) and Rosenberg and Raphael (1986) studied landscapes that were far less fragmented than the redwood forests we examined. The smallest stand examined by Lehmkuhl et al. (1991) was 51 ha, and most of the area around the stands (2,025 ha) consisted of less than 50% clearcut. Few (4/46) of the stands that Rosenberg and Raphael (1986) studied were true islands (isolated from other mature stands by clearcuts or hardwood forest), and the amount of clearcut forest in the surrounding 1000 ha block varied from 0 to 44%. Thus the lack of evidence for sensitivity to fragmentation in these studies may be because the landscapes were not sufficiently fragmented to affect the bird species they examined. McGarigal and McComb (1995) specifically examined landscapes (250–300 ha) encompassing a wide range of landscape structure based on the proportion of late-seral forest and the spatial configuration of the forest. However, they did not use a patch-centered approach, but rather examined the relationship between landscape characteristics and average bird abundance in all seral stages within those landscapes. Thus, the scale of their analysis was much larger than our study. Schiek et al. (1995) used a similar approach to ours but their sample of patches was small (21), and therefore their ability to detect effects of fragmentation may have been limited.

We found no association between sensitivity to fragmentation and life history characteristics. However, most of the species were residents, which contrasts sharply with similar summaries of birds in the midwestern and eastern United States where species that have been identified as sensitive to fragmentation are more often long-distance migrants (Robbins et al. 1989b, Freemark et al. 1995). Thus, there does not appear

to be any suite of life history traits that makes a species more likely to be negatively affected by fragmentation in these forests. This suggests that attempts to classify sensitivity to fragmentation based on life history traits are likely to be problematical (Hansen and Urban 1992, Hansen et al. 1993).

Two species, Pileated Woodpeckers and Steller's Jays, showed evidence of area sensitivity but not edge sensitivity. Pileated Woodpeckers have large territories (>300 ha) in western coniferous forests (Bull and Holthausen 1993), and therefore small isolated forest patches may be less suitable for nesting and foraging. Hejl (1992) also found that Pileated Woodpeckers showed a threshold response to forest patch area in the northern Rockies and suggested that large stands or aggregates of small stands of late-seral forests are necessary to maintain suitable habitat for this species. Brand and George (2001) found that Steller's Jay abundance declined with distance from edge in redwood forests, which is inconsistent with their area sensitivity. Rosenberg and Raphael (1986) also found that Steller's Jays were more abundant along edges, and that they were weakly negatively associated with an index of insularity. Thus, the evidence for area sensitivity in Steller's Jays is weak in both studies (Rosenberg and Raphael 1986; this study), and therefore their designation as area sensitive may be a statistical artifact.

Eight of ten species that showed sensitivity to fragmentation also showed evidence of edge sensitivity. This suggests that area sensitivity may be related to edge avoidance in these species. Although edge sensitivity is often assumed to be associated with area sensitivity (Whitcomb et al. 1981, Askins et al. 1990, Freemark and Collins 1992), Villard (1998) found a poor cor-

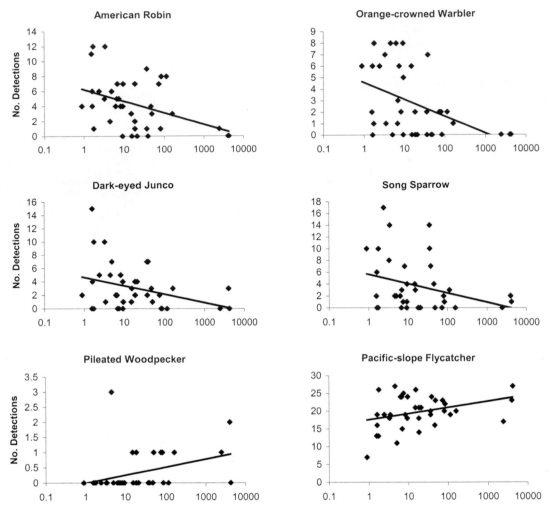

FIGURE 2. Relationship between relative density and patch area for bird species in redwood (*Sequoia sempervirens*) forest patches in northern California. Species that show a positive correlation between patch area and relative abundance are considered area sensitive. Fitted line is best fit Poisson regression with log link function.

relation between edge- and area-sensitive species in studies conducted in the eastern United States.

There are many factors that change between forest edges and interior locations that may influence bird abundance, such as differences in predation (Paton 1994), microclimate (Chen et al. 1993), vegetation structure (Ranney et al. 1981), and insect composition (Shure and Phillips 1991). These factors may act singly or in combination to make forest edges more or less suitable to particular species. For instance, moisture gradients may influence the abundance of ground-dwelling arthropods, which in turn could affect the distribution of ground foraging bird species, as has been suggested for Ovenbirds (*Seiurus aurocapillus*; Gibbs and Faaborg 1990).

Reduced moisture along forest edges may play an important role in the edge avoidance for several of the species. Winter Wrens breed in moist coniferous forests and nest in dense brush, especially along stream banks (Ehrlich et al. 1988). Barrows (1986) found that Winter Wrens in California have broad habitat preferences in fall and winter, but that habitat selection shifts in the breeding season almost exclusively to old-growth forest characterized by a dense, moist understory. Likewise, McGarigal and McComb (1995) found that Winter Wrens are associated with riparian systems in Oregon. The Varied Thrush breeds in moist coniferous forest (George 2000) and song post locations are associated with large diameter trees, on steep slopes, surrounded by a high density of trees

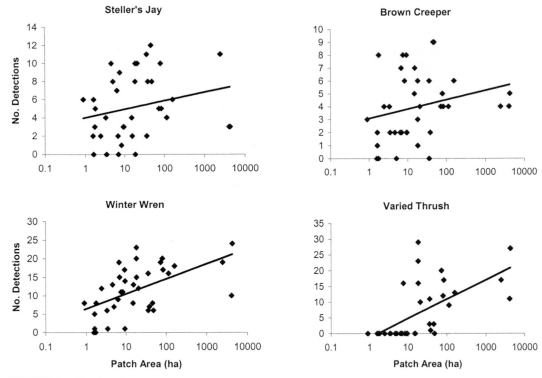

FIGURE 2. Continued.

near streams (Beck and George 2000). Thus, male thrushes prefer moist, shady locations for song posts. The Pacific-slope Flycatcher breeds in forests, especially near water (Ehrlich et al. 1988). Edges receive higher levels of incident radiation (Chen et al. 1993), and thus the microclimate near edges may be unsuitable for these species. Microclimate changes, in turn, could af-

fect vegetation composition and structure as well as prey availability near edges.

Another factor that may cause bird species to avoid edges is predation (Brittingham and Temple 1983). The mechanism is less clear in this case but it could either be a direct response to the presence of potential predators along edges or occur indirectly as unsuccessful nesters move

TABLE 3. BIRD SPECIES IDENTIFIED IN TWO OR MORE STUDIES AS SHOWING EVIDENCE OF SENSITIVITY TO FOREST FRAGMENTATION IN WET CONIFEROUS FORESTS OF THE PACIFIC NORTHWEST

Species	Nest type[a]	Migratory status[b]	Foraging mode[c]	Area sensitive[d]	Edge sensitive[d]
Pileated Woodpecker	Cavity	R	Drill	1, 3, 7	
Pacific-slope Flycatcher	Cup	L	Flycatch	6, 7	1, 8
Steller's Jay	Cup	R	Omnivore	1, 7	
Chestnut-backed Chickadee	Cavity	R	Foliage	1, 3, 5, 6	1, 6
Red-breasted Nuthatch	Cavity	R	Bark	3, 5, 6	1, 8
Brown Creeper	Crevice	R	Bark	3, 4, 7	1, 8
Winter Wren	Crevice	R	Ground	1, 2, 3, 4, 6, 7	1, 2, 8
Golden-crowned Kinglet	Cup	R	Foliage	4, 6, 7	1
Varied Thrush	Cup	S	Ground	3, 5, 6	8
Hermit/Townsend's Warbler	Cup	L/S	Foliage	1, 6	1

[a] Cavity-nest in tree cavities; Crevice-nest in niches and behind bark; Cup-open cup nesters.
[b] L-long-distance migrant; R-resident; S-short distance migrant.
[c] Bark-bark gleaner; Drill-excavates insects from dead wood; Flycatch-sallies for insects from a perch; Foliage-gleans insects from foliage; Ground-gleans insects from ground; Omnivore-feeds on a variety of food types.
[d] Studies included: 1–Rosenberg and Raphael (1986); 2–Lehmkuhl et al. (1991); 3–McGarigal and McComb (1995); 4–Hejl and Paige (1994); 5–Schieck et al. (1995); 6–Manuwal and Manuwal (*this volume*, Table 6); 7–this study; 8–Brand and George (2001).

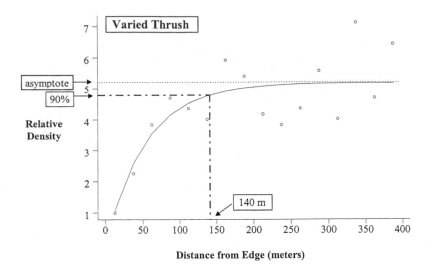

FIGURE 3.   Relative density with respect to distance from the forest edge and estimated edge width for the Varied Thrush. The points represent the band-specific relative density. The smooth curve represents the relative density based on an exponential regression model with one asymptote. The dash-dot line illustrates the edge width, defined as the distance from edge at which 90% of the asymptotic interior relative density has been achieved.

to new locations (Villard 1998). Brand and George (2000) found that predation on artificial nests that mimicked Varied Thrush and Winter Wren nests declined with distance from edge in redwood forest patches and that Steller's Jays were observed preying on the nests on several occasions. These results are consistent with the hypothesis that Winter Wrens and Varied Thrushes avoid forest edges because of higher nest predation. Steller's Jays are also more common on forest edges than forest interior locations (Brand and George 2001) and thus their presence could provide a proximate cue to nesting birds.

Other studies of artificial and natural nests have shown similar patterns with respect to distance from forest edge but there are many exceptions as well (Brand and George 2000, Sisk and Battin *this volume*). In addition, some studies suggest that predation rates on artificial nests may not reflect predation on real nests (Nour et al. 1993, Haskell 1995a, Willebrand and Marcstrom 1988, Wilson et al. 1998, Ortega et al. 1998, King et al. 1999). We found no difference in nesting success between edge (<100 m from forest edge) and interior (>100 m) nests for Winter Wrens, but nesting success of Swainson's Thrushes was lower on edges. Thus the pattern of decreasing nesting success with proximity to forest edge appears to be species-specific and more studies are needed to document the generality of this pattern.

Swainson's Thrush populations may be partic-

ularly vulnerable to increased predation along edges because thrushes are more abundant along edges in redwood forest patches (Brand and George 2001). Thus, thrushes may be experiencing an ecological trap (Gates and Gysel 1978) in this region, which could have severe effects on recruitment and population growth (Donovan and Lamberson 2001). Swainson's Thrush populations may be suffering poor recruitment in other parts of their range. Bednarz et al. (1998) found that Swainson's Thrushes are experiencing low nesting success in central Idaho, which they attributed to high levels of forest fragmentation in the region. Swainson's Thrushes have also been included in a draft list of species of special concern in California because of declines and a shrinkage of their breeding range in the Sierra Nevada mountains (T. Gardali, pers. comm.).

Regardless of the mechanism, edge avoidance has important implications for forest management. Information on the distance over which edge effects occur could provide important management guidelines for minimum widths of forest stands. Brand and George (2001) found that the distance to 90% of asymptotic interior relative density varied from 85 m for the Brown Creeper to 140 m for the Varied Thrush (Fig. 3). The average distance to 90% asymptotic density of the four forest interior species is approximately 115 m. The distance of 115 m from the forest edge also corresponds with the distance at which the probability of predation on artificial nests declines by half (Brand and George 2001). The edge widths estimated in Brand and George (2001) can be used to predict the patch sizes that may be suitable for particular forest interior species. For example, assuming that the average territory size for Varied Thrushes is 4 ha (George 2000), a circular patch of 19.6 ha would provide a 4 ha core with a 140 m buffer. Breeding Varied Thrushes were found to require a minimum patch size of approximately 16 hectares in coast redwood forests (Hurt 1996), close to the predicted size.

Another pattern that has been observed in studies in the eastern U.S. (Wilcove 1985) and Europe (Andrén et al. 1985, Angelstam 1986, Andrén and Angelstam 1988, Andrén 1992), is an increase in nest predation in forest fragments embedded within urban or agricultural landscapes as compared to regenerating forest or other more natural habitats. This may be due to an increase in generalist predators in landscapes that are dominated by agricultural or urban areas (Thompson et al. *this volume*). In redwood forest fragments, however, Brand and George (2000) found that rates of predation on artificial nests adjacent to rural (grassland) edge were significantly higher than nests located adjacent to suburbs, rivers, young forests, or roads. Thus, our results suggest that landscape context has a very different effect on rates of nest predation in the redwood region than in the eastern U.S. and Europe. Our results are consistent with those of Tewksbury et al. (1998) who found that rates of nest predation in riparian forests in Montana were higher in sites adjacent to undisturbed conifer forests than those adjacent to agricultural areas. Thus landscape context may not exert a predictable influence on rates of nest predation in western forests as it does in the eastern U.S. and Europe, perhaps due to the diversity of habitats and associated nest predators in the West. It is also possible that the various landscapes examined by Brand and George (2000) and Tewksbury et al. (1998) were not sufficiently different at the regional level to influence the predator community (Thompson et al. *this volume*).

Predation on artificial nests appears to be substantially lower in redwood forests than other forests. Approximately 69% of the artificial ground nests and 55% of the arboreal nests were intact after 14 days, which is substantially higher than has been found for most other studies conducted in fragmented forests of the eastern U.S. (Wilcove 1985, Yahner and Cypher 1987, Rudnicky and Hunter 1993, Whelan et al. 1994, Fenske-Crawford and Niemi 1997, Yahner and Mahan 1997). This difference may reflect lower overall avian abundance as well as lower predator activity in mature and old-growth redwood forests than in eastern deciduous forests.

Each of the species that showed evidence of area sensitivity in our survey also has been identified as an old-growth associate in one or more regions of the Pacific Northwest (Manuwal and Manuwal *this volume*, Table 2). This suggests that there may be an association between area sensitivity and dependence on old-growth forest habitat among the birds in this region. If this is the case, loss and fragmentation of old-growth forests may have a more severe impact on these species than predictions based on the area of old-growth forest alone.

EAST VS. WEST

The proportion of species showing evidence of sensitivity to habitat fragmentation in redwood forests (6/31 or 19%) is lower than the proportion that has been reported for studies in the eastern U.S. For example, Freemark and Collins (1992) reported that 34/70 or 49% of the species they examined showed evidence of area sensitivity, which is significantly higher than the proportion we observed ($\chi^2 = 7.67$, df $= 1$, P $= 0.006$). The proportions may change depending on what bird orders are included and the studies considered, but the pattern of a higher proportion of area sensitive species in forests of the eastern and midwestern U.S. relative to redwood forests is unlikely to change. In addition, given the overlap in species identified as area sensitive in the studies we examined, it is likely that this pattern holds for all Westside forests. We also found few long-distance migrants among the species that are area sensitive, which is very different from the eastern and midwestern U.S. where long-distance migrants predominate.

Our studies also suggest that the ecological processes that are responsible for area sensitivity among redwood forest birds may differ from those in the eastern U.S. Thompson et al. (*this volume*) have proposed a "top-down" hierarchical model where higher agricultural and human habitation at the regional scale results in increased predator and parasite numbers which in turn reduces the nesting success of birds in these landscapes. Contrary to the predictions of this model, we found that predation on artificial nests was significantly higher along natural grassland edges than suburban edges or roads. In addition, although predation on artificial nests declined with distance from forest edge, this pattern differed among species when we examined natural nests. Parasitism also was not a factor as none of the nests we monitored were parasitized by Brown-headed Cowbirds. Our studies suggest that area sensitivity in some species may be a result of edge avoidance and subsequent decline

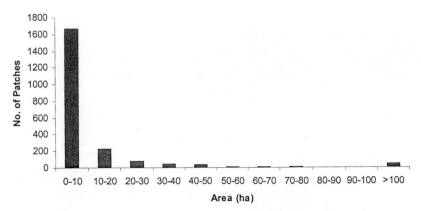

FIGURE 4. Size distribution of mature and old-growth redwood (*Sequoia sempervirens*) forest patches north of Point Reyes National Seashore. Based on Landsat satellite images (Fox 1997).

in small forest patches. This suggests a "bottom-up" mechanism where behavioral responses to edge result in changes in abundance in different sized patches.

MANAGEMENT IMPLICATIONS

Several bird species that breed in coast redwood forests are negatively affected by forest fragmentation. This means that the regional abundance of these species will be affected not only by the amount of mature and old-growth forest but also its distribution across the landscape. Most redwood forests are privately owned and are intensively managed for timber production, and it is unlikely that large amounts of land will be added to parks and reserves (Thornburgh et al. 2000). Thus, the abundance of these species in the region will be greatly influenced by how forest practices affect the distribution of mature forests across the landscape. Presently, 79% of the mature and old-growth redwood forest patches north of Point Reyes National Seashore are less than 10 ha (Fig. 4). This

is below the threshold for breeding occupancy by Varied Thrushes, and many of these patches may be poor or unsuitable habitat for the other species that are sensitive to fragmentation. Changes in forest practice rules that result in larger patches of mature forest on the landscape would greatly benefit these species and should be encouraged.

ACKNOWLEDGMENTS

Special thanks go to M. Hurt, C. Campbell, K. Melody, M. Wuestehube, J. Powell, and D. Kwasny who helped collect data. J. Kranz kindly provided data on nesting success of Swainson's Thrushes and Winter Wrens. S. Elliot helped with the preparation of the manuscript. Public land managers of Prairie Creek Redwoods State Park, Redwood National Park, Humboldt Redwoods State Park, and the Arcata Community Forest, as well as private landowners, were particularly helpful in granting permission to conduct this research. This study was funded by the Humboldt Area Foundation. Support for A. Brand during preparation of this paper was provided by SERDP project CS-1100.

Studies in Avian Biology No. 25:103–112, 2002.

EFFECTS OF HABITAT FRAGMENTATION ON BIRDS IN THE COASTAL CONIFEROUS FORESTS OF THE PACIFIC NORTHWEST

DAVID A. MANUWAL AND NAOMI J. MANUWAL

Abstract. Few studies have been done in the Pacific Northwest on the effects of habitat fragmentation on birds. Comparisons among studies is difficult because of different study designs and possible regional variation in bird response. Timber harvesting and human settlements have greatly fragmented the once vast amounts of old-growth forests. Forest patches of the Pacific Northwest are typically surrounded by forests of different ages rather than agricultural lands, as is found in much of eastern North America. In Washington, one three-year study showed that overall bird species richness and abundance varied little in a managed coniferous forest despite differing degrees of fragmentation. Some individual species, however, increased or decreased with the amount of clearcut area and other landscape variables. Species associated with open habitats or edges increased, while those associated with forests having a well-developed canopy decreased. There is substantial variation in avian response to landscape variables that characterize watersheds. At the stand level, canopy dwellers and cavity nesting species show the most negative response to increasing levels of canopy reduction, whereas species associated with the ground or shrub layer are least affected. Cowbird parasitism is negligible in the mountains of the Pacific Northwest, but apparently is more widespread in the large valleys such as the Puget Sound lowlands and Oregon's Willamette Valley where more farmland and urban, non-forest environments exist. More studies are needed on fragmentation effects on birds and cowbird parasitism in the region.

Key Words: birds; habitat fragmentation; Pacific Northwest.

Natural forces such as fire, floods, and volcanic eruptions have always created natural heterogeneity, but humans have accelerated fragmentation and caused reductions in suitable habitat in some biomes. In the early days of wildlife management, managers were encouraged to create fragmentation and edges since game species thrived in this environment (Leopold 1933, Allen 1962). With more knowledge of the biology of non-game species, we now know that there are edge-sensitive species that often decline in highly fragmented landscapes (Whitcomb et al. 1981, Ambuel and Temple 1983, Wilcove and Whitcomb 1983). The increased concern over the fate of neotropical migrant passerines has resulted in numerous studies in eastern North America (e.g., Howe 1984, Temple and Cary 1988, Robbins et al. 1989a, Terborgh 1989, Wilcove and Robinson 1990, Freemark and Collins 1992, Robinson 1992, Faaborg et al. 1995, King et al. 1998, Friesen et al. 1999, Rosenberg et al. 1999). Thus, most of the published information on this topic for the United States derives from research done east of the Rocky Mountains.

Based on the many studies of birds in the eastern portions of North America, the principal effects of forest fragmentation on birds are: (1) reduction in patch size and change of patch shape appear to negatively affect area-sensitive species, (2) species especially adapted to living in edge habitats increase, and (3) depending on landscape context, the increase in the amount of edge results in elevated predation rates and increased brood parasitism by the Brown-headed Cowbird (*Molothrus ater*). Few studies have been conducted on the effects of forest fragmentation on birds in the Pacific states. Until recently the emphasis has been on relating bird populations to forest age and structural characteristics (e.g., Manuwal and Huff 1987, Carey et al. 1991, Gilbert and Allwine 1991, Hansen et al. 1991, Manuwal 1991, Ralph et al. 1991; Hansen et al. 1995a,b). Our approach in this paper is to evaluate the effects of forest fragmentation on birds by reviewing published as well as unpublished studies of birds in the coniferous forests of western Washington, western Oregon, and northwestern California, and to present new information from three studies in Washington and Oregon.

RESULTS

CHARACTERISTICS OF FOREST FRAGMENTATION IN THE PACIFIC NORTHWEST

Until Euro-American settlement of the area about 150 years ago, forests in the Pacific Northwest were heterogeneous due to natural events such as wildfires. Approximately 50–60% of the forest land base was old-growth forest at the time of settlement (Franklin and Spies 1984, Booth 1991). Due to timber harvesting and other land use activities, only about 20% of the pre-settlement old-growth Douglas-fir (*Pseudotsuga menziesii*) forests remain (FEMAT 1993). Due to different management goals, the remaining forest is fragmented in a variety of ways (Figs. 1 and 2).

The forests of this region are under federal,

FIGURE 1. Typical forest fragmentation in the Oregon and Washington Cascades, Willamette National Forest, Oregon. Photo courtesy of U.S. Forest Service. Photo taken on 12 July 1987.

state, or private management. Private management, which includes forests managed by timber companies, forests owned by private ownership, and forests on Indian lands, traditionally have been harvested for profit as the major objective. This has resulted in large clearcuts, some over 1,000 ha. These large clearcuts are in various stages of regeneration, and some have been converted into plantations, which typically have a rotation time of 40–60 years (Garmen et al. in press). This does not allow for development of structure associated with mature or old-growth forests (>200 years; FEMAT 1993). These lands are regulated by state laws that mandate a riparian zone buffer, but this is generally narrow and

susceptible to edge effects such as windfall and increased insect infestation due to stress on the trees.

The federal lands are managed by agencies with different mandates. The lands administered by the National Park Service, and those designated as wilderness (which in this region are managed by the Forest Service) have a policy of no forest harvesting. Thus, they serve as a refuge for large (>1,000 ha) patches of old-growth forest. These protected forests are often at high elevation, or are bordered by forests that have undergone extensive cutting. The majority of the lands managed by the Forest Service have been harvested by cutting of small patches of

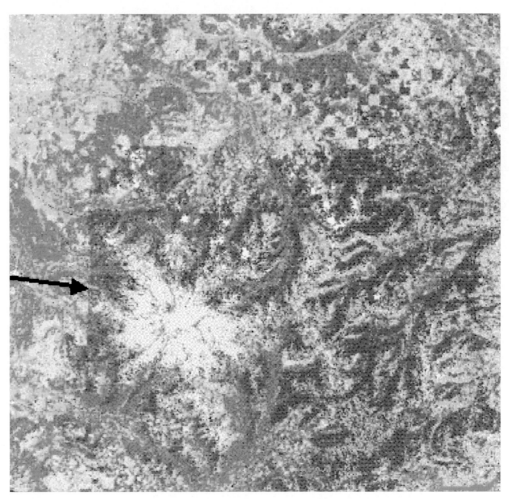

FIGURE 2. Digitized satellite image of western Washington in the Mount Rainier National Park area. Arrow denotes park boundary. Courtesy of C. Grue and K. Dvornich, Washington Gap Analysis.

forest within the old-growth matrix, which has resulted in a checkerboard effect (Franklin and Forman 1987). With time, further cuts between these areas have resulted in different-aged seral forests within the old-growth matrix, causing a loss of large (>1,000 ha) continuous old-growth areas. This technique also results in more edge area than the harvesting practices of the private sector (Spies et al. 1994). The Bureau of Land Management harvesting policy results in mid-sized patches.

The study conducted by Chen et al. (1992) provides insights into the effect of clearcuts on adjacent old-growth forests. They report that these effects include: (1) reduced canopy cover, (2) increased growth rates of Douglas-fir and western hemlock (*Tsuga heterophylla*), (3) elevated rates of tree mortality, and (4) more Douglas-fir and western hemlock seedlings but fewer

of Pacific silver fir (*Abies amabilis*; Chen et al. 1992). The effects of clear-cutting on vegetation characteristics of old-growth Douglas-fir forests ranged from 16 to 137 m for variables related to distance from the edge. Thus, some forest patches, especially those less than 10 ha, may be too small to preserve an interior forest environment (Chen 1991).

In Washington, approximately half of the 9,971,625 ha classed as forest lands are administered by federal agencies (McGinnis et al. 1997). Of this, about 11% is wilderness. In Oregon, Spies et al. (1994) clarified the differing rates of harvest in private and public ownership on a 2,589-km^2 study area. Between 1972 and 1988 the closed forest canopy declined from 71% to 58%. In those areas under private ownership, the decrease was from 50% to 28%, for a net loss of 45%. The non-wilderness lands under federal control declined from 79% to 68%, for a net loss of 13%. The amount of interior forest habitat (habitat not affected by edge factors) decreased from 35% to 12% on private lands, and from 60% to 43% on federally managed lands. Furthermore, internal forest patch size decreased from 160 ha to 62 ha. Internal forests of >1,000 ha comprised 50% of the study area in 1972; by 1988 they comprised only 26%. Contiguous interior forest patches (>5,000 ha) were found only in wilderness and research natural areas (Spies et al. 1994).

OVERVIEW OF SOURCES OF INFORMATION

Our assessment of the effects of fragmentation on birds is based on several studies that have used a wide variety of field methods and analytical approaches. Many studies were not designed specifically to investigate fragmentation effects but nevertheless contain information that is useful in this regard. The studies listed in Table 1 were done in coniferous forests from near sea-level to at least 1,500 m in elevation. The primary zones in which the community studies were conducted were the Douglas-fir/western hemlock zone and the Pacific silver fir zone in the Washington Cascades (Franklin and Dyrness 1988). A variety of landscape metrics were used in these studies to assess landscape-level effects on breeding birds. Areas that were measured varied from 100-ha to 300-ha circles around a surveyed site (Table 1). Other studies were conducted at the stand level.

LANDSCAPE-LEVEL STUDIES

Washington

Birds were surveyed on 24 intensively managed forest stands of different ages on the west slope of the Cascades during 1993–1995 (Aubry et al. 1997; D. A. Manuwal, unpubl. data). Birds detected within 50 m of 12 point count stations were used in this analysis. Each site was visited five times with 8 min count duration at each point (see Aubry et al. 1997 for details). Study sites were located on private industrial forest land in a highly fragmented landscape.

Landscape effects were examined at the individual bird species and community levels. Linear stepwise regressions were calculated for 28 bird species. Only species with at least 30 detections were used in the analysis. Each year was treated separately since there were yearly variations in bird species richness and abundance. Nine FRAGSTAT indices (Table 2; McGarigal and Marks 1995) were entered into the regression equations. Details of the results of these regression analyses for 28 species are in Aubry et al. (1997).

Significant relationships existed between in-

TABLE 1. SELECTED STUDIES IN WASHINGTON, OREGON, AND NORTHWESTERN CALIFORNIA DEALING WITH THE EFFECTS OF EDGE AND FRAGMENTATION ON BIRDS

Scale	Habitat	N	Study length (yrs)	Experimental	Size of unit	Number of landscape indices	Reference
Washington							
Stand	Riparian	18	3	Yes	—	—	Pearson and Manuwal 2001
Stand	Upland	18	3	Yes	—	—	Pearson and Manuwal 2001
Stand	Upland	24	3	No	100 ha	9	Aubry et al. 1997
Stand	Upland	12	3	Yes	—	—	Aubry et al. 1999; D. Manuwal unpubl. data
Oregon							
Landscape	Upland	30	3	No	300 ha	26	McGarigal and McComb 1995
California							
Stand	Upland	—	—	—	—	—	Rosenberg and Raphael 1986

TABLE 2. FRAGSTATS INDICES USED IN LANDSCAPE ANALYSIS OF BIRD SPECIES ABUNDANCE AND COMMUNITY CHARACTERISTICS

Index name (units)	Description[a]
CCAREA (ha)	Total area of clearcuts (3–8 yrs old)
CCED (m/ha)	Total amount of clearcut edge
MAT_AREA (ha)	Total area of mature forest (50–80 yrs old)
PATCHES	Number of patches
ED (m/ha)	Edge density
MNN (m)	Mean nearest neighbor index
SHDI	Shannon's Diversity Index
IJI (percent)	Interspersion and juxtaposition index
CONTAG (percent)	Contagion index

[a] See McGarigal and Marks (1995) for a complete description and definition of each index.

dividual species abundance and six of the nine FRAGSTAT indices. Nine bird species had a positive and eight species had a negative relationship with total clearcut area (CCAREA; Table 3). Virtually all species with a positive response (Table 3) are known to be associated with open, shrubby habitats, so even at the landscape level, these species tend to be most common in a landscape with a large amount of land in clearcuts. All nine bird species typically forage or nest either on the ground or in shrubs and small trees. These species are known as pioneer species and typically are the first ones to colonize recent clearcuts and fire sites. On the other hand, species having negative responses, such as the Winter Wren (*Troglodytes troglodytes*), Golden-crowned Kinglet (*Regulus satrapa*) and Chestnut-backed Chickadee (*Poecile rufescens*), are most often associated with forests with a well-developed canopy, so their response is somewhat predictable.

Eight species were positively correlated with total area of mature forest (MAT_AREA; Table 3). The Pacific-slope Flycatcher (*Empidonax difficilis*), Wilson's Warbler (*Wilsonia pusilla*), Hermit-Townsend's Warbler (either *Dendroica occidentalis* or *D. townsendi* or their hybrids; see Rohwer and Wood 1998), Red-breasted Nuthatch (*Sitta canadensis*), Hairy Woodpecker (*Picoides villosus*), and Evening Grosbeak (*Coccothraustes vespertinus*) all had significant positive responses to the amount of mature forest in the 100 ha circle. The Varied Thrush (*Ixoreus naevius*) and Winter Wren also had negative responses to clearcuts, so these two species may be attracted at the landscape level to more extensive stands of mature forests away from clearcuts.

The Orange-crowned Warbler (*Vermivora celata*) was the only species associated with the amount of clearcut edge. Chestnut-backed Chickadees had a negative association with edge density, indicating that this bird may be an area-sensitive species. The Swainson's Thrush (*Ca-*

tharus ustulatus) was negatively associated with an increasing number of habitat patches. Alternatively, the Dark-eyed Junco (*Junco hyemalis*), White-crowned Sparrow (*Zonotrichia leucophrys*), and Spotted Towhee (*Pipilo maculatus*) were positively associated with interspersion and juxtaposition. This seems to suggest that these species are attracted to habitat patchiness.

At the community level, no significant relationships were found between bird species richness and area of clearcuts or area of mature forests in any of the three years of the study. Similarly, no significant relationships were found between the number of bird detections and area of clearcuts or area of mature forests.

Oregon

McGarigal and McComb (1995) investigated bird community response to landscape structure in the central Oregon Coast Range. They sampled 10 landscapes (250–300 ha) in three basins. Each landscape was characterized by the amount of late-seral forest condition and relative fragmentation. Among the many bird species detected, 12 species were strongly associated with late seral forest condition but were also found in other forest conditions. Three species, the Olive-sided Flycatcher (*Contopus borealis*), Red-tailed Hawk (*Buteo jamaicensis*), and Western Wood-Pewee (*Contopus sordidulus*) were associated with habitats where there was a sharp edge between late-seral and early seral forests. Five species were positively associated with patch size: Gray Jay (*Perisoreus canadensis*), Brown Creeper, Winter Wren, Varied Thrush, and Chestnut-backed Chickadee. The following species were more abundant in fragmented landscapes: Red-breasted Sapsucker (*Sphyrapicus ruber*), Western Wood-Pewee, Olive-sided Flycatcher, and Red-tailed Hawk. The Winter Wren showed the most aversion to fragmented landscapes. Meyer et al. (1998) and Franklin and Gutierrez (*this volume*) examine the relationship

TABLE 3. SUMMARY OF RESPONSES OF BIRD SPECIES TO LANDSCAPE METRICS (SEE TABLE 2 FOR DESCRIPTION OF METRICS)

Variable	Bird species	Response (+ or −)	Variable	Bird species	Response
CCAREA	White-crowned Sparrow	+	MAT_AREA	Pacific-slope Flycatcher	+
	McGillivray's warbler	+		Wilson's Warbler	+
	American Goldfinch	+		Hermit/Townsend's Warbler	+
	Bewick's Wren	+		Varied Thrush	+
	Cedar Waxwing	+		Red-breasted Nuthatch	+
	Song Sparrow	+		Hairy Woodpecker	+
	Spotted Towhee	+		Evening Grosbeak	+
	Willow Flycatcher	+		Winter Wren	+
	Common Yellowthroat	−		Swainson's Thrush	−
	Winter Wren	−		American Robin	−
	Dark-eyed Junco	−		Orange-crowned Warbler	−
	Golden-crowned Kinglet	−		Black-headed Grosbeak	−
	Chestnut-backed Chickadee	−		Song Sparrow	−
	Wilson's Warbler	−			
	Hutton's Vireo	−	IJI2	Dark-eyed Junco	+
	Varied Thrush	−		White-crowned Sparrow	+
	Steller's Jay	−		Spotted Towhee	+
CCED	Orange-crowned Warbler	+			
ED	Chestnut-backed Chickadee	−			
PATCHES	Swainson's Thrush	−			

between habitat fragmentation and Spotted Owls (*Strix occidentalis*).

In general, McGarigal and McComb (1995) found a large amount of variation in response to a wide variety of landscape variables. Part of the difficulty in assessing species responses to habitat variables is the scale at which the comparisons was made. Bird abundance was generally greater in more fragmented landscapes. As is true for many other studies, uncommon species or those with large territories such as the Pileated Woodpecker (*Dryocopus pileatus*), are generally undersampled and their relationship with landscape variables could not be determined.

California

Raphael (1984) and Rosenberg and Raphael (1986) assessed the effects of forest fragmentation in Douglas-fir forests of northwestern California by examining point count survey data relative to 10 fragmentation measures at the plot (N = 136), stand (N = 46), and landscape levels. In general, bird species richness increased in fragmented stands. They also found that bird species richness at the plot and stand levels increased with proximity and extent of adjacent clearcut. They found 20 species associated with edges and 20 other species that avoided edges. Among the common species, only the Olive-sided Flycatcher was detected more often on the edge than in the forest interior. Birds showing the most negative responses to forest fragmentation were the Spotted Owl and Pileated Woodpecker, whereas the Sharp-shinned Hawk (*Accipiter striatus*) and Blue Grouse (*Dendragapus obscurus*) showed less population declines in fragmented areas.

LOCAL AND STAND-LEVEL EFFECTS

Washington riparian zones

In an attempt to determine the response of birds to harvest with two different riparian zone buffer widths, eighteen riparian areas within coniferous forests in the western Washington Cascades were studied in 1993, 1995, and 1996 (Pearson and Manuwal 2001). The clear-cuts created adjacent to the sampled riparian zones caused forest fragmentation and created large amounts of edge along the streams. Ten point count stations were visited where birds were counted for 6 min to determine avian relative abundance. Each study site was visited 5–6 times during the nesting season. All sites were studied for one year before harvest and sampled for two years after harvest to evaluate bird response to the buffer widths.

Species richness was higher after harvest in the uplands compared with unharvested controls. Wider buffer widths had higher species

richness than did unharvested sites. Predictably, species considered to be edge species, for example Dark-eyed Junco, Song Sparrow (*Melospiza melodia*), and Warbling Vireo (*Vireo gilvus*), increased after harvest. Some species, notably the Golden-crowned Kinglet, decreased significantly after harvest.

Washington and Oregon green tree retention

An experimental on-going study initiated in 1992 in the Pacific Northwest, called Demonstration of Ecosystem Management Options (DEMO), is designed to examine the effects of stand-level green tree retention on ecological attributes of the forest. This was a daunting task because of the scale of the study and public concern over continued cutting on National Forest lands. Details of the study design are given by Aubry et al. (1999). In general, it consists of a randomized block design of six treatments representing varying levels of green-tree retention. Each treatment unit is 13 ha in size and leave-trees (trees remaining after harvest) were either clumped (aggregated) or dispersed through the harvested area. Study sites were only in upland areas.

There are four blocks in Oregon and four in Washington. There is substantial variation in elevation between blocks (210–1,710 m), but usually only about 200–300 m variation within a block (Aubry et al. 1999). Birds were surveyed for two years before experimental retention harvests were made and only two blocks in Washington were surveyed after harvest since the other two blocks had not yet been harvested. An overview of this project and preliminary results of pre-treatment sampling is in Lehmkuhl et al. (1999). We report here some preliminary and geographically limited results of the responses of the following groups of birds: cavity-nesters, forest floor-dwellers, and canopy-dwellers (Table 4). Birds were surveyed by both point counts (4 points, 160 m apart, 6 visits) and territory-mapping (11 species only).

Among the three groups of species, forest floor-dwellers appeared to be less impacted by green-tree removal than the other two groups. Bird populations declined in virtually all conditions after harvest, even the control (100% retention) sites. The spring of 1998 was cold and wet in the Washington Cascades and several species of birds either failed in their first nesting attempt or nested late in the season (D. Manuwal, pers. obs.; M. Leu, pers. obs.). This may account for the lower than expected numbers of birds in control sites. Forest floor birds apparently recognize 75% retention sites as little different from untreated (100%) retention sites since there was no change in populations (Table

TABLE 4. PERCENT CHANGE IN NUMBER OF BIRD TERRITORIES TO GREEN-TREE RETENTION LEVELS AFTER HARVEST IN WASHINGTON IN 1998

	Cavity-nesters[a]		Canopy-dwellers[a]		Forest floor-dwellers[a]	
Level of retention	Butte	Paradise Hills	Butte	Paradise Hills	Butte	Paradise Hills
100% Retention (−0%)[b]	−67	−47	−30	−48	−48	−23
75% Aggregated (−25%)	−73	−73	−76	−73	+29	−29
40% Dispersed (−60%)	−64	−91	−66	−95	−26	−47
40% Aggregated (−60%)	−48	−54	−79	−53	−24	−61
15% Dispersed (−85%)	−80	−82	−93	−89	−48	−18
15% Aggregated (−85%)	−79	−85	−87	−91	−51	−50

[a] Cavity-nesters included: Brown Creeper, Chestnut-backed Chickadee and Red-breasted Nuthatch; canopy-dwellers included: Chestnut-backed Chickadee, Hermit Warbler, and Pacific-slope Flycatcher; forest floor-dwellers were: Dark-eyed Junco, Winter Wren, Varied Thrush.
[b] Amount of canopy reduction.

4). It seems clear that both dispersed and aggregated 15% retention offers little habitat for cavity-nesters and canopy-dwellers. The declines in number were close to the decline in green-tree canopy levels. These results and interpretations are preliminary and additional post-treatment sampling may show more definitive trends in bird community and individual species responses.

The adjustment of bird territory placement relative to retention level and dispersion is an especially interesting aspect of the study. Two examples of how birds adjusted their territories are the Dark-eyed Junco and the Hermit Warbler. The junco was a common bird on the study site, having 3 whole territories and 5 partial territories on a single 40% aggregated retention treatment site (Butte) before harvest. After harvest, there were 3 whole territories and 3 partial territories. Each junco territory contained portions of the retention circles as well as cleared area. This fits with the anticipated response of an edge species. Before harvest, the Hermit Warbler was the most abundant species on the study site; there were 12 complete territories and 5 partial territories on the site. After harvest all but 5 territories disappeared and each of those were located such that there was one territory per circular retention patch. Apparently, the patch contained a sufficient amount of canopy and associated insect prey to allow nesting to occur. We have no data on breeding success but all five males were paired. With additional post-harvest sampling in both Oregon and Washington, stronger conclusions can be drawn from this investigation on the response of birds to fragmentation at the stand level.

OTHER INDIVIDUAL SPECIES STUDIES

There are some studies of the effects of fragmentation on species of conservation concern in the Pacific Northwest such as the Spotted Owl (Meyer et al. 1998, Franklin and Gutierrez *this volume*), which is strongly positively associated with several landscape attributes of late successional forests. There are on-going studies of fragmentation effects on the Marbled Murrelet (*Brachyramphus marmoratus*; Raphael et al. *this volume*). As with studies of eastern bird communities, some species such as the Gray Jay, Brown Creeper, Winter Wren, Varied Thrush, and Chestnut-backed Chickadee tend to decrease with fragmentation and are often associated with late successional forests (Rosenberg and Raphael 1986, Manuwal 1991).

A long-term study of Northern Goshawk (*Accipiter gentilis*) demography, breeding behavior, and habitat selection for foraging and nesting on Washington's Olympic Peninsula was initiated in 1995 by Dan Varland and John Marzluff. Together with graduate students Sean Finn and Tom Bloxton, they are investigating the effects of the local- (forest stand) and landscape-level structure, composition, and spatial arrangement of forests on goshawks. The emphasis of the study is to understand how goshawks respond to habitat loss and fragmentation resulting from timber harvest. The first three years of study concentrated on surveying all known occupied nest areas on the Olympic Peninsula (N = 30) to determine if past habitat modification was correlated with current occupancy. Occupied stands differed from unoccupied ones primarily in having greater canopy closure, although the percentage of the surrounding landscape currently comprised of regenerating forest also was negatively correlated with occupancy. Therefore, fragmentation of the mature forest landscape may reduce occupancy of historical nest sites. However, their current research on the foraging and ranging habits of goshawks in fragmented forests suggest that individual pairs are extremely resilient to forest loss and fragmentation. Goshawks forage primarily in mature forests, but make use of regenerating forests and riparian gaps. They are notably unaffected by habitat loss and fragmentation that occurs while they are occupying an area. The working hy-

TABLE 5.   ABUNDANCE OF BROWN-HEADED COWBIRDS IN LOWLAND HABITAT OF WESTERN WASHINGTON FROM BREEDING BIRD SURVEYS (BBS)

BBS route	Name	Years	Mean/year	Population trend[a]
Sea level				
89907	Vashon Island	2	13.0	?
89905	Deception Pass	5	22.6	−
89072	Mukilteo	4	20.5	0
89034	Everett	15	10.5	−
Mean			16.7	
Lowlands, Cascade Foothills				
89111	Carnation	9	19.3	−
89066	Bayview	4	15.8	−
89133	Montesano	11	0.4	0
89078	Pe Ell	3	13.7	0
89059	Raymond	2	7.5	?
Mean			11.3	
Cascades-Low Elevation				
89904	Verlot	6	0.8	−
89902	Cascade River	9	1.2	−
89043	Packwood	19	3.0	−
Mean			1.7	

[a] ? indicates insufficient data; 0 no trend, − decreasing.

pothesis that links these apparently contradictory observations is that specific pairs acclimate and adjust to forest fragmentation in and around their breeding territories, but when these acclimated pairs die, new pairs are less likely to select the formerly occupied habitat for breeding. Lack of continued selection of fragmented habitat by goshawks produces the negative correlation between occupancy and fragmentation, while acclimation to fragmentation allows current territory owners to be unaffected by fragmentation.

BROWN-HEADED COWBIRD PARASITISM

The Brown-headed Cowbird is a relatively recent immigrant to the coastal regions of the Pacific States. It became established in portions of this region only since the 1950s (Rothstein 1994, Morrison and Caldwell *this volume*). In western Washington it may not have become established until a little later since Jewett et al. (1953:592) reported that the cowbird was (referring to the 1940s and 1950s) a "rare migrant and casual winter visitant in western Washington." Since the 1950s, the cowbird has become established as a breeding bird in western Washington but its distribution is clearly restricted to the Puget Trough lowlands. A review of 12 Breeding Bird Survey (BBS) routes in the Puget Sound area indicates that this species is relatively common in the highly fragmented open habitats from sea level up to the foothills of the Cascade Mountains (Table 5). Cowbird abundance decreases with elevation, or at least with a landscape in-

creasingly dominated by coniferous forests. Point count bird surveys in coniferous forests conducted from 1983 to 1998 in the Cascade Mountains at elevations ranging from 300 to 1500 m show that the Brown-headed Cowbird is virtually absent (7 detections out of a total 56,290 bird detections; Table 6) in this landscape even though it is fragmented (Figs. 1 and 2). The cowbirds we detected were in recent clearcuts adjacent to Douglas-fir forests. Factors preventing cowbird colonization of the fragmented coniferous forests in the Washington Cascades are unknown, but it is apparent that cowbird parasitism is not currently impacting potential hosts in the fragmented landscape of the Washington Cascades. Cowbirds are very rare there now but they could become a problem in the future. Cowbirds are relatively common in the Puget Sound Lowlands so parasitism is undoubtedly occurring there, but its extent has not been investigated. The proximity of the presently occupied areas to mountain habitat makes it possible that cowbirds may eventually occupy some of the Cascade and Coast Range montane forests. The effects of predation on songbird communities of the Pacific Northwest is poorly known. A current study by R. Sallabanks is exploring this aspect in managed forests of the Washington Cascades.

CONCLUSIONS

Fragmentation in the mountains of the Pacific Northwest consists of open areas created by clearcut or seed-tree logging in a matrix of for-

TABLE 6. NUMBERS OF BROWN-HEADED COWBIRDS DETECTED IN CONIFEROUS FORESTS OF THE CASCADE MOUNTAINS OF WASHINGTON AND OREGON

Data source[a]	N	Years	Cowbirds detected	Total bird detections
OGWHP	46	2	0	21,962
TFW-RMZ	18	3	0	6,032
TFW-Landscape	24	3	7	20,373
USFS-DEMO-WA	24	2	0	4,446
USFS-DEMO-OR	24	2	0	3,477
Total			7	56,290

[a] Data from point counts within 50 m of points except TFW-RMZ (within 15 m of points). Abbreviations: OGWHP (Manuwal 1991): 12 points, 6 visits, 8 min count duration; 1984, 1985. TFW-RMZ (S. Pearson and D.A. Manuwal, unpubl. data): 10 points, 6 visits, 6 min count duration; 1993, 1995, 1996. TFW-Landscape (Aubry et al. 1997): 12 Points, 6 visits, 8 min count duration, 1993, 1994, 1995. USFS-DEMO-WA (D.A. Manuwal unpubl. data): 4 stations, 6 visits, 8 min count duration; 1995, 1996. USFS-DEMO-OR (D.A. Manuwal unpubl. data): 4 stations, 6 visits, 8 min count duration; 1995, 1996.

ests of various ages. This pattern differs from many areas of eastern North America where forests are located near or adjacent to agricultural lands or human settlements. In the Pacific Northwest, fragmentation appears to be most extensive on private commercial timberlands compared with national forests. The Puget Sound Lowlands have some areas of agriculture, mixed with patches of forests, but this region has not been adequately studied.

The effects of forest fragmentation are not well documented in the Pacific Northwest compared with the many studies in eastern North America [e.g., those cited in Hagan and Johnston (1992) and Martin and Finch (1995)]. Nevertheless, some patterns seem to be emerging from recent studies. Species richness seems to increase in highly fragmented landscapes, chiefly because of the colonization of edge species, which often nest or forage in open, shrubby habitats. However, interior forest birds may be declining under these conditions. The identification of specific landscape variables responsible for this has been difficult to determine, perhaps because birds such as the Winter Wren and Hermit Warbler, which have small territories, respond to stand-level factors rather than large scale ones. There are no long term studies in the Pacific Northwest so we have no information on how fragmentation affects bird abundance. Short-term investigations indicate that some species increase while others decrease with fragmentation, a pattern also observed in the eastern United States.

Brood parasitism and predation have been shown to be a major concern in the fragmented environments of eastern North America (e.g., Robinson et al. 1995b), but there is no evidence that parasitism is an important factor in the coastal mountains of the Pacific Northwest. However, this could become a problem as more forested land is cleared and converted to more open habitat.

Coniferous forests in the Pacific Northwest are naturally heterogeneous because of the effects of fire, wind-throw, floods, and volcanic eruptions. Compared with habitat fragmentation in much of eastern North America, fragmentation in the mountains of the Pacific Northwest is fundamentally different in that forest patches are not surrounded by agricultural land or areas dominated by human development. Instead, forest patches are surrounded by other forest patches of different ages. Late successional forest patches remaining after timber harvesting have become smaller in recent decades and are less suitable for area-sensitive bird species than larger patches. Cowbird brood parasitism is not common in the mountains but does occur in lowland habitats. It is clear that much more research is needed in the Pacific Northwest to determine relationships between birds and forest fragmentation.

ACKNOWLEDGMENTS

We thank S. Garman, T. Spies, and J. Franklin for sharing their information on Pacific Northwest vegetation. C. Grue and K. Dvornich, Washington Cooperative Fish and Wildlife Research Unit, Washington Gap Analysis, provided us with digital maps. S Reutebush provided the aerial photograph of Willamette National Forest. We are grateful to the Washington Department of Natural Resources (Timber, Fish and Wildlife Agreement) for funding the riparian management zone and landscape studies in Washington, and the U.S. Forest Service, Pacific Northwest Forest Experiment Station, Portland, OR, for funding the DEMO project. The efforts of many field ornithologists associated with these projects are gratefully acknowledged.

Studies in Avian Biology No. 25:113–129, 2002.

BIRDS AND CHANGING LANDSCAPE PATTERNS IN CONIFER FORESTS OF THE NORTH-CENTRAL ROCKY MOUNTAINS

SALLIE J. HEJL, DIANE EVANS MACK, JOCK S. YOUNG, JAMES C. BEDNARZ, AND RICHARD L. HUTTO

Abstract. We describe historical and current landscape patterns for the north-central Rocky Mountains, speculate on the expected consequences of human-induced changes in coniferous forest patterns for birds, and examine the evidence related to the expected consequences. The Rocky Mountain region has one of the most heterogeneous landscapes in North America, combining high complexity in abiotic gradients with fire as a major disturbance factor. In recent decades fire suppression has limited this disturbance, resulting in altered stand structures and relatively homogeneous expanses of mid-successional forest where there were once mosaics of different-aged post-fire stands. Elsewhere, historically homogeneous landscapes that rarely burned have become more heterogeneous due to logging. Many forest types are less common than they were historically due to current management. Land conversion to agriculture and development has primarily occurred in low elevations. We speculate that the consequences of these changes include: (1) bird species adapted to historically homogeneous forest landscapes would be negatively affected by landscape heterogeneity created by timber harvest openings; (2) bird species specialized for forest types that were once prevalent but are now uncommon may be negatively affected by decreasing patch size and increasing isolation; and (3) birds that breed in close proximity to human-added landscape features may be negatively affected by brood parasites or nest predators. Brown Creeper (*Certhia americana*) and Golden-crowned Kinglet (*Regulus satrapa*) had the strongest trends of species sensitive to fragmentation indices. Pine Siskin (*Carduelis pinus*), Chipping Sparrow (*Spizella passerina*) and Dark-eyed Junco (*Junco hyemalis*) were positively associated with fragmentation across most studies. Nesting success varied among landscape configurations, and some trends paralleled abundance patterns. Brown-headed Cowbird (*Molothrus ater*) parasitism rates were extremely low (0–3%) where nest success has been studied in coniferous forests of the north-central Rockies. Across extensive and intensive studies, distance to agricultural lands was the strongest predictor of cowbird presence. Therefore, we found evidence for the ideas that birds adapted to homogeneous forest landscapes have been negatively affected by heterogeneity caused by timber harvesting, that patch size is important for some birds in one vanishing habitat (old-growth ponderosa pine, *Pinus ponderosa*), and that cowbirds are more abundant in conifer forests near human-added landscape features. The effects of changes in landscape patterns on birds in the north-central Rockies seem to be less dramatic than in eastern and midwestern North America, and different landscape measures are more relevant to western conifer forests. We need additional research on most aspects of breeding, nonbreeding, and dispersal ecology in relation to landscape patterns and within-stand changes. We offer our proposed consequences as hypotheses upon which to base future tests.

Key Words: birds; fire; fire regimes; fire suppression; forest fragmentation; north-central Rockies; landscape; landscape patterns; wildfire.

Forest fragmentation has clearly affected birds in some landscape configurations in the East and Midwest (Porneluzi et al. 1993, Donovan et al. 1995a, Robinson et al. 1995a). In landscapes where forests are fragmented by agriculture and urbanization, resulting in discrete measurable patches, species richness has been shown to increase with patch area and decrease as patches become more isolated (Whitcomb et al. 1981, Ambuel and Temple 1983, Freemark and Merriam 1986, Blake and Karr 1987). The presence or absence of a species across patches of different sizes suggested minimum area requirements (Temple 1986, Askins et al. 1987, Robbins et al. 1989a). Nesting success declined (Villard et al. 1993, Donovan et al. 1995b), and edge effects (as indicated by nest predation and parasitism) were particularly strong where the landscape matrix had been highly modified (Robinson

1992). These studies identified long-distance migrants as particularly sensitive to area effects.

The effects of landscape changes on bird populations in conifer forests in the West seem to be less dramatic (Rosenberg and Raphael 1986, McGarigal and McComb 1995). Historical and current landscape patterns are quite different in the West than in the East and the Midwest, especially in the mountainous and sparsely populated north-central Rocky Mountains. Conifer forests dominate the mountain slopes of this region, and conversion of lands to agriculture and urban development generally has been restricted to valley bottoms. While the natural heterogeneity of these conifer forests was variable, fire suppression and timber harvest have created landscape patterns with different kinds and levels of heterogeneity. Nonetheless, they remain forested ecosystems that may not present barriers to many native species (McIntyre and Barrett 1992). The response of avian species to this dynamic mosaic may be species-specific and process-specific (Haila 1999). Edge effects may also be substantially different in forest-dominated landscapes than in agricultural ones (Hanski et al. 1996, Bayne and Hobson 1997).

Different measures of landscape patterns are more relevant to landscapes in western conifer forests than those used in the East and Midwest. For example, size and isolation of an individual forest patch is almost impossible to measure in conifer forests of the north-central Rockies because the forest is the matrix rather than the patch, with most stands connected in some way to other conifer forests that may or may not be similar in age, species composition, and structure. The exceptions include rarer forest types, such as old-growth ponderosa pine (*Pinus ponderosa*) or patches of recent fire disturbance. Measures of fragmentation in western conifer forests are thus better achieved by characterizing patterns within a defined landscape, based on relative amounts of forest and amounts and types of edges. More complex variables may be necessary, such as measures of connectivity (Taylor et al. 1993). When patch size is used, patch boundaries often are created somewhat artificially when a user-defined landscape outline is imposed onto the forest matrix for analysis. Because of these constraints, studies in western coniferous forests usually describe the structure of the landscape mosaic in which the forest is embedded (see Wiens 1989) and then relate that structure to avian populations (Rosenberg and Raphael 1986, van Dorp and Opdam 1987, McGarigal and McComb 1995, Schieck et al. 1995).

We investigated whether bird populations are related to landscape changes in north-central Rocky Mountain conifer forests and whether these relationships are similar to what has been reported for other regions. We define the north-central Rockies as that area from eastern Oregon and Washington east through Idaho and western Montana to Wyoming (Fig. 1). We include aspen (*Populus* spp.) in our discussion of conifer forests because it is an integral part of many conifer landscapes. To look at the relationships between birds and landscape patterns, we (1) describe historical landscape patterns and the processes responsible for them; (2) describe current landscape patterns and their causes; (3) discuss implications and potential consequences of human-induced changes between historical and current patterns for coniferous forest birds; (4) examine the current evidence surrounding the expected consequences; and (5) compare our findings for the north-central Rockies to other regions.

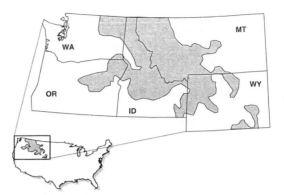

FIGURE 1. The north-central Rocky Mountain geographic area. Rocky Mountain forest type boundaries from Bailey's (1995) ecoregions of the United States, including portions of northern, middle, and southern Rocky Mountain steppe provinces.

HISTORICAL LANDSCAPE PATTERNS

Natural landscape heterogeneity results from the superposition of a disturbance regime onto vegetation patterns created by abiotic gradients (Turner and Romme 1994). Historically, the north-central Rocky Mountain region had one of the most heterogeneous landscapes of any area in North America due to a dry climate and frequent lightning-caused fires, and this disturbance regime was superimposed on complex vegetation patterns resulting from moisture gradients and finely dissected topography.

Characterizing natural or presettlement landscapes can be a very difficult task (Noss 1985, Sprugel 1991). The evidence is scattered and subject to many potential biases (Noss 1985). In the recent bioregional assessment of the interior Columbia River Basin, Hann et al. (1997) used scattered evidence, expert opinion, and simulation models to estimate broad-scale landscape patterns across the region for the 1850–1900 time period. The mid-scale assessment associated with that project (Hessburg et al. 1999) used historical aerial photographs to characterize landscape conditions in sampled watersheds, but historical photos could be found for only the "recent historical" period of the 1930s to 1960s.

Even if accurate historical data could be recovered for one point in time, the dynamic nature of the disturbance regimes diminishes the usefulness of that information. Fire size and severity depend on previous disturbance history (e.g., fuel buildup) as well as cyclic weather patterns (Bessie and Johnson 1995). There is growing evidence that fire disturbance was extremely variable historically and probably not in equilibrium across the landscape (Sprugel 1991, Turner and Romme 1994, Brown et al. 1999). In addition, native Americans altered fire regimes for hundreds of years before Euro-American settlement (Barrett and Arno 1982). Therefore, any characterizations of historical landscape patterns must be considered generalizations and take into account the highly variable nature of the landscape.

ABIOTIC FACTORS

The north-central Rockies are composed of many mountain ranges of varying ruggedness and orientation. Moisture varies with elevation and topography, and there is also a regional gradient in rainfall due to continental climate patterns (Habeck and Mutch 1973, Peet 1988). Finely dissected topography interweaves land units of very different slopes, soils, moisture retention properties, and exposures, and these patterns occur at several spatial scales. Local landscape vegetation patterns are strongly influenced by these abiotic gradients.

Higher elevations have lower temperatures and receive more precipitation. Annual precipitation in the north-central Rockies ranges from less than 380 mm in intermontane valleys to more than 1500 mm at higher elevations (Habeck and Mutch 1973). These local temperature and moisture patterns create zones of forest habitat types based on the physiological requirements and competitive abilities of the various tree species (Daubenmire 1956). For example, in much of the north-central Rockies, the driest and lowest-elevation forests historically were dominated by ponderosa pine, which remains an important early-seral species up into the mid-elevation zone, where Douglas-fir (*Pseudotsuga menziesii*) was typically the major tree species in climax vegetation. The less drought-resistant Engelmann spruce (*Picea engelmanni*) and subalpine fir (*Abies lasiocarpa*) compete for climax status only in the more moist, upper-elevation zones. Each of these zones had different fire regimes (Arno 1980). Fire in many of these regimes maintained large areas dominated by shade-intolerant (early-seral) tree species, including ponderosa pine, lodgepole pine (*Pinus contorta*), western larch (*Larix occidentalis*), sometimes grand fir (*Abies grandis*) and Douglas-fir, and, historically, western white pine (*Pinus monticola*).

Local topography and soils can drastically alter available nutrients, solar radiation, temperature, and water retention (Peet 1988, Swanson et al. 1988). South-facing slopes and ridge tops are much warmer and drier and may support vegetation typical of lower elevations, if soils allow. Sheltered valley bottoms have lower solar radiation and may collect water and cold-air pockets that support vegetation more character-

istic of that nearly 500 m higher on open slopes (Peet 1988). Naturally treeless areas occur wherever slopes are too steep or rocky, or where there is prolonged summer soil drought (Daubenmire 1968). Areas on the east side of the Continental Divide especially have widespread occurrence of forest-grassland-sagebrush mosaics, probably regulated by the availability of moisture (Patten 1963) and the frequency of fire (Arno and Gruell 1983).

In contrast, moist Pacific air reaches a limited area in southeastern British Columbia, northeastern Washington, northern Idaho, and northwestern Montana. The resulting luxuriant forests in this region appear similar to forests in the Cascade Mountains (Peet 1988), with tree species including western hemlock (*Tsuga heterophylla*), western redcedar (*Thuja plicata*), and grand fir (Habeck 1987). The combination of greater precipitation and gentler topography results in relatively continuous forests in this region, including the valley bottoms where there is often no well-defined lower timberline.

DISTURBANCE

Disturbance imposes further heterogeneity on the landscape, at several spatial scales, by producing a mosaic of age classes and successional communities. Fire was historically the most prevalent natural disturbance in the northern Rocky Mountains (Gruell 1983).

The extent and severity of fires in the north-central Rockies depended on the moisture gradient, which varied temporally as well as spatially (Arno 1980). Forests in more mesic areas burned less often (every 50–300 years; Table 1), so they were more likely to reach later successional stages and to accumulate larger amounts of woody fuels, not burning until sufficient fuels and weather conditions produced a stand-replacing crown fire. Forests in drier areas would burn more often (every 5–50 years; Table 1), before sufficient fuels could accumulate to result in a crown fire. These frequent underburns destroyed seedlings of shade-tolerant tree species while causing minimal harm to fire-resistant early-seral trees, thus maintaining non-climax stands of old-growth ponderosa pine and western larch (Arno et al. 1997).

Historically, old-growth ponderosa pine and western larch dominated millions of acres on drier valley bottoms and south facing slopes throughout much of the north-central Rockies (Arno et al. 1997). Although these "fire-dependent" (Habeck 1988) forests could be extensive, complex topography and moisture gradients usually made these forests less homogeneous than in the Southwest (Arno 2000). Heterogeneity could occur at several scales, with grassland-for-

TABLE 1. REPORTED MEAN AND RANGE OF HISTORICAL FIRE INTERVALS IN GENERAL CONIFEROUS FOREST CLASSES

General habitat class[a]	Description	Mean fire intervals[b] (yrs)	Fire interval range[b] (yrs)	Predominant fire regime[c]
Limber pine	Mostly small stands mixed with grass and shrubs on dry or rocky sites	74	variable	Nonlethal?
Warm, dry ponderosa pine or Douglas-fir	Open stands, with grass understory maintained by frequent fire	5–30	2–55	Nonlethal
Warm, moist ponderosa pine	Typically ponderosa pine dominant with an understory of Douglas-fir in the absence of fire	10–49	3–97	Nonlethal
Cool, dry Douglas-fir	Generally open stands of Douglas-fir with sparse understory	35–40	variable?	Nonlethal
Moist Douglas-fir	Douglas-fir often dominates; closed-canopy ponderosa pine, larch, and lodgepole pine common in seral stages	25–30	8–66	Mixed
Grand fir/mixed conifer	Diverse closed-canopy forest; often develops into mixed species stand	13–120	5–150	Mixed-Lethal
Cool lodgepole pine	Pure stands of lodgepole pine or mixed with grand fir and whitebark pine	24–50	1–88	Lethal-Mixed
Subalpine fir and codominant species	Spruce and other firs common in seral stages; stand-replacement fires common	57–153	50–300	Lethal
Moist redcedar and western hemlock	Closed-canopy stands of redcedar and western hemlock	70–120	25–200	Lethal

[a] General classes of forest habitat types employed by U.S. Forest Service (Steele et al. 1981), arranged approximately on a dry to moist gradient.
[b] Fire-interval estimates from Arno 1980, Arno and Gruell 1983; Arno et al. 1995, 1997; Crane and Fischer 1986, Gruell et al. 1982, Gruell 1983.
[c] Historical fire regime thought to occur over most acreage; all habitat types could have all fire types.

est mosaics at the drier extremes and with denser forests created by stand-replacing fires at the wetter extremes. East of the Continental Divide, where it is too dry for larch and too cold for ponderosa pine, Douglas-fir forests often had similar fire regimes (Arno and Gruell 1983). In very dry years, stand-replacement fires may have occurred in any of these areas (Bessie and Johnson 1995, Brown et al. 1999).

In the more mesic areas of the north-central Rockies (maritime-influenced forests, north-facing slopes, and mid- to high-elevation forest types), the predominant fire regime was one of infrequent, stand-replacement fires (Arno and Davis 1980, Romme 1982, Fischer and Bradley 1987, Barrett et al. 1991). In fact, the origin of most Rocky Mountain forest stands can be traced to stand-replacement fires (Arno 1980).

Historically, most individual fires were small (<1 ha; Strauss et al. 1989), because fuels were too moist or sparse to spread the fire. However, most of the area burned by stand-replacement fires was due to a few large fires in dry years (Strauss et al. 1989, Bessie and Johnson 1995), so it was the large fires that created the vegetation mosaic that dominated the landscape until the next extensive fire (Turner and Romme 1994). Large crown fires rarely consumed an entire forest because of local variations in wind, topography, vegetation type, natural fire breaks, and fuel loads (Turner et al. 1994). These factors produced a heterogeneous pattern of burn severity, as well as islands of unburned vegetation (Eberhart and Woodard 1987, DeLong and Tanner 1996). The degree of patchiness depended on the dryness of fuels in the year of the fire (Turner et al. 1994, Turner and Romme 1994).

Data on natural fire intervals in different forest cover types suggest that fire severity and frequency were highly variable prior to current fire suppression activities (Table 1). Frequent nonlethal fires and infrequent stand-replacement fires could occur in the same region depending on weather and fuel accumulations, or individual fires may have been of "mixed severity," with many trees dying and many surviving (Brown 1995, Arno 2000). Mixed-severity fire regimes occurred especially in mid-elevation, mixed-conifer forests, where moisture regimes and topography were variable, and fire-resistant tree species (especially larch and ponderosa pine) occurred. Mixed-severity fires produced heterogeneity at several scales, killing variable amounts of trees within a forest stand and affecting variable numbers of stands within a landscape. The moisture regime influenced this variability in size, with drier areas tending to have smaller patches of lethal burns because fires burned often enough to prevent sufficient fuel accumulation for extensive crown fires (Barrett et al. 1991). This typically left a patchy, erratic pattern on the landscape that fostered development of highly diverse communities (Barrett et al. 1991, Arno 2000, Lyon et al. 2000).

CURRENT TRENDS

In the north-central Rockies, most changes in landscape patterns from historical to current are the result of changes in the disturbance regimes due to fire suppression and timber harvesting. The resulting forests may differ in age, structure, species composition, or landscape pattern, but they remain conifer forests. The little land conversion that has occurred is focused within the lower elevations where forest or grassland has been converted to agricultural land, rural residences, or urban areas.

FIRE SUPPRESSION

Fire suppression has become increasingly effective since the 1930s (Arno 1980, Barrett et al. 1991). Through much of the low and mid-elevation landscapes, fire suppression has altered stand structures and landscape patterns throughout the north-central Rockies (Tande 1979, Arno 1980, Barrett et al. 1991). Because dry, lowland areas had fire-return intervals of 5–50 years, the suppression of low-intensity fires for up to 70 yrs has resulted in abnormal fuel accumulations that make the historically resistant old-growth pine and larch more susceptible to stand-replacement fire.

Hann et al. (1997) estimated that 19% of the interior Columbia River Basin has changed to a lethal fire regime from mixed or non-lethal over the last century. Complex, uneven-aged stands containing fire-resistant trees are being replaced by even-aged post-fire stands that cover large areas of the landscape (Hann et al. 1997). Future fires that burn in this simplified landscape may be larger and more homogeneous, so the homogeneity may be self-perpetuating (Arno 1980, 2000; Barrett et al. 1991).

Many areas naturally had heterogeneous landscapes due to a mosaic of successional stages following stand-replacement fires. Here, fire suppression is converting this mosaic of forest stands from a variety of age classes into a more homogeneous expanse of mid-successional mature forest (Hann et al. 1997). Because succession changes forest structure most rapidly in the earliest age classes, it has taken only a few decades for fire suppression to allow large expanses of closed-canopy, continuous forest to form on the landscape (Tande 1979). However, in areas with stand-replacement fire regimes, the time period of successful fire suppression may not yet be long enough to greatly affect the historical fire-return intervals of 140 to 400 years (Romme 1982, Barrett et al. 1991).

Fire suppression also reduces many unique post-fire habitats on the landscape. Early post-fire patches of standing dead trees are much reduced throughout the region. There also has been a loss of shade-intolerant tree species, such as ponderosa pine, larch, and aspen, as succession advances in the absence of fires (Hann et al. 1997). Fire-maintained old-growth ponderosa pine stands are an obvious example, but western larch also formed large, open stands of fire-maintained old growth (Arno et al. 1997). Larch is restricted to relatively more mesic areas than ponderosa pine, but it is the most shade-intolerant and fire-resistant conifer species in the north-central Rockies (Arno and Fischer 1995), so it is an important early-seral species as well as being an important older-aged component of forests in mixed-severity fire regimes. Aspen is another early-seral tree species that regenerates following fire. In the Centennial Mountains of Idaho, aspen cover has been reduced 80% since 1850, while mature conifer forest increased in area, patch size, and connectivity (Hansen and Rotella 2000). Increasing isolation may be another landscape factor affecting stands of these tree species.

TIMBER HARVEST

With the suppression of fires, timber harvesting is now the most important disturbance returning conifer forests to early successional stages. It is unclear whether the total area involved is similar, however. Hann et al. (1997) estimated that the current areal extent of early-successional stands in moist forests (20%) is at the low end of the historical (pre-1900) range (19–29%), is about the same (18%) as historical in low-elevation dry forests (8–20%), and higher (33%) than historical (23–25%) in upper-elevation cold forests. There are great differences, however, in the landscape patterns and stand structures produced by timber harvest compared with fire (Hann et al. 1997). Whether timber harvest increases or decreases landscape heterogeneity depends on the natural heterogeneity of the area (i.e., fire regime and topography), the harvest methods used, and the spatial scale at which analyses are done.

Timber harvest has greatly reduced the accessible, low-elevation dry forests that historically had non-lethal fire regimes and were dominated by old-growth ponderosa pine or western larch. Accessible forests were preferentially logged first, with more distant ones harvested as technology improved and road systems were created (Hejl 1994). Few old-growth stands remain. In the national forests of eastern Oregon and Washington, where the original low- and mid-elevation ponderosa pine forests may have been about 90% old growth, nearly three-quarters of this old growth had been logged by 1970 (Henjum et al. 1994). In addition, 82% of the remaining old-growth patches are smaller than 100 acres, with only 7 patches over 5,000 acres (Henjum et al. 1994). Fire suppression has resulted in further danger to these patches by allowing the buildup of fuels and converting patches to denser forests with more shade-tolerant tree species. Hann et al. (1997) estimated that the ponderosa pine cover type decreased by 26% throughout the interior Columbia River Basin since 1900. Open-canopy old growth has diminished even more (Henjum et al. 1994). Timber harvesting in combination with fire suppression has also reduced old-growth larch on the landscape. Hann et al. (1997) estimated that the western larch cover type (all ages) has decreased by 36% throughout the interior Columbia River Basin since 1900.

Mid-elevation forest with mixed-severity fire regimes historically had a diversity of stand structures and landscape patterns. Timber harvesting returns some patch heterogeneity to these forests, but generally on a coarser-grained scale than produced by natural fires, with a more regular pattern (Reed et al. 1996a). Clearcuts do not retain the remnant trees or snag structure typical of post-fire forests, nor do they create an environment that could maintain the historical complexity of community composition and structure. Consequently, most of the early-seral forest stands within this type are very different in composition and structure relative to the native conditions (Hann et al. 1997). Harvest methods that retain green trees (e.g., Lehmkuhl et al. 1999) may better mimic some mixed-severity fires, but still lack the snag structure or large, downed woody debris. If the same prescription is always used for this type of cutting, it will produce a relatively simplified and homogeneous landscape.

The most productive forests in this region were the "Cascadian" forests around northern Idaho, where fires were rare and, therefore, large blocks of old growth likely developed. Once fairly homogeneous landscapes have been riddled with clearcuts and other logged conditions. In these and other forests with stand-replacement fire regimes, (e.g., high-elevation lodgepole pine), the creation of many small clearcuts is a departure from the pattern of disturbance created by the natural fire regime (Brown 1995). Similarly, in boreal forests in Canada, DeLong and Tanner (1996) found that wildfires created a more complex landscape pattern than clearcut harvesting practices do, with a greater diversity of patch sizes, more irregular shapes and boundaries, and more patches of mature forest intermixed. These patches may be critical for bird species that require heterogeneity in patch structure. They also provide sources of large trees and snags (legacies) within the young post-disturbance forest (DeLong and Tanner 1996). No cutting method can create the dense snag structure that is produced by a stand-replacement fire.

It is unclear if timber harvest has created more fragmentation than natural disturbance regimes. Reed et al. (1996a) found a substantial increase in patchiness created by clearcutting and roads from 1950 to 1993 in high elevation forests in the Medicine Bow Mountains of southern Wyoming. Quantitative landscape indices suggested a level of fragmentation greater than that found in the Oregon Cascades. However, the disturbance patterns in Wyoming were superimposed on a landscape of natural heterogeneity, and it is unknown what the landscape in either 1950 or 1993 would have been like under a natural fire regime. Tinker et al. (1998) found similar results in the Bighorn Mountains of north-central Wyoming. Old-growth forest patches produced by natural disturbances in western coniferous forests were typically much larger and more continuous than are the remnant patches created by timber harvesting and road building (Tinker et al. 1998). However, they found that roads contributed more to this change in landscape indices than did clearcuts. It is not known if roads are wide enough to cause harmful fragmentation effects for most Rocky Mountain bird species, especially in open forests, but roads are certainly a more permanent disturbance than clearcuts (Reed et al. 1996b).

However atypical the landscape pattern produced by timber harvesting may be, it still leads to forest succession and the retention of natural vegetation. A potentially more serious impact on the forested landscape is the permanent conversion of native habitat to agriculture or residential and urban development (including roads). In the north-central Rockies, this conversion has been concentrated in the valley bottoms. While this limits the amount of fragmentation in the overall landscape, these low elevation areas are also the most productive ecosystems for birds (Hansen and Rotella 1999). As rural development accelerates in the inland west (Knight 1997), we may see much more serious fragmentation and edge effects on birds due to added human features on the landscape (e.g., Friesen et al. 1995).

PROPOSED CONSEQUENCES OF LANDSCAPE CHANGES ON BIRDS

Based on our knowledge of the historical landscape patterns of the region and the changes that have occurred, we speculate about which birds we would expect to be most affected by landscape changes in the past 100 years in north-central Rockies conifer forests. We offer these speculations as a framework from which to examine the data that exist on bird trends and bird relationships with landscape patterns. The proposed consequences of landscape changes on birds are: (1) species that are adapted to moist forest types that historically formed the most homogeneous landscapes (e.g., old-growth cedar/hemlock) would be negatively affected by increased landscape heterogeneity created by timber harvest openings; (2) species specialized for forest types that were once prevalent but are now uncommon or rare (i.e., vanishing habitats: aspen, early post-fire forests, old-growth ponderosa pine, and old-growth larch) may be negatively affected by decreasing patch size and increasing isolation over and above the general loss of habitat; and (3) birds that breed in close proximity to human-added landscape features (such as cows, horses, bird feeders, agricultural land, or residential development) may be negatively affected by brood parasites or nest predators that are attracted to these features. More than one of these consequences could be occurring in any one particular landscape.

HAS FOREST FRAGMENTATION AFFECTED BIRDS OF THE NORTH-CENTRAL ROCKIES?

To evaluate whether and how coniferous forest birds are affected by changes in landscape patterns, we looked for evidence from each of three sources: (1) regional population trends based on the North American Breeding Bird Survey; (2) studies concerning relationships between bird abundance and specific landscape characteristics, including the effects of logging; and (3) studies concerning relationships between nesting success and human-caused landscape modification.

BBS TRENDS

We assumed that if populations of some bird species are declining as the result of changing conditions brought on by fire suppression and intense timber harvesting activities, then the recent 33 years of Breeding Bird Survey (BBS) data (1966–1998) collected from within the region should reflect that fact, although there may be other reasons for any observed declines. Thus, we determined how many conifer forest bird species breed in the north-central Rocky Mountains, which ones are adequately covered by the BBS, and what the BBS data indicated about their recent population trends. We focused our analysis on the Central Rockies region, as defined by Robbins et al. (1986), and the conifer forest habitats within that region. By our own estimate, there are 87 bird species that breed in conifer forest habitats within the region (Table 2), and 39 of those (45%) were abundant enough (>1.0 bird per route) and detected frequently

enough (on more than 14 routes within the region) to obtain reasonably reliable models of their population trends (Sauer et al. 1999). The bird species for which data are too few, and for which we cannot expect the BBS to provide meaningful results in the future, include those that are rarely detected (e.g., diurnal raptors, grouse), those that occur in habitats that are uncommon and poorly sampled by the BBS (e.g., burned forests), and those that are primarily nocturnal (owls).

Only one of the 39 forest bird species for which the BBS provides adequate coverage appears to be declining significantly in the Central Rockies Region—the Olive-sided Flycatcher (Table 2; see table for scientific names of bird species mentioned throughout text). This species is associated with forest openings (natural and human-created) and edges (Altman and Sallabanks 2000), and was most common in harvested and recently burned conifer forest at sites across northern Idaho and western Montana (Hutto and Young 1999). Of these forest types, burned forests have become rarer within the past century. Because several of the species that were not covered well by the BBS are also relatively common in burned forests (woodpeckers), there is even more reason to focus management attention toward the effects of fire suppression and post-fire salvage logging, both of which have undoubtedly affected the more fire-dependent species negatively (Hutto 1995, Kotliar et al. *this volume*).

BIRD ABUNDANCE AND LANDSCAPE FEATURES

Very few studies have been conducted that look specifically at the relationships between changing landscape patterns and birds in forests of the north-central Rockies. We identified five data sets that addressed the relationships between the abundances of bird species and some aspect of landscape configuration. These studies were conducted in different forest types, elevation, and climatic regimes as follows: (1) a region-wide correlational analysis based on 312-ha landscapes centered on bird count points across western Montana and northern Idaho, where conifer forest was defined as one category that included all major conifer types and a wide range of canopy closures within those types (i.e., closed canopy, seed tree, shelterwood, and group selection harvested sites; R. Hutto and J. Young, unpubl. report); (2) a correlational analysis of spatial patterns within 300-ha landscapes in mid-elevation closed-canopy mixed-conifer forest, dominated by grand fir/Douglas-fir/ponderosa pine in west-central Idaho (Evans 1995); (3) a comparison of a continuous 240-ha old-growth landscape with two similar-sized old-

TABLE 2. RECENT POPULATION TRENDS OF CONIFER FOREST BIRD SPECIES IN THE CENTRAL ROCKIES REGION AS DETERMINED FROM BREEDING BIRD SURVEY DATA, 1966–1998

Species	No. routes	BBS trend
Turkey Vulture, *Cathartes aura*		
Sharp-shinned Hawk, *Accipiter striatus*		
Cooper's Hawk, *Accipiter cooperii*		
Northern Goshawk, *Accipiter gentilis*		
Swainson's Hawk, *Buteo swainsoni*		
Red-tailed Hawk, *Buteo jamaicensis*	81	3.4*
American Kestrel, *Falco sparverius*	58	−0.7
Ruffed Grouse, *Bonasa umbellus*	48	−5.4*
Spruce Grouse, *Falcipennis canadensis*		
Blue Grouse, *Dendragapus obscurus*	13	−10.2*
Wild Turkey, *Meleagris gallopavo*		
Flammulated Owl, *Otus flammeolus*		
Great Horned Owl, *Bubo virginianus*		
Northern Pygmy-Owl, *Glaucidium gnoma*		
Barred Owl, *Strix varia*		
Great Gray Owl, *Strix nebulosa*		
Boreal Owl, *Aegolius funereus*		
Northern Saw-whet Owl, *Aegolius acadicus*		
Vaux's Swift, *Chaetura vauxi*		
White-throated Swift, *Aeronautes saxatalis*		
Black-chinned Hummingbird, *Archilochus alexandri*		
Calliope Hummingbird, *Stellula calliope*	39	0.2
Broad-tailed Hummingbird, *Selasphorus platycercus*		
Rufous Hummingbird, *Selasphorus rufus*	57	2.0
Lewis' Woodpecker, *Melanerpes lewis*	11	0.8
Williamson's Sapsucker, *Sphyrapicus thyroideus*		
Red-naped Sapsucker, *Sphyrapicus nuchalis*	**84**	**1.0**
Hairy Woodpecker, *Picoides villosus*	74	2.3
White-headed Woodpecker, *Picoides albolarvatus*		
Three-Toed Woodpecker, *Picoides tridactylus*		
Black-backed Woodpecker, *Picoides arcticus*		
Northern (Red-shafted) Flicker, *Colaptes auratus*	**106**	**0.0**
Pileated Woodpecker, *Dryocopus pileatus*	57	5.4*
Olive-sided Flycatcher, *Contopus cooperi*	**81**	**−4.0***
Western Wood-Pewee, *Contopus sordidulus*	**90**	**−0.3**
Hammond's Flycatcher, *Empidonax hammondii*	**81**	**1.7**
Dusky Flycatcher, *Empidonax oberholseri*	91	−2.0
Cordilleran Flycatcher, *Empidonax occidentalis*	57	2.1
Plumbeous Vireo, *Vireo plumbeus*	9	−9.9*
Cassin's Vireo, *Vireo cassinii*	**72**	**1.5***
Warbling Vireo, *Vireo gilvus*	**103**	**2.2***
Gray Jay, *Perisoreus canadensis*	**67**	**−0.3**
Steller's Jay, *Cyanocitta stelleri*	59	5.4*
Clark's Nutcracker, *Nucifraga columbiana*	**63**	**4.6***
Common Raven, *Corvus corax*	105	2.0
Tree Swallow, *Tachycineta bicolor*	**79**	**1.7**
Violet-green Swallow, *Tachycineta thalassina*	**84**	**4.0**
Northern Rough-winged Swallow, *Stelgidopteryx serripennis*	**64**	**1.3**
Black-capped Chickadee, *Poecile atricapillus*	**94**	**0.7**
Mountain Chickadee, *Poecile gambeli*	**91**	**0.1**
Chestnut-backed Chickadee, *Poecile rufescens*	25	2.4
Red-breasted Nuthatch, *Sitta canadensis*	**104**	**3.1***
White-breasted Nuthatch, *Sitta carolinensis*	32	1.1
Pygmy Nuthatch, *Sitta pygmaea*	15	1.0
Brown Creeper, *Certhia americana*		
Rock Wren, *Salpinctes obsoletus*		
House Wren, *Troglodytes aedon*	62	3.7
Winter Wren, *Troglodytes troglodytes*	**63**	**3.0***
Golden-crowned Kinglet, *Regulus satrapa*	**87**	**0.8**
Ruby-crowned Kinglet, *Regulus calendula*	**92**	**−1.2**
Mountain Bluebird, *Sialia currucoides*	**64**	**1.6**

TABLE 2.   CONTINUED.

Species	No. routes	BBS trend
Townsend's Solitaire, *Myadestes townsendi*	**80**	**−0.5**
Swainson's Thrush, *Catharus ustulatus*	**103**	**0.8**
Hermit Thrush, *Catharus guttatus*	72	1.2
American Robin, *Turdus migratorius*	**111**	**0.5**
Varied Thrush, *Ixoreus naevius*	**68**	**1.4**
Orange-crowned Warbler, *Vermivora celata*	**83**	**1.0**
Nashville Warbler, *Vermivora ruficapilla*		
Yellow-rumped (Audubon's) Warbler, *Dendroica coronata*	**109**	**−0.5**
Townsend's Warbler, *Dendroica townsendi*	**70**	**1.2**
MacGillivray's Warbler, *Oporornis tolmiei*	**96**	**0.9**
Wilson's Warbler, *Wilsonia pusilla*	**77**	**−1.0**
Western Tanager, *Piranga ludoviciana*	97	−0.8
Green-tailed Towhee, *Pipilo chlorurus*	13	−2.9
Spotted Towhee, *Pipilo maculatus*	**55**	**4.5***
Chipping Sparrow, *Spizella passerina*	**111**	**0.1**
Fox Sparrow, *Passerella iliaca*		
Lincoln's Sparrow, *Melospiza lincolnii*	**65**	**6.8***
Dark-eyed (Oregon) Junco, *Junco hyemalis*	**111**	**−0.4**
Black-headed Grosbeak, *Pheucticus melanocephalus*	59	8.9*
Lazuli Bunting, *Passerina amoena*	**61**	**3.4***
Brown-headed Cowbird, *Molothrus ater*	**86**	**−1.1**
Pine Grosbeak, *Pinicola enucleator*		
Cassin's Finch, *Carpodacus cassinii*	**72**	**−0.2**
Red Crossbill, *Loxia curvirostra*	**79**	**0.7**
Pine Siskin, *Carduelis pinus*	**109**	**−0.3**
Evening Grosbeak, *Coccothraustes vespertinus*	62	2.2*

Note: Species without trend information were either too rare (<0.1 bird per route) or detected too infrequently (on fewer than 5 routes) to provide estimates; those without bolded data have either deficient regional abundance (<1.0 birds per route) or route sample size (fewer than 14 routes). Species showing significant declines or increases (P ≤ 0.05) are noted with an asterisk next to the trend value.

growth and selectively-harvested landscapes, each with embedded clearcuts in western red-cedar/western hemlock forests in northern Idaho (Hejl and Paige 1994); (4) a comparison of harvested and unharvested 20–100 ha stands of spruce/fir in southeastern Wyoming (Keller and Anderson 1992); and (5) a patch-based study of old-growth ponderosa pine/Douglas-fir/western larch in western Montana (Aney 1984). Not all of the landscape metrics were evaluated in all studies, and two studies (Keller and Anderson 1992, Hejl and Paige 1994) focused more on the overall comparison of landscapes modified by timber harvesting to unmodified areas (see *Effects of logging patterns*). Bird abundances were based on point counts; point locations usually were within conifer forest and encompassed the natural variability in forest cover around points, and analyses generally included only the most common bird species detected. Thus, information is primarily limited to passerines, because other species are not well-sampled by point counts.

Amount of forest

The amount of forest covering a landscape is a frequently-reported measure of the degree of fragmentation of that landscape (e.g., Robinson

et al. 1995a). It is one metric that can be measured easily in forested landscapes where the forest remains highly interconnected and occurs as the matrix, not as a patch, although it gives no information on the spatial configuration of the remaining habitat. It also is a measure that can be used over large regions when the resolution of the map used to measure forest cover is too coarse to adequately capture other spatial parameters such as patch shape and edge. In the three landscape studies we considered, forest cover was measured at similar extents (within 200–312 ha areas) and at similar resolutions (at the scale of an aerial photograph or 30 m × 30 m pixel). The forest cover of interest ranged from 3–100% across all sampled landscapes, although these measures are not entirely comparable among studies due to different definitions of "forest."

A total of 10 species (five residents, three long-distance migrants, and two short-distance migrants) were consistently positively associated with the amount of forest cover in at least one study (Table 3). The probability of occurrence of seven species increased with increasing amounts of conifer forest in the study in which forest was defined most broadly ("all conifer;" R. Hutto and J. Young, unpubl. report). In

TABLE 3. RELATIONSHIPS BETWEEN CONIFEROUS FOREST BIRD SPECIES AND LANDSCAPE METRICS IN THE NORTH-CENTRAL ROCKY MOUNTAINS

	Amount of forest			Patch size			Edge density		Proximity to edge
	All conifer[a]	Mixed conifer[b]	Cedar/hemlock[c]	All conifer	Mixed conifer	Ponderosa pine[d]	All conifer	Spruce fir[e]	Mixed conifer
Positively associated with elements of continuous landscapes									
Vaux's Swift (LDM, CN[f])				+					
Gray Jay (R, OCN)				(+)					
Chestnut-backed Chickadee (R, CN)	+						−		
Red-breasted Nuthatch (R, CN)	+			+	+		−		−
Brown Creeper (SDM, EN)		+	+	+		+		−	
Winter Wren (R, EN)	+	+	+	+			−		
Golden-crowned Kinglet (R, OCN)	+	+	+	+	+		−		−
Swainson's Thrush (LDM, OCN)	+			(+)			−		
Hermit Thrush (SDM, OCN)				(+)				−	
Varied Thrush (R, OCN)	+			+			−		
Yellow-rumped Warbler (SDM, OCN)		+			+				
Townsend's Warbler (LDM, OCN)	+			+	+		−		−
Black-headed Grosbeak (LDM, OCN)[g]		+							
Pine Grosbeak (R, OCN)				+					
Mixed associations with fragmentation									
Cassin's Vireo (LDM, OCN)	−					+			
Clark's Nutcracker (R, OCN)	−						+		
Western Tanager (LDM, OCN)	−	+		−					
Negatively associated with elements of continuous landscapes									
Hammond's Flycatcher (LDM, OCN)				−					
Dusky Flycatcher (LDM, OCN)[g]					−				
Common Raven (R, OCN)	−			(−)			(+)		
Mountain Chickadee (R, CN)	−			−			+		
Ruby-crowned Kinglet (SDM, OCN)	−			−			+		
Townsend's Solitaire (SDM, OCN)							(+)		
MacGillivray's Warbler (LDM, OCN)[g]				−					
Chipping Sparrow (LDM, OCN)	−			−			+		+
Dark-eyed Junco (SDM, OCN)	−	−				−			+
Cassin's Finch (R, OCN)	−			−			+		
Red Crossbill (R, OCN)				−			+		
Pine Siskin (R, OCN)	−			−			+	+	+

Notes: Forest types described in text. Not all landscape metrics evaluated in all five forest types. Positive association (increased abundance) denoted by +; negative association by −. Responses in parentheses significant at $0.05 < P < 0.10$. All others significant at $P < 0.05$.
[a] R. Hutto and J. Young, unpubl. report. "All Conifer" forest includes seedtree, shelterwood, and group selection harvested sites.
[b] Evans 1995. Mixed conifer is closed canopy mature mixed conifer.
[c] Hejl and Paige 1994.
[d] Aney 1984.
[e] Keller and Anderson 1992.
[f] LDM = long distance migrant, SDM = short distance migrant, R = resident (as defined by Partners in Flight); EN = enclosed nest, OCN = open cup nest, CN = cavity nest.
[g] Black-headed Grosbeak and Dusky Flycatcher classified as riparian by Hutto and Young 1999; MacGillivray's Warbler excluded from "All Conifer" analyses—not restricted to conifer.

closed-canopy mixed conifer forest, five species increased in relative abundance as amount of forest increased (Evans 1995). Three species were more abundant in unharvested cedar/hemlock landscapes than in harvested landscapes, and were less abundant than expected in harvested areas based on the amount of forest remaining (Hejl and Paige 1994). Across these studies, Golden-crowned Kinglet was most frequently associated with forest cover; Brown Creeper and Winter Wren associations appeared in two studies. The relationship between abun-

dance and amount of forest was not tested directly in spruce/fir (Keller and Anderson 1992), but five species were more abundant in continuous forest than in areas interspersed with clearcuts (see *Effects of logging patterns*).

A similar number (9) of species had the opposite association, decreasing in abundance with increasing amounts of forest, suggesting that they would have a positive response to fragmentation. However, this negative association with forest area was examined directly in only two studies, and there was less correspondence between these studies. Dark-eyed Junco was the only species that was negatively associated with forest cover in both studies; Western Tanager had opposing associations. More resident species (five) were negatively associated with increased amount of forest than long- (two) or short-distance (two) migrants.

Patch size

Relationships of abundance with patch size (the area of a continuous block of similar habitat) were tested directly in three studies (Table 3). Most of the species positively associated with larger patch size in the two landscape studies (Evans 1995; R. Hutto and J. Young, unpubl. report) also were associated with amount of forest. The two variables were strongly correlated (r = 0.69) in Hutto and Young's study, as they probably are in many western studies. However, Vaux's Swift, Gray Jay, Hermit Thrush, and Pine Grosbeak were associated with patch size but not to amount of forest in these studies (Evans 1995; R. Hutto and J. Young, unpubl. report). Red-breasted Nuthatch, Golden-crowned Kinglet, and Townsend's Warbler had the most consistent positive associations with patch size between the two studies.

Interpreting Aney's (1984) study in old growth ponderosa pine, we identified two species (Solitary Vireo [now Cassin's Vireo] and Brown Creeper) with possible minimum patch size requirements. These species were absent from stands below a certain size, even though those stands might have been large enough to accommodate at least one territory. Cassin's Vireo (reported territory size of 0.5 ha/pair; Aney 1984) was not detected in stands less than 5 ha (9 of 19 stands examined), but was consistently detected in larger stands. Brown Creeper (territory size ranges from <1 to 6.4 ha/pair; Hejl et al. 2002) was absent from stands less than 4.5 ha (8 of 19 stands). Many species in this study were not detected frequently enough for a pattern of area sensitivity to emerge. In addition, Aney (1984) did not consider annual turnover in assessing presence or absence within patches (Freemark et al. 1995).

Most species (7 of 9) negatively associated with amount of "all conifer" forest across western Montana and northern Idaho (R. Hutto and J. Young, unpubl. report) also were negatively associated with increasing patch size, with the exception of Clark's Nutcracker and Dark-eyed Junco (Table 3). Hammond's Flycatcher and Red Crossbill also were negatively associated with patch size in this study. Only three species decreased in abundance as patch size increased in west-central Idaho (Evans 1995).

Edge

Relationships between birds and edge density or distance from edge were evaluated in three studies. In "all conifer" forests (R. Hutto and J. Young, unpubl. report), all seven of the species that were positively associated with the amount of forest were also negatively associated with edge density (see Table 3; r = −0.048 between these two predictor variables, demonstrating low correlation, and thus reasonable independence, between them). In this instance, edge was defined as the boundary between patches of dissimilar cover, with 15 possible cover classifications (5 forest types, 4 open land types, 3 riparian types, and 3 other classes) within 312-ha landscapes. Two species (Brown Creeper and Hermit Thrush) had a negative association with edge density in spruce/fir (Keller and Anderson 1992). Evans (1995) measured sensitivity to edge directly by comparing abundance across three distances to edge (<50 m, 50–100 m, >100 m). Edges were defined by openings in closed-canopy forest and the juxtaposition of forests of different ages and canopy closure. Red-breasted Nuthatch, Golden-crowned Kinglet, and Townsend's Warbler were significantly more abundant as distance from edge increased (Table 3).

Across studies, 10 species increased in abundance as edge density increased or distance from edge decreased (Table 3). Chipping Sparrow and Pine Siskin were most frequently positively associated with edge across studies.

Effects of logging patterns

Two studies in the north-central Rockies (Keller and Anderson 1992, Hejl and Paige 1994) compared the numbers of birds in landscapes modified by timber harvesting to unmodified areas. In both studies, the modified areas were created by logging (stripcuts, spot cuts, and clearcuts) interspersed within previously unlogged or partially-logged forest. (Partially-logged forest remained as continuous forest, but some trees had been selectively removed previously.) The two studies differed in habitat and methodology. In the high elevation Engelmann spruce/subalpine fir study, Keller and Anderson did not sample clearcut areas because they did not want stand comparisons to reflect avian use of unforested areas compared to forested areas. In the low elevation western redcedar/western hemlock study, Hejl and Paige sampled the complete landscapes, allowing points to fall in clearcuts, on edges, or in forest interior, to see how birds responded to clearcut/forest landscapes as a whole.

Of 16 species detected in spruce/fir and 38 species in cedar/hemlock, 9 species were common to both studies. Of these nine species, three had the same results: Brown Creepers were more abundant in unlogged landscapes, Red-breasted Nuthatches were similarly abundant in logged and unlogged landscapes, and Pine Siskins were more abundant in logged landscapes. Hermit Thrush, American Robin, and Yellow-rumped Warbler had opposite trends in the two studies. Of those species found only in one study but with significant associations, three species were more abundant in unlogged landscapes (Mountain Chickadee, Winter Wren, Swainson's Thrush) and nine in logged landscapes (Northern Flicker, Olive-sided Flycatcher, Townsend's Solitaire, Cassin's Vireo, Warbling Vireo, Orange-crowned Warbler, MacGillivray's Warbler, Western Tanager, and Chipping Sparrow).

In both of these studies, it was difficult to ascertain whether the associations with logged or unlogged landscapes were caused by a simple decrease or increase in suitable habitat caused by logging or by the changes in landscape conditions (i.e., decreased patch size, increased edge). The fact that three species (Brown Creeper, Winter Wren, and Golden-crowned Kinglet) were less abundant in harvested cedar/hemlock landscapes than would be expected based on the amount of forest remaining (see above under *Amount of forest*) suggested that landscape changes could at least be a partial cause of lower numbers in those landscapes. In addition, while most of the species identified in the two studies have similar trends to those resulting from logging in stand-level studies throughout the West (as summarized by Hejl et al. 1995), Gray Jay, Red-breasted Nuthatch, and Pine Siskin do not, indicating potential landscape effects.

Synopsis

Given that there was virtually no replication of any of the conditions among the studies that we summarized, we suggest that the species most or least sensitive to fragmentation, based on their patterns of abundance, are those that show a consistent response in several forest types and geographic regions. Based on this assumption, Brown Creeper clearly had the strongest trend of species sensitive to changes in landscape patterns, as it was associated with at least one variable indicating landscape change (and usually more than one) in four of the five studies examined (Table 3). Golden-crowned Kinglet, Red-breasted Nuthatch, Winter Wren, Hermit Thrush, and Townsend's Warbler also showed consistent results across studies. These species appear as sensitive to disruptions in the pattern of forest cover on the landscape elsewhere in the West. Brown Creeper, Winter Wren, and Red-breasted Nuthatch were correlated with

the amount of forest and/or patch size in coastal Douglas-fir or cedar/hemlock forests (Rosenberg and Raphael 1986, McGarigal and McComb 1995, Schieck et al. 1995), and Red-breasted Nuthatches and Townsend's Warblers avoided edges (Rosenberg and Raphael 1986).

Fewer species had consistent positive associations with elements of more fragmented landscapes in the north-central Rockies. Several species had consistent associations with more than one landscape element within a study, but only three species (Pine Siskin, Chipping Sparrow and Dark-eyed Junco) were consistent across studies. These three species were also more abundant in logged landscapes (Keller and Anderson 1992, Hejl and Paige 1994). Our results were somewhat inconsistent with other western studies. Chipping Sparrow was associated with edges in Douglas-fir forests in California (Rosenberg and Raphael 1986), but Pine Siskin and Dark-eyed Junco were positively associated with larger patches of old-growth Douglas-fir and hemlock forests on Vancouver Island (Schieck et al. 1995).

While the five studies we reviewed differed in methods, particularly in how forest cover was defined, none attempted to define "fragmented" based on a minimum patch size. Thus, inconsistent results among these studies are not attributed to one study considering a 200-ha patch to be a fragment and another considering it continuous forest. Two studies (Evans 1995; R. Hutto and J. Young, unpubl. report) measured fragmentation indices as continuous variables across 300-ha landscapes and related bird abundances in correlation or regression tests. One logging study also based landscape descriptions on 240-ha landscapes (Hejl and Paige 1994). The other logging study used some small (20–40 ha) patches as unmanaged controls (Keller and Anderson 1992), but we used only an edge measure from this study. The old-growth ponderosa pine patch-based study included very small patches (<4 ha) but the only variable discussed from that study was patch size; we used a species' presence or absence across the range of patches as an indication of sensitivity to patch size.

DEMOGRAPHIC RELATIONSHIPS WITH LANDSCAPE FEATURES

Several studies have suggested that the number of individual birds can temporarily increase in areas adjacent to recent cuts due to displacement of birds into the nearest suitable habitat (Schmiegelow et al. 1997, Walters 1998). Over the long term, high abundances can be maintained from source habitats and a population trend would not be apparent (Van Horne 1983, Vickery et al. 1992). Increased densities could have a negative impact on reproductive rates through reduced pairing success, competition for resources, and reproductive failure (Hagen et al. 1996), issues for which demographic studies are needed. Data on the effects of landscape patterns on bird demography are seriously lacking from conifer forest habitats in the north-central Rockies. Several recent studies are beginning to provide information to address this gap.

S. Hejl (unpubl. data) studied nesting success of cavity-nesting and enclosed-nesting species in a continuous old-growth (>170 yr) cedar/hemlock forest landscape (240 ha) and compared results to nesting success from a landscape composed of recent clearcuts in a matrix of old-growth cedar/hemlock in northern Idaho. Nesting success did not differ between landscapes for any of the five focal species (Red-naped Sapsucker, Chestnut-backed Chickadee, Red-breasted Nuthatch, Brown Creeper, and Winter Wren) in 1992–1994, but four species (all but Winter Wren) had trends of lower nesting success in the logged landscape. The sample of nests was limited, and the numbers for some species-landscape combinations may be too low to compute reliable Mayfield estimates (Hensler and Nichols 1981).

D. Evans and colleagues (unpubl. report) studied nesting success of Swainson's Thrushes and Western Tanagers in mixed-conifer forests in west-central Idaho. Data were obtained from 10 separate study plots, four of which were classified as located within relatively continuous forest areas and six of which were classified as relatively fragmented. Stands were classified based on a multivariate analysis of landscape cover within 1 km of the avian demography study plots. Nesting success of neither Swainson's Thrush nor Western Tanager differed between landscape classes, although there was a trend for lower success of Swainson's Thrushes, and higher success of Western Tanagers, in fragmented landscapes. However, overall nest success estimates for both species in either landscape class were substantially below the minimum nest success thresholds suggested as needed to support self-sustaining populations (Martin et al. 1996). Evans et al. (unpubl. report) also found no relationship between nest success and distance to edge for either species. Using survival (recapture and resighting of color-marked individuals) and productivity data collected from mixed-conifer habitats in Idaho, they modeled continuous-landscape and fragmented-landscape populations of Swainson's Thrushes and Western Tanagers. Population trajectories did not differ between continuous and fragmented landscapes for either species, and all populations declined rapidly. Because overall estimates of annual survivorship were relatively high (0.67–0.68 annual survivorship), the authors concluded that the declines in simulated populations were mostly tied to relatively low nesting success.

Sallabanks et al. (1999) initiated a regional study examining the effects of landscape composition on avian nesting success. They monitored replicate plots in managed forest landscapes with both silviculture and agriculture, managed forest landscapes with active silviculture only, and unmanaged forest landscapes with neither agriculture nor silviculture. Although statistical analyses have yet to be conducted, a preliminary examination of the data (2,847 nests of 66 bird species) suggests a mix of results: several species tend to have increasing rates of nest success along a spectrum from managed landscapes with both silviculture and agriculture to unmanaged landscapes (e.g., Warbling Vireo), others appear to be unaffected by landscape composition (e.g., Dusky Flycatcher), and still others have their highest success in the most heavily managed landscapes (e.g., MacGillivray's Warbler; R. Sallabanks, pers. comm.).

The primary cause of landbird nest failures within the north-central Rockies region is predation, as reported elsewhere (Martin 1993). In Idaho, predators destroyed 31–35% of all nests monitored, depending on species and landscape classification (D. Evans et al., unpubl. report). Based on opportunistic observations, these authors recorded evidence of red squirrel (*Tamiasciurus hudsonicus*) predation and speculated that avian predators, such as jays, accounted for some losses. In addition, only one of 202 nests had evidence of cowbird parasitism. Based on one year of data, R. Sallabanks et al. (unpubl. report) reported that 43% of total nests (76% of failures) were destroyed by predators in three regions in Idaho and Montana. In a companion study in west-central Idaho using artificial nests baited with clay eggs, Warner (2000) identified deer mouse (*Peromyscus maniculatus*), yellow-pine chipmunk (*Tamias amoenus*), red squirrel, and northern flying squirrel (*Glaucomys sabrinus*) as the primary predators of nests placed on the ground and in shrubs. Predator assemblages were similar between managed (i.e., with agriculture and/or silviculture) and unmanaged (i.e., without agriculture or silviculture) forest landscapes. Warner (2000) also documented attempted predation on clay eggs by deer, sheep, domestic cattle, coyotes, ground squirrels, beaver, and other songbirds.

Demography data show some consistency with results based on abundance. Abundance data indicated that 14 species are potentially negatively affected by landscape changes caused by timber harvesting (i.e., numbers for these 14 species are either positively correlated with more or larger forests or negatively correlated with edge density or distance to edge; Table 3). For the four of these 14 species for which we have preliminary nesting success data, three (Brown Creeper, Red-breasted Nuthatch, Swainson's Thrush) had lower nesting success trends in logged landscapes. The other species (Winter Wren) had inconsistent nesting success trends. One of the species with a mixed association with landscape changes according to abundance data (Western Tanager) had a trend of greater nesting success in fragmented landscapes. This latter result was consistent with findings by Davis (1999) that Western Tanagers in Idaho were most closely affiliated with relatively open stands of primarily Douglas-fir trees.

Brown-headed Cowbird occurrence

Given that nest parasitism has been shown to be a problem in some fragmented landscapes, we summarized the response of Brown-headed Cowbirds to landscape changes. Studies in the north-central Rockies that have examined cowbird abundance within a landscape context consistently show that proximity to agricultural areas is a strong, if not the strongest, predictor of cowbird occurrence (Hejl and Young 1999, Young and Hutto 1999, Tewksbury et al. 1999). Within conifer forest sites across western Montana and northern Idaho, cowbirds were more likely to be found in xeric forests (especially ponderosa pine), in areas with an abundance of cowbird hosts, close to developed, agricultural, and riparian areas, and less likely to be found in subalpine forests (Young and Hutto 1999). In the Bitterroot Valley, Montana, Brown-headed Cowbird abundances were greatest in riparian areas, less in xeric conifer forest, and least in riparian conifer forests (Tewksbury et al. 1999). Within 518-ha landscapes in xeric ponderosa pine/Douglas-fir forests, landscape context was more important than stand attributes in determining cowbird numbers (Hejl and Young 1999). Cowbirds were more abundant in landscapes with more open land (agricultural land and grassland), deciduous riparian habitat (70–120 yr), and less old growth. Forest cover, logged openings, human residences, and elevation were not important predictors of cowbird numbers in these xeric forests. All of these studies suggest that cowbird distribution is limited by the presence and distribution of largely supplemental food supplied by human activities. In addition, cowbirds may be more abundant in conifer stands near riparian areas (but not in canyons or riparian conifer forests) because they are attracted to riparian habitats that are dense with potential hosts, and venture into adjacent conifer forests secondarily.

Fewer data are available to assess the impact of cowbirds on nest success. From BBIRD sites across the West, forest coverage correlated inversely with nest parasitism within 10-km radius areas, with lower parasitization rates where forest coverage was greater (Hochachka et al. 1999). However, the opposite trend was seen at the 50-km scale. Hochachka et al. (1999) hypothesized that this contrary result suggests that traits other than forest cover, such as human-induced land-use practices that are related to forest cover (see Tewksbury et al. 1998), may be responsible for these results.

Where reproductive success has been studied in coniferous forests of the north-central Rockies, cowbird parasitism rates were extremely low (e.g., 0–3% in varied locations in west-central Idaho, northern Idaho, and western Montana; D. Evans et al., unpubl. data; S. Hejl, unpubl. data; R. Sallabanks, unpubl. data). Parasitism rates are likely to be much higher where cowbirds are more abundant, such as in ponderosa pine forests near residential development and agricultural areas. Overall, however, locations supporting higher parasitism rates currently are relatively rare in the coniferous forest landscape of the north-central Rockies.

DISCUSSION

We found scattered evidence in the few landscape studies from the north-central Rockies supporting our expectations of the birds most affected by landscape changes. We believe that the "Cascadian" forests of northern Idaho historically were continuous, and extensive logging and consequent fragmentation would result in landscape conditions for which species found there are not well adapted. In fact, the two species (Brown Creeper, Golden-crowned Kinglet) that were negatively associated with fragmentation indices in at least three studies in the north-central Rockies were most commonly affiliated with moist, continuous habitats. Additionally, the trend for nesting success of Brown Creepers in a fragmented landscape was half that of continuous forest (although based on a small sample size; S. Hejl, unpubl. data). Other species associated with moist, once-continuous forests (and therefore ones that we would expect to be affected similarly by landscape changes) are: Chestnut-backed Chickadee, Winter Wren, Varied Thrush, and Townsend's Warbler in cedar-hemlock forests. Much of the high-elevation spruce-fir zone also produced large expanses of continuous forest, where the topography permitted, because of the long period between fires (often 300 yr; Romme 1982). For this reason, bird species associated with spruce-fir forests, such as Boreal Owl, Hermit Thrush, and Pine Grosbeak, might be sensitive to fragmentation. Several of the above species had our expected associations with fragmentation indices, but in other forest types. Boreal Owl was not reported in the studies summarized.

Whereas the "Cascadian" forests described here are similar to Pacific Northwest forests in structure, landscape, tree species, and bird communities, these moist forests make up a relatively small proportion of the north-central Rockies as a region. Given the greater natural heterogeneity in the north-central Rockies, it follows that overall, fewer species may exhibit a negative association with fragmentation here than in the Pacific Northwest.

Mid-elevation forests, primarily mixed-conifer types in the Douglas-fir and grand fir zones, had substantial natural heterogeneity historically. Although these landscapes have received considerable logging pressure, the change from historical patterns caused by timber harvest may not be as pronounced as in very moist forests. We are not certain how birds most adapted to using these heterogeneous habitats have been affected by the current level of fragmentation of these landscapes caused thus far by timber harvesting, or if timber harvesting would compensate for changes from fire suppression, either in structure or extent. Most bird species that use Douglas-fir or mixed-conifer forest also use other forest types (Hutto and Young 1999). From the one study conducted in this forest type exclusively, three species (Red-breasted Nuthatch, Golden-crowned Kinglet, and Townsend's Warbler) were negatively associated with more than one fragmentation index (Table 3), but we had classified two of these species as more associated with moist, continuous forests.

Similarly hard to interpret are the consequences of landscape changes in low-elevation dry forests. These forests are likely to have been the most affected by timber harvest, fire exclusion, and proximity to agricultural land and human development, but so many different changes have occurred on each piece of ground that there is no general landscape pattern that has been created. We speculate that low-elevation, dry savannah-like forests with many natural openings (e.g., ponderosa pine) that often are intermixed with grasslands would favor birds that exploit relatively open habitats, and that these birds are less likely to be negatively affected by the intrusion of openings caused by timber harvesting, as long as sufficient amounts of their required habitat elements are available (i.e., above a "habitat loss" threshold; Andrén 1994, Fahrig 1999). Birds associated with ponderosa pine and

many Douglas-fir cover types include Flammulated Owl, Lewis' Woodpecker, White-headed Woodpecker, White-breasted Nuthatch, Cassin's Vireo, and Chipping Sparrow. Chipping Sparrow had a positive association with fragmentation indices in two studies, but Cassin's Vireo had mixed associations. In addition, it recently has been shown that Flammulated Owls are associated with open, edge habitats (Goggans 1986) and with old-growth ponderosa pine interspersed with grasslands at the large landscape scale (Wright 1996). However, in the current era of fire suppression, many low elevation dry forests now support increased tree density and canopy cover (Arno et al. 1997). The consequences of these changes in structure have not been adequately explored, nor have the consequences of human encroachment near these forests.

Patch size was important for some species in remnant patches of old-growth ponderosa pine (Aney 1984). This study, however, is the only one that has examined patch size for the vanishing habitats for which we are concerned, and no one has examined whether patch isolation influences early post-fire, aspen, old-growth ponderosa pine, or old-growth larch patch occupancy by birds. We believe that these issues are especially critical for birds that specialize on these habitats, given the trend of increasingly smaller and more isolated patches.

Three demographic studies (D. Evans et al., unpubl. report; S. Hejl, unpubl. data; R. Sallabanks, unpubl. report) found little to no cowbird parasitism in areas fragmented by logging or in continuous forests. Most of these specific landscapes were far from human-added features with which cowbirds may be associated, but this needs further investigation. Overall, the impact of cowbirds on conifer forest birds in the north-central Rockies currently appears small relative to other factors. Parasitism rates, however, are likely to be high in those conifer forests near agricultural areas or residential development (not well studied), and if human-added features spread throughout conifer forests in the north-central Rockies, then we would expect Brown-headed Cowbird parasitism to increase as well.

There is fairly convincing evidence that assessing the effects of changes in forest landscapes for birds in the north-central Rockies, as elsewhere in the West, requires a different approach from the model developed from more static, fragmented landscapes in the East and Midwest in North America. More extensive forested areas in the East and Midwest may indeed have similar landscape conditions to those most prevalent in north-central Rockies forests, but most fragmentation studies in those regions have dealt with "remnant patches" (sensu Forman and Godron 1986) in the middle of disturbed habitat. In contrast, the natural situation in the north-central Rockies is one of "disturbance patches" (sensu Forman and Godron 1986), such as early post-fire forests or timber harvest openings, in the middle of a less disturbed landscape matrix (Faaborg et al. 1995).

These differences in patterns and processes between regions within North America, and their concomitant differences in avian response, have been reviewed elsewhere. The relationships of increased abundance and species richness with forest fragment size were more pronounced for long-distance migrants and open-cup nesters in eastern and midwestern studies compared with residents or short-distance migrants (Faaborg et al. 1995). In northeastern and central hardwood forests, 72% of species showing area sensitivity in at least some studies were long-distance migrants, compared with 29% in western forests (Freemark et al. 1995). Studies in the north-central Rockies support the conclusion that resident species are equally or perhaps more likely to be negatively affected by fragmentation than migrants. The effect of increasing edge in eastern North America results in greater access of some nest predators into forests (e.g., Brittingham and Temple 1983, Robinson 1992), but this pattern does not necessarily hold in the landscapes of the north-central Rockies. Timber management (e.g., clearcuts) in western coniferous forests introduces few new predators to the biotic community (Marzluff and Restani 1999). In some landscapes of the north-central Rockies, red squirrels and some corvids are at least as abundant in uncut forest as in disturbed areas (Evans and Finch 1994). Thus, we would expect that predator response to changes in western coniferous forest landscapes, and the subsequent effects on nest success, may be better explained by something other than "edge effects." Predator dynamics within these forests have yet to be explored adequately.

Because habitat loss and habitat fragmentation are interdependent (Faaborg et al. 1995, Fahrig 1999), it is difficult to separate the possible consequences of habitat configuration from loss of habitat per se. In modeling thresholds of fragmentation effects, Andrén (1994) proposed that in landscapes with >30% suitable habitat, the amount of habitat was more important than its configuration. Only when suitable habitat was reduced to <30% did patch size and isolation begin to influence bird populations. Most of the studies in the north-central Rockies (and most throughout the West) generally occurred in landscapes with >30% forest cover. Ten landscapes in which nest success was studied by D. Evans et al. (unpubl. report) varied from 32–78% forest

cover, and the authors believed that they may have detected some fragmentation effects in stands at the low end of this range. Given the regional differences in areal extent of forest cover across North America and the types of changes to forests of the north-central Rockies that we describe, it is not surprising that forest size was a dominant influence in midwestern and eastern studies, whereas change of within-stand structure and loss of nest and foraging substrates may predominate in the north-central Rockies.

There are, however, instances when the model of patch size and isolation may be applicable to coniferous forests of the north-central Rockies— specifically for habitats that have become scarcer on the landscape. This includes lower elevation old-growth habitats, which have been heavily harvested and are now disjunct, although perhaps not surrounded by completely dissimilar habitat. Fire disturbance patches, which currently are in decline due to fire suppression, probably represent another example. From a landscape perspective, fire suppression and logging not only decrease potential habitat for old-growth specialists (e.g., Pileated Woodpecker) and post-fire specialists (e.g., Black-backed Woodpecker; Hutto 1995), but also further isolate those habitats, potentially decreasing the viability of populations of such species in the north-central Rockies. What is most important for these birds today is to restore the historical patterns and the processes that created the landscapes for which the birds evolved (Hejl et al. 1995, Hejl 2000).

When not suppressed, stand-replacement fires create well-defined fragments of early successional forest dominated by standing dead trees (Hutto 1995). This is the earliest and most ephemeral condition in post-fire succession. These sites provide nesting opportunities for many primary and secondary cavity nesters, and timber drillers are attracted by the abundant beetle larvae (Hutto 1995). In a literature review, Hutto (1995) noted 15 bird species found equally or more consistently in recently burned forests than in any other vegetation cover type in the northern Rocky Mountains, and some species were nearly restricted to such conditions (Hutto 1995, Hutto and Young 1999). The Black-backed Woodpecker, for example, has been designated a "sensitive species" in several regions by the U.S. Forest Service for precisely that reason. Other species that were most commonly found in burned forests include Three-toed Woodpecker, Hairy Woodpecker, Olive-sided Flycatcher, Mountain Bluebird, American Robin, and Cassin's Finch (Hutto 1995). Early post-fire patches are a naturally fragmented system, but decades of fire suppression have decreased the total area involved and increased the isolation of each burn (Baker 1994). Bird species restricted to such ephemeral, early post-fire patches would have to be adapted to quickly colonize new patches, but increasing isolation may place a strain on individuals finding new patches. In addition, post-fire salvage logging may diminish the suitability of some patches by reducing nest sites and food resources (Caton 1996, Hitchcox 1996, Saab and Dudley 1998).

Finally, BBS data may not be a useful tool for evaluating the effects of landscape changes on birds in these forests. We used BBS to examine regional trends, because we assumed that if landscape changes had greatly affected a species, we would see that reflected in regional trend information. We recognize that our interpretations of these data may be limited because BBS surveys take place on roads and therefore do not sample all landscape situations equally, may sample edge habitat although classified as "forest," do not sample many conifer forest birds well [55% of conifer birds in the north-central Rockies (noted here) and 50% in western North America (Hejl 1994) did not have reliable population trends], and are limited to the most recent 33 years. Indeed, of the 14 species most likely to be negatively affected by fragmentation according to community abundance studies (Table 3), BBS has significant positive trends for two species, indicating either that these species have not been negatively (or may even have been positively) affected by landscape changes in the past 33 years, or that BBS does not sample these birds or issues very well. Alternatively, BBS might be adequate for some of these species or issues, and the general lack of negative trends could indicate that many of these species have not been negatively affected by landscape changes during the past 33 years. We are concerned, however, about the 55% of the species that are not sampled well by BBS. Many of these species are among those most likely to be negatively affected by landscape changes associated with timber harvest and fire exclusion. In general, these species are difficult to study and would benefit from species-specific investigations.

CONCLUSIONS

Overall, our understanding of the relationships between landscape changes and coniferous-forest birds in the north-central Rockies is rudimentary. We have a growing understanding of the landscape issues (current vs. historical patterns and processes), but only scattered in-formation concerning how changes in these landscape patterns may have influenced bird populations, and then only during the breeding season. However, preliminary work suggests that fragmentation is not clearly affecting as many species as in other parts of North America. Differences from fragmentation issues in other regions are due to the kind and degree of fragmentation. In most north-central Rockies conifer forest landscapes, forests are interconnected and far from cowbird feeding sources or predators associated with human residences. Since the effects of some landscape changes in the north-central Rockies are likely to be less dramatic than those that have been documented in the East and Midwest, population responses of species may be subtle and difficult to measure. Large sample sizes are needed to determine if subtle effects are real and biologically significant enough to result in declining populations.

In the future, we need more studies on nesting success, survivorship, dispersal, predator ecology, and parasitism rates in relation to landscape patterns as well as within-stand changes. Research during the nonbreeding season also is needed. We offer our proposed consequences as hypotheses upon which to base future tests. Our greatest concerns are for those species that are associated with habitats that have changed the most, are vanishing, or are near added landscape features that cowbirds use. The loss of fires may be the single greatest continuing threat to birds in these landscapes, via the loss and isolation of critical habitat components (such as snags).

ACKNOWLEDGMENTS

We thank the many committed field assistants who collected bird data for the studies in Idaho and Montana. B. Beringer, C. Clark, C. Davis, J. Holmes, J. Hovis, M. McFadzen, C. Paige, T. Thompson, W. Williams, and the University of Montana Wildlife Spatial Analysis Laboratory were major contributors to the field effort or data analysis. Data, suggestions, encouragement, and other information incorporated into this paper were contributed by T. L. George, C. Hescock, B. Laudenslayer, T. Martin, M. Raphael, R. Sallabanks, F. Samson, M. Slimack, D. Smith, and J. Verner. The field research in Idaho and Montana summarized in this review was supported by the U.S. Forest Service (Regions 1 and 4, Payette and Idaho Panhandle National Forests, Pacific Southwest Research Station, Rocky Mountain Research Station, Pacific Northwest Research Station, and Research Natural Areas Program), U.S. Environmental Protection Agency, Boise Cascade Corporation, Partnerships for Wildlife, Idaho Department of Fish and Game, U.S. Fish and Wildlife Service, Potlatch Corporation, and Arkansas State University. W. Block, D. Dobkin, and an anonymous reviewer provided helpful comments on an earlier version of the manuscript.

Studies in Avian Biology No. 25:130–140, 2002.

EFFECTS OF HABITAT FRAGMENTATION ON PASSERINE BIRDS BREEDING IN INTERMOUNTAIN SHRUBSTEPPE

STEVEN T. KNICK AND JOHN T. ROTENBERRY

Abstract. Habitat fragmentation and loss strongly influence the distribution and abundance of passerine birds breeding in Intermountain shrubsteppe. Wildfires, human activities, and change in vegetation communities often are synergistic in these systems and can result in radical conversion from shrubland to grasslands dominated by exotic annuals at large temporal and spatial scales from which recovery to native conditions is unlikely. As a result, populations of 5 of the 12 species in our review of Intermountain shrubsteppe birds are undergoing significant declines; 5 species are listed as at-risk or as candidates for protection in at least one state. The process by which fragmentation affects bird distributions in these habitats remains unknown because most research has emphasized the detection of population trends and patterns of habitat associations at relatively large spatial scales. Our research indicates that the distribution of shrubland-obligate species, such as Brewer's Sparrows (*Spizella breweri*), Sage Sparrows (*Amphispiza belli*), and Sage Thrashers (*Oreoscoptes montanus*), was highly sensitive to fragmentation of shrublands at spatial scales larger than individual home ranges. In contrast, the underlying mechanisms for both habitat change and bird population dynamics may operate independently of habitat boundaries. We propose alternative, but not necessarily exclusive, mechanisms to explain the relationship between habitat fragmentation and bird distribution and abundance. Fragmentation might influence productivity through differences in breeding density, nesting success, or predation. However, local and landscape variables were not significant determinants either of success, number fledged, or probability of predation or parasitism (although our tests had relatively low statistical power). Alternatively, relative absence of natal philopatry and redistribution by individuals among habitats following fledging or post-migration could account for the pattern of distribution and abundance. Thus, boundary dynamics may be important in determining the distribution of shrubland-obligate species but insignificant relative to the mechanisms causing the pattern of habitat and bird distribution. Because of the dichotomy in responses, Intermountain shrubsteppe systems present a unique challenge in understanding how landscape composition, configuration, and change influence bird population dynamics.

Key Words: *Amphispiza belli*; *Eremophilus alpestris*; habitat fragmentation; landscape ecology; *Oreoscoptes montanus*; shrubsteppe; *Spizella breweri*; *Sturnella neglecta*.

The present rate of fragmentation in Intermountain shrubsteppe landscapes and subsequent conversion to unsuitable habitats is a critical management concern because of its effect on the associated avifauna (Braun et al. 1976, Knopf 1988, Saab and Rich 1997, Rotenberry 1998, Paige and Ritter 1999, Wisdom et al. 2000). Shrubsteppe regions in the Intermountain West, and particularly those at lower elevations in the Snake River Plain and interior Columbia River Basin, represent some of the most endangered ecosystems in North America (Noss and Peters 1995). Similarly, populations of bird species in grassland and shrubland groups have declined more than those in other bird groups during the last 30 years (Knopf 1994, Paige and Ritter 1999, Peterjohn and Sauer 1999). Despite significant habitat losses and declines in bird populations, we still do not adequately understand the mechanisms of bird responses to habitat fragmentation in Intermountain shrubsteppe or, more critically, how to reverse the loss of shrubsteppe habitats (Rotenberry 1998).

Intermountain shrubsteppe historically consisted of large expanses of sagebrush (*Artemisia* spp.), salt desert shrubs (primarily *Atriplex* spp.), and an understory of bunchgrasses interspersed with grassland patches (Hull and Hull 1974, Vale 1975; West 1979, 1983; Wright and Bailey 1982, Billings 1994, Young 1994, West and Young 2000). Shrubsteppe regions contained relatively little natural vegetative heterogeneity compared to other ecosystems in the Intermountain West (Kitchen et al. 1999) because of less pronounced gradients in elevation, moisture, and soil, and were highly susceptible to disturbance (Young and Sparks 1985). Similarly, avian diversity in shrubsteppe communities is low relative to other systems (Wiens and Rotenberry 1981, Wiens 1985a, Dobkin 1994, Rotenberry 1998).

Shrubsteppe birds live in habitats that now have a vastly different disturbance regime from that to which they were adapted. Wildfires, the primary disturbance that destroyed shrubs, historically were frequent but at small-scale, or large but relatively infrequent. Early explorers frequently reported fires in higher elevation, forested regions of the Intermountain West but few fires in the sparsely vegetated sagebrush valleys (Gruell 1985). Aboriginal burning, although common in higher elevation regions, was rare in plains habitats because of scarcity of wild game (Shinn 1980). Estimates of historical fire return intervals range from 20 to >100 years (Houston 1973, Young and Evans 1981, Wright and Bailey 1982). Sparse and patchily distributed fuels created incomplete burns. Thus, the disturbance regime was not severe enough to cause changes in vegetation composition at large scales (Wright 1985). Shrub renewal in disturbed areas was either by dispersal from remaining seed sources within the disturbed area or by regrowth from root crowns (Young and Evans 1978, 1989). The principal heterogeneity consisted of a mosaic of grasslands and different-aged patches of shrubland embedded within a larger shrub-dominated landscape (Young et al. 1979, West and Young 2000).

Exotic annuals, primarily cheatgrass (*Bromus tectorum*), Russian thistle (*Salsola kali*), and tumble mustards (*Descurainia* spp., *Sisymbrium* spp.), became established in the understory around the turn of the 20th century after ground surface disturbance caused by excessive grazing, failed agriculture, and intentional eradication of sagebrush (Vale 1974, Braun et al. 1976, Mack 1981, Yensen 1981). The synergistic pattern of ground disturbance, fire recurrence, and increased dominance by exotic vegetation have caused extensive fragmentation over large spatial scales and converted shrublands that once appeared endless to early settlers in the 1800s (Frémont 1845, Yensen 1982) into vast expanses of exotic annual grasslands (D'Antonio and Vitousek 1992, Young and Longland 1996, Hann et al. 1997, Knick and Rotenberry 1997). Parts of the Snake River Plain now burn every 3–5 years (Whisenant 1990). Using reported extremes for fire return intervals, fires that once impacted <1–5% of the historical landscape now burn 20–33% within some regions in an average year. In shrubland habitats within the Interior Columbia Basin ecosystem (eastern Oregon, eastern Washington, Idaho, northwestern Montana, and northeastern Nevada), the ratio of lethal to nonlethal fires in the current fire regime has increased greatly compared to the historical fire regime (Hann et al. 1997). Consequently, bird species that once experienced little if any habitat change within their home range and life span now live in a system that is undergoing rapid habitat fragmentation and loss (Knick and Rotenberry 2000). The large scale conversion of native shrubsteppe into grasslands dominated by exotic annual species may represent a degradation below a threshold from which recovery to native shrublands is unlikely (West and Young 2000).

In this paper, we discuss the effects of habitat fragmentation on birds living in shrubsteppe systems in the Intermountain West. The pattern of distribution and abundance of these birds is highly correlated at multiple scales with nonspatial measures of vegetative structure and floristics, and with spatial measures such as shrubland patch size, spatial texture, and shrubland-grassland perimeter (Rotenberry and Wiens 1980a, Wiens and Rotenberry 1981, Rotenberry 1985; Wiens 1985a,b; Wiens et al. 1987; Knick and Rotenberry 1995a, 1999, 2000). However, many of the underlying mechanisms of bird behavior and population dynamics that create the pattern of distribution remain unknown (Wiens et al. 1986a; Wiens 1989a,b; Rotenberry 1998, Rotenberry and Knick 1999).

Shrubsteppe systems present a unique challenge to understanding bird population responses to fragmentation. The pattern of distribution and abundance of shrubsteppe birds is highly related to the shrubland-grassland configuration of a region (Knick and Rotenberry 1995a, Vander Haegen et al. 2000). In contrast, mechanisms of disturbance that change habitat composition and configuration, such as fire or livestock grazing, readily cross shrubland-grassland boundaries. Similarly, the relatively slight structural differences between a shrubland patch and an adjacent grassland may have little influence on mechanisms that affect bird population dynamics, such as nest predation or parasitism, compared to boundaries between forest and nonforested habitats (Rotenberry 1998). Thus, fragmentation in shrubsteppe presents a dichotomy in response to habitat boundaries between bird distribution and the mechanisms that create the patterns in habitats and birds. In this review, we first describe the patterns of distribution and abundance of passerine birds in shrubsteppe regions of the Intermountain West. We then examine potential mechanisms by which fragmentation influences population change to produce those patterns.

We make two important assumptions in our review. First, and perhaps too pessimistically, we assume that shrubland fragmentation and loss in low elevation shrubsteppe, unlike other ecosystems in the Intermountain West, may result in degradation below a threshold to a permanent state of exotic annual grasslands from which recovery to a shrubland is not possible without extensive efforts for restoration (Westoby 1981, West and Young 2000). Second, we make untested assumptions about scaling up; that processes and patterns observed at the small spatial and temporal extent of individual studies are present at larger scales throughout the region (Wiens and Rotenberry 1981, Allen and Starr 1982, O'Neill 1989, Wiens 1989c, Levin 1992, Goodwin and Fahrig 1998, Rotenberry and Knick 1999).

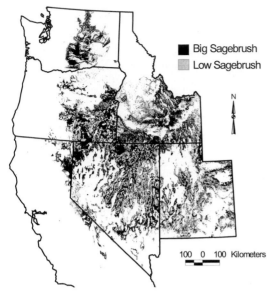

Big Sagebrush

Low Sagebrush

N

100 0 100 Kilometers

FIGURE 1. Distribution of Intermountain sagebrush steppe regions.

TABLE 1. TOTAL AREA (KM²) IN POTENTIAL NATURAL VEGETATION FOR SHRUBSTEPPE CLASSES IN THE INTERMOUNTAIN WEST (KÜCHLER 1964)

Küchler's (1964) potential natural vegetation	Area (km²)
38. Great Basin Sagebrush (*Artemisia*)	128,236
40. Saltbush-greasewood (*Atriplex-Sarcobatus*)	115,630
50. Fescue-wheatgrass (*Festuca-Agropyron*)	20,918
51. Wheatgrass-bluegrass (*Agropyron-Poa*)	36,377
55. Sagebrush steppe (*Artemisia-Agropyron*)	257,610
Total	558,771

Notes: Shrub dominated lands comprise 28–40% of the area within the conterminous western United States (McArther and Ott 1996). We summed estimates within vegetation classes (McArthur and Ott 1996) for Idaho, Utah, Oregon, Nevada, and Washington.

STUDY REGION AND SPECIES

We conducted our review for shrubsteppe regions of Idaho, Oregon, Nevada, Utah, and Washington and including portions of Wyoming and northeastern California (Fig. 1). The areal extent of potential natural vegetation in shrubsteppe habitats in this region, using Küchler's (1964) vegetation classes, is approximately 559,000 km² (Table 1). Within that region, long-term studies of shrubsteppe birds have been conducted in Oregon, Washington, and Idaho. We base much of our discussion on bird and fragmentation dynamics for shrubsteppe systems in the Snake River Plain of southern Idaho and the Interior Columbia Basin, Washington, because they contain studies that specifically addressed habitat fragmentation, and because habitat fragmentation and loss in these areas is most pronounced and may be a harbinger for other shrubsteppe regions of the Intermountain West. We recognize that some regions of the Great Basin, such as eastern Oregon, have the opposite problem of loss of fire, which has led to extensive stands of high density sagebrush. However, our emphasis was on the effects of fragmentation, which are most prevalent in regions currently undergoing high rates of severe disturbance.

The primary species in this review include Horned Larks (*Eremophilus alpestris*), Sage Thrashers (*Oreoscoptes montanus*), Brewer's Sparrows (*Spizella breweri*), Sage Sparrows (*Amphispiza belli*), and Western Meadowlarks (*Sturnella neglecta*). Where available, we also include information on Rock Wrens (*Salpinctes obsoletus*), Loggerhead Shrikes (*Lanius ludovicianus*), Green-tailed Towhees (*Pipilo chlorurus*), Vesper Sparrows (*Pooecetes gramineus*), Grasshopper Sparrows (*Ammodramus savannarum*), Black-throated Sparrows (*Amphispiza bilineata*), and Lark Sparrows (*Chondestes grammacus*). Of these 12 species, 5 are classed by the Partners in Flight Western Working Group as requiring immediate conservation action in at least 1 state or province (Table 2). In addition, 5 of these species exhibit significant population declines in Breeding Bird Surveys conducted throughout the western region (Sauer et al. 1997; Table 2).

SHRUBSTEPPE HABITAT DYNAMICS

HABITAT FRAGMENTATION AND LOSS

Fragmentation and loss of shrubsteppe habitats has been widespread and relatively rapid throughout the Intermountain region largely because of human disturbance (Braun et al. 1976, D'Antonio and Vitousek 1992, Billings 1994, Young 1994, Hann et al. 1997, Mac 1998). More than 10% of the sagebrush steppe in the Intermountain region and 99% of the Palouse Prairie grasslands in eastern Washington, Oregon, and Idaho have been converted to agriculture (Noss et al. 1995). Livestock grazing is pervasive throughout the Intermountain West (Bock et al. 1993), and has influenced >99% of the shrublands and severely altered >30% (West 1996). The change in disturbance regime has facilitated the spread of invasive plants such as cheatgrass, and has altered both the form and function of shrubsteppe regions throughout the Intermountain West (Young 1994). Exotic annual vegetation may indirectly influence bird productivity,

TABLE 2.   STATES AND PROVINCES IN WHICH CONSERVATION ACTION IS RECOMMENDED BY THE PARTNERS IN FLIGHT WESTERN WORKING GROUP AND WESTERN REGIONAL POPULATION TRENDS (% CHANGE/YEAR) IN BREEDING BIRD SURVEYS (SAUER ET AL. 1997) OF PASSERINE BIRDS BREEDING IN INTERMOUNTAIN SHRUBSTEPPE

Species	Conservation action	Population change		
		1966–1996	1966–1979	1980–1996
Horned Lark		−2.1*	−1.7*	−2.6*
Rock Wren		−0.9	1.8	−1.2
Sage Thrasher	BC, ID	0.6	2.7	0.1
Loggerhead Shrike	WA, BC, OR, ID	−4.1*	−8.1*	−1.6
Green-tailed Towhee		−0.1	−1.6	0.7
Brewer's Sparrow	BC, ID, UT	−3.5*	−1.8	−3.0*
Vesper Sparrow		0.0	−0.6	0.7
Lark Sparrow	WA	−1.1	0.9	−0.1
Black-throated Sparrow		−0.8	2.3	−1.2
Sage Sparrow	WA, OR, ID, UT	0.5	−4.9	1.9
Grasshopper Sparrow		0.5	−1.2	3.7
Western Meadowlark		−1.2*	−1.3	−1.5*

* Population trend is significant (α = 0.05).

mortality, and population trends by increasing the severity of disturbance on the habitat and accelerating the rate of fragmentation and shrubland loss.

Fragmentation and loss of shrublands has been particularly pronounced in the Snake River Plain and Columbia River Basin (Whisenant 1990, Dobler et al. 1996). More than 99% of the

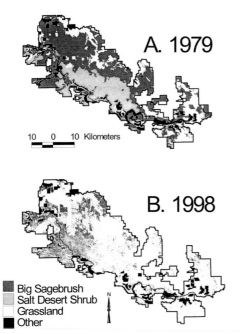

FIGURE 2.   Shrubland loss from 1979 to 1994 in the Snake River Birds of Prey National Conservation Area, southwestern Idaho. The 1979 vegetation map was delineated from aerial photography. The 1994 vegetation map was classified from Landsat satellite imagery (Knick et al. 1997).

basin big sagebrush (*Artemisia tridentata* ssp. *tridentata*) communities in southern Idaho have been converted to agriculture (Noss et al. 1995). Within the 200,000-ha region of the Snake River Birds of Prey National Conservation Area in southwestern Idaho, over 50% of the existing shrublands were destroyed by wildfires between 1979 and 1996 (Fig. 2). During that time, the total area in grasslands, primarily cheatgrass, increased from 17% to 53% (U.S. Dept. Interior 1996). Fire was the primary cause of shrubland loss, exacerbated by disturbance caused by livestock grazing and military training (U.S. Dept. Interior 1996, Knick and Rotenberry 1997). The average fire return interval in the National Conservation Area decreased from 80.5 yr between 1950 (the first year of fire records) to 1979, to 27.5 yr between 1980 to 1994. The fire return interval is as short as 3–5 years in other parts of the Snake River Plain (Whisenant 1990). By comparison, the fire return intervals in the historical disturbance regime, although difficult to reconstruct, were estimated at 60–125 years for nearby sagebrush systems at higher elevation (Wright and Bailey 1982).

Approximately 59% of the historical distribution of shrubsteppe landscapes and 35% of the sagebrush in Washington still exists (Dobler 1994, Dobler et al. 1996, MacDonald and Reese 1998), but more land continues to be converted each year (M. Vander Haegen, pers. comm.). With the exception of three large areas of shrubsteppe remaining in federal management (Yakima Training Center, Hanford Nuclear Site, Yakima Indian Nation), remaining shrubsteppe habitats are largely fragmented within a mosaic dominated by agriculture (Dobler et al. 1996). The primary cause of shrubland loss in the Columbia River Basin, Washington has been large-scale conversion of shrublands to agriculture, although fires also can be significant locally in destroying shrublands (Rickard and Vaughan 1988, Cadwell et al. 1996). Landscapes converted to agriculture are unlikely to be returned to shrublands in the foreseeable future (Dobler et al. 1996, Vander Haegen et al. 2000).

Current distribution compared to historical extent of habitats within the Interior Columbia Basin ecosystem had decreased 33% for big sagebrush, 34% for mountain big sagebrush, and 34% for salt desert shrubs, mostly due to agriculture (Hann et al. 1997). Similarly, areal extent of habitats used by Grasshopper Sparrows had decreased 15%, 19% for Vesper Sparrows, 20% for Western Meadowlarks, 19% for Lark Sparrows, 17% for Sage Thrashers, 15% for Brewer's Sparrows, 21% for Sage Sparrows, 15% for Black-throated Sparrows, and 9% for Loggerhead Shrikes (Wisdom et al. 2000).

HABITAT FRAGMENTATION AND SHRUBSTEPPE BIRDS

FRAGMENTATION AND DISTRIBUTION OF SHRUBSTEPPE BIRDS

Shrubsteppe birds in the Intermountain West are distributed along major gradients between extremes dominated by grassland and shrubland habitats (Rotenberry and Wiens 1980a,b; Wiens and Rotenberry 1981, Wiens et al. 1987, Wiens 1989a). Large scale conversion of shrublands to grassland habitats dominated by exotic annuals likely will result in loss of bird species richness, increased numbers of Horned Larks and Western Meadowlarks, and decreased numbers of shrubland-obligate species (Klebenow and Beall 1977, Rotenberry and Wiens 1978, Castrale 1982, Bock and Bock 1987, McAdoo et al. 1989, Shuler et al. 1993, Dobler 1994, Rotenberry et al. 1995, Bradford et al. 1998).

Few studies have related distribution and abundance of shrubland birds to the composition and configuration of large landscapes (km²; Knick and Rotenberry 1995a, Vander Haegen et al. 2000). Alternatively, measures of spatial heterogeneity taken at small study sites (ha) have not correlated with species abundance or presence and may not reflect the scale at which birds respond to their environment (Wiens 1974a). In southwestern Idaho, we determined the distribution of species in a bird community in the Snake River Birds of Prey National Conservation Area relative to a gradient between shrub and grassland habitats. We used a canonical correspondence analysis (CANOCO; ter Braak 1986, 1988) of species abundances at 134 sites at which we measured local vegetation characteristics and landscape variables (Knick and Ro-

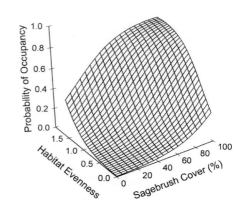

A.

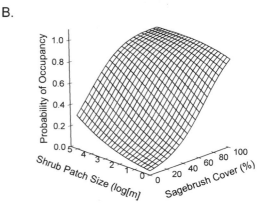

B.

FIGURE 3. Relationship between local and landscape variables and probability of occurrence by Sage Thrashers (A) and Sage Sparrows (B) in southwestern Idaho (Knick and Rotenberry 1995a).

tenberry 1995b). Canonical correspondence analysis is a multivariate direct gradient ordination of species variation relative to environmental variables. The ordination axes of bird species data are constrained to be linear combinations of the environmental variables, but the species are assumed to have a unimodal response to the environmental gradients (ter Braak and Prentice 1988). Shrubland-obligate species, such as Sage and Brewer's sparrows and Sage Thrashers, were associated with Wyoming big sagebrush (*Artemisia tridentata* ssp. *wyomingensis*) communities and landscape variables of increasing shrub patch size and number of shrub cells in the 1-km radius surrounding the sample point (Fig. 3). In contrast, Horned Larks and Western Meadowlarks were associated with disturbed vegetation communities. Predictive maps of Sage Sparrow and Brewer's Sparrow presence, using a resource selection function based on landscape variables and the Mahalanobis distance statistic, again demonstrated the direct re-

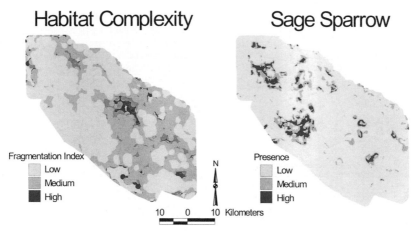

FIGURE 4. Habitat fragmentation within a 5-km radius (average perimeter/area of shrub patches) (top) and probability of Sage Sparrow presence (bottom) in a 200,000-ha shrubsteppe region in southwestern Idaho.

lationship between species presence and large shrubland patches (Fig. 4; Knick and Rotenberry 1999).

The interaction between local vegetation characteristics and landscape measures of fragmentation that determine the probability of bird occupancy carries important implications for our understanding of habitat selection and management. Equal probabilities of occupancy were possible with different combinations of ground cover of sagebrush and patch size (Fig. 3). Moreover, the shape of the selection function changed relative to differences in value of a habitat variable (Rotenberry and Knick 1999). Thus, management questions of minimum areas required by a species may be best answered by a probability of occupancy produced by multiple patch sizes and characteristics. The low probability of occupancy also implies that only a portion of available patches may be occupied, even though the patch may be of sufficient size to encompass multiple territories of individuals (Robbins et al. 1989a).

MECHANISMS UNDERLYING THE DISTRIBUTION PATTERNS

Landscapes generate patterns of species distribution by influencing productivity, mortality, or movements among habitats (Wiens 1976, 1994; Urban and Shugart 1986, Danielson 1992, Pulliam et al. 1992). Many species of birds exhibit a meta-population structure composed of source or sink populations within a region (Pulliam 1988, Hanski 1991, Opdam 1991, Pulliam and Danielson 1991, McCullough 1996). We expected that fragmentation of shrublands facilitated mechanisms that would decrease productivity or increase mortality and thus lower the number and individual contribution of source populations by decreasing and isolating the area of suitable resources, and increasing the amount of edge (Fahrig and Merriam 1994, Wiens 1996). We reviewed studies for evidence that fragmentation resulted in lower nest success or productivity, increased mortality due to predation or parasitism, or influenced movements among habitats.

Productivity

Productivity might be related to fragmentation of shrublands and landscape configuration by differences in breeding density, nest success, or number of young produced. Measures of productivity, as well as microhabitat characteristics of nest placement have been reported for numerous shrubsteppe species (Rich 1980a,b; Reynolds 1981; Petersen and Best 1985a,b; Winter and Best 1985; Rotenberry and Wiens 1980b, 1991). However, few studies have related productivity to large scale measures of spatial characteristics in Intermountain shrubsteppe systems (Knick and Rotenberry 1995b, 1996; Vander Haegen et al. 2000). Of these, only nest success relative to landscape configuration has been measured.

Young were successfully fledged at 11 of 13 Sage Sparrow nests, 27 of 36 Brewer's Sparrow nests, and 8 of 37 Sage Thrasher nests during 1994 and 1995 in southwestern Idaho (Knick and Rotenberry 1996). Local or landscape variables were not associated (P > 0.05) with nesting success of Sage Sparrows. For Brewer's Sparrows, increased nest success was marginally related to increasing landscape heterogeneity (P = 0.098), a trend that was contrary to expectation. Sage Thrasher nests were more successful

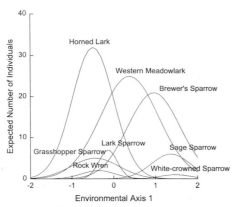

FIGURE 5. Gaussian response curves of bird species along the first environmental axis of a canonical correspondence analysis of bird species and environmental variables. The species response curve was a function of the maximum number of observations (y_o) at a site for the species in the sample, the modal score on the environmental axis (m), and the dispersion (s) along the axis in units of standard deviation. The expected value ($\hat{y}$) then is: $\hat{y} = y_o \cdot \exp\{[-(1/2) \cdot (x - m)^2]/s^2\}$ for any point x of the environmental axis (ter Braak and Looman 1986). Environmental variables were percent ground cover of sagebrush, winterfat, shadscale, and grasslands, and the area, amount of perimeter, and thickness of shrub patches within 1 km of the sampling point.

with increasing shrub patch size (P = 0.064). In Washington, Sage Thrashers, Brewers Sparrows, and Lark Sparrows had lower nest success in fragmented compared to unfragmented regions (M. Vander Haegen, unpubl. data). In eastern Idaho, clutch size and nest success did not differ between an experimentally burned area that reduced sagebrush cover by 50% and control plots, but no spatial characteristics of the landscape were measured (Petersen and Best 1987).

The pattern of species presence along a habitat gradient of decreasing grassland cover and disturbance to increased shrub cover and patch size of shrublands changed from grassland species, such as Grasshopper Sparrows and Horned Larks to shrubland obligates, such as Brewer's and Sage sparrows (Fig. 5). The density of singing males was greatest in unfragmented shrubland habitats for Sage Thrashers, and Brewer's and Sage sparrows (Knick and Rotenberry 1995, 1999). Large-scale habitat changes in southwestern Idaho that increased fragmentation and habitat richness in the landscape were associated with lower densities of Horned Larks, Western Meadowlarks, and Brewer's Sparrows (Knick and Rotenberry 2000). However, bird response was not strongly associated with habitat changes

at small spatial or temporal scales. Densities of Sage and Brewer's sparrows did not differ consistently between plots in controlled fire and unburned areas in eastern Idaho and densities of Sage Thrashers did not change (Petersen and Best 1987, 1999). In Montana, a 50% reduction of sagebrush cover by herbicidal spraying did not affect numbers of breeding pairs of Brewer's Sparrows or Vesper Sparrows the following year, but Brewer's Sparrows declined in the total-kill sagebrush plot (Best 1972). Similarly, prediction of densities of Sage Sparrows and Brewer's Sparrows did not track local habitat changes in eastern Oregon (Wiens and Rotenberry 1985, Wiens et al. 1986b, Rotenberry 1986, Rotenberry and Knick 1999).

Food resources may not limit productivity in shrubsteppe regions except during "ecological crunch" periods (Wiens 1974b, 1989a,b). However, no studies have related food resources in fragmented and unfragmented habitats to differences in nesting success or clutch size. Reduction of arthropod abundance and biomass did not adversely affect productivity of Brewer's Sparrows or Sage Thrashers in Idaho (Howe et al. 1996). Similarly, available biomass of arthropods was >2 orders of magnitude greater than required for bioenergetic demands of a community of shrubsteppe birds breeding in Oregon (Rotenberry 1980).

Predation and parasitism

Edge-related processes that increase predation or parasitism associated with increased fragmentation and decreased patch size can reduce productivity in fragmented habitats relative to larger patches (Urban and Shugart 1986, Wiens et al. 1986a, Temple and Cary 1988, Porneluzi et al. 1993, Paton 1994). Nest predation ranged from 11–100% of the causes of nest failure in Brewer's Sparrows (Reynolds 1979, 1981; Petersen and Best 1987, Rotenberry and Wiens 1989, Rotenberry et al. 1999). Predators included Common Ravens (*Corvus corax*), Black-billed Magpies (*Pica pica*), Loggerhead Shrikes, snakes, long-tailed weasels (*Mustela frenata*), chipmunks (*Tamias* spp.), and ground squirrels (*Spermophilus* spp.). However, no studies have related predation rates to fragmentation in shrubsteppe habitats.

Brown-headed Cowbirds (*Molothrus ater*) parasitize nests of Brewer's and Sage sparrows (Rich 1978, Reynolds 1981, Biermann et al. 1987), but few data exist on the probability of parasitism by cowbirds relative to degree of fragmentation in shrublands. The extent to which cowbirds also may attempt to parasitize Sage Thrasher nests is unknown because Sage

Thrashers reject cowbird eggs (Rich and Rothstein 1985, Reynolds et al. 1999).

The overall parasitism rate on Brewer's and Sage sparrows in the Columbia River Basin, Washington, was <10% (Vander Haegen and Walker 1999), because most nesting attempts by host species were started before cowbirds arrived on the study areas. In addition, the relatively long distance from agriculture developments and cattle feedlots, which provide feeding areas for cowbirds, to shrubsteppe areas in Washington may have accounted for the low parasitism rates (Vander Haegen and Walker 1999). The rate of parasitism in Idaho and Oregon also was low (0–13%) and may reflect the relatively low presence of cowbirds (Rich 1978, Rotenberry and Wiens 1989, Rotenberry et al. 1999). In contrast, cowbirds parasitized 52% of Brewer's sparrow nests in southeastern Alberta (Biermann et al. 1987). Therefore, parasitism by cowbirds increases when shrublands are converted to agriculture or cattle feedlots, providing feeding sites for Brown-Headed Cowbirds from which they can travel into surrounding areas to parasitize nests.

The structural difference between shrubland and grassland to predators or cowbirds may be less significant in producing an edge effect than boundaries between forest and nonforested habitats (Rotenberry 1998). As such, the function of fragmentation may be indirect, by providing homesites, feeding or watering sites, or different plant assemblages in unsuitable fragments that increase the presence or proximity of potential predators or cowbirds (Coker and Capen 1995, Robinson et al. 1995a, Knight et al. 1998).

Redistribution and individual movements

In the absence of habitat-specific differences in productivity or survival to create differences in species abundance relative to habitat fragmentation, the pattern of a species distribution also could result from individuals moving among habitats (Dunning et al. 1992). We expect that adults might exhibit strong site tenacity (Wiens 1985a, Wiens and Rotenberry 1985, Knick and Rotenberry 2000) and return after migration to the same breeding territory as the previous year regardless of any habitat alternation (Rotenberry and Knick 1999; M. Vander Haegen, pers. comm.). In contrast, young birds that previously have not established successful territories may seek new areas either following fledging or upon returning from migration. We do not know if dispersal and migration characteristics, or habitats selected by juveniles differ between those hatched in fragmented or unfragmented shrublands.

Redistribution by individuals following migration and return to the breeding grounds also could account for the pattern of distribution and abundance relative to fragmentation. Many species of shrubsteppe birds migrate seasonally, breeding in the northern Great Basin, and wintering in the southwestern U.S. or northern Mexico. Unfortunately, the considerable majority of detailed research occurs only during the breeding season. There are ample theoretical reasons to expect that events that occur in migration or during winter may play an equal or even greater role in determining population dynamics on the breeding grounds (Dunning and Brown 1982, Knopf 1994, Sherry and Holmes 1995, Herkert and Knopf 1998). Most importantly, the linkage between any specific breeding area and any specific wintering area is unknown for virtually all populations. In essence, then, the breeding grounds of these species represent "open" systems, systems whose properties are affected by events that lie outside the domain of study and, hence, cannot be completely understood without expanding the scale of study.

Linkages within a meta-population are driven by the movements of individual animals, particularly those movements associated with natal dispersal (although post-breeding dispersal may also play a role in some species). Unfortunately, empirical data relating to dispersal are usually lacking, which severely constrains our ability to understand and to adequately model population dynamics in most species. Because many species in fragmented landscapes are potentially threatened, conservation efforts are hampered by the lack of reliable information on dispersal. Patterns of natal dispersal also are relevant to issues of genetic structure and differentiation in populations, which also may have conservation-related consequences. Furthermore, most meta-population models deal only with resident species; little is known about linkages of migrant populations breeding in a fragmented landscape, or whether they even show meta-population structure.

DISCUSSION

The effect of habitat fragmentation and the increased intensity of land use on the biota and its diversity are important considerations in the conservation of the earth's resources (Wilson 1988, Saunders et al. 1991). Increasingly, birds and other animals are forced to live in habitats that have become fragmented in space by the direct or indirect actions of humans. Our understanding of habitat fragmentation and its consequences for bird populations have primarily been developed from forested (Robbins et al. 1989a, Rolstad 1991, Freemark and Collins 1992, Robinson 1992, Robinson et al. 1995a) or grassland regions (Johnson and Temple 1986, Herkert 1994). Yet, fragmentation of shrub-steppe from disturbances such as wildfires, agriculture, or other human-caused land use is equally dynamic and has significant consequences for shrubsteppe birds as well as other taxa (Braun et al. 1976, Knick 1999). Unlike other ecosystems, loss of shrubsteppe may be irreversible once cheatgrass dominates the system because of loss of seed sources, changes in soils, and the increased fire frequency (Westoby 1981, D'Antonio and Vitousek 1992, West and Young 2000).

Populations of shrubsteppe birds are of conservation concern in Intermountain states because of declines over part or most of the Great Basin and Intermountain shrubsteppe regions. In addition to passerines, population declines of Sage Grouse (*Centrocercus urophasianus*) and Columbian Sharp-tailed Grouse (*Tympanuchus phasianellus* ssp. *columbianus*) are linked directly to fragmentation and habitat loss (Swensen et al. 1987, Dobkin 1995, Connelly and Braun 1997, MacDonald and Reese 1998; M. Schroeder et al., unpubl. manuscript). Sage Grouse have recently been petitioned for listing under the Endangered Species Act because of concerns over rangewide declines in numbers, and Columbian Sharp-tailed grouse currently are under status review.

Landscape analyses in shrubsteppe and other arid ecosystems have not been as prevalent as in other major ecosystems largely because mapping and describing habitats over large extents, particularly from satellite imagery, pose difficult technological challenges (Knick et al. 1997). Mapping habitat change by standard remote sensing techniques (Singh 1989, Dunn et al. 1991) also is problematic because of inability of satellite sensors to detect vegetation in sparsely covered shrublands. Appropriate measurement metrics to quantify fragmentation in shrublands are more difficult compared to agricultural and forested systems because of the complex patterns produced by fires (Knick and Rotenberry 1997). Thus, few studies have quantified spatial attributes of composition and configuration of landscapes relative to bird population dynamics in shrubsteppe compared to forested systems.

The process of fragmentation operates at multiple scales of space and time. At large spatial scales in shrublands, fragmentation was associated with distribution and abundance of populations of shrubland species. Declines in populations of Brewer's Sparrows, Western Meadowlarks, and Horned Larks also may be directly related to large-scale fragmentation in Intermountain shrubsteppe. Large-scale fragmentation may influence nesting success or facilitate cowbird movements into previously unsuitable habitats. At smaller scales, we expected that fragmentation would affect individuals within the population to produce the larger pattern. Presence of shrubland birds was influenced by local vegetation characteristics in combination with landscape measures at spatial extents much larger than individual home ranges. However, we did not find convincing evidence that individual productivity or probability of predation was directly related to fragmentation. Thus, the larger regional context in which shrubsteppe birds establish their territories may be more important in determining range-wide patterns than dynamics within that territory once established (Rotenberry and Knick 1999). Cross-scale research is needed to determine appropriate scales at which birds respond to the system (Wiens 1974a, Wiens and Rotenberry 1980, Holling 1992).

Interaction of local and landscape variables in predicting species presence emphasized the difficulty in defining habitat fragmentation in shrubsteppe systems. If fragmentation is defined relative to a species-specific probability of presence, then multiple combinations of local and landscape variables might yield similar probabilities of occupancy by individuals. Similar to defining minimum patch requirements, our understanding of fragmentation must be done in the context of multiple gradients of patch size, perimeter, and the degree of isolation of the patch (Fahrig and Merriam 1994; Wiens 1994, 1996).

The declining populations of Horned Larks and Western Meadowlarks, determined from the North American Breeding Bird Surveys (Sauer et al. 1997), are contrary to our expectations from habitat changes throughout the Intermountain shrubsteppe region. Horned Larks and Western Meadowlarks are grassland species that are common after disturbance and we would predict increases in populations of these two species. However, the exotic-dominated grasslands that result from loss of shrublands throughout much of the Intermountain region are very different from the native grasslands to which Horned Larks and Western Meadowlarks are adapted. Declines in populations of Horned Lark and Western Meadowlark populations indicate that exotic annual grasslands are not ecologically equivalent to native grasslands. Numbers of Western Meadowlarks were lower but those of Horned Larks were higher on transects in cheatgrass compared to sagebrush communities in southcentral Washington (Rogers et al. 1988).

In another apparent discrepancy between species population and habitat trends, numbers of Sage Sparrows observed on Breeding Bird Surveys were increasing, although the trend was statistically insignificant. Possibly, the Breeding Bird Surveys may not be sampling the available habitats, or tracking the habitat changes. We also suggest that for all of these species, dynamics on the wintering grounds may be equally, or even more important in driving population trends than habitat changes on the breeding grounds.

COMPARISON TO MIDWESTERN SHRUBLAND AND GRASSLAND SYSTEMS

Birds living in grassland systems are experiencing a more extreme scenario of habitat fragmentation and loss than birds in shrubland systems. Conversion to agricultural cropland, livestock grazing, and urbanization have altered most of the grassland ecosystems in North America (Knopf 1994, Herkert 1995, Noss et al. 1995, Vickery and Herkert 1999). Habitat loss exceeds 80% of the original distribution of prairie grasslands and is almost complete in areas suitable for agricultural croplands (Samson and Knopf 1994). Other more subtle changes in grassland habitats have resulted from differences in the grazing regime by large herbivores and alteration of historical fire frequencies (Saab et al. 1995). In grasslands, as well as shrublands, restoration of native species and processes remains a significant challenge (Bock et al. 1993, Rotenberry 1998, Vickery et al. 1999).

Fire, grazing, and climate were significant influences in native grasslands but varied in their impact on system processes relative to geographic location. In Great Plains and eastern tallgrass prairies, natural and aboriginal-caused fires were large scale, intense, and frequent (5–30 year return interval), and combined with periodic drought to maintain grasslands and prevent shrub or tree growth (Wright and Bailey 1982, Sims and Risser 2000). Grazing by large herds of bison (*Bison bison*) was locally intensive but highly variable in space and time. In contrast, fire was the dominant disturbance in western grasslands and shrublands because large grazers have been absent since approximately 12,000 years presettlement (Mack and Thompson 1982, West and Young 2000). In all grassland and shrubland systems, fire suppression and control, either by direct intervention or indirectly by human-created fire-breaks, have disrupted successional and cyclic pathways. Similarly, effects of grazing have changed significantly because of reduced native ungulate herds and increased domestic livestock use, often resulting in a more intensive disturbance that is spatially and temporally uniform in the landscape (Bock et al. 1993).

Population trends of grassland birds, as a group, decreased throughout North America from 1966–1996; 13 of 25 species had significant declines and 3 had significant increases during this period (Peterjohn and Sauer 1999). Populations of grassland species also have declined over the past 100 years corresponding to the long-term loss of grasslands (DeSante and George 1994). However, as in shrubland systems, range-wide population changes detected in Breeding Bird Surveys were not well supported by studies at local scales (Herkert and Knopf 1998). In addition, the pattern of distribution and abundance of grassland birds was sensitive to landscape measures, but the mechanisms producing those patterns remain unclear (Herkert and Knopf 1998).

The winter ecology of grassland and shrubland birds is largely unknown, despite potentially having a large influence on sizes of breeding populations (Dunning and Brown 1982). Most western grassland and shrubland bird species are short-distance migrants to southern and southwestern United States and northern Mexico (DeSante and George 1994, Rotenberry 1998, Vickery et al. 1999). Therefore, influences on populations of these species are largely North American processes (Knopf 1994, Herkert 1995, Rotenberry 1998).

The effects of fragmentation in shrubland or grassland systems may be most pronounced when the severity of disturbance results in a highly contrasting mosaic of suitable and unsuitable habitats derived from a previously homogeneous landscape. The structural difference between shrublands and grasslands, or between grasslands and agriculture or urban areas, although slight relative to forest and nonforest boundaries, nonetheless is a significant component to bird distribution and abundance. Where shrublands or grasslands have been fragmented into unsuitable areas, numbers of area-sensitive bird species decline (Johnson and Temple 1986, Herkert 1994, Vickery et al. 1994, Bock et al. 1999, O'Connor et al. 1999, Walk and Warner 1999). Conversely, habitat fragmentation may not be a significant factor in bird dynamics in areas in which habitats remain largely unchanged because the relative severity of disturbance is minimal or infrequent, or in landscapes in which natural heterogeneity of habitats is high. In Colorado foothills containing a high degree of natural heterogeneity, shrubland birds were not sensitive to landscape characteristics (Berry and Bock 1998).

The answer may lie in behavioral mechanisms of habitat selection, particularly the recognition of a suitable place in which to settle for the first time. Prior to the onset of anthropogenically-induced fragmentation, most of the species in this review occurred in (and presumably were adapted to) landscapes dominated by shrublands that were homogeneous over large spatial scales. Perhaps reduction of these vast tracts of shrublands below some minimum, but currently unknown, size to current fragmented landscapes simply represents a poor fit to the habitat template of these birds.

CONCLUSIONS

The distribution of shrubsteppe birds was significantly related to large-scale habitat fragmentation. However, differences in productivity, predation, or parasitism associated with fragmentation of shrublands were either unreported or largely lacking. We suggest that individuals select location of home ranges within a hierarchy of landscape and local vegetation characteristics to produce the range-wide patterns of distribution. However, habitat structure may not be important in influencing mechanisms that affect productivity and mortality among individuals. Thus, patterns of species distribution are the result of individual movements among habitats either post dispersal or after migration. A lag effect due to site tenacity is evident in bird population responses to habitats (Wiens and Rotenberry 1985; Peterson and Best 1987, 1999; Rotenberry and Knick 1999, Knick and Rotenberry 2000). Ultimately, populations of shrubland obligates may not persist in landscapes of increasingly fragmented patches after disturbance (Braun et al. 1976, Rotenberry and Wiens 1980a).

ACKNOWLEDGMENTS

The USGS Forest and Rangeland Ecosystem Science Center, Snake River Field Station, US Department of Interior Global Climate Change Program, University of California, Riverside, and the Bureau of Land Management Challenge Cost Share Program have supported our work on shrubsteppe habitats and passerine birds. We thank F. Howe (Utah Dept. of Wildlife), M. Vander Haegen (Washington Dept. of Fish and Wildlife), and T. Rich (US Bureau of Land Management) for their discussions on shrubsteppe birds, and R. Rosentreter (US Bureau of Land Management), N. West (Utah State University), and J. Young (USDA Agricultural Research Services) for insights into presettlement conditions of shrubsteppe regions. We appreciate reviews of the manuscript by D. Dobkin, T. Rich, and P. Vickery.

Studies in Avian Biology No. 25:141–157, 2002.

HABITAT FRAGMENTATION EFFECTS ON BIRDS IN SOUTHERN CALIFORNIA: CONTRAST TO THE "TOP-DOWN" PARADIGM

DOUGLAS T. BOLGER

Abstract. I review the existing literature on habitat fragmentation and its effects on avian populations in coastal sage scrub and chaparral habitat in coastal southern California. Included in this review is a consideration of the effect of fragmentation on nest predators, brood parasites, food availability, and habitat structure and quality. Fragmentation and the creation of edge are extensive in this region. The primary contemporary fragmenting land-use is residential development. In comparison to forested landscapes in the East and Midwest, fragmentation in this region seems to cause more isolation in bird populations. Local extinctions in isolated habitat fragments are common among some species of the shrub habitat avifauna and colonizations are relatively rare. This difference may be due to more limited dispersal ability in the year-round residents that are characteristic of this region as compared to the long-distance migrants in the East and Midwest. Perhaps due to the semi-arid nature of the region, fragmentation may be accompanied by more habitat degradation than in mesic regions, which could contribute to the lack of successful colonization. In contrast to studies in the East and Midwest, the only demographic study of avian edge effects in this system indicates that nest predation and brood parasitism do not increase near anthropogenically-induced edges. In isolated habitat fragments mammalian mesopredators appear to undergo "mesopredator release" in the absence of coyotes (*Canis latrans*). In habitat fragments the availability of potential arthropod prey is positively related to fragment size and negatively related to fragment age, but does not appear to be a function of distance to edge. In large habitat blocks, however, the abundance of a number of arthropod taxa is lower near edges. A particularly striking edge effect is the invasion of non-native Argentine ants along urban edges. The effect of Argentine ants on native ants is severe but their effect on arthropods that are more important as avian prey is less clear.

Key Words: *Aimophila ruficeps*; Argentine ants; bottom-up; edge effects; habitat fragmentation; *Linepithema humile*; mesopredator release; nest predation; Rufous-crowned Sparrow; southern California; top-down.

Birds display varying degrees of edge and fragment area sensitivity, with abundance of some species declining sharply with fragment area or proximity to fragment edge (Blake and Karr 1987, Soulé et al. 1988, Robbins et al. 1989a, Herkert 1994). The mechanisms generating these sensitivities are often obscure. Since the principal determinant of avian reproductive success is the rate of nest predation (Ricklefs 1969), most mechanistic studies of the effect of fragmentation and edge on birds have focused on the "top-down" effects of nest predation and brood parasitism. In fragmented forests in the East and Midwest of North America nest predation and brood parasitism on neotropical migrant forest birds has been shown to increase with proximity to forest edge and with the degree of fragmentation in the landscape (Paton 1994, Robinson et al. 1995a, Donovan et al. 1997, Hartley and Hunter 1998). Avian and mammalian predators may increase along ecotones in response to increased density of nesting birds attracted to changes in habitat structure (Gates and Gysel 1978), or to resource subsidies provided by human land-use (Wilcove 1985, Andrén 1992). Because of this, highly fragmented landscapes in the Midwest are apparently population sinks (Pulliam 1988) for some neotropical migrant bird species. Their persistence in those landscapes appears dependent upon immigration from large, unfragmented source areas (Robinson et al. 1995a).

These striking findings have led to the current "top-down" paradigm in temperate zone fragmentation studies. However, generalizations derived from these studies may not apply to other species, ecosystems, and land-use types (Wiens 1997, Tewksbury et al. 1998). One land-use that has become increasingly common is urban development (Berry 1990, Roodman 1996). As the world becomes increasingly urban, edge between urban development and natural habitat increases as does the importance of understanding the ecological changes that occur at these interfaces (Babbitt 1999). Urban/natural edges may be especially ecologically active due to high inputs of materials, water, energy, nutrients, human commensal species, and high human population density (McDonnell et al. 1993). Only recently have "bottom-up" effects of habitat fragmentation on avian food availability received attention (Burke and Nol 1998, Zanette et al. 2000).

In coastal southern California, urban residential development is currently the principal land-use that fragments the native shrub habitats, coastal sage scrub and chaparral. Historically, agriculture and grazing also contributed to the pattern of fragmentation. There is a conservation planning effort ongoing for this region (Atwood and Noss 1994) and the reserve system that results from this effort will by necessity be set within an urban matrix. So understanding urban edge and fragmentation effects will be vital to the success of this conservation effort.

In this paper I summarize research on the patterns of distribution and abundance of breeding bird species in these fragmented landscapes and the ecological mechanisms that shape these distributions. I first suggest a conceptual framework describing fragmentation effects and the ecological mechanisms that generate these effects. Original data on bird abundance in the edge and interior of large habitat blocks in San Diego County are also presented. Finally, I review the available literature on fragmentation effects in this region and assess the evidence for a number of ecological mechanisms that might generate the effects. This review is limited to a consideration of species, predominantly passerines, that have coastal sage scrub and/or chaparral as one of their principal breeding habitats or occur in mosaic landscapes with these shrub habitats and non-native grassland.

METHODS

EDGE AND INTERIOR BIRD SURVEYS

To examine the edge sensitivity of the coastal sage scrub avifauna, variable distance point counts (Ralph et al. 1993) were conducted in the spring of 1997, 1998, and 1999 in edge and interior locations of three large coastal sage scrub habitat blocks in San Diego County, CA. Details of the sites are available in Morrison and Bolger (2002). For the analyses below, only detections within 70m of the point count station were used. Most detections of Common Ravens (see Appendix for scientific names of vertebrate species) were beyond 70m so detections up to 150m were allowed for this species. For most species fly-overs were not included in the analyses. However, for species for which most detections were by fly-over, fly-over data were included if the path of flight intercepted a 70-m circle around the point count station. These included Common Raven, Anna's Hummingbird, Costa's Hummingbird, and Western Scrub-Jay.

Point count locations were a minimum of 150m apart and edge locations were at least 70m from the urban edge. A total of 24 locations were surveyed in 1997, 15 in 1998, and 31 in 1999. Three eight-minute counts were conducted per point per year between March 29 and June 13. To achieve statistical independence, locations that were sampled in more than one year were only used in one year in the analyses, producing the final number of locations in Table 1. The choice of locations included in each year's dataset was made to maximize sample sizes.

For common species, the mean number of detections/station/visit was analyzed with two-way ANOVA with year and treatment (edge vs. interior) as the factors. For uncommon species, parametric methods were

not appropriate. Instead, the frequency of presence/absence was analyzed with three-way contingency tables: present/absent × year × treatment. If a species was detected at least once at a location in a given year it was designated present and absent otherwise. The significance of the treatment effect (edge vs. interior) was tested by comparing the chi-square value from the loglinear model that contained all pair-wise interactions to a model that did not contain the treatment × present/absent term. The significance of the treatment × present/absent term was tested by the difference in chi-square value between the models using one degree of freedom.

RESULTS AND DISCUSSION

SOUTHERN CALIFORNIA LANDSCAPES AND AVIFAUNA

There are five primary terrestrial habitats within the coastal zone of southern California: coastal sage scrub, chaparral (mixed and chamise), riparian woodland/scrub, oak woodland, and non-native grassland (Beauchamp 1986). The two shrub habitat types, coastal sage scrub (henceforth CSS) and chaparral, predominate and most research on habitat fragmentation in this region has been conducted in those habitats. The fragmentation studies reviewed below have been conducted in coastal San Diego County (predominantly in CSS habitat), the Palos Verdes Peninsula in Orange County (CSS), and the Santa Monica Mountains in Los Angeles County (chaparral). Most studies cited here were conducted within 20km of the coast, so for the purpose of this review I will define that 20 km band within these three counties as the coastal southern California region.

Coastal sage scrub is a small-statured community of subshrubs and shrubs with average shrub height of 1 m (Mooney 1977) that occurs below 600m elevation in parts of seven southern California counties: San Diego, Riverside, Orange, San Bernardino, Los Angeles, Ventura and Santa Barbara counties (Davis et al. 1995). CSS shrubs are thin-leaved and drought-deciduous. In contrast, chaparral is composed of large, woody sclerophyllous, evergreen shrubs and is geographically more widespread than CSS. It occurs from the coast to the interior Peninsular and Transverse Ranges up to 1500 m elevation.

Coastal sage scrub stands show considerable local (DeSimone and Burk 1992) and regional (Axelrod 1978, Westman 1981) variation in structure and floristics. The most characteristic elements are *Artemisia californica, Eriogonum fasiculatum,* and several *Salvia* species. Regionally, there are at least three recognized subassociations, the southern coastal variety predominantly in San Diego County, the northern coastal variety, and the inland variety primarily in

Riverside County (Axelrod 1978). Local structural variation is due to slope, aspect, substrate, disturbance history, and the influence of non-native grasses.

Undeveloped landscapes in this region are mosaics of patches of the native woody communities and non-native grasslands (Mooney 1977, DeSimone and Burk 1992). Near the coast CSS tends to occur on slopes and generally drier sites, mixed chaparral on steep north-facing slopes, and chamise chaparral on mesa-tops. Disturbance (fire, grazing, and mechanical) contributes to the mosaic because coastal sage scrub is often a successional community following disturbance to chaparral stands. The arrival of widespread non-native grasses and herbs may have exacerbated this patchiness, although there is disagreement over the pre-European extent of native grass and herbaceous stands (Minnich and Dezzani 1998). Frequent or intense fires can type convert CSS and chaparral to non-native grassland (Zedler et al. 1983). CSS in particular is vulnerable to conversion to non-native grassland (Minnich and Dezzani 1998).

There are two gradients of note in this region. First, development, and thus fragmentation, has been most extensive nearest the coast. Consequently, there is an east-west gradient in habitat availability and fragment size in the region (see Figure 2 for an example). There also is a habitat gradient; coastal sage scrub predominates near the coast, and chaparral becomes more common inland and with increasing elevation.

Of the two shrub habitat types, CSS is of greater conservation concern and has been more extensively studied for fragmentation effects. CSS is notable for its restricted range within the U.S. and high diversity of endemic plants and animals (Atwood 1993, Atwood and Noss 1994). CSS is widely reported to have declined to 10–15% of its former range; however, this percentage is based on a disputed assumption of the pre-European cover of coastal sage scrub (Minnich and Dezzani 1998).

There is considerable overlap in the chaparral and coastal sage scrub avifauna (Miller 1951). A number of bird species occur in relatively equal numbers in CSS and chaparral, including Wrentit, Spotted Towhee, California Towhee, Sage Sparrow, Bewick's Wren, California Thrasher, Western Scrub-Jay, Common Bushtit, Lazuli Bunting, and Anna's and Costa's hummingbirds. Several species usually associated with chaparral do breed in CSS, particularly when it is occurs in a mosaic with chaparral, especially Blue-gray Gnatcatcher and Black-chinned Sparrow. Only a few species are restricted to coastal sage scrub. The California Gnatcatcher and Rufous-crowned Sparrow predominantly breed in CSS, occurring only in chaparral that is relatively open or disturbed. Several grassland species occur in open CSS: Western Meadowlark, Grasshopper Sparrow, and Lark Sparrow.

The landscape of coastal southern California consists of four general elements. (1) *The urban matrix*. This land-use is the predominant land-cover in the region and is characterized by high density single-family residential development. Ornamental vegetation ranges from sparse in the higher density neighborhoods to lush in some of the older or more affluent neighborhoods. (2) *Isolated habitat fragments* (ranging from 1 to 1000ha). Fragments occur throughout most of the highly developed portion of the landscape. (3) *The edge of large habitat blocks*; habitat within 250m of the urban edge. (4) *The interior of large habitat blocks*; habitat greater than 250m from the urban edge. These large habitat blocks are either embedded in the urban matrix or are contiguous with the mountainous areas to the east.

CONSERVATION PLANNING IN THE REGION

Partly in response to petitions at the state and federal levels to list the California Gnatcatcher as an endangered species, the state of California initiated the Natural Communities Conservation Planning Program (NCCP; Atwood and Noss 1994). The state coordinates subregional planning processes that prioritize lands based on conservation value. Private landowners voluntarily participate in the planning process. Putative reserves are identified and funding sought for acquisition of lands not currently publicly owned. The eventual listing of the gnatcatcher as a federally threatened species in 1993 gave further impetus to the program as participation in the program gave landowners an avenue to pursue incidental take permits. Planning occurs in 11 subregions with the purpose of designating an interconnected system of reserves, which should result in no reduction in the ability of the region to maintain viable populations of target species (Atwood and Noss 1994). A Central-Coastal Orange County subregional plan has been approved, including 37,000 acres of reserve, and an MSCP subregional plan in San Diego has been approved that includes 170,000 acres of reserves (see http://ceres.ca.gov/CRA/NCCP/updates.htm).

CONCEPTUAL FRAMEWORK

Landscape patterns that suggest fragmentation effects

Conservation biologists often use phrases such as "the effect of habitat fragmentation on birds"; however, exactly what these effects of fragmentation are has been hard to define. Some of the confusion results from confounding the patterns of abundance that result from fragmentation with the ecological processes that generate these patterns. Patterns of abundance or demographic rates in the landscape are often presented as evidence of the effects of fragmentation. These patterns fall into the following categories. (1) *Area sensitivity*—density, probability of occurrence, survival, or reproductive success change with fragment size, or there is a significant difference between those rates in isolated fragments and in large, unfragmented habitat areas. (2) *Age sensitivity*—density, probability of occurrence, survival, or reproductive success changes with fragment age (time elapsed since insularization). (3) *Edge sensitivity*—density, probability of occurrence, survival, or reproductive success changes with proximity to the fragment edge. (4) *Distance sensitivity*—density or probability of occurrence changes in habitat fragments with proximity to other fragments or large habitat blocks.

No directionality of change is implied in these definitions to acknowledge that fragmentation can have positive or negative effects on bird species. These are patterns of abundance or demographic rates in space and time that suggest these parameters change as a consequence of fragmentation. Demonstrating a causal relationship between fragmentation and these patterns requires a consideration of the ecological mechanisms that proximally affect rates of birth, death, immigration, and emigration.

Ecological mechanisms that cause fragmentation effects

How are the patterns of fragmentation sensitivity, as defined above, produced in the landscape? The ecological consequences of habitat fragmentation are complex, diverse, and pervasive because fragmentation affects animal and plant populations via a number of interacting pathways (Wilcove et al. 1986, Robinson et al. 1992, Didham 1997). For example, *area effects* are manifest through the initial sampling effect that determines the initial avian community (Bolger et al. 1991), and through the effect of area on population sizes and rates of extinction. *Isolation effects* occur when the intervening human-modified matrix is relatively impermeable to successful dispersal to isolated patches. This may result in faunal relaxation in fragments, or faunal collapse in the extreme of zero recolonization (Brown 1971, Soulé et al. 1979). *Edge effects* are biotic and abiotic effects derived from the adjacent human-modified matrix that cause gradients in light, moisture, and wind velocity, increased exposure to invasive human commen-

sal species, and increased density of "edge species" (Murcia 1995). Island biogeographic treatments of habitat fragmentation focus on the relationship between stochastic extinction and recolonization (MacArthur and Wilson 1967, Brown 1971). However, when fragmentation is due to the intervention of intense human land uses, such as urbanization, habitat degradation due to edge effects and other anthropogenic disturbance are likely to be significant influences on abundance and extinction rates. The intensity of edge effects may also depend on the relative amount of the developed matrix present in the landscape (Donovan et al. 1997). The direct effects of area reduction, isolation, and edge can lead to *secondary effects* (also called cascading, community, or trophic effects), whereby the direct effects of fragmentation on predators, parasites, competitors, resource species, or mutualists in turn affect species with which these interact. Changes in the abundance of the resource, predator, and parasite species that birds interact with can change bird abundance through their effect on birth and death rates. *Local habitat selection* by birds can affect abundance through changes in immigration and emigration rates. Birds may avoid habitat in small fragments or adjacent to edges due to structural and floristic changes in the vegetation and altered food availability and predator and parasite abundance (Kristan et al. in press). *Landscape-scale habitat selection* occurs when birds choose habitat not only on the basis of local habitat conditions but also on the basis of landscape-scale factors such as patch area, isolation, and edge proximity. As with local habitat selection this mechanism would affect abundance through its effect on relative immigration and emigration rates.

Understanding the consequences of fragmentation has been hampered by our inability to isolate the effects of these different phenomena on the biota. These different effects can act in opposition or in concert. For instance, area and edge effects can be difficult to separate because the percentage of edge-affected habitat increases as fragment area decreases.

FRAGMENTATION PATTERNS IN SOUTHERN CALIFORNIA

Area and age sensitivity

The resident breeding birds of coastal southern California display varying degrees of sensitivity to fragment size and age. Soulé et al. (1988) found that the species richness of a group of eight shrub habitat bird species (Bewick's Wren, Spotted Towhee, California Thrasher, Wrentit, California Quail, Greater Roadrunner,

Cactus Wren, and California Gnatcatcher) showed both area and age effects; richness increased with fragment area (range 0.4–103 ha) and declined with fragment age (range 2–86 years). Quite small fragments (1–5 ha), if they were relatively young (<10 years), supported many species from this group. Species not as restricted to shrub habitat did not show similar sensitivity. These fragments range from 1 km to 15 km from the coast and most were predominated by coastal sage scrub. Some of the fragments also contained stands of mixed or chamise chaparral. Although the fragments are predominantly CSS, Soulé et al. (1988) referred to these generically as "chaparral" habitat fragments following the then popular terms of "soft chaparral" for coastal sage scrub and "hard chaparral" for mixed and chamise chaparral.

The observed decline in species richness with fragment age observed by Soulé et al. (1988) implies relaxation or faunal collapse: non-equilibrium dynamics with local extinctions in excess of infrequent recolonizations across the urban matrix (Brown 1971, Soulé et al. 1979). The existence of this extinction-recolonization imbalance is supported by the observation that species richness in the fragments was significantly lower than that in similar-sized plots in continuous blocks of habitat (Bolger et al. 1991). The species richness in unfragmented plots is an estimate of the species richness initially present in fragments of a similar size. In a recent resurvey of the same fragments ten years later, Crooks et al. (2001) tested the inferences drawn from the static patterns. Consistent with the relaxation conclusion, there were approximately twice as many extinctions (30) as colonizations (12) between 1987 and 1997 among the original group of species considered by Soulé et al. (1988).

Bolger et al. (1991) demonstrated that the distribution patterns in these fragments of the five most common of these species (Bewick's Wren, Spotted Towhee, California Thrasher, Wrentit, California Quail) were nested; species in species-poor fragments were a non-random subset of those in species-rich fragments. They concluded that this pattern was generated by a gradient in extinction vulnerability among the species. Nested occurrence patterns are common in real and virtual islands and can be produced by among-species differences in extinction vulnerability (Patterson and Atmar 1986). This pattern suggested that Wrentit was the most resistant of the five to extinction, Bewick's Wren and Spotted Towhee were intermediate, and California Thrasher and California Quail went extinct most quickly. Consistent with this, Crooks et al. (2001) found that populations of the Wrentit were only now going extinct in the smallest/old-est fragments (5 extinctions, no colonizations). California Quail, the most sensitive species (9 extinctions, no colonizations), underwent additional extinctions in several larger fragments (15–64 ha) as well as a number of small/young fragments (having apparently already gone extinct in the smaller/older fragments). California Thrasher exhibited a similar pattern, going extinct in four small/young fragments and colonizing one. The distribution of the Spotted Towhee changed very little in the intervening years (2 colonizations, no extinctions) and appeared to be in quasi-equilibrium. Soulé et al. (1988) had apparently reached the wrong conclusions about Bewick's Wren, which appears able to recolonize across the urban matrix, experiencing 6 colonizations and only 1 extinction between 1987 and 1997. In this group of five easily surveyed species, extinctions outnumbered colonizations 19 to 9. The results of Crooks et al. (2001) also point out that in this system area-sensitivity cannot be defined independently of fragment age; both variables are important predictors of species distributions in this fragmented landscape (Fig. 1).

Lovio (1996) studied fragments in another part of San Diego and found generally higher diversity in the same species group considered by Soulé et al. (1988) in similar-sized fragments. The differing results are probably the result of differing levels of isolation in the two study areas. The Soulé et al. (1988) and Crooks et al. (2001) study area was in the western part of the county and the fragments were generally isolated canyon fragments embedded in highly developed coastal mesas. Lovio's study area was slightly east and south in the Rancho San Diego area and many of the fragments were portions of slopes and ridgetops that formed a fairly dense network of patches (Lovio 1996). The mean interpatch distances were smaller in Lovio's study area (476 vs. 674 m), and the intervening urban matrix was characterized by a higher cover of mature ornamental vegetation (Weser 1996; D. Bolger, pers. obs.). A number of the fragments were connected to other fragments by narrow habitat strips or areas of disturbed and non-native vegetation (Lovio 1996) and the set of fragments was immediately adjacent to a large unfragmented habitat block. So the difference between Lovio's results and those of Soulé et al. (1988) may be indicative of the importance of the degree of fragment isolation and the permeability of the urban matrix. However, Lovio did not ascertain the age of fragments, so differing fragment ages could also be responsible for the differences between the studies.

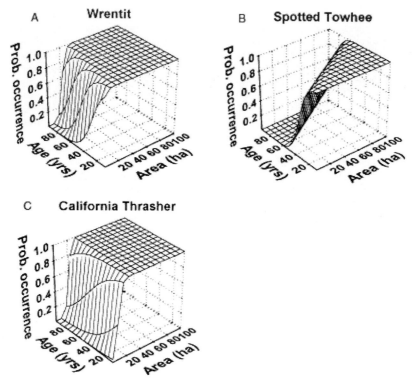

FIGURE 1. Graphical results of multiple logistic regression of the presence/absence of (A) Wrentit, (B) Spotted Towhee, and (C) California Thrasher on fragment area and age. Area sensitivity is a function of fragment age. Larger fragment area is required for persistence in older fragments. From Crooks et al. (2001).

Edge sensitivity

Bolger et al. (1997) analyzed the patterns of abundance of the 20 most common breeding bird species in a 260 sq. km landscape in coastal San Diego County (Fig. 2). This landscape encompassed a land-use gradient that included the interior of a large unfragmented habitat block, its edge, and isolated fragments in the adjacent urban matrix. For 14 of the 20 species, the fit of logistic regression models to bird abundance was improved by the addition of landscape metrics to models containing variables describing local habitat conditions. These landscape metrics described the percentage of CSS and chaparral habitat versus developed land and the amount of urban area and the amount of urban edge in the larger landscape (250 m to 3 km) around each sample point. Based on these analyses and a canonical correspondence analysis, the 20 species were characterized as edge/fragmentation-insensitive (10 species), edge/fragmentation-reduced (6 species) or edge/fragmentation-enhanced (4 species). The finding that half of the common species appear to respond to larger-scale patterns of edge and fragmentation suggests that land-scape structure is a significant determinant of bird abundance in this region.

One surprising result of this study was the elevated abundance of urban-exploiting birds some distance into the non-fragmented habitat block. The abundances of House Finch, Anna's Hummingbird (Fig. 2b), Northern Mockingbird, and Lesser Goldfinch, species common in the urban matrix, were higher in habitat adjacent to the urban edge than further into the patch interior. The region of higher density extended as far as a kilometer in Anna's Hummingbird and House Finch. These results suggest that the urban matrix could be a net source of these species, elevating densities in natural habitat adjacent to the matrix.

In chaparral habitat in the Santa Monica Mountains, Sauvajot et al. (1998) found no correlation between bird abundance and proximity to the urban edge. They also found that bird abundance did not respond to disturbance-induced changes in vegetation structure. In contrast, in inland CSS Kristan et al. (in press) observed strong correlations between bird abundance and edge-proximity that was specifically

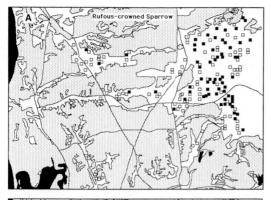

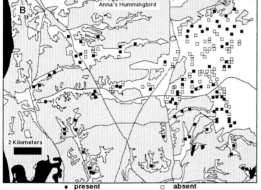

FIGURE 2. The landscape distribution patterns of (A) Rufous-crowned Sparrow and (B) Anna's Hummingbird within a 260 km² study area in coastal San Diego County. Presence/absence denotes either detection or non-detection in a single 8-min point count at each of 202 random locations during the spring of 1993. White areas are the undeveloped habitat mosaic of coastal sage scrub and chaparral. Stippling represents residential and commercial development. From Bolger et al. 1997.

associated with edge-related changes in habitat quality based on known, independent relationships to vegetation composition and structure. The lack of a correlation of disturbance to edge proximity in chaparral may have to do with the differing physical structure of chaparral and CSS vegetation. Dense and robust, chaparral probably rebuffs direct human disturbance along edges better than the smaller statured coastal sage scrub.

In the only demographic study of edge sensitivity in this region I am aware of (Morrison and Bolger 2002), no difference was found in breeding success of Rufous-crowned Sparrows, a ground-nesting year-round resident species, between edge and interior plots. Total reproductive output and daily nest predation rate did not differ between pairs in habitat adjacent to urban development (<200 m from the urban edge) as

compared to those a minimum of 500 m from urban edge during the 1997–1999 breeding seasons. P. Mock (pers. comm.) reported similar results with California Gnatcatchers at one site in San Diego.

EDGE SENSITIVITY

Of 21 species common enough for analysis, 11 differed significantly in abundance between edge and interior plots in CSS in 1997–1999 (Table 1). Anna's Hummingbird, House Finch, Northern Mockingbird, and Western Scrub-Jay were significantly more abundant in edge locations. Common Raven showed a trend of higher abundance in edges, but its abundance was highly variable and the treatment effect was non-significant. Black-chinned Sparrow, California Towhee, Common Bushtit, Lazuli Bunting, Rufous-crowned Sparrow, Spotted Towhee, and Wrentit were significantly less abundant along edges. California Thrasher showed a consistent, but non-significant, trend of lower abundance along edges. In a similar study, Kristan et al. (in press) noted significant negative edge relationships for California Towhee, California Thrasher, and Sage Sparrow, and significant positive effects for Northern Mockingbird and European Starling.

PATTERNS OF LANDSCAPE SENSITIVITY IN THE COASTAL SOUTHERN CALIFORNIA AVIFAUNA

I categorized patterns of landscape sensitivity in the CSS avifauna through a consideration of three factors: (1) area sensitivity, (2) edge sensitivity, and (3) ability to exploit the urban matrix (Table 2). The area sensitivity designations are approximate and not quantitative estimates. Area sensitivity in this system certainly depends on fragment age (Crooks et al. 2001) and possibly on isolation (Lovio 1996), so a simple categorization is not possible. The two categories (10–20 ha and 100–200 ha) represent a qualitative contrast of area sensitivity for patches of CSS between 20 and 60 years old and isolated by at least 500 m of residential development. Species categorized as sensitive to fragmentation at the scale of 10–20 ha are often found in fragments of this size but have been shown to experience local extinction (Soulé et al. 1988, Bolger et al. 1991, Crooks et al. 2001). Species categorized as having 100–200 ha area sensitivity are generally absent or rare in fragments smaller than that size range (Lovio 1996, Bolger et al. 1997; D. Bolger et al., unpubl. data; K. Crooks et al., unpubl. data). Edge sensitivity was derived from a consideration of the relative abundance of species in the interior and near the edge (<250m from urban edge) of large habitat blocks (Fig. 2, Table 1; Bolger et al. 1997). The

TABLE 1. MEAN NUMBER OF DETECTIONS (STANDARD ERROR) WITHIN 70 M OF POINT COUNT STATIONS IN EDGE AND INTERIOR LOCATIONS IN 1997–1999

	1997		1998		1999		F or Chi-square	P
	Edge	Interior	Edge	Interior	Edge	Interior		
N	10	9	7	7	11	7		
California Quail	0.20	0.11	0.29	0.30	0.48	0.43	0.57	0.45
	(0.11)	(0.11)	(0.17)	(0.14)	(0.15)	(0.25)		
Mourning Dove	0.00	0.00	0.10	0.22	0.15	0.12	2.22	0.15
	(0.00)	(0.00)	(0.10)	(0.08)	(0.09)	(0.08)		
Costa's Hummingbird	0.42	0.17	0.05	0.36	0.61	0.57	0.06	0.82
	(0.13)	(0.09)	(0.03)	(0.11)	(0.18)	(0.26)		
Anna's Hummingbird[a]	1.48	1.00	0.97	0.72	1.52	1.01	5.69	0.021
	(0.17)	(0.17)	(0.28)	(0.24)	(0.17)	(0.15)		
Western Scrub-Jay	0.10	0.09	0.24	0.00	1.00	0.05	4.79	0.03
	(0.07)	(0.06)	(0.17)	(0.00)	(0.32)	(0.05)		
Common Raven	0.48	0.20	0.72	0.25	1.00	0.13	0.93	0.37
	(0.14)	(0.17)	(0.29)	(0.14)	(1.00)	(0.10)		
Common Bushtit[a]	1.20	1.28	0.74	1.34	0.88	0.86	0.99	0.033
	(0.28)	(0.29)	(0.34)	(0.36)	(0.22)	(0.28)		
Bewick's Wren	0.28	0.33	0.07	0.04	0.75	0.42	1.83	0.16
	(0.09)	(0.15)	(0.05)	(0.04)	(0.15)	(0.14)		
Northern Mockingbird	1.00	0.19	0.61	0.03	0.26	0.05	6.82	0.009
	(0.29)	(0.08)	(0.22)	(0.03)	(0.10)	(0.05)		
California Thrasher	0.15	0.24	0.22	0.45	0.08	0.27	1.23	0.30
	(0.06)	(0.11)	(0.09)	(0.14)	(0.04)	(0.17)		
Wrentit[a]	0.55	1.28	0.65	1.40	0.51	0.85	13.23	<0.001
	(0.18)	(0.17)	(0.18)	(0.24)	(0.18)	(0.31)		
California Gnatcatcher	0.08	0.17	0.11	0.08	0.03	0.05	0.36	0.60
	(0.06)	(0.07)	(0.07)	(0.08)	(0.03)	(0.05)		
Lesser Goldfinch	0.30	0.52	1.42	0.77	0.76	1.13	0.84	0.37
	(0.16)	(0.20)	(0.59)	(0.25)	(0.26)	(0.28)		
House Finch	1.90	0.22	1.36	0.14	1.64	0.10	20.91	<0.001
	(0.50)	(0.15)	(0.66)	(0.14)	(0.29)	(0.06)		
Lazuli Bunting	0.00	0.15	0.06	0.92	0.00	0.29	14.36	<0.001
	(0.00)	(0.11)	(0.04)	(0.36)	(0.00)	(0.11)		
Spotted Towhee[a]	0.80	0.74	0.42	0.98	0.36	1.01	6.25	0.016
	(0.20)	(0.20)	(0.13)	(0.24)	(0.12)	(0.21)		
California Towhee[a]	2.32	2.81	2.11	2.32	1.64	1.64	0.65	0.042
	(0.37)	(0.41)	(0.36)	(0.24)	(0.32)	(0.38)		
Rufous-crowned Sparrow[a]	0.78	1.17	1.80	3.08	0.23	1.14	15.86	<0.001
	(0.14)	(0.17)	(0.23)	(0.49)	(0.08)	(0.38)		
Black-chinned Sparrow	0.03	0.15	0.00	0.12	0.00	0.17	7.36	0.008
	(0.03)	(0.08)	(0.00)	(0.07)	(0.00)	(0.11)		
Lark Sparrow	0.00	0.17	0.00	0.08	0.00	0.00		
	(0.00)	(0.09)	(0.00)	(0.06)	(0.00)	(0.00)		
Grasshopper Sparrow	0.10	0.06	0.11	0.03	0.00	0.05	0.46	0.50
	(0.10)	(0.06)	(0.11)	(0.03)	(0.00)	(0.05)		

[a] Data from these species were analyzed with 2-way ANOVA; all others were analyzed with three-way contingency tables (see METHODS).

urban-exploiter category includes species that occur in the urban matrix during the breeding season as determined by Lovio (1996) and K. Crooks et al. (unpubl. data). This list includes the species likely to be found in areas of relatively dense, single-family dwellings that support moderate densities of ornamental vegetation. The list of urban-exploiters would probably differ if higher- or lower-density development were considered (Blair 1996). Based on a consideration of these three factors I placed species into three categories: (1) species that appear strongly negatively affected by fragmentation in the landscape, (2) species that appear moderately negatively affected by fragmentation, and (3) species that appear positively affected or neutral (Table 2).

Species in the first category, strongly negatively affected, are generally found only in the largest habitat blocks remaining in the region. These species do not occur in the urban matrix, generally have reduced abundance near urban edges (Table 1; Bolger et al. 1997), and are extremely rare in smaller fragments (K. Crooks et

TABLE 2.   PATTERNS OF LANDSCAPE SENSITIVITY IN THE AVIFAUNA OF COASTAL SOUTHERN CALIFORNIA

Species	Area sensitivity (ha)	Exploits urban matrix	Edge response	Habitat	Migratory status	Nest location
Strongly negative						
Lesser Nighthawk	100–200	No	?	CSS/Chap.	migrant	ground
Blue-gray Gnatcatcher	100–200	No	?	Chap/Woodland	migrant	shrub/tree
Sage Sparrow	100–200	No	negative	CSS/Chap.	resident	shrub
Rufous-crowned Sparrow	100–200	No	negative	CSS	resident	ground
Black-chinned Sparrow	100–200	No	negative	CSS/Chap.	migrant	shrub
Lark Sparrow	100–200	No	negative	Grassland	migrant	ground/shrub
Grasshopper Sparrow	100–200	No	neutral	Grassland	?	ground
Western Meadowlark	100–200	No	negative	Grassland	resident	ground
Moderately negative						
California Quail	10–20	No	neutral	CSS/Chap.	resident	ground
Costa's Hummingbird	10–20	Yes	?	CSS/Chap.	migrant	shrub/tree
Bewick's Wren	10–20	Yes	neutral	CSS/Chap./Rip.	resident	cavity
California Thrasher	10–20	No	negative	CSS/Chap.	resident	shrub
Wrentit	10–20	No	negative	CSS/Chap.	resident	shrub
California Gnatcatcher	10–20	No	neutral	CSS	resident	shrub
Lazuli Bunting	10–20	No	negative	CSS/Chap.	migrant	shrub
Spotted Towhee	10–20	No	negative	CSS/Chap.	resident	ground
Positive or neutral						
Mourning Dove	None	Yes	neutral	Grass/CSS/Chap./Rip.	resident	ground/shrub/tree
Anna's Hummingbird	None	Yes	positive	CSS/Chap.	resident	shrub/tree
Western Scrub-Jay	None	Yes	positive	CSS/Chap.	resident	shrub/tree
American Crow	None	Yes	positive	CSS/Chap./Rip.	resident	tree/cliff
Common Raven	None	Yes	positive	CSS/Chap./Rip.	resident	tree/cliff
Common Bushtit	None	Yes	neutral	CSS/Chap./Rip.	resident	shrub
Northern Mockingbird	None	Yes	positive	CSS/Chap./Rip.	resident	shrub/tree
Lesser Goldfinch	None	Yes	neutral	CSS/Chap.	short dist.	shrub/tree
House Finch	None	Yes	positive	CSS/Chap.	resident	shrub/tree/structure
California Towhee	None	Yes	neutral	CSS/Chap.	resident	shrub

Notes: Classifications of area sensitivity derive from Soulé et al. (1988), Lovio (1996), Bolger et al. (1997), Crooks et al. (2001), and D. Bolger, unpubl. data. Presence in the urban matrix is from Lovio (1996) and Crooks et al. (2001). Edge responses are derived from Bolger et al. (1997) and Table 1. Habitat use is from Bolger et al. (1997) and Unitt (1984). Residency status is from Unitt (1984). Nest locations are from accounts in the *Birds of North America*, Harrison (1979), and D. Bolger, pers. obs.

al., unpubl. data). They are a mixture of resident and migrant species. This is the most problematic category because the fewest data are available and alternative explanations for the landscape patterns of these species need further investigation. Many of these species are primarily grassland or chaparral species that often occur within the coastal habitat mosaic in open CSS habitat and grassland/CSS ecotones or CSS/chaparral ecotones. Their patterns of abundance could reflect the distribution of these less common habitat elements that may be distributed non-randomly with respect to fragment size or edge proximity.

Lark Sparrows, Grasshopper Sparrows, and Western Meadowlarks are primarily associated with grassland but reliably occur in open coastal sage scrub habitat in large habitat blocks. CSS in habitat fragments is generally open, often with a continuous understory of non-native grasses. But these species are rarely present in fragments. Lesser Nighthawks occur in both chaparral and CSS, but require bare ground on mesa tops for breeding and are rare in fragments (Lovio 1996).

Interpretation of the distribution of some of these species, particularly those primarily associated with chaparral, is complicated by historical distribution patterns. The Blue-gray Gnatcatcher and the Black-chinned Sparrow were historically rare in the immediate vicinity of the coast (Unitt 1984), possibly due to an east-west gradient in the cover of chaparral habitat. So their rarity in fragments closest to the coast may not be due to fragmentation sensitivity. Of course, it is possible that those historical patterns already reflected the effects of earlier, agriculturally-induced habitat fragmentation. Lovio (1996) found the Blue-gray Gnatcatcher in his unfragmented control area, but it was absent from all but the largest fragments in the immediately adjacent landscape. The Black-chinned Sparrow does show edge- (Table 2; Bolger et al. 1997) and area-sensitivity (Lovio 1996) within its historical range.

Bolger et al. (1997) found that as a group the Rufous-crowned Sparrow, Lark Sparrow, Black-chinned Sparrow, Sage Sparrow, Western Meadowlark and Costa's Hummingbird displayed an edge-sensitive abundance pattern even when the three habitat types they examined (chamise chaparral, CSS, and mixed chaparral) were considered separately. However, when analyzed individually with regard to habitat, the distribution of Sage Sparrows and Western Meadowlarks suggested their pattern may be driven by the spatial distribution of habitat types. The other four species did display reduced abundance in appropriate habitat near edges. Bolger et al.

(1997) found Sage Sparrows to be associated with chamise chaparral in their study area, but they also occur in CSS (Unitt 1984, Lovio 1996). Lovio (1996) found Sage Sparrows only in the two largest CSS fragments (>150 ha) in his study area.

The species in this group whose pattern most compellingly suggests fragmentation-sensitivity is the Rufous-crowned Sparrow. It is abundant and ubiquitous in unfragmented habitat, but less abundant near edges (Table 1) and rare in isolated habitat fragments (Fig. 2; Bolger et al. 1997; K. Crooks et al., unpubl. data).

I suspect that the distribution of most of the species in this category are determined at least in part by patterns of fragmentation and edge. Yet because of their idiosyncratic distributions and habitat affinities it will be difficult to demonstrate this conclusively. Kristan et al. (in press) constructed interior-based habitat association models for a suite of CSS species using data collected from >200 points throughout southern California. They then applied each model to a new set of points surveyed along an explicit edge-to-interior gradient. Habitat quality (as indexed by predicted probability of a species occurrence at a point) varied significantly for the eight species analyzed (Cactus Wren, California Towhee, California Gnatcatcher, California Thrasher, Sage Sparrow, Western Scrub-Jay, Northern Mockingbird, European Starling). Interestingly, Sage Sparrows and California Thrashers were significantly reduced at edges despite the presence of suitable habitat. Clearly the distribution of these species requires closer examination for evidence of processes producing fragmentation sensitivity. Despite the uncertainties, it is prudent at this time to consider these species very sensitive to fragmentation.

The second category is comprised of species that show area sensitivity in the range of 10–20 ha. A number of these species have been shown to undergo local extinction in habitat fragments (Soulé et al. 1988, Bolger et al. 1991, Crooks et al. 2001). They generally occur at lower abundance in habitat fragments than in unfragmented habitat (K. Crooks et al., unpubl. data). Some of the species show edge sensitivity, others are neutral with regard to edge (Table 1; Bolger et al. 1997). These are generally resident species and are among the common and distinctive species of these habitats. They appear to be shrub habitat generalists occurring abundantly in both CSS and chaparral (Bolger et al. 1997). Most of these species are rarely observed in the urban matrix; however, K. Crooks et al. (unpubl. data) found Costa's Hummingbird to be reasonably abundant in the urban matrix and detected Spotted Towhee and Bewick's Wren there at very low abundance.

The species categorized as neutrally or positively affected by fragmentation are all urban exploiters. They reside and breed within developed habitats in San Diego as well as other disturbed habitats (Unitt 1984; D. Bolger, pers. obs.). All display positive or neutral edge responses (Table 1; Bolger et al. 1997). They vary in abundance in unfragmented habitat and none display obvious area sensitivity; in fact most are more abundant in fragments than in unfragmented habitat (K. Crooks et al., unpubl. data).

MECHANISMS CAUSING FRAGMENTATION EFFECTS IN SOUTHERN CALIFORNIA

Isolation and dispersal limitation

There is currently no direct measure of the ability of most of the species listed in Table 2 to disperse through the urban matrix. However, there is a good deal of correlative evidence for some of the fragmentation-sensitive species that suggests their ability to disperse across the urban matrix is constrained relative to fragmentation-tolerant species.

The relative inability of these species to colonize across the urban landscape is supported by the lack of a relationship between degree of fragment isolation and the distribution of these species. Soulé et al. (1988) found no relationship between fragment isolation and species richness. Crooks et al. (2001) analyzed single species distributions and found only Bewick's Wren's occurrence to be significantly positively correlated with proximity to other fragments. This is consistent with its ability to recolonize fragments, and its occasional detection in the urban matrix (Crooks et al. 2001). Lovio (1996) did find an effect of isolation on species richness; this difference is likely due to the factors mentioned earlier, smaller interpatch distances and a more permeable matrix in his study area. Taken together the results of Lovio (1996) and Soulé et al. (1988) suggest a threshold of isolation and matrix permeability below which dispersal is an important influence on distributions. Bolger et al. (2001) demonstrated that a group of fragmentation-sensitive species (category 2 species) occurred much less frequently in narrow, linear habitat features (ca. 60 m wide and 250 m long) than a group of fragmentation-tolerant species (category 3 species), suggesting the sensitive species have more stringent corridor requirements and that their movements through the urban matrix are more constrained.

One of the striking features of Table 2 is the almost complete correlation of fragmentation-sensitivity with the inability to exploit the urban matrix. This is consistent with the urban matrix as a dispersal barrier for the fragmentation-sensitive species. Clearly, the urban matrix does not provide a barrier to the species that are able to reside there, and in general these species do not show fragmentation sensitivity.

The available evidence suggests that at least in part, fragmentation-sensitive patterns of members of the shrub avifauna are due to the isolating effects of the urban matrix. The matrix is not necessarily a complete barrier to dispersal but it appears to reduce colonization rates below extinction rates for a number of species (Crooks et al. 2001). More direct tests of this hypothesis in the form of dispersal studies or experimental introductions to unoccupied patches are needed.

Two studies have documented dispersal of banded California Gnatcatchers through fragmented landscapes. A banded juvenile was detected 1.3 km from its natal patch, having had to cross a lightly developed landscape of large wooded house lots and parkland (Atwood et al. 1995 cited in Bailey and Mock 1998). Bailey and Mock (1998) also document a number of dispersal events in a heterogeneous landscape in San Diego. A number of these apparently occurred from a large block of habitat through an archipelago of fragments separated by blocks of development up to 1 km wide. This study was conducted in the same landscape as Lovio (1996) with dense ornamental vegetation and sufficient relief to often provide line-of-sight between patches of habitat. This probably facilitates inter-patch movement. So although the California gnatcatcher does show area sensitivity, this may be more related to its large territory requirements (Preston et al. 1998) rather than a strict inability to recolonize isolated fragments. However, even though dispersal through the urban matrix is possible, colonization rates could still be in excess of extinction rates for this species.

Edge effects: habitat degradation/local habitat selection

Fragmentation and the creation of urban edge exposes CSS and chaparral habitat to increased levels of human-induced disturbance. The effect of increasing disturbance in the form of mechanical damage, fire, and exotic plant invasion on vegetation and birds in habitat fragments has not been thoroughly described. Alberts et al. (1993) found that fragments lose native shrub cover through time and native plant diversity declines while exotic plant diversity increases. Disturbance opens up the vegetation in fragments by causing internal fragmentation with stands of shrubs becoming separated by non-native grasses and forbs.

The effect of disturbance-induced changes in vegetation structure on bird communities has not been well-studied in this region. Sauvajot et al. (1998) found that chaparral bird species abundance did not respond to disturbance-induced changes in vegetation structure in chaparral, whereas Kristan et al. (in press) observed significant changes in vegetation, as well as "habitat," in CSS. Bird species clearly assort along a gradient of shrub density from grassland to open CSS to dense CSS and chaparral (Cody 1975, Bolger et al. 1997). By decreasing shrub cover, disturbance should move the bird community along this gradient. However, the relationship of this avifauna to disturbance-induced changes in shrub vegetation structure needs further quantification.

The effect of invasive non-native annual plants has been severe on coastal sage scrub and may be exacerbated by fragmentation. Coastal sage scrub has been exposed to several waves of grass and herbaceous invaders from the Mediterranean and Middle East beginning with species introduced by missionaries in the mid to late 1700s (Mooney et al. 1986, Minnich and Dezzani 1998). Most prominent among these invaders are grasses in the genera *Avena* and *Bromus,* and the annual forb *Brassica nigra.* These plants may invade as a consequence of soil disturbance and intense or frequent fires, and can invade undisturbed CSS from nearby disturbed areas (Zink et al. 1996). Once established these annuals resist native shrub recruitment (Eliason and Allen 1997). The increase in annual biomass increases rates of nutrient cycling (Jackson et al. 1988) and these annuals may decrease fire intervals by increasing fine fuel availability (Zedler et al. 1983).

Coastal sage scrub and chaparral are stable with fire intervals of ten years or more, but degrade to non-native grassland under more frequent fires or particular intense fires (Zedler et al. 1983). Both chaparral and CSS shrubs resprout after fire although resprouting is more complete in chaparral species. Germination from seed caches (*Salvia* spp.) or germination of small wind-dispersed seeds (*Eriogonum fasciculatum, Artemisia californica*) is a more important source of recovery in CSS shrubs than in chaparral species. Frequent fires can deplete the seed bank and stored carbohydrates of root-sprouting species and cause a vegetation type-conversion to non-native grassland.

Non-native invasion is among the most serious threats to the conservation of native plant and animal communities in this region. For example, Minnich and Dezzani (1998) compared historical vegetation data (1929–1934) to recent survey data and concluded that loss of shrub cover of coastal sage scrub shrubs has been extensive in the Perris Plain of Riverside County. Modal shrub cover loss at 78 sites was 40%. This was particularly true on north-facing slopes, which supported high densities of non-native grasses (*Bromus* spp.). Loss of shrub cover occurred even in the absence of fire and grazing, suggesting a competitive exclusion by the non-native grasses, perhaps through competition for moisture (Minnich and Dezzani 1998).

A landscape analysis of the effect of fragmentation and edge on disturbance regimes in this region has not been attempted. Fragmentation and the creation of edge should increase the exposure of native plant communities to humans, exotic invaders, fire, and mechanical disturbance. It seems likely that habitat fragmentation has enhanced plant invasions by disturbing the native shrub vegetation and providing colonization sources of the exotic species. For example, Zink et al. (1996) documented the invasion of undisturbed coastal sage scrub by non-native annuals from a disturbed pipeline right-of-way. Although the effects of non-native annual plant invasion on native grasses, shrubs, and nutrient cycling have been examined, their effects on higher trophic levels has received little attention. The alteration of the physical structure of CSS and chaparral habitat, and changes in seed and arthropod food resources, could affect higher trophic levels including birds.

Landscape-scale habitat selection—patch size and isolation

Feasible observations and experiments to test this hypothesis are elusive, so the only support for this mechanism would be lack of evidence for other mechanisms. This mechanism is perhaps most feasible for the migrant species that would not be expected to have difficulty dispersing across the urban matrix (e.g., Lazuli Bunting). However, this hypothesized mechanism remains speculative.

Secondary effects: top-down—predation and brood parasitism

Morrison and Bolger (2002) found no evidence to suggest that the landscape pattern of the Rufous-crowned Sparrow results from top-down effects near edges. Nest predation rates and breeding productivity did not differ between edge and interior areas. The predation result is surprising considering that some putative nest predators (e.g., Western Scrub-Jays and Common Ravens, Table 1; California ground squirrels, D. Bolger, pers. obs.) are more abundant along edges. Video surveillance and direct observation documented ten predation events, nine of which were by snakes (seven by California kingsnakes, two by gopher snakes), suggesting that snakes are the principal predator on Rufous-crowned Sparrow nests. The rate at which snakes were encountered by field workers was equivalent in edge and interior areas (Morrison and Bolger 2002).

Top-down changes may be important in isolated habitat fragments. Crooks and Soulé (1999) found evidence for mesopredator release in fragments lacking coyotes. They report that the abundance of mesopredators (gray fox, opossum, striped skunk, and domestic cat), as revealed by track stations and scat transects, is negatively correlated with coyote abundance (after accounting for the potential confounding effects of area, age, and isolation). Moreover, mesopredator activity is also higher at times when coyote activity is lower. They found a significant positive correlation between the species richness of shrub-specialist birds and coyote presence and conclude that the presence of coyotes enhances survival and reproduction of these birds through the suppression of mesopredators. Bird species richness showed a non-significant negative trend with increasing mesopredator abundance.

Crooks and Soulé (1999) also presented evidence that the effect of coyotes on domestic cats is particularly marked. Their radio-collared cats often were killed by coyotes, 21% of coyote scat examined contained cat remains, and 46% of cat owners surveyed said they restricted their cats' activities when coyotes were present. The effects of cats can be severe. Based on owner surveys they estimate that a 20-ha fragment would be subject to predation by 35 outdoor cats that together would bring a total of 525 bird prey items to their owners each year. The authors do not report whether the prey items are predominantly common urban species or species residing predominantly in natural habitat.

Brown-headed Cowbirds have been shown to be another important top-down influence in fragmented forest habitat. However, they do not seem to be as significant an influence in fragmented coastal sage scrub vegetation (Ellison 1999). In four years (342 nests, Riverside and San Diego counties) in edge and interior habitat, S. Morrison and D. Bolger (2002; unpubl. data) found no brood parasitism by Brown-headed Cowbirds on Rufous-crowned Sparrows. In two years (same Riverside County site as Morrison and Bolger) Ellison (1999) observed cowbird parasitism in only 3 of 217 nests of Spotted and California towhees and Sage and Rufous-crowned sparrows collectively. Cowbirds were detected in my edge point counts in San Diego, but only infrequently.

In this region, the habitat in which cowbirds are consistently a significant problem is riparian woodland. The endangered Least Bell's Vireo is significantly affected by cowbirds (Kus 1999) as have been other riparian breeding birds. This habitat is naturally patchy, but habitat loss due to development has increased the patchiness as well as patch isolation, and has exposed the habitat to a variety of disturbances. Because breeding habitat for riparian species occurs in relatively small, discrete patches, it has been possible to reduce the local density of cowbirds through trapping programs and reduce parasitism on the Least Bell's Vireo (Kus 1999).

Braden et al. (1997) reported that 32% of California Gnatcatcher nests suffered cowbird parasitism in coastal sage scrub habitat in southwestern Riverside County. Parasitism rates were not analyzed with respect to patch size or distance to edge so it is not possible to interpret these data with regard to fragmentation. However, at least two of Braden's study areas were adjacent to lakes that are fringed by riparian vegetation, which may have attracted the cowbirds (see below). Grishaver et al. (1998) found much lower rates (2%) of parasitism on gnatcatchers at a site in San Diego.

Cowbirds are noted for their large home ranges and the extensive distances they will fly between feeding, roosting, and host nesting areas (Thompson 1994, Robinson et al. 1995a). It is likely then that their abundance in southern California is related to factors distributed at a landscape or regional scale. The effect of urban fragmentation on cowbird abundance is unknown. If cowbirds can exploit resources in the urban matrix, such as seed from feeders, the urban landscape may be highly permeable to them and may enhance cowbird abundance in riparian areas that abut residential development. Further research on the landscape correlates and determinants of cowbird abundance in this region is needed.

Secondary effects: bottom-up

The effect of habitat fragmentation on bird food resources has been relatively understudied (Burke and Nol 1998, Robinson 1998). Bolger et al. (2000) found complex relationships between arthropods and fragment size, age, and edge proximity. Arthropods dwelling on California buckwheat (*Eriogonum fasiculatum*) generally decline in abundance and point diversity with decreasing fragment size and increasing fragment age. Thus food availability for foliage gleaners foraging on buckwheat is potentially lower in smaller and older fragments.

Reponses of the ground-dwelling arthropods are more varied, but are generally similar to the shrub insects. Interestingly, ground spiders increase in abundance and point diversity with decreasing area and increasing age (Bolger et al. 2000). The most abundant ground arthropods in habitat fragments are common non-native species: sowbug (*Armadillidium vulgare*), European earwig (*Forficula auriculatum*), and oriental cockroach (*Blatta orientalis*). There did not seem to be large differences between the edge and interior in the abundance and diversity of ground or shrub arthropods.

In contrast, ground arthropods are generally less abundant in the edge than the interior of large habitat blocks in San Diego (D. Bolger, unpubl. data). Grasshoppers, mites, spiders, jumping bristletails, and native ants were significantly less abundant in edge plots than in interior plots. Beetles, bees and wasps, and flies did not differ between edge and interior plots. No arthropod order was significantly more abundant in edge plots than in interior plots.

The arthropod taxa most vulnerable to fragmentation and edge are the native ants. In San Diego, the non-native Argentine ant (*Linepithema humile*) invades coastal sage scrub habitat from urban edges (Suarez et al. 1998). In isolated habitat fragments (Suarez et al. 1998) and in edge areas of large habitat blocks (D. Bolger, unpubl. data), the abundance and diversity of native ants is strongly negatively correlated with the abundance of the Argentine ant. Argentine ants are invasive human commensals and have become established in Mediterranean climates worldwide (Majer 1994). They have been implicated in the decline of native ants in a number of locations (Erickson 1971, Ward 1987, Majer 1994, Holway 1995, Cammell et al. 1996, Human and Gordon 1996). Argentine ants possess interference and exploitative competitive advantages over native California ants (Human and Gordon 1996, Holway et al. 1998, Holway 1999) and have higher worker densities possibly due to reduced intraspecific competition (Holway et al. 1998).

Several lines of evidence suggest that the availability of water from irrigation and runoff may allow the Argentine ants to invade along edges, and moisture limitation may prevent their invasion of undisturbed interior areas. Tremper (1976) found Argentine ants more vulnerable to desiccation than most native California ants. Also, Argentine ants are able to invade riparian habitat, but only if water flows year-round (Holway 1998a).

Argentine ants are generally smaller than the native ant species they replace, suggesting that they may not be adequate replacements in the diet of ant-eating birds and lizards. Suarez et al. (2000) demonstrated that the ant-specialist coastal horned lizard showed a strong prey pref-

erence for native ants over the Argentine ant. Ants frequently appear in lists of prey consumed by ground-foraging birds, but their relative dietary importance is unclear. Several studies have reported negative correlations of Argentine ants, or other exotic ants, with non-ant arthropods (Porter and Savigno 1990, Cole et al. 1992, Human and Gordon 1997, Bolger et al. 2000), while others have found no relationship (Holway 1998 b). Bolger et al. (2000) found significant partial negative correlations between the abundances of Argentine ants and several non-ant arthropod taxa. The magnitude of the correlations, however, were generally small suggesting the effect of Argentine ants on non-ant arthropods is less severe than their effect on native ants.

Taken together these studies demonstrate that arthropod communities change greatly with fragmentation and edge. In general arthropod abundance and diversity declines in isolated fragments and near the edge of large habitat blocks. Unfortunately, at this time we do not know how these changes in arthropod communities affect bird foraging, reproductive success, and habitat selection.

CONCLUSIONS

The studies reviewed indicate that a significant portion of the avifauna of coastal sage scrub and chaparral habitats in coastal southern California display patterns of abundance that suggest sensitivity to edge and fragmentation caused by urban development. Area, age, and edge sensitivity in bird abundance and presence/absence have been demonstrated in a broad spectrum of the avifauna (Table 1; Soulé et al. 1988, Lovio 1996, Bolger et al. 1997, Crooks et al. 2001). However, so little research has been conducted on mechanisms that it is difficult at this time to generalize about the forces shaping these distributions. Area exerts an influence through an initial sampling effect (Bolger et al. 1991). It may also affect extinction rates through its effect on population size; extinction rates are higher in smaller fragments (Crooks et al. 2001). The available evidence suggests that elevated predation and parasitism along edges are not involved (Morrison and Bolger 2002; P. Mock, pers. comm.). Correlational evidence suggests mesopredator release affects bird species persistence in isolated habitat fragments. However, an effect of mesopredator abundance on nest predation rate or adult or juvenile survival has yet to be demonstrated. Arthropod community composition and abundance varies strongly with fragmentation and edge suggesting that food availability could play a role in shaping these abundance patterns (Suarez et al. 1998, Bolger et al. 2000; D. Bolger, unpubl. data).

The characteristics of the urban matrix and bird species responses to it may be very important. Dispersal limitation imposed by the urban matrix may explain area sensitivity in many fragmentation-sensitive species. Extinction rates of fragmentation-sensitive species exceeded colonization rates in fragments (Crooks et al. 2001). These species generally are not observed to occur in the urban matrix (Table 2). Species that are able to exploit the urban matrix do not show fragment area sensitivity or edge sensitivity (Table 2). Clearly, as shown by the California Gnatcatcher's ability to disperse through developed landscapes, this is not the case for all fragmentation-sensitive species.

The relationship between habitat degradation and extinction and colonization rates in habitat fragments needs clarification. Is fragmented habitat sufficiently degraded to lead to local extinction or cause dispersing birds to pass up fragments? Many fragments lacking particular bird species do not differ in gross habitat characteristics from those that do support them (D. Bolger, pers. obs.). Crooks et al. (2001) found no relationship between extinction rates and percent native shrub cover, an index of habitat degradation. I suspect that, except for the most degraded patches, the absence of species in the "moderately sensitive" category (Table 2) from fragments is due in large part to the inability of these species to successfully disperse through the urban matrix and colonize patches frequently enough to counteract extinction processes. However, studies of dispersal in a variety of species are needed, as are demographic studies in habitat fragments and reintroduction experiments to test the suitability of unoccupied fragmented habitat.

CONTRASTS WITH FRAGMENTATION STUDIES IN THE EAST AND MIDWEST

Several features of the research reviewed here appear in contrast to the work done in the East and Midwest where top-down effects appear to be the most important consequences of fragmentation. Studies in those regions have often documented strong effects of nest predation and brood parasitism near edges or in more fragmented landscapes (Robinson et al. 1995a, Donovan et al. 1997). The evidence for top-down effects in southern California is mixed. Morrison and Bolger (2002) found that rates of nest predation or parasitism were not elevated along developed edges in the Rufous-crowned Sparrow, although Crooks and Soulé (1999) find evidence for mesopredator release in isolated fragments.

Fragment isolation appears to be a more important influence in southern California. In the Midwest, regional-scale dispersal appears to maintain populations of neotropical migrants in

extensive landscape sink areas (Robinson et al. 1995a). In contrast in San Diego, isolation on the scale of 100's of meters appears to prevent rescue of populations of some species in fragments. Either the fragmentation-sensitive species in southern California are poorer dispersers, or they are much better at recognizing and avoiding sink habitat than the neotropical migrants of the Midwest. Of course, it has not been demonstrated that fragments are demographic sinks in southern California as they are for a number of species in the Midwest.

The avifauna in southern California is predominantly composed of year-round resident species as opposed to the neotropical migrant species that dominate the eastern and midwestern avifauna. The generally shorter dispersal distances of residents compared to migrants (Paradis et al. 1998) may help explain the relative importance of isolation. The nature of the intervening urban matrix may also play a role. The urban matrix could be more hostile to dispersal than the agricultural matrix of the Midwest.

Habitat degradation may be a more powerful consequence of fragmentation and edge in the arid West than in the Midwest and East. This degradation may be reflected in changes in physical habitat structure or food availability in habitat fragments. The effect of fragmentation on woody vegetation structure has not been the focus of studies of fragmentation in the East and Midwest, but one study has demonstrated lower food availability in fragments (Burke and Nol 1998).

INFORMATION NEEDS

In addition to those already mentioned there are a number of gaps in our knowledge that limit our ability to understand, predict, and manage the effects of fragmentation on birds in this region. Our understanding of the trophic effects of fragmentation is hindered by the lack of basic autecological data on bird foraging and diet, including adult and nestling food. Nest predation must be investigated on a range of bird species to discover whether the results on the Rufous-crowned Sparrow are generalizable to other species nesting in different strata and with differing landscape sensitivities. We know little about the non-mammalian predator community in fragments. Snakes appear to be quite rare in habitat fragments (D. Bolger, unpubl. data). If this is true what effect does this have on species that are vulnerable to snake predation? Are predation rates lower in fragments or does the effect of increased mammalian mesopredators or other predators compensate for reduced snake predation?

We also need to understand how edge effects

scale with the percentage of the local landscape that is developed (Donovan et al. 1997). Do isolated habitat fragments experience more intense edge effects than larger habitat blocks? Similarly, how does the predation regime in isolated fragments compare with predation in the edge and interior of large habitat blocks? A virtually untouched question is the source status of the urban matrix for bird species that occur in both the urban matrix and natural habitat. Bolger et al. (1997) found elevated densities of some native urban-exploiting birds up to 1km into habitat blocks. The consequences of this density augmentation on avian communities deserves further study.

A landscape perspective on disturbance regimes is urgently needed. How do fragmentation and edge affect non-native plant invasion, fire, and other disturbance regimes. These are among the most severe threats to conservation in this semi-arid region as demonstrated by Minnich and Dezzani's (1998) work. Physical gradients (soil moisture, air temperature, etc.) along edges have not been investigated in this system and may be important. Also the effect of ENSO (El Niño-Southern Oscillation) driven variation in rainfall is essential to understanding avian population fluctuations (Morrison and Bolger in press) that may have important implications for extinction rates in fragments.

CONSERVATION IMPLICATIONS

There is an extensive conservation planning effort ongoing for coastal southern California under the state's Natural Communities Conservation Planning program (NCCP). The reserve system that ultimately results from this effort will by necessity be set within a predominantly urban matrix. A species-by-species evaluation of the conservation implications of the findings reviewed here is beyond the scope of this paper and would require a region-wide evaluation of the abundance and distribution of these species on protected lands (J. Rotenberry et al., unpubl. data). There are, however, a number of general conclusions that can be drawn that are relevant to the management of reserves in these landscapes.

The studies reviewed here suggest that highly isolated shrub habitat patches less than 100 ha provided little conservation value for fragmentation-sensitive species over the long term. However, they do support other members of the regional fauna in abundance (Soulé et al. 1988, Crooks et al. 2001). The limitations of fragmented habitat for conservation are acknowledged in the NCCP reserve selection guidelines that emphasize large, contiguous blocks of habitat (Atwood and Noss 1994). Denser archipel-

agos of fragments probably would support more interpatch movement and higher abundance of these species as suggested by a comparison of Soulé et al. (1988) and Lovio (1996). However, since we do not know whether fragments are sink or source habitat for most species it seems unwise to design landscape to encourage dispersal to fragments from source habitat.

Edge effects on bird abundance (Table 2; Bolger et al. 1997) and the penetration of Argentine ants along edges (Suarez et al. 1998; D. Bolger, unpubl. data) are of concern even in large reserves. We still do not have an adequate understanding of the variety of ecological mechanisms generating edge effects, the extent of their spatial penetration into blocks of habitat or the time course of these effects. Edge effects such as reduced or enhanced abundance of bird species, Argentine ant invasion, and changes in arthropod communities appear to penetrate reserves on the scale of hundreds of meters. Thus these effects can significantly reduce the effective area of even large reserves.

To effectively conserve the coastal southern California biota, it will be necessary to identify the effects of urban fragmentation and understand their ecological mechanisms. There is an understandable desire among land managers and conservation planners for simple geographic answers from ecologists: prescriptions for minimum area requirements, buffer and edge effect distances. However, easy answers are misleading, for although fragmentation and edge effects have a geographic dimension, that is they can be mapped to some degree of resolution, they are primarily community ecological and population ecological phenomena. As such, they are dynamic processes and their spatial dimension is dependent upon the makeup of the local community as well as time. For example, Crooks et al. (2001) demonstrated that area sensitivity is not static but is a function of time. It is likely that the spatial penetration of edge effects is also not static.

Ecologists will only be able to make robust management prescriptions about fragmentation and edge effects when we have more fully examined the range of ecological mechanisms generating these effects. Even then, they will not be simple answers expressed in meters and hectares, but will be time-dependent and conditional on the composition of the local community. So, minimum area requirements will be expressed in general terms for a given range of fragment age and will depend on the condition of the vegetation in the fragment and the composition of the predator community. These answers will not be easy to map, or to explain to policy-makers, but they will be ecologically valid. Of course geographic tools such as buffer distances will continue to be important conservation planning tools. But we cannot allow that fact to convince policy-makers, the public, and ourselves, that conserving the native biota of coastal southern California in the face of a large and growing human population will be as simple as creating buffers of a fixed distance around reserves. Instead, it we will require understanding and actively managing populations and processes, and we are a long way from possessing the neces-

sary knowledge and management capabilities to accomplish that.

ACKNOWLEDGMENTS

The ideas presented here grew out of discussions and collaborations with T. Case, K. Crooks, B. Kus, S. Morrison, J. Rotenberry, T. Scott, M. Soulé, and A. Suarez. I thank D. Dobkin, P. Doran, L. George, P. Mock, and S. Morrison, for helpful feedback on the manuscript. I also acknowledge financial support from the National Science Foundation and the Metropolitan Water District of Southern California.

APPENDIX.   SCIENTIFIC NAME OF ALL VERTEBRATE SPECIES MENTIONED IN TEXT OR TABLES

Birds	
California Quail	*Callipepla californica*
Mourning Dove	*Zenaida macroura*
Lesser Nighthawk	*Chordeiles acutipennis*
Costa's Hummingbird	*Calypte costae*
Anna's Hummingbird	*Calypte anna*
Bell's Vireo	*Vireo bellii*
Western Scrub-jay	*Aphelocoma coerulescens*
Common Raven	*Corvus corax*
American Crow	*Corvus brachyrhynchos*
Common Bushtit	*Psaltriparus minimus*
Bewick's Wren	*Thryomanes bewickii*
Wrentit	*Chamaea fasciata*
Blue-gray Gnatcatcher	*Polioptila caerulea*
California Gnatcatcher	*Polioptila californica*
Northern Mockingbird	*Mimus polyglottos*
California Thrasher	*Toxostoma redivivum*
European Starling	*Sturnus vulgaris*
Lazuli Bunting	*Passerina amoena*
Spotted Towhee	*Pipilo maculatus*
California Towhee	*Pipilo crissalis*
Rufous-crowned Sparrow	*Aimophila ruficeps*
Sage Sparrow	*Amphispiza belli*
Black-chinned Sparrow	*Spizella atrogularis*
Grasshopper Sparrow	*Ammodramus savannarum*
Lark Sparrow	*Chondestes grammacus*
Brown-headed Cowbird	*Molothrus ater*
Western Meadowlark	*Sturnella neglecta*
House Finch	*Carpodacus mexicanus*
Lesser Goldfinch	*Carduelis psaltria*
Reptiles	
coastal horned lizard	*Phrynosoma coronatum*
California kingsnake	*Lampropeltis getula*
gopher snake	*Pituophis melanoleucus*
Mammals	
Virginia oppossum	*Didelphis virginiana*
California ground squirrel	*Spermophilus beechyi*
striped skunk	*Mephitis mephitis*
coyote	*Canis latrans*
grey fox	*Urocyon cinereoargenteus*
domestic cat	*Felis catus*

Studies in Avian Biology No. 25:158–202, 2002.

EFFECTS OF ANTHROPOGENIC FRAGMENTATION AND LIVESTOCK GRAZING ON WESTERN RIPARIAN BIRD COMMUNITIES

Joshua J. Tewksbury, Anne E. Black, Nadav Nur, Victoria A. Saab, Brian D. Logan, and David S. Dobkin

Abstract. Deciduous vegetation along streams and rivers provides breeding habitat to more bird species than any other plant community in the West, yet many riparian areas are heavily grazed by cattle and surrounded by increasingly developed landscapes. The combination of cattle grazing and landscape alteration (habitat loss and fragmentation) are thought to be critical factors affecting the richness and composition of breeding bird communities. Here, we examine the influence of land use and cattle grazing on deciduous riparian bird communities across seven riparian systems in five western states: Montana, Idaho, Nevada, Oregon and California. These riparian systems are embedded in landscapes ranging from nearly pristine to almost completely agricultural. We conducted landscape analysis at two spatial scales: local landscapes (all land within 500 m of each survey location) and regional landscapes (all land within 5 km of each survey location). Despite the large differences among riparian systems, we found a number of consistent effects of landscape change and grazing. Of the 87 species with at least 15 detections on two or more rivers, 44 species were less common in grazed sites, in heavily settled or agricultural landscapes, or in areas with little deciduous riparian habitat. The Veery (*Catharus fuscescens*), Song Sparrow (*Melospiza melodia*), Red-naped Sapsucker (*Sphyrapicus nuchalis*), Fox Sparrow (*Passerella iliaca*), and American Redstart (*Setophaga ruticilla*) were all less common under at least three of these conditions. In contrast, 33 species were significantly more common in one or more of these conditions. Sites surrounded by greater deciduous habitat had higher overall avian abundance and 22 species had significantly higher individual abundances in areas with more deciduous habitat. Yet, areas with more agriculture at the regional scale also had higher total avian abundance, due in large part to greater abundance of European Starling (*Sturnus vulgaris*), American Robin (*Turdus migratorius*), Brown-headed Cowbird (*Molothrus ater*), and Black-billed Magpie (*Pica pica*), all species that use both agricultural and riparian areas. Grazing effects varied considerably among riparian systems, but avian abundance and richness were significantly lower at grazed survey locations. Fifteen species were significantly less abundant in grazed sites while only five species were more abundant therein. Management should focus on (1) preserving and enlarging deciduous habitats, (2) reducing cattle grazing in deciduous habitats, and (3) protecting the few relatively pristine landscapes surrounding large deciduous riparian areas in the West.

Key Words: agriculture; avian abundance and richness; cattle grazing; landscape fragmentation; multi-scale; riparian habitat.

Deciduous riparian areas bordering rivers and streams in the western United States support a higher density of breeding birds than any other habitat type (Carothers and Johnson 1975, Rice et al. 1983, Ohmart and Anderson 1986), and studies explicitly comparing deciduous riparian areas with surrounding upland communities repeatedly have found diversity and density of breeding birds to be greater in riparian communities (Carothers et al. 1974, Johnson et al. 1977, Stamp 1978, Conine et al. 1979, Hehnke and Stone 1979, Knopf 1985; Anderson et al. 1985a,b; Strong and Bock 1990, Cubbedge 1994). The importance of these habitats to the maintenance of avian communities cannot be overemphasized. Deciduous riparian habitat makes up less than 1% of the western land area (Knopf et al. 1988), yet over 50% of western bird species breed primarily or exclusively in deciduous riparian communities (Johnson et al. 1977, Mosconi and Hutto 1982, Johnson 1989, Saab and Groves 1992, Dobkin 1994). Due to

the proliferation of dams, intensive water management practices, and the effects of domestic livestock, riparian areas are considered the most heavily degraded ecosystems in the West (Rosenberg et al. 1991, Dobkin 1994, Ohmart 1994, Saab et al. 1995); some western states have already lost as much as 95% of their historic riparian habitat (Rosenberg et al. 1991, Ohmart 1994). The importance of remaining riparian areas for avian and other wildlife populations is thus greatly magnified.

Two of the primary threats to the quality of remaining deciduous riparian habitats are the conversion of land near riparian areas into agricultural and urban land (Tewksbury et al. 1998, Saab 1999), and cattle grazing within riparian areas (Carothers 1977, Crumpacker 1984, Chaney et al. 1990, Saab et al. 1995, Saab 1998). The effects of these activities on individual rivers have often been studied using different metrics, focusing on different groups of birds, and there have been few attempts to combine data across riparian systems to look for common patterns (Hochachka et al. 1999).

Although it is widely recognized that the richness and composition of breeding bird assemblages are at least partially dependent on the landscape within which they are embedded (Robinson et al. 1995a; Donovan et al. 1995b, 1997; Freemark et al. 1995, Faaborg et al. 1995, Saab 1999), it is not clear what scale or scales are appropriate to use when considering the effects of landscapes on bird populations (Freemark et al. 1995, Donovan et al. 2000). Indeed, given the many factors that can affect the structure of bird communities (nest predation, brood parasitism, competition for food and nesting sites, habitat area limitations), landscapes likely affect bird communities at multiple scales (Wiens 1989, 1995; Urban et al. 1987, Turner 1989, Kareiva 1990, Kotliar and Wiens 1990, Barrett 1992, Andrén 1995, Freemark et al. 1995, Hansson et al. 1995). To date, however, few empirical studies have considered the relative importance of multiple landscape scales (but see Tewksbury et al. 1998, Hochochka et al. 1999, Saab 1999, Donovan et al. 2000), and there has been no attempt to examine the relative effects of multiple land-uses across scales when studying the composition of riparian bird communities.

A focal concern in the western United States is cattle grazing. Domestic cattle graze 70% of the land area in the 11 western states (Crumpacker 1984) causing extensive modifications to vegetation (Holechek et al. 1989). These effects are particularly apparent in deciduous riparian areas (Carothers 1977, Crumpacker 1984, Platts and Nelson 1985, Fleischner 1994, Saab et al. 1995). However, it is not clear which grazing effects are dependent on local factors and levels of grazing intensity, and to what extent grazing effects can be generalized across a broad array of riparian systems and grazing regimes.

Here we examine the influence of regional (within 5 km of each study site) and local (within 500 m of each study site) landscapes and the influence of cattle grazing on the richness and relative abundance of bird communities in seven riparian systems dominated by deciduous trees and shrubs. This work is the result of collaboration by five independent research teams working in five western states over the past decade. By combining efforts, we provide the first meta-analysis of human-induced landscape change and cattle grazing on the avian communities breeding in these critical western habitats in the hope of detecting consistent patterns across the West.

METHODS

RIPARIAN SYSTEMS, SURVEY LOCATIONS, AND LANDSCAPE CHARACTERIZATION

The seven riparian systems included in this work vary considerably in size, physical character, local and regional vegetation patterns, and land use (Fig. 1; Appendix 1), but all possess streamside vegetation dominated by woody deciduous species (see Appendix 1 for detailed descriptions of each riparian system).

We analyzed bird species-abundance data from a total of 437 survey locations (Fig. 1; Table 1). Survey locations were separated by at least 150 m and located in vegetation dominated by cottonwood (*Populus* spp.), aspen (*Populus tremuloides*), or a mixture of species including willow (*Salix* spp.), valley oak (*Quercus lobata*), dogwood (*Cornus* spp.), hawthorn (*Crataegus* spp.), cherry (*Prunus* spp.), alder (*Alnus* spp.), and birch (*Betula* spp.). At each survey location, relative abundance was calculated as the total number of each species detected per visit. Surveys were either fixed-radius point counts (five of the seven systems) or 150-m fixed-width line transects (Table 1). We defined a survey as a single visit to a point or transect location. All studies conducted three surveys per year. The radius of point counts was either 40 m or 50 m, and point duration was either five or 10 min (Table 1).

We defined two spatial scales at each study location: regional landscapes (all land within 5 km of each survey location = 7,854 ha) and local landscapes (all land <500 m of each survey location = 78 ha). Regional landscape character was quantified using state GAP databases (Scott et al. 1993) derived from satellite images (Table 1). Local landscape data were gathered from low elevation aerial photography, ortho-photo quadrangle maps, and high resolution digital data, depending on the riparian system. Using a different data set for local analyses allowed us to include smaller features in analyses, such as linear riparian components and individual buildings that could not be detected at the regional scale. Metrics such as average patch size and edge-to-interior ratios depend on mapping resolution, and our data resolution varied considerably among sources (Table 1). Thus we confined our analyses to the percent cover of four landscape components: forest cover, agriculture, human habitation, and deciduous riparian cover. The first three have been used previously to index landscape fragmentation and habitat conversion (Donovan et al. 1995b, 1997; Robinson et al. 1995a, Young and Hutto 1999). Deciduous riparian cover also has been used in landscape studies. Percent cover blends aspects of patch size and isolation, both of which have been found to affect riparian bird communities (Brown and Dinsmore 1986, Gibbs et al. 1991, Craig and Beal 1992, Saab 1999).

Our decision to compare high-resolution local data with low-resolution regional data also reflects the choice available to land managers, where detailed land-use data are available only at local scales. This approach, however, confounds differences in resolution with differences in scale. Therefore, on three riparian systems (Sacramento, San Joaquin, and Bitterroot rivers), we compared GAP data (used for the regional scale) with aerial photography data (used at the local scale) on the same 500 m local landscapes to examine correlations between estimates derived from different

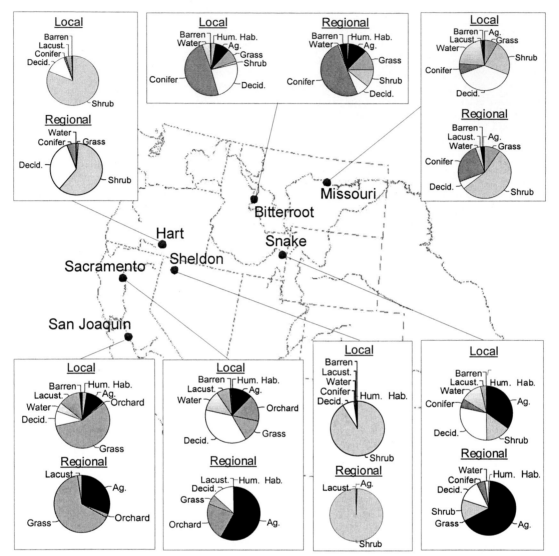

FIGURE 1.   River system locations and general landscape character of each river system. Pie charts are mean percent cover for each landscape component averaged across all survey locations, at both local and regional scales. Hum. Hab. = all human habitations, including houses, farms, commercial developments, and industrial areas. Ag. = all agriculture, including row crops and land used for pasture and row crop, but excluding vineyards and orchards. Orchard = all orchards, primarily fruit and nut trees, and vineyards. Grass = all grasslands. Shrub = all shrublands and juniper woodlands, as bird communities were similar. Decid. = all deciduous habitats. Conifer = Conifer forests. Water = all large bodies of water, including river channels. Lacust. = Lacustrine, partially submerged and wet meadow habitat. Barren = permanent snow, ice, rock, or talus.

data types. For the Bitterroot River, the resolution of GAP data is quite high (Table 1), so we expected some concordance between the two techniques. For the Sacramento and San Joaquin Rivers, the GAP resolution is low, and this shift in resolution could affect results considerably. Because the regional scale contains 100 times the area of the local scale, however, lower resolution at the regional landscape scale should have less effect than lower resolution at the local scale.

LIVESTOCK GRAZING

In five of the seven riparian systems studied, grazing occurred on some but not all of the study sites. Within these five systems, the intensity and timing of grazing differed considerably, from the Missouri River with long term high-intensity grazing on grazed sites and no cattle on rested ("ungrazed") sites for the past 30 years, to the Snake River where grazing intensity dif-

TABLE 1. RIVER SYSTEMS, DATA TYPES, AND SAMPLE SIZES

River system	State	Bird survey type	Duration/ length	Years	Sites	Survey locations	Local landscape		Regional landscape	
							Landscape data source	Minimum mapping unit	Landscape data source	Minimum mapping unit
Sacramento	CA	Point count	5 min	1993–1997[a]	10	55	CWIS[g]	900 m^2	California GAP	100 ha
San Joaquin	CA	Point count	5 min	1995–1997[b]	6	54	CWIS[g]	900 m^2	California GAP	100 ha
Snake	ID	Point count	10 min	1991–1994[c]	46	148[e]	Aerial photos, Ortho-photo Quads.	~650 m^2	Idaho GAP	2 ha, 0.81 ha in riparian
Bitterroot	MT	Point count	10 min	1995–1997[d]	38	120	Aerial photos, Ortho-photo quads.	~650 m^2	MT GAP	2 ha, 0.81 ha in riparian
Missouri	MT	Point count	10 min	1998	9	29	MT GAP	2 ha, 0.81 ha in riparian	MT GAP	2 ha, 0.81 ha in riparian
Sheldon	NV	Transect	150 m long	1991 & 1993	5	10[f]	Aerial photography	~650 m^2	Nevada GAP	100 ha
Hart Mountain	OR	Transect	150 m long	1991 & 1993	7	21[f]	Aerial photography	~650 m^2	Western U.S. GAP[h]	100 ha

[a] Surveys conducted on seven sites (58 points) from 1993–1997, surveys conducted on one site (11 points) from 1994–1997, surveys conducted on one site (three points) from 1995 to 1997, and surveys conducted on one site (nine points) from 1996–1997.
[b] Surveys conducted on one site (15 points) from 1995–1997, surveys conducted on four sites (39 points) from 1996–1997, and surveys conducted on one site (nine points) in 1997 only.
[c] Two surveys at each location in 1991, three at each location in all other years.
[d] Surveys conducted on 16 sites (78 points) from 1995–1997, survey conducted on 22 sites (29 points) in 1996 only.
[e] Bird data were provided for each site (averaged across all points on a site).
[f] Surveys are strip transects (see text) run both in 1991 (grazed) and 1993 (ungrazed) and analyzed separately.
[g] California Wetlands Inventory System map of the Central Valley. Map was classified by the California Department of Fish and Game (1997) from spring and fall 1992/1993 30m satellite images. Available on-line at: http://ceres.ca.gov/wetlands/geo_info/cal_wetland_riparian.html.
[h] The Western GAP is an unreleased GAP cover combining all GAP maps in the western United States; Source: Idaho GAP Lab.

fered considerably among sites and was often moderate or light (Appendix 1). The methods of comparison differ as well; in the Hart Mountain and Sheldon systems, the same sites were surveyed in 1991 and 1993, the first and third growing seasons following cessation of long term livestock grazing. We considered the 1991 surveys "grazed" and the 1993 surveys rested. In all other riparian systems, bird abundance was compared in the same years among different locations, rather than in the same locations among different years. Given all these differences, we expected to find great variation among riparian systems in the effects of grazing, and any consistent effects should represent general effects applicable to a wide variety of riparian ecosystems in the West.

ANALYSIS

Relative abundance data were available for each point count or transect survey except on the Snake River, where data were averaged to the study site level. To accommodate this, we performed analyses at the site level for all riparian systems, and at the survey location level for all areas except the Snake. Both methods gave similar results. However, combining data to the site level resulted in a considerable loss of statistical power, so we present analysis of the survey location data for all rivers except the Snake, which is analyzed at the study site level. Our analysis of species richness includes all areas except the Snake because average richness per survey location could not be calculated from the data available.

All variables were initially screened for deviations from normality using one-sample Kolmogorov-Smirnov tests (Sokal and Rohlf 1995), and transformed where necessary. We used square-root transformations for count data (bird variables), and arcsine square-root transformations for percent data (landscape components). We examined four landscape components—human habitation, agriculture, deciduous forest, and coniferous forest—each at local and regional landscape scales.

Within each riparian system, we examined the effects of landscape differences on the relative abundance of all individual species detected an average of 15 or more times per year on that riparian system. Because we were primarily interested in effects that can be generalized throughout western riparian areas, we limited our analysis to species meeting this criterion on at least two riparian systems (102 species in total). In addition, we examined community level effects by grouping species into different guilds: primary hosts of Brown-headed Cowbirds (see Appendix 2 for scientific names of all species) vs. non-hosts; and long-distance migrants vs. short-distance migrants vs. permanent residents. In examining the effects of grazing, we also divided species into open nesting species vs. primary and secondary cavity nesting species, and low vs. high nesting species. Relative abundance of each species is defined as the average number of individuals detected per survey calculated by averaging values for separate visits within a year and then averaging across years. We also examined overall richness, calculated as the cumulative number of species detected at each location over the three surveys within a single year, averaged across years.

Migratory status followed Sauer et al. (2000). Primary hosts included all species listed as common or frequent cowbird hosts in *The Birder's Handbook* (Ehrlich et al. 1988); species listed as uncommon or rare cowbird hosts were termed secondary hosts (not analyzed in this manuscript). For nest height, we used the mean nest height from nesting studies on the riparian systems in this study, and examined the effect of grazing on the abundance of birds nesting below 2.5 m and above 5 m (Appendix 2).

To control for the large differences in methods among riparian systems, we first tested the effects of each landscape component within each riparian system to maintain consistency in sampling. To assess landscape effects on the avian community, we regressed total relative abundance, richness, and the relative abundance of each avian guild against each of the landscape components at both local and regional scales, using all survey locations within each riparian system for each river-specific analysis. To test for grazing effects we used t-tests within each riparian system, comparing community metrics and individual species between grazed and ungrazed sites. We assumed equal variance among population means unless $P < 0.1$ in Levene tests for equality of variance. Because these analyses are based on overall relative abundance of all species in a guild, the results are heavily influenced by the most common species. To examine landscape and grazing effects on community metrics with all species receiving equal weight, as well as to determine the response of individual species to differences in landscapes, we designated each survey location as low (lower 25%), middle (25 to 75%) or high (upper 25%) with respect to each landscape component within each riparian system. For tests of landscape effects on overall abundance, and the effects of landscapes and grazing on each guild, we coded each species as either more or less abundant in the low sites when compared to the high sites, then used binomial tests to determine if a significant majority of species within each guild were significantly more abundant in the high or low sites. For analysis of individual species, we used Mann-Whitney U-tests to compare the abundance of species in low and high sites for each landscape component within each riparian system and to compare abundance in grazed vs. ungrazed sites. We tested all species on a given riparian system with an average of 15 or greater detections per year. As our purpose was to evaluate the consistency of landscapes and grazing effects across rivers, we limit our results to species tested in at least two riparian systems. This analysis controls for landscape differences among different riparian systems because it compares abundances of birds across the landscape extremes within each riparian system.

To examine landscape and grazing effects across riparian systems, we used Fisher's combined probabilities test (Fisher 1954, Sokal and Rohlf 1995). This test evaluates the P-values from each riparian system against the null hypothesis that there is no general trend of significance across tests (in this case, riparian systems). The value -2 times the sum of the natural logs of all the P values from a group of independent tests of a single hypothesis falls along a cumulative Chi-square distribution with $2k$ degrees of freedom,

TABLE 2. CORRELATIONS AND MEAN DIFFERENCE (1 SE) BETWEEN LANDSCAPE COMPONENTS IDENTIFIED USING HIGH RESOLUTION LOCAL LANDSCAPE DATA AND LOWER RESOLUTION GAP DATA (USED FOR THE REGIONAL SCALE ANALYSIS) BOTH AT THE LOCAL SCALE

	Human habitation		Agriculture		Deciduous riparian		Coniferous forest	
	r	Diff (%)[b]	r	Diff (%)[b]	r	Diff (%)[b]	r	Diff (%)[b]
Bitterroot	0.20*	−5.4 (0.7)	0.78***	−9.0 (1.3)	0.76***	−6.3 (1.2)	0.97***	11.6 (1.0)
Sacramento	—[a]	−1.2 (0.2)	−0.23	5.9 (5.4)	0.11	0.2 (5.7)	—	—
San Joaquin	—[a]	−2.9 (0.3)	0.17	0.8 (3.9)	−0.07	7.6 (3.6)	—	—

Note: * P < 0.05, ** P < 0.01, *** P < 0.005.
[a] Lower resolution data-source picked up no human habitation.
[b] % difference = % component at regional scales (low resolution) − % component at local scales (high resolution).

where k = the number of separate tests (riparian areas) being compared. The combined probabilities test evaluates where the summed value lies along the cumulative Chi-square distribution. Because we are comparing the significance of tests for a general trend in one direction, but trends may be either positive or negative, we had to account for the sign associated with each P value. To do this, we used $-ln$ P for all results whose significance referred to a test opposite in sign from that being evaluated. We evaluated trends in both directions. This procedure produced a more conservative test for an overall pattern across riparian systems, as it is more difficult to reject the null hypothesis of no general effect. Using Fisher's combined probabilities tests also circumvents the problems of combining data with inherent differences in detection probabilities resulting from differences in survey techniques and observers. To determine the most abundant species across river systems, we ranked the abundance of all species within each river system in descending order, and computed mean abundance ranks for all species across rivers (a mean abundance rank of one would mean a species had the highest detection frequency in all rivers it occurred in).

To correct for inflation of significance due to multiple testing, we used sequential Bonferroni adjustment of significance (Rice 1989) for all correlation, regression, and t-tests. Thus for tests of landscape effects, we corrected for a total of 64 tests within each riparian system (four landscape components, two scales, and eight bird community components). We also corrected for 64 tests when examining the significance of the combined probabilities tests across riparian systems. For grazing effects, we corrected for 12 tests (one for each aspect of the bird community examined).

RESULTS

For all studies combined, 180 species were detected across 437 survey locations. Eleven species were detected on all seven river systems. These species, in order of mean abundance rank (lower ranks being more abundant) were the Brown-headed Cowbird, with a mean abundance rank of 7.2; American Robin, 13.7; House Wren, 14.6; Yellow Warbler, 16.1; European Starling, 17.9; Black-headed Grosbeak, 18.9; Bullock's Oriole, 21.3; Mourning Dove, 22.1; Warbling Vireo, 24.1; Brewer's Blackbird, 29.4; and Lazuli Bunting, 30.1. Of the 87 species tested in-

dividually for effects of landscape components and grazing, 44 species were significantly less common either in grazed areas, areas with high human habitation or extensive agriculture, or areas with less deciduous riparian habitat; 33 species were more common under these conditions.

CORRELATIONS AMONG LANDSCAPE COMPONENTS AND BETWEEN DATA RESOLUTIONS

Correlations among landscape components varied considerably among riparian systems, depending on the landscape context within which each stream or river was embedded (Fig. 1). Not surprisingly, both within and between scales, the strongest correlations were found where the four components we examined—human habitation, agriculture, deciduous area, and coniferous forest—dominated the landscape (e.g., Snake and Bitterroot rivers), as opposed to landscapes dominated by shrub or grass (Appendix 3). Landscape components varied considerably in their correlations across scales. Relatively homogeneous and broad land uses, such as agriculture, were always correlated positively across scales, whereas clumped and small land-uses, such as human habitation, were correlated weakly across scales in most riparian systems (Appendix 3). Differences in data resolution also affected correlations across scales. When we controlled for scale and compared both local (high resolution) and regional (low resolution) data at the local scale, we found strong positive correlations on the Bitterroot River (Table 2), where regional analysis was relatively fine grained (Table 1). Even with this higher resolution regional data (minimum mapping unit = 2 ha), however, smaller landscape components were underemphasized compared with dominant landscape components (Table 2). Where regional data were coarse-grained, as on the Sacramento and San Luis rivers, correlations were not significant, and differences had high variance because components identified with the high-resolution local data were either missed entirely, or overemphasized by the low resolution landscape data.

HUMAN HABITATION

At local scales, the majority of all species (62% ± 5% SE, five rivers) had lower relative abundances in areas with high human habitation compared to areas with low human habitation. This trend was particularly apparent in long-distance migrants (66% ± 6% less abundant in areas with high human habitation, five rivers). These relationships were significant for both groups in binomial tests, but because the Brown-headed Cowbird, Yellow Warbler, and the Black-headed Grosbeak (all very common species) were more abundant in areas with high human habitation, there was no relationship between the total number of detections of all species, or detections of long-distance migrants, vs. local human habitation (Table 3). Human habitation was strongly and positively correlated with the number of Brown-headed Cowbirds detected at both scales (Table 3), and the number of non-host species detections was higher in areas with higher regional human habitation, due primarily to the greater abundance of European Starlings, House Wrens, and American Robins in more densely settled areas (Table 4). The five species showing the greatest reduction in frequency in regional landscapes with high proportions of human settlement were Yellow-rumped Warbler, MacGillivray's Warbler, Warbling Vireo, Swainson's Thrush, and Dusky Flycatcher (Table 4). Populations of each of these species are highly vulnerable to cowbird parasitism (Tewksbury et al. 1998).

AGRICULTURE

High abundances of abundant species such as American Robins, Yellow Warblers, and Brown-headed Cowbirds in areas with agriculture (Table 4) led to highly significant positive relationships between total and guild detection frequency and the amount of agriculture at both scales. However, binomial tests for direction of change of all species in each guild were not significant (Table 3; 53% ± 6% of species had higher abundance in areas with more agriculture), and the only river system to show a significant majority of species increasing with regional agriculture was the Bitterroot (Appendix 4). In addition, regional agriculture was significantly, positively correlated with the abundance of Brown-headed Cowbirds, which were twice as abundant in areas with high proportions of agriculture compared with areas with low proportions of agriculture. Primary hosts, although not related to agriculture at the local scale, showed a strong positive relationship with the amount of agriculture regionally. This positive trend was driven almost entirely by Yellow Warblers, the most abundant host. Yellow Warblers were detected far more often in areas with greater amounts of agriculture and human habitation. In contrast, many less abundant cowbird host species, such as Swainson's Thrush, Warbling Vireo, MacGillivray's Warbler, and Yellow-rumped Warbler, were rarely detected at survey locations with high regional agriculture (Table 4). Overall, there was no indication that the majority of hosts were more or less abundant in landscapes dominated by agriculture (Table 3; Appendix 4).

Non-hosts showed a strong positive relationship with agriculture at both scales (Table 3), primarily due to higher abundances of American Robins, House Wrens, European Starlings, Tree Swallows, and Bullock's Orioles in areas with greater proportions of agriculture (Table 4). The effects of human habitation and agriculture appear similar; in total, 24 species were significantly more abundant in areas with high local or regional agriculture, and 17 of these species were also significantly more abundant in areas with high human habitation.

DECIDUOUS RIPARIAN

Across riparian systems, areas with more deciduous riparian habitat tended to have greater avian abundance and diversity. Fifteen species were significantly more abundant in areas with a high proportion of deciduous habitat at the local scale; six of these species were present in at least four riparian systems: Yellow Warbler, Black-headed Grosbeak, Song Sparrow, Western Wood Pewee, Cedar Waxwing, and Orange-crowned Warbler. Only two species were significantly less abundant in areas with greater local deciduous riparian habitat, MacGillivray's Warbler and Townsend's Warbler. Effects at the regional scale were similar (Tables 3 and 4), though almost half of the individual species increasing were different from those increasing at the local scale.

The amount of local deciduous riparian habitat was positively correlated with virtually all avian guilds at both scales. Binomial tests were less convincing of a significant overall effect, where the only significant relationship was between all species and regional deciduous riparian habitat (Table 3; 57% of species ± 4.3%, five rivers). The lack of significant effects in binomial tests at the local scale was caused primarily by effects on the Sacramento River, where greater local deciduous riparian habitat was associated with lower detection frequencies in 67% of all species (Appendix 4).

CONIFEROUS FOREST

At the local scale, the proportion of coniferous forest was not significantly related to total relative abundance, richness, or any guild examined, after correcting for multiple tests. However, at the regional scale, conifer cover had a strong negative effect on cowbird abundance (combined P < 0.001). Cowbirds were detected only half as often at survey locations with high conifer forest when compared to locations with low conifer forest (Table 4). Coniferous cover was also related negatively to the abundance of non-hosts, driven primarily by the low abundance of European Starlings, American Robins, and House Wrens in sites with high coniferous cover. In addition, long-distance migrant abundance was associated positively with percent conifer forest (Table 3), due primarily to many more detections of Warbling Vireo, MacGillivray's Warbler, Townsend's Warbler, Violetgreen Swallow, and Fox Sparrow in areas with more conifers (Table 4). Binomial tests agreed in direction with regressions on total guild abundance, but were non-significant across rivers, showing considerable variation in results among individual rivers (Appendix 4).

GRAZING

The majority of all species (63% ± 5%) were less abundant in grazed locations (Fig. 2A; combined probabilities test χ^2 = 42.8, P < 0.001). After correcting for multiple tests, six species were significantly less abundant at grazed survey locations when all riparian systems were considered, while no species were significantly more abundant at grazed locations (Table 5). In addition, total relative abundance was significantly lower in grazed areas (Fig. 2B; combined probabilities test χ^2 = 48.9, P < 0.001), and species richness showed a non-significant trend to be lower in grazed areas (Fig. 2C; combined probabilities test χ^2 = 19.8, P = 0.01, not significant after correction for multiple tests). The intensity of grazing effects varied greatly among the seven riparian systems. On the Missouri, Sacramento, and Hart systems, 68–73% of species were less abundant in grazed areas (Fig. 2A; binomial tests, P's < 0.007). The Missouri showed the most dramatic effects, with 13 species significantly less abundant in grazed areas and only one more abundant (Appendix 5), and the average detections per count shifted from 36 on ungrazed survey locations to 21 on grazed survey locations. In contrast, on the Snake and Sheldon riparian systems, species were no more likely to be less or more abundant in these areas (Fig. 2A). On the Sheldon, only two species differed significantly between recently grazed and ungrazed sites, with one species more abundant in each condition (Appendix 5).

Cowbird abundances were not significantly different between grazed and ungrazed locations

for any of the five large riparian systems (Fig. 3A). Total primary cowbird hosts, however, were less abundant in grazed areas (Fig. 3B; combined χ^2 = 25.3, P = 0.005), with strong effects on the Missouri River (t = 3.3, P = 0.003) and the Snake River (t = 3.2, P = 0.002; Appendix 5). While the majority of host species were less abundant on grazed sites in all river systems except the Sheldon, the low number of species in the guild precluded significant effects (Fig. 3C). On the Missouri River, the effects of grazing on hosts was driven primarily by lower abundance of Red-eyed Vireo, American Redstart, Lazuli Bunting, Least Flycatcher, and Yellow Warbler in grazed areas (Appendix 5). Lazuli Buntings and Yellow Warblers were also significantly less abundant in grazed sites along the Snake River, as were Veerys and Song Sparrows (Appendix 5). Total non-host abundance showed no consistent response to grazing pressure (Fig. 3D; combined probabilities test χ^2 = 11.3, P = 0.33), but the proportion of species that were more abundant in ungrazed systems was typically higher than expected by chance (Fig. 3E; combined probabilities test χ^2 = 20.0, P = 0.023).

Of the migratory guilds, long-distance migrants were the only group significantly less abundant in grazed areas (Total abundance Fig. 4A: combined probabilities test χ^2 = 47.7, P < 0.001; binomial mean response Fig. 4B: combined probabilities test χ^2 = 26.4, P = 0.003). Across all riparian systems, five of the ten species with significantly lower relative abundances in grazed areas were long-distance migrants (Table 5). The lower relative abundance of long-distance migrants in grazed areas was particularly apparent on the Missouri River, where the average number of long-distance migrants was 21 individuals per survey in ungrazed areas and only 12 per survey in grazed areas (Fig. 4A), and 84% of the species were less abundant in grazed sites (Fig. 4B). In addition to large effects on the Missouri, long-distance migrants were significantly less abundant in grazed sites on the Sacramento (t = 2.1, P = 0.037), and exhibited similar non-significant trends in both Hart Mountain and Snake River systems (P = 0.07 and 0.18, respectively). Residents showed no significant differences between grazed and ungrazed sites for any of the riparian systems (Fig. 4C and 4D). The total abundance of short-distance migrants tended to be lower in grazed areas (Fig. 4E; combined probabilities test χ^2 = 19.3, P = 0.03, not significant after correction for multiple tests) with large differences in detection frequency only on the Missouri River (t = 3.2, P = 0.003). Individual species in this guild were no more likely to be less or more

TABLE 3. EFFECTS OF LANDSCAPE VARIABLES ON TOTAL DETECTIONS, RICHNESS, AND DETECTIONS BY GUILD

Landscape variable	Statistic		All birds[c]	Richness[d]	Cowbirds[e]	Prime hosts[f]	Non-hosts[g]	Long-distance migrant[h]	Residents[i]	Short-distance migrant[j]
Local Human Habitation	Σ[a]	Dir	Neg	Pos	Pos	Pos	Neg	Neg	Neg	Pos
		χ^2	5.25	1.8	28.61	9.21	1.73	11.67	1.79	0.23
		P	0.874	0.985	0.001*	0.512	0.998	0.308	0.998	>0.99
	#[b]	Dir	Neg	N/A	N/A	Neg	Neg	Neg	Neg	Neg
		χ^2	39.8	N/A	N/A	18.4	18.4	25.6	7.12	12.9
		P	<0.001*	N/A	N/A	0.047	0.047	0.004*	0.525	0.231
Regional Human Habitation	Σ	Dir	Pos	Pos	Pos	Neg	Pos	Pos	Pos	Pos
		χ^2	6.36		25.71	10.73	16.18	5.44	9.30	14.26
		P	0.174	0.080[k]	0.001*	0.030	0.002*	0.245	0.054	0.026
	#	Dir	Neg	N/A	N/A	Neg	Neg	Neg	Pos	Neg
		χ^2	9.6	N/A	N/A	2.2	4.5	4.7	1.7	5.1
		P	0.144	N/A	N/A	0.903	0.605	0.585	0.944	0.531
Local Agriculture	Σ	Dir	Pos	Pos	Pos	Pos	Pos	Pos	Pos	Pos
		χ^2	22.94	15.12	34.98	7.67	31.59	7.52	10.90	38.08
		P	0.011*	0.019	<0.001*	0.661	0.001*	0.676	0.366	<0.001*
	#	Dir	Neg	N/A	N/A	Neg	Neg	Neg	Pos	Pos
		χ^2	0.5	N/A	N/A	0.79	0.4	9.8	3.1	0.3
		P	>0.99	N/A	N/A	0.999	>0.99	0.279	0.926	>0.99
Regional Agriculture	Σ	Dir	Pos	Pos	Pos	Pos	Pos	Pos	Pos	Pos
		χ^2	50.66	17.14	56.91	26.72	34.47	14.46	26.96	55.29
		P	<0.001*	0.029	<0.001*	0.003*	<0.001*	0.153	0.003*	<0.001*
	#	Dir	Pos	N/A	N/A	Pos	Pos	Neg	Pos	Pos
		χ^2	14.3	N/A	N/A	7.4	1.9	1.9	1.7	6.2
		P	0.159	N/A	N/A	0.690	0.997	0.997	0.998	0.794
Local Deciduous	Σ	Dir	Pos	Pos	Pos	Pos	Pos	Pos	Pos	Pos
		χ^2	38.01	15.70	31.33	56.87	14.07	16.71	29.28	34.42
		P	<0.001*	0.204	0.005*	<0.001*	0.445	0.272	0.010	0.002*
	#	Dir	Pos	N/A	N/A	Pos	Pos	Neg	Pos	Pos
		χ^2	15.7	N/A	N/A	4.51	10.47	2.3	15.08	0.29
		P	0.334	N/A	N/A	0.991	0.727	>0.99	0.237	>0.99
Regional Deciduous	Σ	Dir	Pos	Pos	Pos	Pos	Pos	Pos	Pos	Neg
		χ^2	12.89	15.12	20.89	20.34	24.25	17.17	28.30	0.62
		P	0.230	0.056	0.022	0.026	0.007*	0.071	0.002*	>0.99
	#	Dir	Pos	N/A	N/A	Pos	Pos	Pos	Pos	Pos
		χ^2	20.4	N/A	N/A	1.1	8.5	7.9	6.9	2.7
		P	0.026*	N/A	N/A	>0.99	0.576	0.635	0.735	0.987
Local Conifer	Σ	Dir	Neg	Neg	Neg	Neg	Neg	Neg	Neg	Neg
		χ^2	18.66	13.73	26.49	7.67	18.64	0.57	23.77	22.38

TABLE 3. CONTINUED

Landscape variable		Statistic	All birds[c]	Richness[d]	Cowbirds[e]	Prime hosts[f]	Non-hosts[g]	Long-distance migrant[h]	Residents[i]	Short-distance migrant[j]
		P	0.017	0.033	0.001*	0.466	0.045	>0.99	0.002*	0.004*
		Dir	Neg	N/A	N/A	Pos	Neg	Pos	Neg	Neg
	#	χ^2	5.1	N/A	N/A	3.0	5.9	12.1	6.2	4.0
		P	0.748	N/A	N/A	0.936	0.655	0.146	0.629	0.857
Regional Conifer	Σ	Dir	Neg	Pos	Neg	Neg	Neg	Pos	Neg	Neg
		χ^2	6.45	7.03	43.87	3.42	23.72	23.30	11.90	21.27
		P	0.597	0.318	<0.001*	0.905	0.003*	0.003*	0.156	0.006*
	#	Dir	Neg	N/A	N/A	Neg	Neg	Pos	Neg	Neg
		χ^2	8.5	N/A	N/A	1.4	8.4	14.2	3.0	10.4
		P	0.383	N/A	N/A	0.994	0.392	0.076	0.932	0.241

Note: Results from combined probabilities tests of linear regression of summed detections of all species in each guild (Σ) and from binomial tests on direction of change of each species in the guild (#).

* Significant (P < 0.05) after Bonferroni correction for multiple tests.

[a] Chi-square value and significance from multiple comparison tests based on regression of landscape value on total abundance within each guild.

[b] Chi-square value and significance from multiple comparison tests based on binomial tests examining the proportion of species more or less abundant in sites with high values for each landscape component.

[c] Average number of all detections per survey.

[d] Average number of species detected per year at a given survey location (3 surveys).

[e] Number of Brown-headed Cowbirds detected.

[f] Number of primary cowbird hosts detected (Appendix 2).

[g] Average number of non-hosts detected (Appendix 2).

[h] Average number of long-distance migrants detected per survey (Appendix 2).

[i] Average number of residents detected per survey (Appendix 2).

[j] Average number of short-distance migrants detected per survey (Appendix 2).

[k] Regression run only on the Bitterroot River; P-value is for regression (Appendix 4).

TABLE 4. INDIVIDUAL SPECIES RESPONSES TO LANDSCAPE COMPONENTS

Landscape component	N	P	Ratio	Bitterroot	Sacramento	San Joaquin	Missouri	Snake	Sheldon	Hart Mountain
High Local Human Habitation										
More Abundant Species										
Bullock's Oriole	4	<0.001*	2.33	0.01/0.11	0.14/0.29	0.30/0.38			0.18/0	
Yellow Warbler	4	<0.001*	3.23	0.18/1.05	0.01/0.01	0.02/0.00			0.73/0.50	
Brown-headed Cowbird	4	<0.001*	1.83	0.40/0.84	0.38/0.59	1.01/1.27			0.82/1.50	
Red-winged Blackbird	4	<0.001*	1.54	0.01/0.20	0.00/0.00	1.22/1.17			1.45/1.25	
Black-headed Grosbeak	4	0.001*	1.62	0.10/0.11	0.42/0.76	0.00/0.11			0.18/0.50	
American Robin	4	0.009	1.79	0.26/0.48	0.10/0.17	0.03/0.05			0.18/0.75	
Western Wood-pewee	3	<0.001*	2.21	0.04/0.27	0.43/0.87				0.45/0.25	
Spotted Towhee	3	0.005*	1.67		0.79/1.30	0.50/0.69			0.09/0.00	
Song Sparrow	3	0.009*	1.99	0.04/0.20		0.60/0.84			0.64/0.50	
Willow Flycatcher	3	0.014	3.13	0.02/0.14	0.01/0.00	0.01/0.00			0.09/0.00	
Downy Woodpecker	3	0.030	1.90	0.03/0.05	0.06/0.14	0.01/0.00				
Red-shafted Flicker	3	0.034	1.68	0.07/0.23	0.05/0.03				0.27/0.00	
Cedar Waxwing	2	<0.001*	2.51	0.08/0.42	0.16/0.0					
Marsh Wren	2	0.042*	13.21			0.0/0.75			0.09/0.0	
Less Abundant Species										
MacGillivray's Warbler	3	<0.001*	4.92	0.52/0.08	0.00/0.00				0.27/0.25	
Townsend's Warbler	3	0.024	107.20	0.25/0.00	0.00/0.01				0.18/0.00	
Ash-throated Flycatcher	2	0.009	1.28		0.51/0.23	0.75/0.70				
Western Scrub-Jay	2	0.011*	2.03		0.26/0.17	0.59/0.17				
High Regional Human Habitation										
More Abundant Species										
European Starling	2	<0.001*	23.12	0.01/0.22				0.11/1.43		
Western Wood-pewee	2	<0.001*	4.70	0.08/0.36				0.02/0.31		
Bullock's Oriole	2	<0.001*	6.46	0.02/0.09				0.18/0.70		
House Wren	2	<0.001*	18.19	0.01/0.04				0.10/1.42		
Red-winged Blackbird	2	<0.001*	6.13	0.03/0.16				0.02/0.15		
Brown-headed Cowbird	2	<0.001*	1.57	0.50/0.77				0.17/0.58		
American Robin	2	0.002*	2.00	0.35/0.49				0.87/1.62		
Yellow Warbler	2	0.003*	2.14	0.39/0.96				2.32/2.39		
Willow Flycatcher	2	0.004*	1.77	0.05/0.11				0.01/0.01		
Downy Woodpecker	2	0.010*	2.30	0.04/0.08				0.03/0.12		
Tree Swallow	2	0.010*	2.99	0.02/0.06				0.12/0.18		
American Goldfinch	2	0.019	3.49	0.01/0.05				0.61/0.96		

TABLE 4. CONTINUED

Landscape component	N	P	Ratio	River system						
				Bitterroot	Sacramento	San Joaquin	Missouri	Snake	Sheldon	Hart Mountain
Less Abundant Species										
Yellow-rumped Warbler	2	<0.001*	4.92	0.10/0.02				0.21/0.02		
MacGillivray's Warbler	2	<0.001*	2.56	0.39/0.19				0.14/0.01		
Warbling Vireo	2	<0.001*	2.00	0.53/0.36				1.07/0.17		
Swainson's Thrush	2	<0.001*	2.39	0.21/0.11				0.04/0.00		
Dusky Flycatcher	2	<0.001*	5.64	0.44/0.08				0.09/0.04		
Ruffed Grouse	2	<0.001*	6.90	0.07/0.01				0.06/0.00		
Red-naped Sapsucker	2	0.006*	2.09	0.14/0.08				0.26/0.06		
Veery	2	0.006*	2.47	0.11/0.03				0.45/0.15		
Song Sparrow	2	0.012	1.34	0.09/0.14				1.01/0.21		
American Crow	2	0.021*	1.43	0.00/0.00				0.26/0.07		
Western Tanager	2	0.023*	3.06	0.07/0.02				0.08/0.03		
High Local Agriculture										
More Abundant Species										
American Robin	4	<0.001*	2.19	0.23/0.65	0.09/0.18	0.07/0.03		1.12/1.90		
Bullock's Oriole	4	<0.001*	2.76	0.00/0.10	0.21/0.37	0.31/0.24		0.29/0.88		
House Wren	4	<0.001*	3.52	0.00/0.05	0.17/0.23	0.79/1.18		0.17/1.53		
European Starling	4	<0.001*	8.28	0.00/0.22	0.11/0.04	0.20/0.08		0.09/1.99		
Brown-headed Cowbird	4	<0.001*	1.75	0.39/0.81	0.35/0.51	0.96/1.38		0.34/0.52		
Yellow Warbler	4	<0.001*	1.97	0.19/1.21	0.03/0.00	0.03/0.03		2.68/2.29		
Great Horned Owl	4	0.004*	N/A	0.00/0.01	0.00/0.02	0.00/0.08		0.00/0.03		
Tree Swallow	4	0.006*	1.33	0.00/0.00	0.68/0.43	0.48/0.55		0.11/0.21		
Black-headed Grosbeak	4	0.006*	1.72	0.10/0.16	0.36/0.80	0.02/0.08		0.25/0.14		
Spotted Sandpiper	4	0.010*	6.94	0.00/0.13	0.01/0.01	0.02/0.00		0.03/0.01		
Downy Woodpecker	4	0.014	2.24	0.04/0.08	0.03/0.12	0.01/0.00		0.04/0.13		
American Goldfinch	4	0.030	1.57	0.00/0.02	0.32/0.28	0.09/0.25		0.79/0.90		
Western Wood-pewee	3	<0.001*	5.26	0.03/0.40	0.29/0.69			0.09/0.42		
Red-winged Blackbird	3	<0.001*	1.26	0.00/0.20		1.18/0.66		0.07/0.05		
Red-shafted Flicker	3	<0.001*	2.02	0.05/0.26		0.04/0.02		0.28/0.15		
Song Sparrow	3	<0.001*	1.73	0.02/0.23		0.72/1.51		0.95/0.12		
Cedar Waxwing	3	0.004*	1.51	0.12/0.36	0.07/0.00			0.36/0.15		
Willow Flycatcher	3	0.014	3.48	0.03/0.13	0.01/0.02			0.00/0.01		
Spotted Towhee	3	0.033	1.98	0.00/0.00	0.02/1.22	0.63/0.96				
Black-billed Magpie	2	0.001*	1.77	0.26/0.40				0.22/0.54		
Eastern Kingbird	2	0.001*	76.67	0.00/0.02				0.00/0.04		
White-breasted Nuthatch	2	0.032*	3.29	0.01/0.03	0.04/0.09					
Less Abundant Species										
Warbling Vireo	3	<0.001*	2.16	0.61/0.41	0.07/0.03			0.74/0.16		
Dusky Flycatcher	3	<0.001*	7.05	0.39/0.06	0.01/0.00			0.06/0.03		

TABLE 4. CONTINUED

Landscape component	N	P	Ratio	River system						
				Bitterroot	Sacramento	San Joaquin	Missouri	Snake	Sheldon	Hart Mountain
Yellow-rumped Warbler	3	0.005*	2.26	0.09/0.06	0.01/0.00			0.16/0.02		
N. Rough-winged Swallow	3	0.017*	N/A		0.02/0.00	0.13/0.00		0.03/0.00		
Townsend's Warbler	3	0.019	46.12	0.29/0.00	0.00/0.01			0.12/0.01		
MacGillivray's Warbler	2	<0.001*	11.87	0.60/0.06		0.00/0.01		0.40/0.07		
Veery	2	0.001*	3.60	0.11/0.04				0.06/0.00		
Ruffed Grouse	2	0.001*	5.29	0.07/0.02						
Nuttall's Woodpecker	2	0.003*	1.87		0.60/0.41	0.31/0.08				
Chipping Sparrow	2	0.005*	9.25	0.10/0.01				0.04/0.01		
Violet-green Swallow	2	0.007*	9.30		0.01/0.00			0.32/0.03		
Ruby-crowned Kinglet	2	0.010*	25.32	0.16/0.01	0.01/0.00					
Red-naped Sapsucker	2	0.012*	1.77	0.12/0.09				0.22/0.05		
Western Scrub-Jay	2	0.017*	1.82		0.28/0.11	0.57/0.35				
Orange-crowned Warbler	2	0.017	7.42	0.13/0.02	0.02/0.00					
High Regional Agriculture										
More Abundant Species										
Brown-headed Cowbird	5	<0.001*	1.97	0.26/0.79	0.32/0.61	0.94/1.44	0.44/0.50	0.25/0.63		
Bullock's Oriole	5	<0.001*	1.59	0.00/0.08	0.19/0.31	0.44/0.27	0.39/0.59	0.20/0.74		
House Wren	5	<0.001*	1.12	0.00/0.07	0.24/0.58	0.99/0.95	2.44/2.45	0.18/1.16		
Yellow Warbler	5	<0.001*	1.35	0.07/0.97	0.02/0.00	0.05/0.03	3.03/3.73	2.10/2.67		
American Robin	5	<0.001*	1.13	0.33/0.65	0.08/0.23	0.03/0.07	2.14/1.36	0.81/1.86		
American Goldfinch	5	<0.001*	1.37	0.00/0.06	0.33/0.37	0.05/0.43	1.78/2.41	0.56/1.32		
European Starling	5	0.002*	2.45	0.00/0.25	0.13/0.01	0.17/0.26	0.44/0.45	0.18/1.26		
Tree Swallow	5	0.015*	1.26	0.00/0.06	0.87/0.48	0.42/0.73	0.03/0.09	0.13/0.30		
Western Wood-pewee	4	<0.001*	1.21	0.04/0.34	0.32/0.99	0.51/0.85	1.78/1.18	0.04/0.39		
Spotted Towhee	4	0.002*	1.55	0.01/0.00	0.62/1.40	0.03/0.24	0.97/1.41			
Common Yellowthroat	4	0.004*	1.04	0.00/0.03	0.05/0.08	0.91/0.84	1.14/1.36			
Red-winged Blackbird	4	0.004*	1.38	0.00/0.13	0.01/0.00		0.33/0.09	0.02/0.16		
Downy Woodpecker	4	0.037	0.92	0.05/0.09	0.04/0.16		0.03/0.09	0.04/0.10		
Black-billed Magpie	3	<0.001*	3.09	0.13/0.66			0.11/0.36	0.36/0.29		
Eastern Kingbird	3	<0.001*	2.81	0.00/0.02			0.72/0.05	0.00/0.03		
Black-capped Chickadee	3	0.003*	1.33	0.13/0.66				0.29/0.30		
Willow Flycatcher	3	0.012	7.40	0.01/0.11	0.01/0.00			0.00/0.01		
Less Abundant Species										
Swainson's Thrush	5	<0.001*	6.17	0.34/0.02	0.00/0.01	0.10/0.04	0.11/0.09	0.07/0.00		
Warbling Vireo	4	<0.001*	4.73	0.59/0.16	0.05/0.01		0.31/0.00	0.96/0.16		
MacGillivray's Warbler	3	<0.001*	8.68	0.52/0.06	0.01/0.00			0.09/0.00		
Violet-green Swallow	3	0.003*	17.63		0.01/0.00		0.14/0.00	0.84/0.05		
American Crow	3	0.004*	8.57	0.01/0.01		0.10/0.02		0.26/0.02		
Yellow-rumped Warbler	3	0.007*	2.98	0.16/0.07				0.17/0.03		

TABLE 4. CONTINUED

Landscape component	N	P	Ratio	River system						
				Bitterroot	Sacramento	San Joaquin	Missouri	Snake	Sheldon	Hart Mountain
Townsend's Warbler	2	<0.001*	166.26	0.47/0.00	0.00/0.01	1.69/0.69				2.00/0.30
Western Kingbird	2	0.015*	2.22		0.38/0.24	0.63/0.33				0.09/0.70
Western Scrub-Jay	2	0.030	1.77		0.27/0.18					0.18/0.00
High Local Deciduous Riparian										
More Abundant Species										
Yellow Warbler	7	<0.001*	1.25	0.03/0.77	0.00/0.01	0.00/0.03	2.71/3.21	1.90/2.81	1.00/0.50	0.27/0.40
Black-headed Grosbeak	7	0.014*	1.80	0.05/0.11	0.72/0.44	0.02/0.17	0.21/0.57	0.08/0.23	0.00/0.33	
Song Sparrow	6	<0.001*	1.85	0.01/0.21		0.53/1.33	0.50/0.79	0.35/0.48	1.00/0.50	
Western Wood-pewee	6	0.015	1.60	0.03/0.21	0.62/0.54		0.71/2.29	0.27/0.24	0.67/0.17	
Cedar Waxwing	4	<0.001*	1.58	0.06/0.25	0.27/0.02		0.36/0.79	0.24/0.34		
Orange-crowned Warbler	4	0.034	2.81	0.12/0.04	0.00/0.02				0.33/0.17	0.00/1.10
Black-capped Chickadee	3	<0.001*	3.48	0.10/0.51			0.00/0.43	0.27/0.36		
Red-eyed Vireo	3	<0.001*	19.60	0.00/0.04			0.07/1.29	0.00/0.01		
Red-naped Sapsucker	3	<0.001*	4.23	0.06/0.21				0.07/0.22		0.09/0.60
Gray Catbird	3	0.007*	3.72	0.00/0.04			0.21/0.57	0.05/0.19		
Veery	2	<0.001*	16.23	0.00/0.08				0.03/0.38		0.00/0.90
Fox Sparrow	2	<0.001*	N/A				0.71/2.50	0.00/0.12		
Least Flycatcher	2	0.006*	3.68	0.00/0.03			0.00/0.43			
American Redstart	2	0.011*	14.27	0.02/0.19						
Bewick's Wren	2	0.031*	1.57		0.49/0.72	0.45/0.75				
Less Abundant Species										
MacGillivray's Warbler	4	0.001*	3.90	0.58/0.13	0.00/0.00			0.04/0.04	0.33/0.17	0.18/0.00
Townsend's Warbler	4	0.004*	12.66	0.40/0.00		0.00/0.01			0.00/0.17	0.18/0.00
Western Kingbird	3	0.026	1.87		0.39/0.14	0.92/0.56			0.00/0.17	
High Regional Deciduous Riparian										
More Abundant Species										
Western Wood-pewee	5	<0.001*	2.23	0.01/0.33	0.51/0.92		1.07/2.00	0.23/0.05		0.20/0.70
American Robin	5	0.020	1.19	0.31/0.65	0.05/0.25		1.36/1.93	1.66/0.94		1.60/1.90
Song Sparrow	4	<0.001*	2.30	0.01/0.20			0.00/0.21	0.45/1.03		0.30/0.00
Yellow Warbler	4	<0.001*	1.27	0.07/0.90			2.43/3.43	2.53/2.13		1.40/0.50
Red-shafted Flicker	4	0.011*	1.47	0.08/0.23			0.79/1.36	0.20/0.32		0.90/0.80
Cedar Waxwing	4	0.012	2.25	0.04/0.23	0.01/0.00		0.29/0.64	0.27/0.32		
Black-capped Chickadee	3	<0.001*	3.14	0.17/0.69			0.29/1.29	0.26/0.26		
Red-eyed Vireo	3	0.004*	67.64	0.00/0.03			0.00/0.71	0.01/0.02		
Willow Flycatcher	3	0.009*	9.86	0.00/0.10				0.01/0.00		
Red-naped Sapsucker	3	0.012*	1.87	0.03/0.09	0.02/0.00			0.12/0.20		0.40/0.70
Red-winged Blackbird	3	0.046	0.45	0.00/0.13				0.15/0.05		0.80/0.00
White-breasted Nuthatch	3	0.046	3.32	0.00/0.03	0.07/0.10		0.00/0.14			

TABLE 4. CONTINUED

Landscape component	N	P	Ratio	Bitterroot	Sacramento	San Joaquin	River system			
							Missouri	Snake	Sheldon	Hart Mountain
Black-billed Magpie	2	<0.001*	2.45	0.17/0.69				0.39/0.34		
Less Abundant Species										
Townsend's Warbler	2	<0.001*	159.60	0.45/0.00						1.10/0.50
Orange-crowned Warbler	2	0.006*	2.33	0.11/0.04	0.00/0.01					
MacGillivray's Warbler	2	0.019	4.52	0.54/0.09				0.05/0.08		
Ruby-crowned Kinglet	2	0.024	4.50	0.18/0.01						0.00/0.10
High Local Conifer Forest										
More Abundant Species										
Swainson's Thrush	4	<0.001*	4.92	0.01/0.31			0.00/0.14	0.00/0.07		0.19/0.20
Warbling Vireo	4	<0.001*	1.96	0.21/0.57			0.00/0.14	0.17/0.71		1.25/1.90
MacGillivray's Warbler	3	<0.001*	13.61	0.05/0.50				0.01/0.11		0.00/0.10
Yellow-rumped Warbler	3	0.007*	2.86	0.03/0.09				0.02/0.12		0.06/0.10
Dusky Flycatcher	3	0.023	0.97	0.02/0.29				0.02/0.03		1.81/1.30
Western Tanager	3	0.034	3.97	0.01/0.08				0.02/0.04		0.06/0.20
Ruffed Grouse	2	<0.001*	11.67	0.01/0.09				0.00/0.06		
Ruby-crowned Kinglet	2	0.007*	6.22	0.01/0.19						0.06/0.10
Veery	2	0.028	2.14	0.02/0.00				0.17/0.59		
Violet-green Swallow	2	0.029	5.30				0.07/0.00	0.05/0.43		
Less Abundant Species										
Western Wood-pewee	4	<0.001*	1.64	0.40/0.03			1.79/1.07	0.33/0.06		0.50/1.00
American Robin	4	<0.001*	1.88	0.72/0.25			2.07/0.93	1.57/0.95		1.94/1.70
House Wren	4	<0.001*	1.60	0.07/0.00			2.50/1.93	1.24/0.05		4.50/4.50
Bullock's Oriole	4	<0.001*	1.90	0.14/0.00			0.64/0.36	0.69/0.25		0.50/0.80
European Starling	4	<0.001*	2.44	0.25/0.00			0.71/0.14	1.27/0.11		0.50/1.40
Yellow Warbler	4	<0.001*	1.41	1.30/0.07			3.21/3.29	2.49/2.80		0.75/1.20
Red-shafted Flicker	4	<0.001*	1.53	0.30/0.06			1.43/0.64	0.17/0.25		1.06/1.10
Downy Woodpecker	4	0.003*	2.11	0.11/0.04			0.00/0.14	0.13/0.03		0.38/0.20
Mourning Dove	4	0.003*	2.01	0.02/0.00			2.21/1.29	0.55/0.14		0.06/0.10
Brown-headed Cowbird	4	0.004*	1.61	0.84/0.36			0.43/0.64	0.54/0.42		1.00/0.70
Cedar Waxwing	3	<0.001*	1.32	0.33/0.08			0.86/0.79	0.19/0.38		
Black-billed Magpie	3	0.009*	1.76	0.44/0.23			0.00/0.14	0.47/0.22		
Black-capped Chickadee	3	0.013	1.74	0.44/0.23			0.64/0.07	0.29/0.32		
American Goldfinch	3	0.024	1.43	0.05/0.00			2.07/1.93	1.08/0.81		
Red-winged Blackbird	2	<0.001*	5.64	0.24/0.00				0.09/0.09		
Willow Flycatcher	2	0.001*	5.14	0.16/0.02				0.01/0.01		
Least Flycatcher	2	0.001*	2.30	0.03/0.00				2.50/1.14		
Spotted Sandpiper	2	0.007*	6.49	0.12/0.00				0.02/0.04		
Great Blue Heron	2	0.017*	8.67	0.04/0.00				0.02/0.01		

TABLE 4. CONTINUED

Landscape component	N	P	Ratio	River system						
				Bitterroot	Sacramento	San Joaquin	Missouri	Snake	Sheldon	Hart Mountain
High Regional Conifer Forest										
More Abundant Species										
Swainson's Thrush	4	<0.001*	1.89	0.01/0.34			0.00/0.14	0.00/0.08		0.42/0.10
Warbling Vireo	4	<0.001*	1.81	0.25/0.65			0.14/0.64	0.14/0.85		1.11/1.30
MacGillivray's Warbler	3	<0.001*	7.25	0.04/0.60				0.00/0.15		0.11/0.00
Dusky Flycatcher	3	<0.001*	1.41	0.02/0.31				0.02/0.06		1.37/2.10
Western Tanager	3	0.002*	1.28	0.01/0.10				0.00/0.04		0.16/0.00
Chipping Sparrow	3	0.003*	6.77	0.01/0.12			0.07/0.00	0.00/0.03		
Pine Siskin	3	0.003*	4.31	0.06/0.35				0.02/0.04		0.05/0.00
Yellow-rumped Warbler	3	0.009*	2.72	0.03/0.17				0.02/0.17		0.11/0.00
Townsend's Warbler	2	<0.001*	7.96	0.00/0.43						0.11/0.00
Orange-crowned Warbler	2	<0.001*	1.73	0.00/0.10						0.53/1.10
Ruffed Grouse	2	0.002*	9.95	0.01/0.09				0.00/0.03		
Violet-green Swallow	2	0.003*	12.60				0.00/0.07	0.04/0.51		
Mountain Chickadee	2	0.008*	N/A	0.00/0.05						0.00/0.30
Ruby-crowned Kinglet	2	0.025	3.03	0.01/0.18						0.11/0.00
Fox Sparrow	2	0.032	2.25					0.05/0.15		0.32/0.80
Less Abundant Species										
Western Wood-pewee	4	<0.001*	1.92	0.47/0.04			1.07/1.57	0.39/0.05		0.58/0.40
Yellow Warbler	4	<0.001*	1.97	1.34/0.05			2.43/3.21	2.75/2.26		1.68/0.30
Bullock's Oriole	4	<0.001*	3.16	0.14/0.00			0.21/0.43	0.75/0.20		0.79/0.30
European Starling	4	<0.001*	11.34	0.25/0.00			1.14/0.00	1.33/0.20		0.63/0.10
Brown-headed Cowbird	4	<0.001*	2.01	0.84/0.23			0.36/0.71	0.63/0.23		1.05/0.90
American Robin	4	<0.001*	1.39	0.73/0.26			1.36/2.79	1.81/1.00		1.95/1.80
House Wren	4	<0.001*	1.37	0.07/0.00			2.21/3.00	1.18/0.11		3.32/3.80
Downy Woodpecker	4	0.012*	2.55	0.10/0.06			0.36/0.00	0.10/0.04		0.32/0.20
Cedar Waxwing	3	<0.001*	1.26	0.31/0.01			0.29/1.00	0.25/0.32		
Red-winged Blackbird	3	<0.001*	38.45	0.24/0.00				0.13/0.03		0.42/0.00
American Goldfinch	3	<0.001*	1.67	0.05/0.00			1.29/1.71	1.25/0.40		
Eastern Kingbird	3	0.003*	3.57	0.02/0.00			0.36/0.14	0.05/0.00		
Willow Flycatcher	2	<0.001*	11.96	0.16/0.01				0.01/0.00		
Spotted Sandpiper	2	0.001*	27.55	0.12/0.00				0.03/0.01		

Notes: Includes all species with study-wide differences in average abundance between the lower 25% of plots (*Low*) and the upper 25% of plots (*High*) when all plots within each river system are ranked from lowest to highest for each landscape variable. The N is the number of rivers in which the species and landscape component were present. P-values are from Fisher's combined probability tests across rivers. We report the ratio of detection frequency (detections per survey) in all of the less abundant class (*Low* or *High*) to detection frequency in all of the more abundant class as 1:x, where x = Ratio. In addition, detection frequency in each river system for *Low* and *High* plots (*Low/High*) is indicated.
* Significant after Bonferroni correction for multiple tests.

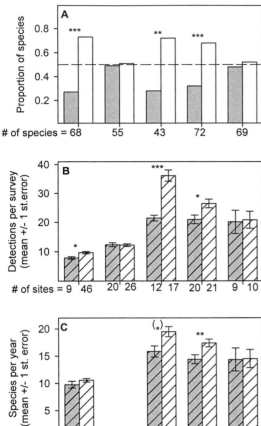

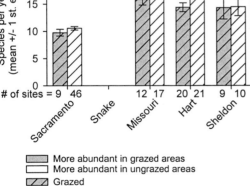

FIGURE 2. Total response of all species to grazing in each riparian system. Proportion of all species more abundant in grazed or ungrazed plots (A), average number of birds detected per survey (B), and the average number of species detected over the course of a single year at a given location (C) for grazed and ungrazed plots in each river system. * P < 0.05, ** P < 0.01, *** P < 0.005. (*) = P-value not significant after correction for multiple tests.

abundant in grazed sites (Fig. 4F; combined probabilities test χ^2 = 7.5, P = 0.679).

Total abundance of open cup nesters was significantly higher in ungrazed survey locations (Fig. 5A; combined probabilities test χ^2 = 46.4, P < 0.0005) and an average of 65% (± 8%) of open-cup nesting species were less abundant in grazed areas (Fig. 5B; combined probabilities test χ^2 = 35.3 P < 0.001). Primary cavity nesting species trended in the same direction (Fig. 5C; combined probabilities test χ^2 = 20.4, P = 0.026, not significant after correction for multiple tests), and secondary cavity nesters showed conflicting patterns on different riparian systems with no overall effect (Fig. 5E; combined probabilities test χ^2 = 4.4, P = 0.92). Binomial tests suggested no overall trend for cavity nesters (Fig. 5D and 5F), though the number of species in each guild was too small for rigorous analysis. On the Missouri, total abundances of open cup and primary cavity nesters were significantly greater on ungrazed sites (t's > 4.2, P's < 0.001) and 22 of 25 open-cup nesting species were more abundant in ungrazed sites. Open-cup nesting abundance was also lower on the Hart Mountain (total abundance; t = 2.6, P = 0.013) and Sacramento River (t = 2.1, P = 0.04) systems, with 30 of 40 species less abundant in grazed areas on Hart Mountain (binomial test P = 0.003) and 27 of 40 species less abundant in grazed locations on the Sacramento (binomial test P = 0.04).

The overall abundance of all species nesting below 2.5 m was significantly lower in grazed sites compared to ungrazed sites (Fig. 6A; combined probabilities test χ^2 = 26.4, P = 0.003) and 67% of species in this category (± 5%) were less abundant in grazed sites (combined probabilities test χ^2 = 17, P = 0.07), with all rivers showing the same trend (Fig. 6B). In contrast, the combined abundance of all species with average nesting heights higher than 5 m showed only a non-significant trend to be lower in grazed areas (Fig. 6C; combined probabilities test χ^2 = 18.6, P = 0.045, not significant after correction for multiple tests), and only 58% (± 9%) of species in this guild were less abundant in grazed sites, with the Snake and Sheldon systems showing either opposite trends or no effect (Fig. 6D; combined probabilities test χ^2 = 5.8, P = 0.23).

DISCUSSION

This synthesis includes seven different western riparian systems, each embedded in a different landscape. In each system, data were gathered by different investigators using similar but not identical methodologies. Despite these differences, our results demonstrate that both landscape character and livestock grazing have some consistent, potentially West-wide effects on bird communities. Although some of these effects are similar to those found in the Midwest (landscape effects on Brown-headed Cowbirds, for example), others will require further study to determine the mechanisms responsible for the patterns (the effects of grazing and agriculture

TABLE 5. SPECIES SHOWING OVERALL TREND IN RESPONSE TO GRAZING

Less common in grazed areas			More common in grazed areas		
Species	Rivers	P	Species	Rivers	P
American Robin	5	0.005*	Dusky Flycatcher	4	0.040
Western Wood-pewee	5	0.031	Western Meadowlark	3	0.056
Black-headed Grosbeak	5	0.080	Brewer's Sparrow	2	0.110
Song Sparrow	4	0.020			
Hairy Woodpecker	4	0.031*			
Mallard	4	0.055			
Red-shafted Flicker	4	0.115			
MacGillivray's Warbler	4	0.129			
Cedar Waxwing	3	0.073			
Cordilleran Flycatcher	2	0.003*			
Red-eyed Vireo	2	0.008*			
Fox Sparrow	2	0.014*			
Green-tailed Towhee	2	0.015*			
Black-capped Chickadee	2	0.017			
Gray Catbird	2	0.032			
Ovenbird	2	0.177			
Turkey Vulture	2	0.197			

Note: Species are ranked by the number of riparian systems included in the analysis (minimum of two) and significance ($P < 0.2$). * Denotes significant after Bonferroni correction for multiple tests.

on Yellow Warblers, for example). Below, we summarize effects of different landscape components and provide a brief synthesis of our findings.

SCALE AND RESOLUTION

Until recently, there has been a significant gap between theoretical work stressing the scale-dependent nature of landscape effects (Wiens 1989, 1995; Dunning et al. 1992) and empirical studies that confine analysis to a single landscape scale (Donovan et al. 1995b, Robinson et al. 1995a, Thompson et al. 2000, Hejl and Young 1999; but see Tewksbury et al. 1998, Young and Hutto 1999, Donovan et al. 2000). The abundance and composition of bird communities are affected by multiple processes across different landscape scales (Dunning et al. 1992, Freemark et al. 1995); even a single process, such as nest predation, acts across multiple scales dependent on the range size and habitat affinities of the primary predators (Andrén 1995, Tewksbury et al. 1998). This variation in the scaling of processes suggests that conservation planning will be best served by examination of multiple scales. Multiple-scale landscape analyses allows the discovery of relationships that are relatively scale-insensitive, and thus more easily applied in management contexts, and it allows determination of appropriate scales when processes such as brood parasitism or nest predation are considered.

Our results show that different landscape components influence bird abundance and diversity at different scales. Overall, 40% of species significantly affected by landscape factors at one scale were not affected by these factors at the other scale (Table 4), suggesting that examination of landscapes at only a single spatial scale may result in loss of considerable information. Importantly, our examination of two landscape scales does not allow us to determine the point when considering more land area decreases rather than increases the explanatory power of a certain landscape variable, as we can only say that a larger landscape is better than a smaller one, or the other way around. Analyses comparing the effect sizes of landscape components at multiple scales would allow estimation of the relative importance of landscape features at different distances from an area of interest.

The appropriate scale is also a function of mapping resolution. Linear landscape components and components that typically have small patch sizes are usually underestimated when mapping resolution is coarse. It is not particularly surprising that we found no significant correlations between data gathered using the low resolution California GAP data and the detailed CWIS data (Table 2), as the resolution of the California GAP data (100 ha minimum patch size) is greater than the entire area of our local landscapes (78 ha). This coarse resolution is inappropriate for local scale habitat mapping, but it may still be appropriate for larger landscape scales as long as the biases are recognized. At our regional scale, where we used these data, we mapped 8000 ha around each survey location, which allowed for a mosaic of patches even

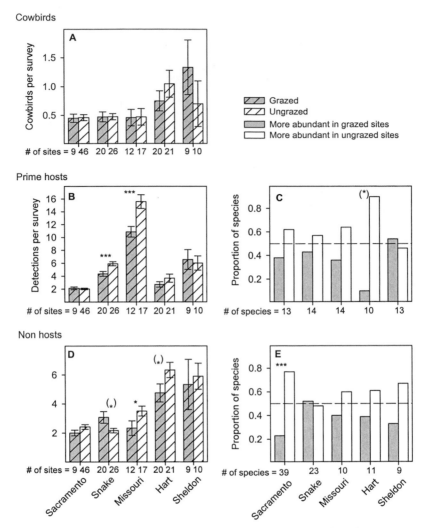

FIGURE 3. Grazing effects on cowbirds, prime hosts, and non-hosts. Total detections per survey on grazed and ungrazed sites (A, B, and D), and proportion of species in each guild more abundant in grazed or ungrazed sites (C and E), for cowbirds (A), prime hosts (B and C), and non-hosts (D and E) in each river system. * P < 0.05, ** P < 0.01, *** P < 0.005. (*) = P-value not significant after correction for multiple tests.

when these patches were 100 ha and larger. At this level, large differences in the regional landscape are fully apparent, but features such as dispersed housing or small riparian areas are not detected. Thus the effect of changing regional agriculture or coniferous forest cover is well represented in the coarse-grained data, while changes in linear deciduous riparian areas may go undetected. As landscape data of higher resolution become more broadly available, comparisons across regions should be possible using the same data sources for all landscape sizes, eliminating the confounding issues of shifting mapping resolution and allowing explicit comparison of scale.

HUMAN HABITATION AND AGRICULTURE

Our finding that overall avian abundance was positively related to regional agricultural abundance runs counter to findings from the East (Croonquist and Brooks 1991, 1993), but is not without precedent in the western United States (Carothers et al. 1974). These results may be better understood by examining the individual species with large differences in abundance, rather than by focusing on guilds (Mannan and Meslow 1984). The high congruence in the species increasing due to agriculture and human habitation is partly a function of the positive correlation that typically exists between agriculture

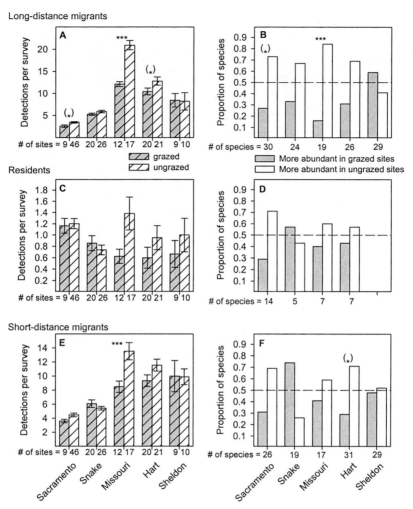

FIGURE 4. Grazing effects on long-distance migrants, residents, and short-distance migrants. Total detections per survey on grazed and ungrazed sites (A, C, and E), and proportion of species within each guild more abundant in grazed or ungrazed sites (B, D, and F), for long-distance migrants (A and B), year-round residents (C and D), and short-distance migrants (E and F) in each river system. * P < 0.05, ** P < 0.01, *** P < 0.005. (*) = P-value not significant after correction for multiple tests.

and houses (Appendix 3). It is likely, however, that many species with higher relative abundance in areas with more agriculture also show similar numerical responses to high human habitation. Brown-headed Cowbirds use both agricultural and farm areas for foraging (Thompson 1994), and European Starlings often forage in suburban and agricultural areas (Fischl and Caccamise 1985). Indeed, most of the species that are more abundant in areas with high agriculture or human habitation often utilize multiple habitats; American Robins, Black-billed Magpies, starlings, and cowbirds are all examples. Increases in starlings may have consequences for other secondary cavity nesters, as starlings can

exclude less aggressive species from cavities (Ingold 1989, 1994, 1998; Nilsson 1984, Kerpez and Smith 1990, Rich et al. 1994, Dobkin et al. 1995). Indeed, densities of Violet-green Swallows were significantly lower in sites with high agriculture at either scale—the same sites in which starlings were significantly more abundant (Table 4).

Higher Brown-headed Cowbird detection frequency in areas with more agriculture has been found previously across both local and regional scales (Conine et al. 1979, Donovan 1997, Tewksbury et al. 1999, Hejl and Young 1999, Hochachka et al. 1999, Young and Hutto 1999). Our finding that the detection frequency of pri-

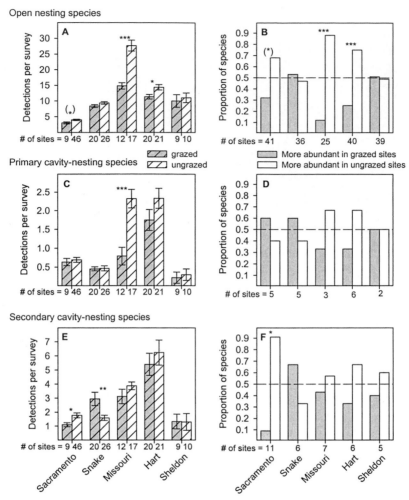

FIGURE 5. Grazing effects on open nesting species, primary cavity nesters, and secondary cavity nesting species. Total detections per survey on grazed and ungrazed sites (A, C, and E), and proportion of species in each guild more abundant in grazed or ungrazed sites (B, D, and F), for open-cup nesting species (A and B), primary cavity nesting species (C and D), and secondary cavity nesting species (E and F) in each river system. * P < 0.05, ** P < 0.01, *** P < 0.005. (*) = P-value not significant after correction for multiple tests.

mary hosts was not lower in areas where cowbirds were common is consistent with other comparisons of cowbird density and host density (Donovan et al. 1997, Tewksbury et al. 1999, Young and Hutto 1999), and does not indicate that cowbirds have no effect on host communities (De Groot et al. 1999). The demographic effect of brood parasitism varies greatly among different host species (Lorenzana and Sealy 1999), and we first expect lower abundances of species that are particularly susceptible to parasitism. Indeed, the Dusky Flycatcher, Swainson's Thrush, Veery, Warbling Vireo, Orange-crowned Warbler, MacGillivray's Warbler, and American Redstart all suffer complete or nearly complete brood loss when parasitized (J. J.

Tewksbury, unpubl. data) and are all less abundant in areas with high human habitation or high agriculture (Table 4), areas where cowbirds are abundant. In contrast, Yellow Warblers are more resistant to the demographic effect of brood parasitism (Clark and Robertson 1981, Sealy 1995), and they were more abundant in areas with high human habitation and agriculture. Importantly, human habitation and agriculture are often concentrated near productive riparian habitat with large flood-plains, areas where many long-distance migrants susceptible to parasitism are more abundant. Thus the trend for Yellow Warblers (more abundant in these areas) may characterize the natural response of other species, as they respond to larger riparian areas, but the ef-

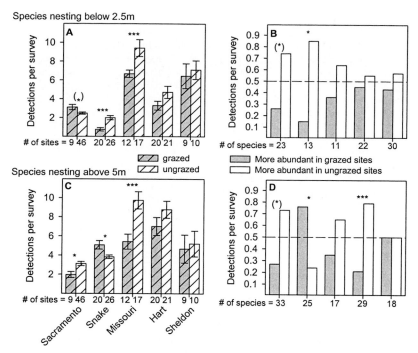

FIGURE 6. Effects of grazing on low and high nesting species. Total detections per survey on grazed and ungrazed sites (A and C), and proportion of species in each guild more abundant in grazed or ungrazed sites (B and D), for species nesting below 2.5m (A and B), and species nesting above 5 m (C and D) in each river system. * P < 0.05, ** P < 0.01, *** P < 0.005. (*) = P-value not significant after correction for multiple tests.

fect of cowbirds may counter this trend. In addition, negative correlations between cowbird and host detection frequencies suggest that rates of brood parasitism are positively related to cowbird detection frequencies. While this assumption is reasonable across most levels of cowbird detection, where cowbird numbers are high, further increases may not change parasitism rates. This may be the case along the Sacramento River, where high-levels of parasitism at all sites may have already caused large regional declines in many species (Gaines 1974), so that current variation in cowbird detection frequency is uncorrelated with parasitism rates.

The largest limitations in understanding the effects of changing landscapes on riparian bird communities are the correlations among components of the landscape. In our study, we cannot separate unambiguously the effects of agriculture and human habitation because of the high correlation between these components (Appendix 3). In some cases, however, correlations between landscape components differ significantly among riparian systems, allowing insights into which relationships are causative, and which are simply due to covariation in landscape components. For example, local deciduous habitat is correlated strongly with higher host abun-

dance (Table 3). In the Bitterroot Valley, agriculture is correlated positively with the amount of local deciduous habitat (Appendix 3; r = 0.47, P < 0.001), and, as a result, we see positive associations between host abundance and regional agriculture. Conversely, along the Snake River, local agriculture and deciduous habitats are negatively correlated (Appendix 3; r = −0.55, P < 0.001), and we see a strong negative relationship between host abundance and agriculture at the local scale (Appendix 4). Thus, changes in host abundance are likely caused by differences in the amount of deciduous habitat, not the amount of agriculture, but the effects are difficult to separate where these components are positively correlated.

DECIDUOUS RIPARIAN AREA

Deciduous riparian area at the local scale is a function of the width of the riparian corridor; thus the positive correlations between avian abundance and deciduous habitat likely are consequences of greater habitat availability and heterogeneity associated with larger riparian corridors (Tyser 1983, Brown and Dinsmore 1986, Dobkin and Wilcox 1986, Craig and Beal 1992, Keller et al. 1993). All of the species that were significantly more abundant at survey locations with high local deciduous habitat are species traditionally considered riparian associates. The guild-level examination of the effects of increasing local deciduous area and increasing regional agriculture suggested similar effects (Table 3), but the individual species responding to these landscape components were quite different (Table 4). Fifteen species had significantly higher abundance in larger deciduous areas, and 17 species were higher in abundance in areas with more regional agriculture. However, only three species were more abundant under both these conditions (Table 4). Thus the bird communities in areas with high agricultural abundance share little in common with the communities in areas with large amounts of deciduous habitat, and guild-based analysis may lead to erroneous conclusions unless the responses of individual species are examined.

Within riparian systems, the breeding bird community found in smaller deciduous tracts was most often a subset of the birds found in larger tracts. Only three species were less abundant in sites with more local deciduous forest, and one of these, the Townsend's Warbler, is typically associated with coniferous habitats. Thus, preserving and restoring large tracts of deciduous habitat likely will do more to preserve riparian-associated species than will any other action. In addition, large deciduous patches also may reduce parasitism in parts of the patch as distance from the nearest cowbird feeding area increases.

CONIFEROUS FOREST

Studies in the Midwest have found that areas with higher conifer abundance, at scales similar to our regional scale, have lower cowbird abundance and parasitism (Donovan et al. 1995b, 1997; Robinson et al. 1995a). Recent work in the western United States, however, has suggested that the abundance of human habitation (Tewksbury et al. 1998), agriculture (Hejl and Young 1999, Young and Hutto 1999, Donovan et al. 2000), and the abundance of suitable hosts (Barber and Martin 1997; Tewksbury et al. 1998, 1999) are better predictors of parasitism pressure than is conifer abundance. Our study supports both bodies of work—cowbirds were not significantly less abundant in areas with more local coniferous forest, but they were related positively to both human habitation and agriculture, and they were also higher in larger riparian areas, where host abundance is also higher. At a regional scale, cowbirds did show a strong negative correlation with the amount of coniferous forest on the landscape, similar to results from the Midwest and East. This relationship at the regional scale is most likely due to

the strong negative correlation between regional coniferous forest cover and agriculture on the Snake and the Bitterroot rivers (Appendix 3), the two rivers where cowbirds and coniferous forest are negatively related (Appendix 4). In the Bitterroot River system, rates of brood parasitism have been directly related to the amount of human habitation on the landscape, not the amount of coniferous forest (Tewksbury et al. 1998). The effects of coniferous forest on individual species were very similar across scales, with over 70% of species affected showing significant effects at both scales.

GRAZING

Variation in the intensity, duration, and timing of grazing has been shown to influence bird communities (Saab et al. 1995), and its effects are particularly apparent in deciduous systems (Fleischner 1994). Our study includes a diversity of grazing regimes, and the effects on bird communities generally match the intensity and duration of the grazing. In the Missouri River, grazed sites have had cattle on them for over 50 years, and ungrazed sites have been free of grazing for over 25 years. This is reflected in the severe effects of grazing on the bird communities. In contrast, grazing-related differences were few in the Sheldon system, where long-term livestock grazing has left a highly degraded set of riparian habitats. Ungrazed survey locations were only in their third year of rest, and the general lack of differences in avian community composition reflected the very limited recovery made by the riparian plant community (D. Dobkin et al., unpubl. data).

Our finding that grazing had no effect on detection frequencies of Brown-headed Cowbirds in any riparian system runs counter to most previous studies (Page et al. 1978, Mosconi and Hutto 1982, Knopf et al. 1988, Schulz and Leninger 1991; but see Taylor 1986). However, we measured grazing pressure on individual study sites, not on the landscape as a whole; thus cowbirds may be foraging in grazed sites but searching for nests in ungrazed sites, where hosts are generally more abundant. Thus grazed and ungrazed sites may offer different resources for cowbirds; previous research in the Bitterroot River system has shown that cowbird abundance is strongly related to host abundance, as well as distance from agriculture (Tewksbury et al. 1999), supporting this possibility.

As cowbirds are not consistently more abundant in grazed areas, the much lower primary host abundance in grazed areas may not be simply the result of higher parasitism pressure, but instead may be due to interactions between vegetation differences and predation rates (Knopf

1985), lack of appropriate settling cues in grazed sites, or indirect interactions between food availability, foraging behavior, and nest predation (Martin 1992). Many primary hosts are also long-distance migrants, and we found that this group was lower in abundance in grazed areas as well. Saab et al. (1995) found the same result after reviewing the literature, and suggested that this could be due to the high proportion of open-cup nesters among long-distance migrants and greater sensitivity of open-cup nesters to grazing. Our data are consistent with this interpretation: open-cup nesters were more heavily affected by grazing than were primary or secondary cavity nesters. Open-cup nesters accounted for 96% of species and 81% of detections for long distance migrants, 82% of species and 28% of detections for short-distance migrants, and only 58% of species and 37% of all detections for residents.

Along the Missouri River, differences in primary cavity nesters between grazed and ungrazed areas were as great as differences in open-cup nesters, a finding that contrasts sharply with previous work (Good and Dambush 1943, Mosconi and Hutto 1982, Medin and Clary 1991). The strong community-wide effects seen on the Missouri may be related to changes in vegetation that take place with continued grazing over long time scales (Ohmart 1994). High-nesting birds and primary cavity nesters may escape the immediate effects of grazing, but as cottonwood and aspen forests age, lack of recruitment of new trees causes a reduction in small and eventually large tree classes, which will affect the density of cavity nesters (Sedgwick and Knopf 1990, Dobkin et al. 1995) and the density of high-nesting species in general. This process may be well advanced in grazed locations along the Missouri, but is unlikely where grazing has been less continuous. Our results comparing low-nesting species to high-nesting species further support this possibility. Low open-cup nesting species have been shown to be particularly sensitive to grazing due to the large effects cattle have on the lower strata of vegetation (Sedgwick and Knopf 1987, Saab et al. 1995, Saab 1998). We also found that while both low and high nesting species had lower detection frequencies in grazed areas, these differences were greater for low nesting species. Along the Missouri, however, equally strong differences were found for both low- and high-nesting species, suggesting that long-term grazing may have affected canopy structure, snag retention, and recruitment of trees into the canopy (Ohmart 1994).

Cowbirds and Landscapes

Cowbirds could pose regional threats to riparian avifaunas due to their ubiquitous nature,

their tendency to reach high densities in riparian areas (Tewksbury et al. 1999, Ward and Smith 2000), and the effects of parasitism both on individual hosts (Pease and Grzybowski 1995, Woodworth 1999) and on community composition (De Groot et al. 1999). Because of this, much work has examined landscape-scale effects on cowbird abundance and parasitism pressure locally (Gustafson and Crow 1994, Coker and Capen 1995, Gates and Evans 1998, Hejl and Young 1999; Tewksbury et al. 1998, 1999; Young and Hutto 1999), regionally (Donovan et al. 1995b, 1997, 2000; Robinson et al. 1995a, Thompson et al. 2000) and nationally (Hochachka et al. 1999). The majority of this work investigated only one or two factors that could limit cowbird abundance, in contrast to our results, which suggest that multiple landscape components may be important in the western United States.

To date, the species that are most often affected by parasitism appear to be extremely habitat limited (Robinson et al. 1995b), suggesting that the primary cause of population decline is not parasitism but habitat loss. With the steady increase in human encroachment upon riparian systems, and the highly mobile nature and generalist feeding strategy of the cowbird (Thompson 1994, Robinson et al. 1995b), we already have lost most of our opportunity to set aside large riparian areas in landscapes that are remote enough to preclude cowbirds altogether. Thus most communities will be affected by cowbirds, and attention should shift to strategies for minimizing the effect of cowbirds at local and regional scales. We suggest that preserving and enhancing the size of deciduous areas that are surrounded by few human habitations and little agriculture will have the greatest benefit for host populations, as cowbirds in these landscapes are likely limited by feeding habitat. In largely agricultural landscapes, cowbirds are more likely limited by availability of host nests, not feeding areas; thus moderate reductions in feeding areas in these areas (feedlots, bird-feeders, corrals, livestock pastures) may have little effect on rates of brood parasitism.

Management Implications and Species of Particular Concern

Our data suggest that the greatest threats to western deciduous riparian systems are (1) continued deciduous habitat loss and reduction in riparian area, (2) continued cattle grazing in remaining deciduous systems, and (3) increasing concentration of homes and farms along major riparian systems in the western United States. All of these factors are likely to have negative effects on bird communities in deciduous riparian areas, but rarely is it possible to extrapolate

TABLE 6. SUMMARY OF ALL SPECIES SIGNIFICANTLY LESS ABUNDANT IN AREAS WITH MORE HUMAN HABITATION, MORE AGRICULTURE, OR LESS DECIDUOUS HABITAT AT EITHER SCALE, OR IN GRAZED HABITATS, TESTED IN AT LEAST TWO RIPARIAN SYSTEMS

Species	More human habitation	More agriculture	Less deciduous	Grazing	Negative responses	Net negative–positive responses	West BBS[a]
Red-naped Sapsucker	0/−	−/0	−/−		4	4	
MacGillivray's Warbler	−/−	−/−	+/+		4	2	
Song Sparrow	+/−	+/0	−/−	−	4	2	**
Western Scrub-jay	−/0	−/−			3	3	
Veery	0/−	−/0	−/0		3	3	
Warbling Vireo	0/−	−/−			3	3	
Red-eyed Vireo			−/−	−	3	3	**
Yellow-rumped Warbler	0/−	−/−			3	3	
Black-capped Chickadee		−0/+	−/−	−	3	2	**
Townsend's Warbler	−/0	−/−	+/+		3	1	
Ruffed Grouse	0/−	−/0			2	2	*
American Crow	0/−	0/−			2	2	
Violet-green Swallow		−/−			2	2	
Swainson's Thrush	0/−	0/−			2	2	
Gray Catbird			−/0	−	2	2	
Fox Sparrow			−/0	−	2	2	
Dusky Flycatcher	0/−	−/0		+	2	1	*
Orange-crowned Warbler		−/0	−/+		2	1	*
Western Wood-pewee	+/+	+/+	−/0	−	2	−2	**
American Robin	+/+	+/+	0/−	−	2	−2	
Cedar Waxwing	+/0	+/0	−/−		2	−2	
Yellow Warbler	+/+	+/+	−/−		2	−2	
Nuttall's Woodpecker		−/0			1	1	
Hairy Woodpecker				−	1	1	
Least Flycatcher			−/0		1	1	
Ash-throated Flycatcher	−/0				1	1	
Cordilleran Flycatcher				−	1	1	
Western Kingbird		0/−			1	1	
Northern Rough-winged Swallow		−/0			1	1	
Bewick's Wren			−/0		1	1	
American Redstart			−/0		1	1	
Western Tanager	0/−				1	1	
Green-tailed towhee				−	1	1	
Chipping Sparrow		−/0			1	1	**
White-breasted Nuthatch		+/0	0/−		1	0	
Ruby-crowned Kinglet		−/0	0/+		1	0	
Black-billed Magpie		+/+	0/−		1	−1	
Black-headed Grosbeak	+/0	+/0	−/0		1	−1	
Red-shafted Flicker	+/0	+/0	0/−		1	−2	*
Red-winged Blackbird	+/+	+/+	0/−		1	−3	**
Willow Flycatcher	+/+	+/+	0/−		1	−3	**

Notes: Significantly ($P = 0.05$) lower detection frequency (−), significantly higher detection frequency (+), and no significant difference in detection frequency (0) are listed for each species in which at least 2 river systems were used in the analysis. Significant effects at local and regional scales are listed (local/regional). Species are ranked by the number of negative responses and the net (negative − positive) responses.
[a] Trend estimates from the Western Breeding Bird Survey region (Sauer et al. 2000). Species with a declining trend ($P < 0.25$) in the past 20 years, or over the course of the entire survey period, are single-starred (*) and species showing significant declines ($P < 0.05$) are marked with double stars (**).

from local studies to regional population trends. The data provided here allow us to highlight consistent trends, and by summarizing the responses to individual land uses we can also identify those species that appear to be at particular risk due to human landscape modification and livestock grazing (Table 6). We ranked each species based on the number of negative responses (lower abundance due to grazing, higher amounts of human habitation or agriculture, or lower amounts of deciduous habitat) making the assumption that species vulnerable to multiple human land-uses should receive greater attention than species vulnerable to only one type of land-use. Ten species had at least three negative responses. Of these, the Veery, MacGillivray's

Warbler, Song Sparrow, Warbling Vireo, and Red-eyed Vireo may be the most at risk, as all but the Warbling Vireo nest lower in dense vegetation (Ehrlich et al. 1988; J. J. Tewksbury unpubl. data) and all frequently suffer brood parasitism (Friedmann et al. 1977; J. J. Tewksbury unpubl. data). These species were all less abundant in landscapes with high human habitation and agriculture or low amounts of riparian habitat, and three respond negatively to livestock grazing. In addition, all of these, as well as the Red-naped Sapsucker, are found almost exclusively in deciduous vegetation. We suggest that these species should be monitored closely in western riparian habitats, and research should be initiated to examine mechanisms behind these patterns.

CONCLUSIONS

Management that focuses on enhancing the size of remaining deciduous riparian areas and reducing cattle grazing on these areas is likely to produce the greatest benefits for bird species dependent on western deciduous riparian habitats. In addition, strict limitations on building in floodplains will reduce the need for absolute flood control on riparian systems, which results in reduced riparian area. Protecting the few areas where riparian systems run through landscapes that are relatively free of human disturbance should be a high conservation priority both to protect the last unaltered pieces of one of the most endangered and important breeding habitats for western birds, and to preserve these few natural landscapes as benchmarks to use in examining the effects of land conversion. Without natural landscapes, we may lose sight of the conditions we are attempting to preserve.

ACKNOWLEDGMENTS

The results summarized here were produced by five independent field teams working over the past decade, and our work would not have been possible without the sharp eyes and strong ears of the many people who conducted surveys in these riparian systems. We thank R. Hutto, B. Kus, and L. George for their comments on earlier drafts of this manuscript.

APPENDIX 1

Descriptions of Individual Riparian Systems

Sacramento

Location: all study sites are between Red Bluff and Colusa, California. Most sites are in remnant forest patches in the Sacramento National Wildlife Refuge.

Vegetation: the floodplain is a complex of early- to late-successional deciduous forests dominated successively by willows (*Salix* spp.) and cottonwood (*Populus* spp.), sycamore (*Platanus* spp.), ash (*Fraxinus* spp.), and valley oak (*Quercus lobata*). Adjacent upper terraces are dominated by valley

oak. See Gaines (1974) for a detailed description of study sites.

Grazing: moderate to heavy cattle grazing for the past 15+ years on grazed sites. Ungrazed sites had been without cattle for at least 3 years before data collection.

San Joaquin

Location: all survey locations are in the northern portion of California's San Joaquin Valley, on levee roads adjacent to riparian stringers, grasslands, and recently (last decade) re-flooded grasslands in the San Luis National Wildlife Refuge.

Vegetation: similar to Sacramento River, dominated by willows and cottonwood, sycamore, ash, and valley oak. Willows and marsh vegetation are more common than valley oak.

Grazing: moderate to heavy cattle grazing for the past 15+ years on grazed sites. Ungrazed sites have been without cattle for at least 3 years before data collection.

Snake

Location: Sites are in an 80-km stretch just downstream of the Idaho/Wyoming border in eastern Idaho. For a detailed description of sites see Saab (1999).

Vegetation: Cottonwood (*Populus angustifolia*) forests. Understory species include dogwood (*Cornus stolonifera*), thin-leafed alder (*Alnus incana*), water birch (*Betula occidentalis*), and willows.

Grazing: moderate to heavy grazing for the past 30+ years on grazed sites. Ungrazed sites have been without cattle for at least three years before data collection.

Bitterroot

Location: survey locations were located along a 40-km stretch of the Bitterroot River and smaller tributaries throughout the Bitterroot Valley between Corvallis to the north and continuing past Darby to the south. See Tewksbury et al. (1998, 1999) for details of study sites.

Vegetation: cottonwood and willow dominate sites along the Bitterroot River, with dogwood, thin-leafed alder, and water birch in smaller quantities. Along tributaries, cottonwood, aspen, and willow are dominant.

Grazing: all study sites were ungrazed or rested for at least five years; thus the Bitterroot River is not included in our analysis of grazing effects.

Missouri

Location: ungrazed survey locations were located on the Charles M. Russell National Wildlife Refuge, and grazed survey locations were in a 40-km stretch of river bordering the refuge to the west.

Vegetation: riparian stands consist of mid- to late-seral riparian vegetation (Hansson et al. 1995) dominated by Great Plains cottonwood (*Populus deltoides*), green ash (*Fraxinus pennsylvanica*), and willow. Floodplains are bounded by the steep, highly eroded "Missouri Breaks," which rise to 300m from the floodplain and support upland vegetation dominated by shrubs.

Grazing: moderate to heavy grazing for the past 30–120 years on grazed sites, ungrazed sites have had no cattle for the past 30 years.

Hart Mountain

Location: all Hart Mountain sites were located in the northwestern Great Basin on the 115,000 ha Hart Mountain National Antelope Refuge (42°25′ N, 119°40′ W) in southeastern Oregon. Data were used from surveys conducted along small streams in five separate drainages.

Vegetation: riparian woodlands occurred as narrow ribbons of riparian habitat, primarily aspen and willows, surrounded by sagebrush (*Artemisia* spp.) steppe, or as dense stands of smaller-stature trees on sideslopes and snowpocket areas in the higher reaches of riparian drainages. For additional details see Dobkin et al. (1995, 1998).

Grazing: in the autumn of 1990, livestock were removed completely from the Hart Mountain refuge, ending continuous livestock use dating back to the 1870s. For this study, we classified data from 1991 (the first growing season following livestock removal) as "grazed," and data from 1993 (the third growing season following livestock removal) as "rested" or "ungrazed." We did not use data for 1992.

Sheldon

Location: all Sheldon sites were on the Sheldon National Wildlife Refuge located in the northwestern corner of Nevada, approximately 55 km southeast of Hart Mountain. Riparian areas occur mostly as narrow valleys and canyons bordered by the steep rimrock of tablelands.

Vegetation: riparian habitat is severely limited at Sheldon, and nearly all riparian habitat in this study consisted of degraded willow-dominated areas.

Grazing: as at Hart Mountain, livestock were removed from the Sheldon Refuge in the autumn of 1990 following continuous livestock use dating back to the 1870s. For this study, we classified data from 1991 (the first growing season following livestock removal) as "grazed," and data from 1993 (the third growing season following livestock removal) as "rested" or "ungrazed." We did not use data for 1992.

APPENDIX 2.   COMMON AND SCIENTIFIC NAMES AND ECOLOGICAL ATTRIBUTES OF ALL SPECIES ANALYZED

Common Name	Scientific Name	Rivers	Mean abundance rank	Migration guild	Host guild	Nest Type	Nest Height
Pied-billed Grebe	*Podilymbus podiceps*	1	61.5		non host		
Western Grebe	*Aechmophorus occidentalis*	1	84		non host		
American White Pelican	*Pelecanus erythrorhynchos*	1	72		non host	open	<2.5m
Double-crested Cormorant	*Phalacrocorax auritus*	1	53		non host	open	<2.5m
American Bittern	*Botaurus lentiginosus*	1	54		non host	open	<2.5m
Great Blue Heron	*Ardea herodias*	4	44.5		non host	open	>5m
Great Egret	*Ardea alba*	1	34		non host	open	>5m
Black-crowned Night-Heron	*Nycticorax nycticorax*	1	47		non host	open	>5m
Turkey Vulture	*Cathartes aura*	3	46	Short-distance	non host	open	<2.5m
Canada Goose	*Branta canadensis*	1	54		non host	open	>5m
Wood Duck	*Aix sponsa*	3	58.5		non host	secondary cavity	<2.5m
Gadwall	*Anas strepera*	2	56		non host	open	<2.5m
Mallard	*Anas platyrhynchos*	6	35.6		non host	open	<2.5m
Green-winged Teal	*Anas crecca*	1	63		non host	open	<2.5m
Cinnamon Teal	*Anas cyanoptera*	1	23		non host	open	<2.5m
Hooded Merganser	*Lophodytes cucullatus*	1	86		non host	secondary cavity	>5m
Common Merganser	*Mergus merganser*	2	59.3		non host	secondary cavity	>5m
Red-breasted Merganser	*Mergus serrator*	1	69		non host		
Osprey	*Pandion haliaetus*	2	61.5	Short-distance	non host	open	>5m
Bald Eagle	*Haliaeetus leucocephalus*	1	81.5	Short-distance	non host	open	>5m
Northern Harrier	*Circus cyaneus*	2	48.3	Short-distance	non host		<2.5m
Sharp-shinned Hawk	*Accipiter striatus*	1	48.5	Short-distance	non host	open	>5m
Cooper's Hawk	*Accipiter cooperii*	2	83.3	Short-distance	non host	open	>5m
Northern Goshawk	*Accipiter gentilis*	2	37	Resident	non host	open	>5m
Red-shouldered Hawk	*Buteo lineatus*	1	50	Short-distance	non host		
Swainson's Hawk	*Buteo swainsoni*	1	45	Long-distance	non host	open	>5m
Red-tailed Hawk	*Buteo jamaicensis*	6	43.1	Short-distance	non host	open	>5m
Golden Eagle	*Aquila chrysaetos*	1	53	Short-distance	non host	open	>5m
American Kestrel	*Falco sparverius*	5	47.8	Short-distance	non host	secondary cavity	>5m
Ring-necked Pheasant	*Phasianus colchicus*	1	23	Resident	non host	open	<2.5m
Ruffed Grouse	*Bonasa umbellus*	2	39	Resident	non host	open	<2.5m
Wild Turkey	*Meleagris gallopavo*	1	69	Resident	non host	open	<2.5m
California Quail	*Callipepla californica*	2	23.5	Resident	non host	open	<2.5m
Virginia Rail	*Rallus limicola*	1	39		non host	open	<2.5m
American Coot	*Fulica americana*	1	51		non host		
Killdeer	*Charadrius vociferus*	4	53.1	Short-distance	non host	open	<2.5m
Solitary Sandpiper	*Tringa solitaria*	1	41		non host		
Spotted Sandpiper	*Actitis macularia*	4	48.1		non host	open	<2.5m
Common Snipe	*Gallinago gallinago*	2	55.8		non host	open	<2.5m

APPENDIX 2. CONTINUED

Common Name	Scientific Name	Rivers	Mean abundance rank	Migration guild	Host guild	Nest Type	Nest Height
Wilson's Phalarope	*Phalaropus tricolor*	1	64		non host	open	<2.5m
Red-necked Phalarope	*Phalaropus lobatus*	2	46.5		non host	open	
Caspian Tern	*Sterna caspia*	1	58	Resident	non host	open	<2.5m
Plain Pigeon	*Columba inornata*	1	86		non host	open	
Mourning Dove	*Zenaida macroura*	7	22.1	Short-distance		open	>5m
Yellow-billed Cuckoo	*Coccyzus americanus*	2	61.5	Long-distance	non host	open	>5m
Great Horned Owl	*Bubo virginianus*	5	49.9	Resident	non host	open	>5m
Barred Owl	*Strix varia*	1	61	Resident	non host	secondary cavity	>5m
Long-eared Owl	*Asio otus*	2	63.5		non host	open	
Short-eared Owl	*Asio flammeus*	1	79	Short-distance	non host	open	<2.5m
Lesser Nighthawk	*Chordeiles acutipennis*	1	61.5	Long-distance	non host	open	<2.5m
Common Nighthawk	*Chordeiles minor*	1	68	Long-distance	non host	open	<2.5m
White-throated Swift	*Aeronautes saxatalis*	2	46	Long-distance	non host	open	>5m
Black-chinned Hummingbird	*Archilochus alexandri*	1	31	Long-distance	non host	open	
Anna's Hummingbird	*Calypte anna*	1	66	Resident	non host	open	
Calliope Hummingbird	*Stellula calliope*	3	53.5	Long-distance	non host	open	<2.5m
Broad-tailed Hummingbird	*Selasphorus platycercus*	3	60	Long-distance	non host	open	
Rufous Hummingbird	*Selasphorus rufus*	2	40	Long-distance	non host	open	>5m
Belted Kingfisher	*Ceryle alcyon*	3	53		non host		
Lewis's Woodpecker	*Melanerpes lewis*	1	80	Short-distance	non host	primary cavity	>5m
Acorn Woodpecker	*Melanerpes formicivorus*	1	45.5	Resident	non host	primary cavity	>5m
Red-naped Sapsucker	*Sphyrapicus nuchalis*	3	17.5	Short-distance	non host	primary cavity	>5m
Red-breasted Sapsucker	*Sphyrapicus ruber*	1	64	Short-distance	non host	primary cavity	>5m
Nuttall's Woodpecker	*Picoides nuttallii*	2	10.5	Resident	non host	primary cavity	
Downy Woodpecker	*Picoides pubescens*	6	35	Resident	non host	primary cavity	>5m
Hairy Woodpecker	*Picoides villosus*	5	36.9	Resident	non host	primary cavity	>5m
Northern Flicker	*Colaptes auratus*	6	20.5	Short-distance	non host	primary cavity	>5m
Pileated Woodpecker	*Dryocopus pileatus*	1	77	Resident	non host	primary cavity	>5m
Olive-sided Flycatcher	*Contopus cooperi*	1	53.5	Long-distance		open	>5m
Western Wood-Pewee	*Contopus sordidulus*	6	13	Long-distance		open	>5m
Willow Flycatcher	*Empidonax traillii*	4	48.6	Long-distance	primary host	open	<2.5m
Least Flycatcher	*Empidonax minimus*	2	34.3	Long-distance		open	
Hammond's Flycatcher	*Empidonax hammondii*	2	51	Long-distance	non host	open	>5m
Gray Flycatcher	*Empidonax wrightii*	1	20.5	Long-distance	non host	open	
Dusky Flycatcher	*Empidonax oberholseri*	5	27.7	Long-distance		open	
Cordilleran Flycatcher	*Empidonax occidentalis*	3	46	Long-distance		open	<2.5m
Pacific-slope Flycatcher	*Empidonax difficulis*	1	45.5	Long-distance		open	<2.5m
Ash-throated Flycatcher	*Myiarchus cinerascens*	2	7	Long-distance	non host	open	
Say's Pheobe	*Sayornis saya*	1	63	Short-distance			

APPENDIX 2. CONTINUED

Common Name	Scientific Name	Rivers	Mean abundance rank	Migration guild	Host guild	Nest Type	Nest Height
Black Phoebe	*Sayornis nigricans*	2	40.5	Resident		open	>5m
Western Kingbird	*Tyrannus verticalis*	3	26.7	Long-distance	primary host	open	>5m
Eastern Kingbird	*Tyrannus tyrannus*	3	47.3	Long-distance	non host	open	
Loggerhead Shrike	*Lanius ludovicianus*	2	34.5	Short-distance		open	>5m
Warbling Vireo	*Vireo gilvus*	7	24.1	Long-distance	primary host	open	>5m
Red-eyed Vireo	*Vireo olivaceus*	4	45	Long-distance	primary host	open	
Gray Jay	*Perisoreus canadensis*	1	90.5	Resident	non host	open	>5m
Steller's Jay	*Cyanocitta stelleri*	1	70	Resident	non host	open	
Western Scrub-Jay	*Aphelocoma californica*	2	12.5	Resident	non host	open	>5m
Clark's Nutcracker	*Nucifraga columbiana*	1	62.5	Resident	non host	open	>5m
Black-billed Magpie	*Pica hudsonia*	5	22	Resident	non host	open	
Yellow-billed Magpie	*Pica nuttalli*	1	21	Resident	non host	open	
American Crow	*Corvus brachyrhynchos*	4	50.8	Short-distance	non host	open	>5m
Common Raven	*Corvus corax*	3	54.3	Resident	non host	open	>5m
Horned Lark	*Eremophila alpestris*	1	53	Short-distance		open	<2.5m
Tree Swallow	*Tachycineta bicolor*	6	20.7	Short-distance		secondary cavity	>5m
Violet-green Swallow	*Tachycineta thalassina*	4	30.8	Long-distance	non host	secondary cavity	>5m
Northern Rough-winged Swallow	*Stelgidopteryx serripennis*	4	44.3	Long-distance	non host		
Bank Swallow	*Riparia riparia*	1	29	Long-distance			
Cliff Swallow	*Petrochelidon pyrrhonota*	6	44.8	Long-distance			
Barn Swallow	*Hirundo rustica*	3	47.5	Long-distance			
Black-capped Chickadee	*Poecile atricapilla*	3	12.8	Resident		secondary cavity	
Mountain Chickadee	*Poecile gambeli*	3	53.2	Resident	non host	secondary cavity	<2.5m
Chestnut-backed Chickadee	*Poecile rufescens*	1	44.5	Resident	non host	secondary cavity	<2.5m
Oak Titmouse	*Baeolophus inornatus*	2	32	Resident			
Bushtit	*Psaltriparus minimus*	1	21	Resident		open	
Red-breasted Nuthatch	*Sitta canadensis*	4	48.3	Short-distance	non host	primary cavity	>5m
White-breasted Nuthatch	*Sitta carolinensis*	3	42	Resident		secondary cavity	>5m
Pygmy Nuthatch	*Sitta pygmaea*	1	60	Resident	non host	primary cavity	>5m
Brown Creeper	*Certhia americana*	1	75.5	Short-distance		open	>5m
Rock Wren	*Salpinctes obsoletus*	1	29	Short-distance			
Bewick's Wren	*Thryomanes bewickii*	2	5	Short-distance		secondary cavity	<2.5m
House Wren	*Troglodytes aedon*	7	14.6	Long-distance		secondary cavity	
Winter Wren	*Troglodytes troglodytes*	1	48	Short-distance	non host		<2.5m
Marsh Wren	*Cistothorus palustris*	2	33	Short-distance		open	<2.5m
Golden-crowned Kinglet	*Regulus satrapa*	1	23	Short-distance		open	>5m
Ruby-crowned Kinglet	*Regulus calendula*	4	37.9	Short-distance		open	>5m

APPENDIX 2. CONTINUED

Common Name	Scientific Name	Rivers	Mean abundance rank	Migration guild	Host guild	Nest Type	Nest Height
Blue-gray Gnatcatcher	*Polioptila caerulea*	1	63	Long-distance	primary host	open	<2.5m
Western Bluebird	*Sialia mexicana*	1	39	Short-distance		secondary cavity	<2.5m
Mountain Bluebird	*Sialia currucoides*	2	34.3	Short-distance		secondary cavity	<2.5m
Townsend's Solitaire	*Myadestes townsendi*	2	73	Short-distance	non host	open	<2.5m
Veery	*Catharus fuscescens*	2	20	Long-distance	primary host	open	<2.5m
Swainson's Thrush	*Catharus ustulatus*	6	32.3	Long-distance		open	
American Robin	*Turdus migratorius*	7	13.7	Short-distance		open	<2.5m
Gray Catbird	*Dumetella carolinensis*	3	34.3	Long-distance		open	
Northern Mockingbird	*Mimus polyglottos*	1	26	Resident		open	
Sage Thrasher	*Oreoscoptes montanus*	1	45	Short-distance		open	<2.5m
Brown Thrasher	*Toxostoma rufum*	1	18	Short-distance		open	<2.5m
California Thrasher	*Toxostoma redivivum*	1	46	Resident	non host	open	<2.5m
European Starling	*Sturnus vulgaris*	7	17.9	Short-distance	non host	secondary cavity	>5m
Cedar Waxwing	*Bombycilla cedrorum*	4	16	Short-distance		open	
Orange-crowned Warbler	*Vermivora celata*	4	32.1	Long-distance		open	<2.5m
Nashville Warbler	*Vermivora ruficapilla*	2	64.5	Long-distance		open	<2.5m
Yellow Warbler	*Dendroica petechia*	7	16.1	Long-distance	primary host	open	>5m
Yellow-rumped Warbler	*Dendroica coronata*	5	33.6	Short-distance	primary host	open	>5m
Townsend's Warbler	*Dendroica townsendi*	5	51.5	Long-distance		open	>5m
Hermit Warbler	*Dendroica occidentalis*	1	58.5	Long-distance		open	>5m
American Redstart	*Setophaga ruticilla*	2	19	Long-distance	primary host	open	<2.5m
Ovenbird	*Seiurus aurocapillus*	2	45	Long-distance	primary host	open	<2.5m
Northern Waterthrush	*Seiurus noveboracensis*	1	51	Long-distance		open	<2.5m
MacGillivray's Warbler	*Oporornis tolmiei*	5	37.4	Long-distance		open	<2.5m
Common Yellowthroat	*Geothlypis trichas*	5	22	Long-distance	primary host	open	<2.5m
Wilson's Warbler	*Wilsonia pusilla*	5	26.6	Long-distance		open	<2.5m
Yellow-breasted Chat	*Icteria virens*	5	38.7	Long-distance	primary host	open	<2.5m
Western Tanager	*Piranga ludoviciana*	6	39.8	Long-distance		open	>5m
Green-tailed Towhee	*Pipilo chlorurus*	2	36	Long-distance		open	<2.5m
Spotted Towhee	*Pipilo maculatus*	5	32.7	Short-distance	primary host	open	<2.5m
California Towhee	*Pipilo crissalis*	2	34	Long-distance		open	<2.5m
Chipping Sparrow	*Spizella passerina*	4	46	Long-distance	primary host	open	<2.5m
Brewer's Sparrow	*Spizella breweri*	2	20.5	Long-distance		open	<2.5m
Vesper Sparrow	*Pooecetes gramineus*	3	45.3	Short-distance	primary host	open	<2.5m
Black-throated Sparrow	*Amphispiza bilineata*	1	35	Short-distance		open	<2.5m
Sage Sparrow	*Amphispiza belli*	1	39	Short-distance		open	<2.5m
Lark Sparrow	*Chondestes grammacus*	3	48	Long-distance		open	<2.5m
Savannah Sparrow	*Passerculus sandwichensis*	2	33.8	Short-distance		open	<2.5m
Fox Sparrow	*Passerella iliaca*	2	20.5	Short-distance		open	<2.5m

APPENDIX 2. CONTINUED

Common Name	Scientific Name	Rivers	Mean abundance rank	Migration guild	Host guild	Nest Type	Nest Height
Song Sparrow	*Melospiza melodia*	6	15.4	Short-distance	primary host	open	<2.5m
White-crowned Sparrow	*Zonotrichia leucophrys*	1	10	Short-distance		open	<2.5m
Golden-crowned Sparrow	*Zonotrichia atricapilla*	2	66	Short-distance		open	
Black-headed Grosbeak	*Pheucticus melanocephalus*	7	18.9	Long-distance		open	
Blue Grosbeak	*Guiraca caerulea*	2	38.5	Long-distance	primary host	open	<2.5m
Lazuli Bunting	*Passerina amoena*	7	30.1	Long-distance	primary host	open	<2.5m
Red-winged Blackbird	*Agelaius phoeniceus*	6	29.1	Short-distance	primary host	open	<2.5m
Tricolored Blackbird	*Agelaius tricolor*	1	52	Resident		open	<2.5m
Western Meadowlark	*Sturnella neglecta*	5	37.2	Short-distance		open	<2.5m
Yellow-headed Blackbird	*Xanthocephalus xanthocephalus*	1	63	Long-distance		open	<2.5m
Brewer's Blackbird	*Euphagus cyanocephalus*	7	29.4	Short-distance	primary host	open	<2.5m
Common Grackle	*Quiscalus quiscula*	1	15	Short-distance		open	
Brown-headed Cowbird	*Molothrus ater*	7	7.21	Short-distance	non host		>5m
Bullock's Oriole	*Icterus bullockii*	7	21.3	Long-distance		open	>5m
Purple Finch	*Carpodacus purpureus*	1	78	Short-distance		open	>5m
Cassin's Finch	*Carpodacus cassinii*	3	35.7	Short-distance	non host	open	>5m
House Finch	*Carpodacus mexicanus*	5	40.4	Short-distance		open	>5m
Red Crossbill	*Loxia curvirostra*	1	9	Short-distance	non host	open	>5m
Pine Siskin	*Carduelis pinus*	4	31.6	Short-distance		open	>5m
Lesser Goldfinch	*Carduelis psaltria*	1	17	Short-distance		open	>5m
American Goldfinch	*Carduelis tristis*	5	17.8	Short-distance	primary host	open	>5m
Evening Grosbeak	*Coccothraustes vespertinus*	1	11	Short-distance		open	>5m
House Sparrow	*Passer domesticus*	1	41	Resident	non host		>5m

Notes: the number of river systems in which the species was detected (Rivers) and the mean rank of each species (Mean abundance rank; 1 = most often detected species on a river). All species were ranked in descending order of detection frequency within each river system. Mean rank abundance is the average rank across all rivers where the species were detected. Species membership in migration, cowbird host, nest type, and nest height guilds is also included.

APPENDIX 3. PEARSON CORRELATIONS (AND P-VALUES) FOR ALL LANDSCAPE VARIABLES WITHIN EACH RIVER SYSTEM (SEE TABLE 1 FOR SAMPLE SIZES)

River system	Landscape variable	Local human habitation	Local agriculture	Local deciduous forest	Local coniferous forest	Regional human habitation	Regional agriculture	Regional deciduous forest
Sacramento	Local agriculture	0.383 (0.004)						
	Local deciduous forest	-0.139 (0.311)	-0.322 (0.016)					
	Local coniferous forest							
	Regional human habitation	-0.220 (0.106)	-0.001 (0.993)	-0.251 (0.064)				
	Regional agriculture	0.714 (<0.001)	0.688 (<0.001)	-0.125 (0.364)		-0.166 (0.227)		
	Regional deciduous forest	0.774 (<0.001)	0.179 (0.190)	-0.239 (0.079)		-0.166 (0.225)	0.630 (<0.001)	
	Regional coniferous forest							
San Joaquin	Local agriculture	0.612 (<0.001)						
	Local deciduous forest	0.275 (0.044)	0.369 (0.006)					
	Local coniferous forest							
	Regional human habitation							
	Regional agriculture	0.215 (0.119)	0.577 (<0.001)	0.213 (0.1216)				
	Regional deciduous forest							
	Regional coniferous forest							
Snake	Local agriculture	0.074 (0.604)						
	Local deciduous forest	-0.304 (0.029)	-0.555 (<0.001)					
	Local coniferous forest	-0.022 (0.876)	-0.706 (<0.001)	0.035 (0.805)				
	Regional human habitation	0.286 (0.040)	0.665 (<0.001)	-0.099 (0.485)	-0.648 (<0.001)			
	Regional agriculture	-0.377 (0.006)	0.589 (<0.001)	0.075 (0.598)	-0.562 (<0.001)	0.596 (<0.001)		
	Regional deciduous forest	0.417 (0.002)	-0.409 (0.003)	-0.114 (0.421)	0.343 (0.013)	-0.410 (0.003)	-0.884 (<0.001)	

APPENDIX 3. CONTINUED

River system	Landscape variable	Local human habitation	Local agriculture	Local deciduous forest	Local coniferous forest	Regional human habitation	Regional agriculture	Regional deciduous forest
Bitterroot	Regional coniferous forest	0.398 (0.003)	−0.546 (<0.001)	−0.094 (0.509)	0.561 (<0.001)	−0.556 (<0.001)	−0.927 (<0.001)	0.798 (<0.001)
	Local agriculture	0.675 (<0.001)						
	Local deciduous forest	0.437 (<0.001)	0.473 (<0.001)					
	Local coniferous forest	−0.623 (<0.001)	−0.851 (<0.001)	−0.688 (<0.001)				
	Regional human habitation	0.242 (0.008)	0.439 (<0.001)	0.335 (<0.001)	−0.581 (<0.001)			
	Regional agriculture	0.470 (<0.001)	0.603 (<0.001)	0.700 (<0.001)	−0.717 (<0.001)	0.561 (<0.001)		
	Regional deciduous forest	0.418 (<0.001)	0.537 (<0.001)	0.690 (<0.001)	−0.651 (<0.001)	0.544 (<0.001)	0.951 (<0.001)	
	Regional coniferous forest	−0.574 (<0.001)	−0.759 (<0.001)	−0.637 (<0.001)	0.869 (<0.001)	−0.623 (<0.001)	−0.909 (<0.001)	−0.833 (<0.001)
Missouri	Local agriculture	·						
	Local deciduous forest	·	0.049 (0.801)					
	Local coniferous forest	·	0.150 (0.438)	−0.575 (0.001)				
	Regional human habitation	·	·	·	·			
	Regional agriculture	·	0.594 (<0.001)	−0.061 (0.754)	0.186 (0.333)	·		
	Regional deciduous forest	·	0.104 (0.593)	0.824 (<0.001)	−0.407 (0.028)	·	−0.003 (0.988)	
	Regional coniferous forest	·	0.201 (0.295)	0.777 (<0.001)	−0.158 (0.413)	·	0.233 (0.2245)	0.809 (<0.001)
Hart	Local coniferous forest	·	·	−0.628 (<0.001)				
	Regional human habitation	·	·	·	·			
	Regional agriculture	·	·	·	·	·		

APPENDIX 3. CONTINUED

River system	Landscape variable	Local human habitation	Local agriculture	Local deciduous forest	Local coniferous forest	Regional human habitation	Regional agriculture	Regional deciduous forest
	Regional deciduous forest			0.226 (0.155)	0.373 (0.016)			
	Regional coniferous forest			0.599 (<0.001)	−0.123 (0.445)			0.433 (0.005)
Sheldon	Local deciduous forest	−0.248 (0.305)						
	Local coniferous forest	0.344 (0.150)		−0.195 (0.424)				
	Regional human habitation							
	Regional agriculture	−0.380 (0.109)		0.924 (<0.001)	−0.199 (0.413)			
	Regional deciduous forest							
	Regional coniferous forest							

APPENDIX 4. EFFECTS OF LANDSCAPE VARIABLES WITHIN INDIVIDUAL RIVER SYSTEMS ON TOTAL DETECTIONS (TOTAL BIRDS), TOTAL RICHNESS (RICHNESS), BROWN-HEADED COWBIRDS, COWBIRD HOST GUILDS, AND MIGRATION GUILDS (SEE APPENDIX 2)

Landscape variable and river system	Statistic	Total birds	Richness	Cowbirds	Prime hosts	Non-hosts	Long-distance migrant	Residents	Short-distance migrant
Local Human Habitation									
Sacramento Σ	Dir	Pos		Pos	Pos	Neg	Pos		
	B	0.13		0.19	0.19	−0.27	0.20		
	R²	0.016		0.036	0.035	0.072	0.039		
	P	0.361		0.166	0.173	0.048	0.150		
#	Dir	Neg			Neg	Neg	Neg	Neg	Neg
	Inc	38%			31%	34%	33%	29%	36%
	P	0.038			0.267	0.074	0.100	0.180	0.230
San Joaquin Σ	Dir			Pos	Pos	Neg		Neg	Pos
	B			0.25	0.26	−0.12		−0.29	0.12
	R²			0.063	0.031	0.015		0.086	0.015
	P			0.062	0.049	0.375		0.028	0.371
#	Dir	Neg				Neg	Neg		
	Inc	43%				41%	35%		
	P	0.313				0.377	0.263		
Snake Σ	Dir	Neg		Neg	Neg	Pos	Neg	Pos	Neg
	B	−0.38		−0.17	−0.52	0.11	−0.44	0.17	−0.23
	R²	0.143		0.029	0.265	0.013	0.187	0.030	0.051
	P	0.005*		0.224	<0.001*	0.415	0.001*	0.211	0.104
#	Dir	Neg			Neg	Neg	Neg	Neg	Neg
	Inc	33%			21%	35%	29%	14%	37%
	P	0.015			0.057	0.210	0.064	0.125	0.359
Bitterroot Σ	Dir	Pos	Pos	Pos	Pos	Pos	Pos	Pos	Pos
	B	0.26	0.15	0.38	0.40	0.25	0.11	0.16	0.19
	R²	0.070	0.021	0.141	0.158	0.060	0.012	0.024	0.035
	P	0.004	0.143	<0.001*	<0.001*	0.007	0.238	0.091	0.040
#	Dir	Pos			Pos	Pos			
	Inc	57%			75%	61%			
	P	0.213			0.077	0.243			
Sheldon Σ	Dir	Neg	Neg		Neg	Neg	Neg	Neg	Neg
	B	−0.51	−0.42		−0.42	−0.43	−0.31	−0.33	−0.39
	R²	0.259	0.176		0.175	0.183	0.099	0.110	0.150
	P	0.026	0.074		0.075	0.068	0.190	0.166	0.101

APPENDIX 4. CONTINUED

Landscape variable and river system	Statistic	Total birds	Richness	Cowbirds	Prime hosts	Non-hosts	Long-distance migrant	Residents	Short-distance migrant
#	Dir	Neg			Neg	Neg	Neg		Neg
	Inc	19%			0%	18%	18%		23%
	P	<0.001			<0.001	0.004	0.001		0.011
Regional Human Habitation									
Snake									
Σ	Dir			Pos	Neg	Pos	Neg	Pos	Pos
	B			0.36	−0.48	0.20	−0.17	0.23	0.23
	R^2			0.126	0.230	0.040	0.034	0.051	0.054
	P			0.009	<0.001*	0.153	0.228	0.105	0.095
#	Dir	Neg				Neg	Neg		
	Inc	40%				35%	38%		
	P	0.178				0.210	0.307		
Bitterroot									
Σ	Dir	Pos	Pos	Pos	Pos	Pos	Neg	Pos	Pos
	B	0.16	0.17	0.33	0.17	0.28	−0.10	0.16	0.24
	R^2	0.026	0.030	0.106	0.030	0.079	0.009	0.024	0.058
	P	0.078	0.080	<0.001*	0.060	0.002	0.289	0.091	0.008
#	Dir								
	Inc								
	P								
Local Agriculture									
Sacramento									
Σ	Dir	Pos	Pos	Pos			Pos		
	B	0.21	0.16	0.24			0.28		
	R^2	0.044	0.025	0.057			0.079		
	P	0.126	0.245	0.080			0.037		
#	Dir					Neg			
	Inc					38%			
	P					0.230			
San Joaquin									
Σ	Dir			Pos	Pos				Pos
	B			0.27	0.24				0.19
	R^2			0.074	0.070				0.035
	P			0.042	0.070				0.167
#	Dir						Neg		
	Inc						38%		
	P						0.381		
Snake									

APPENDIX 4. CONTINUED

Landscape variable and river system	Statistic	Total birds	Richness	Cowbirds	Prime hosts	Non-hosts	Long-distance migrant	Residents	Short-distance migrant
Σ	Dir	Pos		Pos	Neg	Pos	Neg	Pos	Pos
	B	0.23		0.25	−0.54	0.48	−0.13	0.39	0.37
	R^2	0.053		0.063	0.294	0.225	0.013	0.132	0.134
	P	0.097		0.069	<0.001*	<0.001*	0.364	0.004	0.007
#	Dir	Neg				Neg	Neg		
	Inc	40%				36%	26%		
	P	0.310				0.286	0.035		
Bitterroot									
Σ	Dir	Pos	Pos	Pos	Pos	Pos		Pos	Pos
	B	0.26	0.29	0.38	0.33	0.31		0.22	0.33
	R^2	0.068	0.082	0.142	0.106	0.095		0.049	0.109
	P	0.004	0.003	<0.001*	<0.001*	0.001*		0.015	<0.001*
#	Dir	Pos			Pos	Pos		Pos	Pos
	Inc	69%			71%	71%		69%	61%
	P	<0.001*			0.143	0.018		0.210	0.281
Regional Agriculture									
Sacramento									
Σ	Dir	Pos	Pos	Pos			Pos	Pos	Pos
	B	0.34	0.25	0.24			0.27	0.30	0.22
	R^2	0.113	0.063	0.057			0.075	0.091	0.049
	P	0.012*	0.065	0.078			0.044	0.026	0.105
#	Dir			Neg					Neg
	Inc			38%					33%
	P			0.265					0.189
San Joaquin									
Σ	Dir		Neg	Pos		Pos	Neg		Pos
	B		−0.2	0.26		0.15	−0.16		0.33
	R^2		0.041	0.068		0.023	0.037		0.111
	P		0.141	0.052		0.260	0.246		0.012*
#	Dir								
	Inc								
	P								
Snake									
Σ	Dir	Pos		Pos			Pos		Pos
	B	0.51		0.55			0.27		0.51
	R^2	0.256		0.298			0.068		0.260
	P	<0.001*		<0.001*			0.049		<0.001*
#	Dir	Neg				Neg	Neg		

APPENDIX 4. CONTINUED

Landscape variable and river system	Statistic	Total birds	Richness	Cowbirds	Prime hosts	Non-hosts	Long-distance migrant	Residents	Short-distance migrant
Bitterroot									
Σ	Inc	0.4				35%	33%		
	P	0.178				0.210	0.152		
	Dir	Pos	Pos	Pos	Pos	Pos		Pos	Pos
	B	0.23	0.28	0.43	0.33	0.44		0.38	0.30
	R²	0.083	0.081	0.202	0.109	0.191		0.148	0.089
	P	0.001*	0.004	<0.001*	<0.001*	v*		<0.001*	0.001*
#	Dir	Pos			Pos	Pos	Pos	Pos	Pos
	Inc	69%			71%	71%	64%	69%	65%
	P	<0.001*			0.143	0.018*	0.164	0.210	0.170
Missouri									
Σ	Dir	Pos	Pos		Pos	Pos	Pos	Neg	Pos
	B	0.45	0.28		0.45	0.26	0.39	−0.33	0.49
	R²	0.202	0.078		0.203	0.065	0.158	0.111	0.235
	P	0.015*	0.142		0.014*	0.180	0.038	0.078	0.008*
#	Dir	Pos			Pos			Neg	Pos
	Inc	60%			71%			20%	76%
	P	0.222			0.180			0.375	0.049
Local deciduous riparian									
Sacramento									
Σ	Dir	Neg	Neg	Neg		Neg	Neg		Pos
	B	−0.33	−0.31	−0.17		−0.13	−0.41		0.19
	R²	0.107	0.093	0.028		0.017	0.167		0.036
	P	0.015*	0.024	0.218		0.345	0.002*		0.163
#	Dir	Neg			Neg	Neg	Neg		Neg
	Inc	33%			33%	29%	25%		38%
	P	0.007*			0.388	0.038*	0.023*		0.383
San Joaquin									
Σ	Dir	Pos	Pos	Pos	Pos	Pos		Pos	Pos
	B	0.27	0.12	0.13	0.244	0.27		0.28	0.24
	R²	0.073	0.014	0.017	0.059	0.073		0.078	0.056
	P	0.044	0.396	0.343	0.070	0.045		0.038	0.080
#	Dir	Pos			Pos	Pos		Pos	
	Inc	67%			80%	69%		82%	
	P	0.009*			0.109	0.052		0.065	
Snake									
Σ	Dir				Pos	Neg	Pos	Neg	Neg
	B				0.40	−0.42	0.25	−0.25	−0.17
	R²				0.160	0.175	0.053	0.062	0.029

APPENDIX 4. CONTINUED

Landscape variable and river system	Statistic	Total birds	Richness	Cowbirds	Prime hosts	Non-hosts	Long-distance migrant	Residents	Short-distance migrant
#	P				0.003*	0.002*	0.072	0.072	0.224
	Dir	Pos			Pos		Pos		
	Inc	58%			71%		63%		
	P	0.281			0.180		0.307		
Bitterroot									
Σ	Dir	Pos	Pos	Pos	Pos	Pos	Pos	Pos	Pos
	B	0.37	0.34	0.40	0.51	0.34	0.13	0.32	0.30
	R^2	0.140	0.113	0.161	0.259	0.113	0.017	0.100	0.090
	P	<0.001*	0.001*	<0.001*	<0.001*	<0.001*	0.164	<0.001*	0.001*
#	Dir	Pos			Pos	Pos	Pos	Pos	Pos
	Inc	68%			75%	71%	61%	75%	68%
	P	0.001*			0.070	0.015	0.296	0.077	0.089
Missouri									
Σ	Dir	Pos	Pos		Pos	Pos	Pos	Pos	Pos
	B	0.59	0.27		0.34	0.25	0.65	0.37	0.33
	R^2	0.344	0.073		0.117	0.064	0.416	0.139	0.110
	P	0.001*	0.115		0.070	0.187	<0.001*	0.047	0.079
#	Dir	Pos					Pos		
	Inc	63%					72%		
	P	0.144					0.096		
Hart									
Σ	Dir				Neg	Neg		Pos	
	B				−0.43	−0.14		0.27	
	R^2				0.182	0.019		0.071	
	P				0.005*	0.390		0.093	
#	Dir	Neg			Neg			Pos	
	Inc	40%			11%			80%	
	P	0.131			0.039*			0.375	
Sheldon									
Σ	Dir	Pos		Pos	Pos	Pos	Pos		Pos
	B	0.42		0.54	0.50	0.33	0.21		0.62
	R^2	0.180		0.290	0.252	0.110	0.044		0.381
	P	0.071		0.017*	0.028	0.166	0.383		0.005*
#	Dir					Pos	Neg		
	Inc					62%	37%		
	P					0.383	0.248		
Regional deciduous riparian Sacramento									
Σ	Dir	Pos		Pos		Neg	Pos	Pos	

APPENDIX 4. CONTINUED

Landscape variable and river system	Statistic	Total birds	Richness	Cowbirds	Prime hosts	Non-hosts	Long-distance migrant	Residents	Short-distance migrant
	B	0.16		0.17		−0.21	0.26	0.17	
	R²	0.025		0.029		0.045	0.067	0.027	
	P	0.253		0.217		0.122	0.056	0.228	
	Dir				Neg	Neg			
#	Inc				30%	39%			
	P				0.343	0.281			
Snake									
Σ	Dir	Neg		Neg			Neg	Neg	Neg
	B	−0.47		−0.46			−0.31	−0.12	−0.41
	R²	0.221		0.213			0.088	0.014	0.170
	P	<0.001*		0.001*			0.026	0.399	0.002*
	Dir								
#	Inc								
	P								
Bitterroot									
Σ	Dir	Pos	Pos	Pos	Pos	Pos		Pos	Pos
	B	0.26	0.27	0.48	0.32	0.41		0.39	0.25
	R²	0.066	0.073	0.234	0.103	0.167		0.149	0.062
	P	0.005	0.006	<0.001*	<0.001*	<0.001*		<0.001*	0.006
	Dir	Pos			Pos	Pos	Pos	Pos	Pos
#	Inc	68%			71%	71%	63%	69%	65%
	P	0.001*			0.143	0.018	0.216	0.210	0.170
Missouri									
Σ	Dir	Pos	Pos		Pos	Pos	Pos	Pos	Pos
	B	0.61	0.38		0.39	0.34	0.65	0.38	0.33
	R²	0.368	0.146		0.151	0.118	0.413	0.144	0.110
	P	<0.001*	0.041		0.037	0.068	<0.001*	0.043*	0.079
	Dir	Pos				Pos	Pos	Pos	
#	Inc	69%				78%	73%	100%	
	P	0.030				0.180	0.118	0.125	
Hart									
Σ	Dir			Neg	Neg		Pos		Neg
	B			−0.20	−0.15		0.17		−0.24
	R²			0.039	0.023		0.040		0.057
	P			0.213	0.342		0.279		0.134
	Dir						Pos		
#	Inc						63%		
	P						0.359		

APPENDIX 4. CONTINUED

Landscape variable and river system	Statistic	Total birds	Richness	Cowbirds	Prime hosts	Non-hosts	Long-distance migrant	Residents	Short-distance migrant
Local Coniferous Forest									
Snake									
Σ	Dir			Neg	Pos	Neg		Neg	Neg
	B			−0.21	0.45	−0.20		−0.23	−0.17
	R²			0.044	0.202	0.042		0.051	0.030
	P			0.132	0.001*	0.143		0.104	0.217
#	Dir	Pos			Pos		Pos		
	Inc	64%			71%		71%		
	P	0.059			0.180		0.064		
Bitterroot									
Σ	Dir	Neg	Neg	Neg	Neg	Neg		Neg	Neg
	B	−0.29	−0.34	−0.38	−0.40	−0.29		−0.26	−0.29
	R²	0.081	0.116	0.144	0.162	0.084		0.069	0.086
	P	0.002	<0.001*	<0.001*	<0.001*	0.001*		0.004	0.001*
#	Dir	Neg			Neg	Neg		Neg	Neg
	Inc	36%			31%	33%		31%	38%
	P	0.007*			0.210	0.055		0.210	0.265
Missouri									
Σ	Dir	Neg				Neg	Neg	Neg	Neg
	B	−0.31				−0.26	−0.32	−0.37	−0.18
	R²	0.095				0.066	0.090	0.136	0.034
	P	0.103				0.180	0.094	0.049	0.341
#	Dir								
	Inc								
	P								
Hart									
Σ	Dir				Pos		Pos	Neg	Neg
	B				0.18		0.18	−0.15	−0.21
	R²				0.032		0.032	0.024	0.044
	P				0.266		0.250	0.337	0.186
#	Dir						Pos	Neg	
	Inc						76%	17%	
	P						0.027*	0.219	
Regional Coniferous Forest									
Snake									
Σ	Dir	Neg		Neg			Neg		Neg
	B	−0.50		−0.57			−0.35		−0.44
	R²	0.251		0.327			0.118		0.178
	P	<0.001*		<0.001*			0.010		0.002*

APPENDIX 4. CONTINUED

Landscape variable and river system	Statistic	Total birds	Richness	Cowbirds	Prime hosts	Non-hosts	Long-distance migrant	Residents	Short-distance migrant
#	Dir								
	Inc								
	P								
Bitterroot									
Σ	Dir	Neg	Neg	Neg	Neg	Neg	Pos	Neg	Neg
	B	−0.23	−0.27	−0.38	−0.29	−0.35	0.14	−0.28	−0.29
	R^2	0.055	0.072	0.146	0.086	0.124	0.019	0.078	0.084
	P	0.010	0.006	<0.001*	0.001*	<0.001*	0.137	0.002	0.001*
#	Dir	Neg				Neg		Neg	Neg
	Inc	35%				32%		33%	32%
	P	0.004*				0.035		0.302	0.089
Missouri									
Σ	Dir	Pos	Pos	Pos	Pos	Pos	Pos		Pos
	B	0.77	0.69	0.18	0.69	0.19	0.81		0.521
	R^2	0.554		0.034	0.480	0.036	0.664		0.271
	P	<0.001*	<0.001*	0.339	<0.001*	0.325	<0.001*		0.004*
#	Dir	Pos			Pos		Pos		
	Inc	71%			69%		89%		
	P	0.015*			0.267		0.001*		
Hart									
Σ	Dir	Neg	Neg		Neg	Neg	Neg		Neg
	B	−0.25	−0.21		−0.40	−0.32	−0.21		−0.31
	R^2	0.064	0.043		0.160	0.100	0.032		0.097
	P	0.109	0.194		0.010*	0.044*	0.199		0.048*
#	Dir	Neg			Neg	Neg			Neg
	Inc	36%			25%	35%			31%
	P	0.036*			0.289	0.170			0.063

Notes: Results are from linear regression (Σ), with directionality of change (Dir: Pos = higher relative abundance in areas with more of the landscape variable; Neg = lower relative abundance in areas with more of the landscape variable), standardized regression coefficient (B), R^2, and P-value shown; and from Binomial tests across all species in the guild (#) for directionality (more or less abundant) with high amounts of each landscape variable, with directionality of the majority of species (Dir), the percent of species more abundant in areas with high amounts of the landscape variable (Inc), and the P-value for the binomial test shown. All results with a trend (P < 0.4) are shown. * = significant after Bonferroni adjustment for multiple tests.

APPENDIX 5. GRAZING EFFECTS ON INDIVIDUAL SPECIES, BY RIVER

River system	Detection/survey		Mann-Whitney U-test		
	Ungrazed	Grazed	U	W	P
Sacramento					
Less Abundant in Grazed Areas					
Tree Swallow	0.5873	0.0597	66.5	111.5	0.001
Black-headed Grosbeak	0.6412	0.2735	95.5	140.5	0.011
Downy Woodpecker	0.0960	0.0094	105.5	150.5	0.013
American Robin	0.1555	0.0409	123.0	168.0	0.044
California Towhee	0.0406	0.0000	144.0	189.0	0.060
Mourning Dove	0.1550	0.0472	127.5	172.5	0.062
Bank Swallow	0.0821	0.0000	153.0	198.0	0.089
White-breasted Nuthatch	0.0761	0.0189	146.5	191.5	0.122
Turkey Vulture	0.1250	0.0189	155.5	200.5	0.152
European Starling	0.1061	0.0094	157.0	202.0	0.156
Western Wood-pewee	0.5840	0.3741	148.0	193.0	0.179
More Abundant in Grazed Areas					
California Quail	0.0457	0.2169	78.5	1159.5	0.001
Warbling Vireo	0.0341	0.0880	105.5	1186.5	0.004
Wilson's Warbler	0.1370	0.2578	91.0	1172.0	0.007
Bewick's Wren	0.6334	0.8708	116.5	1197.5	0.039
Lazuli Bunting	0.3520	0.4999	123.5	1204.5	0.057
Lesser Goldfinch	0.1702	0.3804	142.5	1223.5	0.130
Snake					
Less Abundant in Grazed Areas					
Veery	0.4791	0.1161	118.0	328.0	0.001
Song Sparrow	0.8020	0.3124	117.0	327.0	0.001
Fox Sparrow	0.1606	0.0131	134.5	344.5	0.002
Black-capped Chickadee	0.3667	0.2178	150.5	360.5	0.015
Lazuli Bunting	0.1176	0.0678	154.0	364.0	0.016
Yellow Warbler	2.7632	2.2466	152.0	362.0	0.017
Mallard	0.0474	0.0118	174.5	384.5	0.029
Black-headed Grosbeak	0.2386	0.1465	162.5	372.5	0.030
Belted Kingfisher	0.0293	0.0091	189.0	399.0	0.041
Gray Catbird	0.1490	0.0763	172.5	382.5	0.047
Cedar Waxwing	0.3268	0.1940	172.0	382.0	0.050
Ruffed Grouse	0.0321	0.0056	203.5	413.5	0.058
Violet-green Swallow	0.2309	0.0971	179.0	389.0	0.059
Broad-tailed Hummingbird	0.0118	0.0022	213.0	423.0	0.096
MacGillivray's Warbler	0.0532	0.0149	196.0	406.0	0.107
Spotted Sandpiper	0.0302	0.0158	198.0	408.0	0.118
Swainson's Thrush	0.0403	0.0068	211.0	421.0	0.147
More Abundant in Grazed Areas					
House Wren	0.4621	1.1689	107.0	458.0	0.001
Mourning Dove	0.2488	0.5509	149.5	500.5	0.014
Pine Siskin	0.0044	0.0529	180.5	531.5	0.019
Black-billed Magpie	0.2475	0.4988	160.0	511.0	0.026
European Starling	0.3474	1.2135	163.5	514.5	0.032
Cassin's Finch	0.0201	0.0326	208.0	559.0	0.167
Missouri					
Less Abundant in Grazed Areas					
Mourning Dove	2.2941	0.7917	19.5	97.5	<0.001
American Robin	2.3824	1.0833	27.0	105.0	0.001
Red-eyed Vireo	0.7059	0.0417	45.5	123.5	0.004
Red-shafted Flicker	1.6765	0.4583	39.0	117.0	0.004
Least Flycatcher	2.1176	1.2083	43.5	121.5	0.008
Brown Thrasher	0.7059	0.1250	48.0	126.0	0.009
Western Wood-pewee	1.8824	1.0833	48.0	126.0	0.011
Lazuli Bunting	1.6765	0.9167	46.0	124.0	0.011
Ovenbird	0.4706	0.0000	60.0	138.0	0.013
House Wren	2.7647	2.0000	54.0	132.0	0.028
Black-headed Grosbeak	0.7353	0.1667	57.5	135.5	0.029
Bullock's Oriole	0.6471	0.2083	57.0	135.0	0.031

APPENDIX 5. CONTINUED

River system	Detection/survey		Mann-Whitney U-test		
	Ungrazed	Grazed	U	W	P
American Redstart	0.4706	0.0833	63.0	141.0	0.034
Yellow Warbler	3.7941	2.5833	58.0	136.0	0.047
Yellow-breasted Chat	2.8529	2.0417	59.0	137.0	0.051
Hairy Woodpecker	0.4118	0.0833	65.0	143.0	0.052
Gray Catbird	0.6176	0.1250	70.5	148.5	0.108
Common Grackle	0.6471	0.3333	76.5	154.5	0.132
Black-capped Chickadee	0.6471	0.2083	74.5	152.5	0.161
American Goldfinch	2.3529	1.5417	72.0	150.0	0.177
More Abundant in Grazed Areas					
Eastern Kingbird	0.1176	0.3333	67.0	220.0	0.048
Spotted Towhee	0.9706	1.3750	67.5	220.5	0.115
Hart					
Less Abundant in Grazed Areas					
Cordilleran Flycatcher	0.3333	0.0000	140.0	350.0	0.005
Hairy Woodpecker	0.4286	0.0500	130.5	340.5	0.005
Green-tailed Towhee	0.5714	0.1500	121.5	331.5	0.006
Rock Wren	0.2619	0.0000	170.0	380.0	0.043
Wilson's Warbler	0.2381	0.0500	170.5	380.5	0.092
Red-tailed Hawk	0.2857	0.1000	171.0	381.0	0.138
More Abundant in Grazed Areas					
Swainson's Thrush	0.1905	0.4000	160.0	391.0	0.091
Black-headed Grosbeak	0.3333	0.6500	154.0	385.0	0.094
Sheldon					
Less Abundant in Grazed Areas					
Western Wood-pewee	0.6000	0.0000	22.5	67.5	0.017
More Abundant in Grazed Areas					
Brewer's Sparrow	0.2000	0.7778	23.0	78.0	0.039
Yellow Warbler	0.3000	0.7778	27.0	82.0	0.096

Notes: Values are mean detections per survey, and results of Mann-Whitney U-test for differences between grazed and ungrazed. All species detected at least 15 times on a given river system with a P < 0.2 from a Mann-Whitney U-test are included.

Studies in Avian Biology No. 25:203–220, 2002.

SPOTTED OWLS, FOREST FRAGMENTATION, AND FOREST HETEROGENEITY

ALAN B. FRANKLIN AND R. J. GUTIÉRREZ

Abstract. The Spotted Owl (*Strix occidentalis*) has been a focal species in the United States in terms of loss and fragmentation of old coniferous forests. Past research has shown a strong association between Spotted Owls and old coniferous forests. Thus, these vegetation types are considered synonymous with Spotted Owl habitat. Past fragmentation of old coniferous forests in the Pacific Northwest, the Sierra Nevada, southern California, and the Southwest has resulted from natural disturbance (e.g., fire), edaphic conditions, and timber harvesting. These processes have occurred at different rates and levels. We reviewed the existing literature on the effects of forest fragmentation and heterogeneity on Spotted Owls at three different scales: a range-wide scale where once-connected populations have been isolated from each other, a population scale where populations with different fragmentation regimes have different demographics, and a territory scale where individuals occupying territories with different fragmentation regimes have different fitness. Studies at the range-wide scale have concentrated on processes, such as juvenile dispersal. There are no published studies on the effects of fragmentation or heterogeneity at the population scale, although the potential exists for examining those effects with current studies. Lack of empirical data on the effects of fragmentation on Spotted Owls led to the development of spatially-explicit simulation models as an aid to reserve design for this species. In addition, some populations of Spotted Owls are naturally disjunct at the range-wide scale. Most empirical studies have concentrated on the territory scale, and most of those studies have examined the effects of fragmentation and heterogeneity on occupancy. We attempted a simple meta-analysis using effect sizes estimated from these studies. However, this analysis was hampered by lack of replicated studies among subspecies and among provinces within subspecies. In addition, studies did not use similar metrics to describe fragmentation and heterogeneity. Thus, empirical studies following simulation models are equivocal in their conclusions. Many questions remain unanswered concerning the effects of forest fragmentation and heterogeneity on Spotted Owls. We provide a set of key questions that need to be addressed to better understand the effects of fragmentation and heterogeneity on Spotted Owls. We also suggest that future research concentrate on understanding natural disturbance regimes and the extent to which timber harvesting is compensatory or additive to natural disturbance regimes. Research on the effects of fragmentation on Spotted Owls should also include alternative hypotheses that some levels of fragmentation and/or heterogeneity may benefit Spotted Owl populations.

Key Words: habitat; habitat fragmentation; meta-analysis; population dynamics; Spotted Owl.

The Spotted Owl (*Strix occidentalis*) occurs in the western United States, Canada, and Mexico, and is comprised of three subspecies: the Northern Spotted Owl (*S. o. caurina*), the California Spotted Owl (*S. o. occidentalis*), and the Mexican Spotted Owl (*S. o. lucida*) (Gutiérrez et al. 1995; Fig. 1). All three subspecies have similar life-history characteristics, with high adult survival, low juvenile survival, and low reproduction (LaHaye et al. 1992, Noon et al. 1992, White et al. 1995, Forsman et al. 1996, Seamans et al. 1999).

Habitat associations of Spotted Owls are variable across and within subspecies. However, all three subspecies have a strong association with older forests for nesting, roosting, and foraging (Forsman et al. 1984, Carey et al. 1990, Solis and Gutiérrez 1990, Call et al. 1992, Gutiérrez et al. 1992; Buchanan et al. 1993, 1995; Ganey and Balda 1994, Seamans and Gutiérrez 1995, Forsman and Giese 1997, LaHaye et al. 1997, Steger et al. 1997, Hershey 1998, Young et al. 1998, LaHaye and Gutiérrez 1999). In general,

these forests are characterized by an overstory of large (≥52 cm dbh) conifers, with a multi-layered understory of conifers and/or hardwood trees and shrubs, and decadence in the form of snags and coarse woody debris. These association have been documented at several scales (see reviews in Gutiérrez et al. 1992, 1995; Ganey and Dick 1995). However, there are exceptions to the association of Spotted Owls with old coniferous forests. Mexican Spotted Owls are found in both old forests and in steep, incised canyon systems with little or no forest cover (Rinkevich and Gutiérrez 1996, Ganey and Dick 1995). Nevertheless, the majority of Mexican Spotted Owl populations are found in areas containing older coniferous forests where they strongly associate with these forests (Ward et al. 1995, Ganey and Dick 1995). In addition, owls frequently inhabit previously logged conifer forests or oak (*Quercus* spp.) forests (Gutiérrez et al. 1992, Folliard 1993). In these latter two situations, residual old trees are often present, the current forest has structural characters similar to

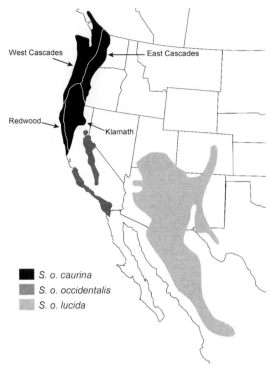

FIGURE 1. Geographic distribution of three subspecies of Spotted Owl (*Strix occidentalis*). Regions shown for Northern Spotted Owl are from Agee and Edmonds (1992).

old forests, and/or microclimates are modified by marine climates or streams.

In addition to differences between subspecies, there are subtle differences in forests used by Spotted Owls within subspecies. For example, Northern Spotted Owls are found in forests composed almost purely of conifers in their northern range. However, in the southern extent of their range many hardwood species dominate the mid- and understories while conifers still dominate the overstory. Despite these and other exceptions, it is generally believed that Spotted Owls associate with older coniferous forests and that these forests provide some key elements for their survival and reproduction.

Both the Northern and Mexican subspecies were listed as threatened under the Endangered Species Act of the United States (U.S. Fish and Wildlife Service 1990, 1993). One criterion that led to listing was habitat loss and fragmentation due to logging and forest management. Existing scientific information at the time of the listing of these two subspecies suggested that these owls were dependant on interior older forest for foraging, roosting, and nesting. Another criterion was the failure of existing regulatory mech-

anisms to control loss and fragmentation of older coniferous forest (U.S. Fish and Wildlife Service 1990, 1993). For similar reasons, the California subspecies was recently petitioned for listing (Center for Biological Diversity 2000).

In this paper, we first review the concepts of fragmentation and heterogeneity as they apply to Spotted Owls. Then, we review simulation models developed to facilitate conservation strategies. Next, we review the existing evidence on the effects of habitat fragmentation on population processes in the three subspecies of Spotted Owls. In particular, we examine habitat fragmentation at three scales: range-wide, population, and territory. The range-wide scale encompasses the geographic range of each subspecies. Habitat fragmentation at this scale may affect meta-population dynamics and gene flow between sub-populations (Gutiérrez and Harrison 1996). The population scale is nested within the range-wide scale. Habitat connectivity is determined by the dispersal ability of young Spotted Owls and local movements of individuals between territories. Potential source-sink population dynamics will be affected by habitat fragmentation and these effects are measurable by variation in rates of population change within populations. The final scale we consider is at the territory level. At this scale, the ability of individual territory holders to move across their territories may be affected by connectivity between blocks of habitat within individual territories. Effects of fragmentation will be expressed in terms of reproductive output and survival of individuals, and by inter-specific interactions such as competition, predation, and hybridization. Clearly, these scales overlap across the three categories (range-wide, population, and territory) that we examined. However, most studies on Spotted Owls encompass one or more of these three scales.

FRAGMENTATION, HETEROGENEITY, AND SPOTTED OWL HABITAT

Mature and old-growth forests are considered synonymous with Spotted Owl habitat. Thus, fragmentation of these forests is considered habitat fragmentation for Spotted Owls. Using the definition of Franklin et al. (*this volume*), habitat fragmentation occurs when habitat becomes discontinuous such that changes occur in population processes. For example, it is unlikely that road cuts (small-scale fragmentation) affects Spotted Owls to the same degree as large catastrophic fires or clearcuts. As Franklin et al. (*this volume*) point out, habitat fragmentation is essentially a binary outcome (habitat versus nonhabitat) whereas heterogeneity is a multi-state outcome. In the context of the scales discussed

Pre-disturbance   **Post-disturbance**

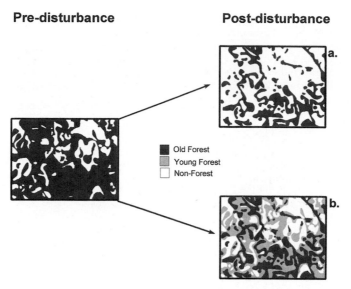

FIGURE 2.   Two hypothetical scenarios in patterns of habitat fragmentation in Spotted Owls: (a) older forest alone is considered Spotted Owl habitat, and (b) older forest in some combination with younger forest is considered Spotted Owl habitat.

in this paper, forest heterogeneity is the diversity of vegetation types and seral stages within a given area.

For older forests to be synonymous with Spotted Owl habitat, these forests must provide the requisite resources and conditions that promote occupancy and allow individuals to survive and reproduce (see definitions in Franklin et al. *this volume*). However, there is evidence that other vegetation types may also contribute to Spotted Owl habitat. This evidence is mostly indirect and relates to abundances of Spotted Owl prey in different vegetation types (Rosenberg and Anthony 1992, Williams et al. 1992, Carey and Peeler 1995, Ward and Block 1995, Zabel et al. 1995, Sureda and Morrison 1998, Ward et al. 1998). Thus, ecotones between older forest and other seral stages may contribute to Spotted Owl habitat, an idea that we will explore further (see HABITAT FRAGMENTATION AT THE TERRITORY SCALE below).

If other seral stages contribute to Spotted Owl habitat as suggested above, then some conversion of older forest to younger seral stages does not necessarily represent habitat fragmentation for Spotted Owls. For example, assume a distribution of old forest shown in Figure 2 prior to disturbance. After disturbance fragments the older forest, a new distribution of young and old forest results. If only old forest is Spotted Owl habitat, then fragmentation of older forest alone, as depicted by scenario A in Figure 2, results in habitat fragmentation for Spotted Owls. However, if young forests in some combination with

older forest constitutes Spotted Owl habitat, as represented by the condition in scenario B in Figure 2, then no habitat fragmentation occurs for Spotted Owls. In the latter scenario, forest fragmentation is represented by heterogeneity of seral stages. Therefore, we acknowledge that other vegetation types may contribute to Spotted Owl habitat (e.g., forest heterogeneity) in our examination of the empirical studies.

MODELS SIMULATING THE EFFECTS OF HABITAT LOSS AND FRAGMENTATION ON SPOTTED OWLS

The Spotted Owl became a conservation issue because of losses of old coniferous forest from logging. Several management plans were developed but empirical data were generally lacking to test the efficacy of these plans. Therefore, simulation models were developed to examine a critical question for management planners—what is the likely persistence of the owl if its habitat continues to be removed? These simulation models ranged from deterministic to stochastic and were used primarily in developing management strategies for the Northern Spotted Owl (Lande 1988, Doak 1989, Lamberson et al. 1992, McKelvey et al. 1992).

The assumption of these models varied but all assumed that (1) habitat in the form of old coniferous forest was either suitable or unsuitable, with no definitions of habitat quality; and (2) juvenile Spotted Owls searched the landscape during dispersal with some specific behavior, e.g., randomly or with some finite number of searches. All of the models predicted that Spotted Owls would not persist with continued loss of old coniferous forest. An early deterministic model (Lande 1988) predicted a critical threshold for Northern Spotted Owls when the proportion of suitable habitat (old coniferous forest) on the landscape fell below 0.21. Other simulation models did not make such explicit predictions because assumptions on how dispersing juvenile owls searched the landscape was critical in determining model results. Nevertheless, all the models clearly predicted the demise of Northern Spotted Owl populations, given the model assumptions and continued loss of old coniferous forest.

All of the models also assumed that habitat fragmentation would be a consequence of loss of old coniferous forest through logging. This was a reasonable assumption given the knowledge at that time concerning Spotted Owl dispersal and harvest unit strategies in western coniferous forests. However, there were few explicit predictions from the models regarding the nature of fragmentation resulting from habitat loss.

CAUSES OF FRAGMENTATION AND HETEROGENEITY

Historically, fire was the major disturbance affecting forested landscapes across the range of all three subspecies (Weatherspoon et al. 1992, Agee 1993, Skinner and Chang 1996, Swetnam and Baisan 1996a, Taylor and Skinner 1998). Before organized fire suppression programs, fire occurred throughout the range of the Spotted Owls at fairly frequent intervals with differing degrees of intensity (Table 1, Fig. 3). California and Mexican Spotted Owls experienced frequent low to moderate intensity fires, whereas Northern Spotted Owls experienced greater variation in fire return intervals (Table 1; see also Skinner and Chang 1996). Owls occurring in the West Cascades, Coast Ranges, and Redwood provinces were probably less affected by fire than in other parts of their range. However, these mesic provinces experienced higher fire intensities less frequently than drier portions of the owl's range. Of the 3,753 owl pairs reported within the range of the Northern Spotted Owl (Gutiérrez 1994), 37% were in the Klamath and Eastern Cascades provinces, which experienced fire regimes characterized by frequent, less-severe fires than those in western Oregon and Washington (Taylor and Skinner 1998).

Fire suppression by humans disrupted natural fire cycles beginning in the 20th century (Fig. 3; Weatherspoon et al. 1992, Agee 1993, Swetnam and Baisan 1996a), but was not relatively effective until the late 1940s (Wills 1991). The effects of fire suppression on landscapes occupied by Spotted Owls have been poorly understood,

TABLE 1. HISTORICAL FIRE REGIMES WITHIN THE RANGE OF THREE SUBSPECIES OF SPOTTED OWLS

Region[a]	Mean interval (years)	Intensity	Source
		Northern Spotted Owl	
West Cascades Province:			
Oregon Coast and Washington Cascades	230–900	moderate–high	Agee and Edmonds 1992, Long et al. 1998
Central Oregon Cascades	95–145	moderate–high	Agee and Edmonds 1992
East Cascades Province	12–52	low–moderate	Agee and Edmonds 1992
Klamath Province	10–50	low–moderate	Taylor and Skinner 1998, Agee and Edmonds 1992
Redwood Province	50–333	low	Veirs 1982
		California Spotted Owl	
Sierra Nevada Mountains	5–30	low–moderate	Weatherspoon et al. 1992
		Mexican Spotted Owl	
Arizona and New Mexico	3–25	low–moderate	Swetnam and Baisan 1996a,b

[a] Locations of provinces for Northern Spotted Owls are shown in Fig. 1.

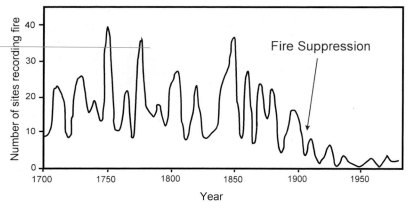

FIGURE 3. Fire occurrence within the range of the Mexican Spotted Owl before and after fire suppression at 63 fire history sites in Arizona and New Mexico (Swetnam and Baisan 1996a).

but several studies suggested that forests prior to fire suppression were less dense and had more openings. Comparing aerial photos from 1944 and 1985, Skinner (1995) found that openings (areas ≥0.1 ha occupied by vegetation less than a third the height of surrounding stands) decreased 39% within unlogged watersheds of the Klamath Province in northern California. In addition, openings became smaller and more dispersed across the landscape after 40 years of fire suppression. Sierran mixed-conifer forests occupied by California Spotted Owls shifted from frequent low- to moderate-severity fires, to long-interval, high-severity, stand-replacing fires after fire suppression (Weatherspoon et al. 1992). This situation probably also applied to forests occupied by Northern and Mexican Spotted Owls. Weatherspoon et al. (1992) also suggested that fire suppression on Sierran forests created more homogeneous landscapes in terms of forested stand configuration. Prior to fire suppression, forests probably were dominated by large, old trees intermixed with a complex array of small, even-aged stands representing a wide range of age- and size-classes (McKelvey and Johnston 1992, Weatherspoon et al. 1992), whereas post-fire suppression forests have become more homogeneous and even-aged. However, there has been considerable disagreement concerning forest conditions under natural fire regimes (Sierra Nevada Ecosystem Project 1996: 63). In either case, the composition and structure of post-fire suppression forests were complicated by logging activities, which have largely replaced fire as the most frequent disturbance to forests occupied by all three subspecies of Spotted Owl.

Coincident with fire suppression, logging began in forests across the range of the Spotted Owl at the turn of the 20th century. However,

logging on publicly-owned forests, and subsequent fire suppression, did not begin until around 1940–1950 (Harris 1984, McKelvey and Johnston 1992). In most parts of the owl's range, logging practices shifted from uneven-aged management to even-aged management (Harris 1984, McKelvey and Johnston 1992, Moir et al. 1995) with clearcut logging as the predominate method. However, in the Sierra Nevada, logging prior to the 1980s rarely used clearcutting; selective logging of the largest trees was the predominant method (McKelvey and Johnston 1992). Habitat fragmentation may have occurred if selective logging degraded the quality of older forests for Spotted Owls. However, the matrix resulting from this type of logging may have different effects than one resulting from clearcut logging. On the other hand, clearcutting began earlier and increased over time within the range of the Northern and Mexican Spotted Owls than in the Sierra Nevada (Harris 1984, Moir et al. 1995). Clearcutting has dramatically altered at least part of the forested landscape used by Spotted Owls (Fig. 4). Ripple et al. (2000) found that prelogging landscapes in the Coast Range of Oregon had significantly greater amounts of old-growth forest (63% of landscape before logging versus 44% after logging). In addition to reducing the amounts of older forest, foresters attempted to disperse 10–20 ha clearcuts, which increased fragmentation of those forests; patch density and edge density increased while mean patch size, largest patch size, and amount of interior forest decreased. However, Ripple et al. (2000) also found that proportions of old-growth forest in pre-logging landscapes were highly variable, ranging from 16–100%, which may have been due to past stand-replacing fires.

Thus, both fire and past logging practices altered landscapes occupied by Spotted Owls.

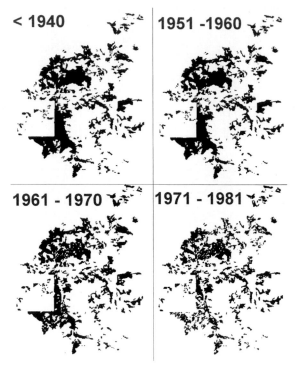

FIGURE 4. Distribution of old-growth forest on the Blue River and McKenzie Ranger Districts of the Willamette National Forest, Oregon (Harris 1984).

While clearcut logging may have been similar to severe stand-replacing fires in that all forest cover is removed, logging did not attempt to mimic natural disturbance regimes, such as fire, under which the owl evolved (McKelvey and Johnston 1992).

HABITAT FRAGMENTATION AT THE RANGE-WIDE SCALE

A number of authors argued that the population process of primary concern with respect to habitat fragmentation across the range of subspecies is juvenile dispersal (Gutiérrez and Harrison 1996, Turchin 1998). This was also recognized in the simulation models discussed previously (Lande 1988, Doak 1989, Lamberson et al. 1992).

Dispersal of juvenile Spotted Owls maintains gene flow and potential demographic connectivity between isolated populations. The importance of juvenile dispersal depends on the dynamics of Spotted Owl populations, e.g., whether population dynamics follow source-sink, meta-population, etc. Regardless of how population dynamics in Spotted Owls are structured, the movement of individual Spotted Owls across the landscape is primarily though juveniles. In general, once Spotted Owls establish a territory,

they are relatively sedentary. Movements of territory holders to other territories is relatively rare and encompasses only short distances; Wagner et al. (1996) estimated that 1.5% of non-juvenile Northern Spotted Owls relocated to new territories each year while moving an average of 6.5 km. An exception was noted for the Mexican Spotted Owl, where an adult female was recovered 187 km from her original territory (Gutiérrez et al. 1996). In contrast to territory holders, juvenile Spotted Owls always disperse from their natal territories (Gutiérrez et al. 1985, Miller 1989, Ganey et al. 1998, Willey and van Riper 2000) and move considerably longer distances (Table 2). In addition, the distributional properties of dispersal distances for juvenile Spotted Owls are quite similar between the Northern and Mexican subspecies (Table 2); no data are available for the California subspecies.

If dispersal maintained demographic continuity, then the degree to which habitat fragmentation affects this connectivity will determine the influences of habitat fragmentation on population processes at the range-wide scale. A key question with respect to dispersal is, does habitat fragmentation affect connectivity between populations and subpopulations of Spotted Owls? Effects can be viewed as either complete disrup-

TABLE 2.   FINAL DISPERSAL DISTANCES REPORTED FOR RADIO-TAGGED JUVENILE NORTHERN AND MEXICAN SPOTTED OWLS

| Subspecies | Region | Final dispersal distance (km)[a] | | | | Source |
		Mean	SD	Range	N	
Northern	California	30.5	23.5	1.0–100.0	23	Gutiérrez et al. 1985
	Oregon	28.1	17.3	3.2–75.8	25	Miller 1989
Mexican	Utah	29.2	22.5	1.7–92.3	26	Willey and van Riper 2000
	Arizona	26.2	22.3	0.6–72.1	17	Ganey et al. 1998

[a] Final dispersal distance is the straight-line distance from the nest to the location farthest from the nest (Ganey et al. 1998).

tion of the connection between populations or reduction in flow of individuals to some threshold point where the connection can be considered severed.

Much of the range of the Northern Spotted Owl and the Sierra Nevada portion occupied by California Spotted Owls has fairly continuous forests considered suitable for occupancy by owls. However, across the range of the Mexican Spotted Owl, the distribution of suitable forests is naturally disjunct (Fig. 5). For the geographic range of the Mexican Spotted Owl to be considered fragmented, connectivity must be affected to a greater degree than normally experienced in the naturally disjunct populations across the range of this subspecies. Although it is tempting to view Mexican Spotted Owl populations as a type of meta-population, there is little support for this (Keitt et al. 1995, Gutiérrez and Harrison 1998). Based on simulation modeling, Keitt et al. (1997) found that the degree to which the range of the Mexican Spotted Owl in the United States (Fig. 5) is connected could be described in terms of dispersal distance; with a dispersal distance of at least 40–50 km, forested patches went from being relatively disconnected to connected. Of 43 juveniles radio-marked by Ganey et al. (1998) and Willey and van Riper (2000), 25.6% dispersed distances at least 40–50 km (Table 3). For comparison, we examined the cumulative distribution of final dispersal distances for 48 radio-marked juvenile Northern Spotted Owls (Gutiérrez et al. 1985, Miller 1989; Table 3). If forested areas within the range of the Northern Spotted Owl were distributed in a manner similar to that of the Mexican Spotted Owl, 27.1% of the dispersing juveniles would be able to move between disjunct populations (Table 3). This suggested that a portion of a given year's juvenile cohort would be capable of connecting a landscape of disjunct habitat patches under the conditions of these studies. However, the question still remains, is this sufficient to maintain connectivity between populations and subpopulations within the geographic range to maintain both demographic processes and gene flow?

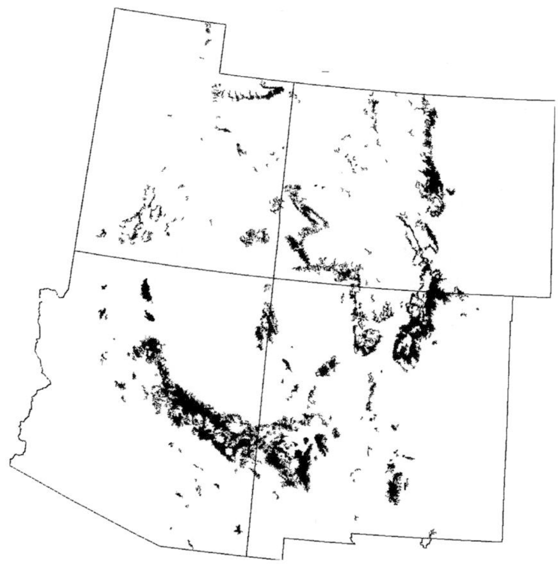

We found few empirical data on the effects of fragmentation on Spotted Owl population processes at the scale of the geographic range. Only one study (Miller et al. 1997) on juvenile Northern Spotted Owl dispersal provided insights on the effect of forest fragmentation on connectivity between populations. First, Miller et al. (1997) found that juveniles used closed-canopy forests more often than expected during dispersal. Second, juveniles selected equally between less fragmented and more fragmented older forests. However, they did observe a negative relationship between net dispersal distance and the proportion of clearcuts on the landscape, suggesting that juveniles encountering more clearcuts during dispersal may be limited in their dispersal distance. Finally, mortality of juveniles appeared to increase with increased use of clearcuts when they temporarily colonized an area, but mortality decreased with increased use of open sapling stands. The openness of clearcuts

FIGURE 5.   Distribution of forested areas within the range of the Mexican Spotted Owl.

TABLE 3. CUMULATIVE DISTRIBUTION OF DISPERSAL DISTANCES OF RADIO-TAGGED JUVENILE MEXICAN AND NORTHERN SPOTTED OWLS

Final dispersal distance $\geq x$ km, where $x =$	% of juveniles dispersing at least x km		Simulated effect on range-wide forested landscape occupied by Mexican Spotted Owls (Keitt et al. 1997)
	Mexican	Northern	
10	74.4	81.3	
20	60.5	64.6	Highly disconnected
30	34.9	41.7	
40	25.6	27.1	Several independent subdivisions
50	14.0	12.5	Most patches joined
60	9.3	6.3	
70	7.0	4.2	
80	4.7	2.1	Highly interconnected

Note: Data on radio-tagged owls are from the sources listed in Table 2.

may make owls more vulnerable to predation or reduce the availability of prey because clearcuts are often dominated by dense, small shrubs. Use of other seral stages may be related to prey, such as the dusky-footed woodrat (*Neotoma fuscipes*), which achieve high abundances in early forest seral stages (Sakai and Noon 1993, Ward et al. 1998). Thus, some degree of fragmentation may not be detrimental to dispersing juvenile Northern Spotted Owls, but the effect of fragmentation of older forest may depend on the intervening matrix (i.e., clearcut versus sapling stands) between forest fragments.

Simulation models examined the potential effects of fragmentation on juvenile dispersal across the range, or portions of the range, of the three subspecies (Doak 1989, McKelvey et al. 1992, Noon and McKelvey 1992, Keitt et al. 1997). However, these models incorporated assumptions about juvenile dispersal behavior because little empirical data existed to parameterize the models. Consequently, these studies provided little real information on how habitat fragmentation affects Spotted Owls. However, the model by Keitt et al. (1997) provided valuable insights into what dispersal capabilities Mexican Spotted Owls require to connect populations across their range, and the models by Lamberson et al. (1994), McKelvey et al. (1992), and Noon and McKelvey (1992) made quantitative predictions about occupancy of habitat blocks containing different numbers of Northern Spotted Owl territories (see also review in Noon and McKelvey 1996). The predictions from these latter models have never been empirically tested.

Habitat fragmentation could potentially affect gene flow as well as population dynamics, which is a major concern of conservation biologists (Frankel and Soulé 1981). Despite the lack of support for a demographic meta-population, there is evidence of past gene flow among Mexican Spotted Owl populations, among Northern

Spotted Owl populations and between Northern and California Spotted Owls (Barrowclough et al. 1999). Further, relatively little gene flow needs to occur to maintain genetic variability (Lande and Barrowclough 1987). Thus, it appears that fragmentation would likely have less effect on gene flow than demography, given what we know of juvenile Spotted Owl dispersal.

HABITAT FRAGMENTATION AT THE POPULATION SCALE

Abundance and reproductive success of Northern Spotted Owls increase with the amount of older forest (Bart and Forsman 1992). However, there are no studies relating metrics measuring forest fragmentation or heterogeneity with population performance. Although there are a large number of populations studies on Spotted Owls (see Noon et al. 1992, White et al. 1995, Forsman et al. 1996, Franklin et al. 1999 for reviews), none relate life-history traits and/or rates of population change (λ) to forest fragmentation or heterogeneity. Such studies would have to employ the population or subpopulation as the unit of comparison rather than the individual or territory (see HABITAT FRAGMENTATION AT THE TERRITORY SCALE below). For example, estimates of λ for Northern Spotted Owls on 15 studies ranged from 0.83 ($\widehat{se}(\hat{\lambda}) = 0.02$) to 0.98 ($\widehat{se}(\hat{\lambda}) = 0.02$), indicating that variation in rates of population change exists among subpopulations (Franklin et al. 1999). Thus, comparisons need to be made with subpopulations of owls inhabiting landscapes having different degrees of habitat fragmentation (e.g., the 15 separate demographic studies in Franklin et al. 1999). In addition, the methods for identifying habitats and quantifying habitat fragmentation would have to be standardized across study areas.

TABLE 4. META-ANALYSIS ON AMOUNTS OF MATURE AND OLD-GROWTH FOREST IN CIRCLES OCCUPIED BY SPOTTED OWLS VERSUS RANDOM CIRCLES ON THE SURROUNDING LANDSCAPE

Subspecies	k^a	$\hat{\bar{d}}$	$\widehat{var(\bar{d})}$	95% CI for $\hat{\bar{d}}$	$\hat{\sigma}^2_{process}$ (95% CI)	$CV_{process}$
Northern	7	0.680	0.011	0.474, 0.886	0.029 (0.000, 0.313)	0.251
California	1	0.352	0.085	0.218, 0.923	—^{b}	—^{b}
Mexican	1	0.466	0.053	0.016, 0.915	—^{b}	—^{b}
All subspecies	9	0.624	0.008	0.449, 0.799	0.022 (0.000, 0.230)	0.236

^{a} Number of studies.
^{b} Not estimable because of insufficient number of studies.

HABITAT FRAGMENTATION AT THE TERRITORY SCALE

Most research on effects of fragmentation and heterogeneity on Spotted Owls has been at the territory scale, and the majority of this work related occupancy to landscape characteristics within territories. In general, researchers examining the effects of habitat fragmentation and heterogeneity compared occupied sites (defined by circles of varying radii around an owl nest or location) with sites of equal size that were randomly placed on the surrounding landscape. Because of the large number of studies, we used some simple meta-analytical techniques to summarize the general findings (see Appendix 1 for methods). In summary, we first estimated effect sizes (d), and their sampling variance (var(d)) for each study. Here, the study was the sampling unit, with each study including 20–100 territories (see Appendix 1). Thus, we were able to estimate sampling variances and 95% confidence intervals of metrics for each study. Effect sizes were measures, in standard deviations, of the difference in metrics (e.g., amount of older forest) between occupied and random sites (Wolf 1986:27, VanderWerf 1992). Ideally, effect sizes should be compared with a distribution of effect sizes derived from published studies (Wolf 1986:27). Because such a distribution was unavailable, we used the rough guidelines of $\hat{d} = 0.2$ for small effects, $\hat{d} = 0.5$ for medium effects, and $\hat{d} = 0.8$ for large effects proposed by Cohen (1987). We used 95% confidence intervals to assess the degree to which effect sizes overlapped zero (no effect) for each study. Where we had ≥ 2 studies with the same metric (e.g., amount of old-growth), we estimated a weighted mean ($\hat{\bar{d}}$), its sampling variance ($\widehat{var(\bar{d})}$), and an estimate of the process variation ($\hat{\sigma}^2_{process}$) of $\hat{\bar{d}}$. This process variation was an estimate of the variation in the metrics across studies and was derived by removing the sampling variation associated with each estimate of d (see Appendix 1). In most cases, there were only 2–3 studies with similar metrics. In these cases, we still estimated the effects size param-

eters and process variation. We recognized these estimates had limited validity for inference but we used them to pose alternative hypotheses and as an example of how a meta-analysis of these parameters would be useful if sufficient studies were available with similar metrics.

We first examined the effects of amounts of mature and old-growth coniferous forest on occupancy. We examined seven studies on the Northern Spotted Owl, ranging from Washington to northern California, one study on the California Spotted Owl, and one study on the Mexican Spotted Owl (Appendix 1). Effect sizes across all subspecies were positive, generally large, and, except for the California Spotted Owl, different from zero, indicating that sites occupied by Spotted Owls had greater amounts of older forest than sites randomly located on the forested landscape (Table 4). In addition, Northern Spotted Owls appeared to have greater effect sizes, suggesting a larger difference between occupied and random sites, than the other two subspecies (Appendix 1). However, the other two subspecies were each represented by only one study and, hence, we did not capture as much geographic variation as for the Northern Spotted Owl. In addition, sites occupied by Northern Spotted Owls on private timber lands in the Redwood Province (Fig. 1) had higher proportions of younger forests (41–60 years) than the other studies (Thome et al. 1999). On these private lands, there were few stands of older forest, but the younger stands often approached the structural characteristics of older conifer forest in the other studies because of higher growth rates in redwood (*Sequoia sempervirens*) forests (Folliard 1993).

Researchers comparing occupied and random sites used 16 different metrics of fragmentation and 6 different measures of heterogeneity (Appendix 1). Unfortunately, none of these metrics were represented by more than three studies, with most used in only a single study. In addition, the majority of the studies were on Northern Spotted Owls. We estimated effect sizes and process variance for six of the metrics examin-

TABLE 5. META-ANALYSIS OF INDICATORS OF FRAGMENTATION AND HETEROGENEITY IN CIRCLES OCCUPIED BY NORTHERN SPOTTED OWLS VERSUS RANDOM CIRCLES ON THE SURROUNDING LANDSCAPE

Metric[a]	k[b]	$\hat{\bar{d}}$	$\widehat{var}(\hat{\bar{d}})$	95% CI for $\hat{\bar{d}}$		$\hat{\sigma}^2_{process}$ (95% CI)	$CV_{process}$
Indicators of Fragmentation							
Mean Patch Area	3	0.865	0.002	0.777,	0.953	0.000 (0.000, 0.341)	0.000
CV Patch Area	2	0.359	0.119	−0.317,	1.035	0.177 (0.000, 250.1)	0.953
Patch Density	2	0.563	0.163	−0.230,	1.354	0.260 (0.000, 338.1)	0.906
Patch Interior	2	0.440	0.045	0.024,	0.856	0.040 (0.000, 110.5)	0.455
Perimeter Density	3	0.289	0.124	−0.401,	0.979	0.342 (0.052, 15.69)	2.024
GISfrag Index	3	−0.638	0.061	−1.122,	−0.154	0.141 (0.000, 8.175)	0.589
Indicators of Heterogeneity							
Shannon-Wiener Index	2	0.272	0.136	−0.451,	0.950	0.220 (0.002, 277.2)	1.676
Dominance	2	−0.307	0.169	−1.113,	0.499	0.285 (0.014, 343.9)	1.442
Contagion	2	0.642	1.147	−1.457,	2.741	0.401 (0.393, 340.3)	2.671

[a] See Appendix 1 for definitions of metrics.
[b] Number of studies.

ing fragmentation (represented by 2–3 studies) and three of the metrics examining heterogeneity (each represented by two studies; Table 5). Effects that appeared to be consistent across studies (i.e., exhibited relatively low CV in spatial process variation) were mean patch area, the amount of patch interior, and the GISfrag index of Ripple et al. (1991a; Table 5). Based on the GISfrag index, Northern Spotted Owls occupied areas having larger patches of older forest (which supported more interior forest) that were more numerous and closer together than the random sites. The effect sizes for these three metrics were different from zero based on 95% confidence intervals (Table 5). The remaining metrics for fragmentation and all the metrics for heterogeneity in Table 5 had large coefficients of spatial process variation, and had effect sizes with confidence intervals including zero. However, in almost all cases the estimates of spatial process variation had extremely large confidence intervals, indicating poor estimation due to inadequate numbers of studies. More importantly, our analysis demonstrates the lack of comparability among studies of Spotted Owl habitat fragmentation because few studies used the same metrics. Thus, there were insufficient samples for most metrics to allow meaningful conclusions.

We also partitioned the data by gross ecological provinces (West Cascades versus Klamath Provinces; Fig. 1) within the range of the Northern Spotted Owl to examine whether large differences between the provinces were responsible for the high coefficients of spatial process variation (Table 6). With the three metrics (mean patch area, interior, and GISfrag) that we considered consistent, effect sizes were similar between the two provinces and were different from zero for each individual study. With the other three metrics of fragmentation (CV patch area,

patch density, and perimeter density), there appeared to be provincial differences that could have accounted for the high degree of spatial process variation observed when provinces were pooled in Table 5. Sites occupied by Northern Spotted Owls in the West Cascades province had less variable patch areas, lower patch density, and inconclusive perimeter densities in relation to random sites. The Klamath province, on the other hand, had more variable patch areas, higher patch densities, and higher perimeter densities than random sites. Only patch density was not different from zero.

Thus, it appears that Northern Spotted Owls occupy sites with greater amounts of older forest that retain higher amounts of interior forest than forested landscapes chosen at random across their range. This appeared to be consistent across provinces. However, the degree of fragmentation in occupied versus random sites in the Klamath province was greater than in the West Cascade province. This was suggested by more variable patch sizes and greater perimeter edge. However, this would only be considered habitat fragmentation if habitat for Northern Spotted Owls in the Klamath province was limited to older forest. If ecotones (represented by the perimeter of other vegetation types with older forest) are also Spotted Owl habitat, then this would not represent habitat fragmentation, but merely an additional component of Spotted Owl habitat (see Franklin et al. *this volume*).

In general, heterogeneity of vegetation types and forest seral stages appears to be higher in occupied than random sites of the Northern and Mexican Spotted Owl, but not the California subspecies (Table 7). For the Northern Spotted Owl in the West Cascades and Klamath provinces, Shannon-Wiener indices of vegetation type or seral stage diversity were higher on occupied sites, Simpson's index was lower, domi-

TABLE 6. PROVINCE DIFFERENCES IN EFFECT SIZES FOR SIX METRICS ASSOCIATED WITH FRAGMENTATION FOR NORTHERN SPOTTED OWLS

Metric	West Cascade Province		Klamath Province	
	Source	d (95% CI)	Source	d (95% CI)
Mean Patch Area	Lehmkuhl and Raphael 1993	0.914 (0.586, 1.243)	Ripple et al. 1997	0.716 (0.059, 1.372)
CV Patch Area	Lehmkuhl and Raphael 1993	0.071 (−0.242, 0.384)	Ripple et al. 1997	0.772 (0.113, 1.432)
Patch Density	Lehmkuhl and Raphael 1993	−0.405 (−0.721, −0.089)	Ripple et al. 1997	0.520 (−0.127, 1.167)
Interior	Johnson 1992	0.302 (0.001, 0.604)	Ripple et al. 1997	0.768 (0.109, 1.428)
Perimeter Density	Lehmkuhl and Raphael 1993	0.213 (−0.101, 0.527)	Ripple et al. 1997	1.028 (0.351, 1.705)
	Johnson 1992	−0.215 (−0.644, 0.085)	—	
GISfrag Index	Lehmkuhl and Raphael 1993	−0.329 (−0.644, −0.014)	Ripple et al. 1997	−1.218 (−1.910, −0.525)
	—		Hunter et al. 1995	−0.591 (−1.036, −0.146)

nance was lower, and contagion was lower. The results from the East Cascades province were opposite in terms of the Shannon-Wiener index, dominance, and contagion. (Morganti 1993; Table 7). However, only contagion was different from zero. In addition, Morganti (1993) only used 3 vegetation types whereas the other researchers used 5–7; increasing vegetation types can affect the direction and the relative magnitude of all the heterogeneity metrics explored here (Morganti 1993, Meyer et al. 1998). Thus, while Spotted Owls may occupy sites with some degree of forest fragmentation in some areas, sites occupied by Northern Spotted Owls appeared to be more consistent in having higher heterogeneity throughout their range. The one study on Mexican Spotted Owls (Peery et al. 1999) had a similar effect size for Simpson's index as for the Northern Spotted Owl in California, indicating that seral stage and vegetation type diversity was higher in occupied than random sites. California Spotted Owls had the opposite trend, with occupied sites having less heterogeneity than random sites.

A few researchers examined the effects of landscape metrics on life-history traits, such as survival and reproduction. Bart (1995) found that survival increased with the amount of older forest within sites occupied by Northern Spotted Owls. However, survival in this study was measured from turnover events of unmarked birds (U. S. Dept. Interior 1992) and may not have been an unbiased measure of survival. Similarly, Ripple et al. (1997) found that a reproductive index was correlated ($r = 0.64$, $P = 0.03$) with amounts of older forest in occupied sites. However, metrics other than the amount of older forest were not included in the analyses in these two studies. In the Redwood province of northern California, Thome et al. (1999) found highest reproductive success in Northern Spotted Owls at sites that had high proportions of 21–40 year old forest stands and lower proportions of older forest. In the Klamath Province of Oregon, average annual reproductive output increased at sites with greater fractal dimension (indicating greater landscape complexity with increased edge), more older forest patches, and greater proportions of hardwood forest (Meyer et al. 1998). Their multiple regression model accounted for 56% of the variation in reproductive output. In the West Cascades province, average annual reproductive output was not explained by any of the habitat and landscape variables measured, but rather by decreased density of owls in the surrounding area, which explained 85% of the variation in reproductive output (Meyer et al. 1998). Finally, Franklin et al. (2000) examined reproductive output, survival, and the

TABLE 7. EFFECT SIZES FOR METRICS OF HETEROGENEITY MEASURED ON SITES OCCUPIED BY SPOTTED OWLS VERSUS RANDOM SITES

Metric[a]	Subspecies	Region[b]	$\hat{d}$	95% CI		Source
Shannon-Wiener Index	Northern	WCAS & KLA (OR)	0.629	0.224,	1.033	Meyer et al. 1998
Shannon-Wiener Index	Northern	ECAS (OR)	−0.109	−0.593,	0.374	Morganti 1993
Simpson's Index	Northern	KLA (CA)	−0.690	−1.147,	−0.233	Hunter et al. 1995
Dominance	Northern	WCAS & KLA (OR)	−0.706	−1.114,	−0.298	Meyer et al. 1998
Dominance	Northern	ECAS (OR)	0.116	−0.374,	0.607	Morganti 1993
Contagion	Northern	WCAS & KLA (OR)	−0.378	−0.778,	0.022	Meyer et al. 1998
Contagion	Northern	ECAS (OR)	1.766	1.189,	2.344	Morganti 1993
Baxter and Wolf Index	California	SIERRA	−0.775[c]	−1.366,	−0.184	two studies
Simpson's Index	Mexican	NM	−0.791	−1.251,	−0.330	Peery et al. 1999

[a] See Appendix 1 for definitions of metrics.
[b] WCAS = West Cascades province, KLA = Klamath province, ECAS = East Cascades province, SIERRA = Sierra Nevada Mountains; state acronyms are in parentheses.
[c] Weighted mean for two studies (Bias and Gutièrrez 1992, Moen & Gutièrrez 1997) in the same area; $\widehat{var}(\hat{d}) = 0.091$.

combination of the two in a measure of habitat-based fitness in relation to landscape habitat variables of sites occupied by Northern Spotted Owls in the Klamath province. They found that reproductive output increased at sites with more edge between older forest and other vegetation types and decreased with the amount of interior forest. Survival, however, increased with more interior older forest and increased edge. Thus, sites with high fitness represented a tradeoff, balancing the amount of interior forest with edge to achieve optimal survival and reproduction (Fig. 6).

DISCUSSION

The effects of habitat fragmentation on species richness and animal population dynamics

have long been of interest to ecologists. Consequently, negative impacts of forest fragmentation on Spotted Owls were assumed without critical examination because this bird's habitat has been highly disrupted by logging over the past century (Gutiérrez 1994). Further, the Spotted Owl is thought to be declining across its range, presumably in response to loss of habitat (and by corollary to increased habitat fragmentation). The loss of habitat, owl population declines, and the federal listing of two subspecies have prompted a plethora of studies on the bird which potentially lends itself to a meta-analysis of fragmentation patterns.

Most of the initial simulation models on Spotted Owls emphasized loss of habitat rather than the explicit effects of habitat fragmentation. As

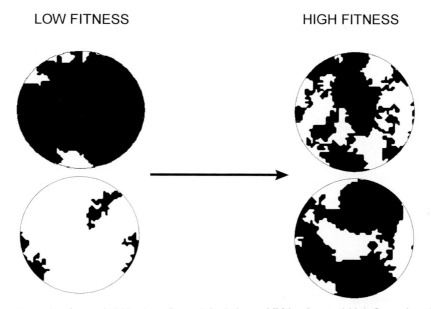

FIGURE 6. Example of occupied Northern Spotted Owl sites exhibiting low and high fitness based on habitat characteristics of those sites (Franklin et al. 2000).

Franklin et al. (*this volume*) point out, habitat loss and habitat fragmentation can have different effects when they are considered separately and at different scales. For example, the model developed by Lande (1988) predicted a threshold amount of suitable Spotted Owl habitat (older forest) below which populations should decline to extinction. This was partially corroborated by empirical studies that found no or few owls in large areas where older forests had been mostly eliminated (Bart and Forsman 1992, Johnson 1992, U. S. Dept. Interior 1992, Gutiérrez 1994). However, these results do not address the issue of critical thresholds for habitat fragmentation in Spotted Owls. Later models became more sophisticated but still only examined loss of suitable habitat (e.g., Doak 1989, Lamberson et al. 1992). The models developed by Lamberson et al. (1994), McKelvey et al. (1992) and Noon and McKelvey (1992) did make quantitative predictions about occupancy by Northern and California Spotted Owls at the range-wide scale in relation to forest patch sizes with different shapes, sizes, and inter-patch distances. However, these predictions have yet to be tested with empirical data. There has been an unfortunate disconnect between theoretical predictions made by simulation models concerning the effects of fragmentation on Spotted Owls and the testing of those predictions with empirical studies. However, this is not unique to Spotted Owls; Doak et al. (1992) argue for better merging of theory and experimentation in understanding habitat fragmentation in general.

At the three scales in the empirical studies that we examined, all three subspecies of Spotted Owl exhibit some degree of association with the structural characteristics of old conifer forest. Even when older forest is not present (e.g., the Redwood Province in the range of the Northern Spotted Owl), Spotted Owls still occupy sites that have forests structurally similar to older forest in other parts of the owl's range. However, at the territory scale there is evidence that early forest seral stages and ecotones (i.e., the interface between conifer forests and other vegetation types) may contribute to Northern Spotted Owl habitat in some areas (Franklin et al. 2000). In particular, early seral stages bordering older forest may provide both abundant and available prey for Northern Spotted Owls in the Klamath province where hardwood trees are important components of the forests occupied by Northern Spotted Owls. Thus, there is some evidence that Spotted Owls in some parts of their range may benefit from forest heterogeneity. Some of this heterogeneity may result from logging or other anthropocentric disturbance. These changes are not necessarily fragmentation (sensu

Franklin et al. *this volume*), but the introduction of openings and peninsulas of different seral stages that provide edge while maintaining interior forest (see Fig. 6) and heterogeneity. The mechanisms that produce potential benefits are still poorly understood but may relate to prey abundance and availability (see Thome et al. 1999, Franklin et al. 2000). This situation may only apply to areas occupied by Northern Spotted Owls (and other subspecies) where forests are mixtures of conifers and hardwoods.

Despite the plethora of habitat-based studies on Spotted Owls, the effects of forest fragmentation and heterogeneity are still poorly understood. Even at the territory scale where most of the studies have been conducted, the many different measures and indices used in the various studies reduced our ability to draw inferences. There is no unified set of metrics for measuring fragmentation of Spotted Owl habitats; an abundance of ad hoc measures exist and often researchers develop their own. However, to understand the effects of habitat fragmentation on Spotted Owls, appropriate metrics need to be developed that can be applied across studies. In the absence of large-scale experiments, reliable knowledge (sensu Romesburg 1981) can only be achieved through replication of observational studies that use similar metrics. Such consistency does not preclude novel approaches by individual investigators. Our attempt to synthesize such studies for Spotted Owls failed in terms of inferences on the effects of fragmentation because researchers did not use similar metrics to quantify habitat fragmentation. That is, each metric of interest was represented by 3 studies at the most. Our sample of studies was also hampered because a number of researchers did not present the requisite information (means and/or standard deviations) to estimate effect sizes. However, the patterns we observed in our meta-analysis can be considered hypotheses that can be tested with more detailed meta-analyses or experimentation.

To understand forest fragmentation, habitat fragmentation, and forest heterogeneity in Spotted Owls, a number of key questions need to be addressed, such as:

1. *What is Spotted Owl habitat?* Older coniferous forest has always been considered synonymous with Spotted Owl habitat but recent studies suggest other vegetation types and landscape attributes may contribute to Spotted Owl habitat as well. Before habitat fragmentation can be assessed and understood, habitat must be properly defined (Franklin et al. *this volume*). In addition, definitions of Spotted Owl habitat can only be achieved

when the mechanisms behind the importance of various components are understood. This probably can only be achieved through analysis of empirical data (particularly of replicated studies) followed by carefully controlled experiments.

2. *Can Northern Spotted Owls and California Spotted Owls maintain viable populations under the same range-wide fragmentation as Mexican Spotted Owls?* While preliminary information on juvenile dispersal, a key process in the effects of fragmentation at the range-wide scale, is available for Northern and Mexican Spotted Owls, this information is still lacking for California Spotted Owls (Verner et al. 1992). In addition, there have been no long-term studies of juvenile dispersal specifically designed to examine the effects of heterogeneity and fragmentation.

3. *Do landscape configurations within subpopulations have the same effect as they do at the territory scale?* This question relates to habitat quality at a population scale, similar to the findings of Franklin et al. (2000) at the territory scale; that is, whether populations can be represented as meta-populations, source/sink populations, etc., with respect to fragmentation and heterogeneity. For example, populations of Spotted Owls may be able to maintain stationary populations in fragmented landscape, but are they bolstered by outside recruitment?

4. *Is timber harvesting compensatory or additive with natural disturbance regimes, such as fire?* Since fire suppression, timber harvesting has become the dominant disturbance causing fragmentation and heterogeneity on landscapes occupied by Spotted Owls. To be completely compensatory, timber harvesting activities would have to impact forests in the same manner as fire, and to be completely additive, timber harvest would have to impact the landscape in a manner very different from fire. Aside from any geochemical differences, the effects of timber harvesting on the landscape probably lie somewhere between these two extremes. Here, we use the terms compensatory and additive similarly to those used in waterfowl harvest (Nichols et al. 1984). The degree to which timber harvest and fire disturbance affect landscapes occupied by Spotted Owls is crucial to understanding land management options and potential strategies. For example, Weatherspoon et al. (1992) argue that a management policy of allowing forest succession to proceed uninterrupted by periodic natural disturbance would likely lead to habitat degradation for California Spotted Owls rather than toward biologically healthy and diverse systems. Rather, they argue management should use natural processes as a guide to management.

RECOMMENDATIONS FOR FUTURE ANALYSES OF FRAGMENTATION EFFECTS ON SPOTTED OWLS

Given the limitations with extant data on studies of fragmentation/landscape characteristics of Spotted Owls we encountered, we recommend the following:

1. Development of stronger theoretical/analytical basis for studies of fragmentation using simulation to understand how fragmentation indices relate to actual landscape configurations (Li and Reynolds 1994).
2. Testing of predictions from simulation models with empirical studies and exposition of explicit predictions from simulation models to allow for such empirical testing.
3. Linkage of useful landscape metrics with life history traits, particularly survival, reproduction, and juvenile dispersal.
4. Inclusion of alternative hypotheses that include a range of effects from positive to negative in terms of fragmentation and heterogeneity.
5. Reporting of mean and standard deviations of landscape metrics used to characterize Spotted Owl habitats.
6. Consistent reporting of useful metrics even if other, better techniques are developed (i.e., researchers should continue to use a baseline of metrics even if they use novel or additional metrics). This has become standard practice with studies of Spotted Owl home range where the Minimum Convex Polygon is consistently used in addition to other estimators even though scientists recognize that it is often biased.
7. Peer referees and editors should recognize the utility and necessity of publishing studies replicating earlier research on the same topic. Clearly, higher standards can be incorporated into replicated studies by sample size requirements (subsequent studies should have a larger or "better" sample than earlier studies), and geographic representation of sampling (studies in areas where there have not been studies previously executed).

We believe that these few recommendations will lead to stronger inference regarding the effect of habitat fragmentation on Spotted Owls. Further, we think these recommendations may serve to advance the understanding of fragmentation on other bird species and the effects of fragmentation on species in general.

ACKNOWLEDGMENTS

We thank T. L. George, D. Dobkin, and J. T. Rotenberry for their editorial contributions. K. McKelvey and J. B. Dunning provided thoughtful reviews. Funding was provided by the U.S. Forest Service, Region 5 (Contract FS 53-91S8-00-EC14).

APPENDIX 1

META-ANALYSIS AND HABITAT METRICS

For each metric measured in each study, we estimated an effect size (d) as:

$$\hat{d} = \frac{\bar{x}_o - \bar{x}_r}{\hat{S}}$$

(Hunter and Schmidt 1990:271) where $\bar{x}_o$ and $\bar{x}_r$ are the estimated mean from occupied and random sites, respectively, and $\hat{S}$ is the estimated pooled standard deviation, calculated as:

$$\hat{S} = \sqrt{\frac{(n_o - 1)(\hat{S}_o)^2 + (n_r - 1)(\hat{S}_r)^2}{n_o + n_r - 2}}$$

(Hunter and Schmidt 1990:271) where n_o, n_r, $\hat{S}_o$, and $\hat{S}_r$ are the sample sizes and standard deviations, respectively, for occupied and random sites within each study. In one case (Lemkuhl and Raphael 1993), standard deviations were not available so we estimated effect size between metrics from reported F-statistics (Wolf 1986:35) as:

$$\hat{d} = \frac{2\sqrt{F}}{\sqrt{df_{error}}}.$$

The sampling variance for $\hat{d}$ was estimated (Hunter and Schmidt 1990) as:

$$\widehat{var}(\hat{d}) = \left(\frac{n_o + n_r - 1}{n_o + n_r - 3}\right)\left(\frac{4}{n_o + n_r}\right)\left(1 + \frac{\hat{d}^2}{8}\right)$$

We estimated a cumulative effect size ($\hat{\bar{d}}$; sensu Rosenberg et al. 2000) across studies as:

$$\hat{\bar{d}} = \frac{\sum_{i=1}^{k} w_i \hat{d}_i}{\sum_{i=1}^{k} w_i} \tag{1}$$

where k is the number of studies, $\hat{d}_i$ is the effect size for the kth study, and $w_i = 1/[\hat{\sigma}^2_{process} + \widehat{var}(\hat{d})]$ and the sampling variance for $\bar{d}$ as:

$$\widehat{var}(\hat{\bar{d}}) = \frac{1}{\sum_{i=1}^{k} w_i} \tag{2}$$

after Burnham et al. (1987:260–266). In this analysis, we partitioned process variance ($\sigma^2_{process}$; the variation across studies) in each metric from the sampling variance associated with estimating the $\hat{d}$ for each study. We estimated process variation by iteratively solving:

$$\frac{1}{n-1} \sum_{i=1}^{n} \left(\frac{1}{\sigma^2_{process} + \widehat{var}(\hat{d}_i)}\right)(\hat{d}_i - \hat{\bar{d}})^2 = 1 \tag{3}$$

after Burnham et al. (1987:260–266). Equations (1) and (2) were solved simultaneously with equation (3) to obtain $\hat{\bar{d}}$ and $\widehat{var}(\hat{\bar{d}})$. These procedures were similar to those proposed by Rosenberg et al. (2000) for random effects modeling of d. To assess the spatial variability in metrics across studies, we used a coefficient of process variation ($CV_{process}$) estimates as:

$$CV_{process} = \frac{\hat{\sigma}_{process}}{\hat{\bar{d}}}.$$

TABLE A1. DATA USED IN META-ANALYSIS

Source	Subspecies	Province[a]	Radius[b] (m)	Grain[c] (ha)	Occupied			Random			Effect size		
					$\bar{x}_o$	S_o	n_o	$\bar{x}_r$	S_r	n_r	$\hat{d}$	$\widehat{\mathrm{var}}(\hat{d})$	95% CI
AMOUNT OF MATURE AND OLD-GROWTH FOREST (area [ha] of mature and old growth forest within the circular samples)													
Lehmkuhl and Raphael 1993	Northern	WA-OLY	3218	1.00	1100.0	—	59	1714.0	—	100	0.405	0.026	0.089, 0.721
Ripple et al. 1991b	Northern	OR-CAS	910	0.56	203.4	30.7	30	164.4	52.6	30	0.907	0.076	0.366, 1.447
Johnson 1992	Northern	OR-CAS	1261	0.56	301.9	94.3	103	266.3	103.7	70	0.362	0.024	0.060, 0.664
Meyer et al. 1998	Northern	OR-W	800	0.25	96.3	58.8	50	49.7	47.3	50	0.874	0.045	0.460, 1.289
Ripple et al. 1997	Northern	OR-SW	1200	0.02	150.8	99.9	20	54.3	71.1	20	1.112	0.122	0.429, 1.796
Hunter et al. 1995	Northern	CA	800	0.09	94.1	26.2	33	71.8	28.1	50	0.815	0.053	0.362, 1.268
Morganti 1993	Northern	OR-S	1951	0.81	609.6	117.2	34	463.8	216.2	32	0.845	0.068	0.334, 1.357
Moen and Gutiérrez 1997	California	Sierras	1207	0.09	68.8	63.6	25	50.4	38.1	25	0.352	0.085	-0.218, 0.923
Peery et al. 1999	Mexican	NM	1000	0.09	64.7	59.5	40	34.1	71.5	40	0.466	0.053	0.016, 0.915
MEAN PATCH AREA (mean area of patches of mature and old-growth forest)													
Lehmkuhl and Raphael 1993	Northern	WA-OLY	3218	1.00	544.0	559.4	59	188.0	238.6	100	0.914	0.028	0.586, 1.243
Meyer et al. 1998	Northern	OR-W	800	0.25	35.1	41.7	50	8.5	14.9	50	0.849	0.045	0.436, 1.263
Ripple et al. 1997	Northern	OR-SW	2400	0.02	167.4	225.8	20	50.1	52.4	20	0.716	0.112	0.059, 1.372
CV PATCH AREA (coefficient of variation for mean area of old-conifer forest patches)													
Ripple et al. 1997	Northern	OR-SW	2400	0.02	1.19	0.54	20	0.72	0.67	20	0.772	0.113	0.113, 1.432
Lehmkuhl and Raphael 1993	Northern	WA-OLY	3218	1.00	1.94	—	59	2.02	—	100	0.071	0.025	-0.242, 0.384
PATCH DENSITY (number of patches of old-conifer forest per km²)													
Lehmkuhl and Raphael 1993	Northern	WA-OLY	3218	1.00	0.23	—	59	0.32	—	100	-0.405	0.026	-0.721, -0.089
Ripple et al. 1997	Northern	OR-SW	2400	0.02	0.31	0.31	20	0.18	0.17	20	0.520	0.109	-0.127, 1.167
INTERIOR (area [ha] of old-conifer forest remaining after subtracting a 105-m [Ripple 1997] or 100-m [Johnson 1992] wide band from the edge of each patch; Ripple et al. 1997)													
Johnson 1992	Northern	OR-CAS	1261	0.56	178.5	105.5	103	146.7	104.6	70	0.302	0.024	0.001, 0.604
Ripple et al. 1997	Northern	OR-SW	2400	0.02	214.6	216.8	20	82.1	111.6	20	0.768	0.113	0.109, 1.428
INTERIOR RATIO (proportion of all patches that are interior old-conifer forest; see Interior definition)													
Ripple et al. 1997	Northern	OR-SW	2400	0.02	0.33	0.13	20	0.17	0.16	20	1.098	0.121	0.415, 1.780
PERIMETER (perimeter [km] of mature/old-growth stands)													
Johnson 1992	Northern	OR-CAS	1261	0.56	10.38	3.65	103	10.34	4.10	70	0.010	0.023	-0.289, 0.310
PERIMETER DENSITY (km of perimeter of old-conifer forest patches divided by the amount of old-conifer forest [km²] within sample circles; referred to as Edge/Area index in Johnson 1992)													
Lehmkuhl and Raphael 1993	Northern	WA-OLY	3218	1.00	2.25	—	59	1.98	—	100	0.213	0.026	-0.101, 0.527
Ripple et al. 1997	Northern	OR-SW	2400	0.02	2.76	1.08	20	1.41	1.51	20	1.028	0.119	0.351, 1.705
Johnson 1992	Northern	OR-CAS	1261	0.56	0.04	0.03	103	0.05	0.02	70	-0.215	0.024	-0.516, 0.085
EDGE (ha of old forest within 100 m of the perimeter interior to a mature/old growth stand)													
Johnson 1992	Northern	OR-CAS	1261	0.56	123.4	41.6	103	119.6	41.0	70	0.092	0.023	-0.208, 0.392
EDGE % (percentage of total edge cells that were between Spotted Owl habitat and other habitats)													
Morganti 1993	Northern	OR-S	1951	0.81	21.6	5.6	34	18.7	6.7	32	0.471	0.064	-0.026, 0.968

TABLE A1. CONTINUED

Source	Subspecies	Province[a]	Radius[b] (m)	Grain[c] (ha)	Occupied $\bar{x}_o$	Occupied S_o	Occupied n_o	Random $\bar{x}_r$	Random S_r	Random n_r	Effect size $\hat{d}$	Effect size $\widehat{var}(\hat{d})$	Effect size 95% CI
EDGE INDEX (Patton [1975] edge index that relates the linear extent of edge for stands of a given type to the perimeter of a circle derived from the area of stands [circles have least perimeter for a given area]; values range from 1, indicating no increase in edge, to >1 indicating proportional increase in edge over that of a circle).													
Lehmkuhl and Raphael 1993	Northern	WA-OLY	3218	1.00	5.22	—	59	5.68	—	100	0.174	0.026	-0.140, 0.487
EDGE/AREA RATIO (index of the proportional deviation of the amount of edge around old-growth patches from the amount of edge expected for old-growth patches containing that much area; values ranged from <0, indicating more edge than expected to >0, indicating less edge than expected for the area of old growth present)													
Meyer et al. 1998	Northern	OR-W	800	0.25	1.03	0.21	50	1.02	0.16	50	0.022	0.041	-0.374, 0.418
PERIMETER/AREA FRACTAL (fractal index based on O'Neill et al. 1988)													
Lehmkuhl and Raphael 1993	Northern	WA-OLY	3218	1.00	1.28	—	59	1.25	—	100	0.160	0.026	-0.154, 0.473
FRACTAL DIMENSION (fractal dimension of all successional stages; values ranged from 1, indicating square patches, to 2, indicating highly convoluted patch perimeters).													
Meyer et al 1998	Northern	OR-W	800	0.25	1.29	0.07	50	1.31	0.07	50	-0.325	0.041	-0.724, 0.073
NEIGHBORHOOD INDEX (index of owl habitat availability within the daily foraging range of an owl; values ranged from 0 to 1)													
Lehmkuhl and Raphael 1993	Northern	WA-OLY	3218	1.00	0.50	0.27	59	0.32	0.22	100	0.751	0.027	0.427, 1.075
DISPERSION SCORE (relative index of how clumped [minimum fragmentation] or dispersed [maximum fragmentation] old-forest stands were distributed; values ranged from −1500, indicating maximally dispersed forest stands, to 1500, indicating maximum clumping of old forest)													
Johnson 1992	Northern	OR-CAS	1261	0.56	-168.0	162.4	103	-153.0	133.9	70	-0.099	0.023	-0.399, 0.201
GISFRAG INDEX (the mean distance to the nearest old-conifer forest patch from each grid cell in the sample area based on Ripple et al. [1991a]; values ranged from near 0, indicating more old-conifer forest patches and shorter distances between patches, to high values, indicating fewer old-conifer forest patches, less connectivity, and longer distances between patches; Hunter et al. [1995] and Lemkuhl and Raphael [1993] used modified version of this index)													
Ripple et al. 1997	Northern	OR-SW	2400	0.02	373.00	272.00	20	1331.0	1079.0	20	-1.218	0.125	-1.91, 0.525
Hunter et al. 1995	Northern	CA	800	0.09	26.30	12.60	33	39.70	27.30	50	-0.591	0.052	-1.036, 0.146
Lehmkuhl and Raphael 1993	Northern	WA-OLY	3218	1.00	0.032	—	59	0.084	—	100	-0.329	0.026	-0.644, -0.014
TAYLOR INDEX (Taylor [1977] index of patchiness that is the probability of encountering a different successional stage when traveling from 1 raster cell to the next along the vertical and horizontal center of the raster map; values ranged from 0, indicating only 1 successional stage encountered, to 1, indicating no 2 adjacent grid points along the axes had the same successional stage)													
Meyer et al. 1998	Northern	OR-W	800	0.25	0.11	0.04	50	0.01	0.05	50	0.304	0.041	-0.095, 0.702
SIMPSON'S INDEX (Simpson [1949] diversity index that provides a measure of vegetation stand and seral stage heterogeneity; values range from 0, indicating highest diversity to 1, indicating no diversity)													
Hunter et al. 1995	Northern	CA	800	0.09	0.64	0.09	33	0.69	0.06	50	-0.690	0.054	-1.147, -0.233
Peery et al. 1999	Mexican	NM	1000	0.09	0.48	0.13	40	0.58	0.13	40	-0.791	0.055	-1.251, -0.331
SHANNON-WIENER DIVERSITY INDEX (combines information on the number of successional stages [s] with evenness of their percent representation; values range from near 0, indicating dominance by one successional stage, to $\log_e[s]$, indicating all successional stages were equally represented; maximum value was $\log_e[7] = 1.95$ and $\log_e [3] = 1.10$ for Meyer et al. [1998] and Morganti [1993], respectively)													
Meyer et al. 1998	Northern	OR-W	800	0.25	1.25	0.25	50	1.05	0.37	50	0.629	0.043	0.224, 1.003
Morganti 1993	Northern	OR-S	1951	0.81	0.96	0.10	34	0.97	0.10	32	-0.109	0.061	-0.593, 0.374

TABLE A1. CONTINUED

Source	Subspecies	Province[a]	Radius[b] (m)	Grain[c] (ha)	Occupied			Random			Effect size		
					$\bar{x}_o$	S_o	n_o	$\bar{x}_r$	S_r	n_r	$\hat{d}$	$\widehat{\mathrm{var}}(\hat{d})$	95% CI
DOMINANCE (scaled index of dominance of forest successional stages; values range from 0, indicating equal representation of all successional stages or vegetation types, to 1, indicating complete dominance by a single seral stage or vegetation type)													
Meyer et al. 1998	Northern	OR-W	800	0.25	0.19	0.11	50	0.30	0.19	50	-0.706	0.043	-1.114, -0.298
Morganti 1993	Northern	OR-S	1951	0.81	0.51	0.05	34	0.50	0.05	32	0.116	0.063	-0.374, 0.607
BAXTER AND WOLF INDEX (count of changes in vegetation along 2 perpendicular transects; Baxter and Wolf 1972)													
Moen and Gutiérrez 1997	California	Sierra	1207	0.09	18.24	4.25	25	23.60	5.08	25	-1.145	0.097	-1.757, -0.533
Bias and Gutiérrez 1992	California	Sierra	1000	0.09	3.85	1.23	52	4.99	2.21	760	-0.529	0.021	-0.812, -0.245
CONTAGION (scaled index of the patchiness of successional stages and vegetation types; values range from 0, indicating numerous small patches, to 1, indicating few, large patches)													
Meyer et al. 1998	Northern	OR-W	800	0.25	0.76	0.07	50	0.79	0.09	50	-0.378	0.042	-0.778, 0.022
Morganti 1993	Northern	OR-S	1951	0.81	0.95	0.01	34	0.93	0.01	32	1.766	0.087	1.189, 2.344

[a] WA = Washington, OR = Oregon, CA = California, NM = New Mexico, OLY = Olympia, CAS = Cascades, W = western, SW = southwestern, S = southern.
[b] Radius of the circle used to define occupied and random sites.
[c] Resolution of smallest patch.

Studies in Avian Biology No. 25:221–235, 2002.

EFFECTS OF FOREST FRAGMENTATION ON POPULATIONS OF THE MARBLED MURRELET

Martin G. Raphael, Diane Evans Mack, John M. Marzluff, and John M. Luginbuhl

Abstract. The Marbled Murrelet (*Brachyramphus marmoratus*) is a threatened seabird that nests on branches of large trees within older coniferous forest in coastal areas of the Pacific Northwest. Surveys suggest that murrelets often nest in continuous stands of mature, complexly structured forest but they also nest in younger forest and in stands varying in size from several to thousands of hectares. We examined how murrelet abundance and reproduction are related to the amount and pattern of nesting habitat at regional, watershed, landscape, and nest site scales. At the regional scale, abundance of murrelets, estimated from offshore surveys, was found to be correlated with amount of nesting habitat in some areas and to a lesser extent with fragmentation of that habitat. We found a similar pattern at the watershed scale. At the scale of nest sites and surrounding landscapes, fragmentation may have greater effect on likelihood of nesting and nest success. Observations of active nests from other studies indicated high failure rates (47 of 71 nests with known outcomes), mostly due to predation (33 of 47 nests). Corvids have been implicated as primary predators. Forest fragmentation can affect the abundance and distribution of corvids, and thus it is possible that fragmentation might lead to higher rates of predation on murrelet nests. Over the past 5 years we have tested this assumption in Washington using artificial nests located in stands of varying structural complexity, levels of fragmentation, and proximity to human activity. Results indicate, first, that a broad suite of predators, including at least 10 mammalian and avian species, prey on simulated eggs and chicks. Second, rates of predation are higher within 50 m of forest edge, but this relationship varies with proximity to human activity and with the structure of the adjacent regenerating forest. Predation increased with proximity to forest edges when the matrix contained human settlements and recreation areas, but not when it was dominated by regenerating forests. Abundance of some predators (e.g., Steller's Jays, *Cyanocitta stelleri*) was greater in more fragmented landscapes, but abundance of other potential predators (e.g., Gray Jays, *Perisoreus canadensis*) was greater in continuous forests, making generalizations about the effects of fragmentation difficult. Research is needed to understand how fragmentation affects both murrelet nest site selection and the risk of nest predation so that managers can provide landscapes able to support large populations of successfully breeding murrelets.

Key Words: *Brachyramphus marmoratus*; corvid; fragmentation; Marbled Murrelet; nesting habitat; nest predation; nest success.

Forest fragmentation has been implicated as an important factor affecting the status and trend of the Marbled Murrelet (*Brachyramphus marmoratus*; U.S. Fish and Wildlife Service 1997a). Forest fragmentation is the process of subdividing continuous forest patches into smaller pieces. In forests of the Pacific Northwest, timber cutting primarily drives this process. For species associated with older forest structures, fragmentation of old-growth habitat leads to a reduction in amount of that habitat as well as a change in its pattern on the landscape. The Marbled Murrelet is unique among other species considered in this volume, as it uses forest patches for nesting but not foraging. It feeds and resides on marine waters for most of the year but nests on large limbs primarily in older forest patches. Therefore, the potential effects of forest fragmentation are limited to those that might affect probability of nesting, nesting success, and survival of adults in transit to or attending nests. For this species, fragmentation will not affect foraging behavior or foraging success. In this paper, we review the potential effects of forest

fragmentation on the murrelet and describe recent experimental evidence of its effects.

BIOLOGY OF THE MARBLED MURRELET

It is important to understand the biology of the Marbled Murrelet as a prelude to reviewing fragmentation effects. The Marbled Murrelet is a small seabird of the family Alcidae whose summer distribution along the Pacific coast of North America extends from the Aleutian Islands of Alaska to Santa Cruz, California. It forages primarily on small fish in the nearshore (0–5 km) marine environment. Unlike other alcids, which nest in colonies on the ground or in burrows at the marine-terrestrial interface, Marbled Murrelets nest solitarily and most often in large trees in coniferous forests, traveling up to ~100 km inland to reach suitable habitat. A small proportion of the Alaska population nests on the ground (Mendenhall 1992, Piatt and Naslund 1995). Tree-nesting Marbled Murrelets do not build a nest, but use a natural platform on which to place their single egg. Both adults share equally in incubation, exchanging once every 24 hr (Nelson and Peck 1995). A few days after hatching the chick is left alone at the nest for the duration of the 30–40 d nestling period, with adults making feeding visits, primarily at dawn and dusk (Nelson and Peck 1995, Nelson 1997). Due to population declines attributed to loss of mature and old-growth forest from logging, low nest success, and mortality at sea, this species was federally listed as threatened in Washington, Oregon, and California in 1992 (U.S. Fish and Wildlife Service 1997a) and is listed as threatened in British Columbia.

The Marbled Murrelet's unusual nesting habitat and secretive behavior during the nesting season kept it one of the least known North American birds of the latter 20th century. The first nest was not discovered on this continent until 1974 (Binford et al. 1975), and many aspects of this species' ecology, at sea and inland, are still unclear. However, in the last 10 years relatively consistent information has emerged on the association of Marbled Murrelets with older coniferous forests and on stand attributes correlated with murrelet activity and nesting. Across the range, sites with the highest likelihood of nesting murrelets have larger trees, more potential nest platforms, and/or greater moss cover on tree limbs than other sites (Grenier and Nelson 1995, Hamer 1995, Kuletz et al. 1995). Nest trees are larger on average than adjacent trees (often the largest tree within a 25–50 m radius), contain more platforms with greater cover than surrounding trees, and often have moderate to heavy epiphyte cover (Jordan and Hughes 1995, Kerns and Miller 1995, Naslund et al. 1995, Manley 1999). Nest trees are often near natural or human-created gaps in the canopy that murrelets use to access nests (Hamer and Nelson 1995, Jordan and Hughes 1995, Kerns and Miller 1995, Naslund et al. 1995, Manley 1999). Large limbs (mean diameter = 32 cm), deformities from mistletoe and other disease, damage, and moss cover create suitable nesting platforms, and these features are most often found in older forests. However, murrelet sites also have been recorded in young (60–70 yr) forests with residual old-growth trees or heavy mistletoe infestations (Nelson 1997). Suitable habitat generally occurs at <1,000 m elevation, as floristics at higher elevations lack the structural features that provide platforms. Manley (1999), however, found nests at elevations up to 1,260 m in the Bunster Range of British Columbia. Older forests at lower elevations had been heavily logged by the time of this study, but it is unknown if nests occurred at higher elevations prior to logging.

Presumably, Marbled Murrelet nesting habitat associations evolved under a regime of large ex-

panses of old-growth conifer forests on the landscape. Wildfire was the primary disturbance agent prior to the 1800s (Agee 1993); extensive, high intensity but low frequency (150–300 yr) fires resulted in large areas of old forest (Garmen et al. 1999). Reduction in extent of old forest in the Pacific Northwest due to logging over the past 100 yr has been implicated in the decline of murrelet populations through reductions in available nesting habitat (Ralph et al. 1995). Loss of conifer forest within the inland limits of the Marbled Murrelet range has been extensive, but actual percentages based on area are difficult to extract from the literature. An estimated 30% of coastal forest remains in British Columbia (Perry 1995). As a site-specific example, 15–25% of old-growth forest in Clayoquot Sound, British Columbia, was logged during 1954–1993, most from low-elevation, large-volume western hemlock forest (Kelson et al. 1995). During the period 1982–1993, the murrelet population declined 40% in Clayoquot Sound, likely as a result of loss of nesting habitat. In western Washington and Oregon, roughly 18% of old-growth forests that occurred before logging remained by the early 1980s (Booth 1991); 5–10% of old-growth redwood forest from the early 1800s remains in California (Carter and Erickson 1992, De Angelos and De Angelos 1998).

POTENTIAL EFFECTS OF HABITAT FRAGMENTATION

Loss of coniferous forests in the Pacific Northwest may affect Marbled Murrelet nesting habitat in multiple ways, including overall decrease in the amount of habitat available and fragmentation of remaining habitat into smaller, discontinuous patches with potentially greater influence of edge phenomena. Edge effects include changes in microclimate at open edges compared with interior sites (Chen et al. 1995, 1999), changes in vegetative species, and changes in predator-prey dynamics (Kremsater and Bunnell 1999). Most studies have difficulty separating the effects of habitat loss, per se, from fragmentation, because habitat loss is a necessary consequence of fragmentation (Fahrig 1999). Fragmentation will lead to reduced area of habitat, including reduced amount of interior habitat, increased number of patches of habitat, reduced sizes of patches, increased amount of edge, and increased isolation of patches. These conditions, in turn, could affect overall population size, likelihood of nesting, survival of adults, and nesting success. These effects could differ over the short run versus the long run. For example, in the short run (say, 10 years), loss and fragmentation of habitat could cause displaced murrelets to locate in remaining patches, nest in marginally suitable habitat, or travel greater distances to locate new, disjunct sites (Divoky and Horton 1995). Although dispersal and colonization mechanisms are unknown, we speculate that if murrelets moved into remaining available habitat, nesting success in marginal or overcrowded habitat may decline over the long run, leading to smaller populations and lower nesting density. In the following sections, we review the evidence for these potential effects over a variety of geographic scales.

REVIEW OF FRAGMENTATION EFFECTS AT MULTIPLE SCALES

REGIONAL SCALE

In a review of Marbled Murrelet population changes, Ralph (1994) observed that, at a broad scale, the species' distribution on the water generally corresponded to amounts of inland old-growth forest. In California and Oregon, the marine distribution was thought to reflect remaining older forests, mostly on federal lands (reviewed by Ralph et al. 1995), with gaps in distribution on the water where older forests no longer occur. This relationship was less evident in Washington and British Columbia, but a systematic comparison of density of murrelets with density of adjacent nesting habitat has not been reported. In Alaska, breeding season concentrations generally coincided with the distribution of coastal old-growth coniferous forest (Piatt and Ford 1993). One exception was Cook Inlet, where there was an abundance of forest cover but few murrelets. The lack of correspondence in this region was explained by poor foraging conditions in Cook Inlet and a dominance of black spruce in the forest cover, which lacks the structural characteristics shared by nest trees.

To examine relationships between offshore numbers of Marbled Murrelets and amount of inland habitat in Washington and Oregon, we compared available vegetation information to published and unpublished murrelet data. As no consistent vegetation map layer was available for both states, we used different datasets but selected for similar attributes as much as possible (see Appendix for details). In Washington, we used a vegetation layer compiled from a number of sources (U.S. Fish and Wildlife Service 1997b). From this we selected late seral habitat (mixed conifer and hardwood, with >70% crown closure of conifer and >10% crown closure from trees >53 cm dbh) to represent potential Marbled Murrelet nesting habitat. At-sea data were summarized from midsummer nearshore (0–400 m) surveys conducted by the Washington Department of Fish and Wildlife in 1997 (C. Thompson, unpubl. data). For Oregon we used a Landsat-based vegetation

map produced by the Western Oregon Digital Image Project (Nighbert et al., unpubl. data). We selected multi-storied stands with mean dbh >48 cm and single-storied stands with mean dbh >74 cm within the Sitka spruce zone (*Picea sitchensis*; Franklin and Dyrness 1973). At-sea data were averaged over 2-km segments from July 1996 nearshore (0–500 m) surveys (C. Strong, unpubl. data). North-south bands were established along the coast based on how the at-sea data were summarized (WA) or to represent approximately 50-km stretches of coastline (OR). Inland boundaries followed Recovery Plan (U.S. Fish and Wildlife Service 1997a) zones (80 km in WA, 56 km in OR), and we established an elevation cutoff of 1,067 m. Habitat was summarized per band as total habitat within the band; murrelet data were summarized as a relative estimate of total numbers of murrelets counted within the band.

We found no correlation between murrelet abundance and estimated amount of nesting habitat at the broad scale over the entire two-state region (Spearman correlation = 0.07, one-tailed $P = 0.391$, $N = 17$ bands; Fig. 1). As summarized in Figure 1, habitat seemed to be most abundant on the Olympic Peninsula of Washington and in southern Oregon. Murrelet abundances were greater in the far northern band of Washington and the central bands of Oregon. Because of the differences in habitat maps between the two states and the perception that relationships between at-sea distributions and inland habitat are not as evident in Washington (Ralph et al. 1995), we also computed correlations for Oregon alone. In that analysis, the correlation was very weak (Spearman correlation = 0.37, one-tailed $P = 0.132$, $N = 11$). Meyer (1999) has argued that habitat closer to shore (within about 25 km) may be more important than habitat further away. In fact, the small concentrations of murrelets off the coast of northern Oregon in 1992 were associated with state parks with old-growth stands near the coast (Strong 1995). Restricting the analysis to habitat within 25 km of shore, the correlations improved slightly (for both states, Spearman correlation = 0.38, one-tailed $P = 0.066$, $N = 17$; for Oregon alone, correlation = 0.38, $P = 0.126$, $N = 11$). We caution that this assessment was conducted at a very broad scale, using indices for habitat and at-sea abundance. Results were entirely a function of the vegetation layer used for mapping, the specific at-sea data used (dates of surveys, single vs. multi-year data, nearshore transects vs. all transects), and the north-south bands we defined. The offshore abundance of murrelets does seem to have a consistent pattern, as the at-sea distribution we depicted for Oregon

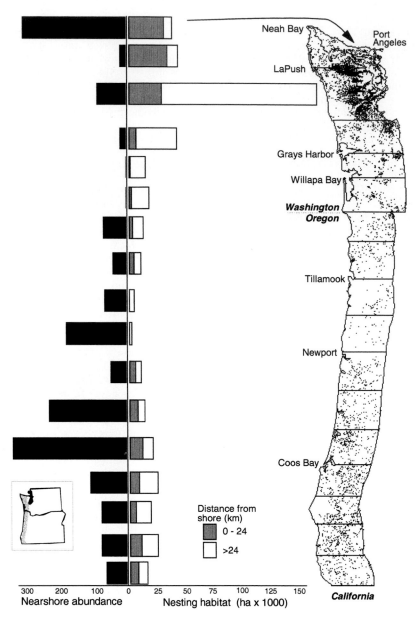

FIGURE 1.   Relative abundance of Marbled Murrelets in nearshore waters within geographic bands of Oregon and Washington in relation to amount of potential nesting habitat (represented as dark polygons on map). Bars represent relative magnitudes in each zone (topmost pair of bars corresponds to northernmost habitat band). Dark bars on the habitat histogram represent habitat within 24 km of the coast; open bars represent remaining inland habitat. See text and Appendix for details and sources of data.

(based on our reanalysis of a subset of C. Strong's data) was very similar to the murrelet distribution he reported for 1992 (Strong 1995, Strong et al. 1995). More refined estimates of murrelet density and available habitat will be forthcoming from various scientists as part of an ongoing murrelet monitoring program. Specifi-

cally, it will be important to obtain consistent estimates of murrelet numbers over the whole region and to develop a more reliable estimate of the amount of nesting habitat using the same sources of data and analytical techniques across all sites.

Meyer (1999) conducted a more quantitative

spatial analysis for southern Oregon and northern California. Within nine 212,000–650,000 ha subregions along the coast, greatest marine densities of murrelets were found offshore of large blocks of consolidated old-growth forest within a matrix of relatively abundant medium-sized, second-growth coniferous or hardwood forests. In subregions with few murrelets, patches of nesting habitat were relatively small, simple-shaped, and scattered. Offshore densities were higher in subregions with more continuous old growth or old growth combined with residual old-growth forest. In fact, this study found that inland habitat variables explained most of the offshore distribution in this region, with marine variables, such as type of shoreline, chlorophyll counts, and sea surface temperature, accounting for little variation (we note, however, that prey densities were not included in her analysis).

WATERSHED SCALE

Several studies have explored relationships between forest landscape patterns and murrelet activity at the watershed scale. On the Olympic Peninsula, Washington, 10 large drainages were sampled with radar for 1–3 yr to compare the numbers of murrelets flying into each drainage with the amount and configuration of habitat available (Raphael et al. 1999, 2002; see Cooper et al. 1991, Hamer et al. 1995, and Burger 1997 for details on the use of radar to sample birds). Mobile radar units were stationed within drainages where the natural topography funneled murrelets flying inland. Late-seral habitat (defined as >70% crown closure with at least 10% from trees >53 cm dbh) occurring below 1,067 m was considered potentially suitable habitat. Late-seral habitat was 1 of 10 land cover types derived from satellite imagery classification (U.S. Fish and Wildlife Service 1997b). In 2000, a year with the largest sample of drainages (N = 10), the maximum number of murrelets detected flying inland was highly correlated with the amount of potentially suitable habitat after accounting for drainage size (partial correlation = 0.86, P = 0.003; Raphael et al. 1999, 2002).

Similar results were found in Clayoquot Sound, Vancouver Island, British Columbia, from 18 watersheds sampled 3 yr with radar. Dawn and dusk radar counts were positively correlated with the size of the drainage and the amount of mature forest, with the strongest correlations between dawn counts and mature forest below 600 m (Burger 2001). In multiple regression models, 60–73% of the variation in dawn counts of murrelets among watersheds was explained by the area of mature forest at elevations <600 m, with another 8% explained by the negative effect of the combined area of logged and immature (<160 yr) forest. In a different study on Vancouver Island, which used audio-visual detections from human observers, there were significantly fewer detections (mean detections per point) in watersheds with <50% old growth compared with those with >50% (Burger 1995).

Whereas relationships between murrelet counts and overall amount of available habitat were strong across studies, relationships with the spatial configuration of habitat at this watershed scale were less revealing. For the Olympic Peninsula study, we used our map of potential nesting habitat and the program FRAGSTATS (McGarigal and Marks 1995) to define patches of potential habitat (a patch is a set of adjacent habitat pixels). We then computed a number of fragmentation metrics and tested whether radar counts of murrelets were correlated with these metrics. Radar counts were not significantly correlated with the density (number/100 ha) of late-seral patches below 1,067 m, average size of patches, or a patchiness index that described a continuum from many small patches to few large patches (Raphael et al. 2002). These results were preliminary and may have been biased somewhat by the artificial patch boundaries created by the elevation cut-off, and by the limitations of the base vegetation map.

NESTING NEIGHBORHOOD

Two studies have examined the spatial characteristics of murrelet habitat within the neighborhood of nest sites, at a landscape scale intermediate between watersheds and nest sites. Both studies found that forest-cover attributes could be useful predictors of murrelet occupancy at the neighborhood scale. Habitat features within 200-ha analysis circles (N = 261) were described around locations occupied and unoccupied by murrelets on the Olympic Peninsula (Raphael et al. 1995). "Occupied" locations were those where behaviors that have been associated with nesting were observed; "unoccupied" locations had no murrelet detections. Locations were screened to include only those surveyed to the Pacific Seabird Group's (PSG) protocol (Ralph et al. 1994). Within the 200-ha circular neighborhoods centered on occupied locations, there was significantly greater area in large sawtimber and old-growth forest compared with neighborhoods centered on locations with no detections. Old growth (but not large sawtimber) occurred in larger patches (mean = 18.6 ha) in "occupied" relative to "no detection" (mean = 8.5 ha) neighborhoods. A landscape pattern index, derived from a combination of variables including number of patches, Shannon's and Simpson's diversity and evenness indices, contagion, and amount of edge (computed using program

FRAGSTATS; see Raphael et al. 1995), differed significantly between occupied and unoccupied neighborhoods. Neighborhoods surrounding occupied locations had a higher landscape pattern index, indicating greater number of patches, greater variety of patch types, smaller average sizes of all patches, and greater amounts of edge. Thus, occupied neighborhoods had more intact patches of old forest but other forest classes within these neighborhoods tended to be patchier and more fragmented. The authors cautioned that the sample of survey locations was somewhat biased, weighted by one intensive study and placed at prospective timber sales.

With a similar approach in northern California and southern Oregon, Meyer (1999) used several map sources and four neighborhood sizes (50–3,217 ha circles) centered on survey stations. Stations with no detections were screened to ensure that they or the stand they were in met the PSG protocol. Analysis circles encompassing more than one station received the highest status of all stations. In general across map layers, there was more old growth, it occurred in larger patches, and was less fragmented in occupied compared with unoccupied locations. The presence of high-contrast edges (natural or clearcuts) did not deter use of a site. In the California portion of the study area, 50-ha neighborhoods were always occupied if they contained >20% old growth with >6% of that as core area (>100 m from an edge), ≥12% of the area in one large patch, a mean patch size ≥11 ha, and mean core area >3 ha.

In support of the influence of habitat fragmentation on murrelet nesting activity, a map of relatively unfragmented old-growth forest in northern California and southern Oregon from the late 1980s was predictive of the current locations of occupied sites (75% correctly predicted in the coast redwood zone of northern California; Meyer 1999). Areas highly fragmented before the late 1980s generally didn't support murrelets in the early 1990s.

NEST SITES

Murrelet nests are difficult to locate, and the sample of active nests on which to assess effects of forest fragmentation on nest fate is relatively small. Early data from small samples from several locations indicated extremely high failure rates and high rates of predation, an interpretation that has been tempered somewhat by larger sample sizes. For example, 100% of 7 nests with known outcome failed in Alaska, 3–4 of which may have been due to predation (Naslund et al. 1995). In Oregon, 6 of 9 (67%) nests failed, with 5 of the 6 failures from predation (Nelson and Peck 1995). Based on the most comprehensive

compilation of nest results to date (9 nests from Alaska, 31 from British Columbia, 4 from Washington, 17 from Oregon, and 10 from California), 66% of 71 nests with known outcome have failed, and 70% of these failures were due to predation (Manley and Nelson 1999). Overall failure rates (not predation only) were similar among the states with larger sample sizes—61% in B.C., 63% in Oregon, and 70% in California—although Alaska nests had complete reproductive failure. Predation rates (% of total nests lost to predation) were more variable but increased from northern to southern latitude—33% in Alaska, 48% in B.C., 53% in Oregon, and 60% in California.

For the subsample of nests from Oregon and B.C., distance to edge (roads, clearcuts) was the most important predictor of nest fate. Successful nests were significantly further from edges ($\bar{X}$ = 141 m) than failed nests ($\bar{X}$ = 56 m, P = 0.02). Nest failure, and predation, were highest within 50 m of an edge compared with >50 m. All nests >150 m from an edge were successful or failed from reasons other than predation.

While there was a trend (P = 0.12) for successful nests in Oregon and British Columbia to occur in larger stands ($\bar{X}$ = 491 ha) compared with unsuccessful nests ($\bar{X}$ = 281 ha), the relatively limited sample of murrelet nests precludes a reliable region-wide analysis of the relationship between stand size and reproductive success. Marbled Murrelet nests and occupied sites have been found in stands ranging in size from 2–565 ha, but stand size is constrained in some geographic areas. For example, average nest stand size in Prince William Sound, Alaska, was smaller than other locations, but reflected what was available (3–63 ha; Naslund et al. 1995). Average stand size of nests in the Bunster Range in British Columbia was 224 ha (Manley 1999).

Changes in habitat configuration in forest landscapes to smaller patch sizes and more edge have been proposed as increasing nest failure by increasing the risk of Marbled Murrelet nests to predation. From observations at active nests, Common Ravens (Corvus corax) are known predators of Marbled Murrelet eggs and adults; Steller's Jays (Cyanocitta stelleri) are known predators of chicks and strongly-suspected predators of eggs (Nelson and Hamer 1995, Manley 1999). Other species implicated but not documented as nest predators include Gray Jay (Perisoreus canadensis), American Crow (Corvus brachyrhynchos), Great Horned Owl (Bubo virginianus), and Cooper's Hawk (Accipiter cooperi; Nelson 1997). Peregrine Falcon (Falco peregrinus), Sharp-shinned Hawk (Accipiter striatus), Northern Goshawk (Accipiter gentilis), and Red-shouldered Hawk (Buteo lineatus) have taken adult murrelets in forests (Marks and Naslund 1994, Singer et al. 1995, Nelson and Hamer 1995; E. Burkett, pers. comm.). It is theorized that adult murrelets' cryptic breeding plumage, limited visits to nests, and timing of visits to coincide with low light levels (dawn and dusk) evolved to minimize predation.

How these potential predators have responded to a changed forest landscape is the best indication of the extent to which the risk of predation at Marbled Murrelet nests has been elevated by forest fragmentation. For increased rates of predation to be linked to fragmentation, predators must increase in numbers or forage extensively along edges or small fragments; the diversity of predators must be highest at forest edges, small fragments, or in fragmented landscapes (Marzluff and Restani 1999); or predators must have greater foraging success along edges compared with interior habitats.

Corvid populations have increased in the western U.S. with increased urbanization, agricultural intensification, and human activity in forests and woodlands (Marzluff et al. 1994). Increases in American Crows, Common Ravens, and Western Scrub-Jays (*Aphelocoma californica*) are especially pronounced. Human refuse, bird feeders, lawns, and road kills appear to be fueling the corvid increase. Recreation sites have similar, but more local, effects in murrelet habitat, leading to large increases in ravens (S. Singer, pers. comm.) and crows (this study).

Several studies have demonstrated that Steller's Jays can be considered an edge species, and thus benefit from increased fragmentation of forest landscapes. In a study combining point counts with telemetry data in potential Marbled Murrelet nesting habitat on Vancouver Island, transects were established in forests and along three types of edges: roads, clearcuts, and rivers (Masselink 1999). The greatest number of jays was detected along clearcut edges, and numbers were higher at all edges compared with interior forest. Among sites sampled with audio-visual surveys along the central B.C. coast, Steller's Jays and American Crows were detected more frequently in sites fragmented by logging compared with unfragmented (unlogged) forest stands (Rodway and Regehr 1999).

However, it should be noted that Steller's Jay response to fragmentation is not unequivocal. In another coastal B.C. study, this species' abundance was not associated with patch size in remnant (left from logging) old-growth Douglas-fir/ western hemlock forest (Schieck et al. 1995). Similarly, there were no significant correlations with landscape variables, including stand size, edge, landscape composition, and patterns in the southern Washington Cascades (Lehmkuhl et al.

1991). In Douglas-fir forest in northwestern California, only 12% of ~2,500 detections were made on edges, abundance decreased with increased proximity and length of clearcut edge, and this species was not associated with the percent of clearcut or length of edge in 1,000-ha landscape blocks (Rosenberg and Raphael 1986). These studies suggest relationships between numbers of predators and fragmentation, but further work is needed to determine whether foraging efficiency of predators is affected by fragmentation.

ARTIFICIAL NEST EXPERIMENTS

METHODS

To specifically address the effects of landscape configuration on the risk of Marbled Murrelet nests to predation and the behavior of potential predators, we conducted an artificial nest experiment for five breeding seasons on the western side of the Olympic Peninsula, Washington (Marzluff et al. 1999, unpubl. data). The study area was adjacent to a major concentration of murrelets in Washington (Varoujean and Williams 1995), and in a landscape used substantially by nesting murrelets (Harrison et al. 1999). Study stands were selected in a randomized block design to investigate the effect of forest structure (simple, complex, and very complex), proximity to human activity (<1 km and >5 km), and landscape fragmentation (stands in continuous forest versus those surrounded on at least 3 sides by 1–15 yr-old regenerating forest). Effects of fragmentation were indicated by the responses of predation and corvid nest predators to: (1) the isolation of stands by regenerating forest, (2) the distance from forest edge, and (3) the interaction of proximity to human activity with stand isolation and distance from forest edge.

Artificial nests were selected for these experiments because of the extreme difficulty in locating a sufficient sample of active nests to design a rigorous experimental study. We are aware of potential biases of using artificial nests (e.g., Major and Kendal 1996, Storaas 1988, Willebrand and Marcström 1988). However, these are minimized in our case because we (1) accurately simulated murrelet nests, eggs, and chicks, and (2) limited our presence around nests (see details below). Additionally, murrelet nests are especially easy to mimic because (1) eggs are laid in simple depressions on moss-covered branches, (2) eggs are sometimes left unattended for several hours during incubation, and (3) nestlings are left alone for much of the day after they reach three days of age (Nelson and Peck 1995, Manley 1999). We explicitly discuss any biases in our use of artificial nests elsewhere (Marzluff et al. 2001, Luginbuhl et al. 2001) and show that rates of predation at our nests are higher, but not significantly higher than those at natural nests. Here we are concerned with comparing rates of nest predation among various treatments. Such comparisons are unbiased because we used the same techniques in all tests and developed ways to assess the importance of all possible nest predators in each treatment (see below).

We climbed trees to place 923 nests in 49 stands of 80- to >200-yr-old forests. We simulated nests at typical heights and locations for murrelets: on moss-covered branches with diameter >11 cm, within the live crown, >15 m above the ground, well covered from above ($\bar{X}$ % overhead cover = 84.1%, SE = 0.39, N = 923), and close to the trunk ($\bar{X}$ distance to bole = 38.9 cm, SE = 0.84, N = 923; Hamer and Nelson 1995, Singer et al. 1995).

To minimize disturbance that might cue predators to the nest's location (i.e., damage to the bark from spurs or human scent trails left from touching the bole or limbs), we climbed trees using 11-mm static climbing rope following Perry (1978); avoided contact with the tree by climbing with ascenders and rappelling to the ground; wore latex or vinyl gloves while taking measurements and preparing the nest; and marked nest trees on the ground with white plastic flagging hung in a random direction approximately 3 m from the tree (Luginbuhl et al. 2001). The entire process of climbing, placing nests, and rappelling took approximately 90 minutes.

Nests were placed in separate trees >50 m apart and only six nests were placed in a given stand at any one time to reduce the effects of area-restricted searching practiced by Common Ravens and American Crows (Marzluff and Balda 1992), and to decrease the possibility that high nest densities may cause predators to associate our activities with food rewards (Sieving 1992, Major et al. 1994). To increase sample size per stand, we replicated experiments from three to five years per stand. No nest trees were used more than one year, but annual replication allowed us to place 18–30 nests in each stand. Each year, two artificial nests (one with an egg and one with a nestling) were placed at each of three distances from the forest edge (<50 m from the edge, approximately 100 m from the edge, and >200 m from the edge).

An important improvement we made over typical artificial nest experiments was to simulate nest contents with plastic eggs and taxidermy mounts of nestlings. We painted eggs to resemble Marbled Murrelet eggs, coated them with wax (household paraffin) to aid with predator identification (Møller 1987, Haskell 1995a), and stored them in cedar chips for >12 hr prior to placement to limit human scent. Plastic eggs were slightly larger than actual Marbled Murrelet eggs (64 mm × 44 mm vs. 59.8 mm × 37.6 mm; Nelson 1997). Nestling models were made from domestic chicken chicks preserved with borax. They were dark-colored (mostly black), approximately 10 cm long, and were placed in a posture that imitated a crouched or sleeping nestling. Although decay of mounted nestlings was limited (they appeared visually unchanged after 30 d), they emitted odor perceptible to humans. However, real Marbled Murrelet nests with a well-developed fecal ring also give off odor perceptible to humans from 2 m away (T. Hamer, pers. comm.). We used eggs and chicks because (1) they represent both life history stages of murrelets vulnerable to nest predation; (2) eggs are highly attractive to corvids (Heinrich et al. 1995) and provide visual cues to their location; and (3) chicks offer olfactory cues as well as visual ones, which may better mimic a real nest and attract scent-oriented predators (Ratti and Reese 1988, Major 1991, Whelan et al. 1994, Darveau et al. 1997). We confirmed the predatory ability of small mammals detected at chick mounts with two years of experimental research (Bradley 2000; J. Bradley and J. Marzluff, unpubl. data). Mice attacked and displaced live pigeon chicks (including those capable of vigorous defense and outweighing mice ten-fold) in captivity and in the wild. Flying squirrels attacked and killed pigeon chicks in captivity. Thus, seemingly "inappropriate" mounted chicks actually accurately indicated the importance of scent-oriented nest predators in our experiments.

The fate of each nest was monitored remotely to avoid continually advertising a nest's location. A motion-sensitive radio transmitter was placed in each model; ground crews could then determine if a nestling or egg was disturbed by checking the transmitter pulse rate (similar to a standard mortality switch). We monitored nests every other day for 30 d, the approximate incubation or brooding period of Marbled Murrelets (DeSanto and Nelson 1995). Remote monitoring allowed determination of predation date (as opposed to simply noting success or failure) while limiting the amount of human presence at the nest sites. Remote monitoring also allowed us to reclimb simulated nests immediately after predation, before other predators or heat from sunlight obscured clues to predator identity left in wax. Occasionally no evidence of predation was found on eggs or chicks despite a change in pulse rate (Luginbuhl et al. 2001). When this occurred, we reset the pulse rate and continued to monitor the nest.

We used a variety of techniques to identify potential predators. In addition to eggs, transmitters inside chicks were coated with household paraffin to record marks left by predators. We monitored 82 artificial nests using 35mm cameras attached to an active infrared motion detection system (Trailmaster® Model TM 1500, Goodson and Assoc., Inc., Lenexa, KS) as described by Hernandez et al. (1997). These cameras imprint photographs with date and time, and are equipped with auto-advance, allowing photography of subsequent predators without researchers re-visiting the nest. They provide an important way to calibrate the predator identification we based on marks in wax. Nests observed with cameras were not included in the determination of predation rate (as indicated by number of days to predation).

We used Kaplan-Meier procedures to estimate the survival rate of nest contents (Pollock et al. 1989). Survival among groups was compared with the log rank test so that all measures of survivorship were weighted equally (Lee 1980). We assumed each nest was independent in survivorship analyses. This allowed us to include covariates accounting for differences in nest microsites and set-up times in the analysis. Inclusion of covariates may better illuminate differences due to design factors (Schueck and Marzluff 1995), but use of nests as experimental units may artificially inflate our sample size (and significance levels) due to pseudoreplication (Hurlbert 1984).

The relative abundance of potential avian nest predators (corvids) was determined from surveys in study stands using a modified point count procedure. These methods are detailed in Luginbuhl et al. (2001).

RESULTS

From our experiments, rates of predation in continuous stands did not differ from rates in

A. All Nests

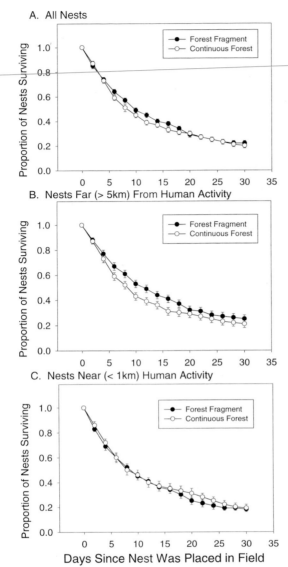

FIGURE 2. Survivorship of artificial Marbled Murrelet nests in fragmented and continuous forest, Olympic Peninsula, WA. Mean survivorship (symbols) ± 1 SE is plotted separately for (A) all forest fragments (N = 524) relative to all continuous forest (N = 399); (B) fragments (N = 249) and continuous forest (N = 179) near campgrounds and small human settlements; and (C) fragments (N = 275) and continuous forest (N = 220) far from human activity centers.

fragmented stands. Roughly 80% of nests were preyed on after 30 d, regardless of whether they were placed in forest fragments or continuous forests (Fig. 2A); the daily pattern of nest loss over the 30-d period of exposure was nearly identical in fragments and continuous forest (Fig. 2A; $\chi^2_{(1)}$ = 0.64, P = 0.42). Proximity to

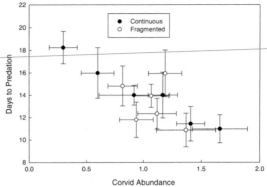

FIGURE 3. Rates of predation (mean days until a nest was depredated) in relation to mean abundance of corvids in fragmented and continuous stands in the Olympic Peninsula, WA. Values are means from 3 to 5 stands ± 1 SE. After Luginbuhl et al. (2001).

human activity affected the influence of forest fragmentation on predation within a stand (interaction between proximity and fragmentation; $F_{(1,849)}$ = 4.7, P = 0.03). Far (>5 km) from human activity, nests in fragments had slower rates of predation than nests in continuous forest (Fig. 2B; $\chi^2_{(1)}$ = 2.45, P = 0.12). In contrast, nests in fragments near (<1 km) human activity had rates of predation similar to nests in continuous forest (Fig. 2C; $\chi^2_{(1)}$ = 0.25, P = 0.65).

In continuous stands, predation rates (as indicated by number of days to predation) increased as abundance of corvids increased (r = −0.98, N = 6, P = 0.001; Fig. 3). In fragmented stands, we found no relationship between corvid abundance and rate of predation (r = −0.35, N = 6, P = 0.500; Fig. 3). The lack of a relation in fragmented stands may be related to edge effects (see below) that may be more important in fragmented stands, or it may reflect the narrow range (0.8–1.4 birds; Fig. 3) of predator abundance in our sample of fragmented stands.

A particular predator did not appear to account for the lack of a fragmentation effect. The effect of fragmentation was minimal regardless of whether we simulated eggs or chicks (interaction between type of mimic and fragmentation; $F_{(1,849)}$ = 0.66, P = 0.80), despite the fact that most predation on eggs was by corvids and most predation on chicks was by mammals (Luginbuhl et al. 2001). Total corvid abundance was similar among stands varying in proximity to human activity and fragmentation (all P-values in ANOVA > 0.48, N = 113 stand years; Fig. 4). Steller's Jay abundance varied as a joint function of proximity to human activity and fragmentation (interaction: $F_{(1,108)}$ = 6.87, P = 0.01), but this species was most abundant in

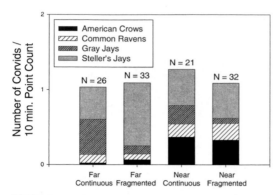

FIGURE 4. Composition of the corvid community determined by point count surveys in stands of varying contiguity and proximity to human activity centers, Olympic Peninsula, WA. Sample sizes are numbers of stands times number of years each stand was surveyed.

fragments far from human activity, which was the condition associated with the slowest (not fastest) rate of predation (Figs. 2 and 4).

The distance of a nest from the edge of the forest-matrix interface was not consistently related to the rate of nest predation. Nests within 50 m of the forest edge tended to be preyed on faster and to a greater extent than nests further into the stand's interior (Fig. 5A; $\chi^2_{(2)}$ = 4.75, P = 0.09). This "edge effect" was consistent and strong near human activity where the edge of the forested stand abutted a campground or small settlement. There, nests within 50 m of the edge were preyed on significantly faster than nests >200 m from the edge (Fig. 5B; $\chi^2_{(2)}$ = 3.96, P = 0.05). However, this "edge-effect" was inconsistent far from human activity where the matrix only included regenerating forest. Here, nests 100 m from the edge fared best, but rates were similar to those 50 m and 200 m from the edge (Fig. 5C; $\chi^2_{(2)}$ = 0.25, P = 0.62).

Corvid nest predators drove the changes in nest predation in relation to distance from the forest fragment edge. In settings far from human activity the relative importance of corvid nest predation was lowest 100 m from the fragment edge (Fig. 6A), the distance associated with the lowest overall rate of predation (Fig. 5B). Likewise, fragments abutting human activity centers had the least predation 200 m from the edge (Fig. 5C), where the relative amount of corvid predation was also lowest (Fig. 6B).

Stand size did not affect predation rates. In an ongoing study in Oregon using similar methods as we report, J. Luginbuhl (unpubl. data) found no difference ($\chi^2_{(1)}$ = 0.23, P = 0.63) in predation rates between large stands (30–60 ha) and small stands (16–28 ha). Stand shape did have a weak affect on predation rates, with higher

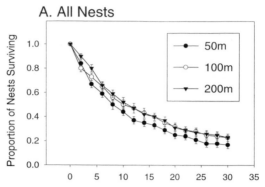

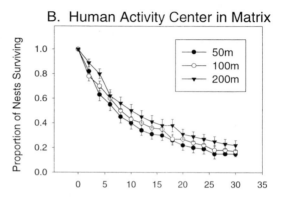

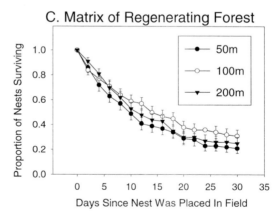

FIGURE 5. Survivorship of simulated murrelet nests at varying distances from the edge of forest fragments, Olympic Peninsula, WA. Survivorship ($\bar{X} \pm 1$ SE) at 50 m, 100 m, and 200 m is evaluated in (A) all stands regardless of proximity to human activity; (B) only in fragments surrounded by 1–15-yr-old clearcuts; and (C) only in fragments adjacent to campgrounds and small settlements. Sample sizes are 208, 204, and 206 for all fragments (A); 116, 113, and 115 for fragments surrounded by clearcuts (B); and 92, 91, and 91 for fragments adjacent to human activity (C) at 50 m, 100 m, and 200 m from the edge, respectively.

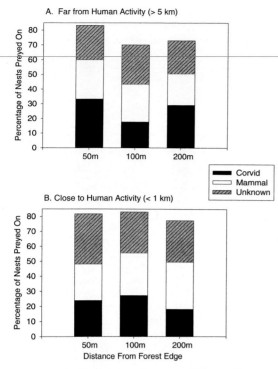

FIGURE 6. Percentage of nests at different distances from the forest edge preyed on by corvids (Gray Jays, Steller's Jays, American Crows, and Common Ravens) versus small mammals (mice, squirrels, and occasionally weasels) when the matrix is (A) far from human activity (>5 km) and (B) close to human activity (<1 km). Sample sizes are given in Fig. 4.

rates of predation in linear versus compact stands ($\chi^2_{(1)}$ = 3.16, P = 0.08).

DISCUSSION

It is apparent that loss of older forest in the Pacific Northwest, primarily due to logging but also through other disturbance processes, has reduced the total area of suitable murrelet nesting habitat and caused remaining habitat to become more fragmented. From examining the evidence of the potential effects of habitat fragmentation on nesting habitat and populations of the Marbled Murrelet at four geographic scales, we found that it is difficult to separate the effects of fragmentation from the concomitant effect of habitat loss. Murrelet response to aspects of fragmentation generally appeared at the smaller scales investigated, including nest stands and nest stand neighborhoods, although at-sea abundances of murrelets were correlated with spatial configurations of habitat in specific locations of southern Oregon and Northern California (Meyer 1999). Marbled Murrelet nests appear particularly vulnerable to human-induced edges (e.g.,

roads and clearcuts) such as those studied in Oregon and British Columbia. Our work with artificial nests supported this conclusion in part, as we did find that rates of predation generally were greater within 50 m of edges, especially in stands close to human activity (recreation sites and small settlements). However, the artificial nest study also demonstrated that relationships between nest success and forest habitat likely are more complex because the composition of the nest predator assemblage is diverse and varies among locations.

The overall lack of an obvious fragmentation effect on artificial nests appears to be due to the diversity of nest predators and to our observations that other factors affecting predator abundance, such as proximity to people and refuse and forest structure, can swamp effects of fragmentation. Among corvids, the total number of individuals remained relatively constant among fragmented and continuous landscapes. This occurred despite variation in the composition of the corvid community (Fig. 4). In particular, the two species of jays showed reciprocal responses to fragmentation that likely equalized the total nest predation risk with respect to fragmentation. Steller's Jays frequented fragmented landscapes, whereas Gray Jays were most abundant in continuous landscapes (Fig. 4). Small mammals were abundant and diverse nest predators in our study area as well, and they were not confined to fragmented or continuous landscapes. This further reduced the relationship between predation and fragmentation (Marzluff and Restani 1999).

Effects of fragmentation on nesting success can vary depending on the forest structures surrounding nesting stands. In remote locations, where forests are fragmented by timber harvest and the matrix surrounding fragments is composed of regenerating forest, nest predation rates from our artificial nest experiment were not elevated, despite increases in Steller's Jay populations in such landscapes. Ongoing research in Oregon suggests that rates of predation are elevated in remote fragments surrounded by young clearcuts with berry-producing shrubs compared with fragments surrounded by clearcuts without berries or by older regenerating forest (Marzluff and Restani 1999; J. Luginbuhl et al., unpubl. data). In contrast, in locations near human settlements and recreation areas where forest fragments abut human activity centers, fragmentation is likely to increase the risk of nest predation (Fig. 5C). A diverse corvid community near human activity (Fig. 4) that feeds on human refuse, offerings at feeders, and berries in exotic plantings and early successional landscapes likely drives this effect. The relative importance of

TABLE 1. POTENTIAL SHORT TERM AND LONG TERM EFFECTS OF FRAGMENTATION OF NESTING HABITAT ON LOCAL POPULATION SIZE AND DEMOGRAPHICS OF THE MARBLED MURRELET IN THE PACIFIC NORTHWEST

Fragmentation effect on nesting habitat	Population size	Adult survival	Number of nests	Nest success
Reduced amount of nesting habitat	0/−[a]	0/0	0/−	−/0
Smaller patch size (reduced area of interior habitat, increased edge)	0/−	0/0	−/−	−/−[b]
Increased number of patches[c]	0/0	0/0	0/0	0/0
Increased isolation of patches	−/−	−/−	0/−	−/0

[a] Symbols to left of slash are short term effects (<10 years); symbols following slash are longer term effects (>10 years but more generally several decades). Symbols are: "−" (negative or deleterious), "0" (neutral), "+" (positive). A negative effect on any demographic parameter is assumed to cause population decline in the longer term.

[b] Effects will vary depending on suite of predators at particular sites. This often depends on the agent of fragmentation and resulting matrix. Some predators are more abundant in continuous forest, others respond to edge (see text).

[c] Effects given for number of patches per se, all else relatively equal. (In larger context of fragmentation, we assume these patches would be smaller, in addition to being more numerous.)

corvids as nest predators declined at nests greater than 200 m from edges abutting human activity (Fig. 6B).

An especially intriguing result (with management implications) is our observation that forests of simple structure are associated with the smallest corvid populations (Marzluff et al. 1999). Maintaining even-aged forests in places of human settlement should therefore be an effective management strategy to reduce regional corvid populations. The siting of recreational development in forested ecosystems also needs to be rethought. Rather than place campsites in structurally complex (aesthetically pleasing) landscapes, placement of campsites in structurally simple landscapes where predator populations are limited and where Marbled Murrelets rarely nest would reduce risk of nest predation.

Based on our review of other studies and our own work, we offer the following speculations on the potential effects of fragmentation on populations of the Marbled Murrelet. The primary effects of fragmentation are a reduction in total area of habitat, smaller average sizes of habitat patches (along with reduced area in interior habitat and increased amount of edge), increased number of patches, and increased isolation of patches. These consequences of habitat loss and fragmentation can affect population size, likelihood of nesting, survival of adults, and nesting success. As shown in Table 1, these effects differ from the short term to long term.

Reduced amount of nesting habitat potentially could result in short term displacement and crowding of nesting birds into remaining patches of habitat, although there is no direct evidence that Marbled Murrelets would respond in this way. Murrelets are thought to exhibit site fidelity (Nelson 1997); if so, birds that had been nesting in former habitat might fail to breed for several years until they either find new habitat or die. In that case, numbers of nests would decline immediately. If displaced birds move to adjacent nesting habitat, then crowding of nests will occur. In either case, population size would not be affected in the short term. However, crowding of nests could result in increased predation and lower nesting success. Assuming short term crowding, we speculate that nesting density in remaining habitat would relax to pre-harvest levels over the longer term, and population size would decrease. Changes in distribution and population declines observed at broad scales along the coast where substantial habitat has been lost (Carter and Erickson 1992, Kelson et al. 1995) support the concept that population declines are associated with loss of habitat.

Smaller patch size and its concomitant reduction in interior habitat and increased edge will result in short term and long term increases in rates of predation on nests (Manley and Nelson 1999; discussed above), although the strength of this effect will vary depending on the suite of predators occurring in the area (Andrén 1992, Nelson and Hamer 1995, Marzluff and Restani 1999). Our artificial nest results suggest that the agent of fragmentation and concomitant development of the matrix around the patches is important to the strength and significance of resultant edge effects. For example, when human settlement or recreational development fragments habitat and surrounds patches, then edge effects may be substantial. Smaller patches also may result in fewer nesting attempts overall, as some areas will no longer be considered suitable habitat and thus not be occupied by murrelets. In northern California, occupied locations contained larger patches and lower edge/area than unoccupied patches (Meyer 1999). Over the longer term these effects will lead to smaller populations if fewer fledglings are recruited into the breeding population. The effect on adult survival is less clear, as the response to fragmentation measures of species known to take adult Marbled Murrelets (see text) is not well documented (but see Rosenberg and Raphael 1986; McGarigal and McComb 1995, 1999).

Increased number of patches is not likely to affect population size or survival in the short or long term, except as an indirect consequence of related effects on patch size and total area of nesting habitat. *Increased isolation of patches* could lead to fewer nesting attempts, as potentially suitable habitat patches >5 km from other active nesting habitat are less likely to be occupied (Meyer 1999). Isolation also could lead to short and long term decrease in adult survival through increased vulnerability of murrelets to predators. Although we know of no direct evidence for this effect, we speculate that a murrelet flying over regenerating forest has greater exposure to avian predators that one flying over mature canopy, but it is also true that most flights to attend nests take place at dusk and dawn when diurnal predators are not active. If this increased risk to predation does occur, the long term result would be a reduction in number of nests and a reduction in population size.

SUMMARY

At the regional scale, we found no correlations between murrelet numbers and amount of nesting habitat at the broad scale along the entire Washington and Oregon coast; we found weak correlations if we restricted our analysis to inland habitat within 25 km of the coast. However, in southern Oregon and northern California, murrelet densities offshore were higher in subregions with more unfragmented and non-isolated old growth or old growth combined with residual old-growth forest.

At the watershed scale, we and other researchers found that numbers of murrelets flying into delineated drainages were strongly correlated with the amount of potential nesting habitat within those drainages, but that indices of fragmentation were not correlated with murrelet abundance.

At the neighborhood scale (~200-ha areas surrounding stands surveyed for murrelets), potential nesting habitat occurred in larger patches and was less fragmented at neighborhoods occupied by murrelets compared with unoccupied neighborhoods, although the entire neighborhood tended to be patchier and more fragmented due to the diversity of patches of younger forest. The presence of high-contrast edges (natural or clearcuts) did not seem to deter use of a site.

At the scale of individual nests, distance to edge was an important influence on nest fate. In Oregon and British Columbia, nest failure (primarily from predation), was highest in nests within 50 m of an edge; nests >150 m from an edge were successful or failed from reasons other than predation. Some evidence suggested that nests were more successful in larger stands (~500 ha) than smaller stands (<300 ha), but successful nests have been observed in a wide range of stand sizes.

Our artificial nest experiments showed similar rates of predation in fragmented and continuous stands; the lack of an obvious fragmentation effect appeared to be due to the diversity of nest predators, the influence of forest structures surrounding nesting stands, and proximity to human activity. Total abundance of avian predators (corvids) was similar in fragmented and continuous stands; predation rates increased with abundance of predators in continuous stands but not in fragmented stands. In remote locations far from human activity, predation rates were greater in continuous stands than in fragmented stands; predation rates were similar in fragmented and continuous stands close to human activity.

Despite the many insights that have emerged from our review of existing studies and our new work with artificial nests, a number of important research questions remain. Understanding trade-offs between predation risk and quality of nesting habitat will require further investigation into how much simple-structured forest in a landscape is enough to reduce predator populations without reducing use of the remaining complex forest for nesting by murrelets. Additional work is certainly needed to better understand how the variety of processes interacts to affect nest site selection, survival, and reproductive success of the murrelet and how these behaviors are influenced by fragmentation of nesting habitat. In particular:

- How do the likelihood of nesting and characteristics of nest sites vary in relation to amount and type of edge?
- How does adult survival, particularly susceptibility to predation, vary with size, shape, and isolation of nesting stands?
- How does fragmentation of continuous nesting habitat affect the behavior of resident murrelets (that is, do displaced resident birds nest in adjacent stands that might be of lower quality, and can they move into stands that are occupied by other nesting murrelets)?
- What is the role and effect of mammalian predators on real nests and how do mammalian predators respond to fragmentation of murrelet nesting habitat?

Although many questions remain, we are heartened that new research is underway, much of it stimulated by requirements for monitoring population and habitat trends of this threatened species. Efforts to better define attributes of nesting habitat and to relate population trends to trends in the amount and pattern of habitat will contribute to conservation of this unique bird.

ACKNOWLEDGMENTS

We thank C. B. Meyer, S. K. Nelson, I. C. Manley, C. W. Thompson, C. S. Strong, and A. Burger for allowing us to use their unpublished data. Our artificial nest experiments were supported by the Sustainable Ecosystems Institute, Rayonier, National Council for Air and Stream Improvement, Washington Department of Natural Resources, Olympic Natural Resources Center, the Pacific Northwest Research Station of the U.S.D.A. Forest Service, U.S. Fish and Wildlife Service, Boise Cascade Corporation, Willamette Industries, and Oregon Department of Forestry; D. E. Varland, L. S. Young, S. P. Horton, S. P. Courtney, J. E. Bradley, and E. A. Neatherlin contributed to that work. We particularly thank the many field assistants who conducted the field experiments and gathered observations. B. Galleher prepared habitat maps and aided with GIS analyses. This manuscript benefited from reviews by S. K. Nelson, T. L. George, and an anonymous reviewer.

APPENDIX

DETAILS OF HABITAT MAPPING FOR FIGURE 1

We used published reports of the characteristics of Marbled Murrelet nest stands to identify potential nesting habitat in Oregon and Washington. Given that nests have been found in smaller-diameter trees with epiphyte cover or deformities that create suitable platforms and in younger stands with remnant old-growth trees (Nelson 1997), but that remnant trees are not easily classified from satellite imagery, we accepted habitat that met the minimum dbh of known nesting stands rather than using dbh of nest trees. This may have inflated our estimates of habitat in some areas. Stands supporting tree nests in Oregon and Washington (N = 26) had a reported mean dbh of 47.7 cm (Hamer and Nelson 1995), although we were unable to discern how many trees were measured to arrive at stand diameter. Five of 9 Oregon nests were located in mature/old-growth stands, with mature trees defined as ≥46 cm dbh (Nelson and Peck 1995). In comparison, minimum nest tree size was 76 cm (N = 45) in OR and 88.5 cm (N = 6) in WA (Nelson 1997). Only potential nesting habitat was extracted from the covers described below. No spatial analyses were performed on these data.

Washington

The vegetation layer was a mosaic compiled from approximately 20 sources that identified Northern Spotted Owl (Strix occidentalis caurina) habitat, including satellite imagery classifications and state, federal and private agency mapping (USFWS 1997b). It included the Washington Department of Natural Resource's owl mosaic (1988–1993), the USDA Forest Service's owl habitat data from Olympic National Park, the WDNR/WDFW habitat map of the western Olympic Peninsula, harvest change data (1989 and 1991), and several private timber industry databases. This was the most up-to-date coverage for all land ownerships within the study area. Late-seral habitat was one of 10 land cover classes, and the only class that included characteristics of suitable murrelet habitat. Late seral was defined as mixed conifer/hardwood with >70% crown closure from conifers and >10% crown closure from trees >53 cm dbh. This class potentially contained some stands that would not have been included as habitat had we been able to specify tree size, composition, and structure. Resolution was 100-m pixels. We further defined suitable habitat as <1,067 m (3,500 ft) elevation. Inland extent of the marbled murrelet zone was defined as 80 km (50 mi; USFWS 1997a). Since the focus of this assessment was coastal distribution of murrelets as related to habitat, we included up to 80 km in from the outer coast, not 80 km from all salt water in WA. We separated the northern portion of the Olympic Peninsula along a watershed boundary to correspond to at-sea data around the tip of the Peninsula into the Strait of Juan de Fuca.

Oregon

The Western Oregon Digital Image Project (WOD-IP) vegetation layer was derived from Landsat TM imagery classification (Nighbert et al., unpubl. data) Resolution of the original data was 25 m, and was resampled to 100-m pixel size. It was comprised of 247 combinations of diameter, canopy closure, number of canopy layers, and species composition. We selected conifer and mixed conifer/hardwood, multi-storied stands with mean dbh >48 cm. We accepted all crown closures, given the range of 12–99% at OR nests (Hamer and Nelson 1995). We dropped down to the >48 cm dbh size, as opposed to including only >74 cm (the largest size class available), to capture younger, potentially suitable habitat and to keep our criteria for OR habitat similar to that used for WA. Given the fire and harvest history in portions of the Sitka spruce (Picea sitchensis) zone (Franklin and Dyrness 1973, Perry 1995), and the difficulty in capturing habitat within this zone (S. K. Nelson, pers. comm.), we also included single-storied stands with mean dbh >74 cm within this narrow corridor along the OR coast. These criteria may have overestimated suitable murrelet habitat in some regions. We set the inland extent of the murrelet zone at 56 km (35 mi), corresponding to the Recovery Zone (USFWS 1997a). For consistency, we applied the same elevation screen as in WA, defining habitat as ≤1,067 m, although this elevation is higher than known nest sites in Oregon.

Murrelet zones from at-sea data

Of the at-sea survey data available, we selected summer surveys from 1997 in Washington (C. Thompson unpubl. data from 1999 report). We included only nearshore transects (<500 m), as these were run more consistently. These data were summarized over variable-length transects (25–105 km), with some sections surveyed multiple times. We selected transects that, pieced together, covered the entire coastline. We used the break points between transects to establish horizontal bands along the coast. The peninsula configuration of the Washington coastline presented a different scenario than Oregon. We opted to include at-sea counts from the north side of the peninsula (the west-

ern Strait of Juan de Fuca), as these birds could potentially be accessing some of the same habitat as birds
on the outer coast. At-sea densities were reported as
the number of murrelets by transect length × 200-m
width. For sections with multiple surveys within our
temporal and spatial criteria (summer months, nearshore distances), we calculated an average density.

Of the Oregon data available (C. Strong, unpubl.
data), 1996 had the more complete coverage of the
coastline. For the 149 2-km stretches of shoreline surveyed in both 1996 and 1997, average nearshore densities did not differ between years (t = 0.216, P =
0.829), so we selected the 1996 data because of its
greater coverage. We selected July nearshore surveys
(400–600 m from shore). Densities were reported for
each 2-km section, and transects were divided into
three regions (north, central, south; Strong et al. 1995).
We maintained regional breaks, and within regions averaged densities over 45–50 km sections. These section
and region breaks established our 11 horizontal bands.

Studies in Avian Biology No. 25:236–270, 2002.

LITERATURE CITED

AGEE, J. K. 1993. Fire ecology of Pacific Northwest forests. Island Press, Washington, D.C.

AGEE, J. K. 1998. The landscape ecology of western forest fire regimes. Northwest Science 72:24–34.

AGEE, J. K., AND R. L. EDMONDS. 1992. Forest protection guidelines for the Northern Spotted Owl. Pp. 419–480 in U.S. Department of Interior. Draft recovery plan for the Northern Spotted Owl. U.S. Department of Interior, Washington, D.C.

AGRESTI, A. 1996. An introduction to categorical data analysis. John Wiley and Sons, New York, NY.

ALBERTS, A. C., A. D. RICHMAN, D. TRAN, R. SAUVAJOT, C. MCCALVIN, AND D. T. BOLGER. 1993. Effects of habitat fragmentation on populations of native and exotic plants in southern California coastal scrub. Pp. 103–110 in J. E. Keely (editor). Interface between ecology and land development in California. Southern California Academy of Science, Los Angeles, CA.

ALLEN, C. D. 1998. A ponderosa pine natural area reveals its secrets. Pp. 551–552 in M. J. Mac, P. A. Opler, C. E. Puckett-Haecker, and P. D. Doran (editors). Status and trends of the Nation's biological resources. Vol. 1. U.S. Geological Survey, Reston, VA.

ALLEN, D. L. 1962. Our wildlife legacy. Funk and Wagnalls, New York, NY.

ALLEN, T. F. H., AND T. B. STARR. 1982. Hierarchy: perspectives for ecological complexity. University of Chicago Press, Chicago, IL.

ALTMAN, B., AND R. SALLABANKS. 2000. Olive-sided Flycatcher (Contopus cooperi). In A. Poole, and F. Gill (editors). The Birds of North America, No. 502. The Academy of Natural Sciences, Philadelphia, PA, and American Ornithologists' Union, Washington, D.C.

AMBUEL, B., AND S. A. TEMPLE. 1982. Songbird populations in southern Wisconsin forests: 1954 and 1979. Journal of Field Ornithology 53:149–158.

AMBUEL, B., AND S. A. TEMPLE. 1983. Area-dependent changes in the bird communities and vegetation of southern Wisconsin forests. Ecology 64:1057–1068.

ANDERSEN, A. N., R. W. BRAITHWAITE, G. D. COOK, L. K. CORBETT, R. J. WILLIAMS, M. M. DOUGLAS, A. M. GILL, S. A. SETTERFIELD, AND W. J. MULLER. 1998. Fire research for conservation management in tropical savannas: introducing the Kapalga fire experiment. Australian Journal of Ecology 23:95–110.

ANDERSON, B. W., R. D. OHMART, AND H. A. ALLEN, JR. 1985a. Riparian birds in the riparian/agricultural interface. Pp. 190–195 in R. E. Warner and K. M. Hendrix (editors). California riparian systems: ecology, conservation, and productive management. University of California Press, Berkeley, CA.

ANDERSON, B. W., R. D. OHMART, J. K. MEENTS, AND W. C. HUNTER. 1985b. Avian use of marshes on the lower Colorado River. Pp. 598–604 in R. E. Warner and K. M. Hendrix (editors). California riparian systems: ecology, conservation, and productive management. University of California Press, Berkeley, CA.

ANDERSON, J. R., E. E. HARDY, J. T. ROACH, AND R. E. WITMER. 1976. A land use and land cover classification system for use with remote sensing data. Professional Paper No. 964. U.S. Geological Survey, Reston, VA.

ANDERSON, S. H., K. MANN, AND H. H. SHUGART. 1977. The effect of transmission-line corridors on bird populations. American Midland Naturalist 97:216–221.

ANDRÉN, H. 1992. Corvid density and nest predation in relation to forest fragmentation: a landscape perspective. Ecology 73:794–804.

ANDRÉN, H. 1994. Effects of habitat fragmentation on birds and mammals in landscapes with different proportions of suitable habitat: a review. Oikos 71:355–366.

ANDRÉN, H. 1995. Effects of landscape composition on predation rates at habitat edges. Pp. 225–255 in L. Hansson, L. Fahrig, and G. Merriam (editors). Mosaic landscapes and ecological processes. Chapman and Hall, London, UK.

ANDRÉN, H. 1999. Habitat fragmentation, the random sample hypothesis and critical thresholds. Oikos 84: 306–308.

ANDRÉN, H., AND P. ANGELSTAM. 1988. Elevated predation rates as an edge effect in habitat islands: experimental evidence. Ecology 69:544–547.

ANDRÉN, H., P. ANGELSTAM, E. LINDSTRÖM, AND P. WIDÉN. 1985. Differences in predation pressure in relation to habitat fragmentation. Oikos 45:273–277.

ANDRÉN, H., A. DELIN, AND A. SEILER. 1997. Population response to landscape changes depends on specialization to different landscape elements. Oikos 80:193–196.

ANEY, W. C. 1984. The effects of patch size on bird communities of remnant old-growth pine stands in western Montana. M.S. thesis. University of Montana, Missoula, MT.

ANGELSTAM, P. 1986. Predation of ground-nesting birds' nests in relation to predator densities and habitat edge. Oikos 47:365–373.

ANGELSTAM, P. 1996. The ghost of forest past—natural disturbance regimes as a basis for reconstruction of biologically diverse forests in Europe. Pp. 287–337 in R. M. DeGraaf and R. I. Miller (editors). Conservation of faunal diversity in forested landscapes. Chapman and Hall, London, U.K.

ANNAND, E. M., AND F. R. THOMPSON, III. 1997. Forest bird response to regeneration practices in central hardwood forests. Journal of Wildlife Management 61:159–171.

ANONYMOUS. 1986. Discussion of standardized breeding codes. Pp. 114–117 in S. M. Sutcliffe, R. E. Bonney, Jr., and J. D. Lowe (editors). Second Northeastern Breeding Bird Atlas Conference, Cornell Lab of Ornithology, Ithaca, NY.

APFELBAUM, S. I., AND A. HANEY. 1981. Bird populations before and after wildfire in a Great Lakes pine forest. Condor 83:347–354.

APFELBAUM, S. I., AND A. HANEY. 1985. Changes in bird populations during succession following fire in northern Great Lakes Wilderness. Pp. 10–15 in R. C. Lucas (editor). Proceedings of the National Wilderness Research Conference: Current Research. USDA Forest Service Gen. Tech. Rep. INT-212. USDA Forest Service, Intermountain Research Station, Ogden, UT.

ARANGO-VÉLEZ, N., AND G. H. KATTAN. 1997. Effects of forest fragmentation on experimental nest predation in Andean cloud forest. Biological Conservation 81:137–143.

ARNO, S. F. 1980. Forest fire history in the Northern Rockies. Journal of Forestry 78:460–465.

ARNO, S. F. 2000. Fire in western forest ecosystems. Pp. 97–120 in J. K. Brown and J. K. Smith (editors). Wildland fire in ecosystems: effects of fire on flora. USDA Forest Service Gen. Tech. Rep. RMRS-GTR-42-vol. 2. USDA Forest Service Rocky Mountain Research Station, Ogden, UT.

ARNO, S. F., AND D. H. DAVIS. 1980. Fire history of western redcedar/hemlock forests in northern Idaho. Pp. 21–26 in M. A. Stokes and J. H. Dieterich (technical coordinators). Proceedings of the fire history workshop. USDA Forest Service Gen. Tech. Rep. RM-81. USDA Forest Service Rocky Mountain Forest and Range Experiment Station, Ft. Collins, CO.

ARNO, S. F., AND W. C. FISCHER. 1995. Larix occidentalis—fire ecology and fire management. Pp. 130–135 in W. C. Schmidt and K. J. McDonald (editors). Ecology and management of Larix forests: a look ahead. USDA Forest Service Gen. Tech. Rep. INT-GTR-319. USDA Forest Service Intermountain Research Station, Ogden, UT.

ARNO, S. F., AND G. E. GRUELL. 1983. Fire history of the forest-grassland ecotone in southwestern Montana. Journal of Range Management 36:332–336.

ARNO, S. F., J. H. SCOTT, AND M. G. HARTWELL. 1995. Age-class structure of old growth ponderosa pine/ Douglas-fir stands and its relationship to fire history. USDA Forest Service Res. Pap. INT-RP-481. USDA Forest Service Intermountain Research Station, Ogden, UT.

ARNO, S. F., H. Y. SMITH, AND M. A. KREBS. 1997. Old growth ponderosa pine and western larch stand structures: influences of pre-1900 fires and fire exclusion. USDA Forest Service Res. Pap. INT-RP-495. USDA Forest Service Intermountain Research Station, Ogden, UT.

ASKINS, R. A., J. F. LYNCH, AND R. GREENBERG. 1990. Population declines in migratory birds in eastern North America. Current Ornithology 7:1–57.

ASKINS, R. A., M. J. PHILBRICK, AND D. S. SUGENO. 1987. Relationship between the regional abundance of forest and the composition of forest bird communities. Biological Conservation 39:129–152.

ATWOOD, J. L. 1993. California gnatcatchers and coastal sage scrub: the biological basis for endangered species listing. Pp. 149–169 in J. E. Keely (editor). Interface between ecology and land development in California. Southern California Academy of Science, Los Angeles, CA.

ATWOOD, J. L., AND R. F. NOSS. 1994. Gnatcatchers and development: a "trainwreck" avoided? Illahee 10:123–130.

AUBRY, K. B., M. P. AMARANTHUS, C. B. HALPERN, J. D. WHITE, B. L. WOODARD, C. E. PETERSON, C. A. LAGOUDAKIS, AND A. J. HORTON., 1999. Evaluating the effects of varying levels and patterns of greentree retention: experimental design of the DEMO Study. Northwest Science 73:12–26.

AUBRY, K. B., S. D. WEST, D. A. MANUWAL, A. B. STRINGER, J. L. ERICKSON, AND S. PEARSON. 1997.

Wildlife use of managed forests: a landscape perspective, vol. 2. Washington Department of Natural Resources, Olympia, WA.

AXELROD, D. 1978. The origin of coastal sage vegetation. American Journal of Botany 65:1117–1131.

BABBITT, B. 1999. Noah's mandate and the birth of urban bioplanning. Conservation Biology 13:677–678.

BAICICH, P. J., AND C. J. O. HARRISON. 1997. A guide to the nests, eggs, and nestlings of North American birds, 2nd ed. Academic Press, San Diego CA.

BAILEY, E. A. AND P. J. MOCK. 1998. Dispersal capability of the California gnatcatcher: a landscape analysis of distribution data. Western Birds 29:351–360.

BAILEY, R. G. 1995. Description of the ecoregions of the United States. 2nd ed. USDA Forest Service Misc. Publ. No. 1391 (rev). USDA Forest Service, Washington, D.C.

BAKER, B. W. 1980. Hair catchers aid in identifying mammalian predators of ground-nesting birds. Wildlife Society Bulletin 8:257–259.

BAKER, W. L. 1992. The landscape ecology of large disturbances in the design and management of nature reserves. Landscape Ecology 7:181–194.

BAKER, W. L. 1993. Spatially heterogeneous multi-scale response of landscapes to fire suppression. Oikos 66:66–71.

BAKER, W. L. 1994. Restoration of landscape structure altered by fire suppression. Conservation Biology 8:763–769.

BÁLDI, A., AND T. KISBENEDEK. 1994. Comparative analysis of edge effect on bird and beetle communities. Acta Zoologica Academiae Scientiarum Hungaricae 40:1–14.

BALL, I. J., R. J. GAZDA, AND D. B. MCINTOSH. 1994. A simple device for measuring survival time of artificial nests. Journal of Wildlife Management 58:793–797.

BARBER, D. R., AND T. E. MARTIN. 1997. Influence of alternate host densities on Brown-headed Cowbird parasitism rates in Black-capped Vireos. Condor 99:595–604.

BARRETT, G. 1992. Landscape ecology: designing sustainable agricultural landscapes. Journal of Sustainable Agriculture 2:83–103.

BARRETT, S. W. 1988. Fire suppression's effects on forest succession within a central Idaho wilderness. Western Journal of Applied Forestry 3:76–80.

BARRETT, S. W., AND S. F. ARNO. 1982. Indian fires as an ecological influence in the northern Rockies. Journal of Forestry 80:647–651.

BARRETT, S. W., S. F. ARNO, AND C. H. KEY. 1991. Fire regimes of western larch—lodgepole pine forests in Glacier National Park, Montana. Canadian Journal of Forest Research 21:1711–1720.

BARROWCLOUGH, G. F., R. J. GUTIÉRREZ, AND J. G. GROTH. 1999. Phylogeography of Spotted Owl (Strix occidentalis) populations based on mitochondrial DNA sequences: gene flow, genetic structure, and a novel biogeographic pattern. Evolution 53:919–931.

BARROWS, C. W. 1986. Habitat relationships of Winter Wrens in northern California. Western Birds 17:17–20.

BART, J. 1995. Amount of suitable habitat and viability

of Northern Spotted Owls. Conservation Biology 9: 943–946.

BART, J., AND E. D. FORSMAN. 1992. Dependence of Northern Spotted Owls *Strix occidentalis caurina* on old-growth forests in the western USA. Biological Conservation 62:95–100.

BAXTER, W. L., AND C. W. WOLF. 1972. Interspersion index as a technique for evaluation of Bob-white Quail habitat. Pp. 158–164 *in* J. A. Morrison and J. C. Lewis (editors). Proceedings of the First National Bobwhite Quail Symposium, Stillwater, OK.

BAYNE, E. M., AND K. A. HOBSON. 1997. Comparing the effects of landscape fragmentation by forestry and agriculture on predation of artificial nests. Conservation Biology 11:1418–1429.

BAYNE, E. M., AND K. A. HOBSON. 1998. The effects of habitat fragmentation by forestry and agriculture on the abundance of small mammals in the southern boreal mixedwood forest. Canadian Journal of Zoology 76:62–69.

BAYNE, E. M., AND K. A. HOBSON. 2000. Relative use of contiguous and fragmented boreal forest by red squirrels (*Tamiasciurus hudsonicus*). Canadian Journal of Zoology 78:35–365.

BAYNE, E. M., K. A. HOBSON, AND P. FARGEY. 1997. Predation on artificial nests in relation to forest type: contrasting the use of quail and plasticine eggs. Ecography 20:233–239.

BEAL, F. E. 1911. Food of the woodpeckers of the United States. USDA Biological Survey Bulletin 37.

BEAUCHAMP, R. M. 1986. A flora of San Diego County. Sweetwater River Press, National City, CA.

BECK, M. J., AND T. L. GEORGE. 2000. Song post and foraging site characteristics of breeding Varied Thrushes in northwestern California. Condor 102: 93–103.

BEDNARZ, J. C., J. C. HOVIS, AND D. M. EVANS. 1998. Ongoing changes in a Swainson's Thrush population related to landscape fragmentation and forest management. Proceedings of the North American Ornithological Conference 6–12 April, St. Louis, MO.

BELLAMY, P. E., S. A. HINSLEY, AND I. NEWTON. 1996a. Factors influencing bird species numbers in small woods in south-east England. Journal of Applied Ecology 33:249–262.

BELLAMY, P. E., S. A. HINSLEY, AND I. NEWTON. 1996b. Local extinctions and recolonisations of passerine bird populations in small woods. Oecologia 108:64–71.

BELSKY, A. J., AND D. M. BLUMENTHAL. 1997. Effects of livestock grazing on stand dynamics and soils in upland forests of the interior West. Conservation Biology 11:315–327.

BENDER, D. J., T. A. CONTRERAS, AND L. FAHRIG. 1998. Habitat loss and population decline: a meta-analysis of the patch size effect. Ecology 79:517–533.

BERG, Å. 1996. Predation on artificial, solitary and aggregated wader nests on farmland. Oecologia 107: 343–346.

BERG, Å., AND T. PÄRT. 1994. Abundance of breeding farmland birds on arable and set-aside fields at forest edges. Ecography 17:147–152.

BERG, Å., S. G. NILSSON, AND U. BOSTROM. 1992. Predation on artificial wader nests on large and small bogs along a south-north gradient. Ornis Scandinavica 23:13–16.

BERRY, B. J. L. 1990. Urbanization. Pp. 103–120 *in* B. L. Turner, II, W. C. Clark, R. W. Kates, J. F. Richards, J. T. Mathews, and W. B. Meyer (editors). The earth as transformed by human action: global and regional changes in the biosphere over the past 300 years. Cambridge University Press, Cambridge, UK.

BERRY, M. E., AND C. E. BOCK. 1998. Effect of habitat and landscape characteristics on avian breeding distribution in Colorado foothills shrub. Southwest Naturalist 43:453–461.

BESSIE, W. C., AND E. A. JOHNSON. 1995. The relative importance of fuels and weather on fire behavior in subalpine forests. Ecology 76:747–762.

BEST, L. B. 1972. First year effects of sagebrush control on two sparrows. Journal of Wildlife Management 36:534–544.

BEST, L. B. 1978. Field Sparrow reproductive success and nesting ecology. Auk 95:9–22.

BEST, L. B., R. C. WHITMORE, AND G. M. BOOTH. 1990. Use of cornfields by birds during the breeding season: the importance of edge habitat. American Midland Naturalist 123:84–99.

BIAS, M. A., AND R. J. GUTIÉRREZ. 1992. Habitat associations of California Spotted Owls in the central Sierra Nevada. Journal of Wildlife Management 56: 584–595.

BIDER, J. R. 1968. Animal activity in uncontrolled terrestrial communities as determined by a sand transect technique. Ecological Monographs 38:269–308.

BIELEFELDT, J., AND R. N. ROSENFIELD. 1997. Reexamination of cowbird parasitism and edge effects in Wisconsin forests. Journal of Wildlife Management 61:1222–1226.

BIERMANN, G. C., W. B. MCGILLIVRAY, AND K. E. NORDIN. 1987. The effect of cowbird parasitism on Brewer's Sparrow productivity in Alberta. Journal of Field Ornithology 58:350–354.

BILLINGS, W. D. 1994. Ecological impacts of cheatgrass and resultant fire on ecosystems in the western Great Basin. Pp. 22–30 *in* S. B. Monsen and S. G. Kitchen (compilers). Proceedings—ecology and management of annual grasslands. USDA Forest Service Gen. Tech. Rep. INT-GTR-313. USDA Forest Service Intermountain Research Station, Ogden, UT.

BINFORD, L. C., B. G. ELLIOTT, AND S. W. SINGER. 1975. Discovery of a nest and the downy young of the Marbled Murrelet. Wilson Bulletin 87:303–440.

BLACKFORD, J. L. 1955. Woodpecker concentrations in burned forest. Condor 57:28–30.

BLAIR, R. B. 1996. Land use and avian species along an urban gradient. Ecological Applications 6:506–519.

BLAKE, J. G. 1982. Influence of fire and logging on nonbreeding bird communities of ponderosa pine forests. Journal of Wildlife Management 46:404–415.

BLAKE, J. G., AND J. R. KARR. 1987. Breeding birds of isolated woodlots: area and habitat relationships. Ecology 68:1724–1734.

BLOCK, W. M., AND L. A. BRENNAN. 1993. The habitat concept in ornithology: theory and applications. Current Ornithology 11:35–91.

BOCK, C. E. 1970. The ecology and behavior of the Lewis' Woodpecker (*Asyndesmus lewis*). University California Publications in Zoology 92:1–100.

BOCK, C. E., AND J. H. BOCK. 1987. Avian habitat occupancy following fire in a Montana shrubsteppe. Prairie Naturalist 19:153–158.

BOCK, C. E., J. H. BOCK, AND B. C. BENNETT. 1999. Songbird abundance in grasslands at a suburban interface on the Colorado high plains. Studies in Avian Biology 19:131–136.

BOCK, C. E., J. H. BOCK, AND H. M. SMITH. 1993. Proposal for a system of federal livestock exclosures on public rangelands in the western United States. Conservation Biology 7:731–733.

BOCK, C. E., AND J. F. LYNCH. 1970. Breeding bird populations of burned and unburned conifer forests in the Sierra Nevada. Condor 72:182–189.

BOCK, C. E., M. RAPHAEL, AND J. H. BOCK. 1978. Changing avian community structure during early post-fire succession in the Sierra Nevada. Wilson Bulletin 90:199–123.

BOLGER, D. T., A. C. ALBERTS, AND M. E. SOULÉ. 1991. Bird species occurrence patterns in habitat fragments: sampling, extinction and nested species subsets. American Naturalist 137:155–166.

BOLGER, D. T., T. A. SCOTT, AND J. T. ROTENBERRY. 1997. Breeding bird abundance in an urbanizing landscape in coastal southern California. Conservation Biology 11:406–421.

BOLGER, D. T., T. A. SCOTT, AND J. T. ROTENBERRY. 2001. Use of corridor-like landscape structures by birds and small mammals. Biological Conservation 102:213–224.

BOLGER, D. T., A. V. SUAREZ, K. R. CROOKS, S. A. MORRISON, AND T. J. CASE. 2000. Arthropods in habitat fragments: effects of area, edge and Argentine ants. Ecological Applications 10:1230–1248.

BOLLINGER, E. K., AND R. G. PEAK. 1995. Depredation of artificial avian nests: a comparison of forest-field and forest-lake edges. American Midland Naturalist 134:200–203.

BOOTH, D. E. 1991. Estimating prelogging old-growth in the Pacific Northwest. Journal of Forestry 89:25–29.

BOULINIER, T., J. D. NICHOLS, J. E. HINES, J. R. SAUER, C. H. FLATHER, AND K. H. POLLOCK. 1998. Higher temporal variability of forest breeding bird communities in fragmented landscapes. Proceedings of the National Academy of Sciences 95:7497–7501.

BOULINIER, T., J. D. NICHOLS, J. E. HINES, J. R. SAUER, C. H. FLATHER, AND K. H. POLLOCK. 2001. Forest fragmentation and bird community dynamics: inferences at regional scales. Ecology 82:1159–1169.

BOWMAN, G. B., AND L. D. HARRIS. 1980. Effect of spatial heterogeneity on ground-nest depredation. Journal of Wildlife Management 44:806–813.

BOYCE, M. S., AND L. L. MCDONALD. 1999. Relating populations to habitats using resource selection functions. Trends in Ecology and Evolution 14:268–272.

BRADEN, G. T., R. L. MCKERNAN, AND S. M. POWELL. 1997. Effects of nest parasitism by the Brown-headed Cowbird on nesting success of the California Gnatcatcher. Condor 99:858–865.

BRADFORD, D. F., S. E. FRANSON, A. C. NEALE, D. T. HEGGEM, G. R. MILLER, AND G. E. CANTERBURY. 1998. Bird species assemblages as indicators of biological integrity in Great Basin rangeland. Environmental Monitoring and Assessment 49:1–22.

BRADLEY, J. B. 2000. The role of arboreal rodents as nest predators. M.S. thesis. University of Washington, Seattle, WA.

BRAND, L. A. 1998. Edge effects in coast redwood forest fragments. M.S. thesis. Humboldt State University, Arcata, CA.

BRAND, L. A., AND T. L. GEORGE. 2000. Predation risks for nesting birds in fragmented coast redwood forest. Journal of Wildlife Management 64:42–51.

BRAND, L. A., AND T. L. GEORGE. 2001. Response of passerine birds to forest edge in coast redwood forest fragments. Auk 118:678–686.

BRAUN, C. E., M. F. BAKER, R. L. ENG, J. S. GASHWILER, AND M. H. SCHROEDER. 1976. Conservation committee report on effects of alteration of sagebrush communities on the associated avifauna. Wilson Bulletin 88:165–171.

BRAWN, J. D., AND S. K. ROBINSON. 1996. Source-sink population dynamics may complicate the interpretation of long-term census data. Ecology 77:3–12.

BREININGER, D. R., AND P. A. SCHMALZER. 1990. Effects of fire and disturbance on plants and birds in a Florida oak/palmetto scrub community. American Midland Naturalist 123:64–74.

BRETT, M. T. 1997. Meta-analysis in ecology. Bulletin of the Ecological Society of America 78:92–94.

BRISKIE, J. V., S. G. SEALY, AND K. A. HOBSON. 1992. Behavioral defenses against avian brood parasitism in sympatric and allopatric host populations. Evolution 46:334–340.

BRITTINGHAM, M. C., AND S. TEMPLE. 1983. Have cowbirds caused forest songbirds to decline? Bioscience 33:31–35.

BROWN, J. H. 1971. Mammals on mountaintops: non-equilibrium insular biogeography. American Naturalist 105:467–478.

BROWN, J. K. 1995. Fire regimes and their relevance to ecosystem management. Pp. 171–178 *in* Proceedings of Society of American Foresters National Convention, Sept. 18–22, 1994, Anchorage, AK. Society of American Foresters, Bethesda, MD.

BROWN, M., AND J. J. DINSMORE. 1986. Implications of marsh size and isolation for marsh bird management. Journal of Wildlife Management 50:392–397.

BROWN, P. M., M. R. KAUFMAN, AND W. D. SHEPPARD. 1999. Long-term, landscape patterns of past fire events in a montane ponderosa pine forest of central Colorado. Landscape Ecology 14:513–532.

BUCHANAN, J. B., L. L. IRWIN, AND E. L. MCCUTCHEN. 1993. Characteristics of Spotted Owl nest trees in the Wenatchee National Forest. Journal of Raptor Research 27:1–7.

BUCHANAN, J. B., L. L. IRWIN, AND E. L. MCCUTCHEN. 1995. Within-stand nest site selection by Spotted Owls in the eastern Washington Cascades. Journal of Wildlife Management 59:301–310.

BULL, E. L. 1980. Resource partitioning among woodpeckers in northeastern Oregon. Ph.D. dissertation. University of Idaho, Moscow, ID.

BULL, E. L., AND R. S. HOLTHAUSEN. 1993. Habitat use and management of Pileated Woodpeckers in northeastern Oregon. Journal of Wildlife Management 57: 335–345.

BULL, E. L., C. G. PARKS, AND T. R. TORGERSEN. 1997. Trees and logs important to wildlife in the Interior Columbia River Basin. USDA Forest Service Gen. Tech. Rep. PNW-GTR-91. USDA Forest Service Pacific Northwest Research Station, Portland, OR.

BUNNELL, F. L. 1995. Forest-dwelling vertebrate faunas and natural fire regimes in British Columbia: patterns and implications for conservation. Conservation Biology 9:636–644.

BUNNELL, F. L. 1999a. What habitat is an island? Pp. 1–31 in J. A. Rochelle, L. A. Lehmann, and J. Wisniewski (editors). Forest fragmentation: wildlife and management implications. Brill Publishers, Leiden, The Netherlands.

BUNNELL, F. L. 1999b. Let's kill a panchestron giving fragmentation a meaning. Pp vii–xiii in J. A. Rochelle, L. A. Lehmann, and J. Wisniewski (editors). Forest fragmentation: wildlife and management implications. Brill Publishers, Leiden, The Netherlands.

BURGER, A. E. 1995. Inland habitat associations of Marbled Murrelet in British Columbia. Pp. 151–161 in C. J. Ralph, G. L. Hunt, Jr., M. G. Raphael, and J. F. Piatt (editors). Ecology and conservation of the Marbled Murrelet. USDA Forest Service Gen. Tech. Rep. PSW-GTR-152. USDA Forest Service Pacific Southwest Research Station, Albany, CA.

BURGER, A. E. 1997. Behavior and numbers of Marbled Murrelets measured with radar. Journal of Field Ornithology 68:208–223.

BURGER, A. E. 2001. Using radar to estimate populations and assess habitat associations of Marbled Murrelets. Journal of Wildlife Management 65:696–715.

BURGER, L. D. 1988. Relations between forest and prairie fragmentation and depredation of artificial nests in Missouri. M.A. thesis. University of Missouri, Columbia, MO.

BURGER, L. D., L. W. BURGER, AND J. FAABORG. 1994. Effects of prairie fragmentation on predation on artificial nests. Journal of Wildlife Management 58: 249–254.

BURGESS, R. L., AND D. M. SHARPE (EDITORS). 1981. Forest island dynamics in man-dominated landscapes. Springer, New York, NY.

BURHANS, D. E. 1997. Habitat and microhabitat features associated with cowbird parasitism in two forest edge cowbird hosts. Condor 99:866–872.

BURHANS, D. E., AND F. R. THOMPSON, III. 1999. Habitat patch size and nesting success of Yellow-Breasted Chats. Wilson Bulletin 111:210–215.

BURKE, D. M., AND E. NOL. 1998. Influence of food abundance, nest-site habitat, and forest fragmentation on breeding Ovenbirds. Auk 115:96–104.

BURKEY, T. V. 1993. Edge effects in seed and egg predation at two neotropical rainforest sites. Biological Conservation 66:139–143.

BURNHAM, K. P., D. R. ANDERSON, G. C. WHITE, C. BROWNIE, AND K. H. POLLOCK. 1987. Design and analysis methods for fish survival experiments based on release-recapture. American Fisheries Society Monograph 5, Bethesda, MD.

BUTCHER, G. S., AND C. R. SMITH. 1986. Breeding bird atlases add zip to summer birding. American Birds 40:419–428.

CADWELL, L. L., J. L. DOWNS, C. M. PHELPS, J. J. NUGENT, L. MARSH, AND L. FITZNER. 1996. Sagebrush restoration in the shrub-steppe of south-central Washington. Pp. 143–145 in J. R. Barrow, E. D. McArthur, R. E. Soesebee, and R. J. Tausch (compilers). Proceedings: shrubland ecosystem dynamics in a changing environment. USDA Forest Service Gen. Tech. Rep. INT-GTR-338. USDA Forest Service Intermountain Research Station, Ogden, UT.

CALL, D. R., R. J. GUTIÉRREZ, AND J. VERNER. 1992. Foraging habitat and home-range characteristics of California Spotted Owls in the Sierra Nevada. Condor 94:880–888.

CAMARGO, J. L. C., AND V. KAPOS. 1995. Complex edge effects in soil moisture and microclimate in central Amazonian forest. Journal of Tropical Ecology 11:205–221.

CAMMELL, M. E., M. J. WAY, AND M. R. PAIVA. 1996. Diversity and structure of ant communities associated with oak, pine, eucalyptus and arable habitats in Portugal. Insect Sociaux 43:37–46.

CANADAY, C. 1997. Loss of insectivorous birds along a gradient of human impact in Amazonia. Biological Conservation 77:63–77.

CAREY, A. B., M. M. HARDT, S. P. HORTON, AND B. L. BISWELL. 1991. Spring bird communities in the Oregon Coast Range. Pp. 123–142 in L. F. Ruggiero, K. B. Aubry, A. B. Carey, and M. H. Huff (editors). Wildlife and vegetation of unmanaged Douglas-fir forests. USDA Forest Service Gen. Tech. Rep. PNW-285. USDA Forest Service Pacific Northwest Research Station, Portland, OR.

CAREY, A. B., AND K. C. PEELER. 1995. Spotted Owls: resource and space use in mosaic landscapes. Journal of Raptor Research 29:223–239.

CAREY, A. B., J. A. REID, AND S. P. HORTON. 1990. Spotted Owl home range and habitat use in southern Oregon coast ranges. Journal of Wildlife Management 54:11–17.

CAROTHERS, S. W. 1977. Importance, preservation, and management of riparian habitats: an overview. Pp. 2–4 in R. R. Johnson and D. A. Jones (editors). Symposium on management of forest and range habitats for nongame birds. USDA Forest Service Gen. Tech. Rep. RM-43. USDA Forest Service Rocky Mountain Research Station, Fort Collins, CO.

CAROTHERS, S. W., AND R. R. JOHNSON. 1975. Water management practices and their effects on nongame birds in range habitats. Pp. 210–222 in D. R. Smith (editor). Symposium on management of forest and range habitats for nongame birds. USDA Forest Service Gen. Tech. Rep. WO-1. USDA Forest Service, Washington, D.C.

CAROTHERS, S. W., R. R. JOHNSON, AND S. W. AITCHISON. 1974. Population structure and social organization of Southwestern riparian birds. American Zoologist 14:97–108.

CARTER, H. R., AND R. A. ERICKSON. 1992. Status and conservation of the Marbled Murrelet in California, 1892–1987. Pp. 92–108 in H. R. Carter and M. L. Morrison (editors). Status and conservation of the Marbled Murrelet in North America. Proceedings of the Western Foundation of Vertebrate Zoology 5.

CASTRALE, J. S. 1982. Effects of two sagebrush control methods on nongame birds. Journal of Wildlife Management 46:945–952.

CATON, E. L. 1996. Effects of fire and salvage logging on the cavity-nesting bird community in northwestern Montana. Ph.D. dissertation. University of Montana, Missoula, MT.

CAVITT, J. F. 1999. Effects of fire and grazing on Brown Thrasher nest predation. Proceedings of the North American Prairie Conference 16:112–119.

CAVITT, J. F. 2000. Fire and a tallgrass prairie reptile community: effects on relative abundance and seasonal activity. Journal of Herpetology 34:12–20.

CENTER FOR BIOLOGICAL DIVERSITY. 2000. Petition to list the California Spotted Owl (Strix occidentalis occidentalis) as a threatened or endangered species. U.S. Department of the Interior, Washington, D.C.

CHACE, J. F., AND A. CRUZ. 1999. Past and present distribution of the Brown-headed Cowbird in the Rocky Mountain region. Studies in Avian Biology 18:89–93.

CHALFOUN, A. D., F. R. THOMPSON, III, AND M. J. RATNASWAMY. 2002. Nest predators and fragmentation: a review and meta-analysis. Conservation Biology 16:1–16.

CHANEY, E., W. ELMORE, AND W. S. PLATTS. 1990. Livestock grazing on western riparian areas. Produced for the Environmental Protection Agency, Eagle, ID.

CHASKO, G. G., AND J. E. GATES. 1982. Avian habitat suitability along a transmission-line corridor in an oak-hickory forest region. Wildlife Monographs 82:1–41.

CHEN, J. 1991. Edge effects: microclimatic pattern and biological responses in old-growth Douglas-fir forests. Ph.D. dissertation. University of Washington, Seattle, WA.

CHEN, J., J. F. FRANKLIN, AND T. A. SPIES. 1992. Vegetation responses to edge environments in old-growth Douglas-fir forests. Ecological Applications 2:387–396.

CHEN, J., J. F. FRANKLIN, AND T. A. SPIES. 1993. Contrasting microclimates among clearcut, edge and interior old-growth Douglas-fir forest. Agricultural and Forest Meteorology 63:219–237.

CHEN, J., J. F. FRANKLIN, AND T. A. SPIES. 1995. Growing-season microclimate gradients from clearcut edges into old-growth Douglas-fir forests. Ecological Applications 5:74–86.

CHEN, J., S. C. SAUNDERS, T. R. CROW, R. J. NAIMAN, L. D. BROSOFSKE, G. D. MROZ, B. L. BROOKSHIRE, AND J. F. FRANKLIN. 1999. Microclimate in forest ecosystem and landscape ecology. BioScience 49:288–297.

CIESLAK, M. 1992. Breeding bird communities on forest edge and interior. Ekologia Polska 40:461–475.

CLARK, J. S. 1988. Effect of climate change on fire regimes in northwestern Minnesota. Nature 334:233–235.

CLARK, K. L., AND R. J. ROBERTSON. 1981. Cowbird (Molothrus ater) parasitism and evolution of antiparasite strategies in the Yellow Warbler (Dendroica petechia). Wilson Bulletin 93:249–258.

CLAWSON, R. L., J. FAABORG, AND E. SEON. 1997. Effects of selected timber management practices on forest birds in Missouri oak-hickory forest: pre-treatment results. Pp. 274–288 in B. L. Brookshire and S. R. Shifley (editors). Proceedings of the Missouri Ozark Forest Ecosystem Project Symposium: an experimental approach to landscape research. USDA Forest Service Gen. Tech. Rep. NC-193. USDA Forest Service North Central Forest Experiment Station, St Paul, MN.

CODY, M. L. 1968. On the methods of resource division in grassland bird communities. American Naturalist 102:107–147.

CODY, M. L. 1975. Towards a theory of continental species diversities. Pp. 214–257 in M. L. Cody and J. M. Diamond (editors). Ecology and evolution of communities. Belknap Press, Cambridge, MA.

CODY, M. L. 1985. An introduction to habitat selection in birds. Pp. 4–46 in M. L. Cody (editor). Habitat selection in birds. Academic Press, San Diego, CA.

COHEN, J. 1969. Natural primate troops and a stochastic population model. American Naturalist 103:455–477.

COHEN, J. 1971. Casual groups of monkeys and men: stochastic models of elemental social systems. Oxford University Press, London, UK.

COHEN, J. 1987. Statistical power analysis for the behavioral sciences. Lawrence Erlbaum Associates, Hillsdale, NJ.

COKER, D. R., AND D. E. CAPEN. 1995. Landscape-level habitat use by Brown-headed Cowbirds in Vermont. Journal of Wildlife Management 59:631–637.

COKER, D. R., AND D. E. CAPEN. 2000. Distribution and habitat associations of Brown-headed Cowbirds in the Green Mountains of Vermont. Pp. 236–243 in J. N. M. Smith, T. L. Cook, S. I. Rothstein, S. K. Robinson, and S. G. Sealy (editors). The biology and management of cowbirds and their hosts. University of Texas Press, Austin, TX.

COLE, F. R., A. C. MEDEIROS, L. L. LOOPE, AND W. W. ZUEHLKE. 1992. Effects of the Argentine ant on arthropod fauna of Hawaiian high-elevation shrubland. Ecology 73:1313–1322.

CONINE, K. H., B. W. ANDERSON, R. D. OHMART, AND J. F. DRAKE. 1979. Responses of riparian species to agricultural habitat conversions. Pp. 248–262 in Strategies for protection and management of floodplain wetlands and other riparian ecosystems. USDA Forest Service Gen. Tech. Rep. WO-12. USDA Forest Service, Washington, D.C.

CONNELLY, J. W., AND C. E. BRAUN. 1997. Long-term changes in sage grouse Centrocercus urophasianus populations in western North America. Wildlife Biology 3:229–234.

COOPER, B. A., R. H. DAY, R. J. RITCHIE, AND C. L. CRANOR. 1991. An improved marine radar system for studies of bird migration. Journal of Field Ornithology 62:367–377.

COTTERILL, S E., AND S. J. HANNON. 1999. No evidence of short-term effects of clearcutting on artificial nest predation in boreal mixedwood forests. Canadian Journal of Forestry Research 29:1900–1910.

COVINGTON W. W., P. Z. FULE, M. M. MOORE, S. C. HART, T. E. KOLB, J. N. MAST, S. S. SACKETT, AND M. R. WAGNER. 1997. Restoring ecosystem health in ponderosa pine forests of the southwest. Journal of Forestry 97:23–29.

COVINGTON, W. W., AND M. M. MOORE. 1994. Southwestern ponderosa pine forest structure: changes since Euro-American settlement. Journal of Forestry 92:39–47.

CRAIG, R. J., AND K. G. BEAL. 1992. The influence of habitat variables on marsh bird communities of the Connecticut River Valley. Wilson Bulletin 104:295–311.

CRANE, M. F., AND W. C. FISCHER. 1986. Fire ecology of the forest habitat types of central Idaho. USDA Forest Service Gen. Tech. Rep. INT-218. USDA Forest Service Intermountain Research Station, Ogden, UT.

CROOKS, K. R. AND M. E. SOULÉ. 1999. Mesopredator release and avifaunal extinctions in a fragmented system. Nature 400:563–566.

CROOKS, K. R., A. V. SUAREZ, D. T. BOLGER, AND M. E. SOULÉ. 2001. Extinction and recolonization of birds on habitat islands. Conservation Biology 15:159–172.

CROONQUIST, M. J., AND R. P. BROOKS. 1991. Use of avian and mammalian guilds as indicators of cumulative impacts in riparian-wetland areas. Environmental Management 15:701–714.

CROONQUIST, M. J., AND R. P. BROOKS. 1993. Effects of habitat disturbance on bird communities in riparian corridors. Journal of Soil and Water Conservation 48:65–70.

CRUMPACKER, D. W. 1984. Regional riparian research and multi-university approach to the special problem of livestock grazing in the Rocky Mountains and Great Plains. Pp. 413–423 in W. E. Warner and K. M. Hendrix (editors). California riparian systems: ecology, conservation, and productive management. University of California Press, Berkeley, CA.

CRUZ, A., W. POST, J. W. WILEY, C. P. ORTEGA, T. K. NAKAMURA, AND J. W. PRATHER. 1998. Potential impacts of cowbird range expansion in Florida. Pp. 313–338, in S. I. Rothstein and S. K. Robinson (editors). Parasitic birds and their hosts: studies in coevolution. Oxford University Press, New York, NY.

CUBBEDGE, A. W. 1994. Comparisons of floodplain forest bird communities adjacent to four land use types at Minnesota Valley National Wildlife Refuge. Ph.D. dissertation. University of Missouri, Columbia, MO.

CURTIS, J. T. 1956. The modification of mid-latitude grasslands and forests by man. Pp. 721–736 in W. L. Thomas (editor). Man's role in changing the face of the earth. University of Chicago Press, Chicago, IL.

DANIELSON, B. J. 1992. Habitat selection, interspecific interactions and landscape composition. Evolutionary Ecology 6:399–411.

DANIELSON, W. R., R. M. DEGRAAF, AND T. K. FULLER. 1997. Rural and suburban forest edges: effect on egg predators and nest predation rates. Landscape and Urban Planning 38:25–36.

D'ANTONIO, C. M., AND P. M. VITOUSEK. 1992. Biological invasions by exotic grasses, the grass/fire cycle, and global change. Annual Review of Ecology and Systematics 23:63–87.

DARVEAU, M., L. BÉLANGER, J. HUOT, É. MELANÇON, AND S. DEBELLEFEUILLE. 1997. Forestry practices and the risk of bird nest predation in a boreal coniferous forest. Ecological Applications 7:572–580.

DASMANN, R. 1981. Wildlife biology. 2nd ed. John Wiley and Sons, New York, NY.

DAUBENMIRE, R. 1956. Climate as a determinant of vegetation distribution in eastern Washington and northern Idaho. Ecological Monographs 26:131–154.

DAUBENMIRE, R. 1968. Soil moisture in relation to vegetation distribution in the mountains of northern Idaho. Ecology 49:431–438.

DAVIS, C. R. 1999. Habitat and territory use by selected neotropical migratory birds in mixed-conifer forests of west-central Idaho. M.S. thesis. Arkansas State University, Jonesboro, AR.

DAVIS, F. W., P. A. STINE, D. M. STOMS, M. I. BORCHERT, AND A. D. HOLLANDER. 1995. Gap analysis of the actual vegetation of California. 1. The southwestern region. Madroño 42:40–78.

DAVIS, G. J., AND R. W. HOWE. 1992. Juvenile dispersal, limited breeding sites, and the dynamics of metapopulations. Theoretical Population Biology 41:184–207.

DAVIS, P. R. 1976. Response of vertebrate fauna to forest fire and clearcutting in south central Wyoming. Ph.D. dissertation. University of Wyoming, Laramie, WY.

DE ANGELOS, H., AND L. DE ANGELOS. 1998. Ancient redwoods and the politics of finance: the hostile takeover of the Pacific Lumber Company. Journal of Financial Economics 47:1919–1925.

DE GROOT, K. L., J. N. M. SMITH, AND M. J. TAITT. 1999. Cowbird removal programs as ecological experiments: measuring community-wide impacts of nest parasitism and predation. Studies in Avian Biology 18:229–234.

DEGRAAF, R. M. 1995. Nest predation rates in managed and reserved extensive northern hardwood forests. Forest Ecology and Management 79:227–234.

DEGRAAF, R. M., AND P. ANGELSTAM. 1993. Effects of timber size-class on predation of artificial nests in extensive forest. Forest Ecology and Management 61:127–136.

DEGRAAF, R. M., AND T. J. MAIER. 1996. Effects of egg size on predation by white-footed mice. Wilson Bulletin 108:535–539.

DEGRAAF, R. M., T. J. MAIER, AND T. K. FULLER. 1999. Predation of small eggs in artificial nests: effects of nest position, edge, and potential predator abundances in extensive forest. Wilson Bulletin 111:236–242.

DELONG, S. C., AND D. TANNER. 1996. Managing the pattern of forest harvest: lessons from wildfire. Biodiversity and Conservation 5:1191–1205.

DESANTE, D. F., AND T. L. GEORGE. 1994. Population trends in the landbirds of western North America. Studies in Avian Biology 15:173–190.

DESANTO, T. L., AND S. K. NELSON. 1995. Comparative reproductive ecology of the auks (Family Alcidae) with emphasis on the Marbled Murrelet. Pp. 33–48 in C. J. Ralph, G. L. Hunt, Jr., M. G. Raphael, and J. F. Piatt (editors). Ecology and conservation of the Marbled Murrelet. USDA Forest Service Gen. Tech. Rep. PSW-GTR-152. USDA Forest Service Pacific Southwest Research Station, Albany, CA.

DESIMONE, S. A., AND J. H. BURK. 1992. Local variation in floristics and distributional factors in Californian coastal sage scrub. Madroño 39:170–188.

DESROCHERS, A., AND S. J. HANNON. 1997. Gap crossing decisions by forest songbirds during the post-fledging period. Conservation Biology 11:1204–1210.

DIAMOND, J. M. 1976. Island biogeography and conservation: strategy and limitations. Science 193:1027–1029.

DIAMOND, J. M. 1978. Niche shifts and the rediscovery of interspecific competition. American Scientist 66:322–331.

DIAMOND, J. M. 1979. Population dynamics and interspecific competition in bird communities. Fortschritte der Zoologie 25:389–402.

DIDHAM, R. K. 1997. The influence of edge effects and forest fragmentation on leaf litter invertebrates in central Amazonia. Pp. 55–70 in W. F. Laurance and R. O. Bierregaard, Jr. (editors). Tropical forest remnants: ecology, management and conservation of fragmented communities. University of Chicago Press, Chicago, IL.

DIJAK, W. D., AND F. R. THOMPSON, III. 2000. Landscape and edge effects on the distribution of mammalian predators in Missouri. Journal of Wildlife Management 64:209–216.

DIVOKY, G. J., AND M. HORTON. 1995. Breeding and natal dispersal, nest habitat loss and implications for Marbled Murrelet populations. Pp. 83–87 in C. J. Ralph, G. L. Hunt, Jr., M. G. Raphael, and J. F. Piatt (editors). Ecology and conservation of the Marbled Murrelet. USDA Forest Service Gen. Tech. Rep. PSW-GTR-152. USDA Forest Service Pacific Southwest Research Station, Albany, CA.

DIXON, R. D., AND V. A. SAAB. 2000. Black-backed Woodpecker (*Picoides arcticus*). *In* A. Poole and F. Gill (editors). Birds of North America No. 509. The Academy of Natural Sciences, Philadelphia, PA, and The American Ornithologists Union, Washington, D.C.

DOAK, D. F. 1989. Spotted Owls and old growth logging in the Pacific Northwest. Conservation Biology 3:389–396.

DOAK, D. F., P. C. MARINO, AND P. M. KAREIVA. 1992. Spatial scale mediates the influence of habitat fragmentation on dispersal success: implications for conservation. Theoretical Population Biology 41:315–336.

DOBKIN, D. S. 1994. Conservation and management of neotropical migrant landbirds in the northern Rockies and Great Plains. University of Idaho Press, Moscow, ID.

DOBKIN, D. S. 1995. Management and conservation of Sage Grouse, denominative species for the ecological health of shrubsteppe ecosystems. USDI Bureau of Land Management, Portland, OR.

DOBKIN, D. S., A. C. RICH, J. A. PRETARE, AND W. H. PYLE. 1995. Nest-site relationships among cavity-nesting birds of riparian and snowpocket aspen woodlands in the northwestern Great Basin. Condor 97:694–707.

DOBKIN, D. S., AND B. A. WILCOX. 1986. Analysis of natural forest fragments: riparian birds in the Toiyabe Mountains, Nevada. Pp. 293–299 in J. Verner, M. L. Morrison, and C. J. Ralph (editors). Wildlife

2000: modeling habitat relationships of terrestrial vertebrates. University of Wisconsin Press, Madison, WI.

DOBLER, F. C. 1994. Washington state shrub-steppe ecosystem studies with emphasis on the relationship between nongame birds and shrub and grass cover densities. Pp. 149–161 in S. B. Monsen and S. G. Kitchen (compilers). Proceedings—ecology and management of annual rangelands. USDA Forest Service Gen. Tech. Rep. INT-GTR-313. USDA Forest Service Intermountain Research Station, Ogden, UT.

DOBLER, F. C., J. EBY, C. PERRY, S. RICHARDSON, AND M. VANDER HAEGEN. 1996. Status of Washington's shrub-steppe ecosystem: extent, ownership, and wildlife/vegetation relationships. Research Report. Washington Department of Fish and Wildlife, Olympia, WA.

DONOVAN, T. M., AND C. H. FLATHER. 2002. Relationships among North American songbird trends, habitat fragmentation, and landscape occupancy. Ecological Applications 12:364–374.

DONOVAN, T. M., P. W. JONES, E. M. ANNAND, AND F. R. THOMPSON, III. 1997. Variation in local-scale edge effects: mechanisms and landscape context. Ecology 78:2064–2075.

DONOVAN, T. M., AND R. H. LAMBERSON. 2001. Area-sensitive distributions counteract negative effects of habitat fragmentation on breeding birds. Ecology 82:1170–1179.

DONOVAN, T. M., R. H. LAMBERSON, A. KIMBER, F. R. THOMPSON, III, AND J. FAABORG. 1995a. Modeling the effects of habitat fragmentation on source and sink demography of neotropical migrant birds. Conservation Biology 9:1396–1407.

DONOVAN, T. M., AND F. R. THOMPSON, III. 2001. Modeling the ecological trap hypothesis: a habitat and demographic sensitivity analysis for migrant songbirds. Ecological Applications 11:871–882.

DONOVAN, T. M., F. R. THOMPSON, III, AND J. FAABORG. 2000. Cowbird distribution at different scales of fragmentation: tradeoffs between breeding and feeding opportunities. Pp. 255–264 in J. N. M. Smith, T. L. Cook, S. I. Rothstein, S. K. Robinson, and S. G. Sealy (editors). The biology and management of cowbirds and their hosts. University of Texas Press, Austin, TX.

DONOVAN, T. M., F. R. THOMPSON, III, J. FAABORG, AND J. R. PROBST. 1995b. Reproductive success of migratory birds in habitat sources and sinks. Conservation Biology 9:1380–1395.

DUNN, C. P., D. M. SHARPE, G. R. GUNTERSPERGEN, F. STEARNS, AND Z. YANG. 1991. Methods for analyzing temporal changes in landscape pattern. Pp. 173–198 in M. G. Turner and R. H. Gardner (editors). Quantitative methods in landscape ecology. Springer-Verlag, New York, NY.

DUNNING, J. B., AND J. H. BROWN. 1982. Summer rainfall and winter sparrow densities: a test of the food limitation hypothesis. Auk 99:123–129.

DUNNING, J. B., B. J. DANIELSON, AND H. R. PULLIAM. 1992. Ecological processes that affect populations in complex landscapes. Oikos 65:169–175.

EBERHART, K. E., AND P. M. WOODARD. 1987. Distribution of residual vegetation associated with large fires in Alberta. Canadian Journal of Forest Research 17:1207–1212.

ECKRICH, G. H., T. E. KOLOSZAR, AND M. D. GOERING. 1999. Effective landscape management of Brown-headed Cowbirds at Ford Hood, Texas. Studies in Avian Biology 18:267–274.

EDENIUS, L., AND K. SJÖBERG. 1997. Distribution of birds in natural landscape mosaics of old-growth forests in northern Sweden: relations to habitat area and landscape context. Ecography 20:425–431.

EHRLICH, P. R., D. S. DOBKIN, AND D. WHEYE. 1988. The birder's handbook: a field guide to the natural history of North American birds. Simon and Schuster, Fireside, New York, NY.

ELIASON, S. A., AND E. B. ALLEN. 1997. Exotic grass competition in suppressing native shrubland re-establishment. Restoration Ecology 5:245–255.

ELLISON, K. 1999. Importance of predation and brood parasitism on nest success in four sparrow species in southern California coastal sage scrub. Studies in Avian Biology 18:191–199.

ERICKSON, J. M. 1971. The displacement of native ant species by the introduced Argentine ant Iridomyrmex humilis (Mayr). Psyche 78:257–266.

EVANS, D. M. 1995. Relationships between landscape pattern and songbird abundance in mixed conifer forests of west-central Idaho. M.S. thesis. Northern Arizona University, Flagstaff, AZ.

EVANS, D. M., AND D. M. FINCH. 1994. Relationships between forest songbird populations and managed forests in Idaho. Pp. 308–314 in W. W. Covington and L. F. Debano (editors). Sustainable ecological systems: implementing an ecological approach to land management. USDA Forest Service Gen. Tech. Rep. RM-247. USDA Forest Service Rocky Mountain Research Station, Fort Collins, CO.

EVANS, D. R., AND J. E. GATES. 1997. Cowbird selection of breeding areas: the role of habitat and bird species abundance. Wilson Bulletin 109:470–480.

FAABORG, J., M. C. BRITTINGHAM, T. M. DONOVAN, AND J. BLAKE. 1993. Habitat fragmentation in the temperate zone: a perspective for managers. Pp. 331–338 in D. M. Finch and P. W. Stangel (editors). Status and management of neotropical migratory birds. USDA Forest Service Gen. Tech. Rep. RM-229. USDA Forest Service Rocky Mountain Research Station, Fort Collins, CO.

FAABORG, J., M. C. BRITTINGHAM, T. M. DONOVAN, AND J. BLAKE. 1995. Habitat fragmentation in the temperate zone. Pp. 357–380 in T. E. Martin and D. M. Finch (editors). Ecology and management of neotropical migratory birds: a synthesis and review of critical issues. Oxford University Press, New York, NY.

FAGAN, W. F., R. S. CANTRELL, AND C. COSNER. 1999. How habitat edges change species interactions. American Naturalist 153:165–182.

FAHRIG, L. 1997. Relative effects of habitat loss and fragmentation on population extinction. Journal of Wildlife Management 61:603–610.

FAHRIG, L. 1998. When does fragmentation of breeding habitat affect population survival? Ecological Modeling 105:273–292.

FAHRIG, L. 1999. Forest loss and fragmentation: which has the greater effect on forest-dwelling animals? Page 87–95 in J. A. Rochelle, L. A. Lehmann, and J. Wisniewski (editors). Forest fragmentation: wildlife and management implications. Brill Publishers, Leiden, The Netherlands.

FAHRIG, L., AND G. MERRIAM. 1994. Conservation of fragmented populations. Conservation Biology 8: 50–59.

FARMER, C. 1999. The density and distribution of Brown-headed Cowbirds: the central coastal California enigma. Studies in Avian Biology 18:62–67.

FAUTH, P. T. 2000. Reproductive success of Wood Thrushes in forest fragments in northern Indiana. Auk 117:194–204.

FEINSINGER, P. 1997. Habitat "shredding." Pp. 270–271 in G. K. Meffe and C. R. Carroll (editors). Principles of conservation biology. Sinauer Associates, Sunderland, MA.

FEMAT, 1993. Forest Ecosystem Management: an ecological, economic and social assessment. Report of the Forest Ecosystem Management Assessment Team. July 1993, Portland, OR. U.S. Government Printing Office, Washington, D.C.

FENSKE-CRAWFORD, T. J., AND G. J. NIEMI. 1997. Predation of artificial ground nests at two types of edges in a forest-dominated landscape. Condor 99:14–24.

FERRIS, C. R. 1979. Effects of Interstate 95 on breeding birds in northern Maine. Journal of Wildlife Management 43:421–427.

FERRY, G. W., R. G. CLARK, R. E. MONTGOMERY, R. W. MUTCH, W. P. LEENHOUTS, AND G. T. ZIMMERMAN. 1995. Altered fire regimes within fire-adapted ecosystems. Pp. 222–224 in E. T. LaRoe, G. S. Farris, C. E. Puckett, P. D. Doran, and M. J. Mac (editors.). Our living resources: a report to the nation on the distribution, abundance, and health of U.S. plants, animals, and ecosystems. USDI National Biological Service, Washington, D.C.

FINCH, D. M., J. L. GANEY, W. YONG, R. T. KIMBALL, AND R. SALLABANKS. 1997. Effects and interactions of fire, logging, and grazing. Pp. 103–136 in W. M. Block and D. M. Finch (editors). Songbird ecology in southwestern ponderosa pine forests: a literature review. USDA For. Serv. Gen. Tech. Rep. RM-292. USDA Forest Service Rocky Mountain Forest and Range Experiment Station, Fort Collins, CO.

FISCHER, W. C., AND A. F. BRADLEY. 1987. Fire ecology of western Montana forest habitat types. USDA Forest Service Gen. Tech. Rep. INT-223. USDA Forest Service Intermountain Research Station, Ogden, Utah.

FISCHL, J., AND D. F. CACCAMISE. 1985. Influence of habitat and season on foraging flock composition in the European starling (Sturnus vulgaris). Oecologia 67:532–539.

FISHER, R. A. 1954. Statistical methods for research workers. 12th Edition. Oliver and Boyd, Edinburgh, UK.

FLAHERTY, P. H. 2000. Effects of pre-disturbance forest vegetation on the impacts of a catastrophic blowdown in a Rocky Mountain subalpine landscape. M.S. thesis. University of Wyoming, Laramie, WY.

FLEISCHNER, T. E. 1994. Ecological costs of livestock grazing in Western North America. Conservation Biology 8:629–644.

FLEMING, K. K., AND W. M. GIULIANO. 1998. Effect of

border-edge cuts on birds at woodlot edges in southwestern Pennsylvania. Journal of Wildlife Management 62:1430–1437.

FLEXNER, S. B., AND L. C. HAUCK (EDITORS). 1987. The Random House dictionary of the English language. 2nd ed. (unabridged). Random House, New York, NY.

FOLLIARD, L. 1993. Nest site characteristics of Northern Spotted Owls in managed forests of northwest California. M.S. thesis. University of Idaho, Moscow, ID.

FORMAN, R. T. T. 1997. Land mosaics: the ecology of landscapes and regions. Cambridge University Press, Cambridge, UK.

FORMAN, R. T. T., AND S. K. COLLINGE. 1996. The 'spatial solution' to conserving biodiversity in landscapes and regions. Pp. 537–568 in R. M. DeGraaf and R. I. Miler (editors). Conservation of faunal diversity in forested landscapes. Chapman and Hall, New York, NY.

FORMAN, R. T. T., A. E. GALLI, AND C. F. LECK. 1976. Forest size and avian diversity in New Jersey woodlots with some land use implications. Oecologia 26:1–8.

FORMAN, R. T. T., AND M. GODRON. 1986. Landscape ecology. John Wiley and Sons, New York, NY.

FORSMAN, E. D., S. DeSTEPHANO, M. G. RAPHAEL, AND R. J. GUTIÉRREZ (EDITORS). 1996. Demography of the Northern Spotted Owl. Studies in Avian Biology No. 17. Cooper Ornithological Society, Los Angeles, CA.

FORSMAN, E. D., AND A. R. GIESE. 1997. Nests of Northern Spotted Owls on the Olympic peninsula, Washington. Wilson Bulletin 109:28–41.

FORSMAN, E. D., E. C. MESLOW, AND H. M. WIGHT. 1984. Distribution and biology of the Spotted Owl in Oregon. Wildlife Monographs 87:1–64.

FOX, L. 1997. Klamath bioregional assessment project GIS maps. Department of Natural Resources, Planning and Interpretation. Humboldt State University, Arcata, CA.

FRANKEL, O. H., AND M. E. SOULÉ. 1981. Conservation and evolution. Cambridge University Press, Cambridge, UK.

FRANKLIN, A. B., D. R. ANDERSON, R. J. GUTIÉRREZ, AND K. P. BURNHAM. 2000. Climate, habitat quality, and fitness in Northern Spotted Owl populations in northwest California. Ecological Monographs 70:539–590.

FRANKLIN, A. B., K. P. BURNHAM, G. C. WHITE, R. J. ANTHONY, E. D. FORSMAN, C. SCHWARZ, J. D. NICHOLS, AND J. HINES. 1999. Range-wide status and trends in Northern Spotted Owl populations. U.S. Geological Survey, Biological Resources Division, Corvallis, OR.

FRANKLIN, J. F., AND C. T. DYRNESS. 1973. Natural vegetation of Oregon and Washington. USDA Forest Service Gen. Tech. Rep. PNW-8. USDA Forest Service Pacific Northwest Research Station, Portland, OR.

FRANKLIN, J. F., AND C. T. DYRNESS. 1988. Natural vegetation of Oregon and Washington. Oregon State University Press, Corvallis, OR.

FRANKLIN, J. F., AND R. T. FORMAN. 1987. Creating landscape patterns by forest cutting: ecological consequences and principles. Landscape Ecology 1:5–18.

FRANKLIN, J. F., AND T. A. SPIES. 1984. Characteristics of old-growth Douglas-fir forests. Pp. 212–229 in Society of American Foresters, New Forests for a Changing World, Bethesda, MD.

FREEMARK, K. E., AND B. COLLINS. 1992. Landscape ecology of birds breeding in temperate forest fragments. Pp. 443–454 in J. M. Hagan, III, and D. W. Johnston (editors). Ecology and conservation of neotropical migrant landbirds. Smithsonian Institution Press, Washington, D.C.

FREEMARK, K. E., J. B. DUNNING, S. J. HEJL, AND J. R. PROBST. 1995. A landscape ecology perspective for research, conservation and management. Pp. 381–427 in T. E. Martin and D. M. Finch (editors). Ecology and management of neotropical migratory birds: a synthesis and review of critical issues. Oxford University Press, New York, NY.

FREEMARK, K. E., AND H. G. MERRIAM. 1986. Importance of area and habitat heterogeneity to bird assemblages in temperate forest fragments. Biological Conservation 36:115–141.

FREEMARK, K. E., J. R. PROBST, J. B. DUNNING, AND S. J. HEJL. 1993. Adding a landscape ecology perspective to conservation and planning. Pp. 346–352 in D. M. Finch and P. W. Stangel (editors). Status and management of neotropical migratory birds. USDA Forest Service Gen. Tech. Rep. RM-229. USDA Forest Service Rocky Mountain Research Station, Ft. Collins, CO.

FRÉMONT, J. C. 1845. Report of the exploring expedition to the Rocky Mountains in the year 1842, and to Oregon and Northern California in the years 1843–44. Gales and Seaton, Washington, D.C.

FRETWELL, S. D., AND H. L. LUCAS, JR. 1970. On territorial behavior and other factors influencing habitat distribution in birds. I. Theoretical development. Acta Biotheoretica 19:16–36.

FRIEDMANN, H. 1963. Host relations of the parasitic cowbirds. U.S. National Museum Bulletin 233:1–276.

FRIEDMANN, H., L. F. KIFF, AND S. I. ROTHSTEIN. 1977. A further contribution to knowledge of the host relations of parasitic cowbirds. Smithsonian Contributions in Zoology 235:1–75.

FRIESEN, L. E., M. D. CADMAN, AND R. J. MACKAY. 1999. Nesting success of neotropical migrant songbirds in a highly fragmented landscape. Conservation Biology 13:33–346.

FRIESEN, L. E., P. F. J. EAGLES, AND R. J. MACKAY. 1995. Effects of residential development on forest-dwelling neotropical migrant songbirds. Conservation Biology 9:1408–1414.

FULE, P. Z., W. W. COVINGTON, AND M. M. MOORE. 1997. Determining reference conditions for ecosystem management of southwestern ponderosa pine forests. Ecological Application 7:895–908.

GAINES, D. 1974. A new look at the nesting riparian avifauna of the Sacramento Valley, California. Western Birds 5:61–80.

GALE, G. A., L. A. HANNERS, AND S. R. PATTON. 1997. Reproductive success of Worm-eating Warblers in a forested landscape. Conservation Biology 11:246–250.

GALLI, A. E., C. F. LECK, AND R. T. T. FORMAN. 1976. Avian distribution patterns in forest islands of different sizes in central New Jersey. Auk 93:356–364.

GANEY, J. L., AND R. P. BALDA. 1994. Habitat selection by Mexican Spotted Owls in northern Arizona. Auk 111:162–169.

GANEY, J. L., W. M. BLOCK, J. K. DWYER, B. E. STROHMEYER, AND J. S. JENNESS. 1998. Dispersal movements and survival rates of juvenile Mexican Spotted Owls in northern Arizona. Wilson Bulletin 110: 206–217.

GANEY, J. L., AND J. L. DICK, JR. 1995. Habitat relationships of the Mexican Spotted Owl: current knowledge. Pp. 1–42 in W. M. Block, F. Clemente, J. F. Cully, J. L. Dick, Jr., A. B. Franklin, J. L. Ganey, F. P. Howe, W. H. Moir, S. L. Spangle, S. E. Rinkevich, D. L. Urban, R. Vahle, J. P. Ward, Jr., and G. C. White. Recovery plan for the Mexican Spotted Owl (Strix occidentalis lucida), volume 2. U.S. Department of Interior, Fish and Wildlife Service, Albuquerque, NM.

GARMEN, S. L., F. J. SWANSON, AND T. A. SPIES. 1999. Past, present, and future landscape patterns in the Douglas-fir region of the Pacific Northwest. Pp. 61–86 in J. A. Rochelle, L. A. Lehmann, and J. Wisniewski (editors). Forest fragmentation: wildlife and management implications. Brill Publishers, Leiden, The Netherlands.

GATES, J. E., AND D. R. EVANS. 1998. Cowbirds breeding in the central Appalachians: spatial and temporal patterns and habitat selection. Ecological Applications 8:27–40.

GATES, J. E., AND N. R. GIFFEN. 1991. Neotropical migrant birds and edge effects at a forest-stream ecotone. Wilson Bulletin 103:204–217.

GATES, J. E., AND L. W. GYSEL. 1978. Avian nest dispersion and fledging success in field-forest ecotones. Ecology 59:871–883.

GEORGE, T. L. 2000. Varied Thrush (Ixoreus naevius). In A. Poole and F. Gill (editors). The Birds of North America, No. 541. The Academy of Natural Sciences, Philadelphia, PA, and The American Ornithologists Union, Washington, D.C.

GERMAINE, S. S., S. H. VESSEY, AND D. E. CAPEN. 1997. Effects of small forest openings on the breeding bird community in a Vermont hardwood forest. Condor 99:708–718.

GIBBS, J. P., AND J. FAABORG. 1990. Estimating the viability of Ovenbird and Kentucky Warbler populations in forest fragments. Conservation Biology 4: 193–196.

GIBBS, J. P., J. R. LONGCORE, D. G. MCAULEY, AND J. K. RINGELMAN. 1991. Use of wetland habitats by selected nongame water birds in Maine. Fish and Wildlife Research No. 9, U.S. Fish and Wildlife Service, Washington D.C.

GILBERT, F. F., AND R. ALLWAINE. 1991. Spring bird communities in the Oregon Cascades Range. Pp. 145–160 in L. F. Ruggiero, K. B. Aubry, A. B. Carey, and M. H. Huff (technical coordinators). Wildlife and vegetation of unmanaged Douglas-fir forests. USDA Forest Service Gen. Tech. Rep. PNW-GTR-285. USDA Forest Service Pacific Northwest Research Station, Portland, OR.

GILES, R. H. 1978. Wildlife management. W. H. Freeman and Company, San Francisco, CA.

GLUCK, M. J., AND R. S. REMPEL. 1996. Structural characteristics of post-wildfire and clearcut landscapes. Environmental Monitoring and Assessment 39:435–450.

GOGGANS, R. 1986. Habitat use by Flammulated Owls in northeastern Oregon. M.S. thesis. Oregon State University, Corvallis, OR.

GOGUEN, C. B., AND N. E. MATHEWS. 1999. Causes and implications of the association between cowbirds and livestock. Studies in Avian Biology 18:10–17.

GOOD, E. E., AND C. A. DAMBACH. 1943. The effect of land use practices in breeding bird populations in Ohio. Journal of Wildlife Management 7:291–297.

GOODWIN, B. J., AND L. FAHRIG. 1998. Spatial scaling and animal population dynamics. Pp. 193–206 in D. L. Peterson and V. T. Parker (editors). Ecological scale: theory and applications. Columbia University Press, New York, NY.

GOTTFRIED, B. M., AND C. F. THOMPSON. 1978. Experimental analysis of nest predation in an old-field habitat. Auk 95:304–312.

GRENIER, J. J., AND S. K. NELSON. 1995. Marbled Murrelet habitat associations in Oregon. Pp. 191–204 in C. J. Ralph, G. L. Hunt, Jr., M. G. Raphael, and J. F. Piatt (editors). Ecology and conservation of the Marbled Murrelet. USDA Forest Service Gen. Tech. Rep. PSW-GTR-152. USDA Forest Service Pacific Southwest Research Station, Albany, CA.

GRISHAVER, M. A., P. J. MOCK, AND K. L. PRESTON. 1998. Breeding behavior of the California gnatcatcher in southwestern San Diego County. Western Birds 29:299–322.

GRUELL, G. E. 1983. Fire and vegetative trends in the Northern Rockies: interpretations from 1871–1982 photographs. USDA Forest Service Gen. Tech. Rep. INT-158. USDA Forest Service Intermountain Forest and Range Experiment Station, Ogden, UT.

GRUELL, G. E. 1985. Fire on the early western landscape: an annotated list of recorded wildfires in presettlement times. Northwest Science 59:97–107.

GRUELL, G. E., W. C. SCHMIDT, S. F. ARNO, AND W. J. REICH. 1982. Seventy years of vegetative change in a managed ponderosa pine forest in western Montana: implications for resource management. USDA Forest Service Gen. Tech. Rep. INT-GTR-130. USDA Forest Service Intermountain Research Station, Ogden, UT.

GUSTAFSON, E. J., AND T. R. CROW. 1994. Modeling the effects of forest harvesting on landscape structure and the spatial distribution of cowbird brood parasitism. Landscape Ecology 9:237–248.

GUTIÉRREZ, R. J. 1994. Changes in the distribution and abundance of Spotted Owls during the past century. Studies in Avian Biology 15:293–300.

GUTIÉRREZ, R. J., A. B. FRANKLIN, AND W. S. LAHAYE. 1995. Spotted Owl (Strix occidentalis). In A. Poole and F. Gill (editors). The Birds of North America, No. 179. The Academy of Natural Sciences, Philadelphia, PA, and The American Ornithologists Union, Washington, D.C.

GUTIÉRREZ, R. J., AND S. HARRISON. 1996. Applying metapopulation theory to Spotted Owl management: a history and critique. Pp. 167–185 in D. R. Mc-

Cullough (editor). Metapopulations and wildlife conservation. Island Press, Washington, D.C.

GUTIÉRREZ, R. J., M. E. SEAMANS, AND M. Z. PEERY. 1996. Intermountain movement by Mexican spotted owls (*Strix occidentalis lucida*). Great Basin Naturalist 56:87–89.

GUTIÉRREZ, R. J., J. VERNER, K. S. MCKELVEY, B. R. NOON, G. N. STEGER, D. R. CALL, W. S. LAHAYE, B. B. BINGHAM, AND J. S. SENSER. 1992. Habitat relations of the California Spotted Owl. Pp. 79–148 *in* J. Verner, K. S. McKelvey, B. R. Noon, R. J. Gutiérrez, G. I. Gould, Jr., and T. W. Beck (editors). The California Spotted Owl: a technical assessment of its current status. USDA Forest Service Gen. Tech. Rep. PSW-GTR-133. USDA Forest Service Pacific Southwest Research Station, Albany, CA.

GUTIÉRREZ, R. J., J. P. WARD, A. B. FRANKLIN, W. S. LAHAYE, AND V. MERETSKY. 1985. Dispersal ecology of juvenile Northern Spotted Owls (*Strix occidentalis caurina*) in northwestern California. Final Report to U.S. Forest Service, Region 6, Portland, OR.

HABECK, J. R. 1987. Present-day vegetation in the northern Rocky Mountains. Annals of the Missouri Botanical Garden 74:804–840.

HABECK, J. R. 1988. Old-growth forests in the northern Rocky Mountains. Natural Areas Journal 8:202–211.

HABECK, J. R., AND R. W. MUTCH. 1973. Fire dependent forests in the northern Rocky Mountains. Quaternary Research 3:408–424.

HADDAD, N. M. 1999. Corridor use predicted from behaviors at habitat boundaries. American Naturalist 153:215–227.

HAGAN, J. M., III, AND D. W. JOHNSTON (EDITORS). 1992. Ecology and conservation of neotropical migrant landbirds. Smithsonian Institution Press, Washington, D.C.

HAGAN, J. M., III, W. M. VANDER HAEGEN, AND P. S. MCKINLEY. 1996. The early development of forest fragmentation effects on birds. Conservation Biology 10:188–202.

HAHN, D. C., AND J. S. HATFIELD. 1995. Parasitization at the landscape scale: cowbirds prefer forests. Conservation Biology 9:1415–1424.

HAHN, D. C., AND R. J. O'CONNOR. 2002. Contrasting determinants of abundance in an invasive brood parasite: ancestral vs. colonized ranges. Pp. 219–228 *in* J. M. Scott, P. J. Heglund, M. L. Morrison, M. Raphael, J. Haufler, and B. Wall (editors). Predicting species occurrences: issues of scale and accuracy. Island Press, Washington, D.C.

HAILA, Y. 1999. Islands and fragments. Pp. 234–264 *in* M. Hunter (editor). Maintaining biodiversity in forest ecosystems. Cambridge University Press, New York, NY.

HALL, L. S., P. R. KRAUSMAN, AND M. L. MORRISON. 1997. The habitat concept and a plea for standard terminology. Wildlife Society Bulletin 25:173–182.

HAMER, T. E. 1995. Inland habitat associations of Marbled Murrelets in western Washington. Pp. 163–189 *in* C. J. Ralph, G. L. Hunt, Jr., M. G. Raphael, and J. F. Piatt (editors). Ecology and conservation of the Marbled Murrelet. USDA Forest Service Gen. Tech. Rep. PSW-GTR-152. USDA Forest Service Pacific Southwest Research Station, Albany, CA.

HAMER, T. E., B. A. COOPER, AND C. J. RALPH. 1995. Use of radar to study the movements of Marbled Murrelets at inland sites. Northwestern Naturalist 76:73–78.

HAMER, T., AND S. K. NELSON. 1995. Characteristics of Marbled Murrelet nest trees and nesting stands. Pp. 49–56 *in* C. J. Ralph, G. L. Hunt, Jr., M. G. Raphael, and J. F. Piatt (editors). Ecology and conservation of the Marbled Murrelet. USDA Forest Service Gen. Tech. Rep. PSW-GTR-152. USDA Forest Service Pacific Southwest Research Station, Albany, CA.

HAMES, R. S. 2001. Habitat fragmentation and forest birds: effects at multiple scales. PhD dissertation. Cornell University, Ithaca, NY.

HAMES, R. S., K. V. ROSENBERG, J. D. LOWE, AND A. A. DHONDT. 2001. Site reoccupation in fragmented landscapes: testing predictions of metapopulation theory. Journal of Animal Ecology 70:182–190.

HANN, W. J., J. L. JONES, M. G. KARL, P. F. HESSBURG, R. E. KEAN, D. G. LONG, J. P. MENAKIS, C. H. MCNICOLL, S. G. LEONARD, R. A. GRAVENMIER, AND B. G. SMITH. 1997. An assessment of ecosystem components in the Interior Columbia Basin and portions of the Klamath and Great Basins, Vol. II. Landscape dynamics of the basin. USDA Forest Service Gen. Tech. Rep. PNW-GTR-405. USDA Forest Service Pacific Northwest Research Station, Portland, OR.

HANNON, S. J., AND S. E. COTTERILL. 1998. Nest predation in aspen woodlots in an agricultural area in Alberta: the enemy from within. Auk 115:16–25.

HANSEN, A. J., S. L. GARMAN, B. MARKS, AND D. L. URBAN. 1993. An approach for managing vertebrate diversity across multiple-use landscapes. Ecological Applications 3:481–496.

HANSEN, A. J., S. L. GARMAN, J. F. WEIGAND, D. L. URBAN, W. C. MCCOMB, AND M. G. RAPHAEL. 1995a. Alternative silvicultural regimes in the Pacific Northwest: simulations of ecological and economic effects. Ecological Applications 5:535–554.

HANSEN, A. J., W. C. MCCOMB, R. VEGA, M. G. RAPHAEL, AND M. HUNTER. 1995b. Bird habitat relationships in natural and managed forests in the West Cascades of Oregon. Ecological Applications 5:555–569.

HANSEN, A. J., AND J. R. ROTELLA. 1999. Abiotic factors and biodiversity. Pp. 161–209 *in* M. Hunter (editor). Maintaining biodiversity in forest ecosystems. Cambridge University Press, New York, NY.

HANSEN, A. J., AND J. J. ROTELLA. 2000. Bird responses to forest fragmentation. Pp. 202–221 *in* R. L. Knight, F. W. Smith, S. W. Buskirk, W. H. Romme, and W. L. Baker (editors). Forest fragmentation in the southern Rocky Mountains. University of Colorado Press, Boulder, CO.

HANSEN, A. J., T. A. SPIES, F. J. SWANSON, AND J. L. OHMANN. 1991. Conserving biodiversity in managed forests. BioScience 41:382–392.

HANSEN, A. J., AND D. L. URBAN. 1992. Avian response to landscape pattern: the role of species' life histories. Landscape Ecology 7:163–180.

HANSKI, I. 1991. Single-species metapopulation dynamics: concepts, models and observations. Biological Journal of the Linnean Society 42:17–38.

HANSKI, I. K., T. J. FENSKE, AND G. J. NIEMI. 1996. Lack of edge effect in nesting success of breeding birds in managed forest landscapes. Auk 113:578–585.

HANSSON, L. 1983. Bird numbers across edges between mature conifer forest and clearcuts in central Sweden. Ornis Scandinavica 14:97–103.

HANSSON, L. 1994. Vertebrate distributions relative to clear-cut edges in a boreal forest landscape. Landscape Ecology 9:105–115.

HANSSON, L., L. FAHRIG, AND G. MERRIAM. 1995. Mosaic landscapes and ecological processes. Chapman and Hall, London, UK.

HARRIS, L. D. 1984. The fragmented forest. University of Chicago Press, Chicago, IL.

HARRIS, L. D. 1988. Edge effects and conservation of biotic diversity. Conservation Biology 2:330–339.

HARRIS, M. A. 1982. Habitat use among woodpeckers in forest burns. M.S. thesis. University of Montana, Missoula, MT.

HARRISON, H. H. 1979. A field guide to western bird nests. Houghton Mifflin, Boston, MA.

HARRISON, P. P., E. G. KUO, AND S. P. HORTON. 1999. Inland Marbled Murrelet surveys in the Olympic Experimental State Forest, Washington, U.S.A. Pacific Seabirds 26:50.

HARTLEY, M. J., AND M. L. HUNTER, JR. 1998. A meta-analysis of forest cover, edge effects, and artificial nest predation rates. Conservation Biology 12:465–469.

HASKELL, D. G. 1995a. A reevaluation of the effects of forest fragmentation on rates of bird-nest predation. Conservation Biology 9:1316–1318.

HASKELL, D. G. 1995b. Forest fragmentation and nest predation: are experiments with Japanese quail eggs misleading? Auk 112:767–770.

HAWROT, R. Y., AND G. J. NIEMI. 1996. Effects of edge type and patch shape on avian communities in a mixed conifer-hardwood forest. Auk 113:586–598.

HAYDEN, T. J., J. FAABORG, AND R. L. CLAWSON. 1985. Estimates of minimum area requirements for Missouri forest birds. Transactions Missouri Academy of Science 19:11–22.

HAZARD, G. C., AND T. L. GEORGE. 1999. Landbird abundance and diversity in different-aged stands of coast redwood forests in northwestern California. Northwestern Naturalist 80:99–109.

HEHNKE, M., AND C. P. STONE. 1979. Value of riparian vegetation to avian populations along the Sacramento River system. USDA Forest Service Gen. Tech. Rep. WO-12:228–235. USDA Forest Service Washington Office, Washington, D.C.

HEINRICH, B., J. M. MARZLUFF, AND B. ADAMS. 1995. Fear and food recognition in naive Common Ravens. Auk 112:499–503.

HEJL, S. J. 1992. The importance of landscape patterns to bird diversity: a perspective from the northern Rocky Mountains. Northwest Environmental Journal 8:119–137.

HEJL, S. J. 1994. Human-induced changes in bird populations in coniferous forests in western North America during the past 100 years. Studies in Avian Biology 15:232–246.

HEJL, S. J. 2000. A strategy for maintaining healthy populations of western coniferous forest birds. Pp. 97–102 in R. Bonney, D. N. Pashley, R. J. Cooper, and L. Niles (editors). Strategies for bird conserva-tion: the Partners in Flight planning process. Proceedings of the 3rd Partners in Flight workshop. USDA Forest Service RMRS-P-16.

HEJL, S. J., R. L. HUTTO, C. R. PRESTON, AND D. M. FINCH. 1995. Effects of silvicultural treatments in the Rocky Mountains. Pp. 220–244 in T. E. Martin and D. M. Finch (editors). Ecology and management of neotropical migratory birds: a synthesis and review of critical issues. Oxford University Press, NY.

HEJL, S. J., K. R. NEWLON, M. E. MCFAZDEN, J. S. YOUNG, AND C. K. GHALAMBER. 2002. Brown Creeper (Certia americana). In A. Poole and F. Gill (editors). The Birds of North America, No. 669. The Academy of Natural Sciences, Philadelphia, PA, and The American Ornithologists' Union, Washington, D.C.

HEJL, S. L., AND L. C. PAIGE. 1994. A preliminary assessment of birds in continuous and fragmented forests of western red cedar/western hemlock in northern Idaho. Pp. 189–197 in D. M. Baumgartner and J. E. Lotan (editors). Proceedings of a symposium on interior cedar-hemlock-white pine forests: ecology and management. Washington State University, Pullman, WA.

HEJL, S. J., AND J. S. YOUNG. 1999. Brown-headed Cowbird distribution in conifer forest landscapes in the Northern Rocky Mountains. Studies in Avian Biology 18:73–79.

HELLE, E., AND P. HELLE. 1982. Edge effect on forest bird densities on offshore islands in the northern Gulf of Bothnia. Annales Zoologici Fennici 19:165–169.

HENJUM, M. G., J. R. KARR, D. L. BOTTOM, D. A. PERRY, J. C. BEDNARZ, S. G. WRIGHT, S. A. BECKWITT, AND E. BECKWITT. 1994. Interim protection for late successional forests, fisheries, and watersheds: National Forests east of the Cascade crest, Oregon and Washington. Technical Review 94-2. The Wildlife Society, Bethesda, MD.

HENSLER, G. L., AND J. D. NICHOLS. 1981. The Mayfield method of estimating nesting success: a model, estimators and simulation results. Wilson Bulletin 93:42–53.

HERKERT, J. R. 1994. The effects of habitat fragmentation on Midwestern grassland bird communities. Ecological Applications 4:461–471.

HERKERT, J. R. 1995. An analysis of Midwestern breeding bird population trends. American Midland Naturalist 134:41–50.

HERKERT, J. R., AND F. L. KNOPF. 1998. Research needs for grassland bird conservation. Pp. 273–282 in J. M. Marzluff and R. Sallabanks (editors). Avian conservation: research and management. Island Press, Washington, D.C.

HERNANDEZ, F., D. ROLLINS, AND R. CANTU. 1997. An evaluation of Trailmaster® camera systems for identifying ground-nest predators. Wildlife Society Bulletin 25:848–853.

HERSHEY, K. T. 1998. Characteristics of forests at Spotted Owl nest sites in the Pacific Northwest. Journal of Wildlife Management 62:1398–1410.

HESKE, E. J. 1995. Mammal abundances on forest-farm edges versus forest interiors in southern Illinois: is there an edge effect? Journal of Mammalogy 76:562–568.

HESKE, E. J., S. K. ROBINSON, AND J. D. BRAWN. 2001. Nest predation and neotropical migrant songbirds: piecing together the fragments. Wildlife Society Bulletin 29:52–61.

HESS, K., JR. 1993. Rocky times in Rocky Mountain National Park: an unnatural history. University Press of Colorado, Niwot, CO.

HESSBURG, P. F., B. C. SMITH, S. D. KREITER, C. A. MILLER, R. B. SALTER, C. H. MCNICOLL, AND W. J. HANN. 1999. Historical and current forest and range landscapes in the Interior Columbia River Basin and portions of the Klamath and Great Basins. Part 1: Linking vegetation patterns and landscape vulnerability to potential insect and pathogen disturbances. USDA Forest Service Gen. Tech. Rep. PNW-GTR-458. USDA Forest Service Pacific Northwest Research Station, Portland, OR.

HICKMAN, S. 1990. Evidence of edge species attraction to nature trails within deciduous forest. Natural Areas Journal 10:3–5.

HINES, J. E., AND J. R. SAUER. 1989. CONTRAST: a general program for the analysis of several survival or recovery rate estimates. U.S. Fish and Wildlife Service Technical Report No. 24. Patuxent Wildlife Research Center, U.S. Fish and Wildlife Service, Laurel, MD.

HINSLEY, S. A., P. E. BELLAMY, I. NEWTON, AND T. H. SPARKS. 1995. Habitat and landscape factors influencing the presence of individual breeding bird species in woodland fragments. Journal of Avian Biology 26:94–104.

HITCHCOX, S. M. 1996. Abundance and nesting success of cavity-nesting birds in unlogged and salvage-logged burned forest in northwestern Montana. M.S. thesis. University of Montana, Missoula, MT.

HOBBS, N. T., AND T. A. HANLEY. 1990. Habitat evaluation—do use-availability data reflect carrying-capacity. Journal of Wildlife Management 54:515–522.

HOBSON, K. A., AND E. BAYNE. 2000. Effects of forest fragmentation by agriculture on avian communities in the southern boreal mixedwoods of western Canada. Wilson Bulletin 112:373–387.

HOBSON, K. A., AND J. SCHIECK. 1999. Changes in bird communities in boreal mixedwood forest: harvest and wildfire effects over 30 years. Ecological Applications 9:849–863.

HOBSON, K. A., AND M-A. VILLARD. 1998. Forest fragmentation affects the behavioral response of American Redstarts to the threat of cowbird parasitism. Condor 100:389–394.

HOCHACHKA, W. M., T. E. MARTIN, V. ARTMAN, C. R. SMITH, S. J. HEJL, D. E. ANDERSEN, D. CURSON, L. PETIT, N. MATHEWS, T. M. DONOVAN, E. E. KLAAS, P. B. WOOD, J. C. MANOLIS, K. P. MCFARLAND, J. V. NICHOLS, J. C. BEDNARZ, D. M. EVANS, J. P. DUGUAY, S. GARNER, J. TEWKSBURY, K. L. PURCELL, J. FAABORG, C. B. GOGUEN, C. RIMMER, R. DETTMERS, M. KNUTSON, J. A. COLLAZO, L. GARNER, D. WHITEHEAD, AND G. GEUPEL. 1999. Scale dependence in the effects of forest coverage on parasitization by Brown-headed Cowbirds. Studies of Avian Biology 18:80–88.

HOFFMAN, N. J. 1997. Distribution of Picoides woodpeckers in relation to habitat disturbance within the Yellowstone area. M.S. thesis. Montana State University, Bozeman, MT.

HOGREFE, T. C., R. H. YAHNER, AND N. H. PIERGALLINI. 1998. Depredation of artificial ground nests in a suburban versus a rural landscape. Journal of the Pennsylvania Academy of Science 72:3–6.

HOLECHEK, J. L., R. D. PIPER, AND C. H. HERBEL. 1989. Range management: principles and practices. Prentice-Hall, Englewood Cliffs, NJ.

HOLLING, C. S. 1992. Cross-scale morphology, geometry, and dynamics of ecosystems. Ecological Monographs 62:447–502.

HOLWAY, D. A. 1995. The distribution of the Argentine ant (Linepithema humile) in central California: a twenty year record of invasion. Conservation Biology 9:1634–1637.

HOLWAY, D. A. 1998a. Factors governing rate of invasion: a natural experiment using Argentine ants. Oecologia 115:206–212.

HOLWAY, D. A. 1998b. Effect of Argentine ant invasions on ground-dwelling arthropods in northern California riparian woodlands. Oecologia 116:252–258.

HOLWAY, D. A. 1999. Competitive mechanisms underlying the displacement of native ants by the invasive Argentine ant. Ecology 80:238–251.

HOLWAY, D. A., A. V. SUAREZ, AND T. J. CASE. 1998. Loss of intraspecific aggression in the success of a widespread invasive social insect. Science 282:949–952.

HOOVER, J. P., AND M. C. BRITTINGHAM. 1993. Regional variation in cowbird parasitism of wood thrushes. Wilson Bulletin 105:228–238.

HOOVER, J. P., M. C. BRITTINGHAM, AND L. J. GOODRICH. 1995. Effects of forest patch size on nesting success of wood thrushes. Auk 112:146–155.

HORTON, S. P., AND R. W. MANNAN. 1988. Effects of prescribed fire on snags and cavity-nesting birds in southeastern Arizona pine forests. Wildlife Society Bulletin 16:37–44.

HOUSTON, D. B. 1973. Wildfires in northern Yellowstone National Park. Ecology 54:1111–1117.

HOWE, F. P., R. L. KNIGHT, L. C. MCEWEN, AND T. L. GEORGE. 1996. Direct and indirect effects of insecticide applications on growth and survival of nestling passerines. Ecological Applications 6:1314–1324.

HOWE, R. W. 1984. Local dynamics of bird assemblages in small forest habitat islands in Australia and North America. Ecology 65:1585–1601.

HOWE, R. W., G. J. DAVIS, AND V. MOSCA. 1991. The demographic significance of "sink" populations. Biological Conservation 57:239–255.

HOWELL, C. A., S. C. LATTA, T. M. DONOVAN, P. A. PORNELUZI, G. R. PARKS, AND J. FAABORG. 2000. Landscape effects mediate breeding bird abundance in Midwestern forests. Landscape Ecology 15:547–562.

HUFF, M. H. 1984. Post-fire succession in the Olympic Mountains, Washington: forest vegetation, fuels, and avifauna. Ph.D. dissertation. University of Washington, Seattle, WA.

HUFF, M. H., J. K. AGEE, AND D. A. MANUWAL. 1985. Post-fire succession of avifauna in the Olympic Mountains, Washington. Pp. 8–15 in J. E. Lotan and

J. K. Brown (editors). Fire's effects on wildlife habitat—proceedings. USDA Forest Service Gen. Tech. Rep. INT-186. USDA Forest Service, Intermountain Forest and Range Experiment Station, Ogden, UT.

HUFF, M. H., AND J. K. SMITH. 2000. Fire effects on animal communities. Pp. 35–42 in J. K. Smith (editor). Wildland fire in ecosystems: effects of fire on fauna. USDA Forest Service Gen. Tech. Rep. RMRS-GTR-42-vol. 1. USDA Forest Service, Intermountain Forest and Range Experiment Station, Ogden, UT.

HUHTA, E. 1995. Effects of spatial scale and vegetation cover on predation of artificial ground nests. Wildlife Biology 1:73–80.

HUHTA, E., J. JOKIMÄKI, AND P. RAHKO. 1998. Distribution and reproductive success of the Pied Flycatcher *Ficedula hypoleuca* in relation to forest patch size and vegetation characteristics: the effect of scale. Ibis 140:214–222.

HUHTA, E., T. MAPPES, AND J. JOKIMÄKI. 1996. Predation on artificial ground nests in relation to forest fragmentation, agricultural land and habitat structure. Ecography 19:85–91.

HULL, A. C., JR., AND M. K. HULL. 1974. Presettlement vegetation of Cache Valley, Utah and Idaho. Journal of Range Management 27:27–29.

HUMAN, K. G., AND D. M. GORDON. 1996. Exploitation and interference competition between the invasive Argentine ant, *Linepithema humile,* and native ant species. Oecologia 105:405–412.

HUMAN, K. G., AND D. M. GORDON. 1997. Effects of Argentine ants on invertebrate biodiversity in northern California. Conservation Biology 11:1242–1248.

HUNTER, J. E., R. J. GUTIÉRREZ, AND A. B. FRANKLIN. 1995. Habitat configuration around Spotted Owl sites in northwestern California. Condor 97:684–693.

HUNTER, J. E., AND F. L. SCHMIDT. 1990. Methods of meta-analysis: correcting error and bias in research findings. Sage Publications, Beverly Hills, CA.

HUNTER, M. L. 1993. Natural fire regimes as spatial models for managing boreal forests. Biological Conservation 65:115–120.

HURLBERT, S. H. 1984. Pseudoreplication and the design of ecological field experiments. Ecological Monographs 54:187–211.

HURT, M. 1996. Breeding distribution of Varied Thrushes (*Ixoreus naevius*) in redwood forest patches. Thesis, Humboldt State University, Arcata, California, USA.

HUTTO, R. L. 1985. Habitat selection by nonbreeding, migratory land birds. Pp. 455–476 in M. L. Cody (editor). Habitat selection in birds. Academic Press, New York, NY.

HUTTO, R. L. 1995. Composition of bird communities following stand-replacement fires in Northern Rocky Mountain (U.S.A.) conifer forests. Conservation Biology 9:1041–1058.

HUTTO, R. L., AND J. S. YOUNG. 1999. Habitat relationships of landbirds in the Northern Region, USDA Forest Service. USDA Forest Service Gen. Tech. Rep. RMRS-GTR-32. USDA Forest Service Rocky Mountain Research Station, Ogden, UT.

IMHOFF, M. L., T. D. SISK, A. MILNE, G. MORGAN, AND T. ORR. 1997. Remotely sensed indicators of habitat heterogeneity: use of synthetic aperture radar in mapping vegetation structure and bird habitat. Remote Sensing and Environment 60:217–227.

INGOLD, D. J. 1989. Nesting phenology and competition for nest sites among Red-headed and Red-bellied woodpeckers and European Starlings. Auk 106:209–217.

INGOLD, D. J. 1994. Influence of nest-site competition between European Starlings and woodpeckers. Wilson Bulletin 106:227–241.

INGOLD, D. J. 1998. The influence of starlings on flicker reproduction when both naturally excavated cavities and artificial nest boxes are available. Wilson Bulletin 110:218–225.

JACKSON, L. E., R. B. STRAUSS, M. K. FIRESTONE, AND J. W. BARTHOLOME. 1988. Plant and soil nitrogen dynamics in California annual grassland. Plant and Soil 110:9–17.

JEWETT, S. G., W. P. TAYLOR, W. T. SHAW, AND J. W. ALDRICH. 1953. Birds of Washington State. University of Washington Press, Seattle, WA.

JOHNSON, A. S. 1989. The thin green line: riparian corridors and endangered species in Arizona and New Mexico. Pp. 35–46 in G. Mackintosh (editor). In defense of wildlife: preserving communities and corridors. Defenders of Wildlife, Washington, D.C.

JOHNSON, D. H. 1979. Estimating nest success: the Mayfield method and an alternative. Auk 96:651–661.

JOHNSON, D. H. 1980. The comparison of usage and availability measurements for evaluating resource preference. Ecology 61:65–71.

JOHNSON, D. H. 1992. Spotted Owls, Great Horned Owls, and forest fragmentation in the central Oregon Cascades. M.S. Thesis. Oregon State University, Corvallis, OR.

JOHNSON, E. A., G. I. FRYER, AND M. J. HEATHCOTT. 1990. The influence of man and climate on frequency of fire in the interior wet belt forest, British Columbia. Journal of Ecology 78:403–412.

JOHNSON, N. K. 1975. Controls on number of species on montane islands in the Great Basin. Evolution 29:545–567.

JOHNSON, N. K. 1994. Pioneering and natural expansion of breeding distributions in western North America. Studies in Avian Biology 15:27–44.

JOHNSON, R. A., AND D. W. WICHERN. 1982. Applied multivariate statistical analysis. Prentice-Hall, Englewood Cliffs, NJ.

JOHNSON, R. G., AND S. A. TEMPLE. 1986. Assessing habitat quality for birds nesting in fragmented tallgrass prairies. Pp. 245–249 in J. A. Verner, M. L. Morrison, and C. J. Ralph (editors). Wildlife 2000: modeling habitat relationships of terrestrial vertebrates. University of Wisconsin Press, Madison, WI.

JOHNSON, R. G., AND S. A. TEMPLE. 1990. Nest predation and brood parasitism of tallgrass prairie birds. Journal of Wildlife Management 54:106–111.

JOHNSON, R. R., L. T. HAIGHT, AND J. M. SIMPSON. 1977. Endangered species vs. endangered habitats: a concept. Pp. 86–79 in R. R. Johnson and D. A. Jones (editors). Importance, preservation, and management of riparian habitat: a symposium. USDA Forest Service Gen. Tech. Rep. RM-43. USDA Forest Service, Rocky Mountain Forest and Range Experiment Station, Fort Collins, CO.

JOHNSON, T. H., AND R. H. WAUER. 1996. Avifaunal response to the 1977 La Mesa fire. Pp. 70–94 in C. D. Allen (editor). Fire effects in Southwestern forests: proceedings of the second La Mesa Fire Symposium, Los Alamos, NM, March 29–31, 1994. USDA Forest Service Rocky Mountain Forest and Range Experiment Station, Ft. Collins, CO.

JOHNSSON, K., S. G. NILSSON, AND M. TJERNBERG. 1993. Characteristics and utilization of old Black Woodpecker *Dryocopus martius* holes by hole-nesting species. Ibis 135:410–416.

JOHNSTON, V. R. 1947. Breeding birds of the forest edge in Illinois. Condor 49:45–53.

JORDAN, K. M., AND S. K. HUGHES. 1995. Characteristics of three Marbled Murrelet tree nests, Vancouver Island, British Columbia. Northwestern Naturalist 76:29–32.

KAREIVA, P. 1990. Population dynamics in spatially complex environments: theory and data. Philosophical Transactions of the Royal Society of London B Biological Sciences 330:175–190.

KARR J. R., AND R. R. ROTH. 1971. Vegetation structure and avian diversity in several New World areas. American Naturalist 105:432–435.

KEITT, T., A. B. FRANKLIN, AND D. L. URBAN. 1995. Landscape analysis and metapopulation structure. Chapter 3 in U.S. Fish and Wildlife Service, Mexican Spotted Owl Recovery Plan, Volume II. U.S. Fish and Wildlife Service, Albuquerque, NM.

KEITT, T. H., D. L. URBAN, AND B. T. MILNE. 1997. Detecting critical scales in fragmented landscapes. Conservation Ecology online (http://www.consecol.org/vol1/iss1/art4/).

KELLER, C. M. E., S. R. CHANDLER, AND S. H. JEFF. 1993. Avian communities in riparian forests of different widths in Maryland and Delaware. Wetlands 13:137–144.

KELLER, M. E., AND S. H. ANDERSON. 1992. Avian use of habitat configurations created by forest cutting in southeastern Wyoming. Condor 94:55–65.

KELSON, J. D., I. A. MANLEY, AND H. R. CARTER. 1995. Decline of the Marbled Murrelet in Clayoquot Sound, British Columbia: 1982–1993. Northwestern Naturalist 76:90–98.

KENDEIGH, S. C. 1944. Measurement of bird populations. Ecological Monographs 14:67–106.

KENDEIGH, S. C. 1982. Bird populations in east central Illinois: fluctuations, variations, and development over a half-century. Illinois Biological Monographs No. 52.

KERNS, S. J., AND R. A. MILLER. 1995. Two Marbled Murrelet nest sites on private commercial forest lands in northern California. Northwestern Naturalist 76:40–42.

KERPEZ, T. A., AND N. S. SMITH. 1990. Competition between European Starlings and native woodpeckers for nest cavities in saguaros. Auk 107:367–375.

KEYSER, A. J., G. E. HILL, AND E. C. SOEHREN. 1998. Effects of forest fragment size, nest density, and proximity to edge on the risk of predation to ground-nesting passerine birds. Conservation Biology 12:986–994.

KING, D. I., R. M. DEGRAAF, AND C. R. GRIFFIN. 1998.

Edge-related nest predation in clearcut and groupcut stands. Conservation Biology 12:1412–1415.

KING, D. I., R. M. DEGRAAF, C. R. GRIFFIN, AND T. J. MAIER. 1999. Do predation rates on artificial nests accurately reflect predation rates on natural bird nests? Journal of Field Ornithology 70:257–262.

KING, D. I., C. R. GRIFFIN, AND R. M. DEGRAAF. 1996. Effects of clearcutting on habitat use and reproductive success of the ovenbird in forested landscapes. Conservation Biology 10:1380–1386.

KING, D. I., C. R. GRIFFIN, AND R. M. DEGRAAF. 1997. Effect of clearcut borders on distribution and abundance of forest birds in northern New Hampshire. Wilson Bulletin 109:239–245.

KING, J. R., AND L. R. MEWALDT. 1987. The summer biology of an unstable insular population of White-crowned Sparrows in Oregon. Condor 89:549–565.

KITCHEN, S. G., E. D. MCARTHUR, AND G. L. JORGENSEN. 1999. Species richness and community structure along a Great Basin elevational gradient. Pp. 59–65 in E. D. McArthur, W. K. Ostler, and C. L. Wambolt (compilers). Proceedings: shrubland ecotones. USDA Forest Service Proc. RMRS-P-11. USDA Forest Service Rocky Mountain Research Station, Ogden, UT.

KLEBENOW, D. A., AND R. C. BEALL. 1977. Fire impacts on birds and mammals on Great Basin rangelands. Pp. 1–13 in Proceedings rangeland management and fire symposium. Joint Rocky Mountain Fire Council and Intermountain Fire Research Council. Journal Series 392, Nevada Agricultural Experiment Station, Reno, NV.

KNICK, S. T. 1999. Forum: requiem for a sagebrush ecosystem? Northwest Science 73:47–51.

KNICK, S. T., AND J. T. ROTENBERRY. 1995a. Landscape characteristics of fragmented shrubsteppe habitats and breeding passerine birds. Conservation Biology 9:1059–1071.

KNICK, S. T., AND J. T. ROTENBERRY. 1995b. Habitat relationships and breeding passerine birds on the Snake River Birds of Prey Area. Idaho Bureau of Land Management Technical Bulletin No. 95-5. Boise, ID.

KNICK, S. T., AND J. T. ROTENBERRY. 1996. Habitat relationships and breeding passerine birds on the Snake River Birds of Prey National Conservation Area. Report to Bureau of Land Management, Boise District Office. Idaho Bureau of Land Management, Boise, ID.

KNICK, S. T., AND J. T. ROTENBERRY. 1997. Landscape characteristics of disturbed shrubsteppe habitats in southwestern Idaho. Landscape Ecology 12:287–297.

KNICK, S. T., AND J. T. ROTENBERRY. 1999. Spatial distribution of breeding passerine bird habitats in southwestern Idaho. Studies in Avian Biology 19:104–111.

KNICK, S. T., AND J. T. ROTENBERRY. 2000. Ghosts of habitat past: the relative contribution of landscape change to current habitat associations of shrubsteppe birds. Ecology 81:220–227.

KNICK, S. T., J. T. ROTENBERRY, AND T. J. ZARRIELLO. 1997. Supervised classification of Landsat thematic mapper imagery in a semi-arid rangeland by nonparametric discriminant analysis. Photogrammetric Engineering and Remote Sensing 63:79–86.

KNIGHT, R. L. 1997. Subdividing the West. Pp. 272–274 in G. K. Meffe and C. R. Carroll (editors). Principles of conservation biology, 2nd ed. Sinauer Associates, Sutherland, MA.

KNIGHT, R. L. 2000. Forest fragmentation in the southern Rocky Mountains. University Press of Colorado, Boulder, CO.

KNIGHT, R. L., R. J. CAMP, AND H. A. L. KNIGHT. 1998. Ravens, cowbirds, and starlings at springs and stock tanks, Mojave National Preserve, California. Great Basin Naturalist 58:393–395.

KNOPF, F. L. 1985. Significance of riparian vegetation to breeding birds across an altitudinal cline. Pp. 105–111 in R. R. Johnson, C. D. Ziebell, D. R. Patton, P. F. Folliott, and R. H. Hamre (editors). Riparian ecosystems and their management: reconciling conflicting issues. First North American riparian conference. USDA Forest Service Gen. Tech. Rep. RM-120. USDA Forest Service Rocky Mountain Forest and Range Experiment Station, Ft. Collins, CO.

KNOPF, F. L. 1988. Conservation of steppe birds in North America. Pp. 27–41 in P. D. Goriup (editor). Ecology and conservation of grassland birds. ICBP Technical Publication No. 7. International Council for Bird Preservation, Cambridge, UK.

KNOPF, F. L. 1994. Avian assemblages on altered grasslands. Studies in Avian Biology 15:247–257.

KNOPF, F. L., J. A. SEDGWICK, AND R. W. CANNON. 1988. Guild structure of a riparian avifauna relative to seasonal cattle grazing. Journal of Wildlife Management 52:280–290.

KOPLIN, J. R. 1969. The numerical response of woodpeckers to insect prey in a subalpine forest in Colorado. Condor 71:436–438.

KOTLIAR, N. B., AND J. A. WIENS. 1990. Multiple scales of patchiness and patch structure: a hierarchical framework for the study of heterogeneity. Oikos 59: 253–260.

KREISEL, K. J., AND S. J. STEIN. 1999. Bird use of burned and unburned coniferous forests during winter. Wilson Bulletin 111:243–250.

KREMSATER, L., AND F. L. BUNNELL. 1999. Edge effects: theory, evidence and implications to management of western North American forests. Pp. 117–153 in J. A. Rochelle, L. A. Lehmann, and J. Wisniewski (editors). Forest fragmentation: wildlife and management implications. Brill Publishers, Leiden, The Netherlands.

KRISTAN, W. B., III, A. J. LYNAM, M. V. PRICE, AND J. T. ROTENBERRY. In press. Alternative causes of edge-abundance relationships in birds and small mammals of California coastal sage scrub. Ecography.

KROODSMA, R. L. 1982. Edge effect on breeding forest birds along a powerline corridor. Journal of Applied Ecology 19:361–370.

KROODSMA, R. L. 1984a. Ecological factors associated with degree of edge effect in breeding birds. Journal of Wildlife Management 48:418–425.

KROODSMA, R. L. 1984b. Effect of edge on breeding forest bird species. Wilson Bulletin 96:426–436.

KROODSMA, R. L. 1987. Edge effect on breeding birds along power-line corridors in east Tennessee. American Midland Naturalist 118:275–283.

KRÜGER, S. C., AND M. J. LAWES. 1997. Edge effects at an induced forest-grassland boundary: forest birds in the Ongoye Forest Reserve, KwaZulu-Natal. South African Journal of Zoology 32:82–97.

KÜCHLER, A. W. 1964. Manual to accompany the map, potential natural vegetation of the conterminous United States. American Geographical Society Spec. Publ. No. 36. American Geographical Society, New York, NY.

KUITUNEN, M., AND P. HELLE. 1988. Relationship of the common treecreeper Certhia familiaris to edge effect and forest fragmentation. Ornis Fennica 65: 150–155.

KULETZ, K. J., D. K. MARKS, N. L. NASLUND, AND M. B. CODY. 1995. Marbled Murrelet activity relative to forest characteristics in the Naked Island area, Prince William Sound, Alaska. Northwestern Naturalist 76:4–11.

KUS, B. E. 1999. Impacts of Brown-headed Cowbird parasitism on productivity of the endangered Least Bell's Vireo. Studies in Avian Biology 18:160–166.

LAHAYE, W. S., AND R. J. GUTIÉRREZ. 1999. Nest sites and nesting habitat of the Northern Spotted Owl in northwestern California. Condor 101:324–330.

LAHAYE, W. S., R. J. GUTIÉRREZ, AND D. R. CALL. 1992. Demography of an insular population of Spotted Owls (Strix occidentalis occidentalis). Pp. 803–814 in D. R. McCullough and R. H. Barrett (editors). Wildlife 2001: populations. Elsevier Applied Science, London, UK.

LAHAYE, W. S., R. J. GUTIÉRREZ, AND D. R. CALL. 1997. Nest-site selection and reproductive success of California Spotted Owls. Wilson Bulletin 109:42–51.

LAMBERSON, R. H., B. R. NOON, C. VOSS, AND K. S. MCKELVEY. 1994. Reserve design for territorial species: the effects of patch size and spacing on the viability of the Northern Spotted Owl. Conservation Biology 8:185–195.

LAMBERSON, R. H., K. S. MCKELVEY, B. R. NOON, AND C. VOSS. 1992. A dynamic analysis of Northern Spotted Owl viability in a fragmented forest landscape. Conservation Biology 6:505–512.

LANDE, R. 1988. Demographic models of the Northern Spotted Owl (Strix occidentalis caurina). Oecologia 75:601–607.

LANDE, R., AND G. F. BARROWCLOUGH. 1987. Effective population size, genetic variation, and their use in population management. Pp. 87–123 in M. E. Soulé (editor). Viable populations for conservation. Cambridge University Press, Cambridge, UK.

LARSEN, C. J. 1991. A status review of the Marbled Murrelet (Brachyramphus marmoratus) in California. Pp. 1–29 in Department of Candidate Species Status Report 91-1. Wildlife Management Division, California Department of Fish and Game, Sacramento, CA.

LATTA, S. C., J. WUNDERLE, M. JOSEPH, E. TERRANOVA, AND M. PAGÁN. 1995. An experimental study of nest predation in a subtropical wet forest following hurricane disturbance. Wilson Bulletin 107:590–602.

LAURANCE, W. F., AND E. YENSEN. 1991. Predicting the

impacts of edge effects in fragmented habitats. Biological Conservation 55:77–92.

LAY, D. 1938. How valuable are woodland clearings to birdlife? Wilson Bulletin 50:254–256.

LEE, E. T. 1980. Statistical methods for survival data analysis. Lifetime Learning, Belmont, CA.

LEENHOUTS, B. 1998. Assessment of biomass burning in the conterminous United States. Conservation Ecology online (http://www.consecol.org/vol2/iss1/art1).

LEHMKUHL, J. F., AND M. G. RAPHAEL. 1993. Habitat pattern around Northern Spotted Owl locations on the Olympic Peninsula, Washington. Journal of Wildlife Management 57:302–315.

LEHMKUHL, J. F., L. F. RUGGIERO, AND P. A. HALL. 1991. Landscape-scale patterns of forest fragmentation and wildlife richness and abundance in the southern Washington Cascade range. Pp. 425–442 in K. B. Aubrey, L. F. Ruggiero, A. B. Carey, and M. H. Huff (editors). Wildlife and vegetation of unmanaged Douglas-fir forests. USDA Forest Service Gen. Tech. Report PNW-GTR-285. USDA Forest Service Pacific Northwest Research Station, Portland, OR.

LEHMKUHL, J. F., S. D. WEST, C. L. CHAMBERS, W. C. McCOMB, D. A. MANUWAL, K. B. AUBRY, J. L. ERICKSON, R. A. GITZEN, AND M. LEU. 1999. An experiment for assessing vertebrate response to varying levels and patterns of green-tree retention. Northwest Science 73:45–63.

LEIMGRUBER, P., W. J. McSHEA, AND J. H. RAPPOLE. 1994. Predation on artificial nests in large forest blocks. Journal of Wildlife Management 58:254–260.

LEOPOLD, A. 1933. Game management. Charles Scribner Sons, New York, NY.

LEVIN, S. A. 1992. The problem of pattern and scale in ecology. Ecology 73:1943–1972.

LI, H., AND J. F. REYNOLDS. 1994. A simulation experiment to quantify spatial heterogeneity in categorical maps. Ecology 75:2446–2455.

LINDER, E. T., AND E. K. BOLLINGER. 1995. Depredation of artificial Ovenbird nests in a forest patch. Wilson Bulletin 107:169–174.

LINDER, K. A., AND S. H. ANDERSON. 1998. Nesting habitat of Lewis' woodpeckers in southeastern Wyoming. Journal of Field Ornithology 69:109–116.

LISSOWAY, J. D. 1996. Remembering the La Mesa fire. Pp. 7–10 in C. D. Allen (editor). Fire effects in Southwestern forests: proceedings of the second La Mesa Fire Symposium, Los Alamos, NM, March 29–31, 1994. USDA Forest Service Rocky Mountain Forest and Range Experiment Station, Ft. Collins, CO.

LONG, C. J., C. WHITLOCK, P. J. BARTLEIN, AND S. H. MILLSPAUGH. 1998. A 9000-year fire history from the Oregon Coast Range, based on high-resolution charcoal study. Canadian Journal of Forestry Research 28:774–787.

LORD, J. M., AND D. A. NORTON. 1990. Scale and the spatial concept of fragmentation. Conservation Biology 4:197–202.

LORENZANA, J. C., AND S. G. SEALY. 1999. A meta-analysis of the impact of parasitism by the Brown-headed Cowbird on its hosts. Studies in Avian Biology 18:241–253.

LOVEJOY, T. E., R. O. BIERREGAARD, JR., A. B. RYLANDS, J. R. MALCOLM, C. E. QUINTELA, L. H. HARPER, K. S. BROWN, JR., A. H. POWELL, G. V. N. POWELL, H. O. R. SCHUBART, AND M. B. HAYS. 1986. Edge and other effects of isolation on Amazon forest fragments. Pp. 257–285 in M. E. Soulé (editor). Conservation biology: the science of scarcity and diversity. Sinauer Associates, Sunderland, MA.

LOVIO, J. C. 1996. The effects of habitat fragmentation on the breeding bird assemblage in California coastal sage scrub. M.S. thesis. San Diego State University, San Diego, CA.

LOWE, P. O., P. F. FOLLIOTT, J. H. DIETERICH, AND D. R. PATTON. 1978. Determining potential wildlife benefits from wildfire in Arizona ponderosa pine forests. USDA Forest Service Gen. Tech. Rep. RM-52. USDA Forest Service Rocky Mountain Forest and Range Experiment Station, Fort Collins, CO.

LOWTHER, P. E. 1993. Brown-headed Cowbird (Molothrus ater). In A. Poole and F. Gill (editors). The Birds of North America, No. 47. The Academy of Natural Sciences, Philadelphia, PA, and The American Ornithologists Union, Washington, D.C.

LUGINBUHL, J. M., J. M. MARZLUFF, J. E. BRADLEY, M. G. RAPHAEL, AND D. E. VARLAND. 2001. Determination and quantification of corvid relative abundance affects its relationship to nest predation. Journal of Field Ornithology 72:556–572.

LYNN, S., M. L. MORRISON, A. J. KUENZI, J. C. C. NEAL, B. N. SACKS, R. HAMLIN, AND L. S. HALL. 1998. Bird use of riparian vegetation along the Truckee River, California and Nevada. Great Basin Naturalist 58:328–343.

LYON, L. J., M. H. HUFF, R. G. HOOPER, E. S. TELFER, D. S. SCHREINER, AND J. K. SMITH. 2000. The effects on animal populations. Pp 25–34 in J. K. Smith (editor). Wildland fire in ecosystems: effects of fire on fauna. USDA Forest Service Gen. Tech. Rep. RMRS-GTR-42-vol. 1. USDA Forest Service Rocky Mountain Research Station, Ogden, UT.

LYON, L. J., M. H. HUFF, AND J. K. SMITH. 2000. Fire effects on fauna at landscape scales. Pp. 43–49 in J. K. Smith (editor). Wildland fire in ecosystems: effects of fire on fauna. USDA Forest Service Gen. Tech. Rep. RMRS-GTR-42-vol. 1. USDA Forest Service Rocky Mountain Research Station, Ogden, UT.

MAC, M. J., P. A. OPLER, E. P. HAECKER, AND P. D. DORAN. 1998. Status and trends of the nation's biological resources. Vol. 2. U.S. Department of Interior, U.S. Geological Survey, Reston, VA.

MACARTHUR, R. M. 1958. Population ecology of some warblers of northeastern coniferous forests. Ecology 39:599–619.

MACARTHUR, R. M., AND J. W. MACARTHUR. 1961. On bird species diversity. Ecology 42:594–598.

MACARTHUR, R. M., J. W. MACARTHUR, AND J. PREER. 1962. On bird species diversity. American Naturalist 96:167–174.

MACARTHUR, R. H., AND E. O. WILSON. 1967. The theory of island biogeography. Princeton University Press, Princeton, NJ.

MACDONALD, M. W., AND K. P. REESE. 1998. Landscape changes within the historical distribution of

Columbian Sharp-tailed Grouse in eastern Washington: is there hope? Northwest Science 72:34–41.

MACK, R. N. 1981. Invasion of *Bromus tectorum* L. into western North America: an ecological chronicle. Agro-Ecosystems 7:145–165.

MACK, R. N., AND J. N. THOMPSON. 1982. Evolution in steppe with few large, hooved mammals. American Naturalist 119:757–773.

MADANY, M. H., AND N. E. WEST. 1983. Livestock grazing-fire regime interactions within montane forests of Zion National Park. Ecology 64:661–667.

MAJER, J. D. 1994. Spread of Argentine ants (*Linepithema humile*), with special reference to Western Australia. Pp. 163–173 *in* D. F. Williams (editor). Exotic ants: biology, impact, and control of introduced species. Westview, Boulder, CO.

MAJOR, R. E. 1991. Identification of nest predators by photography, dummy eggs, and adhesive tape. Auk 108:190–195.

MAJOR, R. E., AND C. E. KENDAL. 1996. The contribution of artificial nest experiments to understanding avian reproductive success: a review of methods and conclusions. Ibis 138:298–307.

MAJOR, R. E., G. H. PYKE, M. T. CHRISTY, G. GOWING, AND R. S. HILL. 1994. Can nest predation explain the timing of the breeding season and the pattern of nest dispersion of New Holland honeyeaters? Oikos 69:364–372.

MANLEY, I. A. 1999. Behaviour and habitat selection of Marbled Murrelets nesting on the Sunshine Coast. M.S. thesis. Simon Fraser University, Vancouver, BC.

MANLEY, I. A., AND S. K. NELSON. 1999. Habitat characteristics associated with nest success and predation at Marbled Murrelet nest trees. Pacific Seabirds 26: 40.

MANNAN, R. W., AND E. C. MESLOW. 1984. Bird populations and vegetation characteristics in managed and old-growth forests, northeastern Oregon (USA). Journal of Wildlife Management 48:1219–1238.

MANUWAL, D. A. 1991. Spring bird communities in the Southern Washington Cascade Range. Pp. 161–174 *in* L. F. Ruggiero, K. B. Aubry, A. B. Carey, and M. H. Huff (technical coordinators). Wildlife and vegetation of unmanaged Douglas-fir forests. USDA Forest Service Gen. Tech. Rep. PNW-GTR-285. USDA Forest Service Pacific Northwest Research Station, Portland, OR.

MANUWAL, D. A., AND M. H. HUFF. 1987. Seasonal differences in bird species, abundance, and guild structure in a Douglas-fir forest sere. Journal of Wildlife Management 51:586–595.

MARINI, M., AND C. MELO. 1998. Predators of quail eggs, and the evidence of the remains: implications for nest predation studies. Condor 100:395–399.

MARINI, M. A., S. K. ROBINSON, AND E. J. HESKE. 1995. Edge effects on nest predation in the Shawnee National forest, southern Illinois. Biological Conservation 74:203–213.

MARKS, D. K., AND N. L. NASLUND. 1994. Sharp-shinned Hawk preys on a Marbled Murrelet nesting in old-growth forest. Wilson Bulletin 106:565–567.

MARTIN, T. E. 1992. Interaction of nest predation and food limitation in reproductive strategies. Current Ornithology 9:163–197.

MARTIN, T. E. 1993. Nest predation among vegetation layers and habitat types: revising the dogmas. American Naturalist 141:897–913.

MARTIN, T. E., I. J. BALL, AND J. TEWKSBURY. 1996. Environmental perturbations and rates of nest predation in birds. Transactions of the North American Wildlife and Natural Resources Conference 61:43–49.

MARTIN, T. E., AND D. M. FINCH (EDITORS). 1995. Ecology and management of neotropical migratory birds: a synthesis and review of critical issues. Oxford University Press, New York, NY.

MARTIN, T. E., C. R. PAINE, C. J. CONWAY, W. M. HOCHACHKA, P. ALLEN, AND J. W. JENKINS. 1997. BBIRD field protocols. Montana Cooperative Wildlife Research Unit, University of Montana, Missoula, MT (http://pica.wru.umt.edu/bbird/protocol/protocol.htm).

MARZLUFF, J. M., AND R. P. BALDA. 1992. The Pinyon Jay. T. and A. D. Poyser, London, UK.

MARZLUFF, J. M., R. B. BOONE, AND G. W. COX. 1994. Native pest bird species in the West: why have they succeeded where so many have failed? Studies in Avian Biology 15:202–220.

MARZLUFF, J. M., M. G. RAPHAEL, J. E. BRADLEY, J. M. LUGINBUHL, AND D. E VARLAND. 1999. Diverse communities of nest predators: implications for murrelet breeding success. Pacific Seabirds 26:40.

MARZLUFF, J. M., M. G. RAPHAEL, AND R. SALLABANKS. 2001. Understanding the effects of forest management on avian species. Wildlife Society Bulletin 28: 1132–1143.

MARZLUFF, J. M., AND M. RESTANI. 1999. The effects of forest fragmentation on avian nest predation. Pp. 155–169 *in* J. A. Rochelle, L. A. Lehmann, and J. Wisniewski (editors). Forest fragmentation: wildlife and management implications. Brill Publishers, Leiden, The Netherlands.

MASSELINK, M. N. M. 1999. Steller's Jay ecology in fragmented forests of coastal BC, with implications for Marbled Murrelets. Pacific Seabirds 26:40.

MAURER, B. A. 1986. Predicting habitat quality for grassland birds using density–habitat correlations. Journal of Wildlife Management 50:556–566.

MAYFIELD, H. F. 1961. Nesting success calculated from exposure. Wilson Bulletin 73:255–261.

MAYFIELD, H. F. 1965. The Brown-headed Cowbird, with old and new hosts. Living Bird 4:13–28.

MAYFIELD, H. F. 1975. Suggestions for calculating nest success. Wilson Bulletin 87:456–466.

MCADOO, J. K., W. S. LONGLAND, AND R. A. EVANS. 1989. Nongame bird community responses to sagebrush invasion of crested wheatgrass seedings. Journal of Wildlife Management 53:494–502.

MCARTHUR, E. D., AND J. E. OTT. 1996. Potential natural vegetation in the 17 conterminous western United States. Pp. 16–28 *in* J. R. Barrow, E. D. McArthur, R. E. Sosebee, and R. J. Tausch (compilers). Proceedings: shrubland ecosystem dynamics in a changing environment. USDA Forest Service Gen. Tech. Rep. INT-GTR-338. USDA Forest Service Rocky Mountain Research Station, Ogden, UT.

MCCULLAGH, P., AND J. A. NELDER. 1989. Generalized linear models. 2nd ed. Chapman and Hall, London, UK.

MCCULLOUGH, D. R. (EDITOR). 1996. Metapopulations

and wildlife conservation. Island Press, Washington, D.C.

McDonnell, M. J., S. T. A. Pickett, and R. V. Pouyat. 1993. The application of the ecological gradient paradigm to the study of urban effects. Pp. 175–189 in M. J. McDonnell and S. T. A. Pickett (editors). Humans as components of ecosystems: the ecology of subtle human effects and populated areas. Springer-Verlag, New York, NY.

McGarigal, K., and B. J. Marks. 1995. FRAGSTATS: spatial pattern analysis program for quantifying landscape structure. USDA Forest Service Gen. Tech. Rep. PNW-GTR-351. USDA Forest Service Pacific Northwest Research Station, Portland, OR.

McGarigal, K., and W. C. McComb. 1995. Relationships between landscape structure and breeding birds in the Oregon coast range. Ecological Monographs 65:235–260.

McGarigal, K., and W. C. McComb. 1999. Forest fragmentation effects on breeding bird communities in the Oregon Coast Range. Pp. 223–246 in J. A. Rochelle, L. A. Lehmann, and J. Wisniewski (editors). Forest fragmentation: wildlife and management implications. Brill Publishers, Leiden, The Netherlands.

McGinnis, W. J., R. H. Phillips, T. L. Raettig, and K. P. Connaughton. 1997. County Portraits of Washington State. USDA Forest Service Gen. Tech. Rep. PNW-GTR-400. USDA Forest Service Pacific Northwest Research Station, Portland, OR.

McIntyre, S., and G. W. Barrett. 1992. Habitat variegation, an alternative to fragmentation. Conservation Biology 6:146–147.

McKelvey, K. S., and J. D. Johnston. 1992. Historical perspectives on forests of the Sierra Nevada and the transverse ranges of southern California: forest conditions at the turn of the century. Pp. 79–148 in J. Verner, K. S. McKelvey, B. R. Noon, R. J. Gutiérrez, G. I. Gould, Jr., and T. W. Beck (editors). The California Spotted Owl: a technical assessment of its current status. USDA Forest Service Gen. Tech. Rep. PSW-GTR-133. USDA Forest Service Pacific Southwest Research Station, Albany, CA.

McKelvey, K. S., B. R. Noon, and R. H. Lamberson. 1992. Conservation planning for species occupying fragmented landscapes: the case of the Northern Spotted Owl. Pp. 424–450 in P. Kareiva, J. Kingsolver, and R. Huey (editors). Biotic interactions and global change. Sinauer Associates, Sunderland, MA.

McKelvey, K. S., C. N. Skinner, C. Chang, D. C. Erman, S. J. Husari, D. J. Parsons, J. W. von Wagtendonk, and C. P. Weatherspoon. 1996. An overview of fire in the Sierra Nevada. Pp. 1033–1040 in Sierra Nevada Ecosystem Project: final report to Congress, vol. II, Assessments and scientific basis for management options. Centers for Water and Wildland Resources, University of California, Davis, CA.

Medin, D. E., and W. P. Clary. 1991. Breeding bird populations in a grazed and ungrazed riparian habitat in Nevada. USDA Forest Serv. Intermountain Res. Sta. Res. Pap. INT-441:1–7.

Meffe, G. K., and C. R. Carroll. 1997. Principles of conservation biology. 2nd ed. Sinauer Associates, Sunderland, MA.

Mendenhall, V. M. 1992. Distribution, breeding records, and conservation problems of the Marbled Murrelet in Alaska. Pp. 5–16 in H. R. Carter and M. L. Morrison (editors). Status and conservation of the Marbled Murrelet in North America. Proceedings of the Western Foundation of Vertebrate Zoology 5.

Mengel, R. M. 1964. The probable history of species formation in some northern wood warblers (Parulidae). Living Bird 3:9–43.

Meyer, C. B. 1999. Marbled Murrelet use of landscapes and seascapes during the breeding season in California and southern Oregon. Ph.D. dissertation. University of Wyoming, Laramie, WY.

Meyer, J. S., L. L. Irwin, and M. S. Boyce. 1998. Influence of habitat abundance and fragmentation on Northern Spotted Owls in western Oregon. Wildlife Monographs 139:1–51.

Miles, R. K., and D. A. Buehler. 1999. An evaluation of point-count and playback techniques for censusing Brown-headed Cowbirds. Pp. 63–68 in J. N. M. Smith, S. I. Rothstein, S. K. Robinson, S. G. Sealy, and T. L. Cook (editors). The ecology and management of cowbirds. University of Texas Press, Austin, TX.

Miller, A. H. 1951. An analysis of the distribution of the birds of California. University of California Publications in Zoology 50:531–624.

Miller, C. K., and R. L. Knight. 1993. Does predator assemblage affect reproductive success in songbirds? Condor 95:712–715.

Miller, G. S. 1989. Dispersal of juvenile Northern Spotted Owls in western Oregon. M.S. thesis. Oregon State University, Corvallis, OR.

Miller, G. S., R. J. Small, and E. C. Meslow. 1997. Habitat selection by Spotted Owls during natal dispersal in western Oregon. Journal of Wildlife Management 61:151–158.

Millspaugh, S. H., and C. Whitlock. 1995. A 750-year fire history based on lake sediment records in central Yellowstone National Park, USA. The Holocene 5:283–292.

Minnich, R. A., and R. J. Dezzani. 1998. Historical decline of coastal sage scrub in the Riverside-Perris Plain, California. Western Birds 29:366–391.

Mitchell, W. B., S. C. Guptill, K. E. Anderson, R. G. Fegeas, and C. A. Hallam. 1977. GIRAS—a geographical information and analysis system for handling land use and land cover data. Professional Paper No. 1059. U.S. Geological Survey, Reston, VA.

Mladenoff, D. J., M. A. White, J. Pastor, and T. R. Crow. 1993. Comparing spatial patterns in unaltered old-growth and disturbed forest landscapes. Ecological Applications 3:294–306.

Moen, C. A., and R. J. Gutiérrez. 1997. California Spotted Owl habitat selection in the central Sierra Nevada. Journal of Wildlife Management 61:1281–1287.

Moir, W. H., J. L. Dick, Jr., W. M. Block, J. P. Ward, Jr., R. Vahle, F. P. Howe, and J. L. Ganey. 1995. Conceptual framework for recovery. Pp. 59–75 in U.S. Fish and Wildlife Service Mexican Spotted

Owl Recovery Plan, Vol. I. U.S. Fish and Wildlife Service, Albuquerque, NM.

MOONEY, H. A. 1977. Southern coastal scrub. Pp. 471–489 in M. G. Barbour and J. Major (editors). Terrestrial vegetation of California. Wiley, New York, NY.

MOONEY, H. A., S. P. HAMBURG, AND J. A. DRAKE. 1986. The invasions of plants and animals into California. Pp. 250–272 in H. A. Mooney and J. A. Drake (editors). Ecology of the biological invasions of North America and Hawaii. Springer-Verlag, New York, NY.

MORGANTI, R. 1993. Landscape patterns in wildlife habitat: the landscape ecology of Northern Spotted Owl habitat in the eastern high Cascade Mountains of southern Oregon. M.S. thesis. University of Oregon, Eugene, OR.

MORRIS, D. L., AND F. R. THOMPSON, III. 1998. Effects of habitat and invertebrate density on abundance and foraging behavior of Brown-headed Cowbirds. Auk 115:376–385.

MORRISON, M. L., AND M. G. RAPHAEL. 1993. Modeling the dynamics of snags. Ecological Applications 3:322–330.

MORRISON, M. L., B. G. MARCOT, AND R. W. MANNAN. 1992. Wildlife-habitat relationships: concepts and applications. University of Wisconsin Press, Madison, WI.

MORRISON, M. L., B. G. MARCOT, AND R. W. MANNAN. 1998. Wildlife-habitat relationships: concepts and applications. 2nd ed. University if Wisconsin Press, Madison, WI.

MORRISON, S. A., AND D. T. BOLGER. 2002. Lack of an urban edge effect on reproduction in a fragmentation-sensitive sparrow. Ecological Applications 12: 398–411.

MORRISON, S. A., AND D. T. BOLGER. In press. Variation in a sparrow's reproductive success with rainfall: food and predator mediated processes. Oecologia.

MORSE, S. F., AND S. K. ROBINSON. 1999. Nesting success of a neotropical migrant in a multiple-use forested landscape. Conservation Biology 13:327–337.

MORTON, E. S. 1989. What do we know about the future of migrant land birds? Pp. 579–589 in J. M. Hagan, III, and D. W. Johnston (editors). Ecology and conservation of neotropical migrant landbirds. Smithsonian Institution Press, Washington, D.C.

MOSCONI, S. L., AND R. L. HUTTO. 1982. The effects of grazing on land birds of western Montana riparian habitat. Pp. 221–233 in J. M. Peek and P. D. Dalke (editors). Wildlife livestock relationships symposium. University of Idaho, Forest and Wildlife Range Experiment Station, Moscow, ID.

MURCIA, C. 1995. Edge effects in fragmented forests: implications for conservation. Trends in Ecology and Evolution 10:58–62.

MURPHY, E. C., AND W. A. LEHNHAUSEN. 1998. Density and foraging ecology of woodpeckers following a stand-replacement fire. Journal of Wildlife Management 62:1359–1372.

MØLLER, A. P. 1989. Nest site selection across field-woodland ecotones: the effect of nest predation. Oikos 56:240–246.

MØLLER, A. P. 1987. Egg predation as a selective factor for nest design: an experiment. Oikos 50:91–94.

NASLUND, N. L., K. J. KULETZ, M. B. CODY, AND D. K. MARKS. 1995. Tree and habitat characteristics and reproductive success at Marbled Murrelet tree nests in Alaska. Northwestern Naturalist 76:12–25.

NELSON, S. K. 1997. Marbled Murrelet (Brachyramphus marmoratus). In A. Poole and F. Gill (editors). The Birds of North America, No. 276. The Academy of Natural Sciences, Philadelphia, PA, and The American Ornithologists Union, Washington, D.C.

NELSON, S. K., AND T. E. HAMER. 1995. Nest success and the effects of predation on Marbled Murrelets. Pp. 89–97 in C. J. Ralph, G. L. Hunt, Jr., M. G. Raphael, and J. F. Piatt (editors). Ecology and conservation of the Marbled Murrelet. USDA Forest Service Gen. Tech. Rep. PSW-GTR-152. USDA Forest Service Pacific Southwest Research Station, Albany, CA.

NELSON, S. K., AND R. W. PECK. 1995. Behavior of Marbled Murrelets at nine nest sites in Oregon. Northwestern Naturalist 76:43–53.

NICHOLS, J. D., M. J. CONROY, D. R. ANDERSON, AND K. P. BURNHAM. 1984. Compensatory mortality in waterfowl populations: a review of the evidence and implications for research and management. Transactions of the North American Wildlife and Natural Resources Conference 49:535–554.

NIEMUTH, N. D., AND M. S. BOYCE. 1997. Edge-related nest losses in Wisconsin pine barrens. Journal of Wildlife Management 61:1234–1239.

NILSSON, S. G. 1984. The evolution of nest-site selection among hole-nesting birds: the importance of nest predation and competition. Ornis Scandinavica 15:167–175.

NOLAN, V., JR. 1978. The ecology and behavior of the Prairie Warbler, Dendroica discolor. Ornithological Monographs 26:1–595.

NOON, B. R., AND K. S. MCKELVEY. 1992. Stability properties of the Spotted Owl metapopulation in southern California. Pp. 187–206 in J. Verner, K. S. McKelvey, B. R. Noon, R. J. Gutiérrez, G. I. Gould, Jr., and T. W. Beck (editors). The California Spotted Owl: a technical assessment of its current status. USDA Forest Service Gen. Tech. Rep. PSW-GTR-133. USDA Forest Service Pacific Southwest Research Station, Albany, CA.

NOON, B. R., AND K. S. MCKELVEY. 1996. Management of the spotted owl: a case history in conservation biology. Annual Review of Ecology and Systematics 27:135–162.

NOON, B. R., K. S. MCKELVEY, D. W. LUTZ, W. S. LAHAYE, R. J. GUTIÉRREZ, AND C. A. MOEN. 1992. Estimates of demographic parameters and rates of population change. Pp. 175–186 in J. Verner, K. S. McKelvey, B. R. Noon, R. J. Gutiérrez, G. I. Gould, Jr., and T. W. Beck (editors). The California Spotted Owl: a technical assessment of its current status. USDA Forest Service Gen. Tech. Rep. PSW-GTR-133. USDA Forest Service Pacific Southwest Research Station, Albany, CA.

NOON, B. R., AND J. R. SAUER. 1992. Population models for passerine birds: structure, parameterization, and analysis. Pp. 411–464 in D. R. McCullough and R. H. Barrett (editors). Wildlife 2001: populations. Elsevier Applied Science, London, UK.

NOSS, R. F. 1985. On characterizing presettlement vegetation: how and why. Natural Areas Journal 5:5–19.

NOSS, R. F. 1990. Indicators for monitoring biodiversity: a hierarchical approach. Conservation Biology 4:355–364.

NOSS, R. F. 1991. Effects of edge and internal patchiness on avian habitat use in an old-growth hammock. Natural Areas Journal 11:34–47.

NOSS, R. F., AND A. COOPERRIDER. 1994. Saving nature's legacy: protecting and restoring biodiversity. Island Press, Covelo, CA.

NOSS, R. F., E. T. LaROE, III, AND J. M. SCOTT. 1995. Endangered ecosystems of the United States: a preliminary assessment of loss and degradation. National Biological Service Biological Report 28. Washington, D.C.

NOSS, R. F., AND R. L. PETERS. 1995. Endangered ecosystems. A status report on America's vanishing habitat and wildlife. Defenders of Wildlife, Washington, D.C.

NOUR, N., E. MATTHYSEN, AND A. A. DHONDT. 1993. Artificial nest predation and habitat fragmentation: different trends in bird and mammal predators. Ecography 16:111–116.

O'CONNOR, R. J., M. T. JONES, R. B. BOONE, AND T. B. LAUBER. 1999. Linking continental climate, land use, and land patterns with grassland bird distribution across the conterminous United States. Studies in Avian Biology 19:45–59.

O'NEILL, R. V., J. R. KRUMMEL, R. H. GARDNER, G. SUGIHARA, B. JACKSON, D. L. DEANGELIS, B. T. MILNE, M. G. TURNER, B. ZYGMUNT, S. W. CHRISTENSEN, V. H. DALE, AND R. L. GRAHAM. 1988. Indices of landscape pattern. Landscape Ecology 1:153–166.

ODUM, E. P. 1958. Fundamentals of ecology. W. B. Saunders Company, Philadelphia, PA.

OHMART, R. D. 1994. The effects of human-induced changes on the avifauna of western riparian habitats. Studies in Avian Biology 15:273–285.

OHMART, R. D., AND B. W. ANDERSON. 1986. Riparian Habitat. Pp. 169–199 in A. Y. Cooperrider, R. J. Boyd, and H. R. Stuart (editors). Inventory and monitoring of wildlife habitat. U.S. Bureau of Land Management Service Center, Denver, CO.

O'NEILL, R. V. 1989. Perspectives in hierarchy and scale. Pp. 140–156 in J. Roughgarden, R. M. May, and S. A. Levin (editors). Perspectives in ecological theory. Princeton University Press, Princeton, NJ.

OPDAM, P. 1991. Metapopulation theory and habitat fragmentation: a review of holarctic breeding bird studies. Landscape Ecology 5:93–106.

ORTEGA, C. 1998. Cowbirds and other brood parasites. University of Arizona Press, Tucson, AZ.

ORTEGA, C. P., J. C. ORTEGA, C. A. RAPP, AND S. A. BACKENSTO. 1998. Validating the use of artificial nests in predation experiments. Journal of Wildlife Management 62:925–932.

ÖZESMI, U., AND W. J. MITSCH. 1997. A spatial habitat model for the marsh-breeding red-winged blackbird Agelaius phoeniceus L. in coastal Lake Erie wetlands. Ecological Modeling 101:139–152.

PAGE, J. L., N. DODD, T. O. OSBORNE, AND J. A. CARSON. 1978. The influence of livestock grazing on non-game wildlife. California Nevada Wildlife 1978:159–173.

PAIGE, C., AND S. A. RITTER. 1999. Birds in a sagebrush sea: managing sagebrush habitats for bird communities. Partners in Flight Western Working Group, Boise, ID.

PARADIS, E., S. R. BAILLIE, W. J. SUTHERLAND, AND R. D. GREGORY. 1998. Patterns of natal and breeding dispersal in birds. Journal of Animal Ecology 67:518–536.

PASITSCHNIAK-ARTS, M., AND F. MESSIER. 1995. Risk of predation on waterfowl nests in the Canadian prairies: effects of habitat edges and agricultural practices. Oikos 73:347–355.

PASITSCHNIAK-ARTS, M., AND F. MESSIER. 1996. Predation on artificial duck nests in a fragmented prairie landscape. Ecoscience 3:436–441.

PATON, P. W. 1994. The effect of edge on avian nest success: how strong is the evidence? Conservation Biology 8:17–26.

PATTEN, D. T. 1963. Vegetational pattern in relation to environments in the Madison Range, Montana. Ecological Monographs 33:375–406.

PATTERSON, B. D., AND W. ATMAR. 1986. Nested subsets and the structure of insular mammalian faunas and archipelagos. Biological Journal of the Linnean Society 28:65–82.

PATTON, D. R. 1975. A diversity index for quantifying habitat "edge." Wildlife Society Bulletin 3:171–173.

PAYNE, R. B. 1973. The breeding season of a parasitic bird, the Brown-headed Cowbird in Central California. Condor 75:80–99.

PAYNE, R. B. 1977. The ecology of brood parasitism in birds. Annual Review of Ecology and Systematics 8:1–28.

PEARSON, S. F., AND D. A. MANUWAL. 2001. Breeding bird response to riparian buffer width in managed Pacific Northwest Douglas-fir forests. Ecological Applications 11:840–853.

PEASE, C. M., AND J. A. GRZYBOWSKI. 1995. Assessing the consequences of brood parasitism and nest predation on seasonal fecundity in passerine birds. Auk 112:343–363.

PEDLAR, J. H., L. FAHRIG, AND H. G. MERRIAM. 1997. Raccoon habitat use at two spatial scales. Journal of Wildlife Management 61:102–112.

PEERY, M. Z., R. J. GUTIÉRREZ, AND M. E. SEAMANS. 1999. Habitat composition and configuration around Mexican Spotted Owl nest and roost sites in the Tularosa Mountains, New Mexico. Journal of Wildlife Management 63:36–43.

PEET, R. K. 1988. Forests of the Rocky Mountains. Pp. 63–101 in M. G. Barbour and W. D. Billings (editors). North American terrestrial vegetation. Cambridge University Press, New York, NY.

PERRY, D. A. 1994. Forest ecosystems. Johns Hopkins University Press, Baltimore, MD.

PERRY, D. A. 1995. Status of forest habitat of the Marbled Murrelet. Pp. 381–383 in C. J. Ralph, G. L. Hunt, Jr., M. G. Raphael, and J. F. Piatt (editors). Ecology and conservation of the Marbled Murrelet. USDA Forest Service Gen. Tech. Rep. PSW-GTR-152. USDA Forest Service Pacific Southwest Research Station, Albany, CA.

PERRY, D. R. 1978. A method to access into the crowns of emergent and canopy trees. Biotropica 10:155–157.

PETERJOHN, B. G., AND J. A. SAUER. 1999. Population status of North American grassland birds from the North American Breeding Bird Survey, 1966–1996. Studies in Avian Biology 19:27–44.

PETERJOHN, B. G., J. R. SAUER, AND S. SCHWARTZ. 2000. Temporal and geographic patterns in population trends of Brown-headed Cowbirds. Pp. 21–34 in J. N. M. Smith, T. L. Cook, S. I. Rothstein, S. G. Sealy, and S. K. Robinson (editors). Ecology and management of cowbirds. University of Texas Press, Austin, TX.

PETERS, R. H. 1991. A critique for ecology. Cambridge University Press, Cambridge, UK.

PETERSEN, K. L., AND L. B. BEST. 1987. Effects of prescribed burning on nongame birds in a sagebrush community. Wildlife Society Bulletin 15:317–325.

PETERSEN, K. L., AND L. B. BEST. 1999. Design and duration of perturbation experiments: implications for data interpretation. Studies in Avian Biology 19:230–236.

PETERSEN, K. P., AND L. B. BEST. 1985a. Nest-site selection by sage sparrows. Condor 87:217–221.

PETERSEN, K. P., AND L. B. BEST. 1985b. Brewer's sparrow nest-site characteristics in a sagebrush community. Journal of Field Ornithology 56:23–27.

PETERSON, S. R. 1982. A preliminary survey of forest bird communities in northern Idaho. Northwest Sciences 56:697–713.

PFISTER, A. R. 1980. Postfire avian ecology in Yellowstone National Park. M.S. thesis. Washington State University, Pullman, WA.

PIATT, J. F., AND N. L. NASLUND. 1995. Abundance, distribution, and population status of Marbled Murrelets in Alaska. Pp. 285–294 in C. J. Ralph, G. L. Hunt, Jr., M. G. Raphael, and J. F. Piatt (editors). Ecology and conservation of the Marbled Murrelet. USDA Forest Service Gen. Tech. Rep. PSW-GTR-152. USDA Forest Service Pacific Southwest Research Station, Albany, CA.

PIATT, J. F., AND R. G. FORD. 1993. Distribution and abundance of Marbled Murrelets in Alaska. Condor 95:662–669.

PICMAN, J. 1988. Experimental study of predation on edges of ground-nesting birds: effects of habitat and nest distribution. Condor 90:124–131.

PICMAN, J., M. L. MILKS, AND L. MICHELLE. 1993. Patterns of predation on passerine nests in marshes: effects of water depth and distance from edge. Auk 110:89–94.

PLATTS, W. S., AND R. L. NELSON. 1985. Streamside and upland vegetation use by cattle. Rangelands 7:5–7.

POLLOCK, K. H., S. R. WINTERSTEIN, C. M. BUNCK, AND P. D. CURTIS. 1989. Survival analysis in telemetry studies: the staggered entry design. Journal of Wildlife Management 53:7–15.

PORNELUZI, P., J. C. BEDNARZ, L. J. GOODRICH, N. ZAWADA, AND J. HOOVER. 1993. Reproductive performance of territorial ovenbirds occupying forest fragments and a contiguous forest in Pennsylvania. Conservation Biology 7:618–622.

PORTER, S. D., AND D. A. SAVIGNANO. 1990. Invasion of polygyne fire ants decimates native ants and disrupts arthropod community. Ecology 71:2095–2106.

PÖSYÄ, H., M. MILONOFF, AND J. VIRTANEN. 1997. Nest predation in hole-nesting birds in relation to habitat edge: an experiment. Ecography 20:329–335.

POWELL, H. D. W. 2000. The influence of prey density on post-fire habitat use of the Black-backed Woodpecker. M.S. thesis. University of Montana, Missoula, MT.

PRESTON, K. L., P. J. MOCK, M. A. GRISHAVER, E. A. BAILEY, AND D. F. KING. 1998. California gnatcatcher territorial behavior. Western Birds 29:242–257.

PROBST, J. R., AND J. P. HAYES. 1987. Pairing success of Kirtland's Warblers in marginal versus suitable habitat. Auk 104:234–241.

PULLIAM, H. R. 1988. Sources, sinks and population regulation. American Naturalist 132:652–661.

PULLIAM, H. R., AND B. J. DANIELSON. 1991. Sources, sinks, and habitat selection: a landscape perspective on population dynamics. American Naturalist 137:S50–S66.

PULLIAM, H. R., J. B. DUNNING, JR., AND J. LIU. 1992. Population dynamics in complex landscapes: a case study. Ecological Applications 2:165–177.

PURCELL, K. L., AND J. VERNER. 1999. Abundance and rates of nest parasitism by Brown-headed Cowbirds over an elevational gradient in the southern Sierra Nevada. Studies in Avian Biology 18:97–103.

RALPH, C. J. 1994. Evidence of changes in populations of the Marbled Murrelet in the Pacific Northwest. Studies in Avian Biology 15:286–292.

RALPH, C. J., G. R. GEUPEL, P. PYLE, T. E. MARTIN, AND D. F. DESANTE. 1993. Handbook of field methods for monitoring landbirds. USDA Forest Service Gen. Tech. Rep. PSW-GTR-144. USDA Forest Service Pacific Southwest Research Station, Albany, CA.

RALPH, C. J., G. L. HUNT, JR., M. G. RAPHAEL, AND J. F. PIATT. 1995. Ecology and conservation of the Marbled Murrelet in North America: an overview. Pp. 3–22 in C. J. Ralph, G. L. Hunt, Jr., M. G. Raphael, and J. F. Piatt (editors). Ecology and conservation of the Marbled Murrelet. USDA Forest Service Gen. Tech. Rep. PSW-GTR-152. USDA Forest Service Pacific Southwest Research Station, Albany, CA.

RALPH, C. J., S. K. NELSON, M. M. SHAUGHNESSY, S. L. MILLER, AND T. E. HAMER. 1994. Methods for surveying Marbled Murrelets in forests: a protocol for land management and research. Pacific Seabird Group, Marbled Murrelet Technical Committee. March 1994.

RALPH, C. J., P. W. C. PATON, AND C. A. TAYLOR. 1991. Habitat association patterns of breeding birds and small mammals in Douglas-fir/hardwood stands in northwestern California and southwestern Oregon. Pp. 379–393 in L. F. Ruggiero, K. B. Aubry, A. B. Carey, and M. H. Huff (technical coordinators). Wildlife and vegetation of unmanaged Douglas-fir forests. USDA Forest Service Gen. Tech. Rep. PNW-GTR-285. USDA Forest Service Pacific Northwest Research Station, Portland, OR.

RANNEY, J. W., M. C. BRUNER, AND J. B. LEVENSON. 1981. The importance of edge in the structure and dynamics of forest islands. Pp. 67–95 in R. L. Burgess, and D. M. Sharpe (editors). Forest island dynamics in man-dominated landscapes. Springer-Verlag, New York, NY.

RAPHAEL, M. G. 1984. Wildlife diversity and abundance in relation to stand age and area in Douglas-fir forests of Northwestern California. Pp. 259–274 in W. R. Meehan, T. R. Merrell, Jr., and T. A. Hanley (editors). Fish and wildlife relationships in old-growth forests. American Institute of Fishery Research Biologists, Morehead City, NC.

RAPHAEL, M. G., D. M. EVANS, AND B. A. COOPER. 1999. Correlating forest habitat distribution with murrelet radar counts: is there a connection at the drainage scale? Pacific Seabirds 26:43.

RAPHAEL, M. G., D. E. MACK, AND B. A. COOPER. 2002. Landscape-scale relationships between abundance of Marbled Murrelets and distribution of nesting habitat. Condor 104:331–342.

RAPHAEL, M. G., AND M. WHITE. 1984. Use of snags by cavity-nesting birds in the Sierra Nevada. Wildlife Monographs 86:1–66.

RAPHAEL, M. G., M. L. MORRISON, AND M. P. YODER-WILLIAMS. 1987. Breeding bird populations during twenty-five years of postfire succession in the Sierra Nevada. Condor 89:614–626.

RAPHAEL, M. G., J. A. YOUNG, AND B. M. GALLEHER. 1995. A landscape-level analysis of Marbled Murrelet habitat in western Washington. Pp. 177–189 in C. J. Ralph, G. L. Hunt, Jr., M. G. Raphael, and J. F. Piatt (editors). Ecology and conservation of the Marbled Murrelet. USDA Forest Service Gen. Tech. Rep. PSW-GTR-152. USDA Forest Service Pacific Southwest Research Station, Albany, CA.

RAPPOLE, J. H., E. S. MORTON, AND M. A. RAMOS. 1989. Density, philopatry, and population estimates for songbird migrants wintering in Veracruz. Pp. 337–344 in J. M. Hagan, III, and D. W. Johnston (editors). Ecology and conservation of neotropical migrant landbirds. Smithsonian Institution Press, Washington, D.C.

RATTI, J. T., AND K. P. REESE. 1988. Preliminary test of the ecological trap hypothesis. Journal of Wildlife Management 52:484–491.

REED, R. A., J. JOHNSON-BARNARD, AND W. L. BAKER. 1996a. Fragmentation of a forested Rocky Mountain landscape, 1950–1993. Biological Conservation 75:267–277.

REESE, K. P., AND J. T. RATTI. 1988. Edge effects: a concept under scrutiny. Transactions of the North American Wildlife and Natural Resource Conference 53:127–136.

REYNOLDS, T. D. 1979. Impact of Loggerhead Shrikes on nesting birds in a sagebrush environment. Auk 96:798–800.

REYNOLDS, T. D. 1981. Nesting of the Sage Thrasher, Sage Sparrow, and Brewer's Sparrow in southeastern Idaho. Condor 83:61–64.

REYNOLDS, T. D., T. D. G. RICH, AND D. A. STEPHENS. 1999. Sage Thrasher (Oreoscoptes montanus). In A. Poole and F. Gill (editors). The Birds of North America, No. 463. The Academy of Natural Sciences, Philadelphia, PA, and The American Ornithologists Union, Washington, D.C.

RICE, J., R. D. OHMART, AND B. W. ANDERSON. 1983. Turnovers in species composition of avian communities in contiguous riparian habitats. Ecology 64:1444–1455.

RICE, W. R. 1989. Analyzing tables of statistical tests. Evolution 43:223–225.

RICH, A. C., D. S. DOBKIN, AND L. J. NILES. 1994. Defining forest fragmentation by corridor width: the influence of narrow forest-dividing corridors on forest-nesting birds in southern New Jersey. Conservation Biology 8:1109–1121.

RICH, T. D. G. 1978. Cowbird parasitism of sage and Brewer's sparrows. Condor 80:438.

RICH, T. D. G. 1980a. Nest placement in sage thrashers, sage sparrows, and Brewer's sparrows. Wilson Bulletin 92:362–368.

RICH, T. D. G. 1980b. Territorial behavior of the sage sparrow: spatial and random aspects. Wilson Bulletin 92:425–438.

RICH, T. D. G., AND S. I. ROTHSTEIN. 1985. Sage thrashers reject cowbird eggs. Condor 87:561–562.

RICKARD, W. H., AND B. E. VAUGHAN. 1988. Plant community characteristics and responses. Pp. 109–179 in W. H. Rickard, L. E. Rogers, B. E. Vaughan, and S. F. Liebetrau (editors). Shrub-steppe: balance and change in a semi-arid terrestrial ecosystem. Elsevier Press, Amsterdam, The Netherlands.

RICKLEFS, R. E. 1969. An analysis of nesting mortality in birds. Smithsonian Contributions to Zoology 9:1–48.

RICKLEFS, R. E. 1973. Fecundity, mortality, and avian demography. Pp. 336–435 in D. S. Farner (editor). Breeding biology of birds. National Academy of Sciences, Philadelphia, PA.

RIES, L. 1998. Butterflies in the highly fragmented prairies of central Iowa: how the landscape affects population isolation. M.S. thesis. Iowa State University, Ames, IA.

RINKEVICH, S. E., AND R. J. GUTIÉRREZ. 1996. Mexican Spotted Owl habitat characteristics in Zion National Park. Journal of Raptor Research 30:74–78.

RIPPLE, W. J., G. A. BRADSHAW, AND T. A. SPIES. 1991a. Measuring forest landscape patterns in the Cascade range of Oregon, USA. Biological Conservation 57:73–88.

RIPPLE, W. J., K. T. HERSHEY, AND R. G. ANTHONY. 2000. Historical forest patterns of Oregon's central Coast Range. Biological Conservation 93:127–133.

RIPPLE, W. J., D. H. JOHNSON, K. T. HERSHEY, AND E. C. MESLOW. 1991b. Old-growth and mature forests near Spotted Owl nests in western Oregon. Journal of Wildlife Management 55:316–318.

RIPPLE, W. J., P. D. LATTIN, K. T. HERSHEY, F. F. WAGNER, AND E. C. MESLOW. 1997. Landscape composition and pattern around Northern Spotted Owl nest sites in southwest Oregon. Journal of Wildlife Management 61:151–158.

ROBBINS, C. S., D. BYSTRAK, AND P. H. GEISSLER. 1986. The Breeding Bird Survey: its first fifteen years, 1965–1979. USDI Fish and Wildlife Service Resource Publication 157:1–196.

ROBBINS, C. S., D. K. DAWSON, AND B. A. DOWELL. 1989a. Habitat area requirements of breeding forest birds of the Middle Atlantic states. Wildlife Monographs 103:1–34.

ROBBINS, C. S., J. R. SAUER, R. S. GREENBERG, AND S. DROEGE. 1989b. Population declines in North American birds that migrate to the Neotropics. Proceedings of the National Academy of Sciences 86:7658–7662.

ROBERTSON, R. J., AND R. F. NORMAN. 1977. The function and evolution of aggressive host behavior towards the Brown-headed Cowbird (*Molothrus ater*). Canadian Journal of Zoology 55:508–518.

ROBINSON, G. R., R. D. HOLT, M. S. GAINES, S. P. HAMBURG, M. L. JOHNSON, H. S. FITCH, AND E. A. MARTINKO. 1992. Diverse and contrasting effects of habitat fragmentation. Science 257:524–526.

ROBINSON, S. K. 1992. Population dynamics of breeding neotropical migrants in a fragmented Illinois landscape. Pp. 408–418 *in* J. M. Hagan, III, and D. W. Johnston (editors). Ecology and conservation of neotropical migrant landbirds. Smithsonian Institution Press, Washington, D.C.

ROBINSON, S. K. 1998. Another threat posed by forest fragmentation: reduced food supply. Auk 115:1–3.

ROBINSON, S. K. 1999. Introduction to Section I: Cowbird ecology: factors affecting the abundance and distribution of cowbirds. Studies in Avian Biology 18:4–9.

ROBINSON, S. K., J. D. BRAWN, S. F. MORSE, AND J. R. HERKERT. 1999. Use of different habitats by breeding Brown-headed Cowbirds in fragmented Midwestern landscapes. Studies in Avian Biology 18:52–62.

ROBINSON, S. K., S. I. ROTHSTEIN, M. C. BRITTINGHAM, L. J. PETIT, AND J. A. GRZYBOWSKI. 1995b. Ecology and behavior of cowbirds and their impact on host populations. Pp. 428–460 *in* T. E. Martin and D. M. Finch (editors). Ecology and management of neotropical migratory birds: a synthesis and review of critical issues. Oxford University Press, New York, NY.

ROBINSON, S. K., F. R. THOMPSON, III, T. M. DONOVAN, D. R. WHITEHEAD, AND J. FAABORG. 1995a. Regional forest fragmentation and the nesting success of migratory birds. Science 267:1987–1990.

ROBINSON, S. K., AND D. S. WILCOVE. 1994. Forest fragmentation in the temperate zone and its effects on migratory songbirds. Bird Conservation International 4:233–249.

ROBINSON, W. D. AND S. K. ROBINSON. 1999. Effects of selective logging on forest bird populations in a fragmented landscape. Conservation Biology 13:58–66.

RODWAY, M. S., AND H. M. REGEHR. 1999. Inland inventory: Marbled Murrelet activity and structural characteristics of old-growth forest in Clayoquot Sound, British Columbia, 1995–97. Pp. 119–236 *in* T. A. Chatwin, A. E. Burger, and L. E. Jones (editors). Inventory of Marbled Murrelets in Clayoqout Sound 1997. Report to B.C. Ministry of Environment, Lands, and Parks, Vancouver Island Regional Office, Nanaimo, B. C.

ROGERS, C. M., AND M. J. CARO. 1998. Song sparrows, top carnivores and nest predation: a test of the mesopredator release hypothesis. Oecologia 116:227–233.

ROGERS, L. E., R. E. FITZNER, L. L. CADWELL, AND B. E. VAUGHAN. 1988. Terrestrial animal habitats and population responses. Pp. 181–256 *in* W. H. Rickard, L. E. Rogers, B. E. Vaughan, and S. F. Liebetrau

(editors). Shrub-steppe: balance and change in a semi-arid terrestrial ecosystem. Elsevier Press, Amsterdam, The Netherlands.

ROHWER, S., AND C. WOOD. 1998. Three hybrid zones between Hermit and Townsend's Warblers in Washington and Oregon. Auk 115:284–310.

ROLSTAD, J. 1991. Consequences of forest fragmentation for the dynamics of bird populations: conceptual issues and the evidence. Biological Journal of the Linnean Society 42:149–163.

ROMESBURG, H. C. 1981. Wildlife science: gaining reliable knowledge. Journal of Wildlife Management 45:293–313.

ROMME, W. H. 1982. Fire and landscape diversity in subalpine forests of Yellowstone National Park. Ecological Monographs 52:199–221.

ROMME, W. H., AND D. G. DESPAIN. 1989. The long history of fire in the Greater Yellowstone Ecosystem. Wildlands 15:10–17.

ROODMAN, D. M. 1996. Rapid urbanization continues. Pp. 94–95 in L. R. Brown, C. Flavin, and H. Kane (editors). Vital signs 1996: the trends that are shaping our future. Worldwatch Institute, New York, NY.

ROSENBERG, D. K., AND R. G. ANTHONY. 1992. Characteristics of northern flying squirrel populations in young second- and old-growth forests in western Oregon. Canadian Journal of Zoology 70:161–166.

ROSENBERG, K. V., AND M. G. RAPHAEL. 1986. Effects of forest fragmentation on vertebrates in Douglas-fir forests. Pp. 263–272 in J. Verner, M. L. Morrison, and C. J. Ralph (editors). Wildlife 2000: modeling habitat relationships of terrestrial vertebrates. University of Wisconsin Press, Madison, WI.

ROSENBERG, K. V., J. D. LOWE, AND A. A. DHONDT. 1999. Effects of forest fragmentation on breeding tanagers: a continental perspective. Conservation Biology 13:568–583.

ROSENBERG, K. V., R. D. OHMART, W. C. HUNTER, AND B. W. ANDERSON. 1991. Birds of the lower Colorado River Valley. University of Arizona Press, Tucson, AZ.

ROSENBERG, M. S., D. C. ADAMS, AND J. GUREVITCH. 2000. MetaWin: statistical software for meta-analysis, version 2.0. Sinauer Associates, Sunderland, MA.

ROTENBERRY, J. T. 1980. Bioenergetics and diet in a simple community of shrubsteppe birds. Oecologia (Berlin) 46:7–12.

ROTENBERRY, J. T. 1985. The role of habitat in avian community composition: physiognomy or floristics? Oecologia 67:213–217.

ROTENBERRY, J. T. 1986. Habitat relationships of shrubsteppe birds: even "good" models cannot predict the future. Pp. 217–221 in J. Verner, M. L. Morrison, and C. J. Ralph (editors). Wildlife 2000: modeling habitat relationships of terrestrial vertebrates. University of Wisconsin Press, Madison, WI.

ROTENBERRY, J. T. 1998. Avian conservation research needs in western shrublands: exotic invaders and the alteration of ecosystem processes. Pp. 262–272 *in* J. M. Marzluff and R. Sallabanks (editors). Avian conservation: research and management. Island Press, Washington, D.C.

ROTENBERRY, J. T., R. J. COOPER, J. M. WUNDERLE, AND K. G. SMITH. 1995. When and how are populations limited? The roles of insect outbreaks, fire, and other natural perturbations. Pp. 55–84 *in* T. E. Martin and D. M. Finch (editors). Ecology and management of neotropical migratory birds. Oxford University Press, New York, NY.

ROTENBERRY, J. T., AND S. T. KNICK. 1999. Multiscale habitat associations of the Sage Sparrow: implications for conservation biology. Studies in Avian Biology 19:95–103.

ROTENBERRY, J. T., M. A. PATTEN, AND K. L. PRESTON. 1999. Brewer's sparrow (*Spizella breweri*). *In* A. Poole and F. Gill (editors). The Birds of North America, No. 390. The Academy of Natural Sciences, Philadelphia, PA, and The American Ornithologists Union, Washington, D.C.

ROTENBERRY, J. T., AND J. A. WIENS. 1978. Nongame bird communities in northwestern rangelands. Pp. 32–46 *in* R. M. DeGraaf (technical coordinator). Proceedings: workshop on nongame bird habitat management in the coniferous forests of the western United States. USDA Forest Service Gen. Tech. Rep. PNW-64. USDA Forest Service Pacific Northwest Research Station, Portland, OR.

ROTENBERRY, J. T., AND J. A. WIENS. 1980a. Habitat structure, patchiness, and avian communities in North American steppe vegetation: a multivariate analysis. Ecology 61:1228–1250.

ROTENBERRY, J. T., AND J. A. WIENS. 1980b. Temporal variation in habitat structure and shrubsteppe bird dynamics. Oecologia 47:1–9.

ROTENBERRY, J. T., AND J. A. WIENS. 1989. Reproductive biology of shrubsteppe passerine birds: geographical and temporal variation in clutch size, brood size, and fledging success. Condor 91:1–14.

ROTENBERRY, J. T., AND J. A. WIENS. 1991. Weather and reproductive variation in shrubsteppe sparrows: a hierarchical analysis. Ecology 72:1325–1335.

ROTHSTEIN, S. I. 1975. Evolutionary rates and host defenses against avian brood parasitism. American Naturalist 109:161–176.

ROTHSTEIN, S. I. 1994. The cowbird's invasion of the far west: history, causes and consequences experienced by host species. Studies in Avian Biology 15:301–315.

ROTHSTEIN, S. I., M. A. PATTEN, AND R. C. FLEISCHER. 2002. Phylogeny, specialization, and brood parasite-host coevolution: some possible pitfalls of parsimony. Behavioral Ecology 13:1–10.

ROTHSTEIN, S. I., AND S. K. ROBINSON. 1988. Parasitic birds and their hosts, studies in coevolution. Oxford University Press, New York, NY.

ROTHSTEIN, S. I., J. VERNER, AND E. STEVENS. 1984. Radio-tracking confirms a unique diurnal pattern of spatial occurrence in the parasitic Brown-headed Cowbird. Ecology 65:77–88.

ROTHSTEIN, S. I., D. A. YOKEL, AND R. C. FLEISCHER. 1986. Social dominance, mating and spacing systems, female fecundity, and vocal dialects in captive and free-ranging Brown-headed Cowbirds. Current Ornithology 3:127–185.

RUDNICKY, T. C., AND M. L. HUNTER, JR. 1993. Avian nest predation in clearcuts, forests, and edges in a forest-dominated landscape. Journal of Wildlife Management 57:358–364.

SAAB, V. A. 1998. Effects of recreational activity and livestock grazing on habitat use by breeding birds in cottonwood forests along the South Fork Snake River. USDI Bureau of Land Management Tech. Bull. No. 98-17, BLM/ID/PT-99/004-1150. USDI Bureau of Land Management, Boise, ID.

SAAB, V. A. 1999. Importance of spatial scale to habitat use by breeding birds in riparian forests: a hierarchical analysis. Ecological Applications 9:135–151.

SAAB, V. A., C. E. BOCK, T. D. G. RICH, AND D. S. DOBKIN. 1995. Livestock grazing effects in western North America. Pp. 311–353 *in* T. E. Martin and D. M. Finch (editors). Ecology and management of neotropical migratory birds: a synthesis and review of critical issues. Oxford University Press, New York, NY.

SAAB, V., R. BRANNON, J. DUDLEY, L. DONOHOO, D. VANDERZANDEN, V. JOHNSON, AND H. LACHOWSKI. 2002. Selection of fire-created snags at two spatial scales by cavity-nesting birds. *In* P. J. Shea, W. F. Laudenslayer, Jr., B. Valentine, C. P. Weatherspoon, and T. E. Lisle (editors). Proceedings of the Symposium on the ecology and management of dead wood in western forests, November 2–4, 1999, Reno, Nevada. USDA Forest Service Gen. Tech. Rep. PSW-GTR-181. USDA Forest Service, Pacific Southwest Research Station, Albany, CA.

SAAB, V. A., AND J. G. DUDLEY. 1998. Responses of cavity-nesting birds to stand-replacement fire and salvage logging in ponderosa pine/Douglas-fir forests of southwestern Idaho. SDA Forest Service Res. Pap. RMRS-RP-11. USDA Forest Service Rocky Mountain Research Station, Fort Collins, CO.

SAAB, V. A., AND C. R. GROVES. 1992. Idaho's migratory landbirds: description, habitats and conservation. Idaho Department of Fish and Game Nongame Wildlife Leaflet No. 10. Idaho Department of Fish and Game, Boise, ID.

SAAB, V. A., AND T. D. G. RICH. 1997. Large-scale conservation assessment for neotropical migratory landbirds in the Interior Columbia River Basin. USDA Forest Service Gen. Tech. Rep. PNW-GTR-399. USDA Forest Service Pacific Northwest Research Station, Portland, OR.

SAKAI, H. F., AND B. R. NOON. 1993. Dusky-footed woodrat abundance in different-aged forests in northwestern California. Journal of Wildlife Management 57:373–382.

SALLABANKS, R., P. J. HEGLUND, J. B. HAUFLER, B. A. GILBERT, AND W. WALL. 1999. Forest fragmentation of the inland west: issues, definitions, and potential study approaches for forest birds. Pp. 187–199 *in* J. A. Rochelle, L. A. Lehmann, and J. Wisniewski (editors). Forest fragmentation: wildlife and management implications. Brill Publishers, Leiden, The Netherlands.

SAMSON, F., AND F. KNOPF. 1994. Prairie conservation in North America. BioScience 44:418–421.

SANDSTRÖM, U. 1991. Enhanced predation rates on cavity bird nests at deciduous forest edges—an experimental study. Ornis Fennica 68:93–98.

SANTOS, T., AND J. L. TELLERIA. 1992. Edge effects on nest predation in Mediterranean fragmented forests. Biological Conservation 60:1–5.

SARACCO, J. F., AND J. A. COLLAZO. 1999. Predation on artificial nests along three edge types in a North Carolina bottomland hardwood forest. Wilson Bulletin 111:541–549.

SARGENT, R. A., J. C. KILGO, B. R. CHAPMAN, AND K. V. MILLER. 1998. Predation of artificial nests in hardwood fragments enclosed by pine and agricultural habitats. Journal of Wildlife Management 62:1438–1442.

SAS INSTITUTE. 1989. SAS/STAT User's Guide, Release 6.03. SAS Institute, Inc., Cary, NC.

SAS INSTITUTE. 1996. SAS/STAT Software: changes and enhancements through Release 6.11. SAS Institute, Inc., Cary, NC.

SAS INSTITUTE. 1998. SAS version 6.11. SAS Institute, Carey, NC.

SAS INSTITUTE. 1999. SAS/STAT User's Guide, Version 8. SAS Institute, Inc., Cary, NC.

SAUER, J. R., AND S. DROEGE. 1992. Geographic patterns in population trends of neotropical migrants in North America. Pp. 26–42 in J. M. Hagan, III, and D. W. Johnston (editors). Ecology and conservation of neotropical migrant landbirds. Smithsonian Institution Press, Washington, D.C.

SAUER, J. R., J. E. HINES, AND J. FALLON. 2001. The North American Breeding Bird Survey: results and analysis 1966–2000. Version 2001.2. USGS Patuxent Wildlife Research Center, Laurel, MD.

SAUER, J. R., J. E. HINES, G. GOUGH, I. THOMAS, AND B. G. PETERJOHN. 1997. The North American Breeding Bird Survey: results and analysis. Version 96.4. USGS Patuxent Wildlife Research Center, Laurel, MD.

SAUER, J. R., J. E. HINES, I. THOMAS, J. FALLON, AND G. GOUGH. 1999. The North American Breeding Bird Survey: results and analysis 1966–1998. Version 98.1. USGS Patuxent Wildlife Research Center, Laurel, MD.

SAUER, J. R., J. E. HINES, I. THOMAS, J. FALLON, AND G. GOUGH. 2000. The North American Breeding Bird Survey: results and analysis 1966–1999. Version 98.1. USGS Patuxent Wildlife Research Center, Laurel, MD.

SAUER, J. R., AND B. K. WILLIAMS. 1989. Generalized procedures for testing hypotheses about survival or recovery rates. Journal of Wildlife Management 53:137–142.

SAUNDERS, D. A., R. J. HOBBS, AND C. R. MARGULES. 1991. Biological consequences of ecosystem fragmentation: a review. Conservation Biology 5:18–32.

SAUVAJOT, R. M., M. BUECHNER, D. A. KAMRADT, AND C. M. SCHONEWALD. 1998. Patterns of human disturbance and response by small mammals and birds in chaparral near urban development. Urban Ecosystems 2:279–297.

SAWYER, J. O., J. GRAY, G. J. WEST, D. A. THORNBURGH, R. F. NOSS, J. H. ENGBECK, JR., B. G. MARCOT, AND R. RAYMOND. 2000. History of redwood and redwood forests. Pp. 7–38 in R. F. Noss (editor). The redwood forest. Island Press, Washington, D.C.

SCHIECK, J., K. LERTZMAN, B. NYBERG, AND R. PAGE. 1995. Effects of patch size on birds in old-growth montane forests. Conservation Biology 9:1072–1084.

SCHMIEGELOW, F. K. A., C. S. MACHTANS, AND S. J. HANNON. 1997. Are boreal birds resilient to forest

fragmentation? An experimental study of short-term community responses. Ecology 78:1914–1932.

SCHUECK, L. S., AND J. M. MARZLUFF. 1995. Influence of weather on conclusions about effects of human activities on raptors. Journal of Wildlife Management 59:674–682.

SCHULZ, T. T., AND W. C. LEININGER. 1991. Nongame wildlife communities in grazed and ungrazed montane riparian sites. Great Basin Naturalist 51:286–292.

SCOTT, J. M., F. DAVIS, B. CSUTI, R. NOSS, B. BUTTERFIELD, C. GROVES, H. ANDERSON, S. CAICCO, F. D'ERCHIA, T. C. EDWARDS, JR., J. ULLIMAN, AND R. G. WRIGHT. 1993. Gap analysis: a geographic approach to protection of biological diversity. Wildlife Monographs 57:1–41.

SEALY, S. G. 1995. Burial of cowbird eggs by parasitized Yellow Warblers: an empirical and experimental study. Animal Behavior 49:877–889.

SEAMANS, M. E., AND R. J. GUTIÉRREZ. 1995. Breeding habitat of the Mexican Spotted Owl in the Tularosa Mountains, New Mexico. Condor 97:944–952.

SEAMANS, M. E., R. J. GUTIÉRREZ, C. A. MAY, AND M. Z. PEERY. 1999. Demography of two Mexican Spotted Owl populations. Conservation Biology 13:744–754.

SEDGWICK, J. A. 1994. Hammond's Flycatcher (Empidonax hammondii). In A. Poole and F. Gill (editors). The Birds of North America, No. 109. The Academy of Natural Sciences, Philadelphia, PA, and The American Ornithologists Union, Washington, D.C.

SEDGWICK, J. A., AND F. L. KNOPF. 1987. Breeding bird response to cattle grazing of a cottonwood bottomland. Journal of Wildlife Management 51:230–237.

SEDGWICK, J. A., AND F. L. KNOPF. 1990. Habitat relationships and nest site characteristics of cavity-nesting birds in cottonwood floodplains. Journal of Wildlife Management 54:112–124.

SEITZ, L. C., AND D. A. ZEGERS. 1993. An experimental study of nest predation in adjacent deciduous, coniferous, and successional habitats. Condor 95:297–304.

SHERRY, T. W., AND R. T. HOLMES. 1992. Population fluctuations in a long-distance neotropical migrant: demographic evidence for the importance of breeding season events in the Redstart. Pp. 431–442 in J. M. Hagan, III, and D. W. Johnston (editors). Ecology and conservation of neotropical migrant landbirds. Smithsonian Institution Press, Washington, D.C.

SHERRY, T. W., AND R. T. HOLMES. 1995. Summer versus winter limitation of populations: what are the issues and what is the evidence? Pp. 85–120 in T. E. Martin and D. M. Finch (editors). Ecology and management of neotropical migratory birds. Oxford University Press, New York, NY.

SHINN, D. A. 1980. Historical perspective on range burning in the inland northwest. Journal of Range Management 33:415–422.

SHINNEMAN, D. J., AND W. L. BAKER. 1997. Nonequilibrium dynamics between catastrophic disturbances and old-growth forests in ponderosa pine landscapes of the Black Hills. Conservation Biology 11:1276–1288.

SHULER, C. A., W. H. RICKARD, AND G. A. SARGEANT.

1993. Conservation of habitats for shrubsteppe birds. Environmental Conservation 20:57–64.

SHURE, D. J., AND D. L. PHILLIPS. 1991. Patch size of forest openings and arthropod populations. Oecologia 86:325–334.

SIERRA NEVADA ECOSYSTEM PROJECT. 1996. Status of the Sierra Nevada, Volume I: Assessment summaries and management strategies. University of California Wildland Resources Center Report No. 37, Davis, California.

SIEVING, K. E. 1992. Nest predation and differential insular extinction among selected forest birds of central Panama. Ecology 73:2310–2328.

SIMBERLOFF, D. S., AND L. G. ABELE. 1976. Island biogeography theory and conservation practice. Science 191:285–286.

SIMBERLOFF, D. S., AND L. G. ABELE. 1982. Refuge design and island biogeographic theory: effects of fragmentation. American Naturalist 120:41–50.

SIMPSON, E. H. 1949. Measurement of diversity. Nature 163:688.

SIMS, P. L., AND P. G. RISSER. 2000. Grasslands. Pp. 323–356 in M. G. Barbour and W. D. Billings (editors). North American terrestrial vegetation. 2nd Edition. Cambridge University Press, Cambridge, UK.

SINGER, S. W., D. L. SUDDJIAN, AND S. A. SINGER. 1995. Fledging behavior, flight patterns, and forest characteristics at Marbled Murrelet tree nests in California. Northwestern Naturalist 76:54–62.

SINGH, A. 1989. Review article: Digital change detection techniques using remotely-sensed data. International Journal of Remote Sensing 10:989–1003.

SISK, T. D. 1992. Distributions of birds and butterflies in heterogeneous landscapes. Ph.D. dissertation. Stanford University, Stanford, CA.

SISK, T. D., AND C. R. MARGULES. 1993. Habitat edges and restoration: methods for quantifying edge effects and predicting the results of restoration efforts. Pp. 57–69 in D. Saunders, R. J. Hobbs, and P. R. Ehrlich (editors). Nature conservation 3: reconstruction of fragmented ecosystems. Surrey Beatty and Sons, Sydney, Australia.

SISK, T. D., AND N. M. HADDAD. 2002. Incorporating the effects of habitat edges into landscape models: effective area models for cross-boundary management. In J. Liu and W. W. Taylor (editors). Integrating landscape ecology into natural resource management. Oxford University Press, Oxford, UK.

SISK, T. D., N. M. HADDAD, AND P. R. EHRLICH. 1997. Bird assemblages in patchy woodlands: modeling the effects of edge and matrix habitats. Ecological Applications 7:1170–1180.

SISK, T. D., AND J. ZOOK. 1996. Influence of landscape composition on the distribution of Swainson's thrush, *Catharus ustulatus,* migrating through Costa Rica. Vida Silvestre Neotropical 5:120–125.

SKINNER, C. N. 1995. Change in spatial characteristics of forest openings in the Klamath Mountains of northwestern California. Landscape Ecology 10: 219–228.

SKINNER, C. N., AND C-R. CHANG. 1996. Fire regimes, past and present. Pp. 1041–1069 in Sierra Nevada Ecosystem Project. Status of the Sierra Nevada, Volume II: Assessment and scientific basis for manage-ment options. University of California Wildland Resources Center Report No. 37, Davis, California.

SMALL, M. F., AND M. L. HUNTER. 1988. Forest fragmentation and avian nest predation in forest landscapes. Oecologia 76:62–64.

SMALL, M. F., AND M. L. HUNTER. 1989. Response of passerines to abrupt forest-river and forest-powerline edges in Maine. Wilson Bulletin 101:77–83.

SMITH, B. E., P. L. MARKS, AND S. GARDESCU. 1993. 200 years of forest cover changes in Tompkins County, New York. Bulletin of the Torrey Botanical Club 120:229–247.

SMITH, J. N. M., AND I. H. MYERS-SMITH. 1998. Spatial variation in parasitism of Song Sparrows by Brown-headed Cowbirds. Pp. 296–312 in S. I. Rothstein and S. K. Robinson (editors). Parasitic birds and their hosts, studies in coevolution. Oxford University Press, New York, NY.

SOKAL, R. R., AND F. J. ROHLF. 1981. Biometry, 2nd ed. W. H. Freeman and Co., New York, NY.

SOKAL, R. R., AND F. J. ROHLF. 1995. Biometry. W. H. Freeman and Co., New York, NY.

SOLIS, D. M., AND R. J. GUTIÉRREZ. 1990. Summer habitat ecology of Northern Spotted Owls in northwestern California. Condor 92:739–748.

SONERUD, G. A., AND P. E. FJELD. 1987. Long-term memory in egg predators: an experiment with a Hooded Crow. Ornis Scandinavica 18:323–325.

SONG, S. J., AND S. J. HANNON. 1999. Predation in heterogeneous forests: a comparison at natural and anthropogenic edges. EcoScience 6:521–530.

SOULÉ, M. E. 1988. Conservation biology: the science of scarcity and diversity. Sinauer Associates, Sunderland, MA.

SOULÉ, M. E., D. T. BOLGER, A. C. ALBERTS, R. SAUVAJOT, J. WRIGHT, M. SORICE, AND S. HILL. 1988. Reconstructed dynamics of rapid extinction of chaparral requiring birds in urban habitat islands. Conservation Biology 2:75–92.

SOULÉ, M. E., B. A. WILCOX, AND C. HOLTBY. 1979. Benign neglect: a model of faunal collapse in the game reserves of East Africa. Biological Conservation 15:259–272.

SOUTHWOOD, T. R. E. 1977. Habitat, templet for ecological strategies? Presidential address to British Ecological Society, 5 January 1977. Journal of Animal Ecology 46:337–365.

SPIES, T. A., W. J. RIPPLE, AND G. A. BRADSHAW. 1994. Dynamics and patterns of a managed coniferous forest landscape in Oregon. Ecological Applications 4: 555–568.

SPRUGEL, D. G. 1991. Disturbance, equilibrium, and environmental variability: what is "natural" vegetation in a changing environment? Biological Conservation 58:1–18.

STACEY, P. B., AND M. TAPER. 1992. Environmental variation and the persistence of small populations. Ecological Applications 2:18–29.

STAMP, N. E. 1978. Breeding birds of riparian woodland in south-central Arizona. Condor 80:64–71.

STEELE, R., R. D. PFISTER, R. A. RYKER, AND J. A. KITTAMS. 1981. Forest habitat types of central Idaho. USDA Forest Service Res. Pap. INT-114. USDA Forest Service Intermountain Research Station, Ogden, UT.

STEGER, G. N., T. E. MUNTON, K. D. JOHNSON, AND G. E. EBERLEIN. 1997. Characteristics of nest trees and nest sites of California Spotted Owls in coniferous forests of the southern Sierra Nevada. Transactions of the Western Section of the Wildlife Society 33: 30–39.

STEVENSON, H. M., AND B. H. ANDERSON. 1994. Florida birdlife. University of Florida Press, Gainesville, FL.

STEWART, O. C. 1956. Fire as the first great force employed by man. Pp. 115–133 in W. L. Thomas (editor). Man's role in changing the face of the earth. University of Chicago Press, Chicago, IL.

STORAAS, T. 1988. A comparison of losses in artificial and naturally occurring capercaillie nests. Journal of Wildlife Management 52:123–126.

STORCH, I. 1991. Habitat fragmentation, nest site selection, and nest predation risk in Capercaillie. Ornis Scandinavica 22:213–217.

STRAUSBERGER, B. M., AND M. V. ASHLEY. 1997. Community-wide patterns of parasitism of a host "generalist" brood-parasitic cowbird. Oecologia 112: 254–262.

STRAUSS, D., L. BEDNAR, AND R. MEES. 1989. Do one percent of forest fires cause ninety-nine percent of the damage? Forest Science 35:319–328.

STRELKE, W. K., AND J. G. DICKSON. 1980. Effect of forest clear-cut edge on breeding birds in east Texas. Journal of Wildlife Management 44:559–567.

STRIBLEY, J. M., AND J. B. HAUFLER. 1999. Landscape effects on cowbird occurrences in Michigan: implications to research needs in forests of the inland west. Studies in Avian Biology 18:68–72.

STRONG, C. S. 1995. Distribution of the Marbled Murrelet along the Oregon Coast in 1992. Northwestern Naturalist 76:99–105.

STRONG, C. S., B. S. KEITT, W. R. MCIVER, C. J. PALMER, AND I. GAFFNEY. 1995. Distribution and population estimates of Marbled Murrelets at sea in Oregon during the summers of 1992 and 1993. Pp. 339–352 in C. J. Ralph, G. L. Hunt, Jr., M. G. Raphael, and J. F. Piatt (editors). Ecology and conservation of the Marbled Murrelet. USDA Forest Service Gen. Tech. Rep. PSW-GTR-152. USDA Forest Service Pacific Southwest Research Station, Albany, CA.

STRONG, T. R., AND C. E. BOCK. 1990. Bird species distribution patterns in riparian habitats in southeastern Arizona. Condor 92:866–885.

STROUD, D. A., T. M. REED, AND N. J. HARDING. 1990. Do moorland breeding waders avoid plantation edges? Bird Study 37:177–186.

SUAREZ, A. V., D. T. BOLGER, AND T. J. CASE. 1998. The effects of fragmentation and invasion on the native ant community in coastal southern California. Ecology 79:2041–2056.

SUAREZ, A. V., K. S. PFENNIG, AND S. K. ROBINSON. 1997. Nesting success of a disturbance-dependent songbird on different kinds of edges. Conservation Biology 11:928–935.

SUAREZ, A. V., J. Q. RICHMOND, AND T. J. CASE. 2000. Prey selection in horned lizards following the invasion of Argentine ants in southern California. Ecological Applications 10:726–743.

SUREDA, M., AND M. L. MORRISON. 1998. Habitat use by small mammals in southeastern Utah, with reference to Mexican Spotted Owl management. Great Basin Naturalist 58:76–81.

SWANSON, F. J., T. K. KRANTZ, N. CAINE, AND R. G. WOODSMANSEE. 1988. Landform effects on ecosystem pattern and processes. BioScience 38:92–98.

SWENSEN, J. E., C. A. SIMMONS, AND C. D. EUSTICE. 1987. Decrease of Sage Grouse Centrocercus urophasianus after ploughing of sagebrush steppe. Biological Conservation 41:125–132.

SWETNAM, T. W., AND C. H. BAISAN. 1996a. Historical fire regime patterns in the southwestern United States since AD 1700. Pp. 11–32 in C. D. Allen (editor). Fire effects in southwestern forests: proceedings of the second La Mesa fire symposium, Los Alamos, New Mexico, March 29–31, 1994. USDA Forest Service General Technical Report RM-GTR-286.

SWETNAM, T. W., AND C. H. BAISAN. 1996b. Fire histories of montane forests in the Madrean borderlands. Pp. 15–36 in P. F. Ffolloitt, L. F. DeBano, M. B. Baker, G. J. Gottfried, G. Solis-Garza, C. B. Edminster, D. G. Neary, L. S. Allen, and R. H. Hamre (technical coordinators). Effects of fire on Madrean province ecosystems—a symposium proceedings. USDA Forest Service General Technical Report RM-GTR-289.

SWETNAM, T. W., AND J. L. BETANCOURT. 1990. Fire-southern oscillation relations in the Southwestern United States. Science 249:1017–1020.

SWETNAM, T. W., B. E. WICKMAN, H. G. PAUL, AND C. H. BAISAN. 1995. Historical patterns of western spruce budworm and Douglas-fir tussock moth outbreaks in the northern Blue Mountains, Oregon, since A.D. 1700. USDA Forest Service Papers PNW-RP-484. USDA Forest Service Pacific Northwest Research Station, Portland, OR.

SWETNAM, T. W., C. D. ALLEN, AND J. L. BENTACOURT. 1999. Applied historical ecology: using the past to manage for the future. Ecological Applications 9: 1189–1206.

TANDE, G. F. 1979. Fire history and vegetation pattern of coniferous forests in Jasper National Park, Alberta. Canadian Journal of Botany 57:1912–1931.

TAYLOR, A. H., AND C. N. SKINNER. 1998. Fire history and landscape dynamics in a late-successional reserve, Klamath Mountains, California, USA. Forest Ecology and Management 111:285–301.

TAYLOR, D. L., AND J. BARMORE. 1980. Post-fire succession of avifauna in coniferous forests of Yellowstone and Grand Teton National Parks, Wyoming. Pp. 130–145 in R. M. DeGraaf and N. G. Tilghman (editors). Management of western forests and grasslands for nongame Birds: workshop proceedings. USDA Forest Service Gen. Tech. Rep. INT-86. USDA Forest Service, Intermountain Research Station, Ogden, UT.

TAYLOR, D. M. 1986. Effects of cattle grazing on passerine birds nesting in riparian habitat. Journal of Range Management 39:254–258.

TAYLOR, M. W. 1977. A comparison of three edge indexes. Wildlife Society Bulletin 5:192–193.

TAYLOR, P. D., L. FAHRIG, K. HENEIN, AND G. MERRIAM. 1993. Connectivity is a vital element of landscape structure. Oikos 68:571–573.

TEMPLE, S. A. 1986. Predicting impacts of habitat fragmentation on forest birds: a comparison of two models. Pp. 301–304 *in* J. Verner, M. L. Morrison, and C. J. Ralph (editors). Wildlife 2000: modeling habitat relationships of terrestrial vertebrates. University of Wisconsin Press, Madison, WI.

TEMPLE, S. A. AND J. R. CARY. 1988. Modeling dynamics of habitat-interior bird populations in fragmented landscapes. Conservation Biology 2:340–347.

TER BRAAK, C. J. F. 1986. Canonical correspondence analysis: a new eigenvector method for multivariate direct gradient analysis. Ecology 67:1167–1179.

TER BRAAK, C. J. F. 1988. CANOCO—a FORTRAN program for canonical community ordination by [partial] [detrended] [canonical] correspondence analysis, principal components analysis and redundancy analysis. Agricultural Mathematics Group, Ministry of Agriculture and Fisheries Tech. Rep. LWA-88-02.

TER BRAAK, C. J. F., AND C. W. N. LOOMAN. 1986. Weighted averaging, logistic regression, and the Gaussian response model. Vegetatio 65:3–11.

TER BRAAK, C. J. F., AND I. C. PRENTICE. 1988. A theory of gradient analysis. Advances in Ecological Research 18:271–317.

TERBORGH, J. 1989. Where have all the birds gone? Princeton University Press, Princeton, NJ.

TERBORGH, J. 1976. Island biogeography and conservation: strategy and limitations. Science 193:1029–1030.

TEWKSBURY, J. J., S. J. HEJL, AND T. E. MARTIN. 1998. Breeding productivity does not decline with increasing fragmentation in a western landscape. Ecology 79:2890–2903.

TEWKSBURY, J. J., T. E. MARTIN, S. J. HEJL, T. S. REDMAN, AND F. J. WHEELER. 1999. Cowbirds in a western valley: effects of landscape structure, vegetation and host density. Studies in Avian Biology 18:23–33.

THINGSTAD, P. G. 1995. Variation in a subalpine passerine bird community in the surroundings of an established hydroelectric reservoir. Fauna Norvegica Serie C. Cinclus 18:63–80.

THOMAS, J. W., E. D. FORSMAN, J. B. LINT, E. C. MESLOW, B. R. NOON, AND J. VERNER. 1990. A conservation strategy for the Northern Spotted Owl. U.S. Government Printing Office, Washington, D.C. 1990-791-171/20026.

THOME, D. M., C. J. ZABEL, AND L. V. DILLER. 1999. Forest stand characteristics and reproduction of Northern Spotted Owls in managed north-central California forests. Journal of Wildlife Management 63:44–59.

THOMPSON, F. R., III. 1993. Simulated responses of a forest-interior bird population to forest management options in central hardwood forests of the United States. Conservation Biology 7:325–333.

THOMPSON, F. R., III. 1994. Temporal and spatial patterns of breeding in Brown-headed Cowbirds in the Midwestern United States. Auk 111:979–990.

THOMPSON, F. R., III, AND W. D. DIJAK. 2000. Differences in movements, home range, and habitat preferences of female brown-headed cowbirds in three Midwestern landscapes. Pp. 100–109 *in* J. N. M. Smith, T. L. Cook, S. I. Rothstein, S. K. Robinson,

and S. G. Sealy (editors). The biology and management of cowbirds and their hosts. University of Texas Press, Austin, TX.

THOMPSON, F. R., III, W. D. DIJAK, AND D. E. BURHANS. 1999. Video identification of predators at songbird nests in old fields. Auk 116:259–264.

THOMPSON, F. R., III, W. D. DIJAK, T. G. KULOWIEC, AND D. A. HAMILTON. 1992. Breeding bird populations in Missouri Ozark forests with and without clearcutting. Journal of Wildlife Management 56: 23–30.

THOMPSON, F. R., III, S. J. LEWIS, J. GREEN, AND D. EWERT. 1992. Status of Neotropical migrant landbirds in the Midwest: identifying species of management concern. Pp. 145–158 *in* D. M. Finch and P. W. Stangel (editors). Status and management of neotropical migratory birds. USDA Gen. Tech. Rep. RM-229. USDA Forest Service Rocky Mountain Research Station, Ft. Collins, CO.

THOMPSON, F. R., III, J. R. PROBST, AND M. G. RAPHAEL. 1995. Impacts of silviculture: overview and management recommendations. Pp. 201–219 *in* T. E. Martin and D. M. Finch (editors). Ecology and management of neotropical migratory birds. Oxford University Press, New York, NY, New York.

THOMPSON, F. R., III, S. K. ROBINSON, T. M. DONOVAN, J. FAABORG, AND D. R. WHITEHEAD. 2000. Biogeographic, landscape, and local factors affecting cowbird abundance and host parasitism levels. Pp. 271–279 *in* J. N. M. Smith, T. L. Cook, S. I. Rothstein, S. K. Robinson, and S. G. Sealy (editors). The biology and management of cowbirds and their hosts. University of Texas Press, Austin, TX.

THORNBURGH, D. A., R. F. NOSS, D. P. ANGELIDES, C. M. OLSEN, F. EUPHRAT, AND H. H. WELSH, JR. 2000. Managing redwoods. Pp. 229–261 *in* R. F. Noss (editor). The redwood forest. Island Press, Washington, D.C.

TIEDEMANN, A. R., J. O. KLEMMEDSON, AND E. L. BULL. 2000. Solution of forest health problems with prescribed fire: are forest productivity and wildlife at risk? Forest Ecology and Management 127:1–18.

TINKER, D. B., C. A. C. RESOR, G. P. BEAUVAIS, K. F. KIPFMUELLER, C. I. FERNANDES, AND W. L. BAKER. 1998. Watershed analysis of forest fragmentation by clearcuts and roads in a Wyoming forest. Landscape Ecology 13:149–165.

TREMPER, B. D. 1976. Distribution of the Argentine ant, *Iridomyrmex humilis* Mayr, in relation to certain native ants of California: ecological, physiological, and behavioral aspects. Ph.D. dissertation. University of California, Berkeley, CA.

TRINE, C. L. 1998. Wood thrush population sinks and implications for the scale of regional conservation strategies. Conservation Biology 12:576–585.

TRINE, C. L., W. D. ROBINSON, AND S. K. ROBINSON. 1998. Consequences of Brown-headed Cowbird brood parasitism for host population dynamics Pp. 273–295 *in* S. I. Rothstein and S. K. Robinson (editors). Parasitic birds and their hosts: studies in coevolution. Oxford University Press, New York, NY.

TRZCINSKI, M. K., L. FAHRIG, AND G. MERRIAM. 1999. Independent effects of forest cover and fragmentation on the distribution of forest breeding birds. Ecological Applications 9:586–593.

TURCHIN, P. 1998. Quantitative analysis of animal movements: measuring and modeling population redistribution in animals and plants. Sinauer Associates, Sunderland, MA.

TURNER, M. G. 1989. Landscape ecology—the effect of pattern on process. Annual Review of Ecology and Systematics 20:171–197.

TURNER, M. G., AND R. H. GARDNER (EDITORS). 1991. Quantitative methods in landscape ecology. Springer-Verlag, New York, NY.

TURNER, M. G., W. H. HARGROVE, R. H. GARDNER, AND W. H. ROMME. 1994. Effects of fire on landscape heterogeneity in Yellowstone National Park, Wyoming. Journal of Vegetation Science 5:731–742.

TURNER, M. G., AND W. H. ROMME. 1994. Landscape dynamics in crown fire ecosystems. Landscape Ecology 9:59–77.

TYSER, R. W. 1983. Species-area relations of cattail marsh avifauna. Passenger Pigeon 45:125–128.

U.S. DEPARTMENT OF INTERIOR. 1992. Draft recovery plan for the Northern Spotted Owl. U.S. Department of Interior, Washington, D.C.

U.S. DEPARTMENT OF INTERIOR. 1996. Effects of military training and fire in the Snake River Birds of Prey National Conservation Area. BLM/IDARNG Research Project Final Report. U.S. Geological Survey, Biological Resources Division, Snake River Field Station, Boise, ID.

U.S. DEPARTMENT OF INTERIOR, AND U.S. DEPARTMENT OF AGRICULTURE. 1998. USDI and USDA Forest Service Joint Fire Science Plan. USDI and USDA Forest Service, Washington, D.C.

U.S. FISH AND WILDLIFE SERVICE. 1990. 50 CFR Part 17 Endangered and threatened wildlife and plants; determination of threatened status for the Northern Spotted Owl; final rule. Federal Register 55:26114–26194.

U.S. FISH AND WILDLIFE SERVICE. 1993. Endangered and threatened wildlife and plants; final rule to list the Mexican Spotted Owl as a threatened species. Federal Register 58:14248–14271.

U.S. FISH AND WILDLIFE SERVICE. 1997a. Recovery plan for the threatened Marbled Murrelet (Brachyramphus marmoratus) in Washington, Oregon, and California. U.S. Fish and Wildlife Service Region 1, Portland, OR.

U.S. FISH AND WILDLIFE SERVICE. 1997b. Final environmental impact statement for a 4d rule for the conservation of the Northern Spotted Owl on nonfederal lands. U.S. Fish and Wildlife Service, Office of Technical Support for Forest Resources, Portland, OR.

UNITT, P. 1984. The birds of San Diego County. San Diego Society of Natural History, San Diego, CA.

URBAN, D. L., R. V. O'NEILL, AND H. H. SHUGART. 1987. Landscape ecology. BioScience 37:119–127.

URBAN, D. L., AND H. H. SHUGART, JR. 1986. Avian demography in mosaic landscapes: modeling paradigm and preliminary results. Pp. 273–280 in J. Verner, M. L. Morrison, and C. J. Ralph (editors). Wildlife 2000: modeling habitat relationships of terrestrial vertebrates. University of Wisconsin Press, Madison, WI.

VALE, T. R. 1974. Sagebrush conversion projects: an element of contemporary environmental change in the western United States. Biological Conservation 6:274–284.

VALE, T. R. 1975. Presettlement vegetation in the sagebrush-grass area of the Intermountain West. Journal of Range Management 28:32–36.

VAN DORP, D., AND P. F. M. OPDAM. 1987. Effects of patch size, isolation, and regional abundance on forest bird communities. Landscape Ecology 1:59–73.

VAN HORN, M. A., R. M. GENTRY, AND J. FAABORG. 1995. Patterns of ovenbird Seiurus aurocapillus pairing success in Missouri forest tracts. Auk 112:98–106.

VAN HORNE, B. 1983. Density as a misleading indicator of habitat quality. Journal of Wildlife Management 47:893–901.

VANDER HAEGEN, W. M., AND R. M. DEGRAAF. 1996a. Predation on artificial nests in forested riparian buffer strips. Journal of Wildlife Management 60:542–550.

VANDER HAEGEN, W. M., AND R. M. DEGRAAF. 1996b. Predation rates on artificial nests in an industrial forest landscape. Forest Ecology and Management 86:171–179.

VANDER HAEGEN, W. M., F. C. DOBLER, AND D. J. PIERCE. 2000. Shrubsteppe bird responses to habitat and landscape variables in eastern Washington, USA. Conservation Biology 14.

VANDER HAEGEN, W. M., AND B. WALKER. 1999. Parasitism by Brown-headed Cowbirds in the shrubsteppe of eastern Washington. Studies in Avian Biology 18:34–40.

VANDERWERF, E. 1992. Lack's clutch size hypothesis: an examination of the evidence using meta-analysis. Ecology 73:1699–1705.

VAROUJEAN, D. H., II, AND W. A. WILLIAMS. 1995. Abundance and distribution of Marbled Murrelets in Oregon and Washington based on aerial surveys. Pp. 339–352 in C. J. Ralph, G. L. Hunt, Jr., M. G. Raphael, and J. F. Piatt (editors). Ecology and conservation of the Marbled Murrelet. USDA Forest Service Gen. Tech. Rep. PSW-GTR-152. USDA Forest Service Pacific Southwest Research Station, Albany, CA.

VEBLEN, T. T. 2000. Disturbance patterns in central Rocky Mountain forests. Pp. 33–56 in R. L. Knight, F. W. Smith, S. W. Buskirk, W. H. Romme, and W. L. Baker (editors). Forest fragmentation in the southern Rocky Mountains. University Press of Colorado, Niwot, CO.

VEBLEN, T. T., K. S. HADLEY, M. S. REID, AND A. J. REBERTUS. 1991. The response of subalpine forests to spruce beetle outbreak in Colorado. Ecology 72:213–231.

VEBLEN, T. T., T. KITZBERGER, AND J. DONNEGAN. 2000. Climatic and human influences on fire regimes in ponderosa pine forests in the Colorado Front Range. Ecological Applications 10:1178–1195.

VEBLEN, T. T., AND D. C. LORENZ. 1991. The Colorado Front Range: a century of ecological change. University of Utah Press, Salt Lake City, UT.

VEIRS, S. D., JR. 1982. Coast redwood forest: stand dynamics, successional status, and the role of fire. Pp. 119–141 in J. E. Means (editor). Forest succession and stand development research in the northwest. Forest Research Laboratory, Corvallis, Oregon.

VERNER, J. 1985. Assessment of counting techniques. Current Ornithology 2:247–302.

VERNER, J. 1986. Summary: effects of habitat patchiness and fragmentation—the researcher's viewpoint. Pp. 327–329 in J. Verner, M. L. Morrison, and C. J. Ralph (editors). Wildlife 2000: modeling habitat relationships of terrestrial vertebrates. University of Wisconsin Press, Madison.

VERNER, J., AND A. S. BOSS. 1980. California wildlife and their habitats: western Sierra Nevada. USDA Forest Service Gen Tech. Rep. PSW-37. USDA Forest Service, Pacific Southwest Forest and Range Experiment Station, Berkeley, CA.

VERNER, J., K. S. MCKELVEY, B. R. NOON, R. J. GUTIÉRREZ, G. I. GOULD, JR., AND T. W. BECK. 1992. The California Spotted Owl: a technical assessment of its current status. U.S. Forest Service General Technical Report PSW-GTR-133. USDA Forest Service Pacific Southwest Research Station, Albany, CA.

VERNER, J., AND L. V. RITTER. 1983. Current status of the Brown-headed Cowbird in the Sierra National Forest. Auk 100:355–368.

VICKERY, P. D., AND J. R. HERKERT (EDITORS). 1999. Ecology and conservation of grassland birds of the Western Hemisphere. Studies in Avian Biology No. 19. Cooper Ornithological Society, Los Angeles, CA.

VICKERY, P. D., M. L. HUNTER, AND S. M. MELVIN. 1994. Effects of habitat area on the distribution of grassland birds in Maine. Conservation Biology 8:1087–1097.

VICKERY, P. D., M. L. HUNTER, AND J. V. WELLS. 1992. Is density an indicator of breeding success. Auk 109:706–710.

VICKERY, P. D., M. L. HUNTER, AND J. V. WELLS. 1992. Evidence of incidental nest predation and its effects on nests of threatened grassland birds. Oikos 63:281–288.

VICKERY, P. D., P. L. TUBARO, J. M. C. SILVA, B. G. PETERJOHN, J. R. HERKERT, AND R. B. CAVALCANTI. 1999. Conservation of grassland birds in the western hemisphere. Studies in Avian Biology 19:2–26.

VILLARD, M.-A. 1998. On forest-interior species, edge avoidance, area sensitivity, and dogmas in avian conservation. Auk 115:801–805.

VILLARD, M.-A., K. FREEMARK, AND G. MERRIAM. 1992. Metapopulation theory and neotropical migrant birds in temporal forests: an empirical investigation. Pp. 474–482 in J. M. Hagan, III, and D. W. Johnston (editors). Ecology and conservation of neotropical migrant landbirds. Smithsonian Institution Press, Washington, D.C.

VILLARD, M.-A., P. R. MARTIN, AND C. G. DRUMMOND. 1993. Habitat fragmentation and pairing success in the Ovenbird (Seiurus aurocapillus). Auk 110:759–768.

VILLARD, M.-A., G. MERRIAM, AND B. A. MAURER. 1995. Dynamics in subdivided populations of neotropical migratory birds in a fragmented temperate forest. Ecology 76:27–40.

VILLARD, M.-A., AND P. D. TAYLOR. 1994. Tolerance to habitat fragmentation influences the colonization of new habitat by forest birds. Oecologia 98:393–401.

VILLARD, M.-A., M. K. TRZCINSKI, AND G. MERRIAM. 1999. Fragmentation effects on forest birds: Relative influence of woodland cover and configuration on landscape occupancy. Conservation Biology 13:774–783.

WAGNER, F. F., E. C. MESLOW, G. M. BENNETT, C. J. LARSON, S. M. SMALL, AND S. DESTEFANO. 1996. Demography of Northern Spotted Owls in the southern Cascades and Siskiyou mountains, Oregon. Studies in Avian Biology 17:67–76.

WAGNER, M. R., W. M. BLOCK, B. W. GEILS, AND K. F. WEGNER. 2000. Restoration ecology: a new forest management paradigm, or another merit badge for foresters? Journal of Forestry 98:22–27.

WALK, J. W., AND R. E. WARNER. 1999. Effects of habitat area on the occurrence of grassland birds in Illinois. American Midland Naturalist 141:339–344.

WALTERS, J. R. 1998. The ecological basis of avian sensitivity to habitat fragmentation. Pp. 181–192 in J. M. Marzluff and R. Sallabanks (editors). Avian conservation: research and management. Island Press, Covelo, CA.

WANDER, S. A. 1985. Comparative breeding biology of the Ovenbird in large vs. fragmented forests: implications for the conservation of neotropical migrant birds. Ph.D. dissertation. Rutgers University, New Brunswick, NJ.

WARD, D., AND J. N. M. SMITH. 2000. Inter-habitat differences in parasitism frequencies by Brown-headed Cowbirds in the Okanagan Valley, British Columbia. Pp. 210–219 in J. N. M. Smith, T. L. Cook, S. I. Rothstein, S. K. Robinson, and S. G. Sealy (editors). The biology and management of cowbirds and their hosts. University of Texas Press, Austin, TX.

WARD, J. P., JR. AND W. M. BLOCK. 1995. Mexican Spotted Owl prey ecology. Pp. 1–42 in W. M. Block, F. Clemente, J. F. Cully, J. L. Dick, Jr., A. B. Franklin, J. L. Ganey, F. P. Howe, W. H. Moir, S. L. Spangle, S. E. Rinkevich, D. L. Urban, R. Vahle, J. P. Ward, Jr., and G. C. White (editors). Recovery plan for the Mexican Spotted Owl (Strix occidentalis lucida), volume 2. U.S. Department of Interior, Fish and Wildlife Service, Albuquerque, NM.

WARD, J. P., JR., A. B. FRANKLIN, S. E. RINKEVICH, AND F. CLEMENTE. 1995. Distribution and abundance of Mexican Spotted Owls. Pp. 1–42 in W. M. Block, F. Clemente, J. F. Cully, J. L. Dick, Jr., A. B. Franklin, J. L. Ganey, F. P. Howe, W. H. Moir, S. L. Spangle, S. E. Rinkevich, D. L. Urban, R. Vahle, J. P. Ward, Jr., and G. C. White (editors). Recovery plan for the Mexican Spotted Owl (Strix occidentalis lucida), volume 2. U.S. Department of Interior, Fish and Wildlife Service, Albuquerque, NM.

WARD, J. P., JR., R. J. GUTIÉRREZ, AND B. R. NOON. 1998. Habitat selection by Northern Spotted Owls: the consequences of prey selection and distribution. Condor 100:79–92.

WARD, P. S. 1987. Distribution of the introduced Argentine ant (Iridomyrmex humilis) in natural habitats of the lower Sacramento Valley and its effects on the indigenous ant fauna. Hilgardia 55:1–16.

WARNER, K. S. 2000. Artificial nests, their predators,

and their ability to represent real nests. M.S. thesis. Boise State University, Boise, ID.

WEATHERSPOON, C. P., S. J. HUSARI, AND J. W. VAN WAGTENDONK. 1992. Fire and fuels management in relation to owl habitat in forests of the Sierra Nevada and southern California. Pp. 247–260 *in* J. Verner, K. S. McKelvey, B. R. Noon, R. J. Gutiérrez, G. I. Gould, Jr., and T. W. Beck (editors). The California Spotted Owl: a technical assessment of its current status. U.S. Forest Service General Technical Report PSW-GTR-133. USDA Forest Service Pacific Southwest Research Station, Albany, CA.

WEINBERG, H. J., AND R. R. ROTH. 1998. Forest area and habitat quality for nesting Wood Thrushes. Auk 115:879–889.

WESER, O. E. 1996. San Diego County 1995–96 aerial foto-map book. Aerial Fotobank, Inc., San Diego, CA.

WEST, N. E. 1979. Basic synecological relationships of sagebrush-dominated lands in the Great Basin and the Colorado Plateau. Pp. 33–41 *in* The sagebrush ecosystem: a symposium. Utah State University, College of Natural Resources, Logan, UT.

WEST, N. E. 1983. Western intermountain sagebrush steppe. Pp. 351–374 *in* N. E. West (editor). Ecosystems of the world. Elsevier Scientific Publishing Co., Amsterdam, The Netherlands.

WEST, N. E. 1996. Strategies for maintenance of and repair of biotic community diversity on rangelands. Pp. 326–346 *in* R. C. Szaro and D. W. Johnston (editors). Biodiversity in managed landscapes: theory and practice. Oxford University Press, New York, NY.

WEST, N. E., AND J. A. YOUNG. 2000. Intermountain valleys and lower mountain slopes. Pp. 255–284 *in* M. G. Barbour and W. D. Billings (editors). North American terrestrial vegetation. 2nd ed. Cambridge University Press, Cambridge, UK.

WESTMAN, W. E. 1981. Diversity relations and succession in Californian coastal sage scrub. Ecology 62: 170–184.

WESTOBY, M. 1981. Elements of a theory of vegetation dynamics in arid rangelands. Israel Journal of Botany 28:169–194.

WHELAN, C. J., M. L. DILGER, D. ROBSON, N. HALLYN, AND S. DILGER. 1994. Effects of olfactory cues on artificial-nest experiments. Auk 111:945–952.

WHISENANT, S. G. 1990. Changing fire frequencies on Idaho's Snake River plains: ecological and management implications. Pp. 4–10 *in* E. D. McArthur, E. M. Romney, S. D. Smith, and P. T. Tueller (editors). Proceedings Symposium on cheatgrass invasion, shrub die-off, and other aspects of shrub biology and management. USDA Forest Service, Intermountain Research Station, Ogden, UT.

WHITCOMB, B. L., R. F. WHITCOMB, AND D. BYSTRAK. 1977. Long-term turnover and effects of selective logging on the avifauna of forest fragments. American Birds 31:17–23.

WHITCOMB, R. F., C. S. ROBBINS, J. F. LYNCH, B. L. WHITCOMB, K. KLIMKIEWICZ, AND D. BYSTRAK. 1981. Effects of forest fragmentation on avifauna of the eastern deciduous forest. Pp. 125–205 *in* R. L. Burgess and D. M. Sharp (editors). Forest island dynamics in man-dominated landscapes. Springer-Verlag, New York, NY.

WHITE, G. C., A. B. FRANKLIN, AND J. P. WARD, JR. 1995. Population biology. Pp. 1–25 *in* W. M. Block, F. Clemente, J. F. Cully, J. L. Dick, Jr., A. B. Franklin, J. L. Ganey, F. P. Howe, W. H. Moir, S. L. Spangle, S. E. Rinkevich, D. L. Urban, R. Vahle, J. P. Ward, Jr., and G. C. White (editors). Recovery plan for the Mexican Spotted Owl (*Strix occidentalis lucida*), volume 2. U.S. Department of Interior, Fish and Wildlife Service, Albuquerque, NM.

WIENS, J. A. 1973. Pattern and process in grassland bird communities. Ecological Monographs 43:237–270.

WIENS, J. A. 1974a. Habitat heterogeneity and avian community structure in North American grasslands. American Midland Naturalist 91:195–213.

WIENS, J. A. 1974b. Climatic instability and the "ecological saturation" of bird communities in North American grasslands. Condor 76:385–400.

WIENS, J. A. 1976. Population responses to patchy environments. Annual Review of Ecology and Systematics 7:81–120.

WIENS, J. A. 1985a. Habitat selection in variable environments: shrub-steppe birds. Pp. 227–251 *in* M. L. Cody (editor). Habitat selection in birds. Academic Press, San Diego, CA.

WIENS, J. A. 1985b. Vertebrate responses to environmental patchiness in arid and semiarid ecosystems. Pp. 169–193 *in* S. T. A. Picket and P. S. White (editors). The ecology of natural disturbance and patch dynamics. Academic Press, New York, NY.

WIENS, J. A. 1989a. The ecology of bird communities. Vol. 1. Foundations and patterns. Cambridge University Press, Cambridge, UK.

WIENS, J. A. 1989b. The ecology of bird communities. Vol. 2. Processes and variations. Cambridge University Press, Cambridge, UK.

WIENS, J. A. 1989c. Spatial scaling in ecology. Functional Ecology 3:385–397.

WIENS, J. A. 1994. Habitat fragmentation: island vs. landscape perspectives on bird conservation. Ibis 137:S97–S104.

WIENS, J. A. 1995. Landscape mosaics and ecological theory. Pp. 1–26 *in* L. Hansson, L. Fahrig, and G. Merriam (editors). Mosaic landscapes and ecological processes. Chapman and Hall, London, UK.

WIENS, J. A. 1996. Wildlife in patchy environments: metapopulations, mosaics, and management. Pp. 53–84 *in* D. R. McCullough (editor). Metapopulations and wildlife conservation. Island Press, Washington, D.C.

WIENS, J. A. 1997. Metapopulation dynamics and landscape ecology. Pp. 43–60 *in* I. A. Hanski and M. E. Gilpin (editors). Metapopulation biology. Academic Press, San Diego, CA.

WIENS, J. A., C. S. CRAWFORD, AND J. R. GOSZ. 1986a. Boundary dynamics: a conceptual framework for studying landscape ecosystems. Oikos 45:421–427.

WIENS, J. A., AND J. T. ROTENBERRY. 1980. Bird community structure in cold shrub deserts: competition or chaos? International Ornithological Congress 17: 1063–1070.

WIENS, J. A., AND J. T. ROTENBERRY. 1981. Habitat associations and community structure of birds in shrubsteppe environments. Ecological Monographs 51:21–41.

WIENS, J. A., AND J. T. ROTENBERRY. 1985. Response of breeding passerine birds to rangeland alteration in a North American shrubsteppe locality. Journal of Applied Ecology 22:655–668.

WIENS, J. A., J. T. ROTENBERRY, AND B. VAN HORNE. 1986b. A lesson in the limitations of field experiments: shrubsteppe birds and habitat alterations. Ecology 67:365–376.

WIENS, J. A., J. T. ROTENBERRY, AND B. VAN HORNE. 1987. Habitat occupancy patterns of North American shrubsteppe birds: the effects of spatial scale. Oikos 48:132–147.

WILCOVE, D. S. 1985. Nest predation in forest tracks and the decline of migratory songbirds. Ecology 66:1211–1214.

WILCOVE, D. S., C. M. MCLELLAN, AND A. P. DOBSON. 1986. Habitat fragmentation in the temperate zone. Pp. 237–256 in M. E. Soulé (editor). Conservation biology: the science of scarcity and diversity. Sinauer Associates, Sunderland, MA.

WILCOVE, D. S., AND S. K. ROBINSON. 1990. The impact of forest fragmentation on bird communities in eastern North America. Pp. 319–331 in A. Keast (editor). Biogeography and ecology of forest bird communities. SPB Academic Publishing, The Hague, The Netherlands.

WILCOVE, D. S., AND R. F. WHITCOMB. 1983. Gone with the trees. Natural History 9/83:82–91.

WILCOX, B. A. 1980. Insular ecology and conservation. Pp. 95–117 in M. E. Soulé and B. A. Wilcox (editors). Conservation biology: an evolutionary-ecological perspective. Sinauer Associates, Sunderland, MA.

WILLEBRAND, T., AND V. MARCSTRÖM. 1988. On the danger of using dummy nests to study predation. Auk 109:378–379.

WILLEY, D. W., AND C. VAN RIPER, III. 2000. First-year movements by juvenile Mexican Spotted Owls in the Canyonlands of Utah. Journal of Raptor Research 34:1–7.

WILLIAMS, D. F., J. VERNER, H. F. SAKAI, AND J. R. WATERS. 1992. General biology of major prey species of the California Spotted Owl. Pp. 207–221 in J. Verner, K. S. McKelvey, B. R. Noon, R. J. Gutiérrez, G. I. Gould, Jr., and T. W. Beck (editors). The California Spotted Owl: a technical assessment of its current status. U.S. Forest Service General Technical Report PSW-GTR-133. USDA Forest Service Pacific Southwest Research Station, Albany, CA.

WILLS, R. D. 1991. Fire history and stand development of Douglas-fir/hardwood forests in northern California. M.S. thesis. Humboldt State University, Arcata, CA.

WILLSON, M. F. 1974. Avian community organization and habitat structure. Ecology 55:1017–1029.

WILSON, E. O. (EDITOR). 1988. Biodiversity. National Academy Press, Washington, D.C.

WILSON, G. R., AND M. C. BRITTINGHAM. 1998. How well do artificial nests estimate success of real nests? Condor 100:357–364.

WINKER, K., J. H. RAPPOLE, AND M. A. RAMOS. 1995. The use of movement data as an assay of habitat quality. Oecologia 101:211–216.

WINTER, B. M., AND L. B. BEST. 1985. Effect of prescribed burning on placement of Sage Sparrow nests. Condor 87:294–295.

WINTER, M., AND J. FAABORG. 1999. Patterns of area sensitivity in grassland-nesting birds. Conservation Biology 13:1424–1436.

WISDOM, M. J., R. S. HOLTHAUSEN, D. C. LEE, B. C. WALES, W. J. MURPHY, M. R. EAMES, C. D. HARGIS, V. A. SAAB, T. D. G. RICH, F. B. SAMSON, D. A. NEWHOUSE, AND N. WARREN. 2000. Source habitats for terrestrial vertebrates of focus in the Interior Columbia Basin: broad-scale trends and management implications. USDA Forest Service Gen. Tech. Rep. PNW-GTR-485. USDA Forest Service Pacific Northwest Research Station, Portland, OR.

WITH, K. A., R. H. GARDNER, AND M. G. TURNER. 1997. Landscape connectivity and population distributions in heterogeneous environments. Oikos 78:151–169.

WOLF, F. M. 1986. Meta-analysis: quantitative methods for research synthesis. Sage University Paper series on Quantitative Applications in the Social Sciences 07-001. Sage Publications, Beverly Hills, CA.

WOODWARD, A. A., A. D. FINK, AND F. R. THOMPSON, III. 2001. Edge effects and ecological traps: effects on shrubland birds in Missouri. Journal of Wildlife Management 65:668–675.

WOODWORTH, B. L. 1999. Modeling population dynamics of a songbird exposed to parasitism and predation and evaluating management options. Conservation Biology 13:67–76.

WRIGHT, H. A. 1985. The effect of fire on grasses and forbs in sagebrush-grass communities. Pp. 12–21 in K. Sanders and J. Durham (editors). Rangeland fire effects. USDI Bureau of Land Management, Boise, ID.

WRIGHT, H. A., AND A. W. BAILEY. 1982. Fire ecology. John Wiley and Sons, New York, NY.

WRIGHT, V. 1996. Multi-scale analysis of Flammulated Owl habitat use: owl distribution, habitat management, and conservation. M.S. thesis. University of Montana, Missoula, MT.

YAHNER, R. H. 1995. Habitat use by wintering and breeding bird communities in relation to edge in an irrigated forest. Wilson Bulletin 107:365–371.

YAHNER, R. H. 1996. Forest fragmentation, artificial nest studies, and predator abundance. Conservation Biology 10:672–673.

YAHNER, R. H. 1997. Historic, present, and future status of Pennsylvania vertebrates: some issues of conservation concern. Journal of the Pennsylvania Academy of Science 71:47–51.

YAHNER, R. H., AND B. L. CYPHER. 1987. Effects of nest location on depredation of artificial arboreal nests. Journal of Wildlife Management 51:178–181.

YAHNER, R. H., AND C. G. MAHAN. 1996. Depredation of artificial ground nests in a managed, forested landscape. Conservation Biology 10:285–288.

YAHNER, R. H., AND C. G. MAHAN. 1997. Effects of logging roads on depredation of artificial ground nests in a forested landscape. Wildlife Society Bulletin 25:158–162.

YAHNER, R. H., T. E. MERRELL, AND J. S. RACHAEL.

1989. Effects of edge contrast on depredation of artificial avian nests. Journal of Wildlife Management 53:1135–1138.

YAHNER, R. H., AND D. P. SCOTT. 1988. Effects of forest fragmentation on depredation of artificial avian nests. Journal of Wildlife Management 52:158–161.

YAHNER, R. H., AND A. L WRIGHT. 1985. Depredation on artificial ground nests: effects of edge and plot age. Journal of Wildlife Management 49:508–513.

YAMASAKI, M., T. M. McCLELLAN, R. M. DeGRAAF, AND C. A. COSTELLO. 2000. Effects of land-use and management practices on the presence of brown-headed cowbirds in the White Mountains of New Hampshire and Maine. Pp. 311–319 in J. N. M. Smith, T. L. Cook, S. I. Rothstein, S. K. Robinson, and S. G. Sealy (editors). The biology and management of cowbirds and their hosts. University of Texas Press, Austin, TX.

YENSEN, D. 1982. A grazing history of southwestern Idaho with emphasis on the Birds of Prey Study Area. U.S. Bureau of Land Management Snake River Birds of Prey Research Project Report. USDI Bureau of Land Management, Boise, ID.

YENSEN, D. L. 1981. The 1900 invasion of alien plants into southern Idaho. Great Basin Naturalist 41:176–183.

YOAKUM, J. D. 1980. Habitat improvement techniques. Pp. 329–403 in J. Schemnitz (editor). Wildlife management techniques manual. The Wildlife Society, Washington, D.C.

YOSEF, R. 1994. The effects of fencelines on the reproductive success of Loggerhead Shrikes. Conservation Biology 8:281–295.

YOUNG, A., AND N. MITCHELL. 1994. Microclimate and vegetation edge effects in a fragmented podocarp-broadleaf forest in New Zealand. Biological Conservation 67:63–72.

YOUNG, J. A. 1994. History and use of semiarid plant communities—changes in vegetation. Pp. 5–8 in S. B. Monsen and S. G. Kitchen (compilers). Proceedings—ecology and management of annual grasslands. USDA Forest Service Gen. Tech. Rep. INT-GTR-313. USDA Forest Service, Intermountain Research Station, Ogden, UT.

YOUNG, J. A., R. E. ECKERT, AND R. A. EVANS. 1979. Historical perspectives regarding the sagebrush ecosystem. Pp. 1–13 in The sagebrush ecosystem: a symposium. Utah State University, College of Natural Resources, Logan, UT.

YOUNG, J. A., AND R. A. EVANS. 1978. Population dynamics after wildfires in sagebrush grasslands. Journal of Range Management 31:283–289.

YOUNG, J. A., AND R. A. EVANS. 1981. Demography and fire history of a western juniper stand. Journal of Range Management 34:501–506.

YOUNG, J. A., AND R. A. EVANS. 1989. Dispersal and germination of big sagebrush (Artemisia tridentata) seeds. Weed Science 37:201–206.

YOUNG, J. A., AND W. S. LONGLAND. 1996. Impact of alien plants on Great Basin rangelands. Weed Technology 10:384–391.

YOUNG, J. A., AND B. A. SPARKS. 1985. Cattle in the cold desert. Utah State University Press, Logan, UT.

YOUNG, J. S., AND R. L. HUTTO. 1999. Habitat and landscape factors affecting cowbird distribution in the Northern Rockies. Studies in Avian Biology 18:41–51.

YOUNG, K. E., R. VALDEZ, P. J. ZWANK, AND W. R. GOULD. 1998. Density and roost site characteristics of Spotted Owls in the Sierra Madre Occidental, Chihuahua, Mexico. Condor 100:732–736.

ZABEL, C. J., K. S. McKELVEY, AND J. P. WARD, JR. 1995. Influence of primary prey on home-range size and habitat-use patterns of Northern Spotted Owls (Strix occidentalis caurina). Canadian Journal of Zoology 73:433–439.

ZANETTE, L., P. DOYLE, AND S. M. TRÉMONT. 2000. Food shortage in small fragments: evidence from an area-sensitive passerine. Ecology 81:1654–1666.

ZEDLER, P. H., C. R. GAUTIER, AND G. S. McMASTER. 1983. Vegetation change in response to extreme events: the effect of a short interval between fires in California chaparral and coastal sage scrub. Ecology 64:809–818.

ZINK, T. A., M. F. ALLEN, B. HEINDL-TENHUNEN, AND E. B. ALLEN. 1996. The effect of a disturbance corridor on an ecological reserve. Restoration Ecology 3:304–310.